The RCRA Practice Manual

SECOND EDITION

Theodore L. Garrett, editor

Section of Environment, Energy, and Resources
Book Publications Committee, 2003–2004
Sam Kalen, *Chair*
Donald C. Baur
Kathleen Marion Carr
James W. Checkley, Jr.
John P. Manard, Jr.
Jay G. Martin
Cary R. Perlman
Mark Squillace
Karen Wardzinski

Cover design by ABA Publishing

The publications of the Section of Environment, Energy, and Resources have a commitment to quality. Our authors and editors are outstanding professionals and active practitioners in their fields. In addition, prior to publication, the contents of all of our books are rigorously reviewed by the Section's Book Publications Committee and outside experts to ensure the highest quality product and presentation.

The materials contained herein represent the opinions of the authors and editors and should not be construed to be the action of either the American Bar Association or the Section of Environment, Energy, and Resources unless adopted pursuant to the bylaws of the Association.

Nothing contained in this book is to be considered as the rendering of legal advice for specific cases, and readers are responsible for obtaining such advice from their own legal counsel. This book and any forms and agreements herein are intended for educational and informational purposes only.

© 2004 American Bar Association. All rights reserved. No part of this publication may be reproduced, stored in a retrieval system, or transmitted in any form or by any means, electronic, mechanical, photocopying, recording, or otherwise, without the prior written permission of the publisher. For permission contact the ABA Copyrights & Contracts Department, copyright@abanet.org or via fax at 312-988-6030.

Printed in the United States of America.

08 07 06 05 04   5 4 3 2 1

Library of Congress Cataloging-in-Publication Data

The RCRA practice manual / by Theodore L. Garrett [editor].—2nd ed.
    p. cm.
  Includes bibliographical references and index.
  ISBN 1-59031-288-0
  1. United States. Resource Conservation and Recovery Act of 1976. 2. Hazardous wastes--Law and legislation—United States. 3. Hazardous waste treatment facilities—Law and legislation—United States. I. Garrett, Theodore L. II. American Bar Association.

  KF3946.R387   2004
  344.7304'62—dc22

               2004001468

Discounts are available for books ordered in bulk. Special consideration is given to state bars, CLE programs, and other bar-related organizations. Inquire at Book Publishing, ABA Publishing, American Bar Association, 321 N. Clark, Chicago, Illinois 60610-4714.

www.ababooks.org

CONTENTS

Preface xiii

About the Editor xv

About the Authors xvii

INTRODUCTION

CHAPTER 1
An Overview of RCRA 1
Theodore L. Garrett
    Introduction 1
    Definition of Hazardous Waste 2
    Obligations of Generators 4
    Transport of Hazardous Waste 5
    Treatment, Storage, and Disposal 6
    Corrective Action 9
    Underground Storage Tanks 11
    Disposal of Nonhazardous Waste 12
    Conclusion 13

CHAPTER 2
RCRA's Relationship to Other Laws 15
Daniel H. Squire
    Overview of RCRA Jurisdiction 15
    RCRA's Relation to Other Regulatory Statutes 17
    RCRA's Relation to the Superfund Cleanup Statute 26
    Conclusion 31

iv Contents

THE SCOPE OF HAZARDOUS WASTE

CHAPTER 3
Recycling and the Definition of Solid Waste 33
Kenneth M. Kastner
　Introduction 33
　Physical Form of a Solid Waste 33
　"Discarded" Material 34
　Specific Exclusions from the Definition of Solid Waste 41
　Regulation of "Recyclable" Materials 42
　Regulation of Used Oil 42
　Conclusion 43

CHAPTER 4
Definition of Hazardous Waste 45
Lynn L. Bergeson
　Introduction 45
　Listed Hazardous Wastes 47
　Characteristic Hazardous Wastes 49
　The Mixture and Derived-from Rules and the Contained-in Policy 52
　HWIR-Media 57
　Mixed Waste Exemption 57
　Universal Waste Rule 58
　Residues of Waste in Empty Containers 59
　Conclusion 60

GENERATORS AND TRANSPORTERS

CHAPTER 5
The Obligations of Generators 61
John A. McKinney Jr., Vito A. Pinto, and Anthony J. Del Piano
　Introduction 61
　Who Qualifies as a "Generator" of Hazardous Waste? 62
　Hazardous Waste Determination 64
　Accumulation and Storage Requirements 65
　Notification to EPA of Hazardous Waste Activities 69
　EPA Identification Number 69
　The Manifest System 70
　Pretransportation Requirements 73
　Record-Keeping and Reporting Requirements 73
　Waste Minimization 77

Contents v

Exemptions from the Regulations 80
Import of Hazardous Waste 84
Export of Hazardous Waste 85
Conclusion 89
Appendix A: EPA Notification of Regulated Waste Activity
(Form 8700-12) 90
Appendix B: EPA Uniform Hazardous Waste Manifest; continuation
sheet (Forms 8700-22 and -22A) 93
Appendix C: EPA 1999 Hazardous Waste Report
(Form 8700-13A/B) 95
Appendix D: The EPA Manual for Waste Minimization Opportunity
Assessments (1988) (excerpts) 97

CHAPTER 6
Transport of Hazardous Waste 103
John R. Jacus and Dean C. Miller
Introduction and Scope 103
Regulation of Hazardous Waste Transporters under RCRA 104
DOT's Hazardous Material Regulations: A Summary 111
DOT's Authority and Coordination with EPA 114
Federal Preemption of Local and State Regulation of Hazardous
Waste Transport 115
Commerce Clause Limitations on State and Local Regulation of
Hazardous Waste Transport 118
Conclusion 120
Appendix A: Department of Transportation Definition of "Public
Highway" 121

TREATMENT, STORAGE, AND DISPOSAL

CHAPTER 7
Permit Requirements 125
David E. Preston, Andrew J. Kok, and Matthew B. Eugster
What Is a RCRA Permit? 125
Determining Permit Applicability 127
Obtaining a RCRA Permit 130
Processing of Permit Applications 133
The Permit 134
Special Permits 136
Permit Denial 138
Permit Modifications 138

Permit Duration and Renewal   142
Permit Termination   142
Interim Status   143
"Inadvertent" TSDF Status   145
Postclosure Permits   146
Permitting Reference Materials   146
Conclusion   147
Appendix A: List of Guidance Documents Released by EPA's Office
of Solid Waste   148
Appendix B: EPA Hazardous Waste Permit Application, Part A
(Form 8700-23)   153

CHAPTER 8
**Operating and Design Standards for Treatment, Storage,
and Disposal Facilities   161**
Janet L. McQuaid
Introduction   161
Subpart A: General Scope   162
Subpart B: General Facility Standards   163
Subpart C: Preparedness and Prevention   170
Subpart D: Contingency Plan and Emergency Procedures   172
Subpart E: Manifest System, Record Keeping, and Reporting   174
Conclusion   180
Appendix: Uniform Hazardous Waste Manifest
(EPA Form 8700-22)   181

CHAPTER 9
Closure, Postclosure, and Financial Responsibility   183
Robert F. Wilkinson and Michael D. Montgomery
Introduction   183
Closure   184
Postclosure   189
Specific Closure and Postclosure Requirements   195
Financial Assurance   199
Conclusion   215

CHAPTER 10
**Standards for Containers, Tanks, Incinerators, Boilers,
and Furnaces   217**
Susan J. Sadler
Introduction   217
Containers   218

Contents vii

Tank Systems 222
Incinerators 232
Boilers and Industrial Furnaces 240
Conclusion 249
Appendix: Tables from EPA's *Technical Implementation Document for EPA's Boiler and Industrial Furnace Regulations* 250

LAND DISPOSAL AND CORRECTIVE ACTION

CHAPTER 11
Land Disposal Facilities 255
Michael D. Montgomery and Robert F. Wilkinson
Introduction 255
Minimum Technological Requirements 256
Groundwater Monitoring 257
Technical Standards 269
Conclusion 287

CHAPTER 12
Land Ban Disposal Restrictions 289
Steven Silverman
Relevant Statutory and Regulatory Provisions 290
The Section 3004(m) Treatment Standards 293
Temporary and Permanent Alternatives to Treatment 297
Interface between the LDR Rules and Other Statutory and Regulatory Programs 300

CHAPTER 12 (UPDATED)
Land Ban Disposal Restrictions 305
Steven Silverman
Introduction 305
Resolution of Issues Relating to LDR Applicability: Update of *Chemical Waste Management v. EPA* 305
Standardization of Treatment Standards 309
Assuring that LDRs Do Not Lead to Environmentally Inappropriate Results and Modifying LDRs to Encourage Aggressive Remediation 312

CHAPTER 13
Corrective Action Requirements 319
James T. Price and Karl S. Bourdeau
Overview of the Statutory Scheme and Regulatory Background 319
Jurisdictional Reach of the Program 321

viii Contents

The Corrective Action Process   327
Implementation of the Corrective Action Program   332
Managing Remediation Wastes   337
Other Technical Issues   341
Expediting Corrective Action   343
Conclusion   344

UNDERGROUND STORAGE TANKS AND NONHAZARDOUS WASTE

CHAPTER 14
Regulation of Underground Storage Tanks   345
John C. Chambers, Chris S. Leason, Michael D. Hockley,
and Benjamin T. Clark
Introduction   345
EPA Underground Storage Tank Regulations   348
Performance Standards, Operating Requirements, and
   Release Detection   350
Notification Requirements   358
Release Reporting and Response   359
Closure   361
Financial Responsibility for Petroleum Underground Storage
   Tank Systems   362
Financial Responsibility for Hazardous Substance Underground
   Storage Tank Systems   372
Lender Liability   373
Authorization of State Programs   374
The USTfields Program   375
Enforcement   375
Using the Internet to Research UST Issues   379
Conclusion   379

CHAPTER 15
Regulation of Nonhazardous Waste under RCRA   381
Robert B. McKinstry Jr.
Introduction   381
State Planning and Open Dumping Requirements of Subtitle D   384
The Substantive Requirements of the Open Dumping Criteria   390
Bevill/Bentson Wastes   395
Resource Recovery: Recovery of Energy and Materials
   from MSW   399

Planning Restrictions on Interstate Flow of Waste and Waste
   Flow Control for Financing and the Commerce Clause   405
Other Nonhazardous Wastes to Which Special Handling
   Requirements Apply   409
Special Issues in Enforcement of Subtitle D Requirements and Other
   Requirements Relating to Nonhazardous Waste   413
Conclusion   415

ENFORCEMENT AND IMPLEMENTATION

CHAPTER 16
Civil and Criminal Enforcement   417
Michael W. Steinberg and Kenneth D. Woodrow
   Introduction   417
   The Enforcing Agencies   420
   Information Gathering   424
   Civil Enforcement Proceedings   425
   Criminal Enforcement   432
   Imminent and Substantial Endangerment   436
   Citizen Suits   437
   Federal Facility Enforcement   441
   Conclusion   442

CHAPTER 17
The Federal-State Relationship under RCRA   443
Marcie R. Horowitz and Michael T. Scanlon
   Introduction   443
   Authorization of State Hazardous Waste Programs   444
   The Hazardous and Solid Waste Amendments of 1984   447
   Effects of State Authorization on EPA Enforcement Power   448
   Citizen Suits in Authorized States   451
   Constitutional Issues   453
   Conclusion   457

Table of Cases   459

Table of Statutes   465

Table of Regulations   469

Index   487

Section of Environment, Energy, and Resources 2003–04

Book Publications Committee

Sam Kalen, *Chair*

Donald C. Baur
Kathleen Marion Carr
James W. Checkley, Jr.
John P. Manard, Jr.
Jay G. Martin
Cary R. Perlman
Mark Squillace
Karen Wardzinski

The Book Publications Committee
would like to thank the following reviewers of
The RCRA Practice Manual, Second Edition

Deborah Brown
Gerald Pels

PREFACE

I had the pleasure of launching the book publications program of the section, serving as editor of its first book, *The Environmental Law Manual*. As an officer and chair of the section, I was proud to see the section's book program blossom to encompass a substantial and growing library of publications covering a broad array of environment, energy, and resources law topics.

The RCRA Practice Manual was first published in 1994. It was designed to provide a detailed, practice-oriented overview of the law in this complex and important area.

Numerous judicial developments have occurred since the first edition of the manual, including cases involving the definition of hazardous waste, Environmental Protection Agency over-filing, citizen suits, imminent and substantial endangerment, cost recovery, preemption, and civil and criminal enforcement.

Regulatory developments have similarly been numerous. A review of some of the developments just during the past three years illustrates the dynamic nature of this area. In 2000 EPA published its determination that fossil fuel combustion wastes are not warranted under Subtitle C, issued RCRA reform draft guidance documents entitled *Handbook of Groundwater Policies for RCRA Corrective Action* and *Results-Based Approaches to Corrective Action*, and issued final guidance entitled *Institutional Controls: A Site Manager's Guide*. In 2001 EPA promulgated regulations to reduce the regulatory burdens on certain mixed-waste generators, published final standards for Corrective Action Management Units (CAMUs) for on-site management of hazardous wastes, issued a set of cleanup reforms known as "Reforms II" to focus on the achievement of results, entered into the first prospective purchaser agreement under RCRA, and published a *Handbook of Groundwater Protection and Cleanup Policies*. In 2002 EPA published amendments to the CAMU regulations, promulgated standards for hazardous air pollutants for hazardous waste combusters, and published regulations regarding fertilizers made from hazardous secondary materials.

The dynamic nature of RCRA warrants this second edition. Indeed, it is overdue. These developments have resulted in numerous changes to

xiv Preface

The RCRA Practice Manual. Every chapter was rewritten to reflect the new judicial and regulatory interpretations of RCRA.

I was fortunate to be able to build on the solid foundation of the first edition. I would like to thank all of the authors of chapters of this book for their efforts and expertise. Thanks also to Deborah Brown, the liaison for this book from the section's Book Publications Committee. I would also like to thank Rick Paszkiet at the ABA for his efforts on this book and the section's overall book publications program. Finally, I would like to thank my law firm for its support.

Theodore L. Garrett
Covington & Burling
Washington, D.C.

ABOUT THE EDITOR

Theodore L. Garrett is a partner with the law firm Covington & Burling in Washington, D.C. He has been extensively involved in litigation, administrative proceedings, and counseling in environmental law matters for over 25 years. Mr. Garrett was chair of the ABA Section of Environment, Energy, and Resources in 2000–2001 and has served in several section leadership positions, including the council and executive committee. He currently serves as section liaison to the ABA Standing Committee on Environmental Law and contributing editor to *Trends*. Mr. Garrett is a frequent speaker at environmental law conferences and has written extensively on environmental law topics. He is editor of the *Environmental Law Manual* and *RCRA Policy Documents* and is a contributing author of *The Clean Water Act Handbook, Environmental Litigation,* and *Practice under the Federal Sentencing Guidelines.* A graduate of Yale College and Columbia Law School, Mr. Garrett served as a law clerk for Supreme Court Chief Justice Warren Burger.

ABOUT THE AUTHORS

Lynn L. Bergeson is a founder and shareholder of Bergeson & Campbell, a law firm concentrating on chemical product approval, regulation, product litigation, and associated business issues. Ms. Bergeson is vice chair of the ABA Section of Environment, Energy, and Resources and serves on the board of the Environmental Law Institute. She serves on the editoral boards of, among others, *Pesticide & Toxic Chemical News* and the *EPA Administrative Law Reporter.* She is coauthor of *The TSCA Basic Practice Book* (ABA, 2000) and author of *The FIFRA Basic Practice Book* (ABA, 2000), *Pesticides Law Handbook* (Government Institutes, 1999), and *Avoiding Liability for Hazardous Waste: RCRA, CERCLA and Related Corporate Law Issues* (Bureau of National Affairs, Corporate Practice Series, 1999). Ms. Bergeson received her B.A. with high honors from Michigan State University and her J.D. from the Columbus School of Law, Catholic University of America, where she was a member of the law review.

Karl S. Bourdeau is a principal in the Washington, D.C., office of Beveridge & Diamond, which specializes in handling complex environmental matters. Mr. Bourdeau is engaged primarily in a regulatory, transactional, and litigation practice related to hazardous substance and hazardous waste issues, focusing on matters arising under RCRA and CERCLA. He has negotiated corrective action orders and permits, challenged corrective action permits, and engaged in advocacy on behalf of clients with respect to federal corrective action rule making and guidance documents. Mr. Bourdeau has represented clients in negotiating remedial action settlements under CERCLA, in private cost recovery actions under that statute, and in advocating reforms considered by EPA to expedite property cleanups and make them more cost-effective. He has written and lectured extensively on solid and hazardous waste regulatory issues and on liabilities associated with hazardous substance contamination. He serves on the board of advisors of the National Brownfields Association. He received his B.S. degree with highest honors from Muhlenberg College and his J.D. from Harvard University.

About the Authors

John C. Chambers was, before his death in December 2000, a partner with the firm of McKenna & Cuneo in Washington, D.C., where he specialized in environmental counseling and litigation with emphasis on hazardous waste regulation under RCRA and CERCLA. He wrote extensively on related topics. Before joining the firm, Mr. Chambers served as in-house counsel for CONOCO in Houston, Texas. From 1981 to 1984, he was principal RCRA attorney for the American Petroleum Institute and was elected chair of its RCRA task force in 1985. He received a B.A. degree from the University of Pennsylvania and his J.D. from the Washington College of Law, the American University.

Benjamin T. Clark is on sabbatical from his practice with Spencer Fane Britt & Browne to serve as a judicial clerk with the Honorable Dean Whipple in the United States District Court for the Western District of Missouri. Mr. Clark received his law degree from the University of Iowa College of Law, where he was elected to the Order of the Coif.

Anthony J. Del Piano is associate general counsel at HSBC Holdings, where he concentrates on insurance and financial services. Formerly, he was an associate at McCarter & English, where he practiced general liability/environmental insurance coverage litigation and environmental compliance. He has written for several legal publications, including *Environmental Law Section Newsletter, Criminal Justice* magazine, the New Jersey Institute for Continued Legal Education, the International Bridge, Tunnel and Turnpike Association, and West Group, Inc. Mr. Del Piano earned his undergraduate degree from Seton Hall University and his J.D. from the University of Notre Dame.

Matthew B. Eugster is an associate at Varnum Riddering Schmidt & Howlett in Grand Rapids, Michigan, where he concentrates on environmental law. He is an associate with the regulatory practice group. Mr. Eugster received his B.S. from Aquinas College, his M.A. in political science with high honors from Western Michigan University, and his J.D. from Wayne State University Law School, where he was a member of the law review.

Michael D. Hockley is a partner in the environmental practice group of Spencer Faine Britt & Browne in Kansas City, Missouri, and serves on the firm's executive committee. His practice concentrates on environmental law with an emphasis on environmental litigation and regulatory enforcement proceedings. In addition to representing individual clients in hazardous waste, Clean Air Act, and multimedia enforcement and permitting proceedings, Mr. Hockley has chaired Superfund site steering committees and served as group counsel to steering committees and industry groups in environmental litigation. He also counsels clients on environmental compliance issues. Mr. Hockley is the chair of the Superfund and Hazardous Waste Committee of the ABA Section of Environment, Energy, and Resources and is a subcommittee chair for the Litigation Section's Committee on Environmental Law. He received his undergraduate degree from the United States Military Academy and his law degree from the University of Nebraska College of Law.

Marcie R. Horowitz is of counsel at Farer Fersko in Westfield, New Jersey. With a background in geology, she counsels clients on environmental issues associated with real estate and business transactions. She also has extensive experience in enforcement and regulatory issues related to hazardous waste management, including the negotiation of complex environmental permits and RCRA closure and corrective action issues. Ms. Horowitz received her undergraduate degree from Rutgers University, her law degree from the University of Pennsylvania School of Law, and a master's degree in geology from Bryn Mawr College. She clerked for the Honorable Arlin M. Adams, U.S. Court of Appeals for the Third Circuit.

John R. Jacus is a partner with Davis Graham & Stubbs, Denver, Colorado. He represents clients in complex business transactions with environmental issues, litigation, and administrative proceedings under all major federal environmental statutes and their state law counterparts. Mr. Jacus has represented clients at Superfund and RCRA sites in the Rocky Mountain region and around the country and has served as joint defense group chair, legal committee co-chair, and common counsel for contribution and cost recovery litigation. He is former chair of the Environmental Law Section, Colorado Bar Association (1996–1997) and a former member of Section Council for the ABA Section of Environment, Energy, and Resources (1995–1998). Mr. Jacus received his B.A. in environmental policy from Stanford University and his law degree from the University of Colorado School of Law. He lectures and writes frequently on environmental law and policy.

Kenneth M. Kastner is a partner in the Washington, D.C., office of Hogan & Hartson and a member of the firm's Environmental and Transportation Groups. His prior positions included assistant general counsel of the Chemical Manufacturers Association, currently the American

Chemistry Council, where he developed and advocated for the positions of the chemical industry when EPA was adopting much of its RCRA hazardous waste program and that program was being challenged in court. Mr. Kastner uses this experience to counsel clients on their hazardous waste regulatory requirements, defend them in enforcement actions (including two of the largest RCRA actions ever brought by EPA and the Department of Justice), negotiate and appeal their permits, and advocate their positions in rulemakings, litigation, and legislation. Mr. Kastner has also handled over 50 RCRA corrective actions, closures, and other remedial projects. As national RCRA counsel to several manufacturing clients, Mr. Kastner's practice involves facilities in nearly all of the states and EPA regions.

Andrew J. Kok is a partner with Varnum Riddering Schmidt & Howlett, Grand Rapids, Michigan, where he concentrates on environmental law. His specialties include Clean Air Act compliance, PCB regulatory requirements, hazardous waste regulation, and Superfund site negotiation. Mr. Kok defends clients in PCB and air quality regulation enforcement actions and in civil and administrative enforcement actions of hazardous waste regulations. He assists hazardous waste treatment, storage, and disposal facilities in permitting and compliance issues, counsels industrial clients on harzardous waste regulations applicable to generators, and represents owners, operators, and other PRPs of Superfund sites in negotiating site response activities and liability allocations. He is also involved in reviewing environmental assessments and private-party response activities, assisting in commercial transactions, determining liability of trustees for environmental costs, and advising clients on various environmental record-keeping and reporting requirements. Mr. Kok received his B.A. from Calvin College and his J.D. from the University of Michigan Law School.

Chris S. Leason is a shareholder at Gallagher & Kennedy in Phoenix, Arizona. Mr. Leason specializes in environmental counseling and litigation and food and drug law counseling. Before attending law school, Mr. Leason was employed as a senior environmental compliance engineer at the Department of Energy's Savannah River Site in Aiken, South Carolina. He received his B.S. in chemical engineering from Pennsylvania State University and his J.D. from George Washington University.

John A. McKinney Jr. is a member of Wolff & Samson PC in West Orange, New Jersey, where he concentrates in the area of environmental law. During his legal career in private practice and as in-house counsel, he has handled numerous environmental matters and since 1980 has been active in the RCRA area. Mr. McKinney is a former chair and vice chair of several section committees and is a former chair of the New Jersey State Bar Association's Environmental Law Section. He received his undergraduate degree from Principia College and his J.D. from the College of William and Mary.

Robert B. McKinstry Jr. holds the Maurice K. Goddard Chair in Forestry and Environmental Resources Conservation in the School of Forest Resources of the Pennsylvania State University. He devotes at least half of his time to public service in Pennsylvania on issues relating to environmental and natural resources conservation. He teaches environmental and natural resource law and policy. Mr. McKinstry focuses his research, in particular, on state, local, and private initiatives addressing global environmental concerns, including climate change, biodiversity, and sustainability. He is also of counsel to Ballard Spahr Andrews & Ingersoll, where he was formerly cofounder and co-partner-in-charge of that firm's Environmental Law Practice Group. Before entering private practice, Mr. McKinstry served a two-year clerkship with the Honorable James L. Latchum, Chief Judge of the Federal District Court for the District of Delaware. He is a master in the Delaware Valley Environmental Inn of Court and serves on the boards of the Pennsylvania Chapter of the Nature Conservancy, the Pennsylvania Environmental Council, the Pennsylvania Resources Council, the Clearwater Conservancy, the Pennsylvania Institute for Conservation Education, and Westtown School. He received his J.D. from the Yale Law School and an M.F.S. from the Yale School of Forestry and Environmental Sciences.

Janet L. McQuaid is a partner in the Austin, Texas, office of Fulbright & Jaworski L.L.P., where her practice focuses on environmental law. She has experience in enforcement, litigation, transactions, and counseling involving RCRA, Superfund, and property contamination. She is a frequent author and speaker on environmental topics and is a co-author and editor of the *Texas Environmental Law Handbook* published by Government Institutes. Ms. McQuaid worked for 11 years as an engineer for Exxon before obtaining her law degree. She received a B.S. in chemical engineering from the University of Pittsburgh an a J.D. from the University of Texas.

Dean C. Miller is of counsel with Davis Graham & Stubbs LLP in Denver, Colorado. Mr. Miller assists clients with matters involving the characterization and management of hazardous wastes in a variety of industries, including manufacturing, mining, and oil and gas exploration and production. He also has extensive experience in soil and groundwater contamination, asbestos, and other environmental concerns. Mr. Miller received his B.A. and M.S. degrees in geology from the University of Colorado at Boulder. He received his J.D., *cum laude,* from Southern Illinois University at Carbondale in 1994. Mr. Miller served two years as the law clerk for the Honorable James L. Foreman of the U.S. District Court for the Southern District of Illinois.

Michael D. Montgomery is an associate in the Environmental & Regulatory Practice Group in the St. Louis, Missouri, office of Husch & Eppenberger, where he focuses his practice on all aspects of environmental law with emphasis on hazardous waste management and CERCLA litigation. He counsels clients regarding federal and state environmental issues affecting chemical products and wastes, and advises them on regulatory compliance programs and audits, self-reporting of violations, and enforcement actions. Before attending law school, he worked as an environmental engineer for a major oil company. Mr. Montgomery earned his B.S. in civil engineering from the University of Missouri at Rolla, his M.S. in environmental engineering from Lamar University, and his J.D. from Washington University at St. Louis.

Vito A. Pinto is a partner in the Environmental Practice Group of Schenck, Price, Smith & King in Morristown, New Jersey, where he counsels businesses with respect to compliance with federal and state environmental laws, including RCRA, ISRA, OSHA, CERCLA, the Clean Air Act, and water pollution legislation. He routinely litigates environmental matters in both federal and state courts in the areas of CERCLA and state statute cost recovery, real estate, environmental insurance coverage, and toxic torts. He graduated from Franklin & Marshall College with an undergraduate degree in geology and received his law degree with honors from the George Washington University National Law Center. Before entering private practice, Mr. Pinto was the judicial law clerk to the Honorable James J. Petrella, Presiding Judge, Appellate Division, New Jersey Superior Court.

David E. Preston is a partner with Varnum Riddering Schmidt & Howlett, Grand Rapids, Michigan, where he concentrates on environmental law, including air and hazardous waste regulation. Mr. Preston works in the defense of federal and state environmental enforcement actions involving air quality, harzardous waste, and solid waste issues, asssisting clients with air permitting and related regulator compliance matters

About the Authors xxiii

at state and federal levels. His experience includes remedial investigation and cleanup activities required under RCRA and TSCA. Mr. Preston serves on the board of the West Michigan Chapter of the Air and Waste Management Association. He received B.S. and M.S. degrees from Bowling Green State University and his J.D. with highest honors from the University of Toledo College of Law.

James T. Price is the chair of the Environmental Law Practice Group and a member of the executive committee of Spencer Fane Britt & Browne, Kansas City, Missouri. His practice focuses on a wide array of environmental regulatory and litigation matters, including hazardous waste permitting, enforcement, and cleanup; corrective action and other proceedings under RCRA; litigation and cleanups under CERCLA; brownfields and contaminated property redevelopment; and state-lead cleanups. In the ABA Section of Environment, Energy, and Resources, Mr. Price has served as a member of the council, chair of the Solid and Hazardous Waste Committee, and vice-chair of the Environmental Transactions, Audits, and Brownfields Committee. He is a member of the Brownfields Commission of Kansas City, Missouri, a mayoral appointment. Mr. Price frequently writes and speaks on environmental law issues before a wide range of audiences. He received his undergraduate degree from the University of Missouri–Columbia and his law degree with honors from Harvard Law School.

Susan J. Sadler is a member with the law firm of Dawda, Mann, Mulcahy & Sadler in Bloomfield Hills, Michigan. Her practice includes providing environmental counsel to clients seeking air, waste, and water permits. She has counseled corporations and individuals on the implications of environmental law in their real estate and business transactions and has defended corporations in enforcement actions brought by government agencies. Ms. Sadler received her undergraduate degree from Albion College and her law degree from the College of Law at the University of Toledo.

Michael T. Scanlon is an associate in Barnes & Thornburg's Indianapolis office, where he concentrates his practice in environmental law. Mr. Scanlon also represents clients regarding OSHA compliance issues. Before joining Barnes & Thornburg, he served as the environmental services director for Ulrich Chemical in Indianapolis and worked for the State of Indiana's Department of Environmental Management and the Air Pollution Control Division of the City of Indianapolis. Mr. Scanlon also has served as an adjunct instructor at the School of Public and Environmental

Affairs, Indiana University–Purdue University at Indianapolis, where he taught a course in hazardous materials regulation. He earned his B.S. degree in natural resources with high honors from Ball State University, his master of public affairs degree from Indiana University at Indianapolis, and his J.D. with highest honors from Indiana University School of Law–Indianapolis, where he was an associate editor of the *Indiana Law Review*.

Steven E. Silverman is an attorney with the Environmental Protection Agency in Washington, D.C. As one of EPA's senior counsel on RCRA matters, he helped develop all of the land disposal restriction regulations and represented EPA in all of the major cases involving the land disposal restrictions. Mr. Silverman's work also encompasses matters under the Clean Air Act. Mr. Silverman has three times received EPA's Gold Medal for Superior Service, the agency's highest award. He earned his undergraduate and law degrees from the University of Michigan.

Daniel H. Squire is a partner with Wilmer, Cutler & Pickering in Washington, D.C., where he has represented clients in complicated CERCLA private cost recovery litigation involving issues of lender liability, successor liability, and corporate officer indemnification. Mr. Squire has focused special attention on the treatment of environmental liabilities in bankruptcy. He received his B.A. from Yale University and his J.D. from Harvard Law School.

Michael W. Steinberg is special counsel at Morgan, Lewis & Bockius in Washington, D.C., where he practices exclusively in the field of environmental law, with special emphasis on litigation and counseling regarding RCRA hazardous waste, Superfund, and environmental justice matters. He was formerly assistant chief of the Environmental Defense Section at the U.S. Department of Justice. Mr. Steinberg received his B.A. from Yale University and his J.D. from the University of Pennsylvania Law School. He clerked for the late Judge Alfred L. Luongo, U.S. District Court for the Eastern District of Pennsylvania.

Robert F. Wilkinson is a member of the Environmental & Regulatory Practice Group in the St. Louis, Missouri, office of Husch & Eppenberger. His practice includes environmental compliance, permitting, and enforcement defense. He has extensive experience with air and hazardous waste compliance and has represented clients on wetlands, water, toxic substances (including PCBs), and other issues. Mr. Wilkinson has also represented clients in connection with complex corporate transactions (acquisitions, mergers, and divestitures) and has advised clients on remediation issues. He has represented clients before a number of state regulatory agencies, EPA regional offices, and EPA headquarters. He also has spoken and written on various regulatory issues and has been active in various industry groups and rule-making advocacy efforts. Mr. Wilkinson was formerly an environmental attorney for Monsanto Company, where he had responsibility for air pollution compliance issues and boiler and industrial furnace regulation compliance.

Kenneth D. Woodrow is a trial lawyer in the National Courts Section of the Civil Division of the United States Department of Justice. He joined the Department in May 2003 from the firm of Morgan, Lewis & Bockius LLP in Washington, D.C., where he was an of counsel in the Environmental Law Section of the Litigation Group. Previously, he was a partner in the Washington, D.C., office of Baker & Hosetler LLP, where his practice focused on environmental litigation. Mr. Woodrow received his B.A. from the University of Virginia and his J.D. from Washington & Lee University School of Law.

CHAPTER 1

An Overview of RCRA

THEODORE L. GARRETT

I. Introduction

The Resource Conservation and Recovery Act (RCRA)[1] establishes a cradle-to-grave program regulating the management of hazardous wastes. Directed by the Environmental Protection Agency (EPA) and implemented in significant part by the various states, the program imposes comprehensive obligations and carries significant sanctions for noncompliance. The RCRA program identifies a broad universe of waste materials as hazardous and regulates the handling of these wastes by generators, transporters, and treatment, storage, and disposal facilities. In addition, RCRA imposes corrective action requirements and provides standards for cleanup under the Superfund statute. Unlike the Superfund statute,[2] which focuses on remedying past waste disposal at abandoned sites, RCRA addresses the ongoing management of hazardous wastes at manufacturing plants and other facilities, thus affecting a large segment of businesses engaged in manufacturing.

RCRA was originally enacted in 1976 as amendments to the Solid Waste Disposal Act.[3] Four years later, EPA published its first RCRA regulations for the regulation of hazardous wastes.[4] These regulations, which filled approximately 200 pages in the *Code of Federal Regulations*,

---

[1]42 U.S.C. § 6901 *et seq.*
[2]*Id.* § 9601 *et seq.*
[3]Pub. L. No. 94-580, 90 Stat. 2395.
[4]45 Fed. Reg. 12,722, 33,066 (1980).

2 THE RCRA PRACTICE MANUAL

have, in the 1993 edition, grown to occupy more than 1,000 pages.[5] This vigorous program of RCRA regulation resulted from increased public and congressional concern with hazardous waste beginning with the Love Canal episode, which also led to the passage of the Superfund law in 1980.

In 1984 Congress amended RCRA extensively in the Hazardous and Solid Waste Amendments of 1984 (HSWA).[6] The HSWA authorized the regulation of underground tanks, the cleanup of contaminated areas of industrial sites not covered by the original law, and increased restrictions on the disposal of wastes on land. The amendments contain detailed provisions and establish strict deadlines.

Today RCRA is being implemented primarily at the state level, although some states are not fully authorized to implement RCRA, and EPA has reserved the (controversial) right to overfile enforcement actions even where an authorized state has taken enforcement action.

This chapter is an overview of the principal features of RCRA. Most of the topics discussed here are treated at length in subsequent chapters. You may also wish to check EPA's Web site for developments: http://www.epa.gov.epaoswer.

II. Definition of Hazardous Waste

Subtitle C of RCRA, which regulates hazardous wastes, applies only to "solid waste" that is "hazardous." Although these concepts lie at the core of the statute, they remain difficult and controversial, and they are more fully discussed in Chapters 3 and 4 of this book. The EPA rules have been the subject of litigation, so they must be read in light of several decisions of the D.C. Circuit.

The first step is to determine whether a waste is a solid waste. Under RCRA, solid waste is any garbage, refuse, sludge, or other discarded material, including solid, liquid, or gaseous material that is contained.[7] Although it is clear that a solid waste need not be solid in the conventional sense, it is less clear when a waste is considered discarded. As a result, there has been a good deal of debate on the extent to which secondary materials that are reused or recycled are covered. In 1985 EPA published a detailed rule and regulatory preamble explaining its definition of solid waste.[8] The definition includes secondary materials that are

---

[5]40 C.F.R. §§ 260–281 (1993).
[6]Pub. L. No. 98-616, 98 Stat. 3221.
[7]42 U.S.C. § 6903(27).
[8]50 Fed. Reg. 641 (1985).

Chapter 1: An Overview of RCRA 3

incinerated for energy recovery and disposed of on the ground.[9] The definitions include fine distinctions among types of materials (sludges, by-products) and types of activities (reclamation, reuse, and disposal) and must be reviewed with care.[10] These issues are discussed in Chapter 3.

There are two principal exclusions from the definition of solid waste. The first is industrial wastewater discharges subject to the Clean Water Act permit program, namely mixtures of industrial wastes and domestic sewage that pass through a sewer system to a publicly owned treatment works.[11] The second exemption covers certain recycled materials, such as secondary materials that are returned to the original process and reused.[12]

Once a waste is determined to be a solid waste, the next consideration becomes whether that waste is "hazardous." There are basically two ways in which a waste can fall into this category: (1) the waste exhibits one of four characteristics (ignitability, corrosivity, reactivity, or toxicity), or (2) the waste is specifically listed by EPA as hazardous in the *Code of Federal Regulations*.[13] EPA has implemented this provision of the statute by promulgating four tests for so-called characteristic wastes.[14] The toxicity characteristic, probably the most frequently used, subjects a waste to a procedure (the Toxicity Characteristic Leaching Procedure) that is intended to simulate the leaching that would occur at a municipal landfill.[15]

EPA has also listed several hundred hazardous wastes in three categories: those from nonspecified sources (F-listed), those from specific industrial processes (K-listed), and commercial chemical products and pesticides when discarded or spilled (P and U wastes).[16] Household wastes and agricultural wastes used for fertilizers are exempt.[17] Congress also exempted mining and certain other wastes pending further study by EPA.[18] The agency has decided not to regulate oil and gas industry exploration and production wastes and mineral extraction and beneficiation and certain mineral processing under RCRA Subtitle C.[19]

---

[9]40 C.F.R. §§ 261.2, 261.4.

[10]*See also* Am. Mining Cong. v. EPA, 824 F.2d 1177 (D.C. Cir. 1987) and 907 F.2d 1179 (D.C. Cir. 1990); Am. Petroleum Inst. v. EPA, 906 F.2d 729 (D.C. Cir. 1990); Ass'n of Battery Recyclers v. EPA, 208 F.3d 1047 (D.C. Cir. 2000); Am. Petroleum Inst. v. EPA, 216 F.3d 50 (D.C. Cir. 2000).

[11]40 C.F.R. § 261.4(a)(1).

[12]*Id.* §§ 261.2(e), 261.4(a)(8).

[13]42 U.S.C. § 6921(b).

[14]40 C.F.R. §§ 261.21–.24.

[15]55 Fed. Reg. 11,798 (1990); 40 C.F.R. pt. 261, app. II.

[16]40 C.F.R. §§ 261.31–.33.

[17]*Id.* § 261.4(b)(1), (2).

[18]42 U.S.C. § 6921(b)(2), (3).

[19]53 Fed. Reg. 25,446 (1988); 51 Fed. Reg. 24,496 (1986).

4 THE RCRA PRACTICE MANUAL

Wastes currently listed by EPA as hazardous may be removed by requesting "delisting," which is accomplished in a special rule-making proceeding.[20]

EPA's rules have a catch-22 aspect in the form of the so-called mixture and derived-from rules. A waste that is not listed is hazardous only if its properties fall under one of the four characteristics. However, under EPA's mixture rule, any solid waste that is mixed with a listed hazardous waste remains a hazardous waste no matter what is done to treat it or reduce its concentration.[21] In addition, EPA rules provide that any waste resulting from the treatment, storage, or disposal of any listed waste is a hazardous waste.[22] These long-standing rules were invalidated on procedural grounds in *Shell Oil Co. v. EPA*.[23] EPA's rules were reinstated pending further rule making. EPA issued its final rule in May 2001.[24] These regulations, which are discussed in more detail in Chapter 4, retain the mixture and derived-from rules with certain clarifications and changes.

III. Obligations of Generators

Generators of hazardous waste must notify EPA of the initiation of hazardous waste activities, obtain an EPA identification number, and properly store hazardous wastes. Wastes must be properly labeled and must be in proper containers for shipment pursuant to Department of Transportation requirements.[25] Generators must use a manifest to track hazardous waste shipments, and the manifest must designate a facility as the shipment's final destination.[26] In addition, generators are required to maintain records and submit biennial reports that summarize their waste generation activities. The regulations in 40 C.F.R. part 262 describe the responsibilities of generators of hazardous waste and are discussed in detail in Chapter 5.

The rules provide a "small generator" exemption to reduce the burden on small businesses or facilities handling small quantities of hazardous wastes.[27] Generators that produce no more than 100 kilograms of

---

[20]42 U.S.C. § 6921(f); 40 C.F.R. §§ 260.20, 260.22.

[21]40 C.F.R. § 261.3(a)(2)(iv).

[22]45 Fed. Reg. 33,096 (1980).

[23]950 F.2d 741 (D.C. Cir. 1991).

[24]66 Fed. Reg. 50,532 (2001).

[25]40 C.F.R. §§ 262.30–.33.

[26]*Id.* §§ 262.20–.23.

[27]42 U.S.C. § 6921(d).

hazardous waste per month are exempt from most of the RCRA require-ments for generators.[28] Generators producing no more than 1,000 kilo-grams of hazardous waste per month may accumulate wastes for 180 days and are eligible for certain exemptions, but they must comply with most of the requirements for generators.[29]

Generators may accumulate wastes on site for 90 days without being subject to all of the requirements for treatment, storage, and dis-posal facilities. They must, however, comply with specific requirements, namely, that they store the waste in tanks or containers that meet RCRA standards, that they clearly label the waste as hazardous, and that they note the date when accumulation begins.[30]

Another important provision allows for "satellite" accumulation of 55 gallons or less of any hazardous waste at or near the point of genera-tion. Once the 55-gallon limit is reached, the waste must be moved to the 90-day temporary accumulation area.[31] Generators are also expected to develop programs to minimize the generation of hazardous wastes.[32] EPA has encouraged companies to engage in source reduction and recy-cling in order to minimize wastes, and has asked companies to report on such efforts in their biennial reports.

IV. Transport of Hazardous Waste

Transportation of hazardous waste is governed by EPA as well as by Department of Transportation (DOT) regulations.[33] Transporters must comply with the EPA regulations in 40 C.F.R. part 263, which require that they obtain EPA identification numbers, use proper containers, and implement the hazardous waste manifest system by ensuring that the manifest accompanies the waste to its next point of delivery.[34] In addi-tion, transporters are required to retain records for three years.

A transporter is exempt from the RCRA requirements with respect to storage of hazardous waste, providing that the waste is properly packaged and the storage does not exceed ten days.[35]

---

[28]40 C.F.R. § 261.5(b), (g).
[29]*Id.* §§ 262.34(d), 262.44.
[30]*Id.* § 262.34(a).
[31]*Id.* § 262.34(c).
[32]42 U.S.C. § 6922(b).
[33]*Id.* § 6922(a).
[34]40 C.F.R. § 263.20.
[35]*Id.* § 263.12.

6 THE RCRA PRACTICE MANUAL

Transportation of hazardous wastes on-site at an industrial facility is exempt from RCRA's standards for transporters.[36] The regulations define the scope of the site for purposes of this exemption. They include contiguous properties divided by public or private rights of way.

If a discharge of hazardous waste occurs during transport, the shipper must notify the EPA National Response Center and must take appropriate action to protect human health and the environment, including cleanup of the discharge.[37]

Transporters are extensively regulated by DOT under the Hazardous Materials Transportation Act (HTMA).[38] The DOT regulations applicable to transportation of hazardous waste are contained in 49 C.F.R. part 171 and are discussed in Chapter 6.

V. Treatment, Storage, and Disposal

Unless otherwise exempt, all facilities that treat, store, or dispose of hazardous wastes must obtain a permit.[39] To allow for an orderly permitting process, Congress granted "interim status" to facilities that were operating when EPA's regulations took effect in 1980, provided that the facilities notify EPA and comply with the applicable EPA standards.[40] The statute allows EPA to delegate permitting and enforcement responsibilities to the states, and more than 40 states have such authority.[41] Because EPA has reserved authority to enforce RCRA requirements and because many new requirements have not been incorporated in state programs, EPA retains much authority in this area. A more detailed discussion of RCRA's permit requirements may be found in Chapter 7.

Treatment, storage, and disposal facilities (TSDFs) are subject to several types of operating and design standards: general facility standards, closure and postclosure care standards, and unit-specific standards.[42] These standards, contained in 40 C.F.R. part 264 (permitted facilities) and part 265 (interim status facilities), are discussed more fully in Chapter 8. The general standards require that each TSDF obtain an identification number, obtain or conduct waste analyses, implement security measures, schedule regular inspections, and provide personnel training.[43]

---

[36]*Id.* § 263.10(b).
[37]*Id.* § 263.30–.31.
[38]49 U.S.C. § 1801 *et seq.*
[39]42 U.S.C. § 6925.
[40]*Id.* § 6925(e).
[41]*Id.* § 6926(b).
[42]*Id.* § 6924(a).
[43]40 C.F.R. § 265.11–.16.

Chapter 1: An Overview of RCRA 7

The TSDF must also take special precautions in handling ignitable, reactive, and otherwise incompatible waste and may not locate facilities in floodplains or near seismic faults.[44] TSDFs must implement preparedness and prevention measures to minimize nonsudden releases, and these facilities must comply with various record-keeping requirements. Finally, land disposal units must implement a groundwater-monitoring program, which varies depending on whether the facility is under interim status or is permitted.[45] If groundwater protection levels are exceeded, corrective action may be required.[46] A more detailed discussion of RCRA's treatment, storage, and disposal requirements is contained in Chapter 8.

RCRA's closure, postclosure, and financial responsibility regulations are intended to secure a TSDF so that it does not pose a significant threat of a release. Each facility must have a written closure plan that identifies how each unit will be closed to satisfy EPA standards, including procedures for removing contaminated soil, cleaning equipment, and performing necessary sampling and analysis.[47] Land disposal facilities must develop postclosure care plans where hazardous wastes or constituents are left in place after closure.[48] The plans must provide for continued groundwater monitoring and maintenance of the integrity of any cap or cover for a period of up to 30 years.[49]

The financial assurance regulations require that each TSDF demonstrate its financial ability to meet closure and postclosure obligations as well as third-party liability.[50] The rules allow TSDFs several means to demonstrate financial ability, including self-insurance, insurance policies, surety bonds, and parent company guarantees.[51] Self-insurance is generally the preferred route, and the rules should be reviewed with care. For a more detailed treatment of RCRA's closure, postclosure, and financial responsibility regulations, see Chapter 9.

In addition to the general requirements outlined above, EPA has established specific standards for containers, tanks, land disposal facilities, miscellaneous units, incinerators, furnaces, and boilers. The standards are generally quite complex and detailed, and must be reviewed in detail; they are described more fully in Chapter 10. The standards for permitted container storage areas require containment systems, timely

---

[44]*Id.* §§ 265.17–.18.
[45]*Id.* §§ 265.90–.91.
[46]*Id.* § 264.100.
[47]*Id.* §§ 264.112, 265.112.
[48]*Id.* §§ 264.110(b), 265.110(b).
[49]*Id.* §§ 264.117, 265.117.
[50]*Id.* pts. 264, 265, subpt. H.
[51]*Id.* §§ 264.143–.145, 265.143–.145.

removal of spills, and removal of waste upon closure.[52] Similarly, permitted tank systems used to manage hazardous waste must have secondary containment systems and leak detection.[53] The rules contain detailed design requirements, rules governing maintenance and operation, and rules governing closure.[54]

EPA requires that incinerators demonstrate an ability to meet a destruction efficiency of 99.99 percent of the principal organic hazardous constituent identified in the permit. Incinerators must also achieve standards for other parameters, such as carbon monoxide and fugitive emissions, and are subject to inspection and maintenance requirements.[55] Boilers and industrial furnaces that burn hazardous waste are regulated separately.[56] In addition, there are certain exemptions for boilers and furnaces used for specific purposes, such as smelting furnaces and small-quantity burners.

HSWA directed the EPA to develop regulations establishing technical design standards (minimum technology requirements) for land disposal units.[57] Landfills generally must have double liners, a leachate collection system, and groundwater monitoring.[58] Bulk or free-liquid containing wastes may not be placed in a landfill. After closure, the owner or operator must conduct postclosure care for a period specified in the permit. Surface impoundments, including lagoons and ponds, also are subject to detailed regulations.[59] The regulations require double liners and leachate collection systems. For surface impoundments, groundwater monitoring also must be conducted. Land disposal facilities are discussed in greater detail in Chapter 11.

In the 1984 HSWA legislation, Congress directed that wastes not be disposed of on land unless they are treated to meet standards promulgated by EPA.[60] This provision is known as the "land ban" because it would prohibit all land disposal if EPA were to fail to meet the statutory dates for promulgating treatment standards. After treatment to best-demonstrated available technology (BDAT), waste can be disposed of in land disposal units meeting applicable requirements.[61] The BDAT standards have been the subject of considerable controversy, with litiga-

---

[52]*Id.* § 264.175.
[53]*Id.* §§ 264.191–.196, 265.191–.196.
[54]*Id.* §§ 264.193–.194, 264.197.
[55]*Id.* §§ 264.343–.347.
[56]42 U.S.C. § 6924(q)(1); 40 C.F.R. § 266.100.
[57]42 U.S.C. §§ 6924(o), 6925(j).
[58]40 C.F.R. §§ 264.301, 265.301.
[59]*Id.* §§ 264.220, 266.220.
[60]42 U.S.C. § 6924(d), (e)(1), (g)(5).
[61]*Id.* § 6924(m), (o).

tion centering on the level of control and the point at which treatment must cease.[62] Since the first edition of this book, Congress has clarified that LDRs do not apply to characteristic wastes that are decharacterized before disposal and then managed in certain land-based treatment systems. EPA developed universal treatment standards in 1994. The agency has also promulgated rules attempting to minimize disincentives to active remediation. These rules include treatment variances and alternative standards for contaminated soils. EPA in 1993 promulgated rules for corrective action management units (CAMUs) for on-site treatment, storage, and disposal of hazardous wastes managed for implementing cleanup, but the agency later tightened these rules in a manner that limits the utility of CAMUs. The land disposal restrictions are discussed in detail in Chapter 12.

The land disposal standards are subject to several exceptions. EPA has authority to grant national capacity variances based on a finding that there is insufficient alternative protective treatment, recovery, or disposal capacity for the wastes.[63] This provision has been used in a number of cases. EPA may also grant one-year extensions, renewable for another year, of a prohibition effective date. Surface impoundments are subject to special provisions.[64] Untreated wastes may be placed in surface impoundments provided that the impoundments meet the technology requirements and sludges are removed within one year.[65] Finally, wastes may be placed without treatment in a "no migration" unit, typically an underground injection well, based on a showing to EPA that there will be no migration of hazardous constituents.[66]

VI. Corrective Action

Before the enactment of HSWA, corrective action had fairly limited scope under RCRA. EPA had authority under RCRA Section 7003 to require persons to take action necessary to address an "imminent and substantial endangerment to health or the environment."[67] Although this provision was used in some early cases to address past contamination at abandoned landfills, its use at such sites was limited once the Superfund statute was enacted in 1980.

---

[62]55 Fed. Reg. 22,520 (1990); *See* Chem. Waste Mgmt. v. EPA, 976 F.2d 2 (D.C. Cir. 1992).
[63]42 U.S.C. § 6924(h)(2).
[64]*Id.* § 6925 (j)(11).
[65]40 C.F.R. § 268.4.
[66]*Id.* § 268.6.
[67]42 U.S.C. § 6973.

10 THE RCRA PRACTICE MANUAL

HSWA dramatically changed the thrust of RCRA in 1984 by adding three important new provisions. Section 3004(u) of RCRA allows EPA to require corrective action for releases from solid waste management units for any person seeking a RCRA permit after 1984, regardless of when the waste was placed in the unit.[68] Section 3004(v) authorizes EPA to require corrective action beyond the boundary of a TSDF where necessary to protect human health and the environment.[69] In addition, Section 3008(h) authorizes EPA to require corrective action for interim-status facilities.[70] These provisions have enormous financial and practical implications for industry that may overshadow the Superfund program. Corrective action is discussed further in Chapter 13.

Sections 3004(u) and 3008(h) apply to facilities that must obtain a RCRA permit or interim status. Thus generators, transporters, and persons accumulating wastes for no more than 90 days are not subject to corrective action. On the other hand, where there is ongoing waste management at a facility, EPA has interpreted the statute to require corrective action anywhere within the contiguous plant boundary.[71]

In July 1990, EPA published a proposed corrective-action rule.[72] This rule proposes the concept of a conditional remedy that allows on-site contamination not meeting cleanup levels to remain provided that certain conditions are met. EPA's proposal sets forth cleanup goals and standards in the form of "action" or trigger levels and "target" or media protection standards. These levels are generally based on promulgated health and environmental standards. EPA has not yet promulgated final regulations. This rule was never finalized; instead, it was withdrawn in October 1999.[73] EPA's 1999 announcement stated that the agency intends to implement issues addressed in the proposal as guidance.

Companies conducting corrective action often must manage contaminated soil and other residues as hazardous waste. EPA is developing a rule that may exempt many such remedial residues from hazardous waste status. Otherwise, the treatment of such remedial residues can be subject to hazardous waste permitting and their redisposal may invoke land disposal restrictions. In May 1998, EPA issued RCRA land disposal treatment standards for contaminated soils.[74] In early 1993, EPA promulgated a rule setting forth the concept of a "corrective action management

---

[68]*Id.* § 6924(u).

[69]*Id.* § 6924(v).

[70]*Id.* § 6928(h).

[71]United Techs. Corp. v. EPA, 821 F.2d 714 (D.C. Cir. 1987).

[72]55 Fed. Reg. 30,798 (1990).

[73]64 Fed. Reg. 54,604 (1999).

[74]63 Fed. Reg. 28,556 (1998).

unit" (CAMU) that allows remediation wastes to be managed without triggering land disposal or minimum technology restrictions.[75] CAMUs will be established by Section 3004(u) permits or Section 3008(h) orders. As noted above, in December 2002, EPA's administrator signed a rule establishing a new framework for wastes placed in corrective action management units. EPA is considering additional approaches that will facilitate and encourage voluntary corrective action.

VII. Underground Storage Tanks

The 1984 Hazardous and Solid Waste Amendments established a comprehensive program for regulating underground storage tanks (USTs) in Subtitle I of RCRA. The statute regulates tanks containing regulated substances such as petroleum products and hazardous substances under the Comprehensive Environmental Response, Compensation, and Liability Act (CERCLA) but excluding hazardous wastes under RCRA.[76] EPA defines an underground tank as a tank or series of tanks and connected piping in which the volume of regulated substances is 10 percent or more beneath the surface of the ground.[77] States with approved programs may implement and enforce the UST standards.[78]

Each owner of a UST was required to notify the appropriate agency of the existence, location, type, and uses of its tank within 18 months of HSWA's enactment.[79] Under the statute and EPA regulations, owners of USTs are required to construct them to maintain structural integrity, install leak detection systems, report releases of regulated substances, take corrective action for releases, and demonstrate financial responsibility.[80] The requirements vary depending on whether the tank is new or old and whether the tank contains petroleum or hazardous substances. A more extensive discussion of these requirements appears in Chapter 14.

The statute contains several exemptions. These include farm or residential tanks of 1,100 gallons or less for storing motor fuel, tanks used to store heating oil for consumptive use on the premises where stored, pipeline tanks regulated under federal laws, surface impoundments, and storage tanks in an underground area such as a basement that are above the surface of the floor.[81]

---

[75]58 Fed. Reg. 8658 (1993); 40 C.F.R. § 260.10.

[76]42 U.S.C. § 6991.

[77]*Id.* § 6991(1); 40 C.F.R. § 280.12.

[78]40 C.F.R. § 281.10 *et seq.*

[79]42 U.S.C. § 6991(a)(2).

[80]*Id.* § 6991(b); 40 C.F.R. pt. 280.

[81]42 U.S.C. § 6991(1).

12 THE RCRA PRACTICE MANUAL

EPA estimates that the UST program affects more than 2 million tanks used for petroleum products and 0.5 million tanks used for hazardous substances as defined by the Superfund law. The UST regulations affect most manufacturing facilities, and environmental counsel and managers should be familiar with them.

VIII. Disposal of Nonhazardous Waste

Although hazardous wastes have been the primary focus of RCRA, nonhazardous wastes are addressed to a more limited extent in Subtitle D. The statute directs states to develop solid waste management plans and to eliminate the open dumping of solid waste.[82] EPA has published criteria for classifying design criteria and practices that constitute open dumping.[83] Landfills that do not meet these criteria are banned.[84] For a detailed discussion of nonhazardous waste regulation, see Chapter 15.

In 1984 HSWA required EPA to examine whether the previously published Subtitle D criteria were sufficient to protect groundwater.[85] In 1991 EPA published new criteria for landfills receiving municipal solid waste.[86] When RCRA is reauthorized, Congress can be expected to consider ways to strengthen and increase the federal role in the Subtitle D program.

RCRA specifies several kinds of nonhazardous wastes for special regulation. These include medical wastes, used oil, and sewage sludge. Medical wastes are regulated under Subtitle J of RCRA,[87] which requires record keeping and manifesting. EPA does not treat used oil as a hazardous waste.[88] However, the agency has promulgated regulations applicable to generators, transporters, and processors of used oil.[89] Sewage sludge is regulated under Section 405 of the Clean Water Act.[90] EPA has published detailed regulations for the use and disposal of sewage sludge.[91]

---

[82]*Id.* § 6943.
[83]40 C.F.R. pt. 257.
[84]42 U.S.C. § 6945(a).
[85]*Id.* § 6949(a).
[86]40 C.F.R. pt. 258.
[87]42 U.S.C. § 6992 *et seq.*
[88]57 Fed. Reg. 21,524 (1992).
[89]40 C.F.R. pt. 279, subpts. C, E, F.
[90]33 U.S.C. § 1345.
[91]58 Fed. Reg. 9248 (1992); 40 C.F.R. pts. 257, 403, 503.

IX. Conclusion

RCRA has emerged as one of the most complex areas of environmental law. In the past 27 years, Congress has made the statute more comprehensive, and EPA has issued hundreds of major regulations. As EPA continues to amend the rules and issue new rules and guidance documents, tracking down the regulatory preambles that explain various related provisions and EPA guidance has become increasingly challenging. In addition, there are hundreds of unpublished informal EPA interpretations and policy documents, which are described in SONREEL's *RCRA Policy Documents: Finding Your Way through the Maze of EPA Guidance on Solid and Hazardous Waste,* published in 1993.

Our goal in publishing this manual is to make RCRA more comprehensible to the practitioner. The chapters that follow were prepared by experts in the field to give lawyers and environmental managers insights into the meaning and implications of the law. It is important to keep in mind, however, that this area of law continues to change, and practitioners must keep up-to-date with changes in the statute and with EPA and state regulations and policies.

CHAPTER 2

RCRA's Relationship to Other Laws

DANIEL H. SQUIRE

I. Overview of RCRA Jurisdiction

As complex as the Resource Conservation and Recovery Act (RCRA) and its regulations are, a complete understanding of the RCRA scheme requires reference to the other federal environmental statutes as well. Three basic types of industrial discharges are addressed by the three major federal statutes imposing environmental regulation: water discharges, covered by the Federal Water Pollution Control Act (the Clean Water Act);[1] air emissions, covered by the Clean Air Act;[2] and waste disposal, covered by the Solid Waste Disposal Act, as amended by RCRA.

The regulatory regimes under RCRA and these other two statutes are not mutually exclusive. Some wastes may be subject to the jurisdiction of both RCRA and either the Clean Water Act or Clean Air Act. In particular, there is no statutory provision that automatically exempts from RCRA all wastes associated with or resulting from water discharges covered by the Clean Water Act or from air emissions covered by the Clean Air Act. Consider in this connection the very definition of "solid waste" under RCRA, which means

> any garbage, refuse, *sludge from a waste treatment plant, water supply treatment plant, or air pollution control facility* and other discarded

---

[1]33 U.S.C. § 1251 *et seq.*
[2]42 U.S.C. § 7401 *et seq.*

16 THE RCRA PRACTICE MANUAL

material, including solid, *liquid*, semisolid, *or contained gaseous material* resulting from industrial, commercial, mining and agricultural operations, . . .[3]

Conversely, there is no statutory provision that exempts RCRA wastes from the Clean Water Act (if they result in water discharges) or the Clean Air Act (if they cause air emissions).

There also is overlap between RCRA and some of the "lesser" environmental regulatory statutes, including the Safe Drinking Water Act (SDWA),[4] the Toxic Substances Control Act (TSCA),[5] and the Hazardous Materials Transportation Act.[6]

Equally important, there is substantial overlap between RCRA and the primary federal cleanup statute, the Comprehensive Environmental Response, Compensation, and Liability Act (CERCLA or Superfund).[7] The definition of "hazardous substance" under CERCLA includes, but is much broader than, the definition of "hazardous waste" under RCRA. One effect of these overlapping definitions is that all sites subject to corrective action under RCRA could be subject alternatively to response action under CERCLA. Although the processes for addressing sites under RCRA and CERCLA are similar, the decision to proceed under one statute or the other can have important practical consequences. Even in CERCLA cleanups, however, RCRA standards—including land disposal restrictions—are often applied.

Notwithstanding (or, perhaps, because of) the overlapping jurisdiction of these federal statutes, a provision in RCRA requires the Environmental Protection Agency (EPA) to integrate that law with other regulatory statutes "for purposes of administration and enforcement" and to "avoid duplication."[8] As described below, EPA has adopted a number of approaches through regulations and other policies to place primary regulatory responsibility for a particular waste management activity under one regulatory program or another.

Apart from these integration concerns, EPA considers the cross-media impacts of new regulations under RCRA to assess their overall impact on the environment. For example, when EPA promulgated its land disposal restrictions, the agency analyzed their impact on a host of environmental programs, including the Clean Water Act; the Marine

---

[3]*Id.* § 6903(27) (emphasis added).
[4]*Id.* § 300(f) *et seq.*
[5]15 U.S.C. § 2601 *et seq.*
[6]49 U.S.C. § 1801 *et seq.*
[7]42 U.S.C. § 9601 *et seq.*
[8]*Id.* § 6905(b).

Protection, Research, and Sanctuaries Act,[9] the Safe Drinking Water Act; the Clean Air Act; CERCLA; the Federal Insecticide, Fungicide, and Rodenticide Act (FIFRA),[10] and TSCA.[11] Among EPA's specific concerns were that new treatment requirements for hazardous waste prior to land disposal would generate additional air emissions from the treatment process and might create incentives to discharge wastewaters to publicly owned treatment works in order to avoid direct treatment costs.

The balance of this chapter is devoted to a more detailed discussion of the relation between RCRA and other federal regulatory statutes, and a comparison of the federal cleanup programs established under RCRA and CERCLA.

II. RCRA's Relation to Other Regulatory Statutes

A. RCRA and the Clean Water Act

The Clean Water Act regulates the discharge of pollutants into surface waters and publicly owned treatment works (POTWs). Industrial facilities that discharge pollutants directly into surface waters must obtain and comply with a permit issued pursuant to Section 402 of the Clean Water Act, which sets facility-specific pollutant discharge limits. Industrial facilities that discharge wastewaters into a POTW must comply with pretreatment standards established under Section 307(b) of the Clean Water Act, as well as with local permit limits set by the POTW regulatory authority.

RCRA intersects with the Clean Water Act in at least three ways. First, certain wastewater streams that are subject to regulation under the Clean Water Act are excluded from regulation under RCRA. In particular, "domestic sewage" and "industrial discharges which are subject to permits" issued under Section 402 of the Clean Water Act are excluded from the definition of "solid waste" for purposes of RCRA.[12] EPA's implementing regulations take these definitions one step further by providing that the domestic sewage exclusion covers "[a]ny mixture of domestic sewage and other wastes that passes through a sewer system to a publicly-owned treatment works for treatment."[13] EPA exempted these mixtures from regulation under RCRA because it determined that

---

[9]33 U.S.C. § 1401 *et seq.*

[10]7 U.S.C. § 136 *et seq.*

[11]55 Fed. Reg. 22,520, 22,676–78 (1990).

[12]42 U.S.C. § 6903(27).

[13]40 C.F.R. § 261.4(a)(1)(ii).

once the waste enters the sewer system, it is adequately regulated under the Clean Water Act.[14]

This is not true, however, before the wastewater is discharged to the sewer system, and the regulations emphasize that the industrial discharge exclusion "applies only to the actual point source discharge. It does not exclude industrial wastewaters while they are being collected, stored, or treated before discharge. . . ."[15] As EPA explained:

> The obvious purpose of the industrial point source discharge exclusion in Section 1004(27) [of RCRA] was to avoid duplicative regulation of point source discharges under RCRA and the Clean Water Act. . . . These considerations do not apply to industrial wastewaters prior to discharge since most of the environmental hazards posed by wastewaters in treatment and holding facilities—primarily groundwater contamination—cannot be controlled under the Clean Water Act or other EPA statutes.[16]

Thus, before they qualify for the Clean Water Act domestic sewage or Section 402 permit exclusion, hazardous wastes in the form of industrial wastewaters are subject to regulation under Subtitle C of RCRA. Such wastewaters include those that are specifically listed as hazardous wastes (for example, hazardous waste code F032)[17] and those that exhibit a hazardous waste characteristic (for example, a D002 corrosive solution).

A second intersection between RCRA and the Clean Water Act involves the status under RCRA of certain wastewater treatment systems that are already regulated under the Clean Water Act. To comply with Sections 402 and 307(b) of the Clean Water Act, most industrial facilities have to treat their wastewaters in some way before discharging them to surface water or a POTW. If the wastewater being treated is a hazardous waste, the permit and related requirements that apply to hazardous waste treatment facilities under RCRA might be expected to apply. However, the RCRA regulations exempt owners or operators of certain types of "wastewater treatment units" from these requirements.[18] For purposes of the exemption, the term "wastewater treatment unit" is defined to include any *tank* or *tank system* (as defined by RCRA) that (1) is "part of a waste-water treatment facility . . . subject to regulation under either section 402 or 307(b) of the Clean Water Act . . ." and

---

[14]45 Fed. Reg. 33,084, 33,097 (1980).
[15]40 C.F.R. § 261.4(a)(2) comment.
[16]45 Fed. Reg. 33,098.
[17]40 C.F.R. § 261.31.
[18]*Id.* §§ 264.1(g)(6), 270.1(c)(2)(v).

(2) treats or stores hazardous waste influent, or produces, treats, or stores hazardous waste sludge.[19] Other wastewater treatment units, notably surface impoundments, remain subject to the full panoply of RCRA permit and related treatment facility requirements if the waste streams being treated are hazardous wastes.

A third intersection between RCRA and the Clean Water Act involves the RCRA land disposal restrictions program (LDR). This program generally prohibits land disposal of hazardous waste, unless the waste has been treated so as to "substantially diminish the toxicity of the waste or substantially reduce the likelihood of migration of hazardous constituents from the waste so that short-term and long-term threats to human health and the environment are minimized."[20] This statutory criterion is embodied in treatment standards promulgated by EPA. Under the LDR regulations, dilution is generally prohibited as a method of meeting these treatment standards. However, because placement of wastes in surface impoundments constitutes "land disposal," EPA predicted that full compliance with the antidilution provision "would create significant regulatory disruption" for facilities that treat wastewaters in surface impoundments before discharge in compliance with the Clean Water Act requirements.[21]

To minimize the potential disruption, EPA modified the antidilution rule in the case of characteristically hazardous wastewaters for which a particular method has not been specified as the treatment standard under the LDR program. Under the modified rule, such wastewaters could be aggregated and diluted in tanks to remove the hazard characteristic before the "decharacterized" wastewater is placed in a surface impoundment for further treatment as part of an integrated Clean Water Act wastewater treatment train.[22]

This modification of the antidilution rule was challenged by certain treatment industry and environmental groups as being inconsistent with the statutory LDR requirements. In *Chemical Waste Management, Inc. v. EPA*,[23] the D.C. Circuit acknowledged the need to "accommodate" the RCRA and the Clean Water Act regulatory programs, and held that allowing such "decharacterized" wastewaters to be placed in a Clean Water Act surface impoundment after the hazard characteristic has been removed through aggregation and dilution in tanks is a reasonable accommodation, even though placement in a surface impoundment is

---

[19]*Id.* § 260.10.
[20]42 U.S.C. § 6924(m)(1).
[21]55 Fed. Reg. 22,657.
[22]40 C.F.R. § 268.3(b).
[23]976 F.2d 2 (D.C. Cir. 1992), *cert. denied,* 113 S. Ct. 1961 (1993).

20 THE RCRA PRACTICE MANUAL

"technically a form of 'land disposal.'"[24] However, because such a "decharacterized" waste stream might still contain significant levels of hazardous constituents, the court required that "whenever wastes are put in CWA surface impoundments before they have been treated pursuant to RCRA to reduce the toxicity of all hazardous constituents, these wastes must be so treated before exiting the CWA treatment facilities."[25]

EPA interprets *Chemical Waste Management* as remanding, rather than vacating, EPA's rule allowing facilities to dilute certain hazardous wastewaters before placement in a surface impoundment subject to Clean Water Act regulation.[26] Therefore, the rule remains in effect until EPA modifies it in accordance with the D.C. Circuit's decision.

B. RCRA and the Clean Air Act

The Clean Air Act is a complex statute designed to curb the emission of pollutants into the air. As far as its intersection with RCRA is concerned, the most significant provision of the Clean Air Act is Section 112, which seeks to control the emission of hazardous air pollutants (HAPs). In the Clean Air Act Amendments of 1990, Congress significantly revamped Section 112 and expressly required EPA "to the maximum extent practicable and consistent with the provisions of . . . section [112], [to] ensure that the requirements of . . . subtitle [C of RCRA] and . . . section [112] are consistent."[27]

Although air emissions from industrial facilities may exhibit hazard characteristics and may be viewed as "wastes," they ordinarily would not be "solid wastes" within the meaning of RCRA, thus avoiding an overlap in the Clean Air Act and RCRA regulatory programs. However, the Clean Air Act and RCRA do have a practical impact on each other, and as suggested above, there is one important area where Clean Air Act jurisdiction and RCRA jurisdiction do overlap.

The practical impact is that air pollution control devices installed to meet Clean Air Act requirements produce dusts and sludges that may be subject to regulation as hazardous waste under RCRA. When Congress enacted RCRA, it expressly included "refuse [or] sludge from . . . [an] air pollution control facility" in the definition of solid waste.[28] Several types of waste from air pollution control devices, such as K061 emission control dust/sludge from the primary production of steel in electric furnaces,

---

[24]*Id.* at 20.

[25]*Id.* at 22.

[26]58 Fed. Reg. 29,860, 29,863 (1993).

[27]42 U.S.C. § 7412(n)(7) (West Supp. 1990).

[28]*Id.* § 6903(27).

have been listed by EPA as hazardous wastes.[29] RCRA also regulates wastes from air pollution control devices that exhibit a hazard characteristic. As a result, an industrial facility may have to install air pollution control devices to satisfy the Clean Air Act and then handle and dispose of wastes from those devices in compliance with RCRA.

Jurisdictional overlap exists in the case of air emissions from hazardous waste treatment, storage, or disposal (TSD) facilities. Section 3004(a) of RCRA[30] directs EPA to "promulgate regulations establishing such performance standards, applicable to owners and operators of [hazardous waste TSD facilities] . . . as may be necessary to protect human health and the environment." EPA has interpreted this language as conferring authority to regulate air emissions from hazardous waste TSD facilities, where necessary to protect health and the environment. Furthermore, in the Hazardous and Solid Waste Amendments of 1984, Congress directed EPA to

> promulgate such regulations for the monitoring and control of air emissions at hazardous waste treatment, storage, and disposal facilities, including but not limited to open tanks, surface impoundments, and landfills, as may be necessary to protect human health and the environment.[31]

Currently, RCRA regulations govern the release of air emissions from incinerators that burn hazardous wastes,[32] from boilers or industrial furnaces (BIFs) that process or burn hazardous wastes,[33] and from process vents and equipment leaks associated with certain types of TSD facilities.[34] These emission sources also are potential subjects of regulation under Section 112 of the Clean Air Act. When EPA issued the BIF regulations in 1991, it recognized this point explicitly, stating that Section 112 of the Clean Air Act "potentially addresses many of the same sources that would be regulated under today's rule."[35] The agency found it "premature" to state whether the boilers and industrial furnaces regulated under the BIF rule would have to comply with Clean Air Act Section 112 regulations as well.[36] Indeed, the prospect of possible Clean Air Act regulation was one of the reasons given for exempting certain metals recovery furnaces from the BIF rule.[37]

---

[29] 40 C.F.R. § 261.32.
[30] 42 U.S.C. § 6924(a).
[31] *Id.* § 6924(n).
[32] 40 C.F.R. pt. 264, subpt. O.
[33] *Id.* pt. 266, subpt. H.
[34] *Id.* pt. 264, subpts. AA, BB.
[35] 56 Fed. Reg. 7134, 7137 (1991).
[36] *Id.*
[37] *Id.*

22 THE RCRA PRACTICE MANUAL

As EPA implements Section 112 of the Clean Air Act in the future, it will have to make sure that the resulting HAP rules are "consistent" with the existing RCRA regulations. For example, there is a potential overlap between RCRA's TSD process vent and equipment leak rules[38] and the so-called Hazardous Organics Standard that is to be promulgated under Section 112 of the Clean Air Act.[39] Moreover, EPA will have to be careful not to apply technology-based Clean Air Act emissions limits to combustion devices that it is purporting to regulate under the health-based regulatory authorities of RCRA. As announced in May 1993, EPA's Draft Hazardous Waste Combustion Strategy appeared to do just that, prompting an immediate court challenge and a somewhat defensive backtracking by the agency.

C. RCRA and the Safe Drinking Water Act

The Safe Drinking Water Act attempts to protect the quality of public drinking water in two ways. First, it directs EPA to set national drinking water regulations for contaminants in public drinking water systems. These maximum contaminant levels (MCLs) for the various chemicals are set as close to the health-based maximum contaminant level goals (MCLGs) as is feasible. Second, SDWA prohibits the underground injection of pollutants except in compliance with an underground injection control (UIC) permit. There is a relationship between RCRA and both aspects of the SDWA regulatory program.

First, MCLs and MCLGs promulgated under SDWA serve as the health-based reference value for many aspects of the RCRA regulatory program. Thus, MCLs are used as the criteria for setting action levels in water under the proposed rule to establish comprehensive procedures and technical standards for conducting corrective actions under RCRA.[40] MCLs also are used as the health basis for setting the toxicity characteristic levels (TCLs) that cause a waste to be identified as a hazardous waste.[41] Similarly, MCLs are applied as the health-based value in evaluating delisting petitions under RCRA.[42] They also serve as the basis for calculating generic exclusion levels for certain high-temperature metals recovery residues under the RCRA derived-from rule.[43]

---

[38]40 C.F.R. pt. 264, subpts. AA, BB.
[39]57 Fed. Reg. 62,608 (1992).
[40]55 Fed. Reg. 30,798, 30,817 (1990).
[41]40 C.F.R. § 261.24.
[42]*Id*. § 260.22.
[43]*Id*. § 261.3(c)(2).

Chapter 2: *RCRA's Relationship to Other Laws* 23

RCRA's relationship to SDWA's UIC program is more complex. By defining the term "land disposal" to include the placement of hazardous waste in an injection well, Congress subjected hazardous waste injection wells to RCRA regulation as well as SDWA regulation.[44] (In addition, Section 3020 of RCRA expressly prohibits the disposal of hazardous waste by underground injection into or above a formation that contains an underground source of drinking water within one-quarter mile of the relevant well.[45]) Therefore, EPA has had to integrate the two regulatory schemes.

To avoid duplication, RCRA regulations exempt the owner or operator of a hazardous waste disposal injection well from RCRA's TSD facility requirements, provided the owner or operator complies with certain SDWA regulations.[46] The SDWA regulations, in turn, require the owner or operator of a hazardous waste disposal injection well to comply with the notification, manifest/reporting, personnel training, and certification of closure requirements applicable to TSD facilities under Part 264 of the RCRA regulations.[47] Both regulatory schemes require that the owner or operator of a hazardous waste injection well obtain a permit, but RCRA grants the owner or operator a permit-by-rule if the owner or operator already possesses a UIC permit and complies with certain other conditions.[48]

EPA's attempt to coordinate SDWA and RCRA regulation of injection wells has proved less successful in the case of the land disposal restriction program. In 1990, EPA issued regulations allowing the owners or operators of deep "class I" injection wells to dilute certain characteristic hazardous wastes, and then inject the "decharacterized" wastes into a well.[49] EPA claimed that this exception to the LDR antidilution ban was "appropriate," because the ban would cause "considerable disruption" at facilities that currently dilute the wastes in compliance with the SDWA UIC program.[50]

In the *Chemical Waste Management* decision discussed previously, the D.C. Circuit rejected EPA's rationale and held that before a "decharacterized" hazardous waste may be disposed of in a class I injection well, it must be treated to meet the "minimize threat" standard set forth in Section

---

[44]42 U.S.C. § 6924(k).
[45]*Id.* § 6939b(a).
[46]40 C.F.R. § 264.1(d).
[47]*Id.* § 144.14.
[48]*Id.* § 270.60(b).
[49]*Id.* §§ 148.1(d), 268.1(c)(3).
[50]55 Fed. Reg. 22,658–59.

24   THE RCRA PRACTICE MANUAL

3004(m)(1) of RCRA.[51] Unless this is done, the court stated, EPA's rule would fail to achieve the "balance" that Congress had in mind when it called for integrating RCRA and other statutes in Section 1006(b)(1) of RCRA.[52] EPA has determined that class I wells may continue to receive decharacterized wastes following dilution until EPA issues a rule, on remand, in accordance with the court's opinion.[53]

D. RCRA and the Toxic Substances Control Act

The Toxic Substances Control Act authorizes EPA to impose a variety of reporting requirements and controls on the manufacture, processing, distribution, use, and disposal of chemical substances. Hazardous wastes generally fall within TSCA's definition of "chemical substance" and therefore potentially are subject to the full range of TSCA regulation. However, EPA has exempted most hazardous wastes from key TSCA requirements.

For example, Section 5 of TSCA[54] imposes "premanufacture notification" and other requirements on manufacturers, importers, and processors of chemical substances. The Section 5 regulations do not, however, apply to "by-products," a term that encompasses many (but not all) hazardous wastes. It is important to note that importers of hazardous waste are subject to the regulations implementing Section 13 of TSCA,[55] which require certification that imported substances comply with TSCA. In addition, constituents of hazardous wastes may be subject to reporting rules under Section 8 of TSCA[56] in certain circumstances.

One provision of TSCA expressly directs EPA to regulate polychlorinated biphenyls (PCBs).[57] Pursuant to that directive, EPA has adopted elaborate rules which generally prohibit the manufacture, processing, and distribution in commerce of PCBs, prohibit their use except as authorized by EPA, and impose strict requirements on their disposal.[58]

Because they are regulated so comprehensively under TSCA, PCBs have not had to be regulated as closely under RCRA. For example, EPA has not listed any solid waste as a hazardous waste because it contains PCBs, and it has not established a toxicity characteristic for PCBs. Fur-

---

[51]*Chemical Waste Management, supra* note 23, 976 F.2d at 25.
[52]*Id.*
[53]58 Fed. Reg. 29,860, 29,864 (1993).
[54]15 U.S.C. § 2604.
[55]*Id.* § 2612.
[56]*Id.* § 2607.
[57]*Id.* § 2605(e).
[58]40 C.F.R. pt. 761.

Chapter 2: RCRA's Relationship to Other Laws 25

thermore, EPA has expressly exempted the disposal of "PCB-containing dielectric fluid and electric equipment containing such fluid" from most RCRA regulatory requirements, provided they are regulated under TSCA and are hazardous only because they exhibit the characteristic of toxicity for certain organic constituents.[59] When EPA promulgated this exception, it stated that "new regulation of these wastes under RCRA may be disruptive to the mandatory phaseout of PCBs in certain electrical transformers and capacitors . . . [and] regulation of these wastes under TSCA is adequate to protect human health and the environment."[60]

PCB-contaminated wastes are not excluded entirely from regulation under RCRA. The toxicity characteristic exemption in 40 C.F.R. Section 261.8 applies only to dielectric fluid and associated electric equipment; other PCB-contaminated wastes, such as hydraulic fluid, are subject to RCRA regulation because they are not fully regulated under TSCA.[61] Moreover, RCRA's LDR requirements subject the land disposal of some PCB-contaminated wastes to regulation under RCRA as well as TSCA. For example, wastes that contain a mixture of PCBs and a "P" or "U" code-listed hazardous waste must be incinerated in compliance with both statutes. Moreover, the residual ash from such incineration must be disposed of in compliance with RCRA's LDR requirements.[62] Finally, the category of so-called California-listed wastes under RCRA expressly includes liquid hazardous wastes containing PCBs in concentrations equal to or greater than 50 parts per million, and liquid hazardous wastes containing halogenated organic compounds, including certain PCBs, in concentrations between 1,000 milligrams per liter and 10,000 milligrams per liter.[63] These PCB-contaminated wastes cannot be land disposed until they have been treated to comply with RCRA's LDR requirements.

E. RCRA and the Hazardous Materials Transportation Act

Materials that are hazardous wastes under RCRA are also likely to be hazardous materials for purposes of the Hazardous Materials Transportation Act. Generators and transporters of hazardous waste must, therefore, comply with Department of Transportation (DOT) regulations and requirements, as well as with separate requirements imposed by EPA under RCRA. Recognizing this overlap, EPA has expressly incorporated applicable DOT requirements (for example, packaging, labeling,

---

[59]*Id.* § 261.8.
[60]55 Fed. Reg. 11,798, 11,841 (1990).
[61]*Id.*
[62]*Id.* at 22,678.
[63]40 C.F.R. § 268.32(a)(2)–(3).

marking, placarding, and discharge reporting) into the RCRA regulations.[64] According to EPA, its "adoption of these DOT regulations ensures consistency with the requirements of DOT and thus avoids the establishment of duplicative or conflicting requirements."[65]

III. RCRA's Relation to the Superfund Cleanup Statute

RCRA jurisdiction is much closer to that of CERCLA, commonly known as the Superfund statute, than it is to that of the Clean Water Act, the Clean Air Act, or the other federal environmental statutes. Both RCRA and CERCLA deal primarily with waste sites. In broad terms, RCRA is a prospective regulatory statute that imposes management standards for the handling of hazardous waste, whereas CERCLA is a retroactive liability statute imposing cleanup responsibility. There is some regulatory overlap between the two statutes, however, and increasingly there is overlap between the emerging corrective action program under RCRA and response action under CERCLA.

Based on the expansive definition of "hazardous substances" covered by CERCLA,[66] it is generally stated that CERCLA jurisdiction is broader than that of RCRA. A CERCLA hazardous substance is defined to include all RCRA hazardous wastes, as well as a long list of substances designated under Sections 307 and 311 of the Clean Water Act, Section 112 of the Clean Air Act, Section 7 of TSCA, or otherwise designated by EPA under CERCLA. At the same time, the universe of RCRA hazardous wastes is expanding, for example, through the addition of hazardous constituents subject to the leaching procedure for defining the RCRA toxicity characteristic. Further, the corrective action program under RCRA (once triggered by the existence of a hazardous waste management unit) applies not only to hazardous wastes, but also to a broader list of hazardous constituents, which contains many of the CERCLA hazardous substances. The reach of both statutes, therefore, is substantial.

A. Regulatory Overlap between RCRA and CERCLA

Although CERCLA contains few purely regulatory provisions, there is some regulatory overlap between the two statutes. For example, Section 103 of CERCLA requires the person in charge of a vessel or facility to notify the National Response Center immediately in the event of a

---

[64]*Id.* §§ 262.30–.33, 263.30(c)(2).
[65]*Id.* § 263.10(a) comment.
[66]42 U.S.C. § 9601(14).

Chapter 2: RCRA's Relationship to Other Laws 27

release of a hazardous substance exceeding the established reportable quantity. CERCLA provides a reporting exemption, however, for releases of hazardous wastes reported to the National Response Center pursuant to the emergency procedures for RCRA facilities. The emergency procedures under RCRA require the owner/operator of a TSD facility to notify the National Response Center (or the government's designated on-scene coordinator) whenever there is a release "which could threaten human health, or the environment, outside the facility."[67]

Another area of regulatory overlap between RCRA and CERCLA concerns the storage of hazardous materials in underground storage tanks (USTs). The RCRA standards applicable to owners/operators of TSD facilities include special provisions governing the storage of RCRA hazardous wastes in tanks.[68] In addition, RCRA contains a separate scheme addressing the much larger universe of underground storage tanks containing petroleum or CERCLA hazardous substances (but excluding RCRA hazardous wastes).[69]

The UST program establishes technical requirements for the installation and operation of USTs containing petroleum and hazardous substances, and corrective action requirements for releases from USTs. With respect to petroleum releases, there is no overlap between the UST program and CERCLA, because the latter expressly exempts petroleum (and natural gas) from the definition of hazardous substances. With respect to releases of hazardous substances from USTs, however, there is a potential for overlap between corrective action under the UST program and response action under CERCLA. As a practical matter, only the largest releases from USTs may attract government attention under CERCLA, especially if they are being addressed adequately under RCRA. The potential overlap between RCRA and CERCLA cleanups, discussed below, is more likely to occur at RCRA TSD facilities with substantial environmental contamination.

B. RCRA Corrective Action versus CERCLA Response Action

1. Covered Sites

There are two primary reasons that the universe of sites subject to potential CERCLA cleanup is larger than the universe of sites subject to RCRA corrective action. First, as discussed earlier, the definition of a CERCLA hazardous substance is broader than that of a RCRA hazardous waste, although the distinction is narrowing.

---

[67]40 C.F.R. § 264.56(d).
[68]*Id.* pt. 264, subpt. J.
[69]*Id.* pt. 280.

28 THE RCRA PRACTICE MANUAL

Second, only permitted TSD facilities are subject to corrective action under RCRA. Specifically, to trigger RCRA corrective action, a facility must have treated, stored, or disposed of a RCRA hazardous waste after November 19, 1980, and have failed to certify closure for each hazardous waste unit by January 26, 1983.[70] Once corrective action is triggered, however, all solid waste management units (SWMUs)—including any discernible unit at which solid wastes containing hazardous constituents have been placed at any time—must be addressed. By way of contrast, any site containing a CERCLA hazardous substance (including a few thousand TSD facilities, but also including tens of thousands of other sites) is a potential Superfund site.

Where EPA has jurisdictional authority to address a site under both RCRA and CERCLA, the agency has expressed a general policy preference for pursuing RCRA corrective action, at least where the owner/operator of the TSD is financially viable.[71] There may be competing considerations, however, such as the involvement of off-site waste generators that EPA can more easily pursue under CERCLA than under RCRA. Additionally, EPA may proceed under CERCLA in order to address contamination that does not meet the definition of a SWMU subject to RCRA corrective action, or to address areawide contamination that is not limited to the RCRA facility. Where EPA does decide to proceed under CERCLA, however, a facility may also be required to take cleanup action required by the state under its own hazardous waste laws or act pursuant to an EPA delegation of authority under RCRA.[72]

In some instances, the responsible private party may be able to influence the selection of the statutory cleanup authority, which can have important procedural and substantive consequences.

2. Enforcement Scheme and Cost Recovery

Under RCRA, the owner/operator of the TSD facility is responsible for corrective action. The facility's operating or postclosure permit is the procedural vehicle for addressing most TSD requirements, including corrective action.[73] During the permit process, the permittee is provided procedural due process with a right to a hearing, an administrative

---

[70]*Id.* § 270.1(c).

[71]55 Fed. Reg. 30,853.

[72]United States v. Colorado, 990 F.2d 1565 (10th Cir. 1993) (United States Army obligated to comply with state compliance order requiring additional work at CERCLA site being addressed by EPA).

[73]40 C.F.R. § 270.14.

Chapter 2: RCRA's Relationship to Other Laws 29

appeal, and judicial review.[74] EPA may enforce permit requirements by issuing an administrative compliance order or initiating an enforcement action in court.

Under CERCLA, on the other hand, there is a broader range of liable parties: the current owner/operator of the facility, as well as the owner/ operator at the time of the disposal, and any transporters or generators of waste disposed of at the facility. Instead of a RCRA permit, the procedural vehicle for requiring response action under CERCLA is a unilateral administrative order issued by EPA under Section 106 or a negotiated agreement in the form of an administrative consent order or a judicial consent decree. There is no right to judicial review of a Section 106 order upon issuance; Section 113(h) of CERCLA contains a ban on "preenforcement review," which allows challenges only if EPA chooses to enforce the order in court or to initiate a cost recovery action. In addition to statutory penalties under CERCLA, including treble damages for noncompliance with a Section 106 order, a consent order or consent decree typically will include a schedule of stipulated penalties for noncompliance.

Whether EPA or a private party undertakes cleanup pursuant to RCRA or, instead, pursuant to CERCLA may affect its right to recover costs from (other) responsible parties. Under CERCLA, a party incurring response costs has an express right to cost recovery and to contribution under Sections 107 and 113. It is less certain whether a party incurring cleanup costs under RCRA can recover those costs under CERCLA, although there is some judicial precedent.[75]

The government may recover costs under CERCLA, however, only to the extent those costs are "not inconsistent with" the National Contingency Plan (NCP),[76] the blueprint for CERCLA cleanup action. A private party may recover only those costs that are "consistent with" the NCP. Any private response action carried out in compliance with a Section 106 order issued by EPA or a consent decree will be deemed to be consistent with the NCP.[77] Otherwise, a private cleanup will be consistent with the NCP if it is in "substantial compliance" with certain procedural

---

[74]*Id.* pt. 124; 42 U.S.C. § 6976.

[75]United States v. Rohm & Haas Co., No. 92-1517 (3d Cir. Aug. 12, 1993) (allowing EPA recovery of RCRA costs as CERCLA response costs but denying recovery of oversight costs); Chem. Waste Mgmt. v. Armstrong World Indus., 669 F. Supp. 1285 (E.D. Pa. 1987) (allowing private party recovery of RCRA costs as CERCLA response costs); Mardan Corp. v. CGC Music, Ltd., 600 F. Supp. 1049 (D. Ariz. 1984), *aff'd*, 804 F.2d 1454 (9th Cir. 1986) (same).

[76]40 C.F.R. pt. 300.

[77]*Id.* § 300.700(c)(3).

30 THE RCRA PRACTICE MANUAL

requirements and results in a "CERCLA-quality cleanup."[78] Accordingly, a RCRA owner/operator contemplating an action against other responsible parties needs to ensure compliance with CERCLA requirements, even if they impose greater costs than the RCRA permitting requirements alone.

3. Cleanup Process

While the formal process for investigating and remediating a facility under RCRA is distinct from that employed under CERCLA, there are certain similarities. Whereas the RCRA process is set forth in the proposed corrective action rule, the CERCLA process is set forth in the NCP. The RCRA Facility Assessment (RFA) is analogous to the Preliminary Assessment/Site Investigation (PA/SI) under CERCLA. The RCRA Facility Investigation (RFI) and the Corrective Measures Study (CMS) under RCRA are similar to the Remedial Investigation and Feasibility Study (RI/FS) under CERCLA.

In choosing the remedy for a facility subject to RCRA corrective action, EPA considers the following factors: (1) long-term reliability and effectiveness; (2) reduction of toxicity, mobility, or volume; (3) short-term effectiveness; (4) implementability; and (5) cost.[79] The criteria for selecting a CERCLA remedy are similar, but potentially more stringent: (1) overall protection of human health and the environment; (2) compliance with applicable or relevant and appropriate requirements (ARARs); (3) long-term effectiveness and permanence; (4) reduction of toxicity, mobility, or volume through treatment; (5) short-term effectiveness; (6) implementability; (7) cost; (8) state acceptance; and (9) cost acceptance.[80] Generally, the RCRA criteria may provide greater flexibility in remedy selection than those set forth under CERCLA. Given that remedy selection under both RCRA and CERCLA is a site-by-site process, however, the CERCLA criteria might actually be applied in a more flexible manner at a particular site, or the same result might be reached whether the CERCLA or RCRA criteria are applied.

Indeed, the substantive cleanup standards at RCRA and CERCLA sites are frequently the same. At each site, CERCLA requires EPA to define and then to comply with ARARs, which are typically defined to include RCRA standards. For example, if the waste material at a CERCLA site is characterized as a RCRA hazardous waste, any cap required as part of the remedy must be a "RCRA cap" in accordance with the standards

---

[78]*Id.*
[79]55 Fed. Reg. 30,824.
[80]40 C.F.R. § 300.430(e)(9).

Chapter 2: RCRA's Relationship to Other Laws 31

applicable to TSD facilities. Similarly, LDRs promulgated for RCRA facilities are applied to CERCLA sites that contain RCRA hazardous waste, which can increase remedial costs substantially. To address concerns about applying LDRs to CERCLA sites, EPA has issued a series of directives labeled Superfund LDR Guidance, which, among other things, provide for a treatability variance from LDRs at some sites. In addition, EPA will apply its new rule relaxing RCRA regulatory requirements within corrective action management units (CAMUs) to CERCLA sites as well.[81] EPA also is attempting to rationalize the application of LDRs to both RCRA and CERCLA cleanups by establishing more appropriate LDRs for contaminated debris and contaminated soil.

In short, there are both important similarities and differences between RCRA and CERCLA cleanup actions. Some of the more subtle differences—such as the relative reasonableness of EPA personnel in the RCRA and CERCLA programs within a particular EPA region, or the potential negative public perception associated with designation as a CERCLA site—may take on greater importance in a particular situation. Especially in instances where EPA has not yet determined whether to address a site under RCRA or CERCLA, an interested party who understands the differences may be able to affect the outcome. Even where EPA already has chosen to proceed under RCRA or CERCLA, however, the increasing overlap between the programs requires an understanding of both.

IV. Conclusion

Understanding and providing advice on the RCRA scheme requires reference to the other federal environmental statutes, including the primary regulatory statutes (the Clean Water Act, the Clean Air Act, the Safe Drinking Water Act, the Toxic Substances Control Act, and the Hazardous Materials Transportation Act) and the primary liability statute (CERCLA). The regulatory regimes under RCRA and the other regulatory statutes are not mutually exclusive, and to an increasing extent, there is substantial overlap between the corrective action program under RCRA and the cleanup process under CERCLA. For the environmental practitioner called upon to analyze a problem under RCRA, this means that sound advice can be provided only after a thorough consideration of the possible implications suggested by a wide range of environmental laws.

---

[81] 58 Fed. Reg. 8658 (1993).

CHAPTER 3

Recycling and the Definition of Solid Waste

KENNETH M. KASTNER

I. Introduction

The first step in determining whether material is subject to regulation under the Resource Conservation and Recovery Act (RCRA) is to decide whether it is a "solid waste." If the material is not a solid waste, it is not regulated under RCRA. If it is a solid waste, it may be regulated as a nonhazardous waste or as a hazardous waste depending on whether it either is listed as a hazardous waste or exhibits a hazardous-waste characteristic—issues discussed in chapter 4.

To be regulated as a solid waste, a material must meet three criteria: (1) it must have the physical form of a solid waste; (2) it must be a "discarded" material; and (3) it must not be excluded from regulation under one of the solid waste exclusions. These three qualifying factors are discussed in this chapter, along with some important judicial decisions on Environmental Protection Agency (EPA) recycling rules.

II. Physical Form of a Solid Waste

A material can be a RCRA solid waste if its physical form is either a solid, semisolid (for example, gel or sludge), liquid, or contained gas.[1] By "contained gas," EPA means a gas that is contained in a cylinder or

---

[1] 42 U.S.C. § 6903(27).

other non-flow-through containment system.[2] In contrast, an uncontained gas, such as a gas flowing through a pipe, column, or tank, is not a solid waste. Since uncontained gases are not solid wastes and therefore cannot be hazardous wastes, as a general matter, units that manage uncontained gases are not regulated under RCRA. To date, EPA has identified two exceptions, however. First, certain valves and pressure relief devices in gas service are regulated under EPA's Subpart BB rules at 40 C.F.R. Parts 264 and 265, Sections .1054 and .1057. Second, a carbon filtration system that filters gases is not itself a waste unit. But if the spent carbon bed exhibits a hazardous waste after the gaseous contaminants become entrained on the carbon, or if the bed contains entrained contaminants that emanated from a listed hazardous waste, thermal regeneration of the spent carbon is considered to be a regulated activity.[3]

III. "Discarded" Material

The most complex criterion for defining a solid waste is that it must be a "discarded" material.[4] EPA defines "discarded" in its rules very broadly as any material that is "abandoned," "recycled," or "inherently waste-like."[5]

A. Inherently Waste-Like and Abandoned Materials

The rules identify "inherently waste-like" materials as certain feedstock to a halogen acid furnace and certain very toxic "F-listed" wastes that contain dioxins and/or furans.[6] These wastes are considered to contain constituents that are so unwanted that they would never be legitimately recycled.

"Abandoned" materials are those that have been disposed of, burned, or incinerated or stored before such actions.[7] EPA has issued several interpretations regarding abandoned materials. First, a spilled commercial chemical product that is fully recovered is not a solid waste, since the material has not been abandoned. There must be objective indicators that all of the spilled product is being recovered, however. If the spilled product is not completely recovered from the spill area, the unre-

---

[2]*See* 56 Fed. Reg. 7200 (Feb. 21, 1991); *See also* letter from M. Williams to S. Wassersug, RPPC #9442.1986(03), Faxback #12632 (Apr. 2, 1986).

[3]*See* 56 Fed. Reg. 7200 (Feb. 21, 1991).

[4]*See* 42 U.S.C. § 6903(27).

[5]*See* 40 C.F.R. § 261.2(a)(2).

[6]*See id.* § 261.2(d).

[7]*See id.* § 261.2(b).

covered, now-abandoned product is a waste that is contained in the soil, gravel, surface water, or other media. If the commercial chemical product is on the "U" or "P" hazardous waste list or if the contaminated media exhibits a hazardous waste characteristic, the contaminated media would have to be managed as a hazardous waste.[8] Note also that if a waste is spilled, it remains a waste whether recovered or not. However, EPA applies a somewhat different rule with respect to abandoned buildings. A building and its contaminated residue, such as lead paint that has been sandblasted from it, are not considered to be solid wastes until the building is demolished or the contaminated residues are removed and further managed.[9]

B. Recycled Materials

As noted, EPA rules begin with the counterintuitive presumption that a secondary material that is beneficially reused and recycled is nonetheless considered to be "discarded" and therefore potentially a solid waste.[10] To avoid overregulation of recycled materials, EPA has crafted complex exclusions to the solid waste definition that attempt to reflect the agency's twin objectives of not regulating reuse and recovery of valuable materials in ongoing manufacturing processes but, at the same time, regulating activities that more closely resemble treatment or disposal of unwanted materials. In an attempt to accomplish these objectives, EPA's recycle exclusions involve fine distinctions among various terms (sludges, spent materials, by-products, co-products, commercial chemical products) and among various activities (direct reuse, closed-loop reclamation, speculative accumulation, use constituting disposal). These distinctions are highly dependent on the facts associated with a particular recycling activity and material, and on whether the recycling resembles "in-process" use of materials or "ex-process" reuse of secondary materials. The recycle rules are further complicated by several important court decisions that call into serious question the validity of EPA's current recycle rules. Yet the RCRA rules clearly place the burden of proof in an enforcement action on the generator to substantiate his or her claim that a particular recycled material is excluded from regulation.[11] This demanding and confusing regulatory program requires that generators involved in recycling be particularly careful in their analysis of the applicable rules.

---

[8]*See* 55 Fed. Reg. 22,671 (June 1, 1990).
[9]*See* letter from M. Shapiro to K. Kastner, Faxback #11841 (June 3, 1994).
[10]*See* 40 C.F.R. § 261.2(a)(2)(ii).
[11]*See id.* § 261.2(f).

36 THE RCRA PRACTICE MANUAL

Care is essential because if a secondary material is recycled and does not meet a recycling exclusion, the material is a solid waste. If that solid waste also meets a hazardous waste listing description or exhibits a hazardous waste characteristic, it must be managed as hazardous waste. Such recycled hazardous wastes are referred to in the regulations as "recycled materials."[12] The generation, storage, and transportation of a recycled material before the recycling unit is generally subject to all hazardous waste management standards.[13] Note, however, that the unit that is used to recycle the recyclable material (for example, a distillation unit) is not subject to hazardous waste permits or other management standards, except RCRA air emission controls when the unit is at a permitted or interim status treatment, storage, or disposal facility.[14] With this background, we turn to the questions that should be asked to determine whether materials that are recycled are solid wastes.

C. Generic Recycle Exclusions

In determining whether a particular material that is recycled or reused is a solid waste, the first question is whether the material is a secondary material. Although not defined in EPA rules, a secondary material is essentially any residual from a manufacturing process or other ancillary process (like cleaning or coating) that has left the process. In contrast, secondary materials do not include the product, co-product, unreacted raw material, or used but not spent ingredient. Although these materials may have exited the process, they are not residuals.

Once the material has been identified as a secondary material, the next question is to determine whether the secondary material and the manner in which it is recycled fit within a recycle exclusion to the definition of solid waste. Nearly 20 statutory and regulatory exclusions apply to specific materials, such as nuclear materials and "home" scrap. These specific exclusions are covered in the next section of this chapter. There are also two groups of generic exclusions: one group for any secondary material that is directly used or reused "as is," and one group for secondary materials that are reclaimed. A secondary material is reclaimed if it is processed to remove the unwanted material and recover the usable material or if it is regenerated. Reclamation activities include filtering, distillation, dewatering, and essentially any other operation that changes the chemical composition or physical form of the material or regenerates it.

---

[12]*See id.* § 261.6(a)(1).
[13]*See id.* § 261.6(b), (c); *but see* certain exemptions at *id.* pt. 266, subpts. C, F, G, M.
[14]*See id.* § 261.6(c).

A secondary material that must be reclaimed before it is used or reused can be excluded from solid waste regulation only under one of four exclusions. First, under the closed-loop reclamation exclusion at 40 C.F.R. Section 261.4(a)(8), a secondary material may be reclaimed and returned for reuse as a feedstock, ingredient, or reactant in the production process from which it was generated or in an integrated process. The secondary material must be conveyed to the reclamation unit through a closed-loop system of tanks and/or pipes or similar enclosed means of conveyance. In other words, the material may not be conveyed to the reclamation unit in a drum, truck, or other portable container. Note that this is the only exclusion from the definition of solid waste that is available for a spent material that must be reclaimed before it can be reused.[15]

A second reclamation exclusion is for a reclaimed by-product that would exhibit a hazardous waste characteristic and not be a listed hazardous waste.[16] "By-products" are defined to include process residues, such as slags and distillation column bottoms. They are not the primary products and not solely or separately produced by the production process.[17]

A third reclamation exclusion is for reclaimed sludges that, like the by-products, would only exhibit a hazardous waste characteristic and not be a listed hazardous waste.[18] Sludges are defined as any residue from a pollution control device, such as sludge from a wastewater treatment system, baghouse dust from an air pollution control device, or a filter and filter media from water purification.[19]

The fourth reclamation exclusion covers reclaimed commercial chemical products.[20] Commercial chemical products are unused products, raw materials, and intermediates that may be out-of-date, off-spec, or unneeded. Despite narrow regulatory language, EPA interprets this exclusion broadly to extend to (1) commercial chemical products that are listed *or* that exhibit a characteristic, and (2) commercial products that are not commonly viewed as chemicals (for example, circuit boards).[21]

Secondary materials that are directly used "as is" without reclamation may be excluded from regulation as a solid waste if they are: (1) reused in

---

[15]*See id.* § 261.2(c), tbl.1.
[16]*See id.*
[17]*See id.* § 261.1(c)(3).
[18]*See id.* § 261.2(c), tbl.1.
[19]*See id.* § 260.10.
[20]*See id.* § 261.2(c), tbl.1.
[21]Final Monthly Report—RCRA/Superfund Hotline for August 1991, RPPC #9441.1991(14), Faxback #13490 (Oct. 15, 1991).

an industrial process to make a product; (2) used or reused as an effective substitute for a commercial product; and (3) reused as a substitute for a feedstock in the original process from which the secondary material was generated.[22] These are referred to as the "direct use" exclusions.

All the above direct-reuse and reclamation exclusions are lost if the secondary material is handled in any of the following ways.[23] First, the material cannot be used in a manner constituting disposal—that is, applied to the land or used to make a product that is applied to the land—unless the material is a U- or P-listed commercial chemical product and land application is the product's intended use. Second, the exclusions are lost if the material is burned for energy recovery or reused to produce fuel, except for material that: (1) meets the comparable fuel requirements at 40 C.F.R. Section 261.38; (2) is "recovered oil"; or (3) is a U- or P-listed commercial chemical product that is itself a fuel. Third, the exclusions are lost if the material is "inherently waste-like," which, as mentioned earlier, includes certain feedstock to a halogen acid furnace and certain very toxic F-listed wastes that contain dioxins and/or furans. Fourth, the exclusions are lost if the material, except for commercial chemical products, is speculatively accumulated. Speculative accumulation occurs if 75 percent of the material that is being accumulated for recycle is not actually recycled within the calendar year.[24]

Finally, the recycling exclusions can be relied upon only if the recycling activity involves "legitimate" material recovery, as opposed to "sham" treatment of unwanted constituents. These limitations on sham recycling are not in EPA's rules, but rather are the result of discussions in *Federal Register* notices and EPA guidance. Although this may put EPA on somewhat weak ground when it seeks to enforce based on a claim that the recycling is sham, such enforcement has been upheld.[25]

The "sham" criteria are best articulated in an April 26, 1989, memorandum to EPA regions from Sylvia Lowrance, then director of EPA's Office of Solid Waste. Ms. Lowrance advises the EPA regions to consider the following criteria in determining whether the recycling is legitimate:

- the secondary material that is being reused should be similar in effectiveness and constituent composition to the virgin raw material that would otherwise have been used;
- reuse should be possible without significant reclamation of the secondary material;

---

[22]*See* 40 C.F.R. § 261.2(e).

[23]*See id.* § 261.2(c)–(e).

[24]*See id.* §§ 261.2(c)(4), 261.1(c)(8), 261.2(c), tbl.1.

[25]*See, e.g.,* Marine Shale Processors Inc. v. EPA, 81 F.3d 1371 (5th Cir. 1996).

Chapter 3: Recycling and the Definition of Solid Waste 39

- the secondary material should be valuable;
- there should be a market for the end product;
- the secondary material should be handled in a manner consistent with the raw material it replaces; and
- any toxic constituents in the secondary material that are not in the virgin material should be performing a function in the reuse, as opposed to being "along for the ride."

This memorandum does not indicate how to weigh or evaluate the "sham" recycling criteria, and the few EPA interpretations since then provide little guidance on how to apply this policy.

D. Court Cases on the Recycle Exclusions

In five court cases discussed below, the U.S. Court of Appeals for the D.C. Circuit has reviewed EPA's recycling exclusions and has addressed the extent to which the agency can legally regulate recycling.

American Mining Congress v. EPA (AMC I)[26] is the first and still most important recycle decision. In it, the U.S. Court of Appeals for the D.C. Circuit reversed EPA's 1985 definition of a solid waste rule relating to when recycled materials are subject to RCRA regulatory jurisdiction as solid wastes. The court held that EPA had gone too far in regulating secondary materials that are recycled in an ongoing manufacturing or industrial process by the generating industry. It is against this standard that all other court challenges have been judged.

In the second case, *American Petroleum Institute v. EPA*,[27] the D.C. Circuit explained that not all recycling is "in-process" and therefore beyond EPA jurisdiction. Specifically, the court held that EPA could regulate as a solid and hazardous waste K061 (emission control dust from the primary production of steel in electric furnaces) that is sent off-site to a metals reclamation facility to recover the valuable metal components. The court reasoned that the K061 material had left the primary steel manufacturing process, had been discarded, and was being reclaimed to meet the waste treatment requirements in EPA's land disposal restriction rules. Since the material had exited the manufacturing process, the court reasoned that it could be regulated as a "discarded" solid waste.

In the third case, *American Mining Congress v. EPA (AMC II)*,[28] the D.C. Circuit held that EPA had jurisdiction to regulate as solid waste sludges that had formed in the earthen wastewater impoundments at

---

[26]824 F.2d 1177 (D.C. Cir. 1987).
[27]906 F.2d 729 (D.C. Cir. 1990).
[28]907 F.2d 1179 (D.C. Cir. 1990).

40 THE RCRA PRACTICE MANUAL

smelter facilities, even if the smelter operators purportedly were storing the sludges in the impoundments for possible future reclamation. The court reasoned that the sludges derive from the wastewater that was in the surface impoundment rather than from the production process; therefore, they are discarded residual materials, not part of the ongoing production activity. The court also noted that EPA had concluded that storage of sludges in surface impoundments could result in contaminants leaching into groundwater. Since leaching contaminants are discarded materials, the court held that the sludges were solid wastes.

The fourth case, *Association of Battery Recyclers v. EPA*,[29] involved a challenge to an EPA rule that would have regulated as solid waste any mineral-processing secondary material that is stored on the land for any period of time before being recycled. The D.C. Circuit set aside EPA's rule saying that storage of a secondary material on the land before its reuse in mineral processing is not an act of discarding the material and, therefore, that such material is not a solid waste.

The fifth case involved the recovery of residual hydrocarbon streams from petroleum refineries and colocated chemical plants. The hydrocarbons were reused to make various petroleum-refining products.[30] EPA had excluded from regulation the hydrocarbons from the refinery's collected residual waters but only after the oil was recovered. EPA considered the collected waters to be solid wastes. The D.C. Circuit rejected EPA's attempt to regulate the water streams. The court reasoned that the refiners were not discarding their oil-bearing water streams before separating off the oil. On the separate issue of colocated plants, unlike recovered oil from refineries, EPA's rules also regulated the recovered oil from chemical plants, except for such oil that (1) would be hazardous only due to ignitability or benzene, (2) came from a colocated chemical plant, and (3) was not speculatively accumulated. EPA justified this rule and its exceptions on the grounds that other recovered oil from chemical plants might contain extraneous, toxic constituents. The D.C. Circuit upheld this rule and considered EPA's justification to be reasonable.

Together, the five decisions generally support the proposition that material should not be subject to RCRA regulation as a solid waste if the material is legitimately recovered (with or without reclamation) and reused in the process from which it was generated or in certain related processes. As such, certain federal recycling rules appear to be too restrictive. For example, the closed-loop reclamation exclusion should

---

[29]208 F.3d 1047 (D.C. Cir. 2000).
[30]*See* Am. Petroleum Inst. v. EPA, 216 F.3d 50 (D.C. Cir. 2000).

probably be broadened to include non-closed-loop reclamation—for example, where secondary materials are stored in drums or transferred in trucks instead of through closed-loop pipes. As another example, EPA rules that exclude reclaimed characteristic sludges and by-products but not listed sludges and by-products are probably too narrow. Nonetheless, EPA has not revised its unauthorized rules to reflect the court's view in many respects. This leaves generators in an unenviable position: they can follow the letter of EPA's recycle rules, even though some are too restrictive, or they can follow the court decisions and in an enforcement action argue that EPA's rules themselves are illegal.

IV. Specific Exclusions from the Definition of Solid Waste

In addition to the generic recycle exclusions discussed above for secondary materials that are directly used and those that are reclaimed, the RCRA statute and rules exclude specific materials from solid waste regulation. Two important statutory exclusions are for (1) industrial wastewaters that are discharged into a sewer, mix with domestic sewage, and pass through to a publicly owned treatment works (POTW); and (2) wastewaters that are discharged to surface waters under a National Pollutant Discharge Elimination System (NPDES) permit.[31] It is important to note that only the material that is discharged is excluded from regulation; before discharge into a POTW's sewer or into a river, the wastewaters generally are regulated as solid wastes. Other important statutory exclusions cover domestic sewage and radioactive residuals that are source, special nuclear, or by-product materials as defined in the Atomic Energy Act.[32] EPA rules also exclude from solid waste regulation many specific materials, including in situ mining materials, reused pulping liquors, reused spent sulfuric acid, irrigation return flows, reclaimed spent wood-preserving solutions and wastewaters, certain reused wastes from coking operations, and certain condenser dross residue from metal recovery operations of electric arc furnace dust.[33] EPA regularly amends its rules to exclude other materials from solid waste regulation and in recent years has excluded comparable fuels, recovered oil used in petroleum refining, certain spent caustics, circuit boards and "processed," "home," and "prompt" scrap.[34]

---

[31]*See* 40 C.F.R. § 261.4(a)(1)(ii), (2).
[32]*See id.* § 261.4(a)(1)(i), (4).
[33]*See, generally, id.* § 261.4(a).
[34]*Id.*

V. Regulation of "Recyclable" Materials

As noted earlier, a recycled material that fails to meet a recycling exclusion is a solid waste. If it is listed as a hazardous waste or exhibits a hazardous waste characteristic, it is referred to as a hazardous waste "recyclable material." Some recyclable materials are exempt from all hazardous waste regulation, while others are subject to special 40 C.F.R. Part 266 requirements, and others are subject to full RCRA regulation.[35]

Examples of recyclable materials that are exempt from all hazardous waste regulation include reclaimed industrial ethyl alcohol; scrap metal; and fuel, reclaimed oil, and hazardous waste fuel from petroleum refining that are reintroduced in the process. In contrast, hazardous wastes that are burned in boilers and industrial furnaces are recyclable materials and are subject to full RCRA regulation.[36] As a midground, certain recyclable materials are subject to special 40 C.F.R. Part 266 standards. These materials include recyclable materials used in a manner constituting disposal, reclaimed precious metals, and reclaimed spent lead-acid batteries.[37] The midground 40 C.F.R. Part 266 standards typically include certain design and operating standards for the recycling units, specifications for the recyclable materials, and record-keeping requirements, but permits are generally not required.[38]

VI. Regulation of Used Oil

EPA regulation of recycled used oil depends on a number of factors. First, used oil is subject to full RCRA regulation if it is mixed with listed hazardous waste (except from conditionally exempt small-quantity generators, or CESQGs) or with characteristic hazardous waste (except from CESQGs or where the mixture no longer exhibits the characteristic) and if it is reused for energy or materials recovery. If the materials are burned for their energy value, they are subject to the 40 C.F.R. Part 266, Subpart H boiler and industrial furnace standards.

Second, used oil is subject to generator, aggregation center, transporter, and processor/re-refiner standards if it only exhibits a hazardous characteristic, is not mixed with hazardous waste (except for CESQG waste or with only characteristic hazardous waste where the mixture ceases to exhibit the characteristic), and is reused for materials recovery

---

[35]*See id.* § 261.6(a).
[36]*See id.* pt. 266, subpt. H.
[37]*See id.* pt. 266, subpts. C, F, G.
[38]*Id.*

(for example, blended and marketed). These standards appear in a new Part 279, Subparts C–F.

Third, used oil is subject only to new analysis and record-keeping requirements if it is burned for energy recovery, only exhibits a characteristic, is not mixed with hazardous waste (except for CESQG waste or only characteristic hazardous waste where the mixture ceases to exhibit the characteristic), and meets the four metal limits and two other parameters at new 40 C.F.R. Section 279.11 (that is, "on-specification used oil").

Fourth, used oil is subject to new standards in 40 C.F.R. Part 279, Subparts G and H if it is burned for energy recovery, is only hazardous due to a characteristic, is not mixed with hazardous waste (except for hazardous waste from a CESQG or with only characteristic hazardous waste where the mixture ceases to exhibit the characteristic), and exceeds the metal limits and other parameters in new 40 C.F.R. Section 279.11 (that is, "off-specification used oil"). These standards include notification, analysis, record keeping, storage (including secondary containment), marketing, tracking, and a requirement to use permitted or interim status boilers, industrial furnaces, or incinerators.

Finally, used oil that is not blended or burned but rather disposed of must meet the full requirements of Subtitle C if the used oil was mixed with a listed hazardous waste or exhibits a characteristic. Note also that used oil cannot be used as a dust suppressant, except in approved states.[39]

VII. Conclusion

In defining a solid waste and its appropriate level of regulation, EPA has two objectives: to promote recycling that involves legitimate reuse of valuable constituents and, at the same time, to regulate recycling that resembles treatment or discarding of unwanted constituents. EPA rules attempt to meet these objectives by drawing fine distinctions among various types of materials and how they are recycled. Extreme care must be taken when evaluating and relying on these very complex and sometimes counterintuitive rules, which often regulate what the layperson would consider to be legitimate recycling.

---

[39]*See id.* pt. 279, subpt. I.

CHAPTER 4

Definition of Hazardous Waste

LYNN L. BERGESON

I. Introduction

In determining whether a material is a hazardous waste, the first step is to determine whether it is a solid waste. The next step is to determine whether the waste is a "hazardous waste" by evaluating whether it is specifically excluded from the Resource Conservation and Recovery Act (RCRA) regulation, a "listed" hazardous waste, or a "characteristic" waste. The first step is crucial since hazardous wastes are a subset of solid wastes: a material must first be a solid waste before it is a hazardous waste under RCRA.

Section 1004(5) of RCRA defines the term "hazardous waste" to mean:

> a solid waste, or combination of solid wastes, which because of its quantity, concentration, or physical, chemical, or infectious characteristics may
> a. cause, or significantly contribute to an increase in mortality or an increase in serious irreversible, or incapacitating reversible, illness; or
> b. pose a substantial present or potential hazard to human health or the environment when improperly treated, stored, transported, or disposed of, or otherwise managed.

Congress excluded several classes of solid waste from regulation as hazardous waste. It did so not because the materials in these classes are inherently different from other materials that are deemed solid waste, but because it lacked data enabling it to determine whether these materials should be regulated as hazardous. The Environmental Protection Agency (EPA) has evaluated and narrowed the statutory list. In some cases, EPA excluded a solid waste from regulation as hazardous waste after determining it would be impractical, unfair, or otherwise undesirable to regulate the waste as hazardous. The excluded wastes are

- household wastes;
- certain agricultural and animal wastes used as fertilizer or soil conditioner;
- mining overburden overlying a mineral deposit returned to the mine site;
- certain fossil fuel combustion wastes;
- crude oil, natural gas, and geothermal energy exploration, development, or production wastes;
- solid waste from the extraction and beneficiation of ores and minerals, 20 specific mineral processing wastes, and on a conditional basis, lightweight air pollution control dust, and sludge;
- most cement kiln dusts;
- for end-users but not manufacturers, certain types of treated wood;
- certain chromium-containing wastes, including specific wastes generated by the tanning industry;
- certain petroleum-contaminated media and debris from underground storage tanks;
- certain types of injected groundwater reinjected as part of hydrocarbon recovery operations;
- spent chlorofluorocarbon refrigerants reclaimed for further use;
- certain used oil filters;
- used oil re-refining distillation bottoms when used as feedstock in asphalt paving and roofing materials;
- certain leachate or gas condensate from landfills containing specific petroleum refinery listed wastes;
- specific raw material, product, and process unit wastes where the waste remains in the unit;
- on a limited basis, waste characterization and treatability study samples; and
- certain dredged material.

EPA has the authority to expand the list of exclusions and does so from time to time.

Chapter 4: Definition of Hazardous Waste 47

II. Listed Hazardous Wastes

A. The "F," "K," "P," and "U" Lists

Under RCRA subtitle C, a solid waste may be a hazardous waste in one of two ways. First, a solid waste that is "listed"—that is, appears on one of three lists found in 40 C.F.R. Part 261, Subpart D—is a hazardous waste unless excluded as the result of a petition to delist filed by an interested party. Second, a solid waste that is not listed may still be considered hazardous if it exhibits one of four characteristics: ignitability, corrosiveness, reactivity, and toxicity.

Currently, there are three lists of hazardous waste:

1. *Hazardous Wastes from Nonspecific Sources*—found at Section 261.31 and commonly called the "F list" because the waste codes begin with an *F*. These wastes generally consist of spent solvents and electroplating wastes.
2. *Hazardous Wastes from Specific Sources*—found at Section 261.32 and commonly called the "K list." These wastes generally are residues from manufacturing and wastewater treatment processes.
3. *Unused Discarded Commercial Chemical Products*—found at Section 261.33. These wastes include off-specification species, container residues, and spill residues thereof. This list, referred to as the "P and U list," consists of two parts: acutely hazardous wastes (the P list), and nonacutely hazardous wastes (the U list).

EPA's initial 1980 list included 16 F-listed, 69 K-listed, and 122 P- and U-listed hazardous wastes. EPA has added to and deleted from the list since 1980. Not long after EPA issued the core RCRA rules in 1980, it initiated a major data-gathering program to identify potential candidate waste streams in several industries for listing. This information-gathering effort, known as the Industries Studies Program, focused on the organic chemicals, dyes and pigments, wood-preserving, and petroleum-refining industries. Based on the information and data obtained from this study, EPA has added or proposed to add a number of wastes to the listings.

Each listing is accompanied by a background document, which describes EPA's basis for listing the waste. These background documents often are helpful in determining the applicability of a listing.

EPA's priority has been listing wastes that contain the toxic constituents listed in Appendix VIII of 40 C.F.R. Part 261. A waste that contains significant concentrations of toxic constituents is likely to be listed, unless

EPA concludes that the constituents are unlikely to migrate in significant concentrations if the waste is mismanaged, or that the constituents are not mobile. The mere presence of a toxic constituent in a waste, therefore, does not automatically mean that EPA will list it as a hazardous waste. This point has been the subject of confusion over the years, and EPA reiterated it in a *Federal Register* notice issued on January 2, 1992.[1]

The waste listings are quite specific, and it often is difficult to determine whether a certain listing includes a particular waste. For example, the listings in Section 261.31 for spent solvents generally apply to specific solvents only if (1) before use, the solvent contained 10 percent or more of one of the specifically listed solvents; (2) the solvent was used for its solvent properties (that is, to solubilize, dissolve, or mobilize); and (3) the solvent is spent (meaning it has been used for its solvent properties, is contaminated, and as a result of that contamination, can no longer serve the purpose for which it was produced).

A second example of the complexity and specificity of the hazardous waste listings appears in the P and U listings. The P and U listings apply to a listed chemical compound only when it is the unused, pure compound, is a technical grade chemical, or exists in a formulation as the sole active ingredient. For example, if a generator of hazardous waste is disposing of a quart bottle of unused, commercially pure methylene chloride, the compound would meet the U080 listing. A generator disposing of an unused product containing methylene chloride as the sole active ingredient in the product also would meet the U080 listing. The P and U listings do not cover mixtures of compounds, where a sole active ingredient does not exist. EPA at one point considered capturing such mixtures in the Subtitle C program but to date has declined to do so.[2]

B. Delisting Hazardous Wastes

Once a waste is "listed," it remains listed regardless of what is done to it. Not all wastes, however, to which a specific listing applies are truly toxic. Some facilities may use different processes or raw materials than other facilities within the same industry and thus generate waste streams of listed hazardous waste that are relatively innocuous.

EPA provided a process for obtaining an administrative "out" for such waste streams, known as the "delisting" process. Under 40 C.F.R. Section 260.22, waste generators may petition EPA to delist their wastes.

---

[1]57 Fed. Reg. 12 (Jan. 2, 1992).
[2]51 Fed. Reg. 5472 (Feb. 13, 1986).

They must demonstrate that the wastes are not hazardous based on the original listing criteria and that the wastes do not contain any other Appendix VIII constituents or exhibit any of the hazardous waste characteristics.

In evaluating delisting petitions, EPA uses a groundwater transport model that attempts to simulate a worst-case land disposal scenario, disposal of the waste in an unlined municipal landfill. Based on a number of assumptions, the model calculates the concentrations of toxic constituents that might occur in a nearby well as a result of disposing of a specific annual quantity of the listed hazardous waste in question. The concentrations of toxic constituents in leachate from the waste are calculated based on standard chemical-specific partition coefficients. Wastes that the model predicts will not cause exposures above an allowable level may be eligible for delisting. If delisted, the waste stream at issue is administratively excused from regulation as a Subtitle C hazardous waste when disposed.

Preparing a delisting petition is time-consuming and costly. Delisting petitions can take as long as three years to process, with no guarantee that a delisting petition will be approved.

III. Characteristic Hazardous Wastes

Solid wastes that are not listed may still be hazardous if they exhibit one or more of the hazardous waste characteristics: ignitability, corrosivity, reactivity, and toxicity. The first three characteristics refer to properties of the waste itself, while the fourth evaluates a waste's potential to release certain hazardous constituents when disposed.

A. Ignitability Characteristic

A waste is ignitable if it meets any of the following criteria:

- it is a liquid, other than an aqueous solution containing less than 24 percent alcohol, and has a flash point below 140 degrees Fahrenheit;
- it is an ignitable compressed gas;
- it is a solid that is capable of causing fire through friction, absorption of moisture, or spontaneous chemical changes and, when ignited, burns so vigorously and consistently that it creates a hazard; or

50 THE RCRA PRACTICE MANUAL

- it is an oxidizer as defined by Department of Transportation regulations.

Ignitable hazardous wastes are assigned a waste code of D001.

B. Corrosivity Characteristic

A waste is corrosive if:

- it is aqueous and has a pH less than or equal to 2.0, or greater than or equal to 12.5; or
- it is a liquid capable of corroding steel at a specified rate and temperature.

Corrosive hazardous wastes are, essentially, acids and bases. The waste code assigned to corrosive hazardous wastes is D002.

Solid (that is, nonliquid) materials cannot be corrosive hazardous wastes. By definition, a material must be aqueous and have a pH within the specified range, or be a liquid that corrodes steel at the specified rate, to be deemed corrosive for RCRA purposes. This is because standard pH measurements can be performed only in the presence of significant amounts of water (pH is the measure of the concentration of hydronium ions in water).

C. Reactivity Characteristic

There are eight criteria for defining a waste as a reactive hazardous waste. These criteria, found at 40 C.F.R. Section 261.23, are:

1. the waste is normally unstable and readily undergoes violent change without detonating;
2. the waste reacts violently with water;
3. the waste forms potentially explosive mixtures with water;
4. when mixed with water, the waste generates toxic gases, vapors, or fumes in a quantity sufficient to present a danger to human health and the environment;
5. the waste is cyanide- or sulfide-bearing and, when exposed to pH conditions between 2.0 and 12.5, can generate toxic gases, vapors, or fumes in a quantity sufficient to present a danger to human health or the environment;
6. the waste is capable of detonation or explosive reaction if subjected to a strong initiating force or if heated under confinement;

Chapter 4: Definition of Hazardous Waste   51

7. the waste is readily capable of detonation or explosive decomposition or reaction at standard temperature and pressure; or
8. the waste is an explosive as defined in Department of Transportation regulations.

With few exceptions, there is no quantitative analysis that can be applied to a waste to determine if it is "reactive." Rather, a generator must use its own knowledge of the waste to make this determination. Reactive hazardous wastes are assigned a waste code of D003.

One issue that has been the subject of concern is EPA's summary withdrawal of guidance governing testing for reactivity. The regulation that addresses the reactivity of a sulfide-bearing (or cyanide-bearing) waste under RCRA[3] provides that such a waste is "reactive" if a representative sample, "when exposed to pH conditions between 2 and 12.5, can generate toxic gases, vapors or fumes in a quantity sufficient to present a danger to human health or the environment." The regulation, however, lacks any implementing protocol or other provisions as to laboratory conditions, sampling methods, or the like for determining whether a specific sulfide-bearing waste is RCRA-reactive. The absence of any such quantitative regulatory test resulted in implementation difficulties that began to surface soon after the regulation was issued in 1980.

In light of these continuing problems, EPA issued an interim guidance document in July 1985 to be used in making regulatory determinations under 40 C.F.R. Section 261.23(a)(5). The 1985 Guidance specifies that sulfide-bearing wastes should be regulated as hazardous if levels of available sulfide, measured as hydrogen sulfide, exceed 500 milligrams per kilogram of waste and also provides laboratory test methods for measuring the amount of hydrogen sulfide released. In early 1998, EPA's Office of Solid Waste (OSW) withdrew the 1985 Guidance in an unpublished memorandum, providing no warning to interested persons and affording no opportunity for public comment on an action with major ramifications. While the OSW Memorandum represented that a *Federal Register* notice announcing the withdrawal of the 1985 Guidance would be prepared "as soon as is feasible," no such notice has been published.

D. Toxicity Characteristic

While the first three characteristics refer to properties of the waste itself, the fourth characteristic, toxicity, considers a waste's potential for release of toxic constituents and any subsequent exposure to those toxic constituents.

---

[3]40 C.F.R. § 261.23(a)(5).

EPA created a TC for potential toxicity that evaluates the presence of both metals and organic toxicants. The TC considers potential mobility of these constituents in a worst-case mismanagement scenario.

When developing this characteristic, EPA intended it to reflect the potential for leaching to groundwater that results from the codisposal of toxic wastes in an actively decomposing municipal landfill generating an acidic leachate. EPA requires the application of an extraction test—the Toxicity Characteristic Leaching Procedure (TCLP)—to determine if a waste leaches any of the 39 specified toxicants above regulatory thresholds. Any leachate sample created using the TCLP that contains a regulated constituent in concentrations at or exceeding its regulatory threshold exhibits the toxicity characteristic and is considered by EPA to be a hazardous waste. Table 1 on page 53 lists the regulated constituents and their respective regulatory thresholds. This table is codified at 40 C.F.R. Section 261.24.

EPA also exempted from the TC certain polychlorinated biphenyl (PCB) wastes because of the effect that such regulation could have on certain PCB-containing material regulated under the Toxic Substances Control Act (TSCA). TSCA requires owners of secondary network higher voltage transformers containing PCBs and located in or near commercial buildings either to remove or reclassify these transformers by October 1, 1990. EPA determined that the regulation of PCB-containing material under the TC could "be disruptive to [this] mandatory phase-out of PCBs." Thus, "PCB-containing dielectric fluid[,] and electric equipment containing such fluid authorized for use and regulated under part 761[,] that are hazardous only because they fail the test for the Toxicity Characteristic . . ."[4] for an organic constituent (waste codes D018–43) are exempted from regulation under the TC.

IV. The Mixture and Derived-from Rules and the Contained-in Policy

A. Overview

If one or more listed hazardous wastes are mixed with a solid waste, the entire mixture is regulated as the listed hazardous waste. This "mixture rule" is found at 40 C.F.R. Section 261.3(a)(2)(iv). Mixtures of a characteristic hazardous waste and a solid waste, however, are hazardous only if the resultant mixture continues to exhibit a hazardous waste characteristic.

Another rule, found at 40 C.F.R. Section 261.3(c)(2)(i), states that any solid waste derived from the treatment, storage, or disposal of a listed

---

[4]40 C.F.R. § 261.8.

Chapter 4: Definition of Hazardous Waste   53

TABLE 1. TCLP Thresholds for Organics

HW. No.	Compound	Level (mg/L)
D018	Benzene	0.5
D019	Carbon tetrachloride	1.0
D020	Chlordane	0.03
D021	Chlorobenzene	100.0
D022	Chloroform	6.0
D023	o-Cresol	200.0
D024	m-Cresol	200.0
D025	p-Cresol	200.0
D026	Cresol	200.0
D027	1,4-Dichlorobenzene	7.5
D028	1,2-Dichloroethane	0.5
D029	1,1-Dichloroethylene	0.7
D030	2,4-Dinitrotoluene	0.13
D031	Heptachlor (and its hydroxide)	.008
D032	Hexachlorobenzene	0.13
D033	Hexachlorobutadiene	0.5
D034	Hexachloroethane	3.0
D035	Methyl Ethyl Ketone	200.0
D036	Nitrobenzene	2.0
D037	Pentachlorophenol	100.0
D038	Pyridine	5.0
D039	Tetrachloroethylene	0.7
D040	Trichloroethylene	0.5
D041	12,4,5-Trichlorophenol	400.0
D042	22,4,6-Trichlorophenol	2.0
D043	Vinyl Chloride	0.2

hazardous waste is a listed hazardous waste unless and until delisted. This is referred to as the "derived-from rule," or the "waste listing carry-through principle." As with the mixture rule, any waste derived from the treatment, storage, or disposal of a characteristic waste is hazardous only if it continues to exhibit a hazardous waste characteristic.

B. Mixture and Derived-from Rules

On May 16, 2001, EPA issued its long-awaited final rule retaining and revising the mixture and derived-from rules.[5] The rule is available at http://www.epa.gov/epaoswer/hazwaste/id/hwirwste/fedreg.htm.

EPA first issued the mixture and derived-from rules in 1980. Under the mixture rule, a mixture of a solid waste with one or more listed hazardous wastes is a hazardous waste. Under the derived-from rule,

---

[5]66 Fed. Reg. 27,266 (May 16, 2001).

54 THE RCRA PRACTICE MANUAL

any solid waste generated from the treatment, storage, or disposal of a listed hazardous waste remains a listed hazardous waste unless and until delisted.

Numerous industries challenged both rules in 1980. In *Shell Oil Co. v. EPA*,[6] the U.S. Court of Appeals for the D.C. Circuit vacated the rules because they had not been issued with adequate notice and comment.

Four issues were addressed in the *Shell Oil Co. v. EPA* decision issued on December 6, 1991. The court vacated and remanded to EPA the derived-from and mixture rules. The court also (1) upheld EPA's authority under RCRA to regulate resource recovery; (2) upheld EPA's RCRA permit-shield provision; and (3) vacated the RCRA requirement that owners or operators of land treatment facilities perform leachate monitoring.

The court vacated the mixture and derived-from rules because it determined that EPA had not complied with the Administrative Procedure Act (APA). Under the APA, adequate notice of what EPA intends to do in a rule making is a necessary component of the rule-making process. The relationship between a proposed rule and the final rule determines the adequacy of notice. Differences between the two will not invalidate the notice, provided the final rule is a logical outgrowth of the proposed rule.

EPA's proposed regulations for identifying hazardous waste did not include the derived-from or mixture rules, nor did EPA discuss these principles in its notice of proposed rule making. The derived-from and mixture rules appeared for the first time in EPA's final rule. Given the absence of any suggestion that the agency was contemplating the derived-from and mixture rules before issuing the final rules, the court reasoned that neither reasonably could be interpreted as logical outgrowths of the notice of proposed rule making.

To avoid the massive disruption that otherwise would have resulted, EPA reinstated the rules on an interim final basis, pursuant to APA Section 553(b)(3)(B).[7] When the D.C. Circuit Court of Appeals remanded the mixture and derived-from rules to EPA in this decision, EPA, Congress, and industry invested large amounts of resources into exploring how to revise the rules. EPA established a Federal Advisory Committee Act Panel to examine regulatory approaches to the rules and make formal recommendations to EPA. EPA's first effort was to propose "HWIR92," a proposal that suggested two different options for curing the over broad mixture and derived-from rules. The first option, concentration-based

---

[6] 950 F.2d 741 (D.C. Cir. 1991).
[7] 57 Fed. Reg. 7628 (Mar. 3, 1992).

Chapter 4: Definition of Hazardous Waste   55

exemption criteria (CBEC), based the type of waste management option on the concentration of hazardous constituents in the waste. The second, an expanded characteristic option (ECHO), greatly expanded the number of RCRA hazardous characteristics.[8] EPA again noted the over breadth of the rules and the increasing problems created by the derived-from rule.

EPA's technically challenging and lengthy proposal was controversial for many reasons, not the least of which was the short time frame that EPA provided for public comment. Congress intervened and prevented EPA from promulgating it until October 1, 1994. Congress also recognized the need to modify the two rules and required EPA to revise the mixture and derived-from rules by that date. EPA instead withdrew HWIR92 and convened a federal advisory committee in July 1993 to help the agency identify options. The advisory committee, however, failed to reach consensus on many key policy issues surrounding establishment of a concentration-based exit system.

Still being required by Congress and court order to modify the mixture and derived-from rules, EPA proposed "HWIR95." This approach also favored a concentration-based exit system. Like its predecessor, HWIR95 was heavily criticized. By virtually all accounts, HWIR95 was technically challenging, overly complicated, and costly to implement.

Although industry has been critical of both rules over the last two decades, EPA's final action retains both rules, with certain changes. Two changes are key.

First, EPA amended the regulations under 40 C.F.R. Section 261.3 for wastes listed in 40 C.F.R. Part 261, Subpart D solely because they exhibit a characteristic of hazardous waste. Under current regulations, these listed wastes, as generated or treated, are considered hazardous waste even when the waste does not exhibit a characteristic, unless they are delisted. Mixtures are considered nonhazardous if the waste no longer exhibits any hazardous characteristic. The final rule clarifies the scope of the exclusion in Section 261.3(g)(1) to include the wastes listed in Part 261, Subpart D only for a characteristic of ignitability, corrosivity, or reactivity.

The final rule also expands the applicability of the exclusion so that derivatives of wastes listed solely for ignitability, reactivity, and/or corrosivity are excluded from hazardous waste regulation if they are decharacterized and meet the appropriate treatment standards. Mixtures of wastes listed solely for the characteristics of ignitability, reactivity, and/or corrosivity that no longer exhibit any characteristic of hazardous waste continue to be excluded. The effect of the rule is to make eligible for the exclusion most waste listed as F003, and also certain K-, P-, and

---

[8]*Id.* at 21,450 (May 20, 1992).

U-listed wastes. The exclusion is self-implementing, and no additional record-keeping or reporting requirements apply.

Second, with respect to the applicability of LDRs under part 268, EPA clarified that when a waste has been listed solely because it exhibits a characteristic of ignitability, corrosivity, and/or reactivity, and that waste does not exhibit any hazardous waste characteristic at the point of generation, then that waste is not subject to the LDR requirements. Wastes that are characteristic at the point of generation but are subsequently decharacterized are still subject to LDR requirements, however.

On October 3, 2001, EPA issued a direct final rule that made two revisions to the final mixture rule issued on May 16, 2001.[9] The first revision reinserts certain exemptions to the mixture rule that were inadvertently deleted in the May final rule. The second revision clarifies that certain wastes (Bevill wastes) and listed hazardous wastes that have been listed solely for the characteristic of ignitability, corrosivity, and/or reactivity are exempt once the character for which the hazardous waste was listed has been removed. This direct final rule was effective on February 1, 2002.

The May 16, 2001, mixture and derived-from rules became effective on August 14, 2001. EPA did not provide a longer lead time because the agency believed the rules were essentially already in effect. The *Federal Register* notice explains in significant detail EPA's response to the many comments it received on the proposed rule. In June 2001, the American Chemistry Council filed suit in the United States Court of Appeals in the District of Columbia Circuit challenging the final HWIR as it relates to the mixture and derived-from rules. The U.S. Court of Appeals for the D.C. Circuit upheld the rule, and denied the petition in 2003.[10]

C. Contained-in Policy

The mixture and derived-from rules are limited in that they apply solely to solid wastes mixed with or derived from hazardous wastes. To address materials that are not "solid waste," such as environmental media and debris, but are nonetheless contaminated with or contain a hazardous waste, EPA applies the "contained-in" policy. Under this policy, EPA considers such material to "contain" a hazardous waste and requires it to be managed as a hazardous waste as long as it contains the hazardous waste.

The contained-in policy for environmental media is not specifically codified. EPA can grant a determination that an environmental medium no longer contains a listed hazardous waste on a site-specific basis with-

---

[9]66 Fed. Reg. 50,332.

[10]*See* American Chemistry Council v. EPA, 337 F.3d 1060 (D.C. Cir. 2003).

out any regulatory procedure. EPA considers environmental media to cover soil, sediments, and groundwater.

EPA codified the policy for debris at Section 261.3(f). That section specifies methods to demonstrate that the debris is nonhazardous. Debris includes larger manufactured and naturally occurring objects (such as dismantled construction materials, decommissioned industrial equipment, and naturally occurring items such as tree trunks and boulders) that are routinely discarded.

EPA first articulated the contained-in policy in a 1986 memorandum issued by EPA's OSW. EPA also addressed the policy in a May 17, 1988, *Federal Register* notice.[11]

V. HWIR-Media

HWIR for Contaminated Media (HWIR-Media) was finalized in late 1998 as part of the March 1994 environmental regulatory reform initiative. HWIR-Media governs hazardous waste remediation wastes treated, stored, or disposed of during cleanup actions. It primarily covered the following issues:

- streamlining the permit process for disposing of hazardous remediation wastes;
- finding that such permit holders will not be subject to corrective action;
- creating a unit called a "staging pile" to allow more flexibility;
- excluding certain dredged materials from regulation; and
- simplifying the state authorization process.

VI. Mixed Waste Exemption

In late 1999, EPA proposed changes to its regulations under RCRA to provide a conditional exemption from the definition of "hazardous" for low-level mixed waste (LLMW) for storage and for low-level radioactive waste or naturally occurring and/or accelerator-produced radioactive material (NARM) that is mixed with hazardous waste for transportation and disposal. EPA issued this conditional exemption from RCRA in May 2001.

The treatment and storage exemption requires the use of tanks or containers to store or treat the waste and specifically applies only to

---

[11]53 Fed. Reg. 17,578–86 (May 17, 1988).

LLMW that meets specified conditions and is generated under a single Nuclear Regulatory Commission (NRC) or NRC Agreement State license. The conditions are set forth in 40 C.F.R. Sections 266.225 and 266.230. Under Section 266.225, LLMW is eligible for this conditional exemption if it is generated and managed under a single NRC or NRC Agreement State license. Mixed waste generated at a facility with a different license number and shipped to the facility for storage or treatment requires a permit and is ineligible for this exemption. NARM waste also is ineligible for this exemption. Additional conditions are set forth in Section 266.230.

The final rule also exempts LLMW and hazardous technologically enhanced NARM waste from RCRA manifest, transportation, and disposal requirements when specified conditions are met. EPA believes the final rule will provide increased flexibility to facilities that manage LLMW.

VII. Universal Waste Rule

EPA developed the universal waste rule after realizing that the regulatory burden from recycling certain hazardous wastes discouraged smaller facilities from recycling the wastes. In 1995, the initial universal waste rule was published in the *Federal Register* to provide incentives for recycling and ease the regulatory burden. The initial rule covered certain batteries, pesticides, and thermostats. Hazardous waste lamps were added to the universal waste program by a 1999 final rule. In general, for certain, specified wastes, the rule eases certain requirements related to notification, labeling, marking, prohibitions, accumulation time limits, employee training, response to releases, off-site shipments, tracking, exports, and transportation.

Specific universal wastes include the following:

- certain batteries;
- agricultural pesticides that have been recalled or banned from use, are obsolete, have become damaged, or are no longer needed due to changes in cropping patterns or other factors;
- thermostats; and
- certain lamps, including fluorescent, high-intensity discharge (HID), neon, mercury vapor, high-pressure sodium, and metal halide lamps.

States authorized to implement the universal waste rule are allowed to include additional universal wastes.

The universal waste rule is codified at 40 C.F.R. Part 273. The regulations include management standard for handlers, transporters, and universal waste destination facilities.

VIII. Residues of Waste in Empty Containers

Residues of hazardous waste in containers are not subject to regulation if the containers are considered to be empty under the RCRA regulations. Containers holding compressed gases are considered empty when the pressure inside the container approaches atmospheric pressure. Containers holding liquid or solid non-acute hazardous waste must have all waste removed from the container or liner by commonly employed practices, such as pumping, pouring, draining, or aspirating. After all waste that can be removed is removed, the container generally is considered empty if:

- no more than 2.5 centimeters (1 inch) of residue is left;
- the container is less than or equal to 110 gallons, and no more than 3 percent of residue, by weight, of the total capacity of the container remains in the container or inner liner; or
- the container is greater than 110 gallons, and no more than 0.3 percent of residue, by weight, of the total capacity of the container remains in the container.

Containers holding acutely hazardous waste (the P list and all other hazardous wastes with the designated hazard code H) are empty when one of three conditions has been met:

1. the container has an inner liner preventing contact between the waste and the container and the liner has been removed;
2. the container has been triple rinsed using an appropriate solvent; or
3. an alternative method is used, should triple rinsing be inappropriate.

EPA has not defined "triple rinsing" either in its regulations or in any guidance. Triple rinsing is not defined to meet the definition of treatment and is thus not subject to permitting requirements.

Rinsate is an acutely hazardous waste under the mixture rule. If residue is removed from a RCRA "empty" container, however, it is generally not regulated. Whether rinsate of an empty container that exhibits a characteristic is regulated is an issue EPA is currently reviewing.

IX. Conclusion

Once it is determined that a material is a solid waste, it must be determined whether the material is a hazardous waste. This is a contextual analysis that requires a thorough understanding of the physical properties of the material, the way it was generated, and the way it will be managed. This exercise requires an understanding of these facts and the applicable RCRA regulations, as well as any embellishments set forth in EPA "guidance" or other clarifying documents. Lastly, it is important to note that the federal RCRA rules may not be identical to their state counterparts.

As for the future of RCRA, EPA has envouraged discussion on the future of the RCRA program and identified trends that could affect the future of waste management. On November 20, 2001, for example, EPA circulated a draft white paper entitled *Beyond RCRA: Prospects for Waste and Materials Management in the Year 2020*. The paper is intended to jump-start a discussion on the future of the nation's waste management program under RCRA. The draft white paper is a thoughtful look at the current waste management program with a view toward satisfying the needs of the future. Public meetings were convened to discuss it. A copy of the draft white paper is available on EPA's Web site, http://www.epa.gov.

CHAPTER 5

The Obligations of Generators

JOHN A. MCKINNEY JR., VITO A. PINTO,
AND ANTHONY J. DEL PIANO

I. Introduction

To ensure the cradle-to-grave tracking and control of hazardous waste, federal law comprehensively regulates the person whose act creates the hazardous waste—the generator—as well as the hazardous waste transporter and any treatment, storage, and disposal facility (TSD facility) handling the hazardous waste. Section 3002 of the Resource Conservation and Recovery Act (RCRA) authorizes the Environmental Protection Agency (EPA) to promulgate standards governing the generation of hazardous wastes. The regulations at Subtitle C establish pervasive standards governing the responsibilities of generators.[1] A generator's failure to fully comprehend the panoply of regulatory requirements may create significant liability.

This chapter presents an overview of the often-confusing federal requirements governing hazardous waste generators. Generally, the regulations require a generator to

- determine if its wastes are regulated as hazardous wastes;
- notify EPA of the initiation of hazardous waste activities and obtain an EPA identification number;
- properly store hazardous wastes and appropriately label containers used to store or transport hazardous wastes;

---

[1] 40 C.F.R. pt. 262.

62   THE RCRA PRACTICE MANUAL

- use a manifest to track hazardous waste shipments from the site of generation to their final destination;
- maintain records and file reports with EPA;
- institute waste minimization procedures to reduce the amount and toxicity of hazardous wastes; and
- follow specified procedures when importing or exporting hazardous wastes.

Although this chapter analyzes the federal standards, most states are now authorized to administer their own programs in lieu of the federal program as long as the state standards are at least as stringent as the federal regulations.[2] Many states precisely duplicate the federal regulations; others regulate additional wastes and impose stricter standards than the federal program. As an initial matter, each generator must ascertain whether the state in which it is located (and the state receiving the shipped waste) requires adherence to the state's own regulatory program, and if so, it must comply with those specific standards. Some portions of the federal program are not subject to state regulation. The standards governing the exportation of hazardous waste to another country, for example, cannot be administered by a state. This is discussed in greater detail in Section XIII of this chapter.

This chapter does not address other regulations that may apply to a generator, such as the standards governing the use of hazardous substances promulgated pursuant to the Occupational Safety and Health Act (OSHA). These standards may be found at 29 C.F.R. Part 1910, Subpart H.

Between the first and second editions of this chapter, the Internet has become an excellent source of information for generators.[3]

II. Who Qualifies as a "Generator" of Hazardous Waste?

Although RCRA does not define the term "generator," the regulations broadly define the term to include:

> any person, by site, whose act or process produces hazardous waste identified or listed in part 261 of this chapter or whose act first causes a hazardous waste to become subject to regulation.[4]

A "person" is defined in the regulations as:

> an individual, trust, firm, joint stock company, Federal Agency, corporation (including a government corporation), partnership,

---

[2]*Id.* pt. 271.
[3]*See* http://www.epa.gov/epaoswer/osw.
[4]40 C.F.R. § 260.10.

Chapter 5: The Obligations of Generators 63

association, State, municipality, commission, political subdivision of a State, or any other interstate body.[5]

The definition of generator is site-specific. In other words, the term applies to each site where hazardous wastes are generated. A company with several facilities, for example, is deemed a generator at each facility that produces a hazardous waste and may have to comply with the generator requirements for each facility. For example, a company that treats several separate locations in a town as a single plant for management purposes may be a generator at each of those locations and may be required to obtain an EPA identification number (EPA ID number) and comply with other generator requirements at each of those facilities.

The definition of generator is broad enough to apply to several different entities associated with a single hazardous waste stream. EPA has published detailed guidance to assist the regulated community in determining which entity must comply with the generator responsibilities where more than one entity may be responsible for the hazardous waste. Much of this guidance is based on the preamble to the initial RCRA regulations published on October 30, 1980.[6] For example, if hazardous wastes are generated in a stationary product or raw material storage tank, EPA will require the operator of the tank to perform the generator responsibilities. For hazardous wastes generated by a manufacturing process unit, EPA initially will look to the operator of the unit. When hazardous wastes are removed at a central facility operated for the purpose of removing sediments and residues from vehicles or vessels, the agency initially will require the operator of the central facility to perform the generator duties.

EPA has stated it will encourage and respect arrangements between private parties assigning generator responsibilities to one of the various entities handling the waste. However, the agency takes the position that all entities are jointly and severally liable for compliance with the generator obligations and reserves the right to take enforcement action against any of the parties, provided that such enforcement is equitable and in the public interest.[7] EPA therefore broadly reads the definition of generator to include an entity that removes hazardous waste from a tank, manufacturing process unit, or other storage vessel.

It is important to note that neither the definition of generator in the regulations, nor the statute itself, provides any exemption for facilities that generate hazardous waste on an accidental or infrequent basis.

---

[5]*Id.*
[6]45 Fed. Reg. 72,026–28 (1980).
[7]*Id.* at 71,026–27.

There are, however, significant exemptions from the regulations for generators that generate no more than 100 kilograms of hazardous waste in a calendar month and for generators producing less than 1,000 kilograms in a calendar month; see Sections XI.A and XI.B of this chapter. Additionally, certain specific wastes, such as household wastes, for example, are exempt from regulation.[8]

III. Hazardous Waste Determination

A generator's initial obligation is to ascertain if the wastes it is generating are deemed hazardous and subject to regulation. The regulations provide a step-by-step analysis to help a generator ascertain if its wastes are regulated as hazardous wastes.[9]

Because a hazardous waste must first be a solid waste to be regulated, a generator must initially consult the definition of solid waste at 40 C.F.R. Section 261.2. The generator must then determine if its waste falls within the scope of the definition of hazardous waste at 40 C.F.R. Section 261.3. If the waste is not specifically excluded from regulation by 40 C.F.R. Section 261.4 (which excludes certain materials from the solid waste classification and certain solid wastes from the hazardous waste classification), the generator must consult 40 C.F.R. Section 261, Subpart D to determine if the waste is a listed hazardous waste. Finally, if the waste is neither excluded nor listed, the generator must determine whether it has one or more hazardous characteristics (ignitability, corrosivity, reactivity, or toxicity). To make this determination, the generator must either test the waste as required[10] or apply its knowledge of the hazardous characteristics of the waste based on the raw materials and processes used to produce the waste.[11] If the generator deems its waste to be hazardous, it must consult 40 C.F.R. Parts 264 and 265 to determine whether its management of the specific waste is subject to TSD facility standards[12] and 40 C.F.R. Part 268 to determine whether it must comply with certain land disposal restrictions.[13]

Certain recycled wastes may be exempt from regulation as solid wastes[14] or subject to specific regulations for recyclable materials.[15] The

---

[8]40 C.F.R. § 261.4(b)(1).
[9]*Id.* § 262.11.
[10]*Id.* § 261.10(a)(2)(i).
[11]*Id.* § 261.11(c)(2).
[12]*Id.* § 262.11(d).
[13]*Id.* § 268.1.
[14]*Id.* § 261.2(e).
[15]*Id.* § 261.6.

disposal of solid waste residues in empty containers may not be subject to regulation under certain circumstances.[16]

It is the generator's responsibility to characterize the nature of its waste stream correctly. Failure to correctly identify a waste as hazardous may result in civil penalties and other sanctions. Note that EPA and the states continually modify the universe of regulated wastes. It is, therefore, imperative to obtain the most current list available for the applicable program. A helpful resource in this regard is the RCRA Hotline, (800) 424-9346. Also, certain used oil generators are subject to regulation pursuant to 40 C.F.R. Part 269.

IV. Accumulation and Storage Requirements

In general, unless covered by an exemption, a generator must have obtained a RCRA permit or fully complied with the requirements of RCRA Section 3005(e) and 40 C.F.R. Section 270.10 to obtain interim status until a permit is issued in order to store hazardous waste at its facility. The term "storage" is defined in the regulations as "the holding of hazardous waste for a temporary period, at the end of which the hazardous waste is treated, disposed of, or stored elsewhere."[17] However, EPA recognizes that a generator cannot be expected to dispose of its hazardous waste immediately upon generation and allows certain exemptions regarding hazardous waste storage for all generators. The regulations allow generators to accumulate hazardous waste on-site for up to 90 days without being subject to all of the permit or interim status requirements under 40 C.F.R. Parts 264 and 265. To be eligible for this 90-day exemption, EPA requires that a generator comply with certain technical and administrative operating requirements for TSD facilities.[18] Most generators avail themselves of the 90-day exemption to avoid a permitting or interim status requirement and the corresponding additional regulatory burden.

To be eligible for the 90-day exemption, all hazardous wastes must be stored in suitable containers and tanks or on drip pads that comply with the applicable standards found at 40 C.F.R. Part 265.[19] The storage containers must be labeled clearly with the words "Hazardous Waste" and must note the date that waste accumulation began.[20] Containers must be constructed of materials capable of adequately containing the

---

[16]*Id.* § 261.7.
[17]*Id.* § 260.10.
[18]*Id.* § 262.34.
[19]*Id.* § 262.34(a)(1).
[20]*Id.* § 262.34(a)(2), (3).

stored hazardous wastes and must be maintained in good condition.[21] The containers must remain closed during storage (except when wastes are added or removed) and inspected weekly for leaks and deterioration.[22] If incompatible wastes are stored, the generator must take further precautionary measures to reduce the chance of fire or explosion.[23]

Generators storing materials in tanks for up to 90 days must also comply with most of the standards governing the proper use and management of tanks.[24] The standards governing tanks are found at Subpart J of 40 C.F.R. Section 265. They require secondary containment for tanks of certain age as well as for tanks used to store specific types of hazardous wastes.[25] The standards specify design specifications and installation requirements for both primary containment and secondary vessels and require integrity inspections. In addition, the tank standards specify general operating requirements[26] and require certain action to be taken if a leak or spill should occur.[27] Also required are inspection of the tanks each operating day and records documenting such inspections.[28] The generator need not, however, comply with the interim status tank standards pertaining to postclosure plans for nonexempt tank systems without secondary containment[29] or the regulations pertaining to the analysis of hazardous wastes and tanks that were previously used to store hazardous wastes that are substantially different from hazardous waste previously treated or stored in the tank.[30]

A generator may also choose to store the hazardous waste on drip pads.[31] The drip pads must meet the criteria set out at Subpart W of 40 C.F.R. Section 265, and the generator must maintain specific records pertaining to waste removal.[32] Note that EPA does not allow surface impoundments or other land-type storage facilities to be employed during the 90-day period; 40 C.F.R. Section 262.34 allows only use of containers, drip pads, and tanks.

In addition to meeting the container, tank, and drip pad requirements, generators storing hazardous waste for up to 90 days also must

---

[21]*Id.* §§ 265.171, .172, .173(b).
[22]*Id.* §§ 265.173–.174.
[23]*Id.* § 265.177.
[24]*Id.* § 262.34(a)(1)(ii).
[25]*Id.* § 265.174.
[26]*Id.* § 265.194.
[27]*Id.* § 265.196.
[28]*Id.* § 265.195.
[29]*Id.* § 265.197(c).
[30]*Id.* § 265.200.
[31]*Id.* § 262.34(a)(1)(iii).
[32]*Id.* § 262.34(a)(iii)(A)–(B).

Chapter 5: The Obligations of Generators   67

comply with the requirements for owners or operators in C and D of 40 C.F.R. Part 265 and with 40 C.F.R. Section 265.16.[33] These requirements mandate on-the-job or classroom instruction in hazardous waste management and emergency response for employees managing hazardous waste at the facility (also refer to Occupational Safety and Health standards for use of hazardous materials found at 29 C.F.R. Part 1910, Subpart H). In addition, all equipment necessary to respond adequately to an emergency must be readily accessible and maintained in good working order. The generator must also familiarize local police, fire, and other emergency response entities with the facility and personnel responsible for handling hazardous substances and must prepare a suitable contingency plan (a set of mandated procedures) for responding to an emergency.

If a generator accumulates hazardous waste for more than 90 days, the generator is considered to be operating a storage facility and will be subject to the applicable permitting requirements and management standards governing TSD facilities[34] and may be subject to sanctions for failure to comply. EPA, upon request, may grant an extension of the 90-day time limitation of up to 30 days on a case-by-case basis due to unforeseen, temporary, and uncontrollable circumstances.[35] The generator must also comply with the requirements of 40 C.F.R. Section 268.7(a)(5), which requires a waste-analysis plan for wastes restricted from land disposal.[36]

A generator may accumulate as much as 55 gallons of hazardous waste or 1 quart of acutely hazardous waste as identified at 40 C.F.R. Section 261.33(e) at or near the point of initial generation of the waste (satellite accumulation areas) without triggering the 90-day storage provision (or the necessity of obtaining a permit), provided the generator complies with certain interim status requirements.[37] For example, the generator must mark the container "Hazardous Waste" and comply with some of the container management practices at 40 C.F.R. Section 265, Subpart I.[38] If the 55-gallon limit is exceeded, the generator must mark the container with the date on which the limit was first exceeded and remove the excess amount within three days of that date.[39]

---

[33]*Id.* § 262.34(a)(4).
[34]*Id.* subparts 264, 265, 270.
[35]*Id.* § 262.34(b).
[36]*Id.* § 262.34(a)(4).
[37]*Id.* § 262.34(c)(1).
[38]*Id.* § 262.34(c)(1)(i)–(ii).
[39]*Id.* § 262.34(c)(2).

68 THE RCRA PRACTICE MANUAL

Generators should be aware of the applicable air standards established by EPA to reduce organic emissions from hazardous waste management activities.[40] The standards are known colloquially as the "Subpart CC" standards because they are included in Subpart CC of Parts 264 and 265 of RCRA Subtitle C regulations. The air standards apply to owners and operators of TSD facilities subject to RCRA Subtitle C permitting requirements and to certain hazardous waste generators accumulating waste in on-site tanks and containers. Pursuant to these standards, air emission controls must be utilized for tanks, surface impoundments, and containers in which hazardous waste is placed on or after June 5, 1995, except under certain conditions specified in the rule. As a general matter, the EPA believes it has effectively focused on tanks, containers, and impoundments used to manage hazardous waste which are capable of releasing organic waste constituents at levels that can be harmful to human health and the environment.[41]

Air emission control requirements are also added to the RCRA permit terms and provisions specified for TDS facility miscellaneous units. The standards further establish a new EPA reference test method (Method 25E) to determine the organic vapor pressure of a waste.

40 C.F.R. Section 262.34(g) and (h) provides exceptions to the 90-day storage provision for generators of at least 1,000 kilograms of hazardous waste per month that also generate wastewater treatment sludge from electroplating operations that meet the listing description of RCRA hazardous waste code F006. Under 40 C.F.R. Section 262.34(g), such generators may accumulate F006 waste on-site for up to 180 days without a permit or interim status, provided the generator satisfies the detailed requirements set forth in that section. 40 C.F.R. Section 262.34(h) extends the period to 270 days for such generators that, in addition, must transport the F006 waste over 200 miles for off-site metal recovery, provided the generator satisfies the same requirements set forth in 40 C.F.R. Section 262.34(g).

Generators that accumulate F006 waste on-site for more than 180 days or 270 days (if applicable), or those which accumulate more than 20,000 kilograms of such waste at any one time, are considered operators of a storage facility, subject to the applicable permitting requirements and management standards governing TSD facilities,[42] unless EPA grants them an extension or exception. EPA may grant a 30-day extension of the 180- or 270-day period, or an exception to the 20,000-kilogram

---

[40]59 Fed. Reg. 62,896 (Dec. 6, 1980).
[41]See 61 Fed. Reg. 59,932.
[42]40 C.F.R. subpts. 264, 265, 270.

limitation, in the event of unforeseen, temporary, and uncontrollable circumstances, which the EPA Regional Administrator decides on a case-by-case basis.[43]

V. Notification to EPA of Hazardous Waste Activities

Section 3010(a) of RCRA requires any person who transports, treats, stores, or disposes of hazardous waste to notify EPA before doing so; this includes generators. The form required for notifying EPA of such activity is known as EPA Form 8700-12.[44] This form is reproduced as Appendix A to this chapter.

Form 8700-12 requires certain general information, including: (1) the generator's name and address; (2) the designation of a contact person at the facility; (3) the EPA hazardous waste number for the hazardous waste being managed; and (4) a brief description of the type of regulated activity conducted at the facility. Certain categories of generators are exempt from this requirement. For example, generators that produce no more than 100 kilograms of hazardous waste per month, as well as persons handling certain specified recycled materials, are not required to file Form 8700-12.[45]

VI. EPA Identification Number

The regulations require generators to obtain from EPA an EPA ID number before treating, storing, disposing of, offering for transport, or transporting hazardous waste.[46] The EPA ID number is unique to each generator and serves to identify generators and other entities regulated under RCRA.

A generator obtains an EPA ID number by submitting Form 8700-12 to the EPA regional office having jurisdiction over the area where the hazardous waste activity is carried out.[47] When a generator initially notifies EPA of its hazardous waste activities, it has simultaneously applied for an EPA ID number. A generator is required to use this number on all of its hazardous waste shipping manifests (for a discussion of the manifest system, see Section VII below) and in connection with all other RCRA-regulated activities where the generator must identify itself.

---

[43]*Id.* § 262.34(h).
[44]45 Fed. Reg. 12,746 (1988).
[45]40 C.F.R. §§ 261.5(b), 261.6(a)(3).
[46]*Id.* § 262.12(a).
[47]*Id.* § 262.12(b).

70   THE RCRA PRACTICE MANUAL

Generators are also obligated to ensure that any transporter or TSD facility handling the hazardous waste also has obtained an EPA ID number.[48] These requirements, in effect, require a generator to inquire into the status of all transporters and TSD facilities handling its wastes. A separate EPA ID number is required for each facility where hazardous wastes are generated, but a single EPA ID number will suffice for a facility where hazardous wastes are generated or stored at more than one location within the facility.

VII. The Manifest System

Consistent with RCRA's cradle-to-grave management of hazardous waste, the regulations require generators to track closely the hazardous wastes they generate. To implement this regulatory scheme, the regulations require the generator to prepare a manifest form for each shipment of hazardous waste before it is taken off-site.[49] The manifest must accompany the hazardous waste from the moment it leaves the generator's facility until it reaches its final destination at the TSD facility. A generator may face both civil and criminal liability for failing to provide a manifest when required to do so or for knowingly making a false material statement or representation on the manifest.[50]

While authorized states are free to formulate and adopt their own manifest forms, EPA has developed a Uniform Hazardous Waste Manifest, EPA Form 8700-22, and its continuation sheet, EPA Form 8700-22A. Copies of both appear as Appendix B. Instructions for filling out Form 8700-22 are in the appendix to 40 C.F.R. Part 262. Most states have adopted the Uniform Hazardous Waste Manifest. Because EPA does not print copies of the Uniform Hazardous Waste Manifest, the generator must obtain copies from the applicable state or, if not required from an applicable state, from any source (such as a printing company).[51] In addition, the Uniform Hazardous Waste Manifest provides for optional information that the individual states may require, such as the generator's, transporter's, and TSD facility's state identification numbers, state hazardous waste identification numbers, and additional descriptions of the waste being transported. This information may be required by the state in which the hazardous waste was generated and by the state in which the TSD facility is located.

---

[48]*Id.* § 262.12(c).
[49]*Id.* § 262.20.
[50]42 U.S.C. 6928(d).
[51]40 C.F.R. § 262.21(c).

A. Contents of the Manifest

The manifest must include such general information as (1) the generator's name, address, telephone number, and EPA ID number; (2) the name and EPA ID number of all transporters; (3) the name, address, and EPA ID number of the designated and alternate TSD facilities; (4) the manifest document number; (5) the Department of Transportation (DOT) name and handling code of the hazardous waste being shipped; (6) the quantity of the waste being shipped; and (7) a description of the type and number of containers being used to ship the waste, along with any special handling instructions.[52]

The manifest must indicate the generator's designation of the facility that will store, treat, or dispose of the waste (the primary designated facility).[53] Additionally, the generator may also designate an alternate facility in the event that an emergency prevents delivery of the hazardous wastes to the primary designated facility.[54] The generator may also direct that the hazardous waste be transported to a third facility or returned to the site of generation if the transporter is unable to deliver the hazardous waste to either the designated facility or the alternative facility.[55]

B. Certifications Required by the Manifest

The manifest requires the generator to certify that it has (1) accurately and completely described the wastes; (2) properly classified, packed, labeled, and marked the waste for shipment; and (3) assured that the waste is in proper condition for transportation.[56]

The generator also is required to certify that it has implemented a waste minimization program to reduce the volume and toxicity of its waste to the extent economically practicable and that it has selected the method of treatment, storage, and disposal that minimizes the present and future threat to human health and the environment. For a discussion of waste minimization, see Section X of this chapter.

C. Using the Manifest

The generator must retain a copy of the manifest and provide the initial transporter with enough copies that each subsequent transporter and

---

[52]Form 8700-22.
[53]40 C.F.R. § 262.20(b).
[54]*Id.* § 262.20(c).
[55]*Id.* § 262.20(d).
[56]*Id.* § 262.23(a)(1); form 8700-22.

72 THE RCRA PRACTICE MANUAL

TSD facility designated on the manifest will have a copy for its files and a copy to return to the generator.[57] The initial transporter is obligated to obtain the signature of the subsequent transporter (or that of the TSD facility if only one transporter is involved) and to give the remaining copies of the manifest to the subsequent transporter before relinquishing control of the hazardous waste shipment. Upon receiving the waste, the TSD facility must itself sign the manifest, retain a copy for its own records, and forward a copy to the generator. Some states require a copy of the manifest to be filed with the state environmental agency.

A generator is obligated to inquire as to the status of its shipments of hazardous waste if it does not receive a signed copy of the manifest from the TSD facility within 35 days of the time the generator first relinquished the hazardous waste to the initial transporter.[58] If the generator has not received a copy of the manifest from the designated facility within 45 days from the date of relinquishing the waste to the initial transporter, the generator must prepare and file an exception report with EPA.[59] Record-keeping and reporting requirements are discussed in greater detail in Section IX of this chapter.

The regulations specify special manifest requirements when the hazardous waste is transported by water or by rail. The generator must send at least three copies of the dated and signed manifest to the designated TSD facility or last water or rail transporter that handles the hazardous waste in the United States. It is not necessary to obtain the signatures of intermediary water or rail transporters unless the hazardous waste will also be shipped by a nonrail or nonwater transporter.[60]

Manifests create the majority of the regulatory problems commonly encountered by generators. Very often, the DOT names and handling codes are subject to varying interpretations. Given that the hasty completion of manifest forms on the loading dock only invites problems, the responsibility for filling out manifests should be placed in the hands of well-trained personnel.

D. Determining Which Manifest to Use

Generators shipping hazardous waste out of state must ensure that they are using the appropriate manifest. A generator is required to use the manifest of the state to which the waste is shipped (the consignment state) if a manifest is supplied by that state and the state requires its

---

[57]*Id.* § 262.22.
[58]*Id.* § 262.42(a)(1).
[59]*Id.* § 262.42(a)(2).
[60]*Id.* § 262.23(c)–(d).

use.[61] If the consignment state does not supply its own manifest but the state in which the generator is located does supply one and requires its use, the generator must use the manifest of its home state.[62] If neither the generator state nor the consignment state supplies and requires the use of its own manifest, the generator may obtain a manifest from any source.[63]

VIII. Pretransportation Requirements

Before shipping hazardous wastes off-site, the generator must ensure that the shipment is properly packaged, labeled, marked, and placarded.[64] EPA has adopted by reference the regulations promulgated by the DOT governing proper packaging,[65] labeling, and marking[66] of hazardous waste, and placarding of the transportation vehicle.[67] The DOT regulations[68] require that containers used to transport hazardous waste containing 110 gallons or less must be specifically labeled with the generator's name and address, the manifest document number, and the following words:

> HAZARDOUS WASTE—Federal Law Prohibits Improper Disposal. If found contact the nearest police or public safety authority or the U.S. Environmental Protection Agency.
> Generator's Name and Address _____.
> Manifest Document Number _____.[69]

DOT provides technical assistance in complying with these sometimes confusing requirements. To obtain assistance, contact the Office of Hazardous Materials Safety at (202) 366-4488.

IX. Record-Keeping and Reporting Requirements

Reporting and record-keeping requirements allow EPA, consistent with RCRA's comprehensive cradle-to-grave policy, to obtain information

---

[61]*Id.* § 262.21(a).
[62]*Id.* § 262.21(b).
[63]*Id.* § 262.21(c).
[64]*Id.* §§ 262.30–.33.
[65]49 C.F.R. pts. 173, 178, 179.
[66]*Id.* pt. 172.
[67]*Id.* pt. 172, subpt. F.
[68]*Id.* § 172.304.
[69]40 C.F.R. § 262.32.

74 THE RCRA PRACTICE MANUAL

regarding the quantities and types of hazardous wastes generated as well as the movement of hazardous waste shipments. Because EPA believes these reporting and record-keeping obligations are an important aspect of RCRA's successful implementation, failure to comply may result in significant liability.

A. Record-Keeping Requirements

Generators are required to maintain four types of records: (1) manifests; (2) exception reports; (3) biennial reports; and (4) laboratory test data.[70] In addition, EPA, as it deems necessary under RCRA Sections 2002(a) and 3002(b), may require generators to submit "additional reports concerning the quantities and disposition of" hazardous wastes.[71]

The generator must retain a copy of each signed manifest for a minimum of three years after the date the initial transporter accepted the waste or until the generator receives a signed copy from the designated TSD facility that received the waste. The manifest signed by the designated TSD facility must be retained for at least three years from the time the waste was accepted by the initial transporter.[72] Copies of all exception reports and biennial reports required to be filed with EPA (see the discussion in the following section) also must be maintained for three years from the date the report is required to be filed.[73] Generators must also retain records of any laboratory or test results, waste analysis, or any other determinations that a waste is hazardous (see Section III above) for at least three years from the date that the waste was last sent to a TSD facility.[74]

The retention periods for all records are automatically extended throughout the duration of any unresolved EPA enforcement action with respect to the regulated activity or as otherwise required by the agency.[75]

B. Reporting Requirements

Generators are required to submit certain reports to EPA. These include: (1) biennial reports describing all hazardous waste activities conducted by the generator during the past year; (2) exception reports for hazardous waste shipments when a signed copy of the manifest is not received by

---

[70]*Id.* § 262.40.
[71]*Id.* § 262.43.
[72]*Id.* § 262.40(a).
[73]*Id.* § 262.40(b).
[74]*Id.* § 262.40(c).
[75]*Id.* § 262.40(d).

the generator within the specified time period; and (3) annual reports of hazardous waste exports.[76] (For a discussion of annual reports for hazardous waste exports, see Section XIII.C of this chapter.)

1. Biennial Reports

On March 1 of every even-numbered year, generators that have shipped any hazardous waste off-site to a TSD facility in the United States must submit a biennial report to the Regional Administrator of EPA detailing all hazardous waste management activities conducted during the prior year. This report must be submitted on EPA Form 8700-13A.[77] A copy of this form is reproduced as Appendix C.

Biennial reports must include the following information: (1) the generator's name, address, and EPA ID number; (2) the calendar year covered by the report; (3) the EPA ID number for each transporter that was used during the calendar year; (4) the name, address, and EPA ID number of each off-site TSD facility to which the generator's hazardous wastes were shipped during the calendar year; and (5) certain information regarding the types of hazardous wastes shipped off-site, including the EPA hazardous waste number, DOT hazard class, and quantity of each hazardous waste shipped off-site.[78] Many of the authorized states require reporting on a more frequent (usually annual) basis.

Generators are also required to describe their waste minimization efforts during the year to reduce the volume and toxicity of the waste generated, along with a description of the changes in volume and toxicity of waste actually achieved during the year as compared with previous years.[79] Generators must certify as to the truth and accuracy of the information contained within the biennial report.[80]

The regulations also require any generator that treats, stores, or disposes of hazardous wastes on-site to submit a biennial report regarding those wastes in accordance with the provisions of 40 C.F.R. Parts 270, 264, 256, and 266.[81]

2. Exception Reports

To track closely the hazardous waste shipment until it reaches its final destination at the TSD facility, EPA requires generators to report instances where the shipment appears to have been mismanaged or mislocated.

---

[76]*Id.* pt. 262, subpt. D; *id.* § 262.56.

[77]*Id.* § 262.41(a).

[78]*Id.* § 262.41(a)(1)–(5).

[79]*Id.* § 262.41(a)(6)–(7).

[80]*Id.* § 262.42(a)(8).

[81]*Id.* § 262.41(b).

76 THE RCRA PRACTICE MANUAL

For purposes of this requirement, the regulations distinguish among generators based on the volume of hazardous waste produced.

If a generator of more than 1,000 kilograms of hazardous waste per calendar month does not receive a signed copy of the manifest from the TSD facility within 45 days from the time the initial transporter accepted the waste, that generator must file an exception report with the EPA Regional Administrator for the region in which the generator is located.[82] The exception report required for the generator of more than 1,000 kilograms of waste per month consists of a legible copy of the manifest accompanied by a cover letter signed by the generator or its authorized representative detailing the generator's efforts to locate the waste shipment.[83]

If a generator of greater than 100 but less than 1,000 kilograms of hazardous waste in a calendar month does not receive the signed copy of the manifest from the TSD facility within 60 days of the date that the waste was accepted by the initial transporter, that generator must file an exception report with the EPA Regional Administrator for the region in which the generator is located.[84] The exception report required for these generators must include a legible copy of the manifest accompanied by some indication that the generator has not received confirmation of delivery of the waste by the TSD facility.[85] This indication may simply consist of a handwritten or typed note on the manifest itself or on an attached sheet of paper.[86]

Generators of no more than 100 kilograms of hazardous waste per month are not required to file exception reports; see Section XI.A of this chapter.

3. Emergency Reporting

Although neither RCRA itself nor the regulations interpreting the act contain any emergency reporting provisions, generators should be mindful of reporting requirements mandated by other statutes. The Comprehensive Environmental Response, Compensation, and Liability Act (CERCLA)[87] requires reporting for any release of a hazardous substance in quantities equal to or greater than its reportable quantity.[88] Generators must report such occurrences immediately by calling the National Response Center at (800) 424-8802.

---

[82]*Id.* § 262.42(a)(2).
[83]*Id.* § 262.42(a)(2)(i)–(ii).
[84]*Id.* § 262.42(b).
[85]*Id.*
[86]Editorial comment to *id.* § 262.42(b).
[87]42 U.S.C. § 9601 *et seq.*
[88]40 C.F.R. § 302.6.

Chapter 5: The Obligations of Generators 77

X. Waste Minimization

The 1984 amendments to RCRA require generators to develop programs to minimize the amount and toxicity of hazardous wastes they produce. As noted earlier, the biennial report requires the generator to describe waste minimization efforts undertaken during each year and to compare the results with those of previous years. The manifest requires the generator to certify that:

> If I am a large quantity generator, I certify that I have a program in place to reduce the volume and toxicity of waste generated to the degree I have determined to be economically practicable and I have selected the practicable method of treatment, storage, or disposal currently available to me which minimizes the present and future threat to human health and the environment, OR, if I am a small quantity generator, I have made a good faith effort to minimize my waste generation and select the best waste management method that is available to me and that I can afford.

EPA has published extensive guidance for implementing waste minimization policies, many of which are available at its Web site.[89] The guidance is extremely valuable in helping generators establish individualized waste minimization programs as well as in addressing specific issues regarding minimization efforts. Published guidance on waste minimization from EPA also appeared in 58 Fed. Reg. 31,114 (1993). In it, EPA confirmed its commitment to a national policy for hazardous waste management that "places highest priority on waste minimization."[90] EPA states that a waste minimization plan should incorporate six elements: (1) top management support; (2) characterization of waste generation and waste management costs; (3) periodic waste minimization assessments; (4) appropriate cost allocation; (5) encouragement of technology transfer; and (6) program implementation and evaluation. EPA urged that each of these elements, if possible, be incorporated in the waste minimization plan. In addition, EPA advised that the plan or program be documented in writing (so that it is available to interested parties) and signed by the corporate officer responsible for ensuring compliance with RCRA.

The 1988 edition of *The EPA Manual for Waste Minimization Opportunity Assessments*,[91] portions of which are reproduced as Appendix D,

---

[89]http://www.epa.gov/epaoswer/hazwaste/minimize/index-htm.
[90]58 Fed. Reg. 31,114 (1993).
[91]EPA/600/S2-88/025.

78 THE RCRA PRACTICE MANUAL

states that a successful waste minimization program will consist of a systematic, continuous, and comprehensive effort to diminish the quantity and toxicity of the hazardous waste to the extent economically practicable. Economic practicability is a subjective standard and, according to EPA, is to be viewed in light of each generator's particular circumstances. Generally, waste minimization consists of two elements: (1) source reduction, defined as any activity that reduces or eliminates the generation of waste at the source (usually within a process), and (2) recycling, defined as the recovery and/or reuse of what would otherwise be a waste material.

EPA has deemed the following practices to constitute sufficient waste minimization under RCRA:

- reuse of some of the hazardous waste generated on-site and shipment of the remaining waste off-site for recycling;
- participation in waste exchange programs if that reduces the generator's volume or toxicity of hazardous waste; and
- a TSD facility accepting waste solvents and oils from off-site, blending them on-site, then recycling and reusing them in an economically beneficial manufacturing program.[92]

The mere transformation of waste from one medium to another, however, does not constitute sufficient waste minimization according to EPA. For example, the removal of organics from wastewater using activated carbon will not satisfy waste minimization requirements because the contaminants are merely converted from wastewater to carbon, a solid waste.

Generally, the generator should engage in source reduction or recycling to obtain the result of reducing the volume and/or toxicity of the waste produced on-site. Source reduction can take the form of technology changes, input material changes, and product changes. Recycling can take the form of reuse and reclamation. The *EPA Manual for Waste Minimization Opportunity Assessments* is extremely helpful in furnishing specific examples of successful waste minimization methods. Some of these methods are:

- *Technological changes:* A manufacturer of fabricated metal products cleaned nickel and titanium wire in an alkaline chemical bath before using the wire in its product. The company later began to experiment with a mechanical abrasive system. The

---

[92]*Id.*

Chapter 5: The Obligations of Generators   79

wire was passed through the system, which uses silk and carbide paths and pressure to brighten the metal. The system worked but required passing the wire through the unit twice for complete cleaning. The following year, the company bought a second abrasive unit and installed it in series with the first unit. This system allowed the company to eliminate the need for the chemical bath.

- *Input material changes:* An electronics manufacturing facility originally cleaned printed circuit boards with solvents. The company found that it could maintain the same operating conditions and workloads by switching from a solvent-based cleaning system to an aqueous-based system. The aqueous-based system was found to clean six times more effectively. This resulted in a lower product reject rate and eliminated the hazardous waste.

- *Product changes:* In the paint-manufacturing industry, water-based coatings are finding increased applications where solvent-based paints were used before. These products do not contain toxic or flammable solvents that make solvent-based paints hazardous when they are disposed of. Also, cleaning the applicators with solvent is not necessary. The use of water-based paints instead of solvent-based paints also greatly reduces emissions of volatile organic compounds into the atmosphere.

- *Reuse:* A printer of newspaper advertising in California purchased an ink-recycling unit to produce black newspaper ink from its various waste inks. The unit blends the different colors of waste ink together with fresh black ink and black toner to create the black ink. This ink is then filtered to remove flakes of dried ink and used in place of fresh black ink, eliminating the need for the company to ship waste ink off-site for disposal. The price of the recycling unit was paid off in 18 months based only on the savings in fresh black ink purchases. The payback improved to 9 months when the cost for disposing of ink as a hazardous waste was included.

- *Reclamation:* A photo-processing company uses an electrolytic deposition cell to recover silver out of the rinse water from film-processing equipment. The silver is then sold to a small recycler. Because the company removes the silver from this wastewater, it can discharge the wastewater to the sewer without additional pretreatment. This unit will pay for itself in less than two years with the value of silver recovered. The company also collects unused film and sells it to the same recycler. The recycler burns the film and collects the silver from the residual ash. Because the recycler removes the silver from the ash, the ash becomes non-hazardous.

80 THE RCRA PRACTICE MANUAL

Additional case studies are discussed in The Waste Minimization National Plan developed by EPA, dated November 1994, and are available for downloading at EPA's Web site.

Several states have adopted waste minimization strategies and have passed laws encouraging waste minimization in a variety of ways, including requiring certain sectors of the regulated community to develop recycling and source reduction programs.

The goals and policies of a waste minimization program are typically established by the company's management. For a program to succeed, management must be committed to those goals and must create a task force to implement them. From the generator's standpoint, many incentives exist for creating a waste minimization program. These include avoiding the increases in the cost of landfill disposal and the high costs of alternative treatment methods, substantial savings in manufacturing costs and raw materials, and reduction in liability for potential environmental contamination. From the standpoint of EPA, the driving force behind waste minimization is EPA's preference that generators find ways to reduce the production of waste, rather than generating waste and subsequently treating it.[93]

XI. *Exemptions from the Regulations*

Generators producing 1,000 kilograms or more of hazardous waste per calendar month (or more than 1 kilogram of acutely hazardous waste per month) must generally comply with all of the generator regulations set forth at 40 C.F.R. Part 262. EPA, however, provides some exemptions from the full panoply of regulations for generators producing hazardous waste in smaller quantities. The following defined categories of generators are eligible for certain exemptions: (1) conditionally exempt small-quantity generators, and (2) small-quantity generators.

A. Conditionally Exempt Small-Quantity Generators

Generators that produce no more than 100 kilograms of hazardous waste per month (or no more than 1 kilogram of acutely hazardous waste) are considered to be conditionally exempt small-quantity generators (CESQGs) and are exempt from most of the RCRA requirements applicable to generators of hazardous waste. The regulations are quite specific as to how a generator determines if it has met or exceeded the

---

[93]*Id.* For further discussion, see 54 Fed. Reg. 3845 (1989); 56 Fed. Reg. 7849 (1991); 58 Fed. Reg. 4802 (1993).

Chapter 5: The Obligations of Generators   81

100-kilogram quantity. Some hazardous wastes are not included in such determination.[94] (For purposes of illustration, 100 kilograms is the equivalent of 220.5 pounds. For water, 100 kilograms would equal approximately 26.4 gallons or slightly less than half a 55-gallon drum.) CESQGs are exempt from the notification, manifest, storage, record-keeping, and reporting requirements. Additionally, the 1-kilogram weight limitation on the generation of acutely hazardous waste in a calendar month does not apply to any residue or contaminated soil resulting from a cleanup of a spill of acutely hazardous waste.[95]

The exemptions granted CESQGs are conditioned on their compliance with four requirements. First, CESQGs must determine if their waste is hazardous.[96] Second, CESQGs must not exceed the 100-kilogram hazardous waste limitation or, except with respect to spills, more than 1 kilogram of acutely hazardous waste, at any time.[97] Third, CESQGs may not accumulate more than 1,000 kilograms of hazardous waste on-site at any time.[98] Fourth, CESQGs must treat or dispose of their hazardous waste either in an on-site facility or at an off-site U.S. TSD facility that meets certain requirements.[99] Facilities that qualify under this section are those facilities with interim status under 40 C.F.R. Parts 265 and 270, facilities possessing EPA Hazardous Waste permits under 40 C.F.R. Part 270, facilities possessing state permits to manage municipal or industrial solid wastes, facilities authorized by a state to manage hazardous waste where the facility has a waste management program approved under 40 C.F.R. Part 271, or facilities meeting certain recycling requirements.[100]

A CESQG exceeding the 100-kilogram-per-calendar-month hazardous waste limitation may be regulated as a small-quantity generator (discussed further in the following section) if it generates less than 1,000 kilograms of hazardous waste per month. Although the CESQG loses the exemption during a month in which it exceeds the 100-kilogram limitation, the exemption applies again in following months if the limitation is not exceeded. It is important to note that the CESQG exemption is not lost when the hazardous waste is combined with nonhazardous waste to produce a mixture that exceeds the 100-kilogram or 1-kilogram limit, as long as the mixture itself does not display any hazardous characteristics

---

[94] 40 C.F.R. § 261.5.
[95] *Id.* § 261.5(e)–(f).
[96] *Id.* § 261.5(g)(1).
[97] *Id.* § 261.5(a).
[98] *Id.* § 261.5(g)(2).
[99] *Id.* § 261.5(g)(3).
[100] *Id.*

as identified in the regulations.[101] Hazardous waste mixed with used oil, or any material produced from such a mixture, may be subject to regulation if it is burned for energy recovery.[102]

B. Small-Quantity Generators

Generators that produce more than 100 but less than 1,000 kilograms of hazardous waste in a calendar month are deemed small-quantity generators (SQGs) and are eligible for certain exemptions from the generator regulations.[103] (For purposes of illustration, 1,000 kilograms is equivalent to 2,205 pounds. For water, 1,000 kilograms would equal just over 264 gallons or slightly less than five full 55-gallon drums.) Because SQGs generate a greater volume of hazardous waste than do CESQGs but less than generators of 1,000 kilograms or more, SQGs must comply with more regulatory requirements than CESQGs but with fewer than generators of 1,000 kilograms or more.

SQGs must obtain an EPA ID number, use only RCRA-regulated transporters and TSD facilities, and comply with all transport requirements. They are also required to file exception reports if they do not receive a signed copy of the manifest from the designated TSD facility within 60 days (see Section IX.B of this chapter for a discussion of reporting requirements). SQGs must comply with manifest requirements but are exempt from doing so if the hazardous waste is reclaimed pursuant to a contractual agreement in which the type of hazardous waste and frequency of hazardous waste shipments are specified in the agreement and if the vehicle used to transport the hazardous waste to the recycling facility and to deliver the regenerated material back to the generator is owned and operated by the reclaimer of the hazardous wastes. The SQG must also retain a copy of the reclamation agreement in its files for at least three years after expiration of the agreement to qualify for this exemption.[104]

SQGs may accumulate hazardous waste on-site for up to 180 days but may not at any one time accumulate on-site greater than 6,000 kilograms.[105] EPA has established modified storage standards for SQGs that include the container and tank standards (previously discussed in Section IV), waste analysis for land disposal restrictions, and marking and label-

---

[101]*Id.* § 261.5(h).

[102]*Id.* § 261.6(j).

[103]*Id.* § 262.34(d)–(f).

[104]*Id.* § 262.20(e).

[105]*Id.* § 262.34(d).

Chapter 5: The Obligations of Generators 83

ing requirements.[106] In addition, the SQG must meet special emergency preparedness and response requirements contained in the operating standards for TSD facilities with interim status.[107] Generally, these standards require SQGs to ensure that all employees are thoroughly familiar with proper waste-handling and emergency procedures, and require SQGs to designate an employee as an emergency coordinator to respond to emergencies. SQGs must also post information showing the location of emergency response equipment.[108]

The 180-day limitation applicable to SQGs may be extended an additional 90 days by EPA for up to 270 days if the waste must be transported to a TSD facility 200 or more miles from the generator's facility, provided that the SQG complies with all other requirements.[109] EPA may also grant up to a 30-day extension of time to the 180- or 270-day applicable limits on a case-by-case basis if there are unforeseen, temporary, or uncontrollable circumstances that prevent the hazardous waste from being shipped off-site.[110] In addition, certain wastes are excepted, in whole or in part, from regulation. These are identified at 40 C.F.R. Section 261.3(c), (d), and (f) and 40 C.F.R. Section 261.4 and also include residues of hazardous waste in empty containers.[111] PCB wastes are regulated under the Toxic Substances Control Act.[112] "Universal waste," which includes, as of this writing, batteries, pesticides, thermostats, and lamps,[113] is regulated in 40 C.F.R. Part 273, which includes standards for large- and small-quantity handlers, a term that includes generators.

As summarized in the *Federal Register* notice of the final rule,[114] a person who generates or creates a universal waste is referred to as a handler. Handlers include both the person who generates the universal waste by deciding to dispose of it and contractors or other persons performing repairs who decide to remove an item that would be treated as universal waste from service. A small-quantity handler of universal waste (SQHUW) is a person who does not accumulate more than 5,000 kilograms of universal waste at his or her location at any one time. A person who accumulates 5,000 kilograms or more of universal waste is referred to as a large-quantity handler of universal waste (LQHUW).[115]

---

[106]*Id.* § 265.201.
[107]*Id.* § 262.34(d)(5).
[108]*Id.*
[109]*Id.* § 262.34(e).
[110]*Id.* § 262.34(f).
[111]*Id.* § 261.7.
[112]*Id.* § 261.8.
[113]*Id.* § 261.9.
[114]60 Fed. Reg. 25,492 (1995).
[115]40 C.F.R. § 273.9.

84 THE RCRA PRACTICE MANUAL

Handlers are prohibited from disposing of, diluting, or treating universal waste except in specified circumstances. A SQHUW is not required to notify EPA of its universal waste activities or obtain an EPA identification number.[116] However, an LQHUW must.[117]

The regulations[118] detail how SQHUWs and LQHUWs must manage their universal waste. In general, the waste must be handled in a manner that prevents releases to the environment. Specific handling and packaging requirements for universal waste are described. Handlers must label or mark universal waste or containers of universal waste as required.[119] Universal waste is subject to an accumulation time limit of one year unless a longer period of accumulation is required solely to facilitate proper recovery, treatment, or disposal. The handler must demonstrate that its universal waste has not been accumulated for a period longer than provided by the regulations.[120] SQHUWs and LQHUWs are subject to employee training requirements.[121] The regulations also govern response to releases[122] and regulate off-site shipment to limit the sending or taking of universal waste to a place other than a universal waste handler destination facility or foreign destination. If a handler of universal waste self-transports its waste off-site, it becomes a transporter and must comply with the transporter requirements of the universal waste rule. SQHUWs need not track universal waste shipments. However, LQHUWs must.[123] Finally, exports of universal waste require compliance with portions of the hazardous waste rules and consent of the receiving country.[124]

XII. *Import of Hazardous Waste*

Any person who imports hazardous waste from a foreign country must comply with all of the manifest requirements discussed above with some minor exceptions.[125] First, the name and address of the generator and the name, address, and EPA ID number of the importer must be substituted in place of the generator's name, address, and EPA ID number. Second, the U.S. importer and initial transporter must execute the

---

[116]*Id.* § 273.12.

[117]*Id.* § 273.32.

[118]*Id.* §§ 273.13, 273.33.

[119]*Id.* §§ 273.14, 273.34.

[120]*Id.* §§ 273.15, 273.35.

[121]*Id.* §§ 273.16, 273.36.

[122]*Id.* §§ 273.17, 273.37.

[123]*Id.* §§ 273.19, 273.39.

[124]*Id.* §§ 273.20, 273.40.

[125]*Id.* pt. 262, subpt. F.

certification in place of the generator's signature on the certification statement. Finally, the importer must obtain and use the manifest form from the consignment state if that state requires use of its own manifest. If the consignment state does not supply its own manifest, one may be obtained from any source.[126]

It is important to note that "any person" who imports hazardous waste must comply with the generator requirements of the RCRA regulations. EPA has interpreted this language to mean that more than one party may be an "importer" in a given transaction. For example, if a U.S. facility arranges for the importation of hazardous waste, both the U.S. facility and the transporter would be "persons" who "import" hazardous waste. Thus, both parties may be held liable as importers of hazardous waste in the event of a violation.[127]

XIII. Export of Hazardous Waste

RCRA strictly and comprehensively regulates the exportation of hazardous waste.[128] The federal regulations governing the exportation of hazardous wastes will apply whether or not an individual state has an approved program.[129] The regulations require exporters to notify EPA of each step of the exportation process and to comply with special manifesting and other reporting requirements. Exports of hazardous wastes are prohibited until: (1) the exporter properly notifies EPA; (2) the receiving country has consented to the hazardous waste shipment; (3) a copy of the EPA Acknowledgment of Consent accompanies the hazardous waste shipment; and (4) the hazardous waste shipment conforms to the terms of the receiving country's written consent. Exportation of the hazardous waste shipment does not terminate the liability of the primary exporter. EPA takes the position that all entities in the chain of exportation remain liable, including the generator.[130]

A. Notification Requirements

Before exporting hazardous waste, the primary exporter (the entity originating the exportation of the waste) must notify the EPA of the waste shipment and its intended destination.[131] The exporter must retain a

---

[126]*Id.* § 262.60(b).

[127]Internal memorandum from John H. Skinner, Generator Responsibilities for Importation of Hazardous Waste, EPA/Doc. 9455.01(85) (June 25, 1985).

[128]40 C.F.R. pt. 262, subpt. E.

[129]42 U.S.C. § 6938; 51 Fed. Reg. 28,664, 28,682 (1986).

[130]51 Fed. Reg. 28,664, 28,668 (1986).

[131]40 C.F.R. § 262.53.

86 THE RCRA PRACTICE MANUAL

copy of each notification of intent to export and confirmation of delivery for three years from the date on which the waste was accepted by the initial transporter. The written notification must be sent at least 60 days before shipment and must either be mailed to the Office of Enforcement and Compliance Assurance, Office of Compliance, Enforcement Planning, Targeting, and Data Division (2222A), Environmental Protection Agency, 401 M St., SW, Washington, DC 20460, or hand-delivered to the same division at the following address: Ariel Rios Bldg., 12th St. and Pennsylvania Ave., NW, Washington, DC. In either case, the front of the envelope must display prominently the following notice: "Attention: Notification of Intent to Export."[132] The notification must include the following information:

- the primary exporter's name, address, phone number, and EPA identification number;
- a description of the waste and its EPA hazardous waste number;
- the DOT shipping name, hazard class, and identification number;
- the estimated total quantity of waste to be exported;
- the estimated frequency of export and time over which the exporting will occur;
- a description of the means of exportation for each shipment;
- a description of the intended treatment, storage, or disposal methods to be used by the receiving country;
- the name and address of the consignee and any alternate consignees; and
- the name of any country through which the waste will pass in shipment, the length of time of such travel, and its mode of transportation in that country.[133]

This notification may cover export activities extending over a 12-month (or less) period. EPA must be notified in writing of any changes in the quantity of waste being exported or the mode of exportation.[134]

Hazardous waste may not be exported until EPA has notified the receiving country and the receiving country has consented to the shipment. If the receiving country consents to the shipment, EPA forwards an Acknowledgment of Consent to the primary exporter. The Acknowledgment of Consent describes the terms of consent as expressed by the receiving country and also informs the primary exporter of any com-

---

[132]*Id.* § 262.53(b).
[133]*Id.* § 262.53(a).
[134]*Id.* § 262.53(c).

ments received from the countries through which the wastes will pass in transit to the receiving country. At that point, the primary exporter is authorized to complete the waste manifest and institute exportation of the waste.[135] Exports of universal waste require compliance with portions of these rules.[136]

B. Manifest Requirements

As with importers, exporters of hazardous waste must also fulfill special manifest requirements.[137] The primary exporter, including any intermediary who arranges for the export, must fill out the ordinary manifest form with certain substitutions. The primary exporter must substitute the name and address of the consignee in the receiving country in place of the name, site address, and EPA ID number of the designated TSD facility. In place of the name, address, and identification number of an alternate facility, the primary exporter must insert the name and address of an alternate consignee. The primary exporter must also identify the point of departure from the United States and certify that the shipment conforms to the terms of the Acknowledgment of Consent. The primary exporter must attach a copy of the Acknowledgment of Consent to the manifest to accompany the subsequent shipment unless it is exported by rail or water. If water shipment is used, the Acknowledgment of Consent must be attached to the shipping paper. Additionally, the primary exporter must require the consignee to confirm the delivery of the hazardous waste to that facility in writing, and describe any significant discrepancies between the information on the manifest and the Acknowledgment of Consent.[138]

If a shipment cannot be accepted by the designated or alternate consignee, the primary exporter must renotify EPA of the change in conditions and obtain another Acknowledgment of Consent before delivery to the new consignee. Alternatively, the primary exporter may instruct the transporter to return the waste to it or to another designated facility in the United States. The primary exporter must then inform the transporter to revise the manifest in order to incorporate these revisions. The consignee must confirm in writing that the wastes were delivered to the designated facility and also describe any significant discrepancies from the manifest.[139] The term "significant" is defined at 40 C.F.R. Section

---

[135]*Id.* § 262.53(c)–(f).
[136]*See id.* §§ 273.20, 273.40.
[137]*Id.* § 262.54.
[138]*Id.* § 262.54(a)–(d), (f), (h).
[139]*Id.* § 262.54(g).

88 THE RCRA PRACTICE MANUAL

264.72. The primary exporter must provide an extra copy of the manifest to the transporter for delivery to the U.S. Customs official at the point of departure from the United States.[140] The primary exporter must use the manifest form required by its own state, if the state supplies one. If the state does not require the use of its own manifest form, the primary exporter is free to obtain a manifest form from any other source.[141]

C. Reporting Requirements

The regulations also contain special export requirements concerning annual reports, exception reports, record-keeping requirements, and international agreements.[142] The primary exporter must file an exception report with EPA if it has not received a copy of the manifest within 45 days of the time that it was signed by the transporter. This report must generally conform to the requirements of 40 C.F.R. Section 262.42 but must list the date and place of departure from the United States.[143] A primary exporter must also prepare an exception report if its waste is returned to the United States or if it does not receive written notification from the consignee that its wastes were received.

The regulations also require exporters of hazardous waste to file annual reports summarizing the types, quantities, and frequency of hazardous waste exports for the prior year. These reports must be filed on March 1 of each year and must include the following information: (1) the exporter's name, address, and EPA ID number; (2) the name and address of each consignee; and (3) a description of the waste transported, including the EPA hazardous waste number, the DOT hazard class, and the quantity of hazardous wastes shipped. Exporters are required to certify that they are familiar with information contained in the report and that the information contained within the report is complete and accurate. A copy of the annual report must be kept for at least three years from the date of the report.[144]

With respect to international agreements, Subpart H, which governs trans-frontier shipments of hazardous waste for recovery with the Organization for Economic Cooperation and Development (OECD), sets forth notification, consent, tracking, reporting, and other requirements for

---

[140]*Id.* § 262.54(i).
[141]*Id.* § 262.54(e).
[142]*Id.* §§ 262.55–.57.
[143]*Id.* § 262.55.
[144]*Id.* §§ 262.56–.57.

imports and exports of hazardous wastes destined for countries listed in 40 C.F.R. Section 262.58(a)(1).[145] Guidance is available on EPA's Web site.[146]

XIV. Conclusion

Any person shipping hazardous waste off-site must pay close attention to the complex regulations applicable to generators of hazardous waste described in this chapter. Because the regulatory scheme relies upon the generator to first document the off-site shipment of hazardous waste, EPA and the states strictly enforce the generator regulations. Companies that routinely comply with the regulations have management systems in place to ensure that wastes are properly categorized, handled, and shipped to authorized facilities by authorized transporters, and that employees are trained in proper handling of hazardous wastes from the point of generation to the shipping dock. Although the regulations that apply to generators of hazardous waste are complex, a well-managed company can successfully comply with them.

---

[145]See id. §§ 262.80–.89.
[146]See, e.g., http://www.epa.gov/OSWRCRA/hazwaste/state/frs/fr152.pdf; http://www.epa.gov/OSWRCRA/hazwaste/state/clists/c1152.pdf.

APPENDIX A

OMB#: 2050-0175 Expires 12/31/2003

MAIL THE COMPLETED FORM TO: The Appropriate State or EPA Regional Office.	United States Environmental Protection Agency **RCRA SUBTITLE C SITE IDENTIFICATION FORM**	

1. Reason for Submittal (See instructions on page 23) MARK CORRECT BOX(ES)	**Reason for Submittal:** ❑ To provide Initial Notification of Regulated Waste Activity (to obtain an EPA ID Number for hazardous waste, universal waste, or used oil activities). ❑ To provide Subsequent Notification of Regulated Waste Activity (to update site identification information). ❑ As a component of a First RCRA Hazardous Waste Part A Permit Application. ❑ As a component of a Revised RCRA Hazardous Waste Part A Permit Application (Amendment #_____). ❑ As a component of the Hazardous Waste Report.	
2. Site EPA ID Number (See instructions on page 24)	**EPA ID Number:** ⎵⎵⎵ ⎵⎵⎵⎵ ⎵⎵⎵⎵	
3. Site Name (See instructions on page 24)	**Name:**	
4. Site Location Information (See instructions on page 24)	**Street Address:**	
	City, Town, or Village:	**State:**
	County Name:	**Zip Code:**
5. Site Land Type (See instructions on page 24)	**Site Land Type:** ❑ Private ❑ County ❑ District ❑ Federal ❑ Indian ❑ Municipal ❑ State ❑ Other	
6. North American Industry Classification System (NAICS) Code(s) for the Site (See instructions on page 24)	**A.**	**B.**
	C.	**D.**
7. Site Mailing Address (See instructions on page 25)	**Street or P. O. Box:**	
	City, Town, or Village:	
	State:	
	Country:	**Zip Code:**
8. Site Contact Person (See instructions on page 25)	**First Name:** | **MI:**	**Last Name:**
	Phone Number:	**Phone Number Extension:**
9. Legal Owner and Operator of the Site (See instructions on pages 25 to 26)	**A. Name of Site's Legal Owner:**	**Date Became Owner (mm/dd/yyyy):**
	Owner Type: ❑ Private ❑ County ❑ District ❑ Federal ❑ Indian ❑ Municipal ❑ State ❑ Other	
	B. Name of Site's Operator:	**Date Became Operator (mm/dd/yyyy):**
	Operator Type: ❑ Private ❑ County ❑ District ❑ Federal ❑ Indian ❑ Municipal ❑ State ❑ Other	

EPA Form 8700-12 (Revised 5/2002)   Page 1 of 3

OMB#: 2050-0175 Expires 12/31/2003

	EPA ID No.											

10. Type of Regulated Waste Activity (Mark the appropriate boxes for activities that apply to your site. See instructions on pages 26 to 30)

A. Hazardous Waste Activities

1. Generator of Hazardous Waste
(Choose only one of the following three categories.)

☐ a. LQG: Greater than 1,000 kg/mo (2,200 lbs./mo.) of non-acute hazardous waste; or

☐ b. SQG: 100 to 1,000 kg/mo (220 - 2,200 lbs./mo.) of non-acute hazardous waste; or

☐ c. CESQG: Less than 100 kg/mo (220 lbs./mo.) of non-acute hazardous waste

In addition, indicate other generator activities. (Mark all that apply)

☐ d. United States Importer of Hazardous Waste

☐ e. Mixed Waste (hazardous and radioactive) Generator

For Items 2 through 6, mark all that apply.

☐ **2. Transporter of Hazardous Waste**

☐ **3. Treater, Storer, or Disposer of Hazardous Waste (at your site)** Note: A hazardous waste permit is required for this activity.

☐ **4. Recycler of Hazardous Waste (at your site)** Note: A hazardous waste permit may be required for this activity.

5. Exempt Boiler and/or Industrial Furnace

☐ a. Small Quantity On-site Burner Exemption

☐ b. Smelting, Melting, and Refining Furnace Exemption

☐ **6. Underground Injection Control**

B. Universal Waste Activities

1. Large Quantity Handler of Universal Waste (accumulate 5,000 kg or more) [refer to your State regulations to determine what is regulated]. Indicate types of universal waste generated and/or accumulated at your site. (Mark all boxes that apply):

		Generate	Accumulate
a.	Batteries	☐	☐
b.	Pesticides	☐	☐
c.	Thermostats	☐	☐
d.	Lamps	☐	☐
e.	Other (specify) _____	☐	☐
f.	Other (specify) _____	☐	☐
g.	Other (specify) _____	☐	☐

☐ **2. Destination Facility for Universal Waste**
Note: A hazardous waste permit may be required for this activity.

C. Used Oil Activities (Mark all boxes that apply.)

1. Used Oil Transporter - Indicate Type(s) of Activity(ies)
☐ a. Transporter
☐ b. Transfer Facility

2. Used Oil Processor and/or Re-refiner - Indicate Type(s) of Activity(ies)
☐ a. Processor
☐ b. Re-refiner

☐ **3. Off-Specification Used Oil Burner**

4. Used Oil Fuel Marketer - Indicate Type(s) of Activity(ies)
☐ a. Marketer Who Directs Shipment of Off-Specification Used Oil to Off-Specification Used Oil Burner
☐ b. Marketer Who First Claims the Used Oil Meets the Specifications

11. Description of Hazardous Wastes (See instructions on page 31)

A. Waste Codes for Federally Regulated Hazardous Wastes. Please list the waste codes of the Federal hazardous wastes handled at your site. List them in the order they are presented in the regulations (e.g., D001, D003, F007, U112). Use an additional page if more spaces are needed.

EPA Form 8700-12 (Revised 5/2002)   Page 2 of 3

OMB#: 2050-0175 Expires 12/31/2003

EPA ID No.											

B. Waste Codes for State-Regulated (i.e., non-Federal) Hazardous Wastes. Please list the waste codes of the State-regulated hazardous wastes handled at your site. List them in the order they are presented in the regulations. Use an additional page if more spaces are needed for waste codes.

12. Comments (See instructions on page 31)

13. Certification. I certify under penalty of law that this document and all attachments were prepared under my direction or supervision in accordance with a system designed to assure that qualified personnel properly gather and evaluate the information submitted. Based on my inquiry of the person or persons who manage the system, or those persons directly responsible for gathering the information, the information submitted is, to the best of my knowledge and belief, true, accurate, and complete. I am aware that there are significant penalties for submitting false information, including the possibility of fine and imprisonment for knowing violations. **(See instructions on page 31)**

Signature of owner, operator, or an authorized representative	Name and Official Title (type or print)	Date Signed (mm/dd/yyyy)

EPA Form 8700-12 (Revised 5/2002)   Page 3 of 3

APPENDIX B

Please print or type (Form designed for use on elite (12 - pitch) typewriter)

Form Approved. OMB No. 2050 - 0039 Expires 9 - 30 - 91

UNIFORM HAZARDOUS WASTE MANIFEST	1 Generator's US EPA ID No.	Manifest Document No.	2. Page 1 of	Information in the shaded areas is not required by Federal law

3. Generator's Name and Mailing Address

A. State Manifest Document Number

B. State Generator's ID

4. Generator's Phone (   )

5. Transporter 1 Company Name	6.	US EPA ID Number

C. State Transporter's ID

D. Transporter's Phone

7. Transporter 2 Company Name	8.	US EPA ID Number

E. State Transporter's ID

F. Transporter's Phone

9. Designated Facility Name and Site Address	10.	US EPA ID Number

G. State Facility's ID

H. Facility's Phone

11. US DOT Description (Including Proper Shipping Name, Hazard Class, and ID Number)	12. Containers		13. Total Quantity	14. Unit Wt/Vol	I. Waste No.
	No.	Type			
G a.					
E					
N b.					
E					
R c.					
A					
T d.					
O					
R					

J. Additional Descriptions for Materials Listed Above

K. Handling Codes for Wastes Listed Above

15. Special Handling Instructions and Additional Information

16. **GENERATOR'S CERTIFICATION:** I hereby declare that the contents of this consignment are fully and accurately described above by proper shipping name and are classified, packed, marked, and labeled, and are in all respects in proper condition for transport by highway according to applicable international and national government regulations.

If I am a large quantity generator, I certify that I have a program in place to reduce the volume and toxicity of waste generated to the degree I have determined to be economically practicable and that I have selected the practicable method of treatment, storage, or disposal currently available to me which minimizes the present and future threat to human health and the environment; **OR,** if I am a small quantity generator, I have made a good faith effort to minimize my waste generation and select the best waste management method that is available to me and that I can afford.

Printed/Typed Name	Signature	Month	Day	Year

T R A N S P O R T E R

17. Transporter 1 Acknowledgement of Receipt of Materials

Printed/Typed Name	Signature	Month	Day	Year

18. Transporter 2 Acknowledgement of Receipt of Materials

Printed/Typed Name	Signature	Month	Day	Year

F A C I L I T Y

19. Discrepancy Indication Space

20. Facility Owner or Operator: Certification of receipt of hazardous materials covered by this manifest except as noted in item 19.

Printed/Typed Name	Signature	Month	Day	Year

EPA Form 8700 - 22 (Rev. 9 - 88) Previous editions are obsolete.

Please print or type

Form Approved. OMB No. 2050 - 0039 Expires 9 - 30 - 91

UNIFORM HAZARDOUS WASTE MANIFEST (continuation sheet)	21. Generator's US EPA ID No.	Manifest Document No.	22. Page	Information in the shaded areas is not required by Federal law

23. Generator's Name

L. State Manifest Document Number

M. State Generator's ID

24. Transporter____ Company Name	25. US EPA ID Number	N. State Transporter's ID
		O. Transporter's Phone
26. Transporter____ Company Name	27. US EPA ID Number	P. State Transporter's ID
		Q. Transporter's Phone

28. US DOT Description (Including Proper Shipping Name, Hazard Class, and ID Number)	29. Containers No.	Type	30. Total Quantity	31. Unit Wt/Vol	R. Waste No.
a.					
b.					
c.					
d.					
e.					
f.					
g.					
h.					
i.					

G E N E R A T O R

S. Additional Descriptions for Materials Listed Above

K. Handling Codes for Wastes Listed Above

31. Special Handling Instructions and Additional Information

33. Transporter____ Acknowledgement of Receipt of Materials		Date
Printed/Typed Name	Signature	Month Day Year
34. Transporter____ Acknowledgement of Receipt of Materials		Date
Printed/Typed Name	Signature	Month Day Year

T R A N S P O R T E R

35. Discrepancy Indication Space

F A C I L I T Y

EPA Form 8700 - 22A (Rev. 9 - 88) Previous editions are obsolete.

APPENDIX C

FORM IC   OMB#: 2050-0024 Expires 11/30/2000

BEFORE COPYING FORM, ATTACH SITE IDENTIFICATION LABEL
OR ENTER:

SITE NAME: _____

EPA ID NO: |__|__|__| |__|__|__| |__|__|__| |__|__|

**U.S. ENVIRONMENTAL
PROTECTION AGENCY**

1999 Hazardous Waste Report

**FORM
IC**

**IDENTIFICATION AND
CERTIFICATION**

Instructions: Please see the detailed instructions beginning on page 7 of the instructions and forms booklet before completing this form. In addition, the page number for instructions specific to each section is provided below.

Sec. I	Site name and location address. Check the box □ in items A, B, C, E, F, G, and H if same as label; if different, enter corrections. If label is absent, enter information. Instructions page 7.

A. EPA ID No.
Same as label □ or → |__|__|__| |__|__|__| |__|__|__| |__|__|

B. County
Same as label □ or →

C. Site/company name
Same as label □ or →

D. Has the site name associated with this EPA ID changed since 1997?
□ 1 Yes   □ 2 No

E. Street name and number. If not applicable, enter industrial park, building name, or other physical location description.
Same as label □ or →

F. City, town, village
Same as label □ or →

G. State
Same as label □
or → |__|__|

H. Zip Code
Same as label □ or →
|__|__|__|__|__| - |__|__|__|__|

Sec. II	Mailing address of site. Instructions page 7.

A. Is the mailing address the same as the location address?   □ 1 Yes (SKIP TO SEC. III)   □ 2 No (CONTINUE TO BOX B)

B. Number and street name of mailing address

C. City, town, village

D. State
|__|__|

E. Zip Code
|__|__|__|__|__| - |__|__|__|__|

Sec. III	Name, title, and telephone number of the person who should be contacted if questions arise regarding this report. Instructions page 7.

A. Last Name   First name   M.I.

B. Title

C. Telephone Number
|__|__|__| |__|__|__| - |__|__|__|__|
Extension |__|__|__|__|

Sec. IV	"I certify under penalty of law that this document and all attachments were prepared under my direction or supervision in accordance with a system designed to assure that qualified personnel properly gather and evaluate the information submitted. Based on my inquiry of the person or persons who manage the system, or those persons directly responsible for gathering the information, the information submitted is, to the best of my knowledge and belief, true, accurate and complete. I am aware that there are significant penalties under Section 3008 of the Resource Conservation and Recovery Act for submitting false information, including the possibility of fine and imprisonment for knowing violations." Instructions page 8.

A. Last Name   First name   M.I.

B. Title

C. Signature

D. Date of signature
|__|__| |__|__| |__|__|
Month   Day   Year

Over →

EPA Form 8700-13A/B (Revised (8/99))   Page 1 of ___

95

FORM IC | OMB#: 2050-0024 Expires 11/30/2000

EPA ID NO. |__|__|__| |__|__|__| |__|__|__| |__|__|

Sec. V	Generator status. Instructions begin on page 8.

A. 1999 RCRA generator status

(CHECK ONE BOX BELOW)

□ 1 LQG
□ 2 SQG   } SKIP TO SEC. VI
□ 3 CESQG
□ 4 Non-generator (CONTINUE TO BOX B)

B. Reason for not generating

(CHECK ALL THAT APPLY)

□ 1 Never generated
□ 2 Out of business
□ 3 Only excluded or delisted waste
□ 4 Only non-hazardous waste

□ 5 Periodic or occasional generator
□ 6 Waste minimization activity
□ 7 Other (SPECIFY IN COMMENTS BOX BELOW)

Sec. VI	On-site waste management status. Instructions page 10.

A. Storage subject to RCRA permitting requirements

|__|

B. Treatment, disposal, or recycling subject to RCRA permitting requirements

|__|

Comments:

EPA Form 8700-13A/B (Revised (8/99))

Page ___ of ___

APPENDIX D

PB88-21301+
EPA/600 2-88 025
April 1988

The EPA Manual for
Waste Minimization Opportunity Assessments

by

Gregory Lorton, et al
Jacobs Engineering
Pasadena, CA 91101

EPA Contract 68-01-7053

EPA Project Officer
H. Freeman

REPRODUCED BY
U.S. DEPARTMENT OF COMMERCE
NATIONAL TECHNICAL INFORMATION SERVICE
SPRINGFIELD, VA. 22161

HAZARDOUS WASTE ENGINEERING RESEARCH LABORATORY
OFFICE OF RESEARCH AND DEVELOPMENT
U.S. ENVIRONMENTAL PROTECTION AGENCY
CINCINNATI, OH 45268

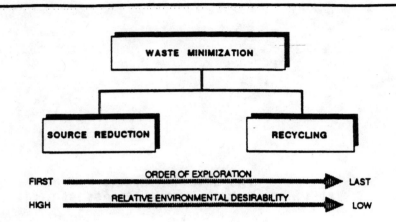

WASTE MINIMIZATION

The reduction, to the extent feasible, of hazardous waste that is generated or subsequently treated, stored or disposed of. It includes any source reduction or recycling activity undertaken by a generator that results in either (1) the reduction of total volume or quantity of hazardous waste or (2) the reduction of toxicity of the hazardous waste, or both, so long as such reduction is consistent with the goal of minimizing present and future threats to human health and the environment (EPA's Report to Congress, 1986, EPA/530-SW-86-033).

SOURCE REDUCTION

Any activity that reduces or eliminates the generation of hazardous waste at the source, usually within a process (op. cit.).

RECYCLING

A material is "recycled" if it is used, reused, or reclaimed (40 CFR 261.1 (c) (7)). A material is "used or reused" if it is either (1) employed as an ingredient (including its use as an intermediate) to make a product; however a material will not satisfy this condition if distinct components of the material are recovered as separate end products (as when metals are recovered from metal containing secondary materials) or (2) employed in a particular function as an effective substitute for a commercial product (40 CFR 261.1 (c) (5)). A material is "reclaimed" if it is processed to recover a useful product or if it is regenerated. Examples include the recovery of lead values from spent batteries and the regeneration of spent solvents (40 CFR 261.1 (c) (4)).

Waste Minimization Definitions

Firm	Waste Minimization Assessment Worksheets	Prepared By
Site		Checked By
Date	Proj. No.	Sheet 1 of 1 Page ___ of ___

WORKSHEET 1 — **ASSESSMENT OVERVIEW**

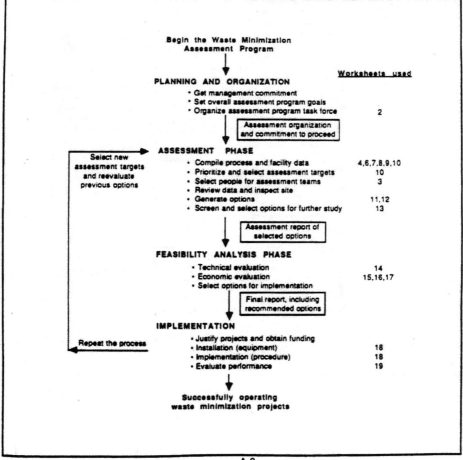

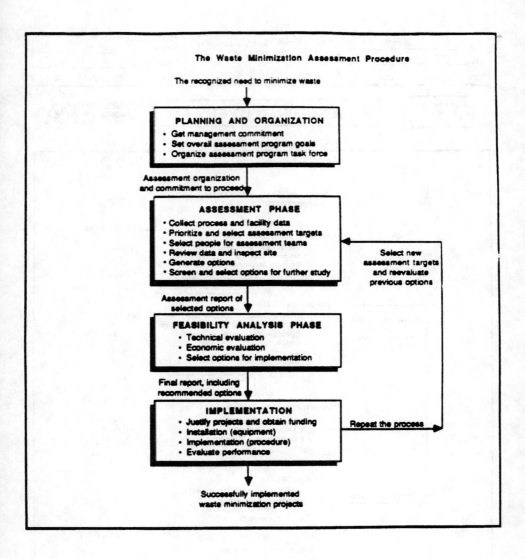

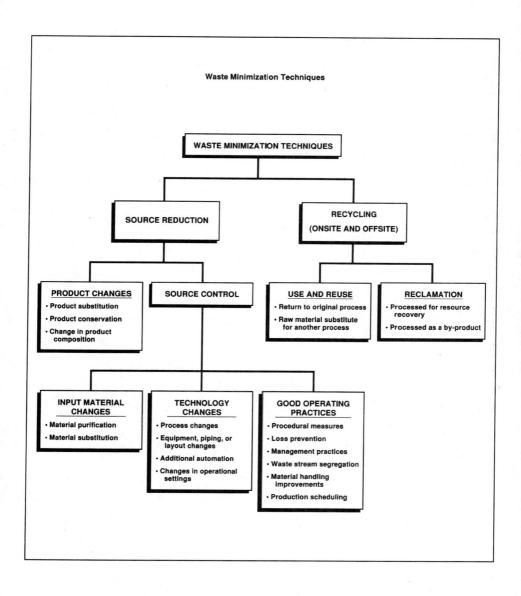

CHAPTER 6

Transport of Hazardous Waste

JOHN R. JACUS AND DEAN C. MILLER

I. Introduction and Scope

Regulating the transport of hazardous waste is key to any system of comprehensive regulation such as that envisioned by Congress in its passage of the Resource Conservation and Recovery Act (RCRA). RCRA's trademark cradle-to-grave regulatory scheme would not be possible without effective, implementable procedures for tracking hazardous waste during transport from its place of origin to its final destination. Considering how vital this component of RCRA's regulatory scheme is to the overall success of the program, it perhaps is surprising to note how few regulations EPA has developed that apply to the transport of hazardous waste. Part 263 of Title 40, C.F.R., is quite sparse compared with the voluminous provisions in RCRA's generator standards or standards for treatment, storage, and disposal (TSD) facilities.

The brevity of EPA's regulations governing transport of hazardous waste is somewhat deceiving. Indeed, the field of hazardous waste transport is an extremely complex one that has undergone substantial changes in recent years by virtue of international and federal regulatory initiatives, as well as through repeated application of federal statutory and constitutional principles attendant to the regulation of commerce.

Although this chapter is limited to subjects falling within the scope of regulation of hazardous waste pursuant to RCRA, any worthwhile review of the regulation of hazardous waste transportation also must touch upon hazardous materials regulations promulgated by the Department of Transportation (DOT) and the statutory and constitutional aspects of intrastate and interstate transportation of hazardous waste. Accordingly, this chapter will review: (1) RCRA regulations affecting transporters of hazardous waste under Subtitle C; (2) the body of regulations promulgated by DOT and adopted by EPA in its regulation of transporters; and (3) constitutional and federal statutory constraints on state and local regulation of hazardous waste transportation.

Subjects discussed elsewhere in this book, including the hazardous waste manifest system and the requirement of obtaining an EPA identification number, also are a part of the body of regulations affecting transporters of hazardous waste. Those subjects will not be discussed in great detail, as they have previously been explained in the context of generator standards under 40 C.F.R. Part 262.

II. Regulation of Hazardous Waste Transporters under RCRA

RCRA standards applicable to transporters of hazardous waste appear at 40 C.F.R. Part 263. Those regulations apply to "persons transporting hazardous waste within the United States if the transportation requires a manifest under 40 CFR Part 262."[1] EPA's transporter standards address use of manifests, obtaining an EPA identification number (EPA ID number), record keeping, hazardous substance incident reporting, and affirmative obligations for response to hazardous waste releases during transport. According to RCRA Section 3003(b),[2] these provisions must be consistent with DOT's hazardous materials regulations.

A. Transporter Identification Numbers and Use of Manifests

Under EPA's transporter standards, a generator of hazardous waste must obtain an EPA ID number prior to transporting hazardous waste or offering such waste for transportation.[3] Additionally, a transporter may not accept hazardous waste from a generator unless the waste is accompanied by a manifest signed in accordance with RCRA's generator standards appearing at 40 C.F.R. Section 262.20.

As noted in the previous chapter, the hazardous waste manifest system requires that before transporting a hazardous waste, the transporter must sign and date the manifest, acknowledging acceptance of the hazardous waste from the generator. The transporter then must return a signed copy of the manifest to the generator before leaving the genera-

---

[1] 40 C.F.R. § 263.10(a).
[2] 42 U.S.C.A. § 6923(b).
[3] 40 C.F.R. § 262.12(a).

Chapter 6: Transport of Hazardous Waste 105

tor's property. Finally, the transporter must ensure that the manifest or its equivalent accompanies the hazardous waste to its next point of delivery, whether that be a transfer facility or a TSD facility.[4] In many cases, a customary shipping paper will satisfy the manifest requirement, provided it contains the necessary information.

Upon delivery of hazardous waste to another transporter or to the designated facility listed on the hazardous waste manifest, the transporter must record the date of delivery and obtain the signature of the next transporter or a representative of the designated facility, retain one copy of the manifest, and forward the remaining copies of the manifest to accompany the waste with the subsequent transporter or the designated TSD facility.[5] As discussed in Section II.A.1–.3 of this chapter, the requirements for bulk shipment via water transporters, shipments involving rail transportation, and exports of hazardous waste leaving the United States have slightly different requirements from the requirements covered in this section.

1. Bulk Shipment by Water Transporter

In the case of transporters of bulk shipments by water, a shipping paper replaces the manifest, provided all manifest-required information, except EPA ID number, generator certification, and signatures, is properly documented. The delivering transporter still must record the date of delivery and obtain the signature of the representative of the designated facility on the shipping paper. Moreover, the person delivering hazardous waste to the initial bulk shipment water transporter must obtain the date of delivery and signature of that transporter on the manifest and then forward it to the designated facility, where it will be joined by the water transporter shipping paper discussed above.[6] A copy of the shipping paper manifest is retained by each bulk shipment water transporter.[7]

2. Shipment by Rail Transport

A shipping paper containing all information required on the manifest, except EPA ID number, generator's certification, and signatures, must accompany the hazardous waste at all times during rail transport. The initial rail transporter must sign and date the manifest, acknowledging acceptance of the hazardous waste, and return a copy of the manifest to the nonrail transporter. The initial rail transporter must then forward at least three copies of the manifest to the next nonrail transporter or the

---

[4] 40 C.F.R. § 263.20(a)–(c).
[5] *Id.* § 263.20(d).
[6] *Id.* § 263.20(e).
[7] *Id.* § 263.22(b).

designated facility, or in the case of export, the last rail transporter designated to handle the waste in the United States.[8] The initial and final rail transporters must retain one copy of the manifest and rail shipping paper in accordance with 40 C.F.R. Section 263.22(c). Waste that is exported must be accompanied by an EPA Acknowledgment of Consent form. Intermediate rail transporters are not required to sign either the manifest or shipping paper.[9]

When delivering hazardous waste to the designated facility or to a nonrail transporter, a rail transporter must record the date of delivery and obtain the handwritten signature of a representative of the designated facility on the manifest or the shipping paper, or of the next nonrail transporter on the manifest, and retain a copy of the manifest or signed shipping paper in accordance with 40 C.F.R. Section 263.22(c).[10] A rail transporter delivering to a nonrail transporter should receive a signed and dated copy of the manifest from the subsequent nonrail transporter.[11]

3. Export and Import of Hazardous Waste

The export of hazardous waste is governed by 40 C.F.R. Section 262, Subpart E. Hazardous waste export is prohibited unless (1) notification in accordance with Section 262.53 has been provided, (2) the receiving country has consented to accept the hazardous waste, (3) a copy of the EPA Acknowledgment of Consent to the shipment accompanies the shipment and, unless exported by rail, is attached to the manifest or shipping paper; and (4) the shipment conforms to the terms of the receiving country's written consent as reflected in the EPA Acknowledgment of Consent.[12] A complete notification, which complies with the requirements of Section 252.53, should be submitted 60 days before the initial shipment is intended to be shipped off-site.[13] A primary exporter must comply with the manifest requirements of 40 C.F.R. Sections 262.20 through 262.23, with some limited exceptions.[14] In addition, primary exporters must file an annual report with the EPA Administrator no later than March 1 each year, summarizing the types, quantities, frequency, and ultimate destination of all hazardous waste exported during the

---

[8]*Id.* § 263.20(f).
[9]*Id.* § 263.20(f)(2).
[10]*Id.* § 263.20(f)(3), (5).
[11]*Id.* § 263.20(f)(4).
[12]*Id.* § 262.52.
[13]*Id.* § 262.53.
[14]*Id.* § 262.54.

previous calendar year.[15] The primary exporter must maintain specific export-related documents for at least three years.[16]

In the case of exported waste, a transporter must indicate on the manifest the date the waste left the United States and must sign the manifest and retain a copy, in accordance with 40 C.F.R. Section 263.22(c).[17] The transporter also must return a signed copy of the manifest to the generator and give another copy of the manifest to a U.S. Customs official at the waste's point of departure from the United States. In accordance with the provisions of 40 C.F.R. Section 262.20, waste being transported for export also must be accompanied by an EPA Acknowledgment of Consent, to be attached to the manifest or shipping paper, except for shipments by rail, discussed above.

Any person who imports hazardous waste from a foreign country into the United States must comply with the requirements of 40 C.F.R. Section 262, Subpart F. This subpart requires compliance with the manifest requirements of Section 262.20(a), with a few minor exceptions.

If hazardous waste destined for a "recovery operation" is imported or exported to or from designated member countries of the Organization for Economic Cooperation and Development (OECD) and is subject to Part 262 manifest requirements or state or federal universal waste management standards of 40 C.F.R. Part 273, the requirements of 40 C.F.R. Section 262, Subpart H apply.[18] "Recovery operations" mean activities leading to resource recovery, recycling, reclamation, direct reuse, or specifically identified alternative uses.[19] The level of control over such imports and exports is indicated by assignment of the waste to a green, amber, or red list.[20] Subpart H establishes requirements for, among other things, notification and consent, waste tracking, reporting, and record keeping.

4. The Reclamation Exemption for Small-Quantity Generators

The RCRA transporter standards provide an important exemption from use of manifests for some waste received for transport from small-quantity generators (SQGs).[21] To qualify for the exemption from compliance with the other requirements of 40 C.F.R. Part 263, the transporter must confirm that the waste is being transported pursuant to a reclamation

---

[15]*Id.* § 262.56.
[16]*Id.* § 262.57.
[17]*Id.* § 263.20(g).
[18]*Id.* § 262.80.
[19]*Id.* § 252.81(k).
[20]*Id.* § 262.82.
[21]*Id.* § 263.20(h).

108   THE RCRA PRACTICE MANUAL

agreement under 40 C.F.R. Section 262.20(e). The transporter then must record on a log or shipping paper the name, address, and EPA ID number of the waste generator, the quantity of waste accepted, all DOT-required shipping information, and the date the waste was accepted. The transporter must carry this informal record when transporting waste to the reclamation facility and retain such record for at least three years after termination or expiration of the reclamation agreement. Note that this limited exemption under RCRA does not relieve generators from complying with DOT regulations if the waste is a hazardous material.

B. Record Retention

Transporters of hazardous waste must keep a copy of manifests signed by the generator, the transporter, and the next recipient of the waste for three years from the date the hazardous waste was accepted by the initial transporter.[22] This document retention period also applies to shipping papers employed in bulk shipment by water transporters and for shipments by rail within the United States. In the case of export of hazardous waste, a transporter must keep a copy of the manifest (indicating that the waste left the United States) for three years from the date the hazardous waste was accepted by the initial transporter. The three-year document retention period applicable to transporters of hazardous waste automatically is extended while any enforcement action regarding transportation of particular wastes is pending, and can also be extended at the request of the EPA Administrator.[23]

C. Relationship to Generator and TSD Requirements

RCRA does not impose the requirements for hazardous waste storage facilities, appearing at 40 C.F.R. Parts 264 and 265, on hazardous waste transporters if the storage of manifested shipments of hazardous waste in containers meeting the requirements of 40 C.F.R. Section 262.30 does not exceed ten days in duration.[24] However, if a transporter brings waste into the United States from abroad or mixes hazardous wastes of different DOT shipping descriptions through placement in a single container, the transporter also must comply with RCRA's generator standards appearing at 40 C.F.R. Part 262.[25]

---

[22]*Id.* § 263.22(a).
[23]*Id.* § 263.22(e).
[24]*Id.* § 263.12.
[25]*Id.* § 263.10(c).

D. On-Site Transportation of Hazardous Waste

RCRA's transporter standards do not apply to on-site transportation of hazardous waste by generators or by owners or operators of TSD facilities.[26] For purposes of this exception, "on-site" is closely related to RCRA's definition of "facility"; see the discussion in Chapter 5. It is important to note, however, that this exception is not completely consistent with DOT's view of the scope of its regulation of hazardous materials transportation.

DOT construes its authority under the Hazardous Materials Transportation Act (HMTA) to extend to any situation where a carrier offers or accepts hazardous materials for transportation in commerce, unless an exemption is obtained.[27] DOT has interpreted "transportation in commerce" to include transportation wholly within private property under certain circumstances.[28] (A copy is reproduced as Appendix A.) So, while in-plant transportation of hazardous waste would not require use of a hazardous waste manifest, it requires compliance with DOT regulations governing packaging and hazard communication (labeling and placarding). The Chief Counsel's Office of the Research and Special Programs Administration (RSPA) has issued interpretations and administrative decisions on a case-by-case basis about whether particular activities constitute "transportation" and therefore are subject to regulation under the hazardous materials regulations. Recently, RSPA proposed implementing an overall rule-making process to clarify which activities are subject to regulation.[29]

E. Substantive Requirements for Transporters of Hazardous Waste

RCRA requires that transporters must deliver the entire quantity of hazardous waste accepted from a generator or transporter to the intended recipient or alternate recipient of the waste.[30] If the waste cannot be delivered in accordance with the specifications on the manifest, the transporter must contact the generator for further directions and must revise the manifest according to the generator's instructions.[31]

If hazardous waste is discharged during transportation, the transporter must give notice to the National Response Center and report in

---

[26]*Id.* § 263.10(b).

[27]49 C.F.R. § 171.2.

[28]DOT Advisory Opinion to Dep't of Energy at p. 2 (Apr. 23, 1991) ("If a road is used by members of the general public . . . without their having to gain access through a controlled access point, transportation on . . . that road is in commerce.").

[29]*See* 66 Fed. Reg. 61,251 (2001).

[30]40 C.F.R. § 263.21(a).

[31]*Id.* § 263.21(b).

110   THE RCRA PRACTICE MANUAL

writing to the Director, Office of Hazardous Materials Regulations, Materials Transportation Bureau, Department of Transportation, Washington, DC 20590.[32] A bulk shipment water transporter that is discharging hazardous waste must give the same notice as required by the National Oil and Hazardous Substance Contingency Plan.[33] These requirements mirror those of DOT.

The transporter standards also impose a broad "general duty" requirement to "take appropriate immediate action to protect human health and the environment"[34] in the event of a release of hazardous waste during transport. Transporter standards give examples of notifying local authorities and diking the discharge area as means of complying with this broad general-duty standard. Additionally, a transporter must clean up any hazardous waste discharge that occurs during transportation, or take such action as may be required or approved by federal, state, or local officials, so that the discharge no longer presents a hazard to human health or the environment.[35] The transporter standards also authorize removal of waste discharged during transportation through use of transporters without EPA ID numbers, and without preparation of a manifest, if a responsible official of a state or local government or a federal agency determines that immediate removal is necessary to protect human health and the environment.[36]

F. EPA Adoption of DOT Regulations

After passage of RCRA in 1976, EPA adopted DOT's hazardous materials regulations (HMRs) as a means of satisfying its mandate to regulate the transport of hazardous waste under RCRA Section 3003,[37] rather than attempting to duplicate much of what DOT had already developed in the way of regulations concerning transport of hazardous materials. Except for transporters of bulk shipments of hazardous waste by water, a transporter that meets all applicable requirements of the HMRs, set forth at 49 C.F.R. Parts 171 through 180, obtains an EPA ID number, and complies with the discharge cleanup requirements of Section 263.31, will be deemed in compliance with RCRA's transporter standards. However, DOT's regulations are voluminous and complex, despite the pursuit of initiatives to standardize and simplify them.

---

[32]*Id.* § 263.30(c).
[33]*Id.* pt. 300.
[34]*Id.* § 263.30(a).
[35]*Id.* § 263.31.
[36]*Id.* § 263.30(b).
[37]42 U.S.C.A. § 6923.

Chapter 6: Transport of Hazardous Waste 111

III. DOT's Hazardous Material Regulations: A Summary

A. History of Regulation

The HMTA, as amended by the Hazardous Materials Transportation Uniform Safety Act of 1990 (HMTUSA), the Hazardous Materials Transportation Authorization Act of 1994 (HMTAA); the Intermodal Safe Container Transportation Amendments Act of 1996 (ISCTAA), and the Federal Transit Act of 1998 (FTA) requires the Secretary of Transportation to promulgate regulations for the safe transport of hazardous materials in intrastate, interstate, and foreign commerce.[38] "Transport" is defined broadly to mean any movement of property and any loading, unloading, or storage incidental to such movement. The Secretary is authorized to designate materials as hazardous when they "pose an unreasonable risk to health and safety or property."[39]

These broad powers and duties of the Secretary of Transportation were first delegated by Congress through passage of the Hazardous Materials Transportation Act of 1975.[40] That act repealed the rule-making authority of various federal agencies in favor of the centralized promulgation of regulations by DOT. The HMTA was passed against a background of piecemeal regulations developed since the turn of the 20th century and the creation of the National Transportation Safety Board to coordinate the efforts addressed by numerous agencies previously involved in regulating hazardous materials transport.

Despite the great improvements brought about under the HMTA and its implementing regulations after 1975, concern continued to grow regarding the body of conflicting state, local, and federal regulations affecting transportation of hazardous materials. To address this concern, Congress enacted the Hazardous Materials Transportation Uniform Safety Act of 1990, substantially amending the HMTA. As noted above, the HMTA has been amended frequently since that time.

B. Scope of HMRs

DOT's hazardous materials regulations (HMRs) regulate the transportation of hazardous materials in intrastate, interstate, and foreign commerce. The regulations define hazardous materials, including hazardous waste, as the substances that have been determined by the Secretary of Transportation to be capable of posing an unreasonable risk to health,

---

[38]49 U.S.C.A. §§ 5101 *et seq.*
[39]*Id.* § 5103(a).
[40]Pub. L. No. 93-633, tit. I, 88 Stat. 2156 (1975).

112   THE RCRA PRACTICE MANUAL

safety, and property when transported in commerce.[41] The regulations define hazardous waste to mean "any material that is subject to the Hazardous Waste Manifest Requirements of the U.S. Environmental Protection Agency specified in 40 C.F.R. Part 262."[42] Those portions of the HMRs of greatest concern to transporters govern shipping papers, labeling, marking, placarding, use of proper containers, and reporting of discharges.

1. Who Is Regulated?

The HMRs apply to three classes of persons: (1) those "offering" hazardous materials for transport, that is, "shippers"; (2) those who transport hazardous materials, known as "carriers," in interstate, intrastate, and foreign commerce, by rail, highway, water, and air; and (3) those who manufacture, fabricate, mark, maintain, recondition, repair, or test containers to be used for transporting hazardous materials.[43] Section 171 of the HMRs sets forth the general information regulations and definitions, some of which are noted above. It also contains the immediate notice and detailed reporting requirements applicable to hazardous materials incidents.[44]

2. Notice Requirements

The notice provisions of the HMRs expressly apply to carriers that transport hazardous materials. Incidents to be immediately reported include those occurring during the course of transportation, including loading, unloading, and temporary storage, in which, as a direct result of hazardous materials, a person is killed, a person receives injuries requiring his or her hospitalization, or property damage exceeding $50,000 is sustained.[45] Other incidents requiring notification involve evacuation of the general public, closure of major transportation arteries or facilities, alteration of the operational pattern of aircraft, or occurrences of breakage, spillage, or suspected contamination involving shipment of radioactive material or etiologic agents.[46]

Following immediate notice of hazardous materials incidents described above, each carrier shall report in writing to DOT within 30 days of the date of discovery of each incident, in accordance with 49 C.F.R. Section 171.15. Additionally, any incident involving an uninten-

---

[41]49 C.F.R. § 171.8.
[42]*Id.*
[43]40 C.F.R. § 171.1.
[44]49 C.F.R. §§ 171.15–.16.
[45]*Id.* § 171.15(a).
[46]*Id.*

Chapter 6: Transport of Hazardous Waste 113

tional release of any quantity of hazardous waste also must be described in the required written report.[47] If a report pertains to a hazardous waste discharge, a copy of the hazardous waste manifest for the waste must be attached to the report, and additional information must be provided, including an estimate of the quantity of the waste removed from the scene, the name and address of the facility to which it was taken, and the manner of disposition of any removed waste.

3. Emergency Response, Training, and Mixtures of Hazardous Materials
Part 172 of the HMRs sets forth a comprehensive hazardous materials table and specifies, among other things, emergency response information required and training requirements. Part 172 applies to each person who offers a hazardous material for transportation and each carrier that transports a hazardous material by air, highway, rail, or water.[48] Part 172 also specifies the manner in which mixtures and solutions of materials comprising a hazardous material identified in the hazardous materials table shall be treated for purposes of compliance with the HMRs.[49]

4. Labeling and Placarding Requirements
Part 172 of the HMRs also addresses the contents of shipping papers, markings, labeling, and placarding. Subpart C governs the contents of shipping papers and specifies what materials require shipping papers for their transport, as well as providing that a RCRA manifest constitutes a DOT shipping paper under the HMRs. Subpart D addresses the general marking requirements for hazardous materials offered for transport. All persons who offer hazardous material for transportation are required to mark each package, freight container, and transport vehicle containing hazardous material in accordance with the requirements of Subpart D.[50]

Subpart E of the HMRs addresses general labeling requirements. This subpart requires that each person who offers hazardous material for transport, or who transports such materials in a variety of packages or containment devices, label packages or containment devices in the manner specified in that subpart.

Finally, Subpart F addresses placarding of containers and vehicles in which hazardous materials are transported. Placarding requirements specified in that subpart do not apply to a number of types of hazardous

---

[47]*Id.* § 171.16(a).
[48]*Id.* § 172.3.
[49]*Id.* § 172.101(c)(10).
[50]*Id.* § 172.300.

114   THE RCRA PRACTICE MANUAL

material, including infectious substances, hazardous materials that are packaged as small quantities, class 9 combustible liquids in nonbulk packaging (a category that includes many RCRA hazardous wastes), and several other categories.[51]

5. General Requirements for Shipments and Packagings

Part 173 of the HMRs contains the general requirements for packaging hazardous materials shipments. Chief among these requirements are the shipper's proper classification of materials based on hazards associated with them and use of proper packaging by the shipper,[52] the shipper's responsibilities generally,[53] and the provisions concerning releases and mixtures of hazardous materials.[54] Other significant provisions of this portion of the HMRs address reuse of containers, transport of empty containers, and special exceptions to the packaging requirements.[55]

Requirements for specific modes of transport are next addressed in Parts 174 through 177. Part 174 governs carriage of hazardous materials by rail; part 175 governs carriage by aircraft; part 176 governs carriage by vessel (water transport); and part 177 addresses carriage by public highway.

IV. DOT's Authority and Coordination with EPA

While EPA and authorized states regulate the transport of hazardous waste under RCRA, DOT regulates transport of hazardous waste and all other "hazardous materials" designated by the Secretary of Transportation pursuant to the HMTA. Because of the obvious overlap in these administrative programs, EPA and DOT signed a memorandum of understanding (MOU) governing their respective enforcement of hazardous material transportation standards.[56] Under the terms of the MOU, DOT and EPA retain authority in areas of overlap between their programs.

Pursuant to the MOU, DOT retains authority to inspect hazardous material transporters to ensure their compliance with HMRs, to investigate EPA reports of suspected violations, to institute appropriate enforcement actions for violations of the HMRs, and to refer suspected violations of RCRA to EPA for follow-up and possible enforcement.

---

[51]*Id.* § 172.500(b).
[52]*Id.* § 173.2–.2a.
[53]*Id.* § 173.22.
[54]*Id.* § 173.24.
[55]*Id.* §§ 173.28, 173.29, 173.3, 173.4, 173.6, 173.12, 173.150–.156, 173.306.
[56]45 Fed. Reg. 51,645 (1980).

The MOU recognizes EPA's continuing authority to pursue enforcement actions when a violation of RCRA's transporter regulations is revealed in the course of EPA's ongoing inspection of generators and operators of TSD facilities for their compliance with RCRA regulations. EPA also will follow up on suspected violations of RCRA referred to it by DOT. Conversely, EPA is obligated under the MOU to refer suspected violations of the HMRs to DOT for its follow-up and possible enforcement. The MOU also requires EPA to provide transporter information to other government agencies, including the Office of Motor Carriers, the Federal Highway Administration (FHWA), and DOT.

The MOU also addresses coordination of enforcement actions between the two agencies. For example, if one agency institutes an enforcement action where both might otherwise proceed, the second agency will not normally take such action, although neither agency is precluded from initiating other legal actions regarding a violation for which the other agency has first sought to enforce its regulations.

V. Federal Preemption of Local and State Regulation of Hazardous Waste Transport

As the HMTA and RCRA have evolved since their passage in 1975 and 1976, respectively, a body of case law has developed concerning the preemptive effect these federal regulatory programs have upon local and state regulation of hazardous materials and hazardous waste transportation. Because these statutes were enacted within a year of each other, and due to the lag in judicial review concerning their preemptive effect, the case law concerning preemption under both statutes can be traced to a handful of cases that first addressed whether RCRA and HMTA preempted local and state regulation of hazardous waste and materials, including their transportation.

Of course, the preemptive effect of any federal statute, including RCRA and the HMTA, is a function of the Constitution's apportionment of powers between the federal government and the several states. In particular, the states' police powers and the supremacy of federal law, including the federal government's authority to regulate commerce among and within the states, come into play whenever a question of statutory preemption is raised. In the areas of environmental protection and public health and safety, these respective constitutional powers of federal and state government have conflicted previously.[57]

---

[57]See generally Paul S. Weiland, Comment, *Federal and State Preemption of Environmental Law: A Critical Analysis*, 24 HARV. ENVTL. L. REV. 237 (2000).

116 THE RCRA PRACTICE MANUAL

The case of *Philadelphia v. New Jersey*[58] was one of the earliest decisions dealing with the preemptive effect of RCRA. In *Philadelphia*, a New Jersey statute prohibiting the importation for disposal of solid and liquid. waste generated outside the state was challenged. Although the case did not cover hazardous waste regulated under Subtitle C of RCRA, the U.S. Supreme Court considered whether RCRA's broad remedial purposes or comprehensive regulatory scheme preempted such regulation at the state level. The Court could find no express congressional intent sufficient to support a finding of RCRA preemption of the New Jersey statute in question, but it invalidated the statute based upon a "dormant commerce clause" analysis, which is discussed in some detail below.

Notwithstanding the *Philadelphia* decision, numerous other courts have, on particular facts, held that RCRA does preempt inconsistent local and state regulations. Some courts have so held, despite the addition of a "savings clause" to RCRA as part of its reauthorization in 1980 that expressly allows states to adopt hazardous waste regulations that are more stringent than those mandated under RCRA.[59]

Similarly, the HMTUSA contains a clause that provides that any state regulation inconsistent with its provisions or regulations promulgated thereunder will be preempted if "(1) complying with a requirement of the State . . . and a requirement of [the HMTA] is not possible; or (2) the requirement of the State . . . as applied or enforced, is an obstacle to accomplishing and carrying out [the HMTA]."[60] However, the HMTUSA allows states to apply to DOT for a waiver of preemption, which may be granted if: (1) the level of protection under the state laws is equal to or greater than the protection under the HMTA, and (2) the state regulation does not unreasonably burden interstate commerce.[61] Recognition of such regulations as not being preempted by the HMRs is discretionary with DOT. In furtherance of both the preemption language

---

[58]437 U.S. 617 (1978).

[59]*See, e.g.,* Rollins Envtl. Servs., Inc. v. Iberville Parish Police Jury, 371 So. 2d 1127 (La. 1979) (finding pre-savings clause RCRA preemption of state regulation of hazardous waste activity); Ensco, Inc. v. Dumas, 807 F.2d 743 (8th Cir. 1986) (invalidating county ordinance prohibiting importation of certain foreign-generated hazardous wastes); Nat'l Solid Waste Mgmt. Assoc. v. Ala. Dep't of Envtl. Mgmt., 729 F. Supp. 792 (N.D. Ala.) (invalidating state statute prohibiting disposal of hazardous waste from states not providing for treatment or disposal facilities within own borders and requiring certain pretreatment of hazardous waste prior to disposal), *vacated,* 910 F.2d 713 (11th Cir. 1990), *modified,* 942 F.2d 1001 (11th Cir.), *cert. denied,* 111 S. Ct. 2800 (1991).

[60]49 U.S.C. § 5125(a).

[61]49 U.S.C.A. § 5125(e).

Chapter 6: Transport of Hazardous Waste   117

and savings clause provisions of the HMTUSA and its predecessor the HMTA, DOT promulgated administrative procedures for determining whether a state or local regulation is considered inconsistent and, therefore, preempted. DOT regularly issues administrative preemption determinations, replacing its earlier practice of making "inconsistency rulings."[62] Pursuant to these procedures, DOT also keeps an index of inconsistency rulings, preemption determinations, waiver-of-preemption determinations, and administrative determinations made to date, and an index to those rulings and determinations by type of state or local regulation or requirement. Such documents can be obtained from the Chief Counsel's Office of the Research and Special Programs Administration (RSPA) of DOT or on the DOT's Web site at http://rspa-atty.dot.gov/ preemptiondet.html.

One preemption issue addressed by RSPA is that of several states' bonding requirements. RSPA reviewed the bonding requirements of Maryland, Massachusetts, and Pennsylvania, which required transporters of hazardous waste to obtain bonds of $10,000 to $60,000 or more for each load of hazardous waste they picked up from or delivered to a facility within those states. RSPA found those bonding requirements constituted "an obstacle to the accomplishment and execution of the HMTA and the HMR," so HMTA preempted them.[63] Massachusetts and Pennsylvania unsuccessfully petitioned RSPA for reconsideration of its initial determination concerning their bonding requirements.[64] The Illinois hazardous waste manifest also was deemed preempted by DOT.[65] RSPA also found that a Michigan requirement requiring the marking of motor vehicles used to transport "liquid industrial wastes" and "hazardous wastes" was preempted.[66] RSPA recently ruled that Missouri's prohibition against recontainerization of hazardous waste at a transfer station was preempted.[67] In similar fashion, New York's prohibition against the transfer or repackaging of hazardous wastes and its requirement that any transfer of hazardous waste from one vehicle to another be indicated on the manifest were found to be preempted by the HMRs.[68]

---

[62]See, e.g., 66 Fed. Reg. 37,089, 37,092 (July 16, 2001).
[63]57 Fed. Reg. 58,848 (1992).
[64]58 Fed. Reg. 32,419 (1993).
[65]38 Fed. Reg. 11,176 (1993).
[66]59 Fed. Reg. 6186 (1994).
[67]66 Fed. Reg. 37,089 (2001).
[68]60 Fed. Reg. 15,970 (1997).

118   THE RCRA PRACTICE MANUAL

The EPA regularly defers to DOT authority under the HMTUSA, as evidenced in EPA's approval of California's RCRA program.[69]

The first judicial opinion addressing HMTUSA preemption is *Colorado Public Utilities Commission v. Harmon*,[70] in which the court invalidated nuclear material transportation regulations adopted in Colorado. This case is particularly instructive in the way the court evaluated DOT's prior preemption determination, the nature of the state requirements at issue, and the courts' application of 49 U.S.C.A. Sections 1804 (covered subject preemption) and 1811(a) (obstacle preemption). Even Colorado's attempt to require proof of mountain-driving training, a matter not addressed by DOT's training requirements, was held to create an obstacle to "the federal purpose of promoting safety through uniformity."[71]

VI. Commerce Clause Limitations on State and Local Regulation of Hazardous Waste Transport

The Commerce Clause of the Constitution reserves to the federal government the power to regulate interstate commerce.[72] Because waste has been recognized as an article of commerce,[73] transport of hazardous waste is a subject reserved for regulation by the federal government under the Commerce Clause. Of course, the tension between the federal government's power to regulate interstate commerce and the states' police powers to regulate matters of local concern, particularly matters such as protection of the environment, human health, and safety, creates the potential for confusion and inconsistent results in this area of the law.[74]

Even when Congress does not expressly legislate pursuant to its power to regulate commerce, state actions affecting interstate commerce may nonetheless be held unconstitutional under a "dormant Commerce Clause" analysis. The dormant Commerce Clause doctrine stands for the proposition that, even where Congress has not specifically authorized

---

[69]57 Fed. Reg. 32,726 (1992). For a good summary of HMTA preemption decisions, see J. Cantrick, *The Hazardous Materials Transportation Act: A Preemption Update*, 22 COLO. LAW. 747 (Apr. 1993). *See also* E. Nolfi, *State or Local Regulation of Transportation of Hazardous Materials as Pre-empted by Hazardous Materials Transportation Act (49 U.S.C. section 1801 et seq.)*, 78 A.L.R. FED. 289 (1985).

[70]951 F.2d 1571 (10th Cir. 1991).

[71]951 F.2d at 1582. *See also* New York *ex rel.* Dep't of Envtl. Conservation v. U.S. Dep't of Transp., 37 F. Supp. 2d 152 (N.D.N.Y. 1999) (holding that HMTA preempted state regulation prohibiting repackaging of hazardous waste).

[72]U.S. CONST. art. I, § 8, cl. 3.

[73]Philadelphia v. New Jersey, *supra* note 57.

[74]*See, e.g.*, J. GABA & D. STEVER, LAW OF SOLID WASTE, POLLUTION PREVENTION AND RECYCLING § 13.03[1][b] (Clark, Boardman, Callaghan 1992).

Chapter 6: Transport of Hazardous Waste   119

state regulation of interstate commerce, there is a negative implication that congressional silence is consistent with a general lack of intent to allow states to so regulate.[75]

The seminal case concerning state regulation of the transport of waste being violative of the dormant Commerce Clause is *Philadelphia v. New Jersey*. While that case involved a prohibition on importation of municipal sol*Id*. waste, not hazardous waste, the constitutional principles enunciated by the U.S. Supreme Court clearly apply to similar attempts at the state and local level to regulate hazardous waste in various ways, including regulation of its transport.[76]

In *Philadelphia v. New Jersey*, the Supreme Court found the New Jersey prohibition on importation of municipal sol*Id*. waste constituted economic protectionism, and was thus a per se violation of the commerce clause. In so holding, the Court distinguished a line of cases, known as the "quarantine cases," that allow for state prohibitions on the transport of articles requiring immediate destruction for public health reasons.[77] In *Chemical Waste Management, Inc. v. Hunt*,[78] the Supreme Court struck down an Alabama statute that imposed an additional fee on all hazardous waste generated outside Alabama and disposed of at Alabama facilities. Quoting *Philadelphia v. New Jersey*, the Court stated that "whatever Alabama's ultimate purpose, it may not be accomplished by discriminating against articles of commerce coming from outside the State unless there is some reason apart from their origin, to treat them differently."[79]

In addition to per se prohibitions on the transport of waste, the courts have overturned state statutes that impose differential fee schedules based on the waste's place of origin, that contain reciprocity requirements for waste importation, that require waste to be processed at a designated facility, and that require health officer certification.[80] Still,

---

[75]*See* H.P. Hood & Sons, Inc. v. DuMond, 336 U.S. 525, 535 (1949).

[76]*See, e.g.*, Hardage v. Atkins, 582 F.2d 1264, 1266–67 (10th Cir. 1978); Nat'l Solid Waste Mgmt. Assoc. v. Alabama Dep't of Envtl. Mgmt., *supra* note 58; *see generally* B. Wynne & T. Hamby, *Interstate Waste: A Key Issue in Resolving the National Hazardous Waste Capacity Crisis*, 32 S. Tex. L. Rev. 601 (Oct. 1991).

[77]437 U.S. at 629; *see also* Clason v. Indiana, 306 U.S. 439 (1939).

[78]504 U.S. 334 (1992).

[79]*Id.* at 344. *See also* C & A Carbone, Inc. v. Town of Clarkstown, N.Y., 511 U.S. 383 (1994) (striking down local ordinance requiring that solid waste processed or handled within town be deposited at town transfer station); Or. Waste Sys., Inc. v. Dep't of Envtl. Quality, 511 U.S. 93 (1994) (striking down state statute imposing differential surcharge on persons disposing of solid waste generated out of state).

[80]*See, e.g.*, U & I Sanitation v. City of Columbus, 205 F.3d 1063 (8th Cir. 2000) (striking down ordinance requiring that waste collected in city destined for in-state disposal be processed at city-owned transfer station).

some states have been successful in regulating the transport of hazardous and other wastes in ways that have only an incidental effect on interstate commerce.[81] These holdings depend upon judicial characterization of the statutes, regulations, or ordinances in question as being "evenhanded." Such characterization by a court allows for application of a type of balancing test established in the case of *Pike v. Bruce Church*.[82] The *Pike* test established that, "[w]here the statute regulates even-handedly to effectuate a legitimate local public interest, and its effects on interstate commerce are only incidental, it will be upheld unless the burden imposed on such commerce is clearly excessive in relation to the putative local benefits."[83]

VII. Conclusion

Despite the substantial efforts to date aimed at simplifying and standardizing the many regulations affecting the transport of hazardous waste, this area of the law will continue to be complex and evolving. Commentators frequently speak of a hazardous waste capacity crisis in this country and propose changes in the courts' application of fundamental legal principles that govern judicial review of hazardous waste regulation, including its transport.[84] EPA continues to work with state and industry representatives on development of a uniform hazardous waste manifest for use in all states to reduce the regulatory burden upon hazardous waste transportation. Future developments in these and other areas are certain to contribute to an altered regulatory landscape that borrows from experience and attempts to improve national and international schemes for regulating the transport of hazardous waste.

---

[81]*See, e.g.*, Houlton Citizens' Coalition v. Town of Houlton, 175 F.3d 178 (1st Cir. 1999) (upholding ordinance requiring generators of residential rubbish to use contractor selected by town or haul it themselves . . . ordinance regulated commerce evenhandedly); Evergreen Waste Sys. v. Metro. Serv. Dist., 820 F.2d 1482 (9th Cir. 1987) (local waste disposal district ban on disposal of municipal solid waste generated outside the district).
[82]397 U.S. 137 (1970).
[83]*Id.*
[84]*See, e.g.*, S. Brietzke, *Hazardous Waste in Interstate Commerce: Minimizing the Problem after City of Philadelphia v. New Jersey*, 24 VAL. U. L. REV. 77 (Fall 1989).

APPENDIX

Letter of April 23, 1991, from
J. Kaleta, Chief Counsel, Department of Transportation, to
S. Denny, Director, Transportation Management Program,
U. S. Department of Energy,
regarding the definition of
"public highway" in the HMTA and HMRS.

APPENDIX

US Department
of Transportation

**Research and
Special Programs
Administration**

Office of the
Chief Counsel

400 Seventh St S W
Washington D C 20590

BRADLEY, CAMPBELL, CARNEY & MADSEN
ATTORNEYS AT LAW
GOLDEN, COLORADO

APR 2 3 1991

JUN 2 1991

FILE:
CLIENT _____
RE _____

Ms. Susan H. Denny
Director
Transportation Management Program
Office of Technology Development
Department of Energy
Washington, DC 20585

Dear Ms. Denny:

I am responding to your March 25 request for a definition of "public highway" in the context of the Hazardous Materials Transportation Act (HMTA), 49 App. U.S.C. 1801 et seq., and the Hazardous Materials Regulations (HMR), 49 C.F.R. Parts 171-180, issued under the HMTA. Because the applicability of the HMTA depends upon the existence of "transportation in commerce" (49 App. U.S.C. 1801, 1803, 1804), I will discuss the issues in terms of whether there is transportation in commerce rather than whether there is transportation on public highways.

On November 16, 1990, the HMTA was amended by the Hazardous Materials Transportation Uniform Safety Act of 1990 (HMTUSA), Public Law 101-615. Section 3 of the HMTUSA added a definition of "person" to 49 App. U.S.C. 1802 that makes it clear that government agencies offering hazardous materials for transportation in commerce or transporting hazardous materials in furtherance of a commercial enterprise are subject to the HMTA. It states:

> The term 'person' means . . . government, Indian tribe, or agency or instrumentality of any government or Indian tribe when it offers hazardous materials in furtherance of a commercial enterprise, but such term does not include (a) the United States Postal Service, or (B) for the purposes of sections 110 and 111 [penalties and specific relief, respectively] of this title, any agency or instrumentality of the Federal Government.

Also, Section 20 of the HMTUSA added 49 U.S.C. App. 1818 to provide that the HMTA applies to contractors with, among others, the Federal Government. It states:

Any person who, under contract with any department, agency, or instrumentality of the executive, legislative, or judicial branch of the Federal government, transports, or causes to be transported or shipped, a hazardous material . . . shall be subject to and comply with all provisions of this title, all orders and regulations issued under this title, and all other substantive and procedural requirements of Federal, State and local governments and Indian tribes (except any such requirements that have been preempted by this title or any other Federal law), in the same manner and to the same extent as any person engaged in such activities that are in or affect commerce is subject to such provisions, orders, regulations, and requirements.

Therefore, the Department of Energy (DOE) is required to comply with the HMR when it offers hazardous materials for transportation or transports them in commerce. DOE, however, is not required to comply with the HMR when it offers or transports hazardous materials in a Government vehicle because those DOE activities are presumed to be for a governmental purpose and thus not in commerce.

DOE's contractors, however, must comply with the HMR even when the transportation is in a Government vehicle -- unless the transportation is not in commerce (a prerequisite to the applicability of the HMTA and the HMR).

Transportation on (across or along) roads outside of Government properties generally is transportation in commerce. Transportation on Government properties requires close analysis to determine whether it is in commerce. If a road is used by members of the general public (including dependents of Government employees) without their having to gain access through a controlled access point, transportation on (across or along) that road is in commerce. On the other hand, if access to a road is controlled at all times through the use of gates and guards, transportation on that road is not in commerce.

One other means of preventing hazardous materials transportation on Government property from being in commerce is to temporarily block access to the section of the road being crossed or used for that transportation. The road would have to be blocked by persons having the legal authority to do so, and public access to the involved section of road would have to be effectively precluded.

3

The following discussion applies these general principles to the situations described in your letter.

Example 1: Road A is located on DOE-owned property and is maintained by DOE. Speed enforcement is by a DOE contractor. The road has unrestricted public access, but there are signs stating that persons are entering DOE property. Analysis: Road A has unrestricted public access, and, therefore, transportation on or across it is subject to the HMR.

Example 2: Road B traverses a DOE site, but is maintained by the State. Speed enforcement is by the State. The DOE cannot unilaterally block the road. There is unrestricted public access, except for times when DOE/State Police physically block public access in order to make special shipments. Analysis: Because there is unrestricted public access to Road B, transportation on or across it is subject to the HMR. However, effective blocking of public access (as described above) by DOE or State officials would avoid application of the HMR.

Example 3: Road C connects two DOE sites, is owned by the city and is maintained by DOE under a legal agreement. Speed enforcement is by the city. The public has unrestricted access. Analysis: Road C is not on Government property; thus, the HMR would apply.

Example 4: Road D is on DOE-owned property and is maintained by DOE. Speed enforcement is by a DOE contractor. The road is posted with a sign restricting usage to those on official government business, but there are no physical barriers. Analysis: Because there is public access to Road D, the HMR would apply there. This result could be changed either by effectively blocking public access or by controlling public use at all times through the use of gates and guards.

As indicated above, transporting a hazardous material across a road or doing so along a road both are subject to the HMR unless the section of the road involved is removed from commerce by one of the above-described actions.

I trust that this information will be useful to you in providing guidance to your operating contractors. Please advise me if additional information or clarification is desired.

Sincerely,

Judith S. Kaleta
Chief Counsel

CHAPTER 7

Permit Requirements

DAVID E. PRESTON, ANDREW J. KOK, AND MATTHEW B. EUGSTER

I. What Is a RCRA Permit?

A. Definition and Purpose

A RCRA hazardous waste treatment, storage, or disposal permit (RCRA permit) is the document that allows a facility to treat, store, or dispose of hazardous waste on-site. RCRA requires any facility that is treating, storing, or disposing of hazardous wastes on-site to have a permit.[1] RCRA does not require facilities that only *generate* hazardous waste to have a permit of this type. EPA or an authorized state reviews and grants or denies RCRA permits. (This chapter refers to EPA as the permitting authority, even though in many cases, states also play an important part in the process.) The RCRA permit program regulations can be found at 40 C.F.R. Parts 124 and 270.

A RCRA permit, in EPA's view, is the mechanism by which an owner or operator of a treatment, storage, or disposal facility (TSDF) demonstrates the ability to comply with the RCRA TSDF performance standards.[2] These performance standards, generally found at 40 C.F.R. Parts 260, 264, 265, and 266, address all aspects of the siting, construction, operation, and monitoring of a TSDF to ensure the protection of public health and safety; they are discussed in detail elsewhere in this book. The RCRA permit sets out the specific performance standards for

---

[1] 42 U.S.C. § 6925.
[2] 40 C.F.R. § 270.4.

126 THE RCRA PRACTICE MANUAL

the TSDF involved. For example, a typical permit describes the construction requirements for the hazardous waste management units at the facility and requirements for testing the waste periodically.

A RCRA permit is an extensive, complicated document that the permit holder must completely understand and comply with. The cost and effort involved in obtaining and complying with a RCRA permit are greater than for permits required by other federal or state environmental regulatory programs. Economic or other justifications must be substantial to support the decision to permit, construct, and operate a TSDF.

B. Effect of a RCRA Permit

With certain exceptions, compliance with a RCRA permit constitutes compliance with Subtitle C (the hazardous waste regulatory portion) of RCRA for purposes of enforcement.[3] In other words, if a TSDF complies with its permit, it is "shielded" from enforcement for failing to comply with a requirement that is not included in its permit.

This "permit shield" does not apply to certain statutory or regulatory requirements. These requirements, which must be complied with whether they are expressly included in the permit or not, are (1) new requirements that become effective by statute; (2) "land disposal restrictions" promulgated under 40 C.F.R. Part 268 (restrictions on placement of hazardous wastes in or on land); (3) certain performance standards under 40 C.F.R. Part 264 for surface impoundments, waste piles, and landfills; and (4) "air emissions" limitations promulgated under 40 CFR Part 265 (AA), (BB), and (CC). These exceptions to the permit shield are set forth at 40 C.F.R. Section 270.4.

Because of the permit shield concept, an EPA permit writer may tend to write permits conservatively, including some potentially unnecessary conditions in the permit. A permit applicant should thus anticipate spending substantial time and effort framing the application appropriately. This may reduce the imposition of unnecessary requirements and minimize the amount of negotiation with the permit writer over the permit conditions.

A feature of the RCRA permit regulations that is related to the permit shield is the duty of the permittee to report all instances of noncompliance with the permit.[4] Thus, while it may be comforting to have a permit shield to rely upon, the permittee will at the same time be subject to increased duties to monitor and report the facility's failure to comply with the permit.

---

[3]*Id.*
[4]*Id.* § 270.30(h)(10).

C. Proposed Standardized RCRA Permit

EPA is proposing revisions to the RCRA hazardous waste permitting program to allow a "standardized permit." The standardized permit would be available to facilities that generate hazardous waste and then manage the waste in units such as tanks, containers, and containment buildings. The RCRA standardized permit would be a document issued by EPA or the authorized state. It would consist of two components: a uniform portion that is included in all permits and a supplemental portion that would be included at EPA's discretion.

EPA (or an authorized state agency) currently issues site-specific RCRA permits to operate hazardous waste management facilities on an individual basis. Each facility applies for a permit, and EPA (or the authorized state agency) writes the site-specific permit.[5] The proposed standardized permit would streamline the permit process by allowing facilities to obtain and modify permits more easily. Standardized permit holders would not have to submit the amount of information needed to support an individual permit application, although they would need to keep the required information at the permitted facility. In addition, the proposed regulations contain new procedures for modifying standardized permits. These new procedures would allow permitted facilities to make certain types of routine changes without prior approval, provided that the permitted facility has informed both the regulatory agency and the public of the changes. For more significant changes, a permitted facility would have to request approval from the regulatory agency.

For more information regarding the EPA's proposed standardized permit visit the EPA's Web site at http://www.epa.gov/epaoswer/hazwaste/permit/std-perm.htm, or see the proposed rules on pages 52,191–52,268 of the October 12, 2001, *Federal Register*.[6]

II. Determining Permit Applicability

When determining whether a facility needs a RCRA permit, a facility owner or operator must generally ask three questions:

1. Will the facility be handling a regulated hazardous waste?
2. Will the hazardous waste be undergoing "treatment," "storage," or "disposal" at the facility, as defined in the regulations?
3. Is an exclusion from the RCRA permit requirements available to the facility?

---

[5]*See id.* pts. 124, 270.
[6]66 Fed. Reg. 52,191.

128 THE RCRA PRACTICE MANUAL

Whether materials handled are "hazardous wastes" is an issue dealt with in earlier chapters. As to whether a facility is engaged in treatment, storage, or disposal activities, a potential applicant should refer to the definitions in the regulations. The key definitions of "facility," "treatment," "storage," and "disposal" are presented at 40 C.F.R. Sections 260.10 and 270.2. In many cases, the applicability of permit requirements will depend on whether an activity or process meets these regulatory definitions. Applicants should also review the *Federal Register* preambles that accompanied the promulgation of these definitions, as well as EPA guidance documents, to fully understand EPA's interpretation of these definitions. A list of these documents appears as Appendix A to this chapter.

A. Regulatory Exclusions from the Permit Requirement

If the waste handled is a regulated hazardous waste and treatment, storage, or disposal activities are present, one must look at the exclusions from the permit requirements. The RCRA regulation specifies activities that are excluded from the treatment, storage, or disposal (TSD) permit requirements. These are set forth in 40 C.F.R. Section 270.1(c)(2) and (3).

The following are not required to obtain a RCRA permit:

- Generators of hazardous waste that temporarily accumulate hazardous waste at their facilities in accordance with 40 C.F.R. Section 262.34.[7]
- Farmers who dispose of waste pesticides from their own use if they follow the disposal requirements set forth in 40 C.F.R. Section 262.70.[8]
- Owners or operators of facilities whose hazardous wastes are excluded from regulation under 40 C.F.R. Sections 261.4 and 261.5 (conditionally exempt small-quantity generators).[9]
- Owners or operators of a "totally enclosed treatment facility" as defined under 40 C.F.R. Section 260.10.[10]
- Owners or operators of "elementary neutralization units" and "wastewater treatment units" as defined under 40 C.F.R. Section 260.10.[11]

---

[7]40 C.F.R. § 270.1(c)(2)(i).
[8]*Id.* § 270.1(c)(2)(ii).
[9]*Id.* § 270.1(c)(2)(iii).
[10]*Id.* § 270.1(c)(2)(iv).
[11]*Id.* § 270.1(c)(2)(v).

Chapter 7: Permit Requirements   129

- A transporter that stores manifested hazardous waste in containers at a transfer facility for no more than ten days.[12]
- A person adding absorbent material to waste in a container or adding waste to absorbent material in a container, at the time the waste is first placed in the container. (This could otherwise be considered "treatment," according to EPA.)[13]
- Universal waste handlers and universal waste transporters managing a listed universal waste.[14]
- A New York State Utility central collection facility consolidating waste in accordance with 40 CFR Section 262.90.
- A person undertaking emergency treatment or containment activities during immediate response activities (spill response).[15] This exclusion should not be confused with the "emergency permit" regulations at 40 C.F.R. Section 270.61, discussed in Section VI of this chapter.

B. Other Exclusions

An owner or operator might not be required to obtain a RCRA permit under the following circumstances:

- An incinerator for polychlorinated biphenyls (PCBs) is not required to obtain a TSD permit if the incinerator is constructed pursuant to an approval under the Toxic Substances Control Act.[16] If the incinerator is used to destroy hazardous waste as well, however, it will require a RCRA permit. This RCRA permit may be applied for after construction of the facility but before use of the incinerator for disposal of hazardous waste.[17]
- In addition to these regulatory exclusions, an owner or operator should be aware that EPA does not apply RCRA retroactively. Thus, wastes that were *disposed of* before becoming regulated by RCRA cannot be subject to the permitting requirements.[18]

---

[12]*Id.* § 270.1(c)(2)(vi).
[13]*Id.* § 270.1(c)(2)(vii).
[14]*Id.* § 270.1(c)(2)(viii).
[15]*Id.* § 270.1(c)(3).
[16]15 U.S.C. § 2601 *et seq.*
[17]42 U.S.C. § 6925(a); 40 C.F.R. § 270.10(f)(3).
[18]55 Fed. Reg. 39,409 (1990); Envtl. Def. Fund v. Lamphier, 714 F.2d 331 (4th Cir. 1990).

III. Obtaining a RCRA Permit

A. Application Procedure

Before *beginning* construction of a new TSDF, a RCRA permit must be obtained. The standard permit application consists of two submittals, which are known as Part A, a short standardized form, and Part B, a lengthy narrative collection of information about the proposed facility. However, the regulations also provide for permits by rule (Section 270.60); emergency permits (Section 270.61); research, development, and demonstration permits (Section 270.65); and special permits for incinerators, injection wells, and other specific facilities (Sections 270.62, .63, .64, and .66). Persons who are covered by RCRA permits by rule under 40 C.F.R. Section 270.60 need not submit an application for a RCRA permit. Emergency permits under 40 C.F.R. Section 270.61 require neither a Part A nor a Part B application. Permits for research, development, or demonstration of TSD technologies under 40 C.F.R. Section 270.65 involve a separate application process. These types of permits are discussed in Section VI of this chapter.

Part A and Part B will be submitted for EPA review concurrently, and must be submitted at least 180 days before proposed construction.[19] The construction of the TSD may not begin until both Part A and Part B applications are submitted and EPA has issued a permit. Existing facilities that become newly regulated as TSD facilities must meet submittal deadlines for both Part A and Part B in order to continue TSD activities. These deadlines are set forth at 40 C.F.R. Sections 270.1(b), .10(e), and .10(f). Figure 1 is a flow chart that illustrates how the owner or operator of an existing facility can determine which of these deadlines apply.

B. Part A Application

The required contents of a Part A application are found at 40 C.F.R. Section 270.13. The standardized Part A application form is relatively simple to prepare (see Appendix B). The Part A application must generally identify the owner and operator of the facility, the type of treatment, storage, or disposal activity that is to be carried on, the type and amount of hazardous waste handled, and the type(s) of units used (waste piles, surface impoundments, etc.).

The regulations require the *operator* of a TSDF to obtain a permit, even if another person owns the facility. However, the owner of the facility also must sign the permit application (both Part A and Part B).[20]

---

[19]40 C.F.R. § 270.10(f)(2).
[20]*Id.* § 270.10(b).

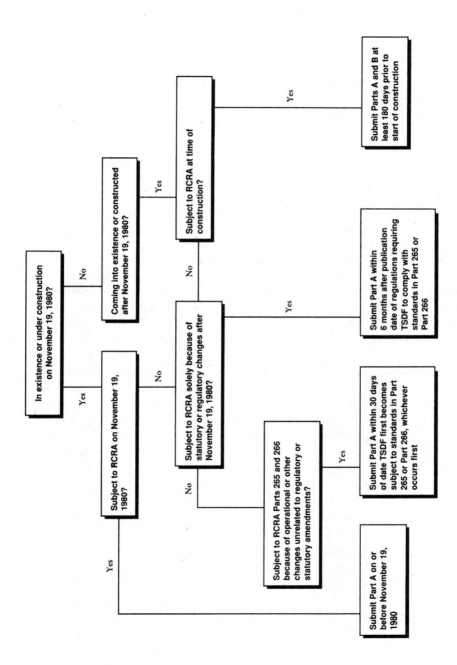

FIGURE I: Flow Chart of RCRA Permit Application Submittal Schedule

C. Part B Application

Part B of the RCRA permit application is as lengthy as Part A is short. While Part A serves mainly a notification purpose, informing EPA that hazardous waste treatment, storage, or disposal activities are or will be occurring at the facility, Part B must give EPA complete information on how the facility intends to comply with *all* of the 40 C.F.R. Part 264 TSD performance standard requirements.

Part B is not prepared on a standard form as is Part A. Rather, Part B consists of specifications, plans and drawings, reports, and other documentation that demonstrate the applicant's ability to comply with the requirements of a RCRA permit.

The contents of Part B vary depending upon the type of TSDF at issue. There are, however, general requirements that apply to all facilities. For example, Part B must describe security measures to be taken at the facility, waste characterization procedures, and so forth. Refer to 40 C.F.R. Section 270.14 for the complete list of these requirements.

Additional Part B requirements specific to containers, tank systems, surface impoundments, waste piles, incinerators, land treatment facilities, landfills, boilers and industrial furnaces burning hazardous waste, miscellaneous units, process vents, and drip pads can be found in 40 C.F.R. Sections 270.15 through .26.

Although RCRA requires that an application for a permit for a new facility be submitted at least 180 days before the planned commencement date of construction, a much greater lead time should be allowed. EPA cannot be expected to expedite the application review process solely to satisfy an applicant's schedule for starting construction or waste-handling activities.

An incomplete or technically deficient Part B will greatly increase the time required to obtain the permit. While processing is pending, Part A or B of the permit application may become partially outdated. An applicant should amend or update the Part A or B submittal as necessary during the processing period. EPA can terminate a permit after issuance if the applicant failed to disclose relevant information during application.[21]

An applicant should consider hiring a consultant to assist in completing the Part B document. A consultant with experience in RCRA permitting should have knowledge of the information that EPA will typically expect to see in a complete Part B submittal. It may also be helpful to obtain and use as a guide copies of recently completed and approved permit applications. These may be available from the reviewing agency through a request submitted under state or federal freedom-

---

[21]*Id.* § 270.10(g).

of-information laws. Finally, EPA makes available guidance documents that specify what Part B of the permit application should include. A list of these documents is provided as Appendix A to this chapter.

An applicant should exercise care in submitting RCRA permit applications, since he or she will be bound by the information they contain. The owner and operator, if different people, must both sign the permit application. An environmental manager cannot normally sign the application; rather, the person signing the application must be a high-level corporate officer or, if delegation procedures set forth in the regulations are followed, facility manager.[22] The regulations express the intent to hold persons with facility management responsibility accountable, and to encourage them to be familiar with the environmental practices at the facility.

D. Corrective Action Considerations

Although corrective action requirements under RCRA are discussed in detail in other chapters, their impact on the RCRA permit process should be mentioned.

If a facility is in the process of obtaining a permit, EPA must address corrective action requirements in the permit before it is issued.[23] This will be part of the process of obtaining the permit. EPA may require the facility to conduct investigations to determine whether corrective action should be required as a condition of the permit. If a facility has already received its permit, EPA may issue a corrective action addendum to the permit. Again, there will normally be a preliminary investigation, or RCRA Facility Assessment (RFA), to determine whether corrective action is necessary at the facility.

Corrective action requirements should be considered before a facility applies for a permit. EPA will closely scrutinize the past on-site waste disposal practices and impacts at the facility. If EPA determines that corrective action is necessary, the permit will require investigations and remediation on a schedule and under terms specified by EPA. The facility should consider and address this possibility before and during the permit application process.

IV. Processing of Permit Applications

Once EPA receives Parts A and B of the permit application, it must review and act on the application in accordance with the procedures set

---

[22]*Id.* § 270.11(a)(1).
[23]RCRA § 3004(u), 42 U.S.C. § 6924(u).

forth in 40 C.F.R. Part 124. An applicant should become familiar with the specifics of these procedures before submitting an application. Although the following is a general summary of the normal process, any number of permutations of this process may occur. The EPA-developed flow chart (Figure 2) gives more specifics and citations to the applicable rules.

The first step in the process is a review by EPA for administrative completeness. A determination that the application is complete is not necessarily a determination that the application is "technically adequate," and EPA may (and, in most cases, will) request additional information from the applicant. Once it has determined that the application is administratively and technically complete, EPA will either prepare a draft permit or tentatively deny the permit. In either case, EPA will prepare a fact sheet regarding its proposed action and will give the applicant, and the public, notice of its proposed action. There is ample opportunity for public comment during the review process, a fact that the applicant should not overlook. Public input can have a major effect on the permit decision.

A facility that wishes to appeal a permit *denial* must follow the informal hearing procedures in 40 C.F.R. Section 124.19. A more formal appeal process for permit or interim status *terminations* is set forth in 40 C.F.R. Sections 124.71 through .91.

V. *The Permit*

The typical RCRA permit is issued in two parts—one part by the state covering hazardous waste regulations that the state is authorized to implement; and a second part by the EPA for any RCRA requirements for which the state does not yet have authorization. Thus, the applicant may have to deal with two different agencies for different parts of its permit.[24]

A. Standard Conditions

All RCRA permits must incorporate, either expressly or by reference, certain conditions set forth in 40 C.F.R. Part 270, Subpart C. These conditions include:

- the duty to comply with the permit;
- the duty to reapply for a permit if activities will continue beyond the expiration of the permit;

---

[24]*See* Ciba-Geigy Corp. v. Sidamon-Eristoff, 3 F.3d 40 (2d Cir. Aug. 12, 1993).

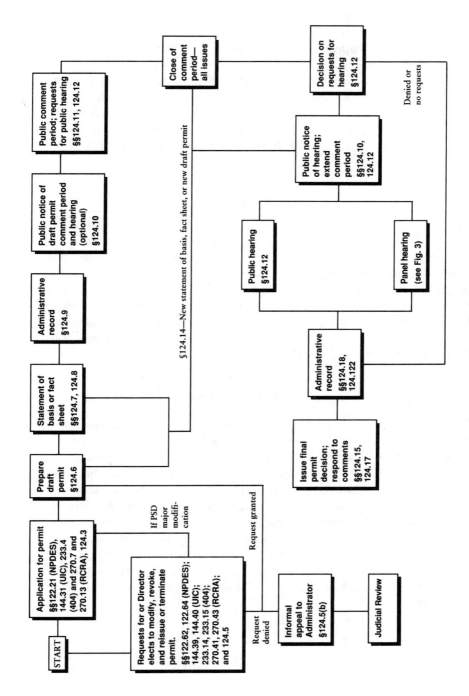

FIGURE 2: Conventional U.S. EPA Permitting Procedures

136 THE RCRA PRACTICE MANUAL

- the duty to operate and maintain the facility properly;
- the duty to provide information to EPA;
- the duty to allow inspection and entry by the EPA or its authorized representative;
- the duty to obtain samples and take measurements for purposes of monitoring and to record the results of those activities; and
- the duty to provide periodic reports and to provide information regarding anticipated noncompliance and other information that may have been omitted from or incorrectly included in a permit application.[25]

B. Case-by-Case Conditions

EPA is mandated by RCRA to include in every permit "conditions . . . necessary to protect human health and the environment."[26] Thus, EPA may include case-by-case terms and conditions in addition to the standard terms and conditions for all RCRA permits. For example, a facility might be required to conduct more environmental monitoring than called for in the regulations, build extra containment structures, and so forth. For this reason, the permit application process can be unexpectedly burdensome. The permit itself may be hundreds of pages long, including attachments and exhibits.

VI. Special Permits

The RCRA regulations allow for alternatives to the standard permitting process in various situations. These "special permits" generally provide an opportunity to avoid the lengthy process of obtaining a standard RCRA permit, but the regulations carefully restrict their availability and conditions. "Permits by rule" and "emergency permits" are discussed further below, but special permits and procedures are also available for hazardous waste incinerators (Section 270.62); land treatment demonstrations (Section 270.63); TSD research, development, and demonstration activities (Section 270.65); and boilers and industrial furnaces burning hazardous waste (Section 270.66). These special permits typically allow a facility to conduct certain trial activities before issuance of the final permit.

---

[25]40 C.F.R. §§ 270.30–.31.
[26]42 U.S.C. § 6925(c).

A. Permits by Rule

Certain facilities, although not excluded from the requirement to obtain a RCRA permit, do not need to go through the standard permit process. These three types of facilities are underground injection well facilities, publicly owned treatment works (POTWs), and ocean disposal vessels. These facilities are deemed by EPA to have obtained a RCRA permit if they comply with the requirements of certain other specified federal environmental statutes. These facilities are not required to submit a RCRA permit application to obtain this "permit by rule."[27]

1. Underground Injection Wells

Hazardous waste injection wells are regulated by the Underground Injection Control (UIC) Program of the Safe Drinking Water Act. However, an owner or operator of an injection well system that has been issued a UIC permit will be deemed to have a RCRA permit *if* the owner or operator complies with the requirements of 40 C.F.R. Section 270.60(b). EPA *may* issue an "interim" permit to this type of facility for up to two years if it has not yet received a UIC permit.[28]

2. Publicly Owned Treatment Works

A publicly owned treatment works (POTW) that treats, stores, or disposes of hazardous waste is not excluded from RCRA permit requirements. However, if the POTW has a permit issued pursuant to the National Pollutant Discharge Elimination System (NPDES) of the Clean Water Act and complies with 40 C.F.R. Section 270.60(c), it will be deemed to have a RCRA permit for its hazardous waste activities.

3. Ocean Disposal Vessels

Barges or vessels engaged in offshore disposal are not excluded from obtaining a TSD permit. However, if the owner or operator of the barge or vessel has a permit for ocean dumping issued under the Marine Protection, Research and Sanctuaries Act and complies with the requirements of Section 270.60(a), it will be deemed to have a RCRA permit for ocean disposal from the barge or vessel.

B. Emergency Permits

EPA can issue emergency permits, which authorize a facility to treat, store, or dispose of hazardous waste in instances where EPA determines it is

---

[27]40 C.F.R. § 270.1(c)(1).
[28]*Id.* § 270.64.

necessary due to an imminent and substantial endangerment to human health or the environment. The emergency permit may be oral or written; if oral, it must be followed by a written permit within five days.[29]

An emergency permit cannot exceed 90 days in duration. It must specify the hazardous waste received, and how and where it will be treated, stored, or disposed of. EPA must issue public notice of the emergency permit.[30] To the extent possible, and consistent with the emergency situation, the permit must incorporate all applicable requirements of Parts 264, 266, and 270. EPA can terminate the emergency permit at any time without offering hearings or other procedures to the applicant if it determines that such action is appropriate to protect human health and the environment.

VII. Permit Denial

40 C.F.R. Part 124 contains procedures for EPA to follow in denying, modifying, revoking, reissuing, and terminating a RCRA permit. 40 C.F.R. Section 270.29 provides that EPA may deny a permit either as to one unit of a hazardous waste management facility or the facility as a whole. The procedures set out in Part 124 are to be employed for a permit application denial, and are illustrated in Figure 3.

VIII. Permit Modifications

The owner or operator of a TSDF will often want to modify the permit due to changes in operations, wastes handled, ownership, and so forth. The modification must be made in accordance with the standards and procedures at 40 C.F.R. Part 270, Subpart D. Permit modifications are categorized generally as class 1, class 2, or class 3 modifications, with different procedures to be followed for each.

Class 1 modifications apply to minor changes that keep the permit current with routine changes to the facility or its operation, and are subject to minimal procedural requirements.

Class 2 modifications are those necessary to enable a permittee to respond to common variations in the types and quantities of the waste managed, to technological advancements, and to changes necessary to comply with new regulations. Class 2 modifications are subject to greater procedural requirements, described below.

---

[29]*Id.* § 270.61.
[30]*Id.* § 270.61(b)(5).

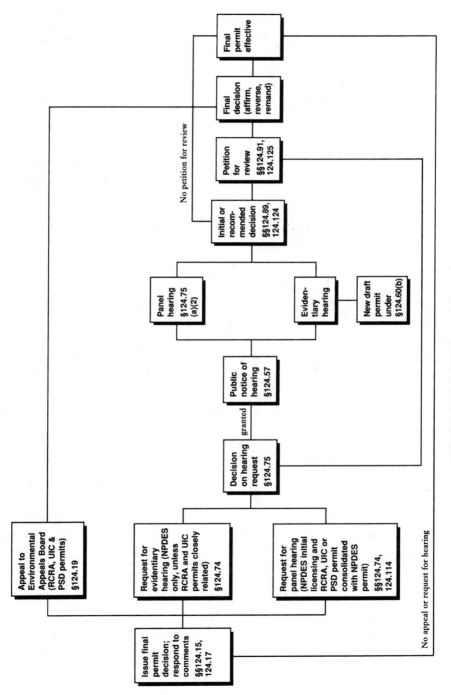

FIGURE 3: U.S. EPA Appeal Procedures

140 THE RCRA PRACTICE MANUAL

Class 3 modifications are those that substantially alter the facility or its operation, such as, for example, changes in compliance schedules or the addition of new waste management units. Procedures for class 3 modifications are also described below. EPA lists examples of class 1, 2, and 3 modifications in Appendix I to 40 C.F.R. Section 270.42.

A. Change in Owner or Operator

A permit can be transferred to a new owner or operator. However, the permit must be modified according to the procedures for class I modifications to reflect the change. At the time of the modification, EPA can add other additional requirements into the permit as well. The old owner or operator is liable for compliance with certain terms of the permit until released by EPA. For example, the old owner or operator must maintain financial assurances for the facility until released by EPA.[31]

B. Class 1 Modifications

Class 1 modifications may be made by the permittee under the conditions set forth in 40 C.F.R. Section 270.42(a). A permittee requesting a class 1 permit modification may elect to follow the procedures for a class 2 permit modification instead if it wishes to allow for public participation in the modification decision. EPA must be notified of this decision.

C. Class 2 Modifications

Section 270.42(b) addresses the procedures for class 2 modifications. A permittee requesting a class 2 modification must submit to EPA a request that describes the exact change to be made, identifies that the modification is a class 2 modification, explains why the modification is needed, and provides the applicable information required by 40 C.F.R. Sections 270.13 through .21, .62, and .63. EPA must respond to a request for a class 2 modification within 120 days, or the modification is automatically authorized on a temporary basis.[32]

D. Class 3 Modifications

A class 3 modification request is very similar to a class 2 modification request. However, the EPA procedure for responding to a class 3 modification request differs from that used to respond to a class 2 request.

---

[31]*Id.* § 270.42.
[32]*Id.* § 270.42(b)(6).

Chapter 7: Permit Requirements   141

40 C.F.R. Section 270.42(c) sets forth the procedures for submitting a class 3 modification request and responding to such a request.

E. Other Modifications

In the case of modifications not listed in Appendix I of Part 270, a permittee desiring a modification to a permit has two options. The permittee may either consider the modification to be class 3 and submit a class 3 modification request, or may request a determination by EPA that the modification should be reviewed and approved as either a class 1 or a class 2 modification.[33]

F. Temporary Modification Authorizations

EPA may grant temporary authorizations for permit modifications of up to two 180-day periods when requested by the owner or operator, provided the criteria set forth in Section 270.42(e) are satisfied. The owner or operator is required to notify all interested persons (on a list kept by EPA) of the temporary authorization request.

G. Appeals of Permit Modification Decisions

The decision to grant or deny either a class 2 or a class 3 permit modification request may be appealed by the permittee, a member of the public, or a state or local government unit pursuant to the procedures of 40 C.F.R. Section 124.19.[34] An automatic authorization that is effective because of EPA's failure to respond to a class 2 modification request in a timely manner may also be appealed by the public or a unit of state or local government. However, the permitted TSDF may continue to operate pursuant to the automatic authorization until the appeal has been granted.[35]

H. Newly Regulated Wastes and Hazardous Waste Management Units

A permitted TSDF is authorized to manage wastes newly listed or identified under Part 261, or to manage hazardous wastes in newly regulated hazardous waste management units, without going through the standard

---

[33]*Id.* § 270.42(d).
[34]*Id.* § 270.42(f)(2).
[35]*Id.* § 270.42(f)(3).

142   THE RCRA PRACTICE MANUAL

modification procedures. The facility must meet the requirements set forth in 40 C.F.R. Section 270.42(g).

IX. Permit Duration and Renewal

RCRA permits are effective for a fixed term that cannot exceed ten years.[36] A TSDF may continue to operate under an expired permit provided certain requirements are satisfied, as described below.

A. EPA-Issued Permits

If EPA has issued the permit and is responsible for reissuance of the permit, the existing permit conditions can remain in effect (and enforceable) until the effective date of the new permit.[37] For this to occur, the application for the new permit must comply with the requirements of 40 C.F.R. Section 270.10(c). The application must be administratively complete and must be submitted at least 180 days before the expiration date of the current permit, unless the EPA has given permission to file on a later date. However, no application may be submitted after the expiration date of the current permit.[38] The existing permit will not continue to be in effect if EPA's failure to issue a new permit before the expiration date of the current permit is due to the fault of the permittee.[39]

B. State-Issued Permits

In the states that have an authorized hazardous waste permit program under 40 C.F.R. Part 271, an expiring EPA-issued permit will be effective and enforceable beyond the expiration date if the permittee has submitted a timely and complete application under applicable state law and regulations. The permit will continue only until the effective date of the state's issuance or denial of a state RCRA permit.[40]

X. Permit Termination

A TSDF that obtains a RCRA permit should also consider how it will eventually "escape" the permitting requirements. A RCRA permit does

---

[36]42 U.S.C. § 6925(c)(3); 40 C.F.R. § 270.50(a).
[37]Administrative Procedures Act, 5 U.S.C. § 558(c); 40 C.F.R. § 270.51.
[38]40 C.F.R. § 270.10(h).
[39]*Id.* § 270.51(a)(2).
[40]*Id.* § 270.51(d).

not expire simply upon the discontinuation of the use of the facility or hazardous waste management unit. Once a facility is subject to the permitting requirements, it must maintain its permit until all hazardous wastes and soil and groundwater impacted by the hazardous materials are either removed or treated. A postclosure permit will be required for surface impoundments, landfills, land treatment units, and waste piles, unless the owner or operator "clean closes" the unit (i.e., removes all hazardous wastes and decontaminates equipment and materials—also known as "closure by removal").[41] For additional discussion of the owner or operator's postclosure responsibilities, see Chapter 9. Once this is complete, the TSDF must obtain a modification to the term of its permit that renders the permit no longer applicable.

EPA may terminate a permit if (1) the permittee fails to comply with a condition of the permit; (2) the permittee fails to fully disclose all relevant facts in the permit application process; (3) the permittee misrepresents a relevant fact at any time; or (4) the permitted activity endangers human health or the environment. In terminating a permit, EPA must follow the procedures of 40 C.F.R. Part 124.[42]

XI. Interim Status

A. Eligibility for Interim Status

RCRA allows certain facilities to operate as "grandfathered" TSDFs without a permit under what is termed "interim status."[43] Interim status is available in two situations for a facility that was not subject to the RCRA permit requirements but becomes newly regulated.

First, EPA (or Congress) may decide that a waste that was nonhazardous should now be considered hazardous. A facility would either have to discontinue treating, storing, or disposing of that waste or obtain interim status until it could either discontinue its activities or obtain a permit.[44]

Secondly, a nonhazardous waste treated, stored, or disposed of by a facility may begin to exhibit hazardous characteristics because of operational changes at the facility. Again, the facility can either discontinue its activities or obtain interim status.[45]

---

[41]*Id.* § 270.1(c)(5).
[42]*Id.* § 270.43.
[43]42 U.S.C. § 6925; 40 C.F.R. subpt. G.
[44]40 C.F.R. § 270.10(e)(i).
[45]*Id.* § 270.10(e)(ii).

144   THE RCRA PRACTICE MANUAL

To obtain interim status, a facility that is newly regulated due to regulatory changes must submit a Part A within six months of the publication of such a regulatory change. A facility that is newly regulated because of process changes at the facility must submit a Part A within 30 days of first treating, storing, or disposing of the hazardous waste.[46]

For interim status, the facility must submit a Part A application and file a RCRA Section 3010(a) Notification of Hazardous Waste Activity. The notification must state the location and general description of hazardous waste activity and the identified or listed hazardous wastes handled by the TSDF. Failure to provide this notification will preclude interim status, whether or not the owner or operator has fully complied with the requirements for submittal of a Part A.

Any facility that has been previously denied a RCRA permit or whose permit has been previously terminated is ineligible for interim status.[47] However, the facility may submit Parts A and B of the RCRA permit application in order to obtain a standard RCRA permit.

Many facilities obtained interim status in 1980, immediately after the effective date of the RCRA regulations. Interim status is no longer available for those facilities, since EPA was obligated to make a final decision on permit applications by certain deadlines. The latest of these deadlines was November 8, 1992.[48]

B. Loss of Interim Status

For a facility that achieved interim status on November 19, 1980, Part B of the permit application did not have to be submitted until it was requested—"called in"—by EPA. Because EPA had difficulty processing the extensive Part Bs, however, relatively few were being called in. Furthermore, EPA did not have the resources to inspect or take enforcement actions to ensure that interim status facilities were in compliance with the 40 C.F.R. Part 265 performance standards. To regulate these interim status facilities more fully, Congress added a provision in the Hazardous and Solid Waste Amendments of 1984 (HSWA) that requires all interim status facilities to certify compliance with the groundwater monitoring and financial assurances requirements of RCRA and submit a Part B application by certain dates. A facility failing to do so loses interim status.[49]

A TSDF that may lose interim status or whose RCRA permit may be denied or terminated should be prepared to discontinue its hazardous

---

[46]*Id.* § 270.10(e); 45 Fed. Reg. 76,633 (1980).
[47]40 C.F.R. § 270.70(c).
[48]42 U.S.C. § 6925(c); 40 C.F.R. § 270.73.
[49]42 U.S.C. § 6925(c).

waste treatment, storage, or disposal activities immediately upon the occurrence of such an event in order to avoid potential EPA enforcement action. This will require planning on the part of the TSDF, since changing a TSDF's processes or waste-handling methods often requires several months or longer.

XII. "Inadvertent" TSDF Status

In some cases, a facility may inadvertently, without a permit or interim status, engage in TSD activities and thus be subject to all of the RCRA permit requirements. This can happen in various ways, including but not limited to:

- accumulating hazardous wastes beyond the 90- or 180-day time limits for accumulation;
- improperly accumulating hazardous wastes;
- discovering hazardous wastes stored or disposed of on-site; and
- failing to timely identify newly regulated hazardous wastes and properly manage them.

If one of these circumstances does occur, EPA will often take the position that the facility operated as an unpermitted TSDF and may seek injunctive relief or penalties.

Perhaps the best response in a situation such as this is to discontinue immediately the TSD activity, to the extent possible. This may include costly measures, such as immediate off-site disposal of hazardous wastes at a permitted facility or excavation of hazardous wastes disposed of on land.

If the facility cannot immediately cease the TSDF activity (for example, if it will take months to remove the hazardous wastes from storage or disposal at the facility), the facility may still be able to obtain interim status. If the waste only recently became regulated because of changes to the RCRA regulations, there is a six-month window of opportunity in which to obtain interim status.[50] If the facility will need a lengthy period of time in which to remove hazardous wastes, it may need to seek full permitted status by submitting a Part B application as well.

Whether a facility in this situation seeks interim status or a full permit, it will need immediately to begin complying with all of the Part 265 TSDF performance standards.

---

[50] 40 C.F.R. § 270.10(e).

XIII. Postclosure Permits

As discussed in Chapter 9, postclosure permits are required for a facility if all hazardous wastes and impacted soil and groundwater are not removed at the time of closure.

As with TSDF operating permits, a facility is required to submit a Part B permit application to EPA. However, the application need not address issues that are not relevant to postclosure responsibilities. The facility needs to submit only the information specified in 40 CFR Section 270.28 for the postclosure permit renewal, unless the permitting agency requires additional information. Among other items, the Part B application for a postclosure permit must address groundwater monitoring, financial responsibility, and corrective action.

The postclosure care period lasts for 30 years after completion of closure, unless the Regional Administrator shortens or extends the postclosure care period in accordance with 40 CFR Sections 264.117(a) and 265.117(a). RCRA permits have a fixed term not to exceed ten years, so owners and operators of facilities that receive postclosure permits must renew their permits at least every ten years during the postclosure care period.[51]

XIV. Permitting Reference Materials

Because the RCRA permitting regulations are so complicated, and because the regulations are unclear with respect to many situations, practitioners will often want to refer to guidance and interpretive materials. Explanatory preambles in the *Federal Register* should be consulted. *Federal Register* citations can generally be found in the *Code of Federal Regulations* after each rule section. Another source of information is EPA's guidance documents, listed in Appendix A. A third source, which contains EPA's own interpretation of its regulations, is the *RCRA Permit Policy Compendium*. This compendium is compiled by the Office of Solid Waste and Emergency Response (OSWER) and can be ordered from the National Technical Information Service. It includes hundreds of EPA responses to inquiries regarding regulatory interpretations.

---

[51]*Id.* § 270.50.

XV. Conclusion

The RCRA permitting regulations are set forth at 40 C.F.R. Parts 270 and 124, and the owners and operators of all treatment, storage, and disposal facilities must comply with them. All owners and operators of facilities generating or handling hazardous wastes should become familiar with the regulations in order to determine when a permit is required and when an exception to the permitting requirements can be claimed.

The RCRA permitting regulations are complex and comprehensive. The process of obtaining a permit and the requirements that must be satisfied to maintain a permit properly are complex and burdensome. Thus, it is important for the potential permittee to determine if a permit is needed and, if so, whether the time and effort necessary to obtain and maintain a permit are warranted. In either case, familiarity with the RCRA permitting regulations is essential.

APPENDIX A

List of Guidance Documents Released by EPA's Office of Solid Waste

Taken from EPA's *Catalogue of Hazardous and Solid Waste Publications*, 16th Edition. To order documents, call (800) 424-9346, or visit http://www.epa.gov/epaoswer/osw/catalog.htm.

Abstracts of Selected Precious Metal Mines' Permits

Alternate Concentration Limit Guidance; Part I: ACL Policy and Information Requirements; Part II: Based on 264.94(B) Criteria; Case Studies

Construction Quality Assurance for Hazardous Waste Land Disposal Facilities; Technical Guidance Document

Criteria for Identifying Areas of Vulnerable Hydrogeology under RCRA (Complete Set)

Environmental Fact Sheet: Amendment to Requirements for Hazardous Waste Incinerator Permits

Environmental Fact Sheet: Changes to Interim Status Facilities; Modifications to Hazardous Waste Permits; Procedures for Postclosure Permitting

Environmental Fact Sheet: Coke Ovens Temporarily Exempted from BIF Rule Provisions

Environmental Fact Sheet: Proposed Rulemaking on Corrective Action for Solid Waste Management Units at Hazardous Waste Management Facilities

Final Interim Status Standards for Surface Impoundments (40 C.F.R. 265.220); Standards Applicable to Owners and Operators of Hazardous Waste Treatment, Storage, and Disposal Facilities Under RCRA, Subtitle C, Section 3004

Financial Requirements (40 C.F.R. 264 and 265, Subpart H); Standards Applicable to Owners and Operators of Hazardous Waste Treatment, Storage, and Disposal Facilities Under RCRA, Subtitle C, Section 3004

Financial Requirements; Interim Status Standards (40 C.F.R. 265, Subpart H); Final Draft Guidance

Chapter 7: Permit Requirements 149

General and Interim Status Standards for Tanks (40 C.F.R. 264 and 265, Subpart J); Interim Status Standards for Chemical, Physical, and Biological Treatment (40 C.F.R. 265, Subpart Q); Standards Applicable to Owners and Operators of Hazardous Waste Treatment, Storage, and Disposal Facilities Under RCRA, Subtitle C, Section 3004

General Facility Standards for Location of Facilities (40 C.F.R. 264, Subpart B, Section 264.18); Standards Applicable to Owners and Operators of Hazardous Waste Treatment, Storage, and Disposal Facilities Under RCRA, Subtitle C, Section 3004

General Issues Concerning Interim Status Standards (40 C.F.R. 265); Standards Applicable to Owners and Operators of Hazardous Waste Treatment, Storage, and Disposal Facilities Under RCRA, Subtitle C, Section 3004

General Waste Analysis (40 C.F.R. 264.13); Interim Status Standards for General Waste Analysis (40 C.F.R. 265.13); Standards Applicable to Owners and Operators of Hazardous Waste Treatment, Storage, and Disposal Facilities Under RCRA, Subtitle C, Section 3004

Groundwater Monitoring (40 C.F.R. 265, Subpart F); Standards Applicable to Owners and Operators of Hazardous Waste Treatment, Storage, and Disposal Facilities Under RCRA, Subtitle C, Section 3004

Groundwater Monitoring Guidance for Owners and Operators of Interim Status Facilities

Guidance Document for Subpart F: Air Emission Monitoring; Land Disposal Toxic Air Emissions Evaluation Guidance

Guidance Document: Seismic Considerations in Hazardous Waste Management Facilities

Guidance for Facility Management Planning; Draft

Guidance for Permit Writers: Facilities Storing Hazardous Waste in Containers

Guidance Manual for Cost Estimates for Closure and Post-Closure Plans (Subparts G and H); Volume I: Treatment and Storage Facilities; Volume II: Land Disposal Facilities; Volume III: Unit Costs; Volume IV: Documentation

Guidance Manual for Hazardous Waste Incinerator Permits; Final Report

Guidance Manual for Research, Development, and Demonstration Permits (40 C.F.R. Section 270.65)

Guidance Manual on Hazardous Waste Land Treatment Closure/Post-Closure (40 C.F.R. Part 265)

150 THE RCRA PRACTICE MANUAL

Guidance on Issuing Permits to Facilities Required to Analyze Groundwater for Appendix VII Constituents

Guidance on Public Involvement in the RCRA Permitting Program

Guide for Preparing RCRA Permit Applications for Existing Facilities

Hazardous Waste Incineration Permitting Study

Hazardous Waste Incineration: Questions and Answers

Hydrologic Simulation on Solid Waste Disposal Sites

Incineration Standards (40 C.F.R. 264 and 265, Subpart O); Standards Applicable to Owners and Operators of Hazardous Waste Treatment, Storage, and Disposal Facilities Under RCRA, Subtitle C, Section 3004

Interim Status Standards and General Status Standards for Closure and Post-Closure Care (40 C.F.R. 264 and 265, Subpart G); Standards Applicable to Owners and Operators of Hazardous Waste Treatment, Storage, and Disposal Facilities Under RCRA, Subtitle C, Section 3004

Interim Status Standards for Land Treatment Facilities (40 C.F.R. 265, Subpart M); Standards Applicable to Owners and Operators of Hazardous Waste Treatment, Storage, and Disposal Facilities Under RCRA, Subtitle C, Section 3004

Interim Status Standards for Landfills (40 C.F.R. 265, Subpart N); Standards Applicable to Owners and Operators of Hazardous Waste Treatment, Storage, and Disposal Facilities Under RCRA, Subtitle C, Section 3004

Interim Status Standards for Thermal Treatment Processes Other Than Incineration and for Open Burning (40 C.F.R. 265, Subpart P); Standards Applicable to Owners and Operators of Hazardous Waste Treatment, Storage, and Disposal Facilities Under RCRA, Subtitle C, Section 3004

Interim Status Surface Impoundments; Retrofitting Variances; Guidance Document

Liability Coverage; Requirements for Owners and Operators of Hazardous Waste Treatment, Storage, and Disposal Facilities; A Guidance Manual

Management of Hazardous Waste Leachate

Model RCRA Permit for Hazardous Waste Management Facilities

Modifying RCRA Permits

No Migration Variances to the Hazardous Waste Land Disposal Prohibitions; A Guidance Manual for Petitioners

Chapter 7: Permit Requirements   151

Permit Applicants' Guidance Manual for Exposure Information Requirements Under RCRA, Section 3019

Permit Applicants' Guidance Manual for Hazardous Waste Land Treatment, Storage, and Disposal Facilities; Final Draft

Permit Applicants' Guidance Manual for the General Facility Standards of 40 C.F.R. 264

Permit Guidance Manual on Hazardous Waste Land Treatment Demonstrations

Permit Guidance Manual on Unsaturated Zone Monitoring for Hazardous Waste Land Treatment Units

Permit Writers' Guidance Manual for Hazardous Waste Land Treatment, Storage, and Disposal Facilities; Phase I: Criteria for Location Acceptability and Existing Applicable Regulations

Permit Writers' Guidance Manual for Hazardous Waste Tank Standards

Permitting Hazardous Waste Incinerators

Permitting of Land Disposal Facilities; Groundwater and Air Emission Monitoring

Permitting of Land Disposal Facilities; Groundwater Protection Standard

Permitting of Land Disposal Facilities; Information Requirements for Permitting Discharges; General Standards Applicable to Owners and Operators of Hazardous Waste Treatment, and Disposal Facilities

Permitting of Land Disposal Facilities; Land Treatment

Permitting of Land Disposal Facilities; Landfills

Permitting of Land Disposal Facilities; Overview; Background Document

Permitting of Land Disposal Facilities; Performance Standards for Land Disposal Facilities

Permitting of Land Disposal Facilities; Surface Impoundments

Permitting of Land Disposal Facilities; Underground Injection; Background Document

Permitting of Land Disposal Facilities; Waste Piles

Plans, Recordkeeping, Variances, and Demonstrations for Hazardous Waste Treatment, Storage, and Disposal Facilities; A Guidance Manual

Procedural Guidance for Reviewing Exposure Information Under RCRA, Section 3019

152 THE RCRA PRACTICE MANUAL

Proposed Additions to Standards for Hazardous Waste Incineration (40 C.F.R. 264.342 and 264.343); Standards Applicable to Owners and Operators of Hazardous Waste Treatment, Storage, and Disposal Facilities Under RCRA, Subtitle C, Section 3004

RCRA Corrective Action Interim Measures Guidance; Interim Final

RCRA Corrective Action Plan; Interim Final

RCRA Groundwater Monitoring Compliance Order Guidance

RCRA Groundwater Monitoring Technical Enforcement Guidance Document (TEGD) (Final)

RCRA Implementation Plans (RIP); Fiscal Years: 1987–1992

RCRA Implementation Plan (RIP); Fiscal Year 1993

RCRA Permit Policy Compendium (Complete Set)

RCRA Permit Policy Compendium Update Package; Revision 1

RCRA Permit Quality Protocol; Draft

Regional Guidance Manual for Selected Interim Status Requirements (Draft)

Response to Comments Background Document for the Third Land Disposal Restrictions Proposed Rule; Volume 1-P; BDAT Related Comments; Leachates

Soil Properties, Classification, and Hydraulic Conductivity Testing

Technical Guidance for Corrective Measures; Determining Appropriate Technology and Response for Air Releases; Draft Final Report

Technical Guidance for Corrective Measures; Subsurface Gas

Technical Implementation Document for U.S. EPA's Boiler and Industrial Furnace Regulations

Technical Resource Document for Obtaining Variances from the Secondary Containment Requirement of Hazardous Waste Tank Systems; Volumes I and II

Technical Resource Document for the Storage and Treatment of Hazardous Waste in Tank Systems

Waste Analysis Plans; A Guidance Manual

APPENDIX B

OMB #: 2050-0034 Expires 10/31/02

United States Environmental Protection Agency
HAZARDOUS WASTE PERMIT INFORMATION FORM

1. Facility Permit Contact (See instructions on page 35)	First Name:		MI:	Last Name:
	Phone Number:			Phone Number Extension:

2. Facility Permit Contact Mailing Address (See instructions on page 35)	Street or P.O. Box:		
	City, Town, or Village:		
	State:		
	Country:		Zip Code:

3. Legal Owner Mailing Address and Telephone Number (See instructions on page 36)	Street or P.O. Box:		
	City, Town, or Village:		
	State:		
	Country:	Zip Code:	Phone Number

4. Operator Mailing Address and Telephone Number (See instructions on page 36)	Street or P.O. Box:		
	City, Town, or Village:		
	State:		
	Country:	Zip Code:	Phone Number

5. Facility Existence Date (See instructions on page 36)	Facility Existence Date (mm/dd/yyyy):

6. Other Environmental Permits (See instructions on page 36)

A. Permit Type (Enter code)	B. Permit Number	C. Description

7. Nature of Business (Provide a brief description; see instructions on page 37)

EPA Form 8700-23 (Revised 5/2002)   Page 1 of 6

OMB #: 2050-0034 Expires 10/31/02

8. Process Codes and Design Capacities (See instructions on page 37)

A. PROCESS CODE - *Enter the code from the list of process codes below that best describes each process to be used at the facility. Thirteen lines are provided for entering codes. If more lines are needed, attach a separate sheet of paper with the additional information. For "other" processes (i.e., D99, S99, T04 and X99), describe the process (including its design capacity) in the space provided in Item 9.*

B. PROCESS DESIGN CAPACITY - *For each code entered in column A, enter the capacity of the process.*

    1. AMOUNT - *Enter the amount. In a case where design capacity is not applicable (such as in a closure/post-closure or enforcement action) enter the total amount of waste for that process.*

    2. UNIT OF MEASURE - *For each amount entered in column B(1), enter the code in column B(2) from the list of unit of measure codes below that describes the unit of measure used. Select only from the units of measure in this list.*

C. PROCESS TOTAL NUMBER OF UNITS - *Enter the total number of units for each corresponding process code.*

PROCESS CODE	PROCESS	APPROPRIATE UNITS OF MEASURE FOR PROCESS DESIGN CAPACITY	PROCESS CODE	PROCESS	APPROPRIATE UNITS OF MEASURE FOR PROCESS DESIGN CAPACITY
	Disposal:		T81	Cement Kiln	Gallons Per Day; Liters Per Day; Pounds
D79	Underground Injection Well Disposal	Gallons; Liters; Gallons Per Day; or Liters Per Day	T82	Lime Kiln	Per Hour; Short Tons Per Hour; Kilograms
D80	Landfill	Acre-feet; Hectare-meter; Acres; Cubic Meters; Hectares; Cubic Yards	T83	Aggregate Kiln	Per Hour; Metric Tons Per Day; Metric
			T84	Phosphate Kiln	Tons Per Hour; Short Tons Per Day; Btu Per
D81	Land Treatment	Acres or Hectares	T85	Coke Oven	Hour; Liters Per Hour; Kilograms Per
D82	Ocean Disposal	Gallons Per Day or Liters Per Day	T86	Blast Furnace	Hour; or Million Btu Per Hour
D83	Surface Impoundment Disposal	Gallons; Liters; Cubic Meters; or Cubic Yards	T87	Smelting, Melting, or Refining Furnace	Gallons Per Day; Liters Per Day; Pounds Per Hour; Short Tons Per Hour; Kilograms
D99	Other Disposal	Any Unit of Measure Listed Below	T88	Titanium Dioxide Chloride Oxidation Reactor	Per Hour; Metric Tons Per Day; Metric Tons Per Hour; Short Tons Per Day; Btu Per
	Storage:		T89	Methane Reforming Furnace	Hour; Gallons Per Hour; Liters Per Hour; or
S01	Container	Gallons; Liters; Cubic Meters; or Cubic Yards	T90	Pulping Liquor Recovery Furnace	Million Btu Per Hour
S02	Tank Storage	Gallons; Liters; Cubic Meters; or Cubic Yards	T91	Combustion Device Used In The Recovery Of Sulfur Values	
S03	Waste Pile	Cubic Yards or Cubic Meters		From Spent Sulfuric Acid	
S04	Surface Impoundment Storage	Gallons; Liters; Cubic Meters; or Cubic Yards		Halogen Acid Furnaces	
S05	Drip Pad	Gallons; Liters; Acres; Cubic Meters; Hectares; or Cubic Yards	T92	Other Industrial Furnaces Listed In 40 CFR §260.10	
S06	Containment Building Storage	Cubic Yards or Cubic Meters	T93		
S99	Other Storage	Any Unit of Measure Listed Below	T94	Containment Building - Treatment	Cubic Yards; Cubic Meters; Short Tons Per Hour; Gallons Per Hour; Liters Per Hour;
	Treatment:				Btu Per Hour; Pounds Per Hour; Short Tons
T01	Tank Treatment	Gallons Per Day; Liters Per Day; Short Tons Per Hour; Gallons Per Hour; Liters Per Hour; Pounds Per Hour; Short Tons Per Day; Kilograms Per Hour; Metric Tons Per Day; or Metric Tons Per Hour			Per Day; Kilograms Per Hour; Metric Tons Per Hour; or Million Btu Per Hour
T02	Surface Impoundment Treatment	Gallons Per Day; Liters Per Day; Short Tons Per Hour; Gallons Per Hour; Liters Per Hour; Pounds Per Hour; Short Tons per Day; Kilograms Per Hour; Metric Tons Per Day; or Metric Tons Per Hour		**Miscellaneous (Subpart X):**	
			X01	Open Burning/Open Detonation	Any Unit of Measure Listed Below
			X02	Mechanical Processing	Short Tons Per Hour; Metric Tons Per Hour; Short Tons Per Day; Metric Tons Per
T03	Incinerator	Short Tons Per Hour; Metric Tons Per Hour; Gallons Per Hour; Liters Per Hour; Btu Per Hour; Pounds Per Hour; Short Tons Per Day; Kilograms Per Hour; Gallons Per Day; Liters Per Day; Metric Tons Per Hour; or Million Btu Per Hour			Day; Pounds Per Hour; Kilograms Per Hour; Gallons Per Hour; Liters Per Hour; or Gallons Per Day
			X03	Thermal Unit	Gallons Per Day; Liters Per Day; Pounds Per Hour; Short Tons Per Hour; Kilograms
T04	Other Treatment	Gallons Per Day; Liters Per Day; Pounds Per Hour; Short Tons Per Hour; Kilograms Per Hour; Metric Tons Per Day; Metric Tons Per Day; Short Tons Per Day; Btu Per Hour; Gallons Per Day; Liters Per Day; Liters Per Hour; or Million Btu Per Hour			Per Hour; Metric Tons Per Day; Metric Tons Per Hour; Short Tons Per Day; Btu Per Hour; or Million Btu Per Hour
			X04	Geologic Repository	Cubic Yards; Cubic Meters; Acre-feet; Hectare-meter; Gallons; or Liters
T80	Boiler	Gallons; Liters; Gallons Per Hour; Liters Per Hour; Btu Per Hour; or Million Btu Per Hour	X99	Other Subpart X	Any Unit of Measure Listed Below

UNIT OF MEASURE	UNIT OF MEASURE CODE	UNIT OF MEASURE	UNIT OF MEASURE CODE	UNIT OF MEASURE	UNIT OF MEASURE CODE
Gallons	G	Short Tons Per Hour	D	Cubic Yards	Y
Gallons Per Hour	E	Metric Tons Per Hour	W	Cubic Meters	C
Gallons Per Day	U	Short Tons Per Day	N	Acres	B
Liters	L	Metric Tons Per Day	S	Acre-feet	A
Liters Per Hour	H	Pounds Per Hour	J	Hectares	Q
Liters Per Day	V	Kilograms Per Hour	R	Hectare-meter	F
		Million Btu Per Hour	X	Btu Per Hour	I

EPA Form 8700-23 (Revised 5/2002)   Page 2 of 6

OMB #: 2050-0034 Expires 10/31/02

8. Process Codes and Design Capacities (Continued)

EXAMPLE FOR COMPLETING Item 8 (shown in line number X-1 below): A facility has a storage tank, which can hold 533.788 gallons.

Line Number	A. Process Code (From list above)			B. PROCESS DESIGN CAPACITY		(2) Unit of Measure (Enter code)	C. Process Total Number of Units	For Official Use Only
				(1) Amount (Specify)				
X 1	S	0	2	5 3 3	. 7 8 8	G	0 0 1	
1					.			
2					.			
3					.			
4					.			
5					.			
6					.			
7					.			
8					.			
9					.			
1 0					.			
1 1					.			
1 2					.			
1 3					.			

NOTE: If you need to list more than 13 process codes, attach an additional sheet(s) with the information in the same format as above. Number the lines sequentially, taking into account any lines that will be used for "other" processes (i.e., D99, S99, T04 and X99) in Item 9.

9. Other Processes (See instructions on page 37 and follow instructions from Item 8 for D99, S99, T04 and X99 process codes)

Line Number (Enter #s in sequence with Item 8)	A. Process Code (From list above)			B. PROCESS DESIGN CAPACITY		(2) Unit of Measure (Enter code)	C. Process Total Number of Units	D. Description of Process
				(1) Amount (Specify)				
X 1	T	0	4		.			In-situ Vitrification
1					.			
2					.			
3					.			
4					.			

EPA Form 8700-23 (Revised 5/2002)   Page 3 of 6

OMB #: 2050-0034 Expires 10/31/02

10. Description of Hazardous Wastes (See instructions on page 37)

A. **EPA HAZARDOUS WASTE NUMBER** - Enter the four-digit number from 40 CFR, Part 261 Subpart D of each listed hazardous waste you will handle. For hazardous wastes which are not listed in 40 CFR, Part 261 Subpart D, enter the four-digit number(s) from 40 CFR Part 261, Subpart C that describes the characteristics and/or the toxic contaminants of those hazardous wastes.

B. **ESTIMATED ANNUAL QUANTITY** - For each listed waste entered in column A, estimate the quantity of that waste that will be handled on an annual basis. For each characteristic or toxic contaminant entered in column A, estimate the total annual quantity of all the non-listed waste(s) that will be handled which possess that characteristic or contaminant.

C. **UNIT OF MEASURE** - For each quantity entered in column B, enter the unit of measure code. Units of measure which must be used and the appropriate codes are:

ENGLISH UNIT OF MEASURE	CODE	METRIC UNIT OF MEASURE	CODE
POUNDS	P	KILOGRAMS	K
TONS	T	METRIC TONS	M

If facility records use any other unit of measure for quantity, the units of measure must be converted into one of the required units of measure, taking into account the appropriate density or specific gravity of the waste.

D. **PROCESSES**

1. **PROCESS CODES:**

   For listed hazardous waste: For each listed hazardous waste entered in column A select the code(s) from the list of process codes contained in Items 8A and 9A on page 3 to indicate the waste will be stored, treated, and/or disposed at the facility.

   For non-listed hazardous waste: For each characteristic or toxic contaminant entered in column A, select the code(s) from the list of process codes contained in Items 8A and 9A on page 3 to indicate all the processes that will be used to store, treat, and/or dispose of all the non-listed hazardous wastes that possess that characteristic or toxic contaminant.

   NOTE: THREE SPACES ARE PROVIDED FOR ENTERING PROCESS CODES. IF MORE ARE NEEDED:

   1. Enter the first two as described above.
   2. Enter "000" in the extreme right box of Item 10.D(1).
   3. Use additional sheet, enter line number from previous sheet, and enter additional code(s) in Item 10.E.

2. **PROCESS DESCRIPTION:** If a code is not listed for a process that will be used, describe the process in Item 10.D(2) or in Item 10.E(2).

   NOTE: HAZARDOUS WASTES DESCRIBED BY MORE THAN ONE EPA HAZARDOUS WASTE NUMBER - Hazardous wastes that can be described by more than one EPA Hazardous Waste Number shall be described on the form as follows:

   1. Select one of the EPA Hazardous Waste Numbers and enter it in column A. On the same line complete columns B, C and D by estimating the total annual quantity of the waste and describing all the processes to be used to treat, store, and/or dispose of the waste.

   2. In column A of the next line enter the other EPA Hazardous Waste Number that can be used to describe the waste. In column D(2) on that line enter "included with above" and make no other entries on that line.

   3. Repeat step 2 for each EPA Hazardous Waste Number that can be used to describe the hazardous waste.

EXAMPLE FOR COMPLETING Item 10 (shown in line numbers X-1, X-2, X-3, and X-4 below) - A facility will treat and dispose of an estimated 900 pounds per year of chrome shavings from leather tanning and finishing operations. In addition, the facility will treat and dispose of three non-listed wastes. Two wastes are corrosive only and there will be an estimated 200 pounds per year of each waste. The other waste is corrosive and ignitable and there will be an estimated 100 pounds per year of that waste. Treatment will be in an incinerator and disposal will be in a landfill.

Line Number		A. EPA Hazardous Waste No. (Enter code)			B. Estimated Annual Quantity of Waste	C. Unit of Measure (Enter code)	D. PROCESSES							(2) PROCESS DESCRIPTION (If a code is not entered in D(1))
							(1) PROCESS CODES (Enter code)							
X	1	K	0 5	4	900	P	T	0	3	D	8	0		
X	2	D	0 0	2	400	P	T	0	3	D	8	0		
X	3	D	0 0	1	100	P	T	0	3	D	8	0		
X	4	D	0 0	2										Included With Above

EPA Form 8700-23 (Revised 5/2002)   Page 4 of 6

OMB #: 2050-0034 Expires 10/31/02

10. Description of Hazardous Wastes *(Continued; use additional sheets as necessary)*

Line Number	A. EPA Hazardous Waste No. (Enter code)	B. Estimated Annual Quantity of Waste	C. Unit of Measure (Enter code)	D. PROCESSES				(2) PROCESS DESCRIPTION (If a code is not entered in D(1))
				(1) PROCESS CODES (Enter code)				
1								
2								
3								
4								
5								
6								
7								
8								
9								
1 0								
1 1								
1 2								
1 3								
1 4								
1 5								
1 6								
1 7								
1 8								
1 9								
2 0								
2 1								
2 2								
2 3								
2 4								
2 5								
2 6								
2 7								
2 8								
2 9								
3 0								
3 1								
3 2								
3 3								

EPA Form 8700-23 (Revised 5/2002)   Page 5 of 6

OMB #: 2050-0034 Expires 10/31/02

10. Description of Hazardous Wastes (*Continued; Additional Sheet*)

Line Number	A. EPA Hazardous Waste No. (Enter code)	B. Estimated Annual Quantity of Waste	C. Unit of Measure (Enter code)	E. PROCESSES			(2) PROCESS DESCRIPTION (If a code is not entered in E(1))
				(1) PROCESS CODES (Enter code)			

EPA Form 8700-23 (Revised 5/2002)   Page __ of __

OMB #: 2050-0034 Expires 10/31/02

11. Map (See instructions on page 38)

Attach to this application a topographic map, or other equivalent map, of the area extending to at least one mile beyond property boundaries. The map must show the outline of the facility, the location of each of its existing and proposed intake and discharge structures, each of its hazardous waste treatment, storage, or disposal facilities, and each well where it injects fluids underground. Include all springs, rivers and other surface water bodies in this map area. See instructions for precise requirements.

12. Facility Drawing (See instructions on page 39)

All existing facilities must include a scale drawing of the facility (see instructions for more detail).

13. Photographs (See instructions on page 39)

All existing facilities must include photographs (aerial or ground-level) that clearly delineate all existing structures; existing storage, treatment and disposal areas; and sites of future storage, treatment or disposal areas (see instructions for more detail).

14. Comments (See instructions on page 39)

EPA Form 8700-23 (Revised 5/2002)   Page 6 of 6

CHAPTER 8

Operating and Design Standards for Treatment, Storage, and Disposal Facilities

JANET L. MCQUAID

I. Introduction

Section 3004(a) of the Resource Conservation and Recovery Act (RCRA) authorizes EPA to promulgate regulations establishing performance standards applicable to owners and operators of facilities for the treatment, storage, or disposal of regulated hazardous wastes, as may be necessary for the protection of human health and the environment.[1] These regulations may include, but are not limited to, provisions regarding record keeping, reporting, monitoring, and inspection; compliance with the hazardous waste shipment manifest system; operating standards for treatment, storage, and disposal of hazardous waste; standards for location, design, and construction of hazardous waste facilities; contingency plans; training; financial responsibility criteria; and permitting.[2] Pursuant to that authority, Part 264 of the rules implementing RCRA sets minimum national standards applicable to most hazardous waste treatment, storage, and disposal activities.[3]

Facilities that treat, store, or dispose of hazardous wastes are referred to in this chapter as hazardous waste facilities. This chapter covers the

---

[1]42 U.S.C. § 6924(a).
[2]*Id.* § 6924(a)(1)–(7).
[3]40 C.F.R. § 264.1 (2001).

162 THE RCRA PRACTICE MANUAL

provisions in Part 264 outlining the general scope and applicability of the regulations (Subpart A) and requiring hazardous waste facilities to comply with general facility standards (Subpart B); with standards relating to preparedness and prevention of fire, explosion, and releases of hazardous waste (Subpart C); with requirements for contingency planning and emergency procedures (Subpart D); and with procedures requiring manifests, record keeping, and reporting (Subpart E). Later chapters of this book address other requirements of Part 264, including remediation of releases (Subpart F), closure of facilities and postclosure care (Subpart G), financial responsibility requirements (Subpart H), and standards that apply to particular types of hazardous waste facilities (Subparts I through X).

II. *Subpart A: General Scope*

Some activities and facilities are exempt from Part 264, but the exemptions are narrow. For example, persons operating a publicly owned treatment works (POTW) or engaging in ocean disposal of hazardous wastes are exempt from the Subpart B requirements except to the extent that these requirements are included in a RCRA permit by rule.[4] The requirements for underground injection of hazardous waste are established by a permit issued pursuant to the Safe Drinking Water Act,[5] not the requirements of Part 264.[6] Although ocean disposal and underground injection are themselves exempt from the Part 264 requirements, persons undertaking these activities cannot completely disregard the requirements of Part 264. Up until the time that hazardous waste is loaded onto an oceangoing vessel or is injected underground, the storage and treatment of the wastes are subject to the Part 264 requirements.[7] The general requirements of Subpart B also do not apply to a hazardous waste facility located in a state that has received authorization from the EPA for its own state RCRA program.[8] This exemption may be more theoretical than real, however, because to obtain authorization for its own program, a state must show that its standards for hazardous waste facilities are equivalent to or provide substantially the

---

[4]*Id.* § 264.1(c), (e).
[5]*Id.* § 144.14.
[6]*Id.* § 264.1(d).
[7]*Id.* § 264.1(c) comment, (e) comment.
[8]*Id.* § 264.1(f).

same degree of protection as the standards in Part 264.[9] Many states simply adopt the Part 264 federal standards by reference.[10]

Section 3004(a) of RCRA also requires EPA, where appropriate, to distinguish in its general hazardous waste facility regulations between requirements appropriate for new facilities and for facilities in existence on the date of the promulgation of the regulations. Facilities in existence as of the date of promulgation of regulations that render the waste hazardous are subject to the interim status provisions of Section 3005(e) of RCRA.[11] Accordingly, Part 265 of EPA's implementing regulations provides a parallel set of requirements that apply to interim status facilities.[12] For the most part, however, these regulations have diminished in importance as the large universe of interim status facilities in existence when RCRA was enacted has diminished over time as a result of either closure or issuance of a final RCRA permit under the permitting program. Nevertheless, some interim status facilities continue to operate, and some continue to come into existence as a result of statutory or regulatory changes, such as new hazardous waste listings, which render previously unregulated facilities subject to the regulations. The Part 265 regulations for interim status facilities cover the same subjects as are covered in Part 264 for permitted facilities and, with respect to the subject matter of this chapter, virtually mirror the Part 264 provisions. Accordingly, this chapter provides specific references and citations to the Part 265 regulations only where the Part 265 and Part 264 regulations differ significantly.

III. Subpart B: General Facility Standards

Certain standards and requirements apply to all types of hazardous waste facilities. Subpart B details these generally applicable requirements.

A. Identification Number

Every hazardous waste facility owner or operator must obtain from the EPA an identification number.[13]

---

[9]*Id.* §§ 271.1(i), 271.4.

[10]*See, e.g.,* 30 TEX. ADMIN. CODE § 335.152 (Texas industrial solid waste regulations incorporating part 264 provisions).

[11]42 U.S.C. § 6925(e).

[12]40 C.F.R. pt. 265.

[13]*Id.* § 264.11.

164   THE RCRA PRACTICE MANUAL

B. Required Notices

The owner or operator of a hazardous waste facility has certain notification obligations. An owner or operator must notify EPA if the facility intends to accept hazardous waste from another country.[14] Before transferring ownership or operation of a hazardous waste facility, an owner or operator must give written notice to the transferee of the requirements of Part 264 and Part 270, the hazardous waste permitting program.[15] In addition, before a hazardous waste facility can accept another generator's wastes from off-site, the owner or operator of the hazardous waste facility must provide written notification to the generator, keeping a copy on file, indicating that the facility has the necessary permits and will accept the waste the generator is shipping.[16]

C. General Waste Analysis

Before accepting a hazardous waste for treatment, storage, or disposal, a facility owner or operator must obtain a detailed chemical and physical analysis of a representative sample of the waste.[17] The owner or operator does not always have to conduct the chemical analysis itself. Instead, the owner or operator may, in many instances, rely on information provided by the generator or on an analysis of similar wastes generated by a similar process.[18] Moreover, the owner or operator need not obtain a detailed analysis of every waste shipment. Hazardous waste facilities accepting off-site wastes must inspect each hazardous waste shipment. The facilities must then analyze the hazardous waste shipment only if the inspection suggests it is necessary to do so.[19] Specific wastes or waste management facilities may have different or additional inspection and analysis requirements.[20]

A chemical analysis must be repeated often enough to keep it accurate and up-to-date. At a minimum, this means that the analysis must be repeated when the owner or operator is notified or has reason to believe that the process or operation generating the waste has changed, or when an inspection of the waste suggests that it is not the same waste

---

[14]*Id.* § 264.12(a).
[15]*Id.* § 264.12(c).
[16]*Id.* § 264.12(b).
[17]*Id.* § 264.13(a)(1).
[18]*Id.* § 264.13(a)(2) comment, 13(a)(1).
[19]*Id.* § 264.13(a)(4).
[20]*Id.* §§ 264.17 (ignitable, reactive, or incompatible wastes), 264.314 (bulk and containerized liquids), 264.341 (incinerators), 264.1032, 264.1034(d) (process vents on certain waste management facilities), 268.7 (land disposal restrictions).

Chapter 8: Operating and Design Standards 165

described on the accompanying manifest.[21] The owner or operator must follow a written waste analysis plan that describes the waste inspection and analysis procedures, including test and sampling methods, the parameters to be analyzed and the corresponding rationale, and frequency of review of the analysis.[22] For facilities accepting off-site wastes, the waste analysis plan must also describe the waste analysis that generators have agreed to supply and the procedures that will be used to inspect and, if necessary, analyze each shipment of hazardous waste received.[23]

D. Security

Hazardous waste facilities must implement security measures, unless direct contact with the wastes is not harmful or disturbance of the waste or equipment will not cause a violation of Part 264.[24] These measures must be adequate to prevent the unknowing entry by persons or livestock onto active portions of a hazardous waste facility and also to minimize the possibility of knowing but unauthorized entry.[25] At a minimum, security measures must include 24-hour surveillance, an artificial or natural barrier that completely surrounds the active portion of the facility, or controlled entry.[26] In addition, a warning sign must be posted at the entrance to each active portion of a facility.[27] The sign must be printed in any language predominant in the area as well as in English.[28]

E. General Inspection Requirements

Hazardous waste facilities must be inspected regularly, and problems must be timely repaired. Inspection records must be kept for three years from the date of the inspection.[29] All equipment must be inspected often enough to identify problems in time to correct them before they harm human health or the environment.[30] In addition, as part of obtaining a Part B permit for the facility, the owner or operator must develop, keep

---

[21]*Id.* § 264.13(a)(3).
[22]*Id.* § 264.13(b).
[23]*Id.* § 264.13(b)(5), (c).
[24]*Id.* § 264.14(a).
[25]*Id.*
[26]*Id.* § 264.14(b).
[27]*Id.* § 264.14(c).
[28]*Id.*
[29]*Id.* § 264.15(d).
[30]*Id.* § 264.15(a).

166   THE RCRA PRACTICE MANUAL

at the facility, and follow a written inspection schedule for certain equipment that is important to preventing, detecting, or responding to environmental or human health problems.[31] The written schedule must describe the frequency of inspection and the types of problems inspectors are to look for—for example, malfunctions of pumps, leaking of fittings, or eroding of dikes.[32] Although the frequency of inspection may vary for different types of equipment, it should be based on the rate of possible deterioration and the probability of environmental or human health harm if a problem goes undetected.[33] Areas subject to spills, such as loading docks, must be inspected daily.[34] In addition, inspection frequencies must comply with the requirements of other sections of Part 264 relating to specific types of waste management facilities or equipment.[35]

F. Personnel Training

Within six months of being assigned to a position involving hazardous waste management, personnel working at hazardous waste facilities must complete a program of classroom or on-the-job training that teaches them to comply with the requirements of Part 264.[36] No employee may be permitted to work unsupervised until completing this training.[37] Each employee must take part in an annual review of the initial training.[38] Records documenting that each employee has completed this training

---

[31]*Id.* § 264.15(b)(1) (listing as critical equipment monitoring equipment, safety and emergency equipment, security devices, and operating and structural equipment, such as dikes and sump pumps).

[32]*Id.* § 264.14(b)(3)–(4).

[33]*Id.* § 264.15(b)(4).

[34]*Id.*

[35]*Id.* §§ 264:174 (*weekly inspections* of areas where containers are stored), 264.195(b) (*daily inspection* of aboveground portions of tank systems, *bimonthly inspection* of sources of impressed current on tank systems, and *annual inspection* of cathodic protection on tank), 264.226(b) (*weekly inspection* of in-service surface impoundments), 264.254(b) (*weekly inspection* of waste piles), 264.303(b) (*weekly inspection* of landfills), 264.347(b), (c) (*daily inspection* of incinerator and associated equipment, *weekly inspection* of incinerator emergency waste feed cut-off system and alarms, *monthly operational testing* of incinerator), 264.602 (*as required* to protect human health and the environment as specified in the permit for miscellaneous unit), 264.1033(f)(3) (*daily inspection* of readings from monitoring instruments on control devices used to comply with the requirements of Part 264), 264.1052(a)(1)–(2) (*weekly visual* and *monthly intensive inspections* of pumps in light liquid service), 264.1053(e)(1) (checking of compressor seal sensors daily at unmanned plant sites or *monthly* at manned plant sites), 264.1058(a) (*monitoring within five days* of problem detection for pumps in heavy liquid service).

[36]*Id.* § 264.16(a)(1), (b).

[37]*Id.* § 264.16(b).

[38]*Id.* § 264.16(c).

Chapter 8: Operating and Design Standards 167

and the annual reviews must be kept on current personnel until the facility is closed and on former employees for at least three years from the date the employee last worked at the facility.[39] As part of its Part B permit, each facility must have a training program approved by EPA.[40] Initial training must be designed to ensure that facility personnel are able to respond effectively to emergencies by familiarizing them with emergency procedures, equipment, and systems, including:

- procedures for using, inspecting, repairing, and replacing facility emergency and monitoring equipment;
- key parameters for automatic waste feed cutoff systems;
- communications or alarm systems;
- response to fires or explosions;
- response to groundwater contamination incidents; and
- shutdown of operations.[41]

G. Ignitable, Reactive, or Incompatible Wastes

The owner or operator of a hazardous waste facility must take special precautions in the handling of ignitable, reactive, or other incompatible wastes. These wastes must be separated and protected from sources of ignition or reactions. While ignitable or reactive waste is being handled, the owner or operator must confine smoking and open flame to specifically designated areas. "No Smoking" signs must be conspicuously displayed wherever there is an ignitable or reactive waste.[42] Owners or operators of facilities that manage ignitable or reactive wastes or mix incompatible wastes or materials must take additional precautions as required by other sections of Part 264.[43]

H. Location Standards

Section 3004(o)(7) of RCRA authorizes EPA to restrict the siting of hazardous waste facilities in environmentally sensitive locations. Under EPA's regulations, new facilities cannot be located within 200 feet of a fault that has had displacement in the Holocene period (10,000 years ago through the present).[44] Facilities located in certain jurisdictions must

---

[39]*Id.* § 264.16(e).
[40]*Id.* § 264.16(a)(1) comment.
[41]*Id.* § 264.16(a)(3).
[42]*Id.* § 264.17(a).
[43]*Id.* § 264.17(b).
[44]*Id.* § 264.18(a).

168   THE RCRA PRACTICE MANUAL

demonstrate compliance with this requirement; in other jurisdictions, compliance is assumed.[45] Jurisdictions for which compliance must be demonstrated include all of California and Nevada, as well as parts of Alaska, Arizona, Colorado, Hawaii (specifically, the island of Hawaii), Idaho, Montana, New Mexico, Utah, Washington, and Wyoming.[46] Procedures for demonstrating compliance with this requirement are described in Part 270, relating to permits.[47] These procedures become more intensive if evidence of a fault is found within 3,000 feet of the facility, requiring a comprehensive geologic analysis of the site and subsurface exploration (trenching) of the area within 200 feet from portions of the facility where treatment, storage, or disposal of hazardous waste will be conducted unless the comprehensive analysis is otherwise conclusive on the absence of a fault within that area.[48] Such trenching is to be performed in a perpendicular direction to known faults (which have had displacement in Holocene time) passing within 3,000 feet of the portions of the facility where treatment, storage, or disposal of hazardous waste will be conducted.[49] This investigation must document the location of faults found with supporting maps and other analyses.[50] For further information, the *Guidance Manual for the Location Standards* provides greater detail on the content of each type of seismic investigation and the appropriate conditions under which each approach or a combination of approaches should be used.[51]

In addition, for most types of hazardous waste facilities located within a 100-year floodplain, special requirements apply.[52] To locate a hazardous waste facility in a 100-year floodplain, the facility must be designed, constructed, and operated to prevent any hazardous waste from washing out of the facility during a 100-year flood.[53] For both new and existing facilities, EPA has the discretion to waive this requirement if the owner or operator demonstrates that procedures are in place that would allow the waste to be removed safely (to a different permitted waste facility) before floodwaters can reach the original facility.[54] EPA

---

[45]*Id.* § 264.18(a) comment.

[46]*Id.* § 264 app. VI.

[47]*Id.* § 270.14(b)(11).

[48]*Id.* § 270.14(b)(11)(ii)(B).

[49]*Id.*

[50]*Id.*

[51]*Id.* § 270.14(b)(11)(ii)(B) comment.

[52]*Id.* §§ 264.18(b), 264.10(b) (applying this requirement to all currently identified types of hazardous waste management facilities except corrective action management units [Subpart X], drip pads [Subpart W], and containment buildings [Subpart DD]).

[53]*Id.* § 264.18(b).

[54]*Id.* §§ 264.18(b)(i), 264.18(b) comment.

Chapter 8: Operating and Design Standards   169

can also waive this requirement for certain existing facilities, such as surface impoundments, waste piles, land treatment units, landfills, and miscellaneous units, if the owner or operator demonstrates that a washout would not result in any harm to human health or the environment based on several characteristics, such as the volume and physical and chemical characteristics of the waste, the concentration of hazardous constituents in surface waters as a result of a washout, and the impact of such concentrations and hazardous constituents on surface waters and their current and/or potential uses, water quality standards, sediments, and soils of the 100-year floodplain.[55]

Finally, placement of noncontainerized or bulk liquid hazardous waste in salt dome formations, salt bed formations, underground mines, or caves is prohibited.[56]

I. Construction Quality Assurance Program

Hazardous waste facilities that include surface impoundments, waste piles, or landfill units subject to the minimum technology requirements discussed in Chapters 10 and 11 of this book must develop a construction quality assurance (CQA) program to ensure that the unit meets or exceeds all design criteria and specifications prescribed in its RCRA permit.[57] The CQA program must be developed and implemented under the direction of a CQA officer, who must be a registered professional engineer.[58] The CQA program must address all physical components of the unit, such as foundations, dikes, liners, geomembranes (flexible membrane liners), leachate collection and removal systems, and final cover systems.[59] The CQA plan must identify the applicable units, the CQA officer and other key personnel in the development and implementation of the CQA program, and the inspection and sampling activities for all unit components that will ensure they meet the design specifications.[60] The prescribed observations, inspections, tests, and measurements must be sufficient to ensure the structural integrity and stability, proper construction, and materials' conformity of the unit components.[61] In particular, unless an equivalent alternative test is approved, test fills must be conducted for compacted soil liners to ensure compliance with

---

[55]*Id.* §§ 264.18(b)(ii)(A)–(D).
[56]*Id.* § 264.18(c).
[57]*Id.* § 264.19.
[58]*Id.*
[59]*Id.* § 264.19(a)(2).
[60]*Id.* § 264.19(b).
[61]*Id.* § 264.19(c).

the specified hydraulic conductivity requirements.[62] Finally, waste may not be received in the unit until the CQA officer has delivered a certified approval of the unit to the Regional Administrator of EPA.[63]

The general facility standards and requirements of Subpart B apply to all hazardous waste management facilities unless specifically exempted.[64] In addition to these general standards, all nonexempt facilities must be constructed and operated to comply with the preparedness and prevention requirements of Subpart C.

IV. Subpart C: Preparedness and Prevention

Subpart C requires that hazardous waste facilities must be designed, constructed, operated, and maintained to minimize the possibility of a fire, explosion, or unplanned sudden or unsudden release of hazardous waste that could threaten human health or the environment.[65] Subpart C spells out the type of emergency equipment required at hazardous waste management facilities, what type of access must be provided to and for the equipment, and the nature of the relationship that must be established with local emergency response authorities.

A. Required Equipment and Testing

Unless an owner or operator demonstrates otherwise in its Part B permit application, a hazardous waste facility must be equipped with the following:

- an internal communications or alarm system capable of providing immediate emergency instruction (voice or signal) to facility personnel;
- a device, such as a telephone (immediately available at the scene of operations) or a handheld two-way radio, capable of summoning emergency assistance from local police departments, fire departments, or state or local emergency response teams;
- portable fire extinguishers, fire control equipment (including special extinguishing equipment, such as that using foam, inert gas, or dry chemicals), spill control equipment, and decontamination equipment; and

---

[62]*Id.* § 264.19(c)(2).
[63]*Id.* § 264.19(d).
[64]*Id.* § 264.10(a).
[65]*Id.* § 264.31.

Chapter 8: Operating and Design Standards 171

- water at adequate volume and pressure to supply water hose streams, or foam-producing equipment, or automatic sprinklers, or spray systems.[66]

This equipment must be tested and maintained as necessary to ensure its proper operation in time of an emergency.[67]

B. Access to Communications or Alarm

When personnel are pouring, mixing, spreading, or otherwise handling hazardous waste, each such employee must have immediate access to an in-plant alarm or emergency communication device, either directly or through visual or voice contact with another employee.[68] At any time there is just one employee on the premises while the facility is operating, that employee must have immediate access to a device capable of summoning emergency assistance from outside the facility.[69] The design of the facility and housekeeping practices must allow aisle space for the unobstructed movement of personnel and emergency equipment to any area of the facility.[70] However, each of these provisions is subject to the Regional Administrator's discretion.[71]

C. Arrangements with State and Local Authorities

The owner or operator of a hazardous waste facility must attempt to make the following arrangements with state and local emergency response organizations, as appropriate for the facility involved:

- arrangements to familiarize police, fire departments, and emergency response teams with the layout of the facility, properties of hazardous waste handled at the facility and associated hazards, places where facility personnel would normally be working, entrances to and roads inside the facility, and possible evacuation routes;
- where more than one police and fire department might respond to an emergency, agreements designating primary emergency authority to a specific police and a specific fire department, and

---

[66]*Id.* § 264.32.
[67]*Id.* § 264.33.
[68]*Id.* § 264.34(a).
[69]*Id.* § 264.34(b).
[70]*Id.* § 264.35.
[71]*Id.* §§ 264.34(a)–(b), 264.35.

agreements with any others to provide support to the primary emergency authority;

- agreements with the state emergency response teams, emergency response contractors, and equipment suppliers; and
- arrangements to familiarize local hospitals with the properties of hazardous waste handled at the facility and the types of injuries or illnesses that could result from fires, explosions, or releases at the facility.[72]

If these organizations will not enter into these arrangements with the hazardous waste facility, the owner or operator must document the refusal in the facility's operating record.[73]

The preparedness and prevention requirements of Subpart C describe requirements designed to minimize the effect of a fire, an explosion, or an unplanned release before it happens. In addition to these preparedness and prevention requirements, all waste management facilities are required to prepare contingency plans and emergency procedures that they will use to minimize the effect of such an event after it happens. These plans and procedures are described in the following section.

V. Subpart D: Contingency Plan and Emergency Procedures

As part of its Part B permit application, every hazardous waste facility, unless specifically exempted from the Part 264 requirements, must have a contingency plan approved by EPA. A copy of this plan must be maintained at the facility and must be provided to any state and local authorities that may be called upon to provide emergency services (for example, police, fire department, hospitals, and state and local emergency response teams).

A. Content of Contingency Plan

The contingency plan must be designed to minimize hazards to human health and the environment from fires, explosions, or unplanned (sudden or unsudden) releases of hazardous waste.[74] This plan describes the emergency procedures that facility personnel will follow immediately upon the occurrence of such an event.[75] In addition, the plan describes

---

[72]*Id.* § 264.37(a).
[73]*Id.* § 264.37(b).
[74]*Id.* § 264.51(a).
[75]*Id.* §§ 264.51(b), 264.52.

Chapter 8: Operating and Design Standards   173

the roles that local police, fire departments, hospitals, contractors, and state and local emergency response teams will play in responding to a fire, explosion, or release at the facility.[76] The contingency plan must include an up-to-date list of names, addresses, and home and office phone numbers of all persons qualified to act as emergency coordinator, as described below.[77] In addition, the plan must include an up-to-date list describing and locating all emergency equipment at the facility, such as fire-fighting systems, spill control equipment, communication and alarm systems, and decontamination equipment.[78] Finally, the contingency plan must include an evacuation plan for all facility personnel, including primary and alternate evacuation routes.[79]

B. Emergency Coordinator

There must at all times be at least one employee, either at the facility or on call (that is, available to reach the facility within a short period of time), with the responsibility for coordinating all emergency response measures and the authority to commit the resources needed to carry out the contingency plan.[80] This employee must be thoroughly familiar with all aspects of the facility's contingency plan, all operations and activities at the facility, the location and characteristics of waste handled, the location of all records within the facility, and the facility layout.[81]

C. Emergency Procedures

In the event of an imminent or actual emergency situation, the emergency coordinator must immediately activate in-plant alarms, notify state and local agencies with designated response roles, identify the character, source, amount, and extent of any release, and assess possible hazards to human health or the environment.[82] If the emergency coordinator determines that there is a threat to human health or the environment outside the facility, the emergency coordinator must immediately notify appropriate local authorities and remain available to help decide whether local areas should be evacuated.[83] In addition, the emergency

---

[76]*Id.* § 264.52(c).
[77]*Id.* § 264.52(d).
[78]*Id.* § 264.52(e).
[79]*Id.* § 264.52(f).
[80]*Id.* § 264.55.
[81]*Id.*
[82]*Id.* § 264.56(a)–(c).
[83]*Id.* § 264.56(d)(1).

coordinator must immediately notify either the government official designated as on-scene coordinator for that geographical area or telephone the National Response Center at its 24-hour number, (800) 424-8802, providing information on the facility involved, the time and type of incident, the name and quantity of materials involved, the extent of injuries, and the possible hazards to human health or the environment outside the facility.[84]

The emergency coordinator must take all reasonable measures to ensure that fires, explosions, or releases do not occur, recur, or spread, including, as necessary, shutting down facility processes and operations, collecting and containing released waste, and removing and isolating containers.[85] If the facility is shut down in response to the emergency, the emergency coordinator must monitor for leaks, pressure buildup, and so on.[86] Immediately after the emergency, the coordinator must provide for the treatment, storage, or disposal of any recovered waste or contaminated material that results from the emergency in accordance with all requirements applying to such wastes.[87] In addition, the emergency coordinator must put the emergency equipment back in order before resuming operations at the facility and complete certain reports to EPA and state and local authorities within a short time after the incident.[88]

VI. Subpart E: Manifest System, Record Keeping, and Reporting

RCRA has been characterized as providing cradle-to-grave control of hazardous wastes. Subpart E of RCRA's implementing regulations is instrumental in allowing the cradle-to-grave monitoring and regulation of hazardous waste.

A. Generators

The "cradle" in the cradle-to-grave scheme is the hazardous waste generator. The standards governing hazardous waste generators are found in Part 262 of the rules implementing RCRA. Part 262 requires most generators to obtain an EPA identification number and comply with its packaging, labeling, marking, placarding, record-keeping, and reporting requirements.[89] Part 262 also requires each generator that ships hazardous waste

---

[84]*Id.* § 264.56(d)(2).
[85]*Id.* § 264.56(e).
[86]*Id.* § 264.56(f).
[87]*Id.* § 264.56(g).
[88]*Id.* § 264.56(h)–(j).
[89]*Id.* §§ 262.12 262.30–.44.

Chapter 8: Operating and Design Standards   175

off-site for treatment, storage, or disposal to prepare a hazardous waste manifest to accompany each shipment with the transporter.[90] The manifest must designate the facility to which the waste is to be shipped.[91] The generator also has the option to designate one alternate facility to handle the waste if an emergency prevents delivery to the primary facility.[92] The manifest must be signed and dated by the generator.[93] A copy of the latest available version of EPA's Uniform Hazardous Waste Manifest Form is reproduced as part of the appendix to this chapter.

States' manifests may impose additional, more restrictive requirements than those called for by the EPA. However, this flexibility has caused problems with inconsistent requirements between states, particularly on interstate shipments of hazardous wastes. In 2001, the EPA proposed a rule to standardize the states' manifests, which is still under consideration as of this writing.[94] In addition to modifying the federal manifest, the agency expects to utilize electronic reporting that would allow generators to report via the Internet.[95]

B. Transporters

As described in Chapter 6 of this manual, when hazardous waste is shipped wholly by rail or wholly by water in bulk shipments to a hazardous waste facility in the United States, the generator of the waste must send three copies of the manifest directly to the designated facility.[96] If the waste is shipped in bulk by a combination of rail and another mode of transportation, three copies of the manifest may be sent to the first nonrail transporter.[97] If the waste is to be exported wholly by rail, the generator must send three copies of the manifest to the last rail transporter to handle the waste in the United States.[98] If the waste is to be exported in bulk by water, the generator must send three copies of the manifest to the last water transporter of the bulk shipment.[99] Exports

---

[90] *Id.* §§ 262.20(a), 262.23(b).

[91] *Id.* § 262.20(b).

[92] *Id.* § 262.20(c).

[93] *Id.* § 262.23(a)(1)–(2).

[94] Modification of the Hazardous Waste Manifest System, 66 Fed. Reg. 28,240 (2001); *see also* Unified Agenda, 68 Fed. Reg. 73,539 (2003) (indicating plans to complete the uniform manifest rule by December 2003).

[95] Establishment of Electronic Reporting; Electronic Records, 66 Fed. Reg. 46,162 (2001); *see also* Unified Agenda, 68 Fed. Reg. 73,539 (2003) (announcing indefinite deferral of the electronic recordkeeping portion of the proposed rule but indicating plans to complete the electronic reporting portion of the proposed rule by August 2004).

[96] 40 C.F.R. § 262.23.

[97] *Id.* § 262.23(d)(1).

[98] *Id.* § 262.23(d)(3).

[99] *Id.* § 262.23(c).

176 THE RCRA PRACTICE MANUAL

must also be accompanied by an EPA Acknowledgment of Consent of the receiving country to the export.[100]

The transporter cannot accept hazardous waste from a generator unless it is accompanied by a signed manifest.[101] The transporter must then pass along the manifest or a shipping paper containing similar information to intermediate transporters and the receiving facility according to the provisions of Part 263 (standards for hazardous waste transporters).[102] These requirements are covered in more detail in Chapter 6 of this manual on standards for hazardous waste transporters.

C. Hazardous Waste Facility Procedures

Every shipment of hazardous waste that ultimately arrives at a hazardous waste facility should be accompanied by either a Hazardous Waste Manifest or a shipping paper. If the hazardous waste facility receives the manifest, the owner or operator must sign and date each copy of the manifest to certify that the hazardous waste covered by the manifest was received.[103] If there are differences between the quantity or type of hazardous waste designated and the type actually received, the owner or operator must record any significant discrepancies on the manifest.[104] If the hazardous waste facility receives only a shipping paper and not the manifest, the facility may nevertheless accept the shipment if the shipping paper contains all the information required by the manifest, excluding only the generator's EPA identification number and the generator's signed certification.[105]

Whether the hazardous waste facility receives a manifest or a shipping paper, it should immediately sign and date each copy of the document to certify that the wastes covered by the document were received, and give a copy to the transporter.[106] Copies of the signed and dated manifest or shipping paper for each waste shipment must be kept at the facility for three years after the date of delivery.[107]

D. Manifest Discrepancies

There may be differences in quantity or type of wastes received versus what is described in the manifest or shipping paper. Significant discrep-

---

[100]*Id.* § 262.52(c).
[101]*Id.* § 263.20.
[102]*Id.* §§ 262.20–.22.
[103]*Id.* § 264.71(a)(1).
[104]*Id.* § 264.71(a)(2).
[105]*Id.* § 264.71(b)(1)–(2).
[106]*Id.* § 264.71(a)(1), (a)(3), (b)(1), (b)(3).
[107]*Id.* § 264.71(a)(5), (b)(5).

ancies must be noted on the manifest or shipping paper.[108] For bulk wastes (such as tanker shipments), discrepancies in quantity are significant if there are differences of more than 10 percent between the manifest and actual weight for bulk wastes.[109] For batch wastes (for instance, shipments in drums), any variation in the number of pieces (such as a difference of one drum in a truckload) is considered significant.[110] Differences in type of waste are significant if there are obvious differences that can be discovered by inspection or waste analysis, such as waste solvent substituted for waste acid, or toxic constituents not reported on the manifest or shipping paper.[111] It is not necessary, however, for facilities whose waste analysis plan would otherwise require sampling to sample and analyze the waste before signing the manifest or shipping paper.[112] Instead, the manifest rules give the hazardous waste facility 15 days after receipt of the waste to reconcile any discrepancy with the generator.[113] If the discrepancy cannot be reconciled within 15 days, the owner or operator of the receiving facility must send a letter to the EPA Regional Administrator describing the discrepancy and the attempts to reconcile, along with a copy of the manifest or shipping paper at issue attached.[114] In addition, within 30 days after delivery of the waste, the receiving facility must send the generator a signed and dated copy of the manifest or shipping paper.[115]

E. Nonmanifested Wastes

If, in spite of the above requirements, a hazardous waste facility receives waste from off-site without an accompanying manifest or shipping paper, it may nevertheless be able to accept the waste if either the waste or the accepting facility meets certain requirements. Waste from conditionally exempt small-quantity generators is exempt from the manifest requirement.[116] The receiving facility should obtain a certification from the generator that the waste qualifies for this or some other exclusion.[117] Even nonexempt waste can be accepted without a manifest or shipping paper.[118] However, such waste may be accepted only if the receiving

---

[108]*Id.* § 264.71(a)(2), (b)(2).
[109]*Id.* § 264.72(a)(1).
[110]*Id.*
[111]*Id.*
[112]*Id.* § 264.71(a)(2) comment, (b)(2) comment.
[113]*Id.* § 264.72(b).
[114]*Id.*
[115]*Id.* § 264.71(a)(4), (b)(4).
[116]*Id.* § 261.5.
[117]*Id.* § 264.76 comment.
[118]*Id.* § 264.76.

178   THE RCRA PRACTICE MANUAL

facility files an Unmanifested Waste Report for the waste delivery that describes the receiving facility; the date the facility received the waste; the generator and transporter to the extent known; the quantity and description of the waste; the method of treatment, storage, or disposal; the manifest certification signed by the owner or operator of the hazardous waste facility; and a brief explanation of why the waste was unmanifested, if known.[119]

F. Operating Record Requirements

In addition to complying with the manifest requirements, the owner or operator of a hazardous waste facility must file certain reports with EPA or the state agency with RCRA authorization from EPA. The owner or operator of a hazardous waste facility must keep a written operating record at the facility for the life of the facility.[120] The operating record must include a description of each hazardous waste received and the methods and dates of its treatment, storage, and disposal; the quantity received; the location of each hazardous waste within the facility; and the quantity at each location.[121] For disposal facilities, the location and quantity of each hazardous waste must be recorded on a map or diagram of each cell or disposal area.[122] If the waste was accompanied by a manifest, all of the required information must be cross-referenced to the manifest documents.[23] In addition, the lifetime operating record must contain the results of waste analyses; summary reports and details of all incidents that require implementing the facility contingency plan; records and results of inspections (kept only three years); and data from monitoring, testing, or analytical data; and where required for any corrective action as well as for surface impoundments, waste piles, land treatment, landfills, incinerators, and on process vents and equipment leaks.[124] For facilities that accept waste from off-site, the operating record must contain copies of notices the facility sends to generators certifying that it has all requisite permits, all closure cost estimates (and for disposal facilities, all postclosure cost estimates), and a certification by the facility permittee at least once every year that it has a waste reduction program in place.[125] The facility's operating record must also con-

---

[119]*Id.* § 264.76(a)–(g).
[120]*Id.* § 264.73(a)–(b).
[121]*Id.* § 264.73(b)(1)–(2).
[122]*Id.* § 264.73(b)(2).
[123]*Id.*
[124]*Id.* § 264.73(b)(3)–(6).
[125]*Id.* § 264.73(b)(7)–(9).

tain certain information about the use of land disposal facilities covered by Sections 268.5 through 268.8 of the RCRA regulations.[126] Finally, the owner or operator must record and maintain any records required under 40 C.F.R. Section 264.1(j)(13), relating to remediation waste management sites.[127] These records must be made available upon request by the EPA or its representative.[128]

G. Biennial Reports

By March 1 of every even-numbered year, the owner or operator of a hazardous waste facility must submit a report on EPA Form 8700-13B to the EPA regional office, covering facility activities for the prior calendar year.[129] This report must provide the EPA identification number, name, and address of the facility; the calendar year covered by the report; for off-site facilities, the EPA identification number of each hazardous waste generator that sent waste to the facility (for imported shipments, the name and address of the foreign generator); a description and quantity of each hazardous waste received during the year (for off-site facilities, this information must be listed by EPA identification number of each generator); the method of treatment, storage, or disposal for each waste; and the most recent closure cost estimates (for disposal facilities, the most recent postclosure cost estimate).[130] For on-site generators, the report must include the waste reduction measures taken, as well as a description of the changes in volume and toxicity of waste actually achieved compared with years prior to 1984 (to the extent such information is available).[131] All facilities must include the manifest certification signed by the owner or operator of the facility.[132]

H. Incidental Reports

In addition to the reports described above, the facility must report to the EPA regional office any releases, fires, and explosions within 15 days after the incident, as well as any facility closures, or as otherwise required by the facility-specific standards discussed elsewhere in this book.[133]

---

[128]*Id.* § 264.73(b)(10)–(16).
[129]*Id.* § 264.73(b)(17).
[130]*Id.* § 264.74(a).
[131]*Id.* § 264.75.
[132]*Id.* § 264.75(a)–(g).
[133]*Id.* § 264.75(h)–(i).
[134]*Id.* § 264.75(j).
[135]*Id.* § 264.77.

VII. Conclusion

This chapter addressed the requirements of Part 264 generally applicable to all facilities: the general facility standards (Subpart B); the standards relating to preparedness and prevention of fire, explosion, and releases of hazardous waste (Subpart C); the requirements for contingency planning and emergency procedures (Subpart D); and the procedures for handling manifests, record keeping, and reporting (Subpart E). The next chapter covers the requirements for closure, postclosure, and financial responsibility for hazardous waste treatment, storage, and disposal facilities.

APPENDIX

Please print or type   (Form designed for use on elite (12 - pitch) typewriter)

Form Approved. OMB No. 2050 - 0039 Expires 9 - 30 - 91

UNIFORM HAZARDOUS WASTE MANIFEST	1 Generator's US EPA ID No.	Manifest Document No.	2. Page 1 of	Information in the shaded areas is not required by Federal law

3. Generator's Name and Mailing Address	A. State Manifest Document Number
	B. State Generator's ID
4. Generator's Phone ( )	

5. Transporter 1 Company Name	6.	US EPA ID Number	C. State Transporter's ID
			D. Transporter's Phone
7. Transporter 2 Company Name	8.	US EPA ID Number	E. State Transporter's ID
			F. Transporter's Phone
9. Designated Facility Name and Site Address	10.	US EPA ID Number	G. State Facility's ID
			H. Facility's Phone

11. US DOT Description (Including Proper Shipping Name, Hazard Class, and ID Number)	12. Containers No.	Type	13. Total Quantity	14. Unit Wt/Vol	I. Waste No.
G a.					
E					
N b.					
E					
R c.					
A					
T d.					
O					
R					

J. Additional Descriptions for Materials Listed Above	K. Handling Codes for Wastes Listed Above

15. Special Handling Instructions and Additional Information

16. **GENERATOR'S CERTIFICATION:** I hereby declare that the contents of this consignment are fully and accurately described above by proper shipping name and are classified, packed, marked, and labeled, and are in all respects in proper condition for transport by highway according to applicable international and national government regulations.

If I am a large quantity generator, I certify that I have a program in place to reduce the volume and toxicity of waste generated to the degree I have determined to be economically practicable and that I have selected the practicable method of treatment, storage, or disposal currently available to me which minimizes the present and future threat to human health and the environment; **OR,** if I am a small quantity generator, I have made a good faith effort to minimize my waste generation and select the best waste management method that is available to me and that I can afford.

Printed/Typed Name	Signature	Month	Day	Year

T 17. Transporter 1 Acknowledgement of Receipt of Materials				
R **A** Printed/Typed Name	Signature	Month	Day	Year
N **S** 18. Transporter 2 Acknowledgement of Receipt of Materials				
P **O** Printed/Typed Name	Signature	Month	Day	Year
R **T** **E** **R**				

F 19. Discrepancy Indication Space
A
C
I
L
I 20. Facility Owner or Operator: Certification of receipt of hazardous materials covered by this manifest except as noted in item 19.
T
Y Printed/Typed Name   Signature   Month Day Year

EPA Form 8700 - 22 (Rev. 9 - 88) Previous editions are obsolete.

CHAPTER 9

Closure, Postclosure, and Financial Responsibility

ROBERT F. WILKINSON AND MICHAEL D. MONTGOMERY

I. Introduction

The RCRA regulations provide very detailed requirements on generators, transporters, and owners and operators of treatment, storage, and disposal facilities. Much attention is typically focused on when and under what circumstances materials enter the RCRA regulatory scheme. Once regulated, a hazardous waste will, in most cases, end up passing through some form of hazardous waste management unit. Once that unit reaches the end of its life, the closure and postclosure requirements dictate how the unit is to be decommissioned, either for nonhazardous use or for dismantling, and whether any long-term supervision and care for that unit may be required in order to protect human health and the environment. Due to the extensive postclosure care period for some units (30 years or more), closure and postclosure requirements will affect the selection and use of various waste management options.

Financial assurance provides an important role in helping to assure the public that owners and operators will be able to meet their closure and postclosure obligations in the future. There is some flexibility in the choice of financial assurance mechanism; however, each mechanism imposes additional costs and burdens on the management of hazardous waste and has, in some cases, driven financially weaker owners and operators out of business.

II. Closure

A. Closure Plan

The general closure standard requires that closure be performed in a manner that minimizes the need for further maintenance of the unit and that controls, minimizes, or eliminates, to the extent necessary to protect human health and the environment, the escape of hazardous waste, constituents, leachate, contaminated runoff, or decomposition products after closure.[1] The general closure and postclosure regulations governing closure plans, the timing of closure, certification of closure, and postclosure are found in Subpart G of the permitted and interim status regulations.[2] The actual closure of a particular hazardous waste management unit is governed by the specific closure regulations established for the various types of regulated waste management units, the written closure plan, and, if applicable, the postclosure plan for the unit.

A facility is required to have a written closure plan that addresses all regulated units at the facility.[3] Closure of fewer than all the units at a facility is considered a "partial closure," even though particular units undergoing closure are considered "closed" for purposes of further RCRA regulation.[4] If a facility closes all of the units subject to the closure requirements, then the facility is considered to have undergone "final closure."[5] The facility may still continue to operate as a generator-only facility and may continue to be subject to postclosure care obligations.

A newly regulated facility is required to have a written closure plan within six months after the facility has one or more hazardous waste management units that are first subject to RCRA regulations.[6] The closure plan for interim status facilities must be available for inspection, but there is no requirement to submit the plan to the EPA Regional Administrator until 45 or 180 days before the owner or operator expects to begin closure, the amount of time depending on the type of unit.[7] If the facility has a permit, the closure plan would have been submitted as part of the permit application and approved as part of the approval and issuance of the permit.[8] An approved closure plan becomes a condition of a RCRA permit.

---

[1] 40 C.F.R. §§ 264.111, 265.111.
[2] *Id.* §§ 264.110–.120, 265.110–.120.
[3] *Id.* §§ 264.112(b)(1), 265.112(b)(1).
[4] *Id.* § 260.10.
[5] *Id.*
[6] *Id.* § 265.112(a).
[7] *Id.* § 265.112(a), (d).
[8] *Id.* § 270.14(b)(13).

Chapter 9: Closure, Postclosure, and Financial Responsibility 185

A closure plan must identify the steps necessary to perform a partial or final closure of the facility at any point during the active life of the facility.[9] The plan must describe how each unit will be closed to meet the general closure performance standard.[10] The description must identify the maximum extent of operations that will be closed during the active life of the facility and provide an estimate of the maximum inventory of hazardous waste on-site at any one time during the active life of the facility.[11] The plan must provide detailed descriptions of the methods to be used to remove, transport, treat, store, or dispose of waste either on-site or off-site. The detailed descriptions must indicate the steps needed to remove or decontaminate all hazardous waste residues and contaminated containment system components, equipment, structures, and soils. The descriptions should set forth the procedure for cleaning equipment, removing contaminated soil, sampling and analysis methods for soils, and criteria for determining extent of decontamination required to meet the closure standard.[12]

The plan must also include additional activities that may be necessary during partial or final closure to satisfy the closure standard, including, but not limited to, groundwater monitoring, leachate collection, and run-on and runoff control.[13] The plan must provide a schedule for closure of each hazardous waste management unit and for final closure of the facility, including a schedule for the time needed to close each unit and the time required for intervening closure activities.[14] The plan must provide an estimate of the expected year of closure if the facility uses a trust fund for its demonstration of financial assurance and (1) the facility is to be closed before the expiration of the permit, or (2) in the case of interim status facilities, the remaining operating life of the facility is less than 20 years or the closure plan has not been approved.[15] Finally, the plan must include any alternative requirements imposed by the Regional Administrator pursuant to 40 C.F.R. Sections 264.90(f), 264.110(c), 264.140(d), 265.90(f), 265.110(d), and/or 265.140(d) or a reference to the enforceable document containing the alternative requirements.[16]

An interim status closure plan that has not been approved by the Regional Administrator can be amended at any time before notification

---

[9]*Id.* §§ 264.112(b), 265.112(b).
[10]*Id.* §§ 264.112(b)(1), 265.112(b)(1).
[11]*Id.* §§ 264.112(b)(2)–(3), 265.112(b)(2)–(3).
[12]*Id.* §§ 264.112(b)(4), 265.112(b)(4).
[13]*Id.* §§ 264.112(b)(5), 265.112(b)(5).
[14]*Id.* §§ 264.112(b)(6), 265.112(b)(6).
[15]*Id.* §§ 264.112(b)(7), 265.112(b)(7).
[16]*Id.* §§ 264.112(b)(8), 265.112(b)(8).

of closure.[17] If there is an approved closure plan, then the owner or operator must submit a written request for a change in the plan.[18] This modification request must include a copy of the amended closure plan. The plan must be amended whenever the owner or operator changes operation or facility design in a manner that affects closure, or if there is a change in the expected year of closure. Requests for changes to approved closure plans must be submitted to the Regional Administrator at least 60 days before a proposed change or within 60 days after an unexpected change in conditions. If during closure or postclosure there is an unexpected change in conditions, the closure plan must be modified within 30 days of the change. A change in a closure plan can require a permit modification depending on the nature of the change. The Regional Administrator can request modifications to closure plans or approve modifications to closure plans; thus, the approved closure plan becomes the plan submitted by the owner with the modifications imposed by the Regional Administrator.

Once the owner or operator has performed all the steps for closure required by the closure plan, an independent registered professional engineer and the owner or operator must certify that the unit was closed in accordance with the approved closure plan.[19] This certification must be submitted by registered mail to the Regional Administrator within 60 days of the completion of closure. The Regional Administrator can request documentation supporting the engineer's certification; in fact, engineers will often prepare a closure report that is automatically supplied to the Regional Administrator along with the closure certification. Once the Regional Administrator accepts the closure certification, the unit is closed, and the Regional Administrator should provide the owner or operator with a written notice informing the owner or operator that financial assurance no longer need be provided for closure of the unit.

No later than the submission of the closure certification, the owner or operator must submit to the local zoning authority (or authority with jurisdiction over local land use) and to the Regional Administrator a survey plat, prepared and certified by a professional land surveyor, indicating the location and dimension of landfill cells and other hazardous waste disposal units relative to permanently surveyed benchmarks. The plat must contain a prominently displayed note stating the owner's or operator's obligation to restrict disturbance of the disposal unit in accordance with applicable RCRA closure (Subpart G) regulations.[20]

---

[17]*Id.* § 265.112(c).
[18]*Id.* §§ 264.112(c), 265.112(c).
[19]*Id.* §§ 264.115, 265.115.
[20]*Id.* §§ 264.116, 265.116.

Chapter 9: Closure, Postclosure, and Financial Responsibility   187

B. Timing of Closure

The owner or operator of a surface impoundment, waste pile, landfill, or land treatment unit who has an approved closure plan for the unit must submit a notice to the Regional Administrator 60 days before the owner or operator "expects to begin closure."[21] Owners or operators with an approved closure plan for tanks, container storage, incinerators, boilers, or industrial furnaces need supply notice only 45 days in advance. The date when the owner or operator "expects to begin closure" is no later than 30 days from the date that the hazardous waste management unit receives the known final volume of hazardous waste or, if there is a reasonable possibility that the unit will continue to receive additional hazardous wastes, within one year of the date when the unit received its last volume of hazardous waste. The one-year time period can, with the approval of the Regional Administrator, be extended. Some units can possibly delay closure and convert from management of hazardous waste to nonhazardous waste, as will be discussed in the next section of this chapter.

The timing for notification of closure is different for an owner or operator who does not have an approved closure plan.[22] If the owner or operator has a land disposal unit (for example, a surface impoundment, waste pile, land treatment unit, or landfill), then the owner or operator must submit a closure plan for the unit 180 days before the expected date of closure. For other types of units, the closure plan must be submitted for approval 45 days before the expected date of closure. If the facility has its interim status terminated, except by reason of having received a permit, or the facility is issued a judicial order to close, then it must submit a closure plan within 15 days of that event.[23] After the closure plan is submitted, the timing of the closure depends largely on how long the reviewing agency takes to approve the closure plan, as closure cannot commence until an approved closure plan is in place. Once a closure plan is submitted, the Regional Administrator will give the owner or operator and the public the opportunity to submit written comments on the plan and to request modifications of the plan within 30 days from the date of newspaper notice announcing the opportunity to comment. The Regional Administrator may also hold a public hearing, upon request or at his own discretion, if such a hearing might clarify one or more issues related to closure. The public must be given 30 days' notice of a hearing. Within 90 days of submission of the plan, the

---

[21]*Id.* §§ 264.112(d), 265.112(d).
[22]*Id.* § 265.112(d).
[23]*Id.* § 265.112(d)(3).

188 THE RCRA PRACTICE MANUAL

Regional Administrator must approve, modify, or disapprove the plan. If the plan is disapproved, the owner or operator must modify the plan or submit a new plan within 30 days, after which the Regional Administrator will approve or modify within 60 days.[24]

The regulations provide for a time for closure to be completed.[25] Within 90 days after receiving the final volume of hazardous waste or 90 days after approval of the closure plan (if no closure plan had been approved before notice of closure), all hazardous waste must be treated, removed, or disposed of as provided in the closure plan. All closure activities must then be completed within 180 days of receipt of the final volume of hazardous waste or the date of approval of the closure plan. Both of these dates can be extended by approval from the Regional Administrator.

C. Delay of Closure

EPA became aware that the pressure RCRA placed on facilities to cease using surface impoundments for the management of hazardous waste threatened the viability of many facilities that generated large volumes of wastewater. EPA realized that it would be very costly and time-consuming for facilities that had relied on large surface impoundments to manage millions of gallons of wastewater to convert to management of this wastewater in large aboveground tanks. EPA promulgated the delay of closure rule, which, under certain circumstances, allows a formerly hazardous waste management unit (normally an impoundment, sometimes a landfill) to accept nonhazardous waste before completing closure.[26]

The facility seeking delay of closure for use of a hazardous unit for the management of nonhazardous waste must demonstrate the following:

- the unit has the design capacity to receive nonhazardous waste;
- there is a reasonable likelihood that nonhazardous waste will be received within one year from the receipt of the last volume of hazardous waste;
- the management of nonhazardous waste will not be incompatible with any remaining hazardous waste;
- closure of the unit would be incompatible with the continued operation of the unit or facility; and
- the owner or operator will continue to operate within the terms of the permit or interim status standards.

---

[24]*Id.* § 265.112(d)(4).
[25]*Id.* §§ 264.113, 265.113.
[26]*Id.* §§ 264.113(b)–(e), 265.113(b)–(e).

Chapter 9: Closure, Postclosure, and Financial Responsibility 189

The conversion to nonhazardous waste management may affect a number of plans and operations, so it is necessary to apply for the appropriate permit modifications (or modify the Part B application if the facility is in interim status) to accommodate those changes. If the unit does not meet the minimum technology requirements for liners and leachate collection systems or have a variance from those requirements, then the facility must submit a contingent corrective measures plan under the groundwater monitoring requirements of Subpart F. Moreover, within 90 days after final receipt of hazardous waste, the facility must remove all hazardous waste from the unit by removing all hazardous liquids and all hazardous sludges to the extent removal can be done without impairing the integrity of the liner. In addition, the unit will be subject to groundwater monitoring requirements and, if groundwater monitoring documents a release from the unit, to corrective action. The unit might continue to receive nonhazardous waste, even if it is subject to corrective action, provided that it can demonstrate that continued receipt of nonhazardous waste would not impede corrective action. If the Regional Administrator finds that the owner or operator has not implemented required corrective measures or that substantial progress has not been made, the Regional Administrator can provide the owner or operator and the public with notice of the requirement for the unit to be closed.[27]

The regulations provide that the final determination of the Regional Administrator under this special summary closure procedure is not subject to administrative appeal.[28] At final closure, when the unit is no longer receiving nonhazardous waste, all the closure standards apply.

III. Postclosure

Postclosure care obligations will be imposed on (1) all hazardous waste disposal facilities; (2) waste piles and surface impoundments that have not been able to achieve "clean closure" because hazardous waste or constituents have been left in place; (3) tank systems that are required by 40 C.F.R. Sections 264.197 or 265.197 to meet the requirements for landfills; and (4) containment buildings that are required by 40 C.F.R. Sections 264.1102 or 265.1102 to meet the requirements for landfills.[29] The presumptive postclosure care period is 30 years, commencing after the completion of closure of the unit.[30] During the 30-year period, the facility

---

[27]*Id.* §§ 264.113(e)(7), 265.113(e)(7).
[28]*Id.* §§ 264.113(e)(7)(v), 265.113(e)(7)(v).
[29]*Id.* §§ 264.110(b), 265.110(b).
[30]*Id.* §§ 264.117(a), 265.117(a).

190 THE RCRA PRACTICE MANUAL

must continue groundwater monitoring and reporting, and maintain and monitor waste containment systems applicable to the type of unit being closed. Postclosure usually means the perpetual care of a capped landfill that, during its operational life, may have been a surface impoundment or a waste pile. This perpetual care would include such activities as continued groundwater monitoring of the unit, leachate collection, if necessary, and the measures necessary to maintain the integrity of the cap. The basic standards for postclosure care are the same for permitted and interim status facilities.

The postclosure care period can be lengthened or shortened from the 30-year presumptive period.[31] If the facility is subject to a permit and the facility owner or operator wishes to shorten the postclosure period, the facility owner will need to apply for a permit modification and demonstrate to the Regional Administrator that the reduced period of postclosure care is protective of human health and the environment. For the same reasons—protection of human health and the environment—the Regional Administrator can lengthen the postclosure care period.

A. Postclosure Plans

An owner or operator of a hazardous waste disposal unit must have a written postclosure plan.[32] Permitted surface impoundments and waste piles that have neither liners nor an exemption from the liner requirements must have a contingent postclosure plan.[33] Permitted and interim status surface impoundments, waste piles, and other hazardous waste management units that are determined to have to close as a landfill because clean closure is not possible must submit a postclosure plan to the Regional Administrator within 90 days of the date that it was determined to close as a landfill.[34] The postclosure plan needs to provide a description of planned monitoring and maintenance activities required as postclosure care. A postclosure plan can be modified in much the same manner as modifying a closure plan. The requirements for modification are basically the same for interim status and permitted facilities in terms of the need to provide the Regional Administrator with a written request for a modification before making changes at the facility that will require the modification.[35] A permitted facility making a change in its postclosure plan must apply for a permit modification because the

---

[31]*Id.* §§ 264.117(a)(2), 265.117(a)(2).
[32]*Id.* §§ 264.118(a), 265.118(a).
[33]*Id.* § 264.228(c)(1)(ii).
[34]*Id.* §§ 264.118(a), 265.118(a).
[35]*Id.* §§ 264.118(d), 265.118(d).

Chapter 9: Closure, Postclosure, and Financial Responsibility 191

postclosure plan submitted with the permit application, once approved, becomes a condition of the permit.

An interim status facility needs to submit a postclosure plan at least 180 days before the date the facility intends to begin partial or final closure of the unit.[36] In addition, the owner or operator must submit a postclosure plan within 15 days if interim status for the facility is terminated other than by having a permit being issued to the facility, or if there is a judicial decree or final order under RCRA Section 3008 ordering the facility to cease receiving waste or to close.

The interim status regulations include a procedure to provide notice to the owner or operator and the public of the postclosure plan and any modifications to the plan by publishing a newspaper notice requesting written comments within 30 days following the notice of intent to approve or modify a postclosure plan.[37] In addition, the Regional Administrator can hold a public hearing on the approval of the postclosure plan or modifications to the plan. The Regional Administrator is to approve, modify, or disapprove of the plan within 90 days of receipt of the plan. If the Regional Administrator does not approve of the plan, the Regional Administrator is directed by the regulations to provide the owner or operator with a written statement of the reasons for the refusal. The owner or operator then must rewrite the plan and submit it within 30 days of receiving the Regional Administrator's comments. The Regional Administrator then has 60 days to approve or modify the revised plan. If the plan is modified by the Regional Administrator, the approved plan that the owner or operator must comply with is the plan as modified by the Regional Administrator. The modification of a postclosure plan for a permitted facility is governed by the procedures established for modifying permit conditions.

B. Postclosure Care

Ordinarily the use of an area of a facility subject to postclosure care "must never be allowed to disturb the integrity of the final cover, liner(s), or any other components of the containment system, or the function of the facility's monitoring system."[38] It may be possible to use the area of the property subject to postclosure care and make a change in the postclosure conditions, if the Regional Administrator is persuaded that the change is necessary to the proposed use of the property and will not increase the potential for the closed area to pose a threat to human health

---

[36]*Id.* § 265.118(e).
[37]*Id.* § 265.118(f).
[38]*Id.* §§ 264.117(c), 265.117(c).

192 THE RCRA PRACTICE MANUAL

or the environment. For a permitted facility, this change would likely involve a permit modification, and for an interim status facility, it would likely entail a change in the postclosure plan and, thus, may be subject to public notice and comment.

After closure is completed, the owner or operator is required to submit to both the local zoning agency with authority over land use and the Regional Administrator a record of the type, location, and quantity of hazardous waste disposed of in each cell of a landfill or in the waste management unit.[39] Further, within 60 days of certification of closure of the first hazardous waste disposal unit and 60 days from the certification of the last hazardous waste management unit, the owner or operator must record a notation on the deed to the facility (or on another type of document used in the jurisdiction for title searching purposes) that "will in perpetuity notify any potential purchaser" that (1) the property was used to manage hazardous waste; (2) its use is restricted under the closure regulations; and (3) a survey plan and record of the type, location, and quantity of hazardous waste have been filed with the zoning board.[40] The owner or operator must submit a certification that this recorded notice has been filed and a copy of the notice has been sent to the Regional Administrator.

If the owner or operator or a subsequent owner of the property wishes to remove the hazardous waste or hazardous waste residues that caused the hazardous waste management unit to be closed as a landfill, the owner can do so by requesting a change in the postclosure permit or in the postclosure plan if there is no postclosure permit.[41] This request must demonstrate that the removal is necessary to the use of the property and is protective of human health and the environment. The regulation warns that this removal of the waste subjects the owner to becoming a generator of hazardous waste because the waste is once again being managed.[42] Following the removal, the owner can petition the Regional Administrator to remove the notation to the deed or have added to the deed a notation that the hazardous waste has been removed.

Certification of the completion of postclosure care is to be submitted no later than 60 days after the completion of the postclosure care period for the unit.[43] The certification is to be signed by the owner or operator and an independent registered professional engineer. The certification

---

[39]*Id*. §§ 264.119(a), 265.119(a).
[40]*Id*. §§ 264.119(b), 265.119(b).
[41]*Id*. §§ 264.119(c), 265.119(c).
[42]*Id*. §§ 264.119(c), 265.119(c).
[43]*Id*. §§ 264.120, 265.120.

Chapter 9: Closure, Postclosure, and Financial Responsibility   193

must state that the postclosure care of the unit was performed in accordance with the requirements of the approved postclosure plan. The Regional Administrator can request supporting documentation of engineer's certification until the Regional Administrator releases the owner or operator from the financial assurance requirements for postclosure care.

C. Postclosure Permits

EPA imposes postclosure care obligations on facilities by means of a postclosure permit.[44] In some instances, postclosure care obligations are imposed on a facility by modifying an existing permit to include postclosure care obligations for a closed unit. If the facility has no operating units subject to a permit, EPA will request that the facility submit a Part B permit application as the basis for issuing a postclosure care permit to the facility. Thus, a facility could conceivably operate a generator-only facility, perhaps even be a small-quantity generator, and still be subject to a postclosure care obligation due to the presence of closed hazardous waste management units. When EPA issues postclosure permits, it typically issues the permit with all of the boilerplate permit provisions found in the Part 270 regulations, even though many of those provisions were drafted to apply to operating facilities, as opposed to a facility subject to a RCRA permit only due to postclosure care. Even more significant is EPA's interpretation that the corrective action obligations imposed by RCRA Section 3004(u) that attend the issuance of a RCRA permit apply to facilities that have only postclosure permits. Thus, a facility that today is only a generator of hazardous waste may have to receive a RCRA permit, which would include provisions to conduct RCRA corrective action, because the facility had closed hazardous waste management units that do not meet the current clean closure standard.

This is particularly significant because of a change in RCRA that occurred as one of the provisions of the Hazardous and Solid Waste Amendments of 1984. Congress realized that a number of land disposal facilities, landfills, surface impoundments, and waste piles were closing under the interim status closure regulations, which at the time were less stringent than the closure performance standards applicable to permitted facilities. For example, the old interim status closure standards provided that a unit could close if it removed all hazardous waste. In the case of many surface impoundments, the only hazardous waste managed was corrosive wastewater. After the installation of upstream neutralization devices (which are likely to be exempted from RCRA permitting as

---

[44]*Id.* § 270.1(c).

treatment units), the incoming waste was no longer hazardous, and it was relatively simple to demonstrate that there was no longer any hazardous waste in the impoundment. The waste stream could have carried organics and metals that are hazardous constituents, yet there was no requirement under the old interim status closure standard to remove those materials in order to demonstrate clean closure. Congress promulgated RCRA Section 3005(i), which requires land disposal facilities that closed under the old interim status closure standards to comply with Subpart F groundwater monitoring. In 1987, EPA modified the interim status closure standards to bring them in line with the permitted standards.[45] EPA allows facilities that closed under interim status the opportunity to demonstrate to EPA's satisfaction that the interim status closure under the old rules was the equivalent of a permitted clean closure.[46] If a facility can meet this equivalency demonstration, it will not be subject to the requirement of Section 3005(i), which EPA imposes by means of a postclosure permit.

Section 3005(i) only directs a facility to comply with the components of the Subpart F groundwater-monitoring program. It does not require that a former hazardous waste management unit in effect reclose if that unit continued to operate after RCRA closure as a nonhazardous facility, as was the case with many formerly hazardous surface impoundments. The hazardous waste management units subject to postclosure obligations by means of Section 3005(i) are obligated to install and operate a Subpart F groundwater-monitoring program and to do so under the auspices of a postclosure permit, which will in turn subject the facility to corrective action obligations. As explained in Section II.C above, continued use of, for example, an impoundment for nonhazardous wastewater management is not necessarily inconsistent with providing Subpart F groundwater monitoring for the impoundment, even if the unit is required to perform corrective action under Subpart F.

In 1998, EPA amended its regulations to provide an optional mechanism for imposing postclosure care requirements on units that close without obtaining a permit.[47] The new mechanism assures that interim status units that close meet the same requirements as those imposed on permitted units that are closed. To impose those requirements, permitting authorities may issue an enforceable document that performs many of the functions of a permit. The process of issuing an enforceable document must include minimum public involvement with notice and an opportunity to comment. An enforceable document can include federal

---

[45]*Id.* § 270.1(c)(5).
[46]*Id.* § 270.1(c)(6).
[47]*Id.* § 265.121.

Chapter 9: Closure, Postclosure, and Financial Responsibility   195

orders issued pursuant to Section 3008(h) of RCRA and Section 106 of CERCLA, as well as various state enforcement orders issued pursuant to authorities authorized by EPA.[48]

An enforceable document may also be used in place of the closure and postclosure requirements where the Regional Administrator determines that (1) a regulated unit is located among solid waste management units (or areas of concern), a release has occurred, and both the regulated unit and one or more of the solid waste management units (or areas of concern) have likely contributed to the release, and (2) the alternative requirements will protect human health and the environment and will satisfy the closure standard.[49] This option is designed to address potentially conflicting requirements between closure and postclosure standards and requirements of corrective action.

IV. Specific Closure and Postclosure Requirements

A. Containers

There are no specified closure standards applicable to hazardous waste container storage pads or areas for interim status container storage areas. For permitted container storage areas, the regulations require that all hazardous waste be removed from the containment system and the containers, liners, bases, and soils containing waste or residues be removed or decontaminated.[50] In practice, these same requirements are applied to interim status container storage areas. The government agency will usually require some soil samples be taken in the area around the pad. If there are documented releases, it may require that samples be taken from cracks in the pad or other areas where the released contents of a container may have flowed. On occasion, regulatory agencies will require a generator to "close" an accumulation storage pad if the generator has inadvertently allowed waste to accumulate over 90 days without approval of an extension.

B. Tanks

The closure standards for interim status tanks and permitted tanks are essentially identical.[51] The owner or operator must remove or decontaminate all waste residues, contaminated containment system components

---

[48]*Id.* § 270.1(c)(7).
[49]*Id.* §§ 264.110(c), 265.110(d).
[50]*Id.* § 264.178.
[51]*Id.* §§ 264.197, 265.197.

(liners, etc.), contaminated soils, structures, and equipment. Because the definition of a tank includes the entire tank system, which includes the piping and related containment systems running into the hazardous waste tank from the point of generation of hazardous waste, the area subject to closure requirements can be quite large. If the tank does not have secondary containment and is not exempt from the requirement to have secondary containment, then the closure plan for the tank must provide for the contingency that the tank will be required to be closed as a landfill due to the inability to remove all the waste at closure.[52] Thus, it is necessary for tanks subject to this contingency also to have prepared a postclosure plan. Closure cost estimates must take into consideration closure and postclosure costs as if the contingency had to be implemented.

C. Surface Impoundments

The closure requirements for interim status and permitted surface impoundments are largely the same, subject to some additional requirements for permitted surface impoundments.[53] The basic requirement is that all waste residues, containment system components (liners, etc.), contaminated subsoils, and structure and equipment be removed or be decontaminated and treated as hazardous waste. Free liquids must be removed, and remaining waste must be solidified or stabilized in order to allow the impoundment to support a final cover. The cover must provide for the long-term minimization of migration of liquids through the impoundment, minimize maintenance, promote drainage and minimize erosion, accommodate settling and subsidence, and have a permeability less than or equal to the permeability of any bottom liner system or natural subsoils present. If waste or residues are left in place after the completion of closure, then the impoundment will be considered to have been closed as a landfill (that is, with waste in place) and, thus, be subject to postclosure care.[54] If the impoundment does not have a liner and is not exempt from the requirement to have a liner, the closure plan for the impoundment must provide for a contingent closure plan and postclosure plan that will take into account the discovery that it is not practical to remove all contaminated soil at closure.[55] If the impoundment is subject to this contingent closure plan, its closure cost estimate must be based on complying with the contingent closure and postclosure plans and need not be based on a cost estimate for a clean closure.

---

[52]*Id.* §§ 264.197(c), 265.197(c).
[53]*Id.* §§ 264.228, 265.228.
[54]*Id.* §§ 264.228(b), 265.228(b).
[55]*Id.* § 264.228(l).

The interim status standards for impoundments do not provide for the contingent closure plan and contingent postclosure plan. Under the interim status closure regulations, if the owner or operator had a closure plan that intended to affect a clean closure and then during the course of closure work it was determined to be impractical, if not impossible, to affect a clean closure, the owner or operator must submit a modified closure plan within 30 days of the determination to close as a landfill, which will also require a postclosure plan for postclosure care of the unit.[56]

D. Waste Piles

The closure requirements for waste piles are essentially the same as for surface impoundments.[57] The difference between the permitted standards and the interim status standards is that the permitted standards require that a contingent closure plan and contingent postclosure plan be submitted whenever the waste pile does not meet the liner requirements or have an exemption from them. The interim status standards would require a closure plan modification to provide for a closure as a landfill. That modification is to be submitted within 30 days of the determination that the unit cannot be clean closed.

E. Land Treatment Facilities

The closure requirements for land treatment units require that the land treatment unit operating requirements be maintained during closure.[58] There are some variations between the closure requirements applicable to interim status land treatment units and permitted units.

The permitted unit must continue to be operated as necessary to maximize degradation, transformation, or immobilization of hazardous constituents during closure.[59] Run-on and runoff control must be maintained, as well as wind dispersal control. Prohibitions on the growth of food-chain crops continue. The permitted unit must continue unsaturated zone monitoring except that soil-pore liquid monitoring may be terminated 90 days after the last application of waste to the treatment zone. A vegetative cover must be maintained on the facility that can grow without excessive maintenance or without interfering with the degradation of the waste.

---

[56]*Id.* § 265.112(l)(2).
[57]*Id.* §§ 264.258, 265.258.
[58]*Id.* §§ 264.280, 265.280.
[59]*Id.* § 264.280(c).

An independent soil scientist instead of an engineer may certify closure of a land treatment unit.[60] The activities required during closure must also be continued during postclosure.[61] The owner or operator can avoid postclosure obligations if the owner or operator can demonstrate to the Regional Administrator that the level of hazardous constituents in the treatment zone soil does not exceed the background value of the constituents by a statistically significant amount.[62] The closure regulations govern in part how the background value is to be determined and how the statistical comparison is to be made between background levels and treatment zone levels of hazardous constituents. Finally, the owner or operator can avoid further groundwater-monitoring requirements if the Regional Administrator finds that there is no statistical increase in hazardous constituents in the treatment zone as compared with background and if unsaturated zone monitoring indicates that hazardous constituents have not migrated beyond the treatment zone during the active life of the unit.

Under the interim status regulations, the owner or operator must have a closure and postclosure plan that takes into account control of run-on and runoff, control of airborne particulates, and compliance with the prohibition of the growth of food-chain crops.[63] The interim status regulations, unlike the permit regulations, list a number of factors that the owner or operator must consider in designing a closure plan and postclosure plan.[64] Under the interim status regulations, the owner or operator is to consider the removal of contaminated soil, the placement of a final cover, and continued groundwater monitoring.[65] The control measures (that is, run-on, runoff) must continue during postclosure. The owner or operator must also continue soil pore monitoring and must restrict access to the unit. There is no provision for ceasing monitoring of the groundwater. The only way to end postclosure obligations for monitoring under the interim status regulations is to apply for a modification of the postclosure obligations.

F. Landfills

When an individual landfill cell or the entire landfill is closed, the owner or operator must cover the landfill with a cover designed and con-

---

[60]*Id.* § 264.280(b).
[61]*Id.* § 264.280(c).
[62]*Id.* § 264.280(d).
[63]*Id.* § 265.280(a).
[64]*Id.* § 265.280(b).
[65]*Id.* § 265.280(l).

Chapter 9: Closure, Postclosure, and Financial Responsibility 199

structed to provide long-term minimization of migration of liquids through the landfill, function with minimum maintenance, promote drainage and minimize erosion or abrasion of cover, accommodate settling and subsidence, and have a permeability less than or equal to the permeability of any bottom liner system or natural subsoils.[66] At final closure, the owner or operator is obligated to provide postclosure care that will maintain the integrity and effectiveness of the final cover, repair the cap as necessary, operate the leachate collection and removal system until leachate is no longer detected, maintain and monitor the groundwater-monitoring system, prevent run-on and runoff from damaging the cover, and protect and maintain surveyed benchmarks. The interim status regulations do not require the maintenance of the leachate collection system because the interim status design standards do not require the installation of a leachate collection system.

G. Other Units

At the closure of an incinerator, thermal treatment, drip pad, or other hazardous waste management unit, the owner or operator must remove all hazardous waste and residues, including ash, scrubber water, and sludges from the site.[67] If the unit cannot be clean closed, it will be subject to closure as a landfill and must have a postclosure care plan. Drip pads used in wood-treating operations must be closed by removing or decontaminating all waste residues, contaminated containment system components (pad, liners, etc.), contaminated subsoils, structures, and equipment. A drip pad that cannot achieve the clean closure standard must be closed as a landfill and, thus, be subject to postclosure care.[68] If the drip pad does not comply with the liner requirements, that drip pad must have a contingent postclosure plan.

V. Financial Assurance

Financial assurance is used to demonstrate the adequacy of financial resources to meet closure and postclosure care obligations and to demonstrate sudden and nonsudden occurrence liability coverage. Financial assurance is demonstrated by the use of one or more financial mechanisms. The requirements for demonstrating financial assurance are found in Subpart H of the Part 264 and Part 265 regulations.

---

[66]*Id.* §§ 264.310, 265.310.
[67]*Id.* §§ 264.351, 264.575, 264.603, 265.351, 265.381, 265.404, 265.445.
[68]*Id.* §§ 264.575(b), 265.445(b).

If a facility is a so-called generator-only or less-than-90-day facility that only accumulates hazardous waste that was generated on-site, it is not subject to financial assurance requirements under the federal rules. This exemption from the financial assurance requirements is made clear in the generator accumulation regulation, which exempts generators from most provisions in Subpart H.[69] In addition, small-quantity generators (those generating between 100 and 1,000 kilograms per month) and conditionally exempt small-quantity generators (those generating less than 100 kilograms per month) do not have to demonstrate financial assurance.[70]

There is one case in which a less-than-90-day generator might have to demonstrate financial assurance. This would arise if the generator were attempting to close a less-than-90-day container accumulation area or less-than-90-day accumulation tank and, due to releases from containers or the tank, was unable to demonstrate "clean closure." In this situation, the generator would be subject to postclosure care requirements, and the former less-than-90-day waste management unit would technically be closed as a RCRA landfill and, thus, have to demonstrate financial assurance for postclosure care.[71]

Hazardous waste management units that have interim status or a permit to treat, store, or dispose of waste are subject to the obligation to have a detailed written closure cost estimate and must demonstrate financial assurance for that closure cost estimate.[72] The rationale for the financial assurance requirements is that a hazardous waste management unit should not be allowed to begin operation unless it can be demonstrated that, at the end of the useful life of the unit, it will be properly decommissioned and cleaned up, not simply abandoned. Further, if waste will be left in place following closure of the unit (for instance, a landfill or a unit that cannot be "clean closed"), that unit must have a written postclosure care estimate and demonstrate financial assurance for postclosure care to ensure that the proper long-term maintenance of waste left in place can be performed.[73]

A. Closure and Postclosure Cost Estimate

The owner or operator of the hazardous waste management unit subject to closure obligations must maintain at the facility a detailed written

---

[69]*Id.* § 262.34(a)(1).
[70]*Id.* §§ 262.34(d), 261.5.
[71]*Id.* § 265.197(b).
[72]*Id.* §§ 264.142, 265.142.
[73]*Id.* §§ 264.144, 265.144.

Chapter 9: Closure, Postclosure, and Financial Responsibility 201

estimate, in current dollars, of the cost to close the facility in accordance with the approved closure plan.[74] The estimated cost must be based on cost of closure at the time in the facility's life when closure would be most expensive. For example, this would be at the end of the useful life of a landfill when it is full to its capacity or, for other hazardous waste management units, the time when they have their maximum inventory of hazardous waste. Second, the cost estimate must be based on hiring third parties to perform the closure activities. A third party is defined to exclude a parent or subsidiary corporation. Thus, the owner or operator cannot make estimates based on using the owner or operator's employees to perform the closure work even if the owner or operator's employees can perform the work at the time of closure. The rationale behind this requirement is that closure might occur at a time when the owner or operator is no longer in business, and the responsibility to effect closure could fall to the government, which would likely have to employ contractors to complete the work. The regulations do allow the closure cost to take into consideration the ability to use on-site disposal, if it can be demonstrated that on-site disposal will be available at the time of closure of the unit. Finally, the closure cost estimate cannot incorporate salvage associated with the closure of the hazardous waste unit, nor can the estimate incorporate a zero cost for handling the hazardous waste at closure on the basis that the wastes associated with the closure will have some economic value.

The closure cost estimate must be adjusted for inflation each year.[75] This adjustment must take place within 60 days before the anniversary date of establishing the financial instrument used for financial assurance or, for a firm using the financial test, within 30 days of the close of the fiscal year (and before submitting the financial test demonstration to the Regional Administrator).

The adjustment for inflation is made by multiplying the closure costs by the implicit price deflator for the gross national product. Dividing the latest published annual deflator by the deflator for the previous year arrives at the inflation factor. In addition to the annual adjustment for inflation, if midyear changes to the closure plan are made that increase the closure costs, then a revised closure cost adjustment must be made within 30 days of the approval of the modification of the closure plan. Since there has been inflation ever since the implementation of the financial assurance regulations, the governmental reviewers examining financial assurance demonstrations expect to see a constant increase in closure

---

[74]*Id.* §§ 264.142, 265.142.
[75]*Id.* §§ 264.142(b), 265.142(b).

202 THE RCRA PRACTICE MANUAL

cost estimates. It is possible for the estimate to drop if, for example, a partial closure takes place at the facility, which reduces the estimated cost to close the facility.

The postclosure cost estimate is calculated and adjusted in much the same way as the closure cost estimate.[76] The postclosure cost estimate is derived by multiplying the annual cost of postclosure care by the number of years of postclosure care. The annual costs must be calculated based on having third parties perform the postclosure care. The postclosure costs must be revised annually by adjusting for inflation in the same manner as closure costs are adjusted for inflation. Likewise, if the postclosure care plan is modified and that modification increases postclosure costs, then the postclosure cost estimate must be revised within 30 days of the change to reflect the higher costs.

In addition to demonstrating financial assurance for closure, hazardous waste management facilities that store, treat, or dispose of hazardous waste pursuant to interim status or a permit must demonstrate financial responsibility for bodily injury and property damage to third parties caused by sudden accidental occurrences arising from the operation of the facility.[77] The owner or operator must have and maintain liability coverage for sudden accidental occurrences in the amount of at least $1 million per occurrence, with an annual aggregate of at least $2 million independent of defense costs. If the facility is a land disposal facility (for example, surface impoundment or landfill), the facility, in addition to having sudden occurrence liability coverage, must also have nonsudden liability coverage for bodily injury and property damage to third parties caused by nonsudden accidental occurrences in the amount of $3 million per occurrence, with an annual aggregate of $6 million independent of legal defense costs. Thus, a facility required to demonstrate financial assurance for both types of liability needs to demonstrate $8 million in coverage.

The amounts and kind of liability coverage that must be demonstrated are subject to adjustment. First, a facility can provide the Regional Administrator with a written variance request seeking to demonstrate a lesser amount of financial assurance coverage required to be demonstrated for a facility.[78] That is, an owner or operator can attempt to make the case that the standard coverage amounts of $1 million/$2 million and $3 million/$6 million are greater than necessary to protect adequately against the risks posed by the facility. The Regional Administrator can

---

[76]*Id.* §§ 264.144, 265.144.
[77]*Id.* §§ 264.147, 265.147.
[78]*Id.* §§ 264.147(c), 265.147(c).

Chapter 9: Closure, Postclosure, and Financial Responsibility 203

request technical and engineering information to be used to determine the appropriate level of financial responsibility. The request for a variance in the liability requirements will be treated as a permit modification, and the Regional Administrator is expressly provided with the discretion to hold a public hearing on the matter. There is no explicit authority granted to the Regional Administrator to waive the liability requirements altogether.

The Regional Administrator has the authority to increase the required amount of the levels of financial responsibility, if the Regional Administrator determines that the default levels provided by the regulations are not consistent with the "degree and duration of the risk associated" with a particular facility.[79] In addition, the Regional Administrator has the authority to impose the requirement to have nonsudden liability coverage on a facility that is not a surface impoundment, landfill, or land treatment unit. Again, any such upward revision to a facility's requirement to demonstrate financial responsibility for liability coverage will be treated as a permit modification and may be the subject of a public hearing at the Regional Administrator's discretion.

There is the potential for some ambiguity in what is meant by the liability requirement terms. The RCRA regulations state that the terms "bodily injury" and "property damage" will have the meanings given those terms by the applicable state law, but the terms do not include liabilities that, "consistent with standard industry practice," are excluded from coverage in liability policies for bodily injury and property damage.[80] EPA has provided definitions of some of the key terms used in the liability section. "Accidental occurrence" is defined as "an accident, including continuous or repeated exposure to conditions, which results in bodily injury or property damage neither expected nor intended from the standpoint of the insured."[81] The term "non-sudden accidental occurrence" is defined as "an occurrence which takes place over time and involves continuous or repeated exposure," whereas "sudden accidental occurrence" is defined as "an occurrence which is not continuous or repeated in nature."[82] The various liability insurance terms and how they are to be interpreted and applied to situations including environmental contamination are the subject of many substantial lawsuits between insureds and their liability insurance carriers.

The documents demonstrating financial assurance for closure and, if necessary, postclosure care and liability insurance must be in place 60

---

[79]*Id.* §§ 264.147(d), 265.147(d).
[80]*Id.* §§ 264.141(g), 265.141(g).
[81]*Id.*
[82]*Id.*

204 THE RCRA PRACTICE MANUAL

days before a new waste management unit that is required to demonstrate financial responsibility first receives hazardous waste.[83] Financial assurance no longer need be maintained after the owner or operator receives a written notice to that effect from the Regional Administrator.[84] The Regional Administrator should provide such notice releasing the owner or operator of the responsibility to demonstrate financial assurance within 60 days after receiving the certification of the completion of closure or postclosure. If the Regional Administrator has reason to believe that final closure or postclosure did not comply with the closure or postclosure plan, then the Regional Administrator will provide the owner or operator with a detailed written statement of why closure or postclosure was not completed in accordance with the approved plan and, thus, why the owner or operator is not being released from the obligation to maintain financial assurance.

RCRA financial responsibility for closure and liability obligations can be demonstrated by using one or more of the six financial mechanisms provided for in the rules. A single facility can use multiple mechanisms to demonstrate financial responsibility, and an owner or operator that owns multiple facilities can use one or more financial mechanisms to demonstrate financial responsibility for all of its facilities.[85] The mechanisms are as follows: trust fund, surety bond, letter of credit, insurance, financial test, and corporate guarantee. While these basic financial mechanisms are available for use to meet closure requirements and for liability requirements, they may operate differently depending on whether they are being used for closure or for liability coverage. The governmental agencies that administer financial assurance can be very strict about the requirement that the documents used for the various financial mechanisms follow exactly the wording and form prescribed by the regulations. In some states, the burden is eased somewhat by the state's adoption of the form that contains the boilerplate wording and that simply requires information to be inserted and attached.

B. Trust Fund

The trust fund is the most commonly used financial mechanism for demonstrating compliance with closure and postclosure financial responsibility.[86] It is the financial mechanism most available to operators of hazardous waste management facilities lacking the financial resources

---

[83]*Id.* § 264.147(a)(1)(i).
[84]*Id.* §§ 264.143(i), 265.143(h).
[85]*Id.* §§ 264.143(g)–(h), 265.143(f)–(g).
[86]*Id.* §§ 264.143(a), 265.143(a).

Chapter 9: Closure, Postclosure, and Financial Responsibility 205

required to exercise the other financial mechanisms, which are more readily available to large organizations. The trust fund allows an owner or operator to meet its financial responsibility obligations by paying over time. The trust fund financial assurance mechanism consists of a trust agreement and a fund for the trust.

The RCRA regulations specify the wording of the trust agreement.[87] The regulations require that the trustee be an entity that has the authority to act as a trustee and whose trust operations are regulated and are examined by a federal or state agency. Typically, the trust is established with the owner or operator's bank. Schedule A to the trust agreement specifies the facility or facilities to which the trust is being used to demonstrate financial responsibility and the current closure and postclosure cost estimates. This schedule must change within 60 days of the annual revision to the closure cost estimates. Schedule B to the agreement reflects the amount of funds in the trust at the time the trust is established. Annually, at least 30 days before the anniversary of the trust fund, the trustee is to provide the hazardous waste facility owner or operator and the Regional Administrator with a statement confirming the amount of funds in the trust.

The trust is irrevocable and can be terminated only by the Regional Administrator, the owner or operator, and the trustee. Only EPA can direct how and to whom funds from the trust can be paid in support of the closure of a unit or the postclosure care of a unit.[88] If funds are left in the trust after closure or postclosure is complete, the trustee, at the direction of EPA, can pay the remaining funds in the trust to the owner or operator.

The facility owner or operator is required to pay into the fund an amount every year such that, at the anticipated time of closing, the fund will have sufficient funds to assure completion of the closure in accordance with the approved closure plan. The annual payment must be made based on a consideration of the expected remaining life of the facility, the current closure cost estimate, and the amount of the funds in the trust. The first payment must be made for a new facility before the initial receipt of waste. The first payment must be at least equal to the current closure cost estimate divided by the number of years in the pay-in period. The pay-in period is the number of years remaining in the life of the facility or 20 years, whichever is less. Subsequent payments are calculated by subtracting the current value of the trust fund from the current closure cost estimate and dividing that amount by the number of years remaining in the pay-in period. If the trust fund is used as a substitute

---

[87]*Id.* § 264.151(a)(1).
[88]*Id.* §§ 264.143(a)(10), 265.143(a)(10).

206 THE RCRA PRACTICE MANUAL

for another financial mechanism, then the first year's payment into the trust fund must be equal to the amount of funds that would have accumulated in the fund if payments had begun before the unit first began to receive hazardous waste.

The trust fund is not often used to demonstrate liability coverage requirement because it requires that the trust fund be funded for the full amount of liability requirement. This would mean that a facility would have to deposit either $2 million or $8 million in the fund, depending on whether the facility was a land disposal facility. For many companies, this mechanism probably ties up too much cash and, thus, is a costly option.

C. Financial Test

The financial mechanism of choice for large corporations is the financial test.[89] This mechanism is based on the use of one of two alternative calculations or tests demonstrating that a corporation's financial condition as reflected on its balance sheet will provide ample financial resources to pay for closure and postclosure costs. This mechanism is also used for demonstrating liability coverage.[90] Both tests require that the owner or operator have a tangible net worth of at least $10 million and have assets located in the United States amounting to at least 90 percent of total assets or at least six times the sum of the current closure and postclosure cost estimates plus plugging and abandonment costs. Plugging and abandonment costs are the rough equivalent of closure costs that apply to underground injection control wells regulated under the Safe Drinking Water Act. Under the first test, in addition to meeting the requirements both tests have in common, the owner or operator must be able to demonstrate two of the following three ratios: "a ratio of total liabilities to net worth less than 2.0; a ratio of the sum of net income plus depreciation, depletion, and amortization to total liabilities greater than 0.1; and a ratio of current assets to current liabilities greater than 1.5."[91] In addition, under the first test, the net working capital and tangible net worth must each be at least six times the sum of closure costs and plugging and abandonment costs.

Under the second test, in addition to the common requirements, the owner or operator needs to have a certain high bond rating and tangible net worth of six times the closure and abandonment costs.[92] If the owner

---

[89]*Id.* §§ 264.143(f), 265.143(e).
[90]*Id.* §§ 264.147(f), 265.147(f).
[91]*Id.* §§ 264.143(f)(1)(i)(A), 265.143(e)(1)(i)(A).
[92]*Id.* §§ 264.143(f)(1)(ii), 265.143(e)(1)(ii).

Chapter 9: Closure, Postclosure, and Financial Responsibility   207

or operator has sufficient balance sheet financial strength to meet one or both of the tests, then the test can be used for both closure and postclosure obligations.

The owner or operator must submit a letter, whose wording is specified in the regulations, signed by the owner or operator's chief financial officer (CFO).[93] The letter must be accompanied by an independent certified public accountant's report on the examination of the firm's financial statements. This is usually accomplished by providing the firm's annual report, which would contain the public accountant's report. Finally, the CFO's letter must be accompanied by a report from the independent certified public accountant stating that the data specified in the CFO's letter were derived from the independently audited year-end financial statement for the latest fiscal year, and that no matters have come to the auditor's attention that suggest a need to adjust the specified data. The CFO's letter must be submitted 60 days before the initial receipt of hazardous waste. Thereafter, a revised letter and test must be submitted within 90 days after the end of the fiscal year. If the firm can no longer meet the test, the firm has 120 days from the end of the close of the previous fiscal year to put in place another financial mechanism.[94]

D. Corporate Guarantee

The ability to use a corporate guarantee to demonstrate financial responsibility recently has been liberalized. An owner or operator requiring financial responsibility can demonstrate such responsibility by use of a guarantee that is received from a direct or higher-tier parent corporation, a firm that shares the same parent corporation as the owner or operator, or a firm that has a "substantial business relationship" with the owner or operator.[95] The term "substantial business relationship" is defined as the extent of a business relationship necessary under applicable state law to make a guarantee contract issued incident to that relationship valid and enforceable. A "substantial business relationship" must arise from a pattern of recent or ongoing business transactions, in addition to the guarantee itself, such that a currently existing business relationship between the guarantor and the owner or operator is demonstrated to the satisfaction of the applicable EPA Regional Administrator.[96]

The guarantor must be able to meet one or the other of the two financial tests. The wording of the guarantee, as well as the letter from the

---

[93]*Id.* § 264.151.
[94]*Id.* §§ 264.143(f)(6), 265.143(c)(6).
[95]*Id.* §§ 264.143(f), 265.143(e).
[96]*Id.* §§ 264.141(h), 265.141(h).

CFO of the guarantor, must be taken verbatim from the regulations.[97] If the owner and operator and the guarantor share the same parent corporation, then the guarantee must describe the value of the consideration provided for the guarantee. For the purposes of maintaining separation between a parent and a subsidiary, in cases where the guarantor is the parent corporation, it may make sense for the parent to receive consideration from the owner or operator for the guarantee, even though the wording of the guarantee does not require that this consideration be recited. If the guarantor is a firm with a "substantial business relationship" with the owner or operator, then that relationship must be described, and the consideration received for the guarantee must be recited.[98]

The guarantee will provide that, if the owner or operator fails to perform the required closure, the guarantor will establish a closure trust fund in the name of the owner or operator. The guarantor can cancel the guarantee only by providing notice by certified mail, return receipt requested, to the owner or operator and to the Regional Administrator 120 days before the intended date to cancel. The owner or operator needs to provide alternative financial assurance that satisfies the Regional Administrator within 90 days of receipt of the guarantor's termination notice. If the owner or operator does not secure alternative financial assurance within the 90 days, which the Regional Administrator must approve in writing, the guarantor must provide some financial mechanism to continue financial assurance in effect for the owner or operator.

E. Surety Bond

Permitted facilities can use a surety bond to guarantee payment into a closure trust fund or to guarantee performance of closure, whereas the interim status regulations provide only for a bond to guarantee payment into a trust fund.[99] The permitted and interim status regulations prescribe the same wording for the surety bond that can be used to demonstrate financial responsibility by guaranteeing payment into a closure trust fund.[100] The surety company issuing the bond must be listed as an acceptable surety on federal bonds in Department of Treasury Circular 570. In conjunction with the use of a surety bond, the owner or operator must also establish a standby trust fund that would be the recipient of the funds from the penal sum of the bond in the event the owner or operator does not perform its closure obligations. The standby trust

---

[97]*Id.* § 264.151(f), (h).
[98]*Id.* §§ 264.143(f)(10), 265.143(e)(10).
[99]*Id.* §§ 264.143(b)–(c), 265.143(b).
[100]*Id.* § 264.151(b).

Chapter 9: Closure, Postclosure, and Financial Responsibility 209

agreement must meet the wording requirements of the trust used for a closure trust fund, but the standby trust does not need to be funded at its establishment or have annual payments made into it.[101] The terms of a bond guaranteeing closure performance must provide that the owner or operator will perform final closure in accordance with the approved closure plan and any applicable permit provisions or will provide alternative financial assurance acceptable to the Regional Administrator within 90 days after notification of cancellation of the bond by the surety.[102] Under this type of bond, the surety is liable to perform the closure guaranteed by the bond if it is determined that the owner or operator failed to perform final closure in accordance with the approved closure plan, or the surety may pay into the standby trust the penal sum of the bond, which must at least equal the current closure cost estimate. The penal sum of the bond must be increased whenever the current closure cost estimate is an amount greater than the penal sum. This adjustment must be made within 60 days of the change. The surety can cancel the bond by providing notice to the Regional Administrator and owner or operator 120 days in advance. The owner or operator may cancel the bond if the owner or operator obtains the approval to do so from the Regional Administrator, or the owner or operator is released from the obligation to maintain financial assurance. The surety is not liable for deficiencies in the closure performance, if the Regional Administrator has released the owner or operator from the requirement to maintain financial assurance.

F. Letter of Credit

The use of an irrevocable letter of credit to demonstrate financial responsibility closely resembles the use of a surety bond.[103] The institution issuing the letter of credit must have the authority to issue such instruments and have its letter-of-credit operations regulated and examined by a federal or state agency. The regulations specify the wording of the letter of credit.[104] The owner or operator must prepare a standby trust agreement, although as with the use of the surety bond, it is not necessary to initially fund or to pay into the trust agreement.[105] The letter of credit must be accompanied by a letter from the owner or operator indicating the number of the letter of credit, the name of the issuing institution,

---

[101]*Id.* § 264.143(b)(3).
[102]*Id.* § 264.143(c).
[103]*Id.* §§ 264.143(d), 265.143(c).
[104]*Id.* § 264.151(d).
[105]*Id.* §§ 264.151(d)(3), 265.151(c)(3).

210   THE RCRA PRACTICE MANUAL

issuance date, information about the facility using the letter of credit, and the amount of funds represented by the letter of credit. The letter of credit must be irrevocable and issued for a period of at least one year, with an automatic provision that it will be extended for another year unless notice is made at least 120 days before the expiration date to cancel the letter of credit. The amount of the letter of credit must be at least equal to the current closure cost and, if the amount drops below the current closure cost, it must be increased within 60 days after the cost increase. Similarly, if the closure cost decreases, the letter of credit may be decreased if approved in writing by the Regional Administrator. If it is determined under Section 3008 of RCRA that the owner or operator has failed to perform final closure in accordance with the closure plan, the Regional Administrator may draw on the letter of credit. The Regional Administrator may also draw on the letter of credit if, following notice of nonrenewal of the letter of credit, the owner or operator fails to put in place another financial mechanism or fails to have the issuing institution extend the letter of credit. The letter of credit will be returned to the issuing institution when the owner or operator secures alternative financial assurance or when the owner or operator is released from the requirement to provide financial assurance.

G. Insurance

The insurer providing the certificate of insurance used to demonstrate financial assurance (which must conform to the language set forth in the regulations) must be licensed to transact the business of insurance, or be eligible to provide insurance as an excess or surplus lines insurer, in one or more states.[105] The face amount of the certificate of insurance must be equal to the current closure cost estimate. The policy may not be canceled, terminated, or not renewed for any reason other than the failure to pay a premium. In addition, the policy must allow assignment to a successor owner or operator, which may be conditioned on the consent of the insurer, provided that such consent is not unreasonably refused. The automatic renewal of the policy must allow the insured the option to renew the face value of the expiring policy. Failure to pay a premium without substituting alternative financial assurance is deemed to be "a significant violation" of RCRA.

The insurer can cancel the policy only for nonpayment of a premium and then only by providing notice 120 days in advance of the intention to cancel for nonpayment. Cancellation, termination, or failure

---

[106]*Id.* §§ 264.143(e), 265.143(d).

Chapter 9: Closure, Postclosure, and Financial Responsibility 211

to renew may not occur, and the policy will remain in effect if, before the policy expires, one of the following events occurs:

- the Regional Administrator determines the facility is abandoned;
- the permit is terminated or revoked or a new permit is denied;
- closure of the facility is ordered by the Regional Administrator or a U.S. district court;
- the owner or operator is undergoing a Title 11 bankruptcy; or
- the premium due is paid.

The face amount of the insurance must be increased within 60 days of the current closure cost estimate exceeding the face amount. With the approval of the Regional Administrator, the face amount can be reduced if the closure costs are reduced.

Providing financial assurance through an insurance policy provides for a different mechanism for paying out during partial or final closure. As the owner or operator (or other person authorized to perform closure) pays for closure activities, that person may request reimbursement for closure expenses by submitting itemized bills to the Regional Administrator. Within 60 days of receiving bills for closure activities, the Regional Administrator will instruct the insurer to make reimbursement in such amounts as the Regional Administrator authorizes in writing. If the Regional Administrator does not instruct the insurer to reimburse the owner or operator, the Regional Administrator will provide a detailed written statement of the reasons. The Regional Administrator may withhold reimbursements if the Regional Administrator determines that reimbursing a partial closure will not provide adequate funds to complete final closure or the Regional Administrator determines that the face amount of the policy is inadequate to complete final closure. In this case, the Regional Administrator may deny requests for reimbursement until the owner or operator completes final closure and is no longer required to maintain financial assurance.

H. Multiple Mechanisms and Multiple Facilities

A facility may use more than one of the different mechanisms to demonstrate financial assurance. Only trust funds, surety bonds, letters of credit, and insurance can be used in combination with one another. If an existing trust fund is used in connection with one mechanism, that same trust can be used as the standby trust for another mechanism.[107]

---

[107]*Id.* §§ 264.143(g), 264.146, 265.143(f), 265.146.

An owner or operator may use a single financial mechanism to demonstrate financial assurance for multiple facilities.[108] Typically, large corporations able to use the financial test to demonstrate financial assurance for all of their facilities in various states do this. The amount of the funds available through this mechanism must be no less than the sum of the funds that would be available if a separate mechanism had been established for each facility. If a single mechanism is used for multiple facilities, then that mechanism must show some information about the other facilities.

I. State Mechanisms

If EPA is administering the part of the RCRA program that requires the owner or operator to maintain financial assurance, but the state where the facility is located has its own hazardous waste regulations that include financial responsibility mechanisms, the owner or operator can seek approval from the Regional Administrator to use a state financial mechanism.[109] The Regional Administrator will consider the certainty of the availability of funds and the amount that will be made available in determining whether the state mechanism is equivalent to the federal mechanism. To seek approval for the use of a state mechanism, the owner or operator must put the state mechanism into effect and provide a letter to the Regional Administrator seeking acceptance of the state mechanism.

J. Financial Assurance for Corrective Action

At the present time, while the regulations require financial assurance for corrective action, EPA has not yet adopted any regulations that specifically address how financial assurance is to be provided for corrective action. In the October 24, 1986, *Federal Register*, EPA proposed how financial assurance would be provided for corrective action obligations. In that proposed rule making, EPA stated that "[w]e have assumed that, in the absence of this regulation, permitted facilities would comply with the section 3004(u) financial assurance requirement by using one of the financial assurance mechanisms currently allowed for demonstration of financial assurance for closure and postclosure care of hazardous waste management facilities."[110] Thus, at the present time, in the absence of specific financial assurance regulations for corrective actions, the issues

---

[108]*Id*. §§ 264.143(h), 265.143(g).

[109]*Id*. §§ 264.149, 265.149.

[110]51 Fed. Reg. 37,854, 37,855 n.2 (1986).

Chapter 9: Closure, Postclosure, and Financial Responsibility   213

of how much financial assurance and how it is to be demonstrated are resolved by the regulators on a case-by-case basis through terms in RCRA permits by applying the existing financial mechanisms.

Even though EPA's proposal is not final, it may be used as guidance by regulators attempting to reach a resolution of these issues. In the proposed rule making, EPA proposed that the trust fund, letter of credit, financial test, and corporate guarantee, with some modifications, would be available to use to demonstrate financial assurance for corrective action. EPA did not think that either a surety bond or insurance would be practical for use in the corrective action context. In fact, EPA stated that it did not think insurance would be available because it would be "analogous to writing fire insurance for a burning building" and that it did not believe that any companies were currently writing insurance for closure and postclosure care.[111] EPA also proposed that the mechanism be used for all known releases to any medium and that the demonstration be required when EPA specifies the appropriate corrective action measures in the permit. The proposed rule would employ most financial mechanisms in much the same manner as used in the context of demonstrating financial assurance for closure and postclosure care.

EPA proposed to make two significant changes to the operation of the trust fund for corrective action so that demonstrating financial assurance would not drive firms into bankruptcy. EPA proposed that the pay-in formula would be the balance remaining (BR) at the end of the pay-in period less the current value (CV) of the trust divided by the number of years (Y) of the pay-in period. This formula takes into consideration that while a facility is paying into the trust fund, that facility is also expending funds for corrective action, so all that is necessary to be in the fund at the end of the pay-in period is an amount sufficient to pay for the work remaining to be completed after the pay-in is completed. The second change EPA proposed would provide for a pay-in period that would be the shorter of 20 years or one-half of the expected corrective action period. EPA rejected the use of the permit term (maximum 10 years) for the pay-in period on the basis that the permit term did not reflect the obligations faced by owners or operators of facilities that identify releases subject to corrective action.

K. Liability Requirements

The requirement to have liability coverage to provide for claims from third parties for bodily injury or property damage due to sudden accidental occurrences can be satisfied by using an insurance policy amended

---

[111]*Id.* at 37,857.

214 THE RCRA PRACTICE MANUAL

by the attachment of the Hazardous Waste Facility Liability Endorsement or by a Certificate of Liability Insurance that meets the regulatory requirements.[112] The insurance policy must be issued by an insurer licensed to transact the business of insurance or eligible to provide insurance as an excess or surplus lines insurer in one or more states. In addition to the use of the insurance certificate, an owner or operator may use the financial test, corporate guarantee, letter of credit, surety bond, trust fund, or a combination of mechanisms to demonstrate liability coverage.[113] An owner or operator cannot combine the financial test with a corporate guarantee unless the financial statement of the owner or operator is not consolidated with the financial statement of the grantor.[114]

The Regional Administrator must be notified within 30 days of any of the following occurrences:

- a claim that reduces the amount of financial assurance provided by an instrument;
- the entry of a Certification of Valid Claim for bodily injury or property damages between an owner or operator and a third party related to bodily injury or property damages caused by a sudden or nonsudden occurrence; or
- a final court order establishing a judgment for bodily injury or property damage caused by a sudden or nonsudden accidental occurrence.[115]

EPA also revised its regulations with respect to the use of a letter of credit in this area, which would allow the creation of a standby trust fund with the designation of an independent trustee as the beneficiary.[116] Thus, the trustee, rather than the issuer of the letter of credit, is responsible for assessing the validity of the claim. Previously, the letter of credit designated third-party claimants as the beneficiary, leaving the issuer of the letter of credit to be faced with the burden of deciding the validity of a claim.

L. Implications of Financial Assurance

In the early years of the RCRA program, the imposition of financial assurance requirements may have driven some owners and operators of hazardous waste management facilities out of business. Some compa-

---

[112]40 C.F.R. §§ 264.147(a), 265.147(a).
[113]*Id.* §§ 264.147(a)(2)–(5), 265.147(a)(2)–(5).
[114]*Id.* §§ 264.147(a)(6), 265.147(a)(6).
[115]*Id.* §§ 264.147(a)(7), 265.147(a)(7).
[116]*Id.* §§ 264.147(h), 265.147(h).

nies (and industries) may continue to have trouble from time to time making their financial assurance demonstrations due to changes in the economic and business cycles. Despite these difficulties, there remains a reasonable assortment of mechanisms for demonstrating financial assurance. In the past few years, moreover, the availability of insurance to provide increasing portions of financial assurance has increased and may provide an effective means to meet the financial assurance obligations as well as manage the financial impact of environmental remediation.

VI. Conclusion

The closure and postclosure requirements, though reasonably objective and straightforward at first glance, are often more arduous than they appear. It often takes a considerable amount of time to complete what otherwise might appear to be a fairly simple closure. In addition, postclosure requirements can be difficult to negotiate and may take considerably longer to complete than originally planned. Owners and operators should be aware that closure and, if required, postclosure care can be difficult and time-consuming processes. EPA's new regulation providing for the use of enforceable documents to meet closure and postclosure requirements can offer a reasonable alternative, particularly for facilities that already face corrective action or CERCLA remediation obligations.

The financial assurance requirements, largely unchanged over the past several years, offer very detailed requirements that, in nearly all cases, must be carefully observed. The potentially staggering costs of corrective action, coupled with drops in the business and economic cycles for various companies, have placed some pressure on the ability to make the required demonstration. Perhaps the increased availability of insurance for demonstrating financial assurance can provide some relief.

CHAPTER 10

Standards for Containers, Tanks, Incinerators, Boilers, and Furnaces

SUSAN J. SADLER

I. Introduction

This chapter discusses the RCRA standards applicable to containers, tanks, incinerators, boilers, and furnaces. The regulations covering "permitted" containers, tanks, and incinerators are found in 40 C.F.R. Part 264. The provisions addressing "interim status" containers, tanks, and incinerators are set forth in 40 C.F.R. Part 265. Standards governing boilers and industrial furnaces are located in a separate regulatory section, 40 C.F.R. Part 266.

This chapter reviews the significant regulations affecting containers, tanks, incinerators, boilers, and industrial furnaces. In discussing each of these devices, the focus will be on the scope of the regulations and exemptions from them. The chapter then discusses the regulatory design requirements, owner and operator maintenance obligations, requirements arising where specific hazardous wastes are stored, and the owner or operator obligations when each device is removed from usage or closed.

Where relevant, this chapter identifies the differences between the regulations applicable to permitted devices and those that apply to interim status devices. Interim status devices are devices that were in existence on the effective date of the regulation. 40 C.F.R. Part 265 governs such interim facilities until final permitting or closure.

II. Containers

A. Overview and Exemptions

Regulation 40 C.F.R. Section 260.10 defines a container as:

> any *portable* device in which a material is stored, transported, treated, disposed of, or otherwise handled.

Containers are generally used for storing rather than disposing of hazardous wastes. Containers represent the most common and generally least expensive method of storing hazardous waste. The definition of containers also extends to storage units that are mobile because they are portable. Thus, a container can be a 55-gallon drum or a tanker truck. The only significant difference between the regulations that govern permitted containers and those covering interim status containers is the requirement that permitted containers possess a secondary containment system.

B. Design Requirements for Containers and Storage Areas

For a container to meet specification, it must be designed to hold and contain its contents. The container must be made of a material that is compatible with its contents. Therefore, if a container is deteriorating or is not intact, it does not meet the requirements of Parts 264 and 265. The container must remain closed during storage, and safety measures must be taken to prevent unauthorized access to the storage area.

The storage area for containers at a permitted facility must possess a secondary containment system pursuant to 40 C.F.R. Section 264.175. The secondary containment system must have a base made of an impervious material, capable of holding leaked and spilled material and accumulated precipitation until the liquids can be removed. The base must also be sloped so that it operates as a drain. This is often accomplished by a poured concrete pad with curbing. A program for removing waste from the secondary containment must be in place. Secondary containment systems around stored containers must be able to hold free liquids equal to or greater than 10 percent of the capacity of all of the containers in the area or the capacity to contain the volume of the largest container in the area, whichever is greater. For example, the secondary containment system around an area holding ten 55-gallon drums must be capable of holding 55 gallons.

Rainwater and other precipitation (run-on) may not enter the containment system unless the systems base possesses excess capacity. The

Chapter 10: Standards for Containers, Tanks, Incinerators, Boilers, and Furnaces 219

regulation does not specify the amount of excess capacity, except to state that it must be sufficient to hold any precipitation that might enter the containment system.

The container storage area need not possess secondary containment if the containers do not hold free liquids (except for certain dioxin wastes). However, in such cases, the storage area must be designed to remove liquids resulting from precipitation and must be sloped toward a drain or designed for collection and removal. The facility owner should first make a proper determination as to whether the materials do or do not contain free liquids.[1] The containers must also be elevated or otherwise protected from contact with liquids. Containers that hold EPA hazardous wastes F020, F021, F022, F023, and F026 must always possess secondary containment. These wastes are described in 40 C.F.R. Part 261.31.

The regulation of areas in which interim status facilities store containers is somewhat less rigorous. The interim status allows the facility to postpone the cost of retrofilling its storage area until it is permitted. The secondary containment requirements placed on permitted facilities do not apply to interim status facilities.

C. Maintenance Requirements

Owners and operators of permitted and interim status containers must satisfy identical maintenance requirements. The owner or operator must visually inspect container storage areas weekly for leaks and signs of corrosion.[2] The results of these weekly inspections and periodic repairs should be recorded in an operator's log. The operator should keep copies of the log for three years. If a container is not in good condition or begins to leak, the owner or operator must immediately transfer the contents to a container that is in good condition. The addition of an absorbent material to a container in response to a leak does not necessarily constitute treatment of a waste. The provision descriptively defines containers that are not in good condition as ones that show severe rusting or apparent structural defects.

Containers must remain closed except when waste is removed or added.[3] This requires owners to confirm the sealing mechanism on all containers remain intact. The regulations prohibit an owner or operator from opening, handling, or storing a container in a manner that may cause it to leak or rupture.

---

[1]*See* EPA Test Method SW-846.
[2]40 C.F.R. §§ 264.174, 265.174.
[3]*Id.* §§ 264.173, 265.173.

220   THE RCRA PRACTICE MANUAL

The regulations also identify maintenance requirements for the secondary containment areas. The owner or operator must remove waste from the secondary containment system's sump or collection area in time to prevent the system from overflowing. The base or floor of the containment storage area must remain impervious and free of cracks.

D. Regulations Pertaining to Specific Wastes

Owners or operators of containers may not mix incompatible materials. Waste is incompatible with a container if it will cause either the container or its inner liner to corrode or decay.[4] Containers must therefore be made of, or lined with, materials compatible with their contents.[5] Incompatible wastes or materials may not be placed in the same container.[6] Wastes are incompatible if mixing of the waste could cause fire, explosion, or heat; release of toxic dust, flammable fumes, or gases; or release of flammable fumes or gases. A container must be emptied and washed (pursuant to regulation) before materials incompatible with its previous contents are placed inside.

Owners and operators must also guard against inadvertent mixing of incompatible wastes that are stored in separate containers located near one another. The containers must be separated by a dike, berm, wall, or other device. As with the other provisions discussed, this provision is aimed at preventing fires, explosions, and other reactions.

E. Handling the "Empty" Container

Waste remaining in empty containers after closure is exempt from 40 C.F.R. Sections 261 through 265, 268, and 270, which govern identification and listing of hazardous wastes, duties of generators and transporters of hazardous wastes, standards for owners and operators of permitted and interim status facilities, and land disposal and hazardous waste permits.[7]

A container is empty if it satisfies certain regulatory criteria. The criteria to be applied depend on whether the container previously held acute hazardous wastes. Acute hazardous wastes are wastes that pose an extreme threat to human health or the environment. These wastes are P-listed hazardous wastes identified in 40 C.F.R. Section 261.33 and other hazardous wastes that are designated with the letter *H*.

---

[4]*Id.* § 260.10.
[5]*Id.* §§ 264.172, 265.172.
[6]*Id.* §§ 264.177, 265.177.
[7]*Id.* § 261.7.

Chapter 10: Standards for Containers, Tanks, Incinerators, Boilers, and Furnaces 221

A container that never held acute hazardous wastes is considered empty (that is, "RCRA empty") if all of the waste that is removable (through common methods) has been removed *and* no more than 2.5 centimeters (1 inch) of residue remains in the container. In addition to these requirements, a container possessing a capacity of less than 110 gallons is empty only if an amount of *waste* equal to or less than 3 percent of its capacity remains in the container. A container with a capacity greater than 110 gallons is empty only if the amount of waste remaining in the container is no more than 0.3 percent, by weight, of its total capacity. By contrast, the Department of Transportation considers a container to be empty if it contains no more than 3 percent of its capacity for containers up to 119 gallons in capacity.

The small residue of material left in a RCRA empty container is exempt from Subtitle C regulation. However, the contents of the container that existed before the container attained RCRA empty status are fully regulated. A container that held acute hazardous waste is empty if the container has been cleaned by triple rinsing with an appropriate solvent, or by another method scientifically demonstrated to be as effective, and the liner is removed. The triple rinsing standard is ambiguous: the regulation does not define triple rinsing, does not identify the amount or type of solvent that must be used in triple rinsing, nor does it articulate a measurable standard against which to confirm the container's empty status. Containers with inner liners forming a complete barrier between the waste and the container are empty once the liner is removed.

The owner or operator that uses triple rinsing to empty a container that held acute hazardous waste may need to dispose of or treat the rinsate as hazardous waste. In such circumstances, the owner or operator may become a generator that is responsible for disposing of the rinsate. Confusion over treating the rinsate for cleaning a container that once stored polychorinated biphenyls (PCBs) is addressed in *Rollins Environmental Services, Inc. v. EPA.*[8] While the cleaning of a container is arguably a treatment activity, doing so does not require a Subtitle C treatment permit. If triple rinsing of an empty container is not appropriate, the regulations do allow for the use of an alternative method.

F. Regulations Governing Closure

The closure of a container storage site is governed by 40 C.F.R. Sections 264.178 and 265.178. To achieve closure, the owner or operator must remove all hazardous wastes, liners, and residues from the secondary

---

[8]937 F.2d 649 (D.C. Cir. 1991).

222   THE RCRA PRACTICE MANUAL

containment system and must remove or decontaminate containers, liners, and bases. Soil containing waste residue must also be decontaminated or removed. The owner or operator will be regulated as a generator of the hazardous wastes removed from the containers in connection with closure activities.

G. Miscellaneous Provisions

Owners or operators of containers may be governed by regulations other than RCRA. For example, standards promulgated by the Department of Transportation govern the labeling, transport, and reuse of containers used in transportation. Specific state laws may also affect the management of containers.

III. Tank Systems

A. Overview and Exemptions

Tank systems used to store or treat hazardous wastes are governed by 40 C.F.R. Sections 264.190 and 265.190. A tank is defined as:

> a stationary device, designed to contain an accumulation of hazardous waste which is constructed primarily of non-earthen materials (e.g., wood, concrete, steel, plastic) which provide structural support to the tank.[9]

The term "tank system" means:

> a hazardous waste storage or treatment tank and its associated ancillary equipment and containment system.

Like the regulations that govern other hazardous waste treatment and storage devices, the regulatory program for hazardous waste tank systems has multiple objectives. These objectives include ensuring system integrity, proper installation, adequate spill response, and proper maintenance and closure.

With a few exceptions, the regulations governing owners and operators of interim status tank systems contain few differences from the regulations governing the owners and operators of permitted tank systems. The major difference between interim status and permitted tank regulations arises in the storage of incompatible wastes.

---

[9]40 C.F.R. § 260.10.

Chapter 10: Standards for Containers, Tanks, Incinerators, Boilers, and Furnaces 223

Interim status requirements may also apply to owners and operators of noninterim status tank systems that use the tank to store between 100 and 1,000 kilograms of hazardous waste for 180 days or less. That provision is discussed in Chapter 7, which deals with issues bearing on the storage and transport of hazardous wastes.

B. Required Design and Components

New tank systems must possess certain design features set forth in 40 C.F.R Sections 264 and 265.192. These regulations include corrosion protection measures for the new tank system and its components. New tank systems in this context include reinstalled, refurbished, and replacement tanks. The operator must be prepared to demonstrate that the tank system and its components contain a sufficient base protection from system failure, rupture, and collapse. The tank's seams and connection points must be sealed, and pressure must be regulated to prevent rupture or explosion. Corrosion protection is achieved by the use of corrosion-resistant material and coatings. In addition, corrosion is prevented by cathodic protection and electrical isolation devices. However, the design features and components required for existing tank systems vary, as do installation requirements.

1. Secondary Containment Requirements

The regulations in 40 C.F.R. Section 264.193 detail secondary containment requirements. If an existing tank does not hold free liquids or is located inside a building with an impermeable floor, it is exempt from secondary containment requirements. All new tank systems must possess secondary containment systems even if they do not hold free liquids or are located in a building. Owners or operators of all other existing tank systems must provide secondary containment according to a timetable that has since lapsed.

Owners and operators of existing tank systems that store certain specified hazardous wastes must have installed secondary containment by January 1989. Other existing tank systems of documented age must possess secondary containment by the time the system becomes 15 years old. If the existing tank system's age is unknown, the owner or operator must install a secondary containment system by January 12, 1995. If the tank system's age is unknown but it is located at a facility that is more than 7 years old, the owner or operator must provide secondary containment before the facility becomes 15 years old or by January 12, 1989, whichever is later.

Where an existing tank's contents are declared hazardous after January 12, 1987, the foregoing time for adding secondary containment starts to run on the date that the waste is declared hazardous. For example, if a system was documented to be 14 years old and its contents were declared hazardous on January 1, 1988, the owner would have been required to install a secondary containment system on or before January 1, 1990.

Where required, the secondary containment system must, at a minimum, prevent wastes and accumulated liquids from escaping. The secondary containment system must also be capable of detecting releases and holding released waste until it can be removed.

Additional design requirements for secondary containment systems are detailed at 40 C.F.R. Sections 264.193 and 265.193. The system must be constructed of or lined with a material compatible with the stored waste, must sit on a foundation strong enough to support it, and must include a leak detection system.

The secondary containment system must include a barrier feature such as an external liner, a vault, a double-walled tank, or an equivalent device. The requirements for each of these devices are specified in 40 C.F.R. Sections 264.193, 265.193, and 260.10. The secondary containment system must also be sloped or otherwise designed to permit drainage. For additional information on technical specifications and design of underground storage tanks obtain a copy of a Steel Tank Institute's Standards for Dual Wall Underground Storage Tanks.

An external liner must have the capacity to hold the contents of the largest tank within its boundary. The liner must prevent liquids from entering the secondary containment system unless it possesses enough capacity to hold both the volume of the largest tank and the volume of a 25-year/24-hour rainfall. The liner must be free of cracks and gaps and must surround the tank completely, covering any ground likely to come into contact with released waste.

Vault systems are used as external liners. The vault must possess the same capacity as liners. If the vault contains joints, each joint must possess a chemical-resistant water stop. The vault must possess an impermeable interior coating or lining that is compatible with the stored waste. Where the tank system holds ignitable or reactive wastes, the vault must include protection against formation and ignition of vapors. Finally, the vault must possess an exterior moisture barrier or must contain some other design feature that prevents moisture from entering the vault.

A double-walled tank is an inner tank fully enveloped by an outer shell. If the double-walled tank is metal, anticorrosion measures must be provided for both the inner and outer shells. If there is a release from the inner tank, the materials must be contained by the outer shell. The double-walled tank must also possess a system for detecting leaks within 24 hours of their occurrence.

Chapter 10: Standards for Containers, Tanks, Incinerators, Boilers, and Furnaces 225

Secondary containment must also be provided for the ancillary components of new tank systems. Ancillary equipment need not possess secondary containment if it is inspected daily. According to the regulation, examples of secondary containment for ancillary components include double-walled piping, trenching, and jacketing. Thus, it is not sufficient to provide backup for only the tank itself. The owner or operator must ensure that all piping and supports that feed into the tank possess secondary containment features.

An owner or operator may obtain a variance from secondary containment requirements if he or she demonstrates to the Regional Administrator of EPA that the tank system's design and operation, combined with the hydrogeological features of the facility (such as the presence of a clay layer), will prevent waste from escaping into the environment just as effectively as a secondary containment system. To secure a variance, the owner or operator must demonstrate that neither human health nor the environment will be substantially harmed if the tank's contents escape, or that the point of the potential release is aboveground and can be visually observed.

The regulation lists numerous factors that the Regional Administrator of EPA must evaluate in deciding whether or not to grant a variance. These factors include water flow and usage patterns, water quality, including the presence of any contamination and current, and the anticipated uses of the water and land.

Owners and operators that secure variances from secondary containment requirements must satisfy additional requirements when responding to spills from the tank system. For example, the owner or operator must decontaminate the soil and prevent waste from migrating after a spill has occurred.[10] The owner or operator may also be required to conduct more frequent inspections following a release incident.

The leak detection system must detect leakage from the tank system or the secondary containment system within 24 hours of its occurrence. The 24-hour requirement may be relaxed if the owner or operator demonstrates that the best available technology will not permit detection within 24 hours.

A leak detection system that operates in conjunction with a secondary containment system allows for immediate response in the event of a release. This means the secondary containment will only be used as an emergency short-term storage area in the events of operational errors, such as spillage and overfilling of tanks. This prevents a release of the materials onto the environment and allows for removal within 24 hours.

---

[10]*Id.* §§ 264.193, 265.193.

The leak detection system should also detect failures in the tank's containment capability.

2. Requirements Applicable to Existing Tank Systems

40 C.F.R. Sections 264.191 and 265.191 govern existing tank systems. The owner or operator must evaluate existing tank systems that lack secondary containment and must obtain a written engineer-certified assessment stating that the tank system is fit for use. The assessment must conclude that the tank system will not fail when it comes into contact with stored hazardous wastes. The assessment must take into account the design standards applied to the tank, corrosion protection measures that exist on the tank, the tank's age, and the results of leak or other integrity examination.

If the existing tank system is underground, cannot be entered for testing, and lacks a secondary containment system, the owner or operator must conduct a leak test that accounts for temperature variations, tank-end deflation, vapor pockets, and the impact of high water tables. If the tank system is underground but may be entered for testing, the owner or operator may substitute another engineer-certified examination that addresses cracks, leaks, corrosion, and erosion.

3. New Tank Systems

Owners and operators of new permitted and interim status tank systems must submit to the EPA Regional Administrator a certification that the tank's design, corrosion protection, and compatibility with the wastes to be stored or treated will ensure that the tank system will not collapse, rupture, or otherwise fail.[11]

This certification must be prepared by an independent registered engineer and must confirm compliance with the design standards applied to installation and operation of the tank and its ancillary equipment. The certification must also identify the hazardous characteristics of the wastes to be stored or treated. If external metal components of the tank system will be in contact with soil or water, the certification must identify factors that will affect corrosion, including the moisture content of the soil. In such cases, the certification must also estimate the type and degree of corrosion protection required. When the tank system is to be located beneath an area traversed by vehicular traffic, the certification must identify measures that will protect it from being damaged by the traffic. After receiving the technical assessment and certification, the Regional Administrator will decide whether to approve the tank system's design.

---

[11]*Id.* §§ 264.192, 265.192.

The new tank system must possess design features enumerated in 40 C.F.R. Sections 264.192 and 265.192. The new tank system must have foundations that will support the tank and, if it is located in a fault or frost zone, anchoring sufficient to protect the tank from becoming dislodged. The tank system must also be designed to withstand the effects of frost heave.

C. Regulations Governing Maintenance and Operation

1. Operating Requirements

General operating requirements for tank systems are identified in 40 C.F.R. Sections 264.194 and 265.195. The provision forbids tank system owners or operators from placing wastes in a tank that will cause the tank to rupture, spill, or otherwise fail. Owners and operators must also undertake practices or establish controls that will prevent spills from occurring. Specifically, the owner or operator must provide for spill overflow prevention controls such as check valves, dry disconnect couplings, overfill prevention controls, level-sensing devices, high-level alarms, an automatic feed cutoff, or a bypass to a standby tank. If the tank is uncovered, the owner or operator must maintain a vertical clearance between the top of the tank and the surface of the waste sufficient to prevent the tank from tipping over.

2. Inspection Requirements

The owner or operator of hazardous waste tanks must regularly inspect the facility's tank system to confirm the integrity of the tank and respond if there is a release. Inspection requirements for permitted tank systems are set forth in 40 C.F.R. Section 264.195, and those for interim status tank systems are located in 40 C.F.R. Section 265.195. The owner or operator of a permitted tank system must inspect overfill controls according to the schedule contained in the permit, while the owner or operator of an interim status tank system must inspect overfill controls daily. The remaining inspection requirements for interim and permitted tank systems are identical.

The owner or operator must conduct daily visual inspections of the aboveground portions of the tank system for signs of corrosion or release and the area surrounding the externally accessible portion of a tank system for signs of erosion, leaks, and other defects. The owner or operator must also review data collected by monitoring or leak detection equipment on a daily basis.

The regulations contain special inspection requirements for cathodic protection systems. Cathodic protection systems prevent corrosion by

228   THE RCRA PRACTICE MANUAL

applying an electrical current to the tank's metallic surface. These devices must be inspected to confirm they are functioning properly within six months following installation and annually thereafter. Sources of impressed mechanisms currently used for cathodic protection systems must be inspected at least bimonthly.

The owner or operator of a tank system lacking secondary containment must meet additional inspection requirements under 40 C.F.R. Section 264.193. Annual leak tests must be conducted on underground tank systems that cannot be entered for inspection. If the underground tank system cannot be entered, the owner or operator may substitute the requirements with an equivalent inspection method undertaken by a registered engineer. This alternative inspection must be adequate to detect obvious cracks, leaks, corrosion, or erosion. The tank's contents must be removed if doing so is necessary to conduct the inspection. The alternative inspection must be conducted according to a schedule sufficient to ensure that any defects will be detected in light of the tank's contents, the system's age, and the rate of corrosion or erosion. For additional guidance on tank inspection, review the American Petroleum Institute's *Practical Guide for Inspection of Refinery Equipment*.

The owner or operator must document all of the foregoing inspections of its hazardous waste tanks. Inspection records must be retained with the facility's operating records for at least three years.

D. Regulations Pertaining to Specific Wastes

An owner or operator may not place ignitable or reactive wastes in a tank system unless the waste is treated so that it no longer meets the definition of ignitable or reactive under 40 C.F.R. Sections 261.21 and 261.23.[12] The owner or operator must undertake other measures to prevent extreme heat, fire, and explosions; production of uncontrolled toxic fumes, dusts, or gases; damage to the tank system or facility's structural integrity; and other types of harm to the environment or to human health. As an alternative to these measures, the owner or operator may take steps to protect the contained waste from coming in contact with other materials or conditions that might cause it to react or ignite. The use of the buffer zone must be in compliance with the National Fire Protection Association's Flammable and Combustible Liquids Code.

If ignitable or reactive waste is stored in a tank system due to special circumstances, it must be kept a safe distance from public areas, such as streets adjoining property, and management areas that are not used for

---

[12]*Id.* §§ 264.198, 265.198.

Chapter 10: Standards for Containers, Tanks, Incinerators, Boilers, and Furnaces   229

storage. Safe distances are identified in the National Fire Protection Association's Flammable and Combustible Liquids Code, which RCRA regulations incorporate by reference. The foregoing requirements do not apply if the owner or operator uses the tank system to store reactive waste only in emergency situations. The regulation does not define what circumstances constitute an emergency.

An owner or operator may place incompatible wastes together in a tank system, or place waste in a tank system that previously held incompatible wastes and has not been decontaminated, only if the owner or operator ensures that the waste, when mixed, will not produce heat, pressure, fires, explosions, or other violent reactions, including toxic mists, dusts, or gases that threaten human health; and will not damage the tank's structural integrity.[13]

If waste to be stored in an interim status tank is substantially different from waste previously stored in the tank system, or if the owner or operator of an interim status facility intends to chemically treat waste by a method substantially different from prior methods used, the owner or operator must satisfy additional requirements.[14] The owner or operator must conduct waste analyses, trial treatment storage tests, and obtain data regarding similar wastes that show that the tank will not rupture, corrode, or otherwise fail. This practice, however, is advisable for owners and operators of all tank systems undergoing content changes.

E. Regulations Governing Closure

When closing a tank system, an owner or operator must perform the acts identified in 40 C.F.R. Sections 264.197 and 265.197. The owner or operator must remove and decontaminate wastes, waste residues, tank system components, and soils. The provision explicitly states that the owner or operator must treat a contaminated tank system including all of its components as hazardous waste. Therefore, for disposal purposes, the tank contents, the tank system and its components may be considered a RCRA hazardous waste. If this closure is undertaken pursuant to these requirements, the tank system will have attained "clean closure" status. This satisfies all postclosure obligations for the tank system. The facility may still have other RCRA closure and financial responsibilities, depending on its operations.

An owner or operator that cannot practicably remove or decontaminate the impacted soils, residues, and components from the site of the

---

[13]*Id.* §§ 264.199, 265.199.
[14]*Id.* § 265.200.

230   THE RCRA PRACTICE MANUAL

tank removal must undertake the postclosure care required for landfill disposal pursuant to 40 C.F.R. Section 264.310. The postclosure requirements for landfills are discussed in Chapter 9. Owners and operators should consider closure mechanisms by following EPA's administrative reforms referred to as RCRA Cleanup Reforms.

Additional closure requirements govern tank systems that lack secondary containment. The owner or operator of such a system must submit both a plan for removing and decontaminating the system and its components and a contingency plan for decontaminating the surrounding soil. The owner or operator must also submit budgets that reflect the costs of the plans and must provide financial assurance to cover estimated closure costs.

F. Miscellaneous Regulations

1. Spill Management and Release Response

In responding to spills and leaks from a hazardous waste tank, an owner or operator must meet the requirements set forth in 40 C.F.R. Sections 264.196 and 265.196. When a release occurs, the owner or operator must immediately remove the tank system from service, prevent waste from entering the system, inspect the system to determine the cause of the release, and stop additional waste from flowing into the system. Specifically, the owner or operator must remove from the tank system enough waste to prevent any further release and to permit inspection. Additionally, the owner or operator must remove any waste that has been collected by the secondary containment system. These acts must be performed within 24 hours after the release. However, if the owner or operator demonstrates that it is not practicably possible to perform these acts within 24 hours, the owner or operator may perform them as soon as is practicably possible. If a release is visible, the owner or operator must immediately conduct a visual inspection of the release, prevent the released waste from migrating into the soils or surface water, and remove and dispose of visibly contaminated soils. Additional remedial activities may be required following these actions.

The owner or operator of a tank system that has received a variance from the secondary containment requirement must take additional steps following a release. The owner or operator must prevent released waste from migrating into the groundwater or surface water and decontaminate or remove contaminated soil.[15] Before returning the system to service, the owner or operator must add a secondary containment system or again request a new variance.

---

[15]*Id.* §§ 264.193, 265.193.

Chapter 10: Standards for Containers, Tanks, Incinerators, Boilers, and Furnaces 231

The owner or operator of the tank must also satisfy reporting requirements after a release has occurred.[16] Releases of waste that are greater than 1 pound or are not immediately controlled and cleaned up must be reported to the EPA Regional Administrator within 24 hours after they occur. Within 30 days after any release is detected, the owner or operator must submit a comprehensive report to the Regional Administrator that identifies the likely route of migration for the waste, soil characteristics at the site, the results of soil sampling and monitoring, and the proximity of the release to drinking water, surface water, and populated areas. The report must also detail all response activities that have been undertaken and those activities that are planned. The owner or operator must also comply with the spill reporting requirements contained in Title III of the Superfund Amendments and Reauthorization Act of 1986 (SARA).[17]

2. Requirements for Returning the Tank to Service

Before a tank system is returned to service following a release, the requirements in 40 C.F.R. Sections 264.136 and 265.196 must be satisfied. If the release has not damaged the tank system's integrity, the owner or operator need simply clean up the spill and conduct necessary repairs. The owner or operator must repair the system if the release was caused by a leak from the primary tank system into the secondary containment system.

If after a release the tank system is determined to be unfit, the tank system must be taken out of service. The release must be stopped, and the contents must be removed before the system can be repaired.

If wastes were released from a component of the tank system and the tank system lacks secondary containment and cannot be visually inspected, the owner or operator must provide secondary containment for the component. Whenever a component is replaced, the owner or operator must satisfy the secondary containment requirements governing new components and new tank systems.

After all major repairs, the tank system cannot be returned to service until a registered independent engineer certifies that the system is adequate to store hazardous waste. The owner or operator must submit this certification to the Regional Administrator of EPA within seven days after returning the system to service. By way of illustration, the regulation states that major repairs include installation of a liner or repair of a ruptured primary or secondary containment vessel.

---

[16]*Id.* §§ 264.196, 265.196.
[17]42 U.S.C. § 11,001 *et seq.*

232   THE RCRA PRACTICE MANUAL

IV. Incinerators

A. Overview and Exemptions

1. Definitions and Overview

An incinerator is defined as an enclosed device that:

> [u]ses controlled flame combustion and neither meets the criteria for classification as a boiler, sludge dryer or carbon regeneration unit, nor is listed as an industrial furnace.[18]

The definition of incinerators also includes devices that meet the definitions of infrared incinerators or plasma arc incinerators. An infrared incinerator is defined as:

> any enclosed device that uses electric powered resistance heaters as a source of radiant heat and which is not listed as an industrial furnace.[19]

A plasma arc incinerator is defined as:

> any enclosed device using a high intensity electrical discharge or arc as a source of heat and which is not listed as an industrial furnace.[20]

Incinerators that burn hazardous waste must be designed, constructed, and maintained to meet certain performance standards. Minimum efficiency standards require the incinerator to destroy 99.99 percent of each principal organic hazardous constituent identified in the permit. To confirm that levels of destruction and removal efficiency are maintained, the incinerator's design must include sufficient detection features. The incinerator's design must include a mechanism to contain and cut off the flow of waste in the event of an operational failure. In addition to satisfying applicable RCRA requirements, the owner and operator of an incinerator must strictly comply with the Clean Air Act.

2. Policy Issues

Despite mixed reactions from the public, there has been an increase in demand for incinerators to treat hazardous waste effectively. Technical capabilities have improved to ensure that high enough temperatures

---

[18]40 C.F.R. § 260.10.
[19]*Id.*
[20]Id.

Chapter 10: Standards for Containers, Tanks, Incinerators, Boilers, and Furnaces   233

(1,500–2,500 degrees Fahrenheit) are maintained for enough time in the destruction chamber, along with proper combination of waste and oxygen so as to burn the hazardous waste efficiently.

In spite of the increasing demand for this technology, EPA's strategy on addressing combustion as a treatment alternative resulted in dampening of some interest. Previously, EPA had announced its strategic goals in EPA Draft Strategy for Combustion of Hazardous Waste in Incinerators and Boilers: Interim Final Guidance on Waste Minimization for Hazardous Waste Generators.[21] These "strategic goals" grew out of health concerns raised by citizens living near incinerators, and a belief that waste reduction methods would better serve community interests. The agency's regulatory approach shifted toward increasing pressure on source reduction programs and a reevaluation of how this affects the need to permit new combustion facilities. This policy affected the permitting of incinerators, boilers, and industrial furnaces and, for practical purposes, froze the permitting of new combustion facilities or expansion of the capacity of existing facilities.

To further investigate these issues, an EPA-State Committee and a National Roundtable were formed to examine developing strategies for aggressive source reduction, improvements in permitting standards, treatment alternatives, and the scientific basis for decision making. EPA had announced a series of short- and long-term actions to complement these concerns. Included among the short-term actions are the upgrading of emissions standards, increasing inspections, requiring greater public participation, and source reduction. EPA began a program of aggressive inspection of existing facilities and issuance of enforcement actions against those facilities out of compliance. Other efforts focused on longer-term actions to increase the rules on emission controls, public participation, and evaluation of risks.

With respect to existing permitted combustion facilities, EPA has a policy of aggressive enforcement of all permit provisions. EPA has pressured permitted facilities to accept waste only from generators that have put into place their own comprehensive waste reduction programs. Segments within society that are greatly dependent on combustion facilities are evaluating how they might reduce their waste volumes.

3. Exemptions

Incinerators are exempt from regulation if they burn wastes identified as hazardous solely because they are ignitable and/or corrosive, or if they burn wastes that are hazardous solely because they are reactive, if the

---

[21]EPA (May 18, 1993).

234 THE RCRA PRACTICE MANUAL

wastes will not be burned while other wastes are present in the reaction zone.[22] Incinerators that burn wastes exhibiting none of the hazardous characteristics ordinarily associated with the waste also are exempt. When the waste to be burned contains insignificant levels of hazardous constituents, the incinerator permit may exempt the incinerator from certain RCRA provisions except for those regulations pertaining to closure and waste analysis requirements.

4. Manner of Implementation

The regulations pertaining to permitted incinerators do not identify specific design and operating requirements, but instead identify performance standards that these incinerators must achieve. The incinerator permit identifies design and operating requirements that are deemed sufficient to satisfy the regulatory performance requirements. The regulations governing interim status incinerators, however, contain specific design and operating requirements. Given the change in this regulatory field, any analysis of applicable incinerator regulations must be confirmed by reviewing the regulation in place at the time of preparing a permit.

B. Required Design, Components, and Permits

1. Waste Analysis

Owners and operators of both permitted and interim status incinerators must conduct a waste analysis pursuant to 40 C.F.R. Section 265.13 before they burn hazardous waste. The focus of the waste analysis, especially where feedstocks may change, is on ensuring consistent and steady operating conditions. This includes a review of the fuel feed and airflow to determine potential emissions.

Owners and operators of interim status incinerators must conduct both the general waste analysis outlined in 40 C.F.R. Section 265.13 and a more specific analysis. The owner or operator must determine heating value, sulfur and halogen content, and lead and mercury concentrations of the waste to be burned.[23] This information is needed to establish normal operating conditions and identify the pollutants that incineration will emit.

The waste analysis must also identify the heat value of the waste to be burned, the viscosity or physical form of the waste, and the hazardous organic constituents found in the waste. The analysis must also identify

---

[22]40 C.F.R. § 264.3.
[23]*Id.* § 265.341.

Chapter 10: Standards for Containers, Tanks, Incinerators, Boilers, and Furnaces 235

what constituents have been excluded from the analysis and state the basis for their exclusion. Finally, the analysis must approximate the volume of the hazardous constituents of the waste to be incinerated.

2. Trial Burn

The design and operating requirements that must be included in the permit are established through a trial burn. The trial burn tests the ability of the incinerator unit to meet operating standards when burning the proposed waste under certain operating conditions. The permit applicant must demonstrate that the waste will be destroyed by combustion while operating in compliance with performance standards under established operating conditions. An incinerator may only burn waste specified in the permit and under the conditions outlined in the permit.

The trial burn must be conducted if it will aid in evaluating the incinerator's performance or in determining what operating requirements need to be included in the permit, so that operation will not present an imminent hazard to human health or to the environment. However, the regulations suggest that the trial burn may not be necessary if the applicant shows that the information sought can be reasonably developed through a method other than a trial burn. Given EPA policy, however, it is doubtful any permitting will occur without a trial burn.

Before securing a permit, the owner or operator must conduct a trial burn according to a trial burn plan. 40 C.F.R. Section 270.62 details the trial burn requirements. The trial burn plan must include the required waste analysis and must identify the design specifications and model of the incinerator, identify IRS manufacturer, describe the procedures and equipment to be used in monitoring and sampling, state a test schedule and protocol, and identify procedures for rapid shutdown of the incinerator. Lastly, the trial burn plan must also include any additional information that the Regional Administrator of EPA finds reasonably necessary.

After the trial burn plan is submitted, the Regional Administrator must identify principal organic hazardous constituents (POHCs) whose destruction and removal efficiencies (DREs) must be calculated during the trial burn. POHCs are indicator chemicals for which thermal combustion is difficult and, therefore, indicate the efficiency of the incinerator.

The owner or operator must submit the results of the trial burn to the Regional Administrator of EPA within 90 days after the trial burn is completed. The results must include analysis of emissions, scrubber water, and the POHCs found in the incinerator waste feed and provide any other information that the Regional Administrator finds necessary.

Public challenges to the permitting of an incinerator often become intense during the trial burn phase. This tension was demonstrated in

236 THE RCRA PRACTICE MANUAL

Greenpeace v. Waste Technologies Industries,[24] wherein Greenpeace sought and was granted a temporary restraining order to prevent a trial burn in East Liverpool, Ohio. This case is the predecessor to EPA's movement toward aggressive source reduction and freezing the permitting of additional combustion facilities. In a subsequent opinion, *Greenpeace v. Waste Technologies Industries*,[25] the court allowed the eight-day proposed test burn to proceed but enjoined operating the incinerator during the period between the trial burn and issuance of the final permitting decision. In November 1993, the Sixth Circuit, in *Greenpeace, Inc. v. Waste Technologies Industries*,[26] reviewed the permit issued to Waste Technologies Industries, and found that Greenpeace lacked standing to bring a RCRA claim against a permitted facility to address the issue of imminent and substantial endangerment. The court indicated that Greenpeace had not taken advantage of opportunities that existed during the permitting process and public comment periods to challenge this facility. The court, in relying upon *Palumbo v. Waste Technologies Industries*,[27] found that Greenpeace's complaint constituted nothing more than an improper collateral attack on a prior permitting decision of EPA to allow for the test burns. In each of these *Greenpeace* decisions, the court gave significant consideration to the risk assessments submitted by the parties.

3. Permit Requirements

The Regional Administrator of EPA uses the results of the trial burn to determine the specific operating requirements to be included in the incinerator permit. The permit requirements are aimed at ensuring that the incinerator will satisfy the performance standards delineated in 40 C.F.R. Section 264.343.

The performance standards focus on several areas, the first of which is confirming the degree and efficiency of incineration. The incinerator must achieve a 99.99 percent rate for destruction and energy recovery (DER) for each POHC identified in the permit. This means that only 1 of every 10,000 molecules of hazardous constituent is allowed to be vented through the incinerator's stack. Where the incinerator burns wastes that contain dioxins and PCBs, the incinerator must achieve a higher DER— 99.9999 percent—for each identified POHC.

As indicated above, POHCs are the organic constituents of the waste that are the most difficult to incinerate. Whether a constituent is designated a POHC depends, in part, on the quantity or concentration in which the constituent is present in the waste to be burned.

---

[24] 1993 W.L. 128,732 (N.D. Ohio, Jan. 21, 1993).
[25] 1993 W.L. 134,861 (N.D. Ohio, Mar. 5, 1993).
[26] 9 F.3d 1174 (6th Cir. 1993).
[27] 989 F.2d 156 (4th Cir. 1993).

Chapter 10: Standards for Containers, Tanks, Incinerators, Boilers, and Furnaces 237

The performance standards also focus on emissions. Hydrogen chloride emissions from an incinerator that emits more than 1.8 kilograms (4 pounds) per hour are limited to 1.8 kilograms per hour or an amount equal to 1 percent of the hydrogen chloride present before emissions are filtered through pollution control equipment, whichever is greater. Furthermore, the incinerator may not emit particulate matter in excess of 180 milligrams per dry cubic meter (0.08 grains per dry standard cubic foot). This level is corrected for the oxygen level in stack gas according to a formula identified in 40 C.F.R. Section 264.343.

Compliance with permit requirements is deemed to satisfy the performance standards. However, EPA may issue permit modification, revocation, or reissuance of a permit where evidence indicates that compliance with permit standards does not guarantee compliance with performance standards.[28]

Activities within EPA suggest that controls on the emissions of particulates, metals, dioxins, and furans will continue to be tightened even on permitted facilities. It is anticipated that EPA will rely on RCRA's provisions granting the EPA omnibus permit authority. Many of these standards will be tied to source performance standards for new municipal waste combusters.

4. Other Permit Limitations

Each incinerator permit must establish the limitations identified in 40 C.F.R. Section 264.345. These include limitations on carbon monoxide emissions, waste feed rate, combustion temperature, combustion gas velocity, variations in incinerator design and operating procedures, and other operating requirements necessary to ensure compliance with applicable performance standards. The incinerator must be shut down if the incinerator exceeds the limits established by the permit.

It is EPA policy that facilities seeking permits must perform site-specific risk assessments before it will issue a permit.

5. Operating Requirements

All permitted incinerators must satisfy the operating requirements established in 40 C.F.R. Section 264.345. While incinerating hazardous waste, the operator must monitor the instruments for combustion and emission rates. Fugitive emissions must be controlled by completely sealing the combustion zone or by maintaining combustion zone pressure at a level lower than atmospheric pressure. The owner or operator may also prevent fugitive emissions through an equivalent alternative method. The incinerator must also possess an automatic waste feed cutoff system.

---

[28]40 C.F.R. § 264.343.

238 THE RCRA PRACTICE MANUAL

The system must cut off the flow of waste into the incinerator if the limitations established in the permit are exceeded.

6. Interim Status Certification Requirements

Owners or operators of interim status incinerators must obtain a certification that the incinerator meets the performance requirements of 40 C.F.R. Section 264.343 before burning EPA hazardous wastes F020, F021, F022, P023, F026, and P027.[29] The regulations governing interim status incinerators do not identify separate operating requirements except to state that the owner or operator cannot feed hazardous waste into an incinerator during start-up or shutdown unless normal operating conditions exist.[30]

C. Maintenance and Inspection Requirements

1. Inspection Requirements

The inspection requirements for permitted and interim status incinerators and ancillary equipment are outlined in 40 C.F.R. Sections 264.347 and 265.347. The requirements for permitted incinerators are different than those for interim status incinerators. Inspections required during operation of the incinerator focus on leaks, spills, emissions, emergency controls, and alarm systems.

Owners and operators of interim status incinerators must monitor instruments that relate to combustion temperature and emission controls at 15-minute intervals. The regulation identifies the instruments as those related to waste feed, auxiliary fuel feed, air flow, incinerator temperature, scrubber flow, scrubber pH, and relevant level controls. The regulation also requires daily inspections of the incinerator and its associated equipment for leaks, spills, and fugitive emissions.

During incineration, the owner or operator of a permitted incinerator must monitor combustion temperature, waste feed rate, and combustion gas velocity. The owner or operator must also continuously monitor the carbon monoxide level. Upon request by the Regional Administrator of EPA, the owner or operator must sample and analyze waste and exhaust emissions.

The owner or operator of a permitted incinerator must also conduct daily inspections of the operating incinerator for leaks, spills, fugitive emissions, and signs of tampering. The emergency waste feed cutoff system must be inspected weekly. However, the weekly inspection require-

---

[29]*Id.* § 265.352.
[30]*Id.* § 265.345.

Chapter 10: Standards for Containers, Tanks, Incinerators, Boilers, and Furnaces 239

ment may be relaxed if the owner or operator demonstrates that weekly inspections are unduly burdensome and that less frequent inspections are adequate. The owner or operator of a permitted incinerator must record the data from the foregoing monitoring and inspections and must retain the data in the incinerator's operating log for three years.

In addition to the maintenance protocols discussed, owners and operators of all incinerators and waste-burning boilers and industrial furnaces should review the effect of the February 14, 2002, final rules set forth in NESHAP: "Standards for Hazardous Air Pollutants for Hazardous Waste Combustors."[31] These final rules may impact a company's emission limits and compliance programs for testing and monitoring the incinerator.

2. Waste-Monitoring Requirements

Owners and operators of permitted incinerators must regularly analyze the waste burned in the incinerator. This analysis must verify that the constituents in the waste meets the limits specified in the incinerator permit. Owners and operators of interim status incinerators need not conduct regular waste analysis.

D. Regulations Governing Closure

The closure of permitted and interim status incinerators is governed by 40 C.F.R. Sections 264.351 and 265.351. These provisions are less detailed than those that govern closure of tanks and containers. Both provisions state simply that the owner or operator must remove hazardous waste and waste residues from the incinerator site.

The comments to both provisions explain that, upon closure, the owner or operator is treated as a generator of hazardous wastes and, when removing materials from the incinerator, is regulated accordingly. In disassembling and removing the incinerator and its components, the owner and operator must ensure compliance with applicable RCRA disposal requirements.

E. Mobile Incinerators

Innovative technologies for remediation at Superfund sites were encouraged by the SARA amendments to CERCLA. As a result, interest in mobile incinerators has increased. A mobile incinerator is advantageous because it may treat wastes at more than one location. This benefit, however, is diminished insofar as the permitting process requires repetitive

---

[31]67 Fed. Reg. 6968, 2002 W.L. 219,779 (F.R.).

240 THE RCRA PRACTICE MANUAL

submittals and expensive public hearings before operation at each new location. Under RCRA, each new location is considered a new facility, so a site-specific permit must be issued before use at each site. Use of trial burn data from previous locations may help to simplify the permitting process. Legislative attempts have been made to develop statewide permits governing issues common to each mobile incinerator site such as waste type and incinerator descriptions. Site-specific issues would then be addressed in separate permits issued before the incinerator is used on each site.

The permitting of mobile incinerators has raised other issues. Specifically, questions remain as to whether public comment requirements would be satisfied when statewide permits are issued. Industries that rely on mobile incinerators have also encountered difficulty with disposing and treating combustion residues.

V. Boilers and Industrial Furnaces

A. Overview and Exemptions

Boilers and industrial furnaces (BIFs) are treated together in a single regulatory subchapter, 40 C.F.R. Section 266.100 *et seq.* This section details those provisions.

The regulations governing BIFs are different from those governing incinerators. These differences in part relate to the previous exemption of BIFs from hazardous waste rules because RCRA treated the activity as recycling. Because BIFs became subject to regulation later than furnaces, they have, in the view of at least one commentator, left incinerators behind in terms of regulatory sophistication. In response to the regulatory differences in the treatment of incinerators and BIFs, an association of commercial hazardous waste incinerators was created to challenge what its members believed were the inequities within RCRA regulations.

The distinction in regulatory treatment is based in part on the fact that incinerators burn hazardous waste for the sole purpose of disposal while boilers and industrial furnaces burn hazardous waste as an energy source. As a result, temperature and destruction of waste constituents may be treated differently. Despite the specific regulatory differences between BIFs and incinerators, the previous discussion regarding the permitting requirements placed on incinerators applies to BIFs.

1. Boilers Defined

Boilers are enclosed devices with a controlled flame. Boilers must meet specific combustion requirements set forth in 40 C.F.R. Section 260.10.

Chapter 10: Standards for Containers, Tanks, Incinerators, Boilers, and Furnaces 241

A boiler must have physical provisions for recovering and exporting thermal energy in the form of steam, heated fuels, or heated gases.

The combustion chamber and primary energy recovery sections must be integrally designed so that the two components function as a single manufactured or assembled unit. To meet the definition of a boiler, the device must maintain at least a 60 percent thermal energy recovery rate. The boiler must annually export and use at least 75 percent of the energy recovered.

The Regional Administrator of EPA may designate combustion devices as boilers even if the device does not otherwise meet the precise criteria and standards identified in 40 C.F.R. Section 260.32. This designation of the combustion device as a boiler is based on the extent to which the unit has energy recovery and export provisions. It may also be considered a boiler if the combustion devices and recovery equipment are integrally designed. The Regional Administrator must also consider the device's energy recovery efficiency, the extent to which recovered energy is utilized, and the extent to which the device is commonly and customarily used as a boiler.

2. Industrial Furnaces Defined

An industrial furnace is any one of a series of enumerated enclosed devices that are integral components of manufacturing processes and that use thermal treatment to accomplish recovery of materials or energy.[32] Industrial furnaces, as enumerated in 40 C.F.R. Section 260.10, include various types of kilns, coke ovens, blast furnaces, smelting, melting, and refining furnaces; titanium dioxide chloride process reactors; methane reforming furnaces; pulping liquor recovery furnaces; combustion devices used to recover sulfur values; and certain halogen acid furnaces.

The EPA Administrator may expand the list of devices that are defined as furnaces after appropriate notice and comment.[33] The provision identifies factors, one or more of which may serve as the basis for this designation. The factors focus on the use of the device to burn materials in producing products.

3. Exemptions

A device that satisfies the foregoing criteria is governed by 40 C.F.R. Section 266.100 *et seq.* That provision, however, identifies various devices that are exempt from regulation. The regulations do not apply where

---

[32]*Id.* § 260.10.
[33]*Id.*

242 THE RCRA PRACTICE MANUAL

exempt used oil or gas recovered from solid waste landfills is burned for energy recovery, where certain exempt hazardous wastes are burned, or where the device is a coke oven that burns EPA hazardous waste K087.

Smelting, melting, and refining furnaces that process waste solely for metal recovery and satisfy certain other conditions specified in the regulation are exempt.[34] To qualify for this exemption, the owner or operator must file with EPA a one-time notice stating that hazardous waste is to be burned for the sole purpose of metal recovery, that the waste contains recoverable levels of metals, and that the owner or operator will continue to sample and analyze feedstocks. The owner or operator must retain documents supporting compliance with the exemption requirements for a minimum of three years.

The scope of the metal recovery furnace exemption is restricted by 40 C.F.R. Section 266.100. That provision identifies characteristics of hazardous wastes that cannot be deemed burned solely for their metal content. The provision also contains special requirements for exempting furnaces that seek to recover the nickel-chromium or metals trapped in baghouse bags. The Regional Administrator of EPA may revoke the metal recovery exemption where the waste used as a fuel poses a threat to human health or the environment.

Furnaces that burn hazardous wastes in order to recover economically significant amounts of precious metals are exempt from all provisions of the subchapter except for Section 266.112. The precious metal recovery exemption requires that the owner or operator file a one-time notice with EPA. The owner or operator must also sample and analyze the hazardous waste in order to document that it is burned for precious metal recovery. Records of this analysis must be retained for a minimum of three years.

Owners or operators of furnaces and boilers that burn a small quantity of hazardous wastes are exempted by 40 C.F.R. Section 266.108. This exemption is commonly referred to as the small-quantity burner exemption. The exemption applies if (1) the hazardous waste burned does not exceed certain maximum levels relative to stack height; (2) the hazardous waste firing rate does not exceed 1 percent of the furnace's or boiler's total fuel requirements; and (3) the hazardous waste possesses a minimum heating value of 5,000 British thermal units per pound (akin to a low-grade coal). This exemption does not apply to EPA hazardous wastes P020, P021, P022, P023, P026, or P027. The owner or operator of a small-quantity burner must comply with the notification and record-keeping requirements similar to those applied to the foregoing exemptions.

---

[34]*Id.* §§ 266.101, 266.112.

Chapter 10: Standards for Containers, Tanks, Incinerators, Boilers, and Furnaces 243

4. Interim Status

Interim status furnaces and boilers are governed by 40 C.F.R. Section 266.103. A boiler or industrial furnace possesses interim status if it was in operation or under construction on or before August 21, 1991. A boiler or industrial furnace is considered under construction for interim status if, on or before August 21, 1991, all necessary approvals and permits were acquired and construction had actually begun on that date, or if the owner or operator had entered into a construction contract before that date. This section details the differences in the regulations that govern permitted and interim status BIFs.

B. Required Design, Components, and Permits

1. Overview of the Permitting Process

Design and operating standards that permitted incinerators or boilers must satisfy are located in 40 C.F.R. Section 266.102. As with incinerators, the regulations focus on performance standards, and permits must specify operating requirements that are sufficient to satisfy the standards. The permit also specifies what hazardous wastes the furnace or boiler may burn.

The terrain and use of the land surrounding the boiler or furnace affect the requirements contained in the permit. The permitting process, for example, considers the relationship between the stack height and the elevation of the surrounding terrain in order to establish emissions requirements.

2. Permit Requirements

The precise operating requirements included in the permit are generally determined in a trial burn or another comparable test. The operating requirements that permits must include are identified in 40 C.F.R. Section 266.102. There is some movement to replace the trial burn with a refined system of continuous emissions monitoring at the burner's stack and data extrapolation to regulate emissions. The first set of requirements seeks to ensure compliance with organic emissions standards. The regulation addresses two specific organic emissions standards: destruction and removal efficiency (DRE) standards and the carbon monoxide and hydrocarbon standards.

A DRE of 99.99 percent is required for most F series hazardous wastes, and a 99.999 percent efficiency rate is required for dioxin listed wastes.[35] The permit must ensure compliance with the DRE standard by

---

[35]*Id.* § 266.104.

establishing limits on the hazardous waste feed rate, minimum and maximum device production rates, appropriate controls for hazardous waste firing, allowable design variations, minimum combustion gas temperatures, and an appropriate indicator of combustion gas velocity.

The permit must also contain requirements that ensure compliance with limits on carbon monoxide emissions. Carbon monoxide emissions may not exceed 100 parts per million by volume except where stack gas concentrations of hydrocarbons do not exceed 20 parts per million by volume.

Permit provisions must ensure compliance with particulate emissions requirements. A boiler or industrial furnace may not emit particulate matter of more than 180 milligrams per dry standard cubic meter (0.08 grains per dry standard cubic foot).[36] To ensure compliance with these requirements, the permit must limit the total amount of ash placed in the boiler or furnace, determine a maximum device production rate, establish appropriate controls for operation and maintenance of the hazardous waste firing system, and establish allowable variation for furnace or boiler design. Permits for cement kilns or lightweight aggregate kilns, however, need not limit ash content.

The permit requirements necessary to ensure compliance with metals and hydrogen chloride (HCl) and chlorine gas (Cl_2) emissions standards vary depending on which of three standards the owner or operator elects to apply. The first standard, known as the tier I standard, is the most conservative. Under it, the owner or operator analyzes the waste feed and it is assumed that all metals, HCl, and Cl_2 contained in the feed are emitted. A permit issued under the tier I standard limits the rate at which metals, HCl, and Cl_2 are fed into the boiler or industrial furnace. A tier I permit must also prescribe a program for sampling and analyzing the waste feed.

Tier II standards apply where the owner or operator conducts emissions testing. The tier II standard is advantageous because it establishes limits based on the amount of metals, HCl, and Cl_2 actually emitted. The owner or operator is forced to elect this standard if metal, HCl, or Cl_2 concentrations in the waste feed exceed tier I limits.

Permits issued under tier II must limit hazardous waste feed rates and the total amount of metals, chlorine, and chloride present in the feedstream. The permit must identify maximum combustion and flue gas temperatures as well as the maximum device production rate, allowable variation in boiler and furnace design, and operation and maintenance controls.

Emissions of metals, HCl, and Cl_2 may also be governed by a tier III standard, the least conservative standard. Tier III applies if the owner or

---

[36]*Id.* § 266.105.

Chapter 10: Standards for Containers, Tanks, Incinerators, Boilers, and Furnaces 245

operator conducts both emissions testing and site-specific dispersion modeling to determine the maximum ground level concentrations of emitted metals, HCl, and Cl_2.

3. Operating Requirements

Every furnace or boiler must satisfy the operating requirements identified in 40 C.F.R. Section 266.102. Owners and operators of furnaces or boilers must prevent fugitive emissions by sealing the combustion zone or by maintaining combustion zone pressure at a level lower than atmospheric pressure. To ensure proper operations of the boiler or furnace, the owner or operator must conduct analysis of the fuel used to ensure the feedstack is within the constituent limits set forth in the permit.

RCRA regulates the method and manner that boilers and industrial furnaces receive a load of fuel. If the fuel source is a hazardous waste fuel, the transfer must be conducted in a manner that reduces the risk of emissions, leakage, rupture, or ignition of the fuel.[37]

The direct transfer of hazardous waste fuel into an industrial furnace or boiler cannot be done from an open container. The hazardous waste is to be pumped from a closed storage unit or container. The direct transfer equipment must be designed with sufficient structural strength and operated in a manner that does not result in failure.

In addition, each boiler or furnace must have a mechanism that cuts off waste feed if operating conditions deviate from those specified in the permit. When the waste feed is cut off, exhaust gases must be directed to the air pollution control system, and the operating parameters established by the permit must continue to be monitored. The minimum combustion temperature established by the permit must also be maintained during the cutoff.

4. Requirements for Interim Status Boilers and Industrial Furnaces

Interim status boilers and industrial furnaces are governed by 40 C.F.R. Section 266.103. Technically, many BIP facilities that burn hazardous wastes are, according to EPA, in interim status and awaiting a final determination on their pending permits. That provision identifies specific requirements for boilers and industrial furnaces that burn hazardous waste for a purpose other than their use as an ingredient in the feedstock. Whether hazardous waste is burned solely as an ingredient is determined based on factors identified in the regulation.

Where a furnace burns hazardous wastes for noningredient purposes, the owner or operator must maintain a minimum combustion gas temperature of 1800 degrees Fahrenheit and must determine that enough oxygen

---

[37]*Id.* § 266.111.

246 THE RCRA PRACTICE MANUAL

is present to combust the organic constituents of the waste. If the furnace is a cement kiln, hazardous waste must be fed directly into the kiln.

Owners and operators must file certifications of precompliance and compliance before specified dates. The provision forbids owners and operators from burning hazardous wastes that possess a heating value of less than 5000 British thermal units per pound before the compliance date. This restriction does not, however, apply, where the waste is burned solely as an ingredient, where the waste is burned for compliance testing for no more than 710 hours, or where the owner or operator documents that, before August 25, 1991, the boiler or furnace was operated as an interim status incinerator, met interim status eligibility requirements, and that waste with a heating value of less than 5000 British thermal units per pound was burned.

The owner or operator must have submitted a precompliance certification on or before August 21, 1991, stating that the device, when operated within specified limits, will not exceed regulatory emissions limits. To secure this certification, the owner or operator must have submitted specified information about the facility operated, estimated emission rates, and emission controls. The certification must limit feed rates for total hazardous wastes and individual metals, chloride, and chlorine, and the maximum device production rate.

The owner or operator of an interim status furnace or boiler were to have submitted a certification of compliance on or before August 21, 1992. This certification is based on the results of actual emissions testing and is used to establish operating parameters and limitations. If an owner or operator failed to obtain a certification of compliance on or before August 21, 1992, it was to cease burning hazardous waste, limit hazardous waste burning to the level permitted for compliance testing, or obtain a case-by-case extension of time. Extensions were granted to the owner or operator if the failure to secure the certification in a timely manner was beyond his or her control or where the owner or operator is seeking a boiler or industrial furnace permit.

A certification of compliance must be renewed every three years. If the owner or operator does not comply with the required renewal schedule, the boiler or furnace must cease operation and may resume operation only pursuant to a permit.

C. Operating and Maintenance Requirements

Owners and operators of both permitted and interim status boilers and furnaces must conduct regular monitoring and inspections. Where the permit specifies, the owner or operator must monitor feed rates, compo-

Chapter 10: Standards for Containers, Tanks, Incinerators, Boilers, and Furnaces   247

sition of feedstocks, and the presence of metals, chlorine, and chloride.[38] The permit may also direct the owner or operator to monitor carbon monoxide, hydrocarbon, and oxygen levels continuously. The owner or operator of an interim status furnace or boiler must always monitor these variables.[39] In addition, the Director of the EPA may request both permitted and interim status operators to sample hazardous waste pursuant to 40 C.F.R. Sections 266.102(b) and 266.103(j).

Both interim and permitted operators must also fulfill inspection requirements under 40 C.F.R. Sections 266.102(b) and 266.103(j). The owner or operator must visually inspect the furnace or boiler for leaks, spills, fugitive emissions, and signs of tampering. The automatic hazardous waste feed cutoff system and alarms must be tested weekly. Both interim and permitted operators must record the results of monitoring and inspections.

D. Regulatory Treatment of Residues

40 C.F.R. Section 266.112 governs treatment of the residues produced by boilers and industrial furnaces and exempts certain hazardous waste residues from regulation. EPA takes the position that the exception is mandated by a 1980 amendment to RCRA,[40] which temporarily exempted from RCRA Subtitle C regulation residues generated primarily from combustion of coal or other fossil fuels, processing of ores and minerals, and cement kiln dust waste. There were efforts to challenge the way in which owners and operators manage cement kiln dust derived from the burning of hazardous materials. EPA's regulatory interpretation of the statutory provision, commonly known as the Bevill amendments,[41] is controversial.

A two-part test determines whether residues produced by a boiler with fuel of at least 50 percent coal, an industrial furnace that processes at least 50 percent ores and minerals, or a cement kiln with a feedstock consisting of normal raw materials are exempt from regulation.[42] Such residues are not exempt if they contain concentrations of toxic compounds that are significantly higher than those found after combustion in the absence of hazardous wastes and if toxins are present in a concentration that poses a significant risk of harm.

---

[38]*Id.* § 266.102(b).
[39]*Id.* § 266.103(j).
[40]42 U.S.C.A. § 6921(3)(A).
[41]First set forth at 56 Fed. Reg. 7134 (1991).
[42]40 C.F.R. § 266.112.

248 THE RCRA PRACTICE MANUAL

In *Louisiana-Pacific Corp. v. Asarco, Inc.*,[43] the court found the slag that is otherwise exempted from RCRA regulation pursuant to the Bevill amendments is not exempt as a hazardous substance from regulation under the Comprehensive Environmental Response, Compensation, and Liability Act (CERCLA).

In *In re Wheland Foundry*,[44] an administrative law judge, in reviewing the treatment of fly ash waste under RCRA, found that the Bevill amendments had exempted the wastes from treatment. This had the effect of absolving the company for its past disposal of fly ash waste. It was understood that Wheland Foundry with respect to future disposal would treat fly ash waste under applicable land ban regulations.

In *Horsehead Resource Development Co. v. EPA*,[45] environmentalists, citizen groups, and members of the hazardous waste treatment industry challenged EPA's interpretation of the Bevill amendments. The environmental petitioners had argued that the Bevill amendments were intended to apply only to the residues left after burning conventional, nonhazardous material.

Initially, to facilitate disposition of the case, EPA in 1993 entered into a settlement agreement to resolve certain issues associated with the scope of the BIF rules on emission standards for boilers, industrial furnaces, and incinerators. In addition, the case addressed the issue of matter and dioxin emissions from boilers, industrial furnaces, and hazardous waste incinerators. The court, in *Horsehead*, severed from the main action the inquiry into those regulations affecting smelting, melting, and refining furnaces that recover metals, small-quantity burners, and the upgrading of incinerator standards. EPA agreed to address those issues through the process of rule making.

As a result, the plaintiffs in *Horsehead* asserted that 40 C.F.R. Section 266.112 could not be expanded to include residues derived from burning hazardous waste fuels. The court held that BIFs that burn fuel consisting of coal, oil and other fossil fuels, and cement kiln dust are subject to RCRA regulation. The court accepted in part EPA's position and found that in some circumstances when the BIF burns fuels that contain hazardous waste, the resultant cement kiln dust and combustion residues can be considered hazardous waste. This opinion relies on the fact that the EPA has authority to regulate the burning of hazardous waste because it is considered "treatment" for RCRA purposes. The residue is then considered hazardous waste as it was "derived from" hazardous waste treatment, unless it can be shown otherwise.

---

[43]6 F.3d 1332 (9th Cir. 1993).

[44]1993 W.L. 426,029 (EPA).

[45]305 U.S. App. D.C. 35, 16 F.3d 1246, 62 U.S.L.W. 2547, 3 P.E.R.C. 1073, 24 Envtl. L. Rep. 20,563 (1994), *cert. denied*, (U.S.) 130 L. Ed. 2d 27, 115 S. Ct. 72, 39 Envtl. L. Rep. 1608 (1994).

Chapter 10: Standards for Containers, Tanks, Incinerators, Boilers, and Furnaces   249

To demonstrate that the residues in a BIF are not a RCRA hazardous waste requires a showing of low hazard or that the residues ("not significantly affected" test) from the waste fuel are sufficiently similar to normal residues. This determination does not mean that the storage units that contain waste fuel are exempt from RCRA obligations.

E. Miscellaneous Regulations

Requirements for the direct transfer of hazardous wastes into a furnace are set forth in 40 C.F.R. Section 266.111. The provision forbids transfer of hazardous wastes from open-top containers into a boiler or furnace. The equipment used to transfer the waste must always be closed except when necessary to transfer the waste. Finally, the owner or operator must transfer waste to a boiler or furnace in a manner that does not cause extreme heat or explosions; produce toxic mists, dust, or fumes; damage the container or transfer equipment; or damage the boiler's or furnace's capability of meeting applicable performance standards. The owner or operator must also avoid spillage of any waste.

The equipment used to transfer the hazardous wastes must be equipped with secondary containment. If the equipment lacks secondary containment, the owner or operator must secure a registered engineer's certification that the design and structural integrity of the equipment are sufficient.

The owner or operator must inspect the equipment used to transfer hazardous waste into the furnace or boiler each hour that the equipment is used. Specifically, the owner or operator must inspect the overfill spill equipment, aboveground portions of direct transfer equipment, data gathered from monitoring and leak detection equipment, and cathodic protection systems. The owner or operator must retain records of the inspections for at least three years.

VI. Conclusion

The RCRA regulation of tanks and containers is far more settled than the regulations associated with incinerators, boilers, and industrial furnaces. As to each of these units, the regulatory concerns are the same. The regulations in each instance focus on the capability to contain a release, prevent emissions, ensure proper closure, maintain continuous inspections, and avoid chemical reactions. In the case of incinerators, boilers, and industrial furnaces, the regulatory scheme is changing and expanding to address public concerns while assessing the potential risks associated with such equipment and encouraging source reduction so as to limit their use.

TABLE 10-1
Documentation Requirements for Existing and New Facilities with Newly Regulated BIFs

Documentation	Existing Facilities					New Facility
	Not Previously Subject to Interim Status or Permit Requirements With BIF Subject to RCRA Regulations for First Time	Interim Status RCRA Facility[a] With Newly Regulated BIF	Permitted RCRA Facility[b] With Newly Regulated BIF	Facility With Permitted and Interim Status RCRA Units[c] on Site and With Newly Regulated BIF	Facility With BIF Unit Under RCRA Incinerator Standards	
3010 Notification (EPA Form 8700-12)	Submit to EPA by May 22, 1991, if facility was handling hazardous waste fuel on February 21, 1991, if not previously submitted	Should have been submitted to EPA before initiation of hazardous waste activity	Should have been submitted to EPA before initiation of hazardous waste activity	Should have been submitted to EPA before initiation of hazardous waste activity	Should have been submitted to EPA before initiation of hazardous waste activity	Not applicable[d]
Part A Permit Application (EPA Form 8700-23)	Submit to EPA by August 21, 1991	Submit revised Part A to EPA by August 21, 1991	Submit Class 1 modification (e.g., could be a revised Part A) to EPA by August 21, 1991	Submit revised Part A or Class 1 modification to EPA by August 21, 1991	If BIF was operating under interim status incinerator standards and/or if BIF not allowed by EPA to continue permit review process, submit revised Part A to EPA by August 21, 1991	Submit to EPA as part of RCRA permit application
Precompliance Certification	Submit to EPA by August 21, 1991	Submit to EPA by August 21, 1991	Submit to EPA by August 21, 1991	Submit to EPA by August 21, 1991	If BIF was operating under interim status incinerator standards and/or if BIF not allowed by EPA to continue permit review process, submit to EPA by August 21, 1991	Not applicable
Compliance Certification	Submit to EPA by August 21, 1992 or as extended	Submit to EPA by August 21, 1992 or as extended	Submit to EPA by August 21, 1992 or as extended, unless permit modification issued by that date	Submit to EPA by August 21, 1992 or as extended, unless permit modification issued by that date	If BIF was operating under interim status incinerator standards and/or if BIF not allowed by EPA to continue permit review process, submit to EPA by August 21, 1992 or as extended	Not applicable

[a] Facility has interim status units that are not BIFs (e.g., storage tanks, thermal treatment units).
[b] Facility has permitted units that are not BIFs (e.g., storage tanks, thermal treatment units).
[c] Facility has interim status and permitted units on site that are not BIFs (e.g., storage tanks, thermal treatment units).
[d] Facility is still required to file for an EPA identification number.

250

APPENDIX

TABLE 10-1 (Continued)
Documentation Requirements for Existing and New Facilities with Newly Regulated BIFs

Documentation	Existing Facilities					New Facility
	Not Previously Subject to Interim Status or Permit Requirements With BIF Subject to RCRA Regulations for First Time	Interim Status RCRA Facility[a] With Newly Regulated BIF	Permitted RCRA Facility[b] With Newly Regulated BIF	Facility With Permitted and Interim Status RCRA Units[c] on Site and With Newly Regulated BIF	Facility With BIF Unit Under RCRA Incinerator Standards	
Part B Permit Application	When requested by EPA, submit by date set (which will be at least 6 months after request)	When requested by EPA, submit by date set (which will be at least 6 months after request)	Submit Class 3 modification to EPA by February 17, 1992	If revised Part A submitted on August 21, 1991, submit Part B by date set by Agency (which will be at least 6 months after EPA request); if Class 1 modification submitted by August 21, 1991, submit Class 3 modification to EPA by February 17, 1992	If revised Part A was submitted on August 21, 1991, submit Part B by date set by Agency (which will be at least 6 months after EPA request); if facility in process of obtaining incinerator permit, continue process if EPA allows; if facility operates under incinerator permit, continue operation until permit is reopened or expires, then submit BIF permit application	Submit to EPA at least 180 days before physical construction expected to begin
Public Notification by Applicant of Request for Permit modification Published in Local Newspaper	Not applicable	Not applicable	Not applicable for Class 1 modification; publish within 7 days before or after submittal of Class 3 modification	Not applicable unless facility submits Class 3 modification in which case within 7 days before or after submittal of Class 3 modification	Not applicable	Not applicable

[a] Facility has interim status units that are not BIFs (e.g., storage tanks, thermal treatment units).
[b] Facility has permitted units that are not BIFs (e.g., storage tanks, thermal treatment units).
[c] Facility has interim status and permitted units on site that are not BIFs (e.g., storage tanks, thermal treatment units).
[d] Facility is still required to file for an EPA identification number.

TABLE 10-2
Contents of a Trial Burn Plan

Trial Burn Plan
Detailed engineering description of the boiler or industrial furnace: • Manufacturer's name, model number. • Type. • Maximum design capacity. • Description of the feed system for the hazardous waste, fuel, and other feedstocks. • Capacity of hazardous waste feed systems. • Description of automatic waste feed cutoff system(s). • Description of stack gas monitoring and any pollution control monitoring systems.
Description of each feed stream and waste that will be burned during the trial burn and a discussion of how they represent the worst-case conditions for the BIF: • Heating value. • Source, composition, and chemical analysis if possible. • Levels of antimony, arsenic, barium, beryllium, cadmium, chromium, lead, mercury, silver, thallium, total chlorine/chloride, and ash. • Viscosity or description of physical form. • Identification of organics pursuant to 40 CFR Part 261, Appendix VIII, testing for hazardous constituents present in the feed stream.

An approximate quantification of 40 CFR Part 261, Appendix VIII hazardous constituents in the hazardous waste.
• Description of blending procedures, if applicable, prior to firing.
• Operating conditions during the trial burn, a discussion of how they represent the worst-case conditions for the BIF, proposed permit operating conditions, and anticipated results from these conditions.
• Description of the air pollution control system, its operating conditions, and a discussion of how the test conditions represent the worst-case conditions for the BIF.
• Test protocol:
  • Operating conditions for emission control equipment.
  • Sampling and monitoring procedures, equipment, frequency, analytical procedures, and proof they will satisfy the requirements of the tests.
  • Quality assurance/quality control (QA/QC) plan.
  • Test schedule.
  • Shutdown procedures in the event of equipment malfunction, including hazardous waste feed cutoffs and emissions controls.

Identification of ranges of hazardous waste feed, feed rates of other fuels and feedstocks, and other parameters affecting the ability of the BIF to meet emissions standards. • Other necessary information.

Taken from EPA, Technical Implementation Document for EPA's Boiler and Industrial Furnace Regulations, PB92-154 947, March 1992.

**Operating Parameters For Which Limits Are Established
During Precompliance, Compliance, and Permit Periods**

Parameter	Operating Limits		
	Interim Status		Permit[a]
	Precompliance	Compliance	
Total feed rate of hazardous waste	✓	✓	✓
Total feed rate of pumpable hazardous waste[b]	✓	✓	✓
Feed rate of each of the 10 BIF-regulated metals in:			
- Total feed streams	✓	✓	✓
- Total hazardous waste feed streams[c,k]	✓	✓	✓
- Total pumpable hazardous waste feed stream[d,k]	✓	✓	✓
Total feed rate of chlorine and chloride in total feed streams	✓	✓	✓
Total feed rate of ash in total feed streams[e]	✓	✓	✓
Maximum production rate when producing normal product	✓	✓	✓
CO concentration in stack gas		✓	✓
HC concentration in stack gas, if necessary[f]		✓	✓
Maximum combustion chamber temperature[b]		✓	✓
Maximum flue gas temperature entering the PM control device[b]		✓	✓
Various APCS-specific operating parameters[g,h]		✓	✓
Minimum production rate when producing normal product, if applicable			✓
Minimum combustion gas temperature[i]			✓
Maximum emission rate for each metal[j]			✓
Maximum emission rate for HCl and for Cl_2[j]			✓
Feed rate of other fuels			✓
Appropriate controls of the hazardous waste firing system			✓
Appropriate indicator of combustion gas velocity			✓
Allowable variation in boiler and industrial furnace system design or operating procedures			✓
Other operating requirements as are necessary to ensure that DRE is met			✓

[a]See §266.102(e) for complete listing and description of permit operating requirements.
[b]Not applicable if complying with Tier I or adjusted Tier I metals feed rate screening limits.
[c]Not applicable during compliance or permit period if complying with Tier I or adjusted Tier I metals feed rate screening limits.
[d]Not applicable during precompliance or permit period if complying with Tier I or adjusted Tier I metals feed rate screening limits.
[e]Not applicable for cement and light-weight aggregate kilns.
[f]HC limit necessary if operating under Tier II controls for PICs or if feeding waste at locations other than the hot end.
[g]Parameters are specified in §266.103(c)(2)(ix-xiii).
[h]Limits not applicable if complying with Tier I or adjusted Tier I for metals and total chlorine and chloride.
[i]During compliance, minimum combustion chamber need only be maintained following a waste feed cutoff, for the duration that the waste remains in the chamber.
[j]Not applicable if complying with Tier I or adjusted Tier I total chloride and chlorine feed rate screening limits.
[k]The final BIF Rule specifies that facilities complying with Tier I or adjusted Tier I metals feed rate screening limits must establish limits for these parameters during interim status (precompliance or compliance, as noted). EPA is considering amending the rule to rescind the requirements for facilities complying with Tier I or adjusted Tier I metals feed rate screening limits to establish limits on these parameters.

Taken from U.S. EPA Publication: Technical Implementation Document for EPA's Boiler and Industrial Furnace Regulations

CHAPTER 11

Land Disposal Facilities

MICHAEL D. MONTGOMERY AND ROBERT F. WILKINSON

I. Introduction

The term "land disposal," as defined in RCRA Section 3004(k), includes any placement of hazardous waste in a landfill, surface impoundment, waste pile, injection well, land treatment facility, salt dome formation, salt bed formation, or underground mine or cave. In 1984, the Congress imposed minimum technology requirements on land disposal units as part of the Hazardous and Solid Waste Amendments of 1984.

Regulations defining unit-specific standards for four of these types of units—landfills, surface impoundments, waste piles, and land treatment units—have been promulgated and are included in Subparts K through N of 40 C.F.R. Parts 264 and 265. Any permitted land disposal unit that is not included in one of these categories is required to meet the performance-based standards defined under Subpart X, Miscellaneous Units.[1] These regulations include standards for design, construction, operation, and closure of the land disposal unit. Land disposal units must also comply with the general facility standards in 40 C.F.R. 264/265 Subparts A–H.

---

[1] 40 C.F.R. pt. 264, subpt. X. 40 C.F.R. Part 265, Subpart R addresses interim status injection wells. While interim status injection wells are subject to the general facility standards of 40 C.F.R. § 265, Subparts A–F, injection wells are primarily regulated under the Safe Drinking Water Act.

II. Minimum Technological Requirements

Land disposal units pose a particular threat of contaminating soil and groundwater. Recognizing this threat, Congress amended Section 3004 of RCRA to impose certain minimum technological requirements on surface impoundments and landfills. Surface impoundments and landfills are required, unless they qualify for an exemption, to have two or more liners with a leachate collection system and groundwater monitoring. The minimum technological requirements apply to units that first received waste after November 8, 1984.[2] Furthermore, surface impoundments that were operating under interim status on November 8, 1984, had four years from that date to either meet the minimum technology requirements or cease receiving waste, which would have triggered the obligation to commence closure.[3]

There are some statutory exemptions to the minimum technological requirements. The minimum technological requirements will not apply if the owner or operator of a surface impoundment or landfill demonstrates to the permitting authority that "alternative design and operating practices, together with location characteristics, will prevent the migration of any hazardous constituents into the groundwater or surface water at least as effectively as [the minimum technological requirements]."[4] A similar exemption for interim status surface impoundments appears at 42 U.S.C. Section 6925(j)(4).[5]

Additionally, the statute provides for three different exemptions from the minimum technological requirements for surface impoundments. The first exemption applies to a surface impoundment that is (1) equipped with one liner (for which there is no evidence that it is leaking); (2) located more than one-quarter mile from an underground source of drinking water; and (3) implementing a groundwater-monitoring program.[6] The second exemption applies to impoundments used for aggressive biological treatment facilities as part of a permitted Clean Water Act system.[7] The third exemption applies to impoundments that can demonstrate to the EPA Regional Administrator's satisfaction that the impoundment is located, designed, and operated so as to assure that there will be no migration of any hazardous constituents into groundwater or surface water. If an impoundment that qualifies for one of these three minimum

---

[2]42 U.S.C. § 6924(o)(1).
[3]*Id.* § 6925(j)(1).
[4]*Id.* § 6924(o)(2). *See also* 40 C.F.R. § 264.221(d).
[5]*See also* 40 C.F.R. § 265.221(c).
[6]42 U.S.C. § 6925(j)(2).
[7]*Id.* § 6925(j)(3).

technology requirement exemptions no longer meets the criteria for exemption due to a change in condition (including the existence of a leak), then the impoundment does not have four years to meet the minimum technological requirements, as it would if it were newly regulated by RCRA. Instead, it has only two years after discovery of the change in condition (or within three years in the case of a surface impoundment subject to the National Pollutant Discharge Elimination System [NPDES] exemption) to meet the minimum technology requirements or cease accepting hazardous waste.[8]

An exemption from the double liner requirement is also available for a monofill that contains only waste from foundry emission controls or metal casting molding sand, provided such wastes are not deemed to be hazardous for any reason other than the toxicity characteristics D004 through D017.[9] The monofill must be equipped with at least one liner. The regulations require that, if this liner is not designed to prevent waste from migrating into the liner, then, upon closure, the liner and all waste residues must be removed or decontaminated.[10] If all contaminated soil is not removed or decontaminated, the owner or operator must comply with all applicable postclosure requirements, including groundwater monitoring and corrective action.[11] In addition, the monofill must be located at least one-quarter mile away from an underground source of drinking water and must comply with groundwater-monitoring requirements.[12]

III. Groundwater Monitoring

Subpart F of the RCRA regulations[13] regulates groundwater monitoring of regulated land-based units that manage hazardous waste (for instance, surface impoundments, landfills, land treatment units) at permitted and interim status facilities. The greatest threat to the environment that may be posed by the use of land-based units for hazardous waste management is the potential for hazardous waste to be released from the unit into the groundwater. The permitted groundwater-monitoring program is more elaborate and facility-specific than the groundwater-monitoring program for interim status facilities. The requirements of the monitoring program for permitted units are specified in permit conditions and are

---

[8]*Id.* § 6925(j)(6)(B).

[9]*Id.* § 6924(o)(3).

[10]40 C.F.R. §§ 264.221(e)(2)(i)(A), 264.302(e)(2)(i)(A).

[11]*Id.*

[12]*Id.* §§ 264.221(e)(2)(i)(B)–(C), 264.302(e)(2)(i)(B)–(C).

[13]*Id.* §§ 264.90–.101, 265.90–.94

258   THE RCRA PRACTICE MANUAL

often based on the groundwater-monitoring data gathered for the facility when the facility had interim status. The major difference between the interim status and the permitted groundwater-monitoring program is that, unlike the interim status groundwater-monitoring regulations, the permitted groundwater-monitoring program specifically provides for corrective action if a release of hazardous waste from a regulated unit is detected.

A. Interim Status Groundwater Monitoring

The interim status groundwater-monitoring program[14] applies to land-based hazardous waste management units, unless the unit qualifies for one of the two exemptions from the requirement to perform groundwater monitoring. Neither exemption requires the approval of EPA's Regional Administrator, but instead relies on certification by a geologist, geotechnical engineer, or "qualified professional" that the facility meets the regulatory requirements for an exemption from monitoring.

The first exemption applies if the owner can demonstrate that there is a low potential for migration of hazardous waste or constituents via the uppermost aquifer to a water well supply or to surface water.[15] This written demonstration must be kept at the facility and be based on a consideration of a number of specified factors related to the facility's geology.

The second exemption applies to surface impoundments that only manage hazardous waste that is hazardous solely due to the corrosivity characteristic.[16] No groundwater monitoring is required for such a facility if a "qualified professional" can certify that, based on the characteristics of the waste, the waste will no longer be corrosive before it could migrate out of the impoundment.

1. General Standards

The general standards for an interim status groundwater-monitoring system are found at 40 C.F.R. Section 265.91. The standards require that such a system consist of at least one well installed hydraulically upgradient of the waste management area and at least three downgradient wells at the limit of the waste management area. The actual number, locations, and depths of the wells must be sufficient to provide groundwater samples that are representative of the background groundwater quality in the uppermost aquifer not affected by the facility and ensure

---

[14]*Id.* §§ 265.90–.94.
[15]*Id.* § 265.90(c).
[16]*Id.* § 265.90(e).

immediate detection of any statistically significant amounts of hazardous waste or constituents migrating from the hazardous waste management unit into the uppermost aquifer.

The owner or operator can place the downgradient wells in an alternative location if the owner or operator can make a written demonstration, certified by a qualified groundwater scientist, that existing physical obstacles prevent monitoring at the limit of the waste management area, that the alternative location is as close to the limit as is practical, and that the alternative location will, as early as possible, detect statistically significant amounts of hazardous waste or constituents migrating from the unit.

If only one hazardous waste management unit is subject to monitoring, the hazardous waste management area is described by the perimeter of the unit. Multiple waste management units can be combined for purposes of monitoring. When multiple units are combined for groundwater-monitoring purposes, the hazardous waste management area is described by the imaginary boundary line that circumscribes the several waste management units.

The regulations also establish technical performance standards for how the wells are to be installed to ensure that the wells both produce adequate groundwater samples and protect the groundwater from being contaminated via the pathway created by an improperly installed well.

2. Sampling and Analysis

The owner or operator must have a written sampling and analysis plan at the facility, pursuant to 40 C.F.R. Section 265.92, that addresses the procedures and techniques for sample collection, sample preservation and shipments, analytical procedure, and chain-of-custody control. EPA has issued a number of technical guidance documents that address these issues.

An interim status groundwater monitoring program needs to analyze groundwater samples for parameters that would characterize the groundwater's suitability as a drinking water supply, parameters that characterize the general quality of the groundwater (chloride, iron, manganese, phenols, sodium, sulfates), and general indicators of groundwater organic and inorganic contamination (pH, specific conductance, total organic carbon, and total organic halogen).

3. Indicator Evaluation Program

During the first year of operation under the indicator groundwater-monitoring program, the owner or operator must establish background concentrations for the prescribed parameters by analyzing the upgradient

260 THE RCRA PRACTICE MANUAL

wells quarterly. Additionally, the owner or operator is required to develop an "outline" of an assessment monitoring program that is a more comprehensive groundwater-monitoring program than the indicator evaluation program required by the regulations in the first year of operation.[17] The more comprehensive assessment program must be able to determine whether hazardous waste or constituents have been released, the rate and extent of migration, and the concentration of any contaminants. If the owner or operator knows or believes that the indicator parameters will show a statistically significant increase over background, the owner or operator can begin at the assessment monitoring phase by submitting an alternative groundwater-monitoring plan to the EPA Regional Administrator.

After the first year, all wells must be sampled for the groundwater quality parameters at least annually and the groundwater contamination indicators at least semiannually.[18] When groundwater samples are taken, the elevation of the groundwater surface must be taken to determine the groundwater flow direction. The owner or operator must evaluate data on groundwater surface evaluation at least annually, to ensure that the wells are properly located to detect a release.[19] If the wells are not properly located, the system must be modified immediately to bring the facility into compliance.[20]

The regulations prescribe the analysis that must be used to determine whether there has been a statistically significant increase in the concentration of the indicator parameters in the downgradient wells when compared with the upgradient well that represents the background concentration.[21] If analysis confirms that the significant increase was not the result of laboratory error, then within seven days of confirmation, the owner or operator must provide the EPA Regional Administrator with written notice that the facility may be affecting groundwater quality. This begins the transition to an assessment groundwater-monitoring program.[22]

4. Assessment Program

Within 15 days of the notification that the facility may be affecting groundwater quality, the owner or owner must develop and submit to the Regional Administrator a groundwater assessment plan, based on

---

[17]*Id.* § 265.93(a).
[18]*Id.* § 265.92(d).
[19]*Id.* § 265.92(e).
[20]*Id.* § 265.93(f).
[21]*Id.* § 265.93(b).
[22]*Id.* § 265.93(d).

the aforementioned outline. This groundwater assessment plan for the facility must be certified by a qualified geologist or geotechnical engineer. It must specify the number, location, and depth of wells; sampling and analytical methods; evaluation procedures; and a schedule for implementation of the assessment program.[23]

The first determination of the rate and extent of migration and concentration of hazardous waste or constituents must be made as soon as technically feasible. Within 15 days of the determination, a written report must be submitted to the EPA Regional Administrator, providing an assessment of groundwater quality. If the assessment program determines that there has been no release, then the owner or operator may reinstate the indicator evaluation program. If the owner or operator reinstates the indicator evaluation program, he or she must notify the Regional Administrator of this within 15 days of this determination. If assessment monitoring confirms a release, then the assessment monitoring must continue to be made on a quarterly basis until final closure of the facility.[24]

5. Record Keeping and Reporting

If an interim status facility is not performing assessment monitoring of a release, then it must keep records of analyses and surface elevations throughout the active life of the facility and throughout the postclosure care period, where appropriate.[25] During the first year, the facility must report to the EPA Regional Administrator the drinking water parameter concentrations within 15 days of the completion of quarterly analysis. After the first year, by March 1 of each year, the owner or operator must report the groundwater quality parameter concentrations and statistical evaluation of the data. Similarly, results of evaluations of surface elevations and any necessary response to an evaluation of that data must be reported annually, no later than March 1.

If the facility is doing assessment monitoring, it also must keep analyses and evaluations throughout the active life of the facility and during any postclosure care period. Annually, by no later than March 1 of the following calendar year, the facility must report to the Regional Administrator the results of the groundwater quality assessment, which would include the calculated or measured rate or migration of hazardous waste or constituents.[26]

---

[23]*Id.*
[24]*Id.* § 265.93(e).
[25]*Id.* § 265.94.
[26]*Id.* § 265.94(b).

B. Permitted Groundwater Monitoring

RCRA permitted facilities are subject to a three-phase program for detecting, characterizing, and responding to releases to the uppermost aquifer from regulated hazardous waste management units.[27] The specifics of a permitted facility's groundwater-monitoring program are found in the conditions of the facility's permit. Thus, changes in the groundwater-monitoring program ordinarily require permit modifications.

The regulations provide for five exemptions from the requirement for a groundwater-monitoring system.[28] The first exemption applies to a facility or operation that is exempted from the substantive requirements of Part 264 and the permit requirements. The second exemption applies to a unit that the EPA Regional Administrator finds meets the following criteria:

- it is an engineered structure;
- it does not receive or contain liquid waste or free liquids;
- it is designed and operated to exclude liquids;
- both an inner and an outer layer of containment enclose the waste;
- a leak detection system is built into each containment layer;
- the owner or operator will provide continuing operation and maintenance of the leak detection system; and
- to a reasonable degree of certainty, hazardous constituents will not migrate beyond the outer containment layer before the end of the postclosure period.

The third exemption applies if the Regional Administrator finds that there is no potential for migration of liquid from the unit to the uppermost aquifer during the active life of the unit and during the postclosure period. This exemption requires a demonstration certified by a qualified geologist or geotechnical engineer and must be based on a prediction that uses assumptions that maximize the rate of liquid migration. The fourth exemption applies to a waste pile that meets the standards of 40 C.F.R. Section 264.250(c), which basically means it is a waste pile of dry materials in a building. Such a waste pile might be reclassified as a containment building and not be subject to the groundwater monitoring requirements. Lastly, there is an exemption from performing groundwater monitoring during the postclosure period that applies if the EPA Regional Administrator finds that a land treatment facility's treatment

---

[27]*Id.* pt. 264, subpart F.
[28]*Id.* § 264.90(b).

Chapter 11: Land Disposal Facilities 263

zone, in accordance with the requirements applicable to land treatment facilities, does not contain levels of hazardous constituents that are above background levels by an amount that is statistically significant, and if the unsaturated-zone-monitoring program has not shown a statistically significant increase in hazardous constituents below the treatment zone during the operating life of the unit. Ordinarily, the groundwater-monitoring requirements will continue into the postclosure care period if the unit is subject to postclosure care.[29] Postclosure groundwater monitoring can be avoided if all waste, waste residues, contaminated containment system components, and contaminated subsoils are removed or decontaminated at closure; this means the unit has been "clean closed," so there is no reason to continue groundwater monitoring.[30] A common requirement that many regulatory agencies impose on facilities, even though not provided for in the RCRA regulations, is that they must continue groundwater monitoring for a limited period of time (for example, three to five years) to verify that the closure was in fact clean.

The first phase of the Subpart F groundwater-monitoring requirements is detection monitoring.[31] It requires that the owner or operator monitor groundwater at the downgradient edge of the waste management boundary for indicator parameters or constituents that indicate the likelihood of a release of hazardous waste or constituents from the regulated unit. If a release is detected, the owner or operator must test for the presence of all Appendix IX constituents. A groundwater protection standard is established for every Appendix IX constituent detected at above background levels.

Confirmation of a release triggers the second, compliance-monitoring, phase of the program. During the compliance-monitoring phase, the owner or operator is required to perform additional investigation to characterize the nature and extent of contamination.[32] Compliance monitoring determines whether the release discovered during detection monitoring exceeds the groundwater protection standard, which means that the release may harm the environment and steps must be taken to address the release.

In the third and final stage, corrective action, the owner or operator is required to remove or treat in place all contaminants present in concentrations above the groundwater protection standard beyond the compliance point.[33]

---

[29]*Id.* § 264.96.
[30]*Id.* § 270.1(c)(5).
[31]*Id.* § 264.98.
[32]*Id.* § 264.99.
[33]*Id.* § 264.100.

Not all permitted facilities begin with the first phase in the permitted groundwater-monitoring program because data submitted with the permit application and obtained during interim status may require that the facility be governed by a later phase of groundwater monitoring.

1. *Groundwater Protection Standards*

The groundwater-monitoring requirements are designed to ensure that measured groundwater parameters are at or below the permit-specified concentration limits (that is, the groundwater protection standard) at the designated point of compliance during the compliance period.[34] The facility permit specifies concentration limits for the particular hazardous constituents that will be used as the facility's groundwater protection standard. These concentration limits will be established based on measurements of background levels of hazardous constituents, the limits established under the Safe Drinking Water Act as drinking water standards for certain groundwater contaminants, or upon a demonstration of the appropriateness of site-specific alternative concentration limits.[35] The point of compliance is where the monitoring wells are to be located. It is a vertical surface located at the hydraulically downgradient limit of the waste management area and extends down into the uppermost aquifer underlying the regulated units.[36] The waste management area is the limit projected in the horizontal plane of the area on which the waste will be placed during the active life in a regulated unit. The waste management area includes the horizontal space taken up by any liner, dike, or other barrier designed to contain waste in a regulated unit. Where the facility contains more than one regulated unit, the waste management area is described by an imaginary line circumscribing the several regulated units.

The compliance period is the number of years equal to the active life of the waste management area, including prepermitting activity and the closure activities.[37] It begins when the owner or operator initiates compliance monitoring. If the owner or operator is engaged in a corrective action program following a compliance period, the compliance period is extended until the owner or operator can demonstrate that the groundwater protection standard has not been exceeded for three consecutive years.

---

[34]*Id.* § 264.92.
[35]*Id.* § 264.94.
[36]*Id.* § 264.95.
[37]*Id.* § 264.96.

Chapter 11: Land Disposal Facilities 265

2. General Standards for Permitted Groundwater-Monitoring Systems

The regulations do not specify the number of wells or their precise locations. Rather, the regulations impose performance standards on what the groundwater-monitoring system must be able to accomplish when the details of the system are incorporated into conditions in the facility's permit.[38] The monitoring system must contain enough wells installed at appropriate locations and depths to yield samples from the upper aquifer that (1) represent the quality of background water that has not been affected by leakage from a regulated unit; (2) represent the quality of groundwater passing the point of compliance; and (3) allow for the detection of contamination when hazardous waste or constituents have migrated from the waste management area. The groundwater-monitoring program must include a groundwater sampling and analysis plan, measurements of groundwater surface elevations, chain-of-custody procedures, and a statistically adequate sampling program to determine background concentrations. The regulations provide for four different types of statistical methods that the owner or operator can choose from, in addition to allowing the owner or operator to propose to the EPA Regional Administrator an alternative statistical method to demonstrate compliance with the groundwater protection standard. The permit will specify when groundwater-monitoring data must be submitted.

Many RCRA facilities use environmental consultants to perform some or all of their RCRA groundwater monitoring. It is advisable to make certain that the consultants have read and understand the facility's permit conditions for groundwater monitoring. Otherwise, consultants might perform the groundwater monitoring and analysis of the data in a manner that does not adhere to the specific requirements of the facility's permit that governs compliance with RCRA. In addition, copies of records associated with the groundwater monitoring required by the permit or regulations must be maintained at the facility, not by the consultant.

3. Detection Monitoring

The first phase of the permitted groundwater-monitoring program[39] measures for the presence of indicator parameters (for example, specific conductance, total organic carbon, or total organic halogen) and waste constituents or reaction products that provide a reliable indication of the presence of hazardous constituents in groundwater. The Regional Administrator will specify the parameters or constituents in the permit, along

---

[38]*Id.* § 264.97.
[39]*Id.* § 264.98.

266 THE RCRA PRACTICE MANUAL

with the frequency of sample collection and what statistical tests will be used to determine whether there is statistically significant evidence of a release from the regulated unit. A sequence of at least four samples from each well (background and compliance wells) must be collected at least semiannually during detection monitoring, with the groundwater flow rate and direction to be determined at least annually. The permit-specified statistical method is used to compare the background data with the compliance point data to determine whether there has been a statistically significant increase that indicates a release. The permit will specify how many days are allowed after data collection to perform the required statistical analysis.

Within seven days of determining that the monitoring data indicate statistically significant evidence of contamination at a compliance point, the owner or operator must notify the EPA Regional Administrator in writing. The notice must include an identification of the constituents or parameters that showed a statistically significant increase. The owner or operator will need to sample all wells immediately to determine whether any wells contain Appendix IX constituents and, if so, to determine the relative concentrations of the constituents. The owner or operator may resample within one month for the Appendix IX compounds found to be present in the earlier sampling. If the results of the second analysis confirm the initial results, then these constituents will form the basis for the second phase of permitted groundwater monitoring—compliance monitoring. If there is no resampling, the initial results are the basis for compliance monitoring.

The owner or operator has 90 days to submit an application for a permit modification to institute a compliance monitoring program. The application must identify the Appendix IX constituents detected, along with any proposed changes to the groundwater-monitoring system, monitoring frequency, sampling and analysis plans, and statistical methods. The application must also state whether the owner or operator intends to apply for alternative concentration limits. Within 180 days, the owner or operator must submit to the EPA Regional Administrator all data necessary to justify an alternative concentration limit and an engineering feasibility plan for a corrective action program. The plan for a corrective action program need not be submitted if the only hazardous constituents detected were the drinking water parameters at concentrations below the drinking water standards, or if the owner or operator has sought alternative concentration levels for the Appendix IX constituents.

The owner or operator may attempt to demonstrate that a source other than the regulated unit is responsible for a statistically significant

Chapter 11: Land Disposal Facilities   267

difference in parameters or constituents at a compliance point, or that the apparently statistically significant number is an artifact caused by an error in sampling, analysis, or statistical evaluation, or is due to natural variation. The owner or operator may make this demonstration in lieu of, or in addition to, submitting a permit modification application. The requirement to submit a permit modification within the 90-day time limit cannot be avoided unless the owner or operator succeeds in demonstrating that the cause of the statistically significant difference is a source other than a release from the regulated unit. Another source may be implicated if, for example, an operating impoundment is located in an area that has closed impoundments and landfills that may contain similar waste materials. Another example would be if certain hazardous constituents are either difficult to analyze accurately or are also found in materials used by the laboratory performing the analysis of the groundwater samples. Within seven days of receiving notice of the statistically significant finding, the owner or operator must notify the Regional Administrator of its intention to demonstrate that the increase in the concentration of a hazardous constituent was due to an alternative source or that the determination is a statistical or analytical error. In addition, within 90 days, the owner or operator must provide a report on the basis for attributing the variance to a source other than the detection of a release from a regulated unit. Also within the 90-day period, the owner or operator must submit a permit modification application to make appropriate changes to the detection monitoring program to prevent incorrectly attributing statistically significant increases of monitoring parameters to the regulated unit.

4. Compliance Monitoring

For a facility subject to compliance monitoring, the permit will specify the list of hazardous constituents and their concentration limits, the compliance point, the compliance period, the sampling and analysis procedures, the statistical procedure, and the frequency of sample collection and statistical analysis.[40] The owner or operator will be required to determine groundwater flow rate and direction at least annually. A sequence of at least four samples from each background and compliance well must be collected semiannually during the compliance period. At least annually, all wells at the compliance point must be analyzed for all Appendix IX constituents to determine whether additional hazardous constituents are present at particular concentrations. If a new constituent appears, the owner or operator can resample within one month and repeat the

---

[40]*Id.* § 264.99.

Appendix IX analysis. If there is a confirmation of the new constituent, a notice of such finding must be made to the Regional Administrator of EPA within seven days. Failure to resample means that notice of the new constituent will be required within seven days of the initial finding. Similarly, if sampling indicates that a concentration limit was exceeded in a compliance well, notice of such must be sent to the Regional Administrator within seven days. A permit modification to establish a corrective action program is due within 180 days. Only 90 days are allowed if an engineering feasibility study has been previously submitted. This permit modification application must provide a detailed description of corrective action that will achieve compliance with the groundwater protection standard, as well as a groundwater monitoring plan that will demonstrate the effectiveness of the corrective action.

As with the detection monitoring program, the owner or operator can demonstrate to the EPA Regional Administrator that the test result in excess of the compliance limit was not properly attributable to a release from a regulated unit. This requires an initial notice to the Regional Administrator within seven days of discovery. Within 90 days, the owner or operator must submit a demonstration of what caused the monitoring variance and a permit modification that will make appropriate changes to avoid a repetition of the incorrect attribution of a statistically significant difference to a release from a regulated unit. If at any time the owner or operator considers that the compliance monitoring program no longer satisfies the requirements of a compliance monitoring program, the owner or operator has 90 days to submit a permit modification to make appropriate revisions to the program.

5. Corrective Action

A corrective action program, pursuant to 40 C.F.R. Section 264.100, will be put in place when necessary to ensure that a regulated unit complies with the groundwater protection standard. The permit will specify a list of constituents, concentrations, compliance points, and the length of the compliance period. The owner or operator will be required to remove hazardous waste constituents or treat them in place so as not to exceed concentration limits. The corrective action must "begin within a reasonable time period after the groundwater protection standard is exceeded."[41] The groundwater-monitoring program during the corrective action period must be able to demonstrate the effectiveness of the corrective action. Corrective action must take place where concentration limits are exceeded between the compliance point and the downgradient

---

[41]*Id.* § 264.100(c).

Chapter 11: Land Disposal Facilities   269

property boundary. Corrective action can also be required of the owner or operator where contamination has migrated beyond the facility boundary, unless the owner or operator can demonstrate an inability to obtain access to neighboring property despite the owner or operator's best efforts to do so. Corrective action must be initiated and completed within a reasonable period of time considering the extent of contamination; it can be terminated once the concentrations are reduced to below the specified limits. If corrective action is being conducted at the end of the compliance period, it must continue as long as necessary to achieve compliance with the groundwater protection standards. Corrective action taken after the compliance period can terminate when three consecutive years of monitoring indicates that levels are within the specified limits. The owner or operator also must provide the Regional Administrator with semiannual reports of the effectiveness of corrective action.

IV. Technical Standards

The RCRA regulations incorporate technical standards for surface impoundments, waste piles, land treatment units, and landfills. The standards include regulations governing applicability, design and operating requirements, monitoring and inspection requirements (except the land treatment subpart), closure and postclosure care requirements, special requirements for ignitable or reactive wastes, special requirements for incompatible wastes, and special requirements for certain listed wastes from nonspecific sources. All or part of the closure requirements, however, can be replaced with alternative requirements set out in an approved closure or postclosure plan or in an enforceable document, where the alternative requirements are protective of human health and the environment and were developed pursuant to corrective action for the unit.[42] In addition, the regulations include specific requirements directed to the specific types of waste units.

A. Surface Impoundments

The permitting standards for surface impoundments are found at 40 C.F.R. Sections 264.220 through 264.232. A surface impoundment is defined as "a natural topographic depression, man-made excavation, or diked area formed primarily of earthen materials . . . which is designed

---

[42]*Id.* §§ 264.110(c), 265.110(d).

270 THE RCRA PRACTICE MANUAL

to hold an accumulation of liquid wastes or wastes containing free liquids."[43] Surface impoundments, commonly referred to as "pits, ponds, or lagoons," are typically used for waste treatment or storage.

As previously discussed, surface impoundments that are not exempted are subject to minimum technological requirements.[44] Two or more liners must be installed with a leachate collection system between such liners for new surface impoundments on which construction commenced after January 29, 1992, each replacement of an existing surface impoundment that is to commence reuse after July 29, 1992, and each lateral extension of an existing surface impoundment unit on which construction commenced after July 29, 1992. In addition, all surface impoundments must be designed, constructed, maintained, and operated to prevent overtopping and must have dikes that are designed, constructed, and maintained so as to prevent massive failure.[45]

The required top liner is to be designed, operated, and constructed in a manner that prevents the migration of any constituent into the liner during the life of the facility (including the postclosure monitoring period). The lower liner must be constructed of two components. The upper component must be constructed to prevent the migration of hazardous constituents into it for the life of the facility (including the postclosure care period). The lower component must be constructed to minimize constituent migration if a breach of the upper component occurs and must be constructed of recompacted soil in a layer that is three feet thick with a hydraulic conductivity rate of no more than 10^{-7} centimeter per second.

Surface impoundments also require a leachate collection system between the two liners. Such system is also to act as a leak detection system that is capable of detecting, collecting, and removing leaks of hazardous constituents at the earliest predictable time. The permit will specify an action leakage rate[46] that, if exceeded, will trigger a response action pursuant to a previously approved response action plan.[47] The action leakage rate is the maximum flow rate that the leak detection system can remove without the fluid head on the bottom liner exceeding one foot including an adequate margin of safety.

The permitting authority may approve alternative design or operating practices to the liner and leachate collection system if the owner or operator is able to demonstrate that alternative design and operating

---

[43]*Id.* § 260.10.
[44]*Id.* § 264.221.
[45]*Id.* § 264.221(g)–(h).
[46]*Id.* § 264.222.
[47]*Id.* § 264.223.

practices and the location of the surface impoundment will prevent the migration of hazardous constituents into the groundwater or surface water and will allow the detection of leaks through the top liner as effectively.[48]

In the Contaminated Debris Rule issued in August 1992, EPA addressed the question of how long an impoundment that does not meet the minimum technology requirements can continue to manage hazardous waste subject to a land disposal restriction.[49] This EPA interpretation reconciles the apparent conflict between the four-year time limit Congress provided for impoundments newly brought into RCRA to upgrade to meet the minimum technology standards (or two years for an impoundment that lost its exemption) and the land disposal restriction requirement that only impoundments that meet the minimum technology requirements can receive hazardous waste subject to a national capacity variance from a land disposal restriction. EPA also addressed the application of the statutory requirement that surface impoundments receiving hazardous wastes that do not meet the land disposal restriction standards must be dredged annually.[50] EPA concluded that "continued use of the impoundment would be allowed during the four-year retrofit/closure period ... use of the impoundment during that time would not be disrupted by a dredging requirement, and the impoundment would be allowed to close with wastes in place."[51]

Liner and cover systems must be inspected during construction for uniformity, damage, and imperfections. Immediately after installation, synthetic liners and covers must be inspected for tight seams and joints and the absence of tears, punctures, and blisters. Soil-based and admixed liner and cover systems must be inspected immediately after installation for imperfections that could cause an increase in the permeability of the liner or cover.[52]

Operation of the surface impoundment must comply with the applicable requirements of the air emission standards in 40 CFR 264 Subparts BB and CC.[53] Additionally, ignitable or reactive wastes may not be placed in a surface impoundment unless the Land Disposal Restrictions are complied with and (1) the waste is treated before placement in the impoundment so that the residue is no longer ignitable or reactive and general requirements for reactive or ignitable wastes are met; (2) the

---

[48]*Id.* § 264.221(d).
[49]57 Fed. Reg. 37,194, 37,218–21 (1992).
[50]42 U.S.C. § 6925(j)(11)(B).
[51]57 Fed. Reg. 37,221.
[52]40 C.F.R. § 264.226.
[53]*Id.* § 264.232.

272 THE RCRA PRACTICE MANUAL

waste is protected from any material or condition that would cause it to ignite or react; or (3) the impoundment is used solely for emergencies.[54] Incompatible wastes may not be placed together in an impoundment unless the general requirements for incompatible waste are met.[55]

Hazardous wastes bearing the waste codes F020, F021, F022, F023, F026, and F027 may not be placed in a surface impoundment without the approval of the permitting authority, taking into account the characteristics of the waste (including migration potential through soil), the attenuative properties of the surrounding soils or material, the mobilizing properties of material in contact with the wastes, and the effectiveness of treatment, design, or monitoring techniques.[56]

During operation, the surface impoundment must be inspected weekly and after storms for evidence of failure of overtopping control systems; sudden drops in the level of material in the impoundment; and severe erosion or deterioration of the dikes or containment system. Before permit issuance and after any period of more than six months during which the impoundment is not in service, a qualified engineer must certify that the impoundment's dike has structural integrity, will withstand the pressure exerted by the amounts and types of wastes in the impoundment, and will not fail due to scouring or piping. Furthermore, the integrity of the dike cannot depend on any liner system installed during construction of the impoundment.

Whenever the level of material in the impoundment suddenly drops for reasons other than changes in the rates of flow of material into or out of the impoundment, or whenever the dike leaks, the impoundment must be taken out of service.[57] In such instance, the flow of waste into the impoundment must be stopped immediately, the leak must be stopped immediately, and any surface leakage must be contained immediately. The owner or operator must also take any other steps that may be necessary to prevent catastrophic failure, and if the leak cannot be located or stopped, the impoundment must be emptied. Finally, the owner or operator is required to notify the permitting authority in writing within seven days after discovery of the problem. The procedures for taking the surface impoundment out of service must be specified in the facility's contingency plan.

Before a surface impoundment can be returned to service after a failure, the failed portion must be repaired, and if the dike failed, its structural integrity must be recertified. If the impoundment was taken out of

---

[54]*Id.* § 264.229.
[55]*Id.* § 264.230.
[56]*Id.* § 264.231.
[57]*Id.* § 264.227.

Chapter 11: Land Disposal Facilities 273

service because of a sudden drop in level, any existing portion of the impoundment that was not required to be lined must be lined with a single liner meeting the criteria described earlier. Also, for any other portion, the liner system must be repaired and certified by a qualified engineer as meeting the design specifications appearing in the permit. If a surface impoundment is not returned to service, it must be closed in accordance with the closure requirements.

Upon closure of a surface impoundment, the owner or operator may either close the impoundment as a landfill with waste residues in place or clean close the impoundment by removing all waste residues, contaminated containment system components, and contaminated structures and equipment.[58] Any material removed during closure may need to be managed as hazardous waste, recognizing that the land disposal restrictions may apply even if the residue is no longer a characteristic hazardous waste. To close with material in place, the owner or operator must (1) eliminate free liquids by removing liquid wastes or solidifying the waste; (2) stabilize the waste sufficiently to support the final cover; and (3) cover the impoundment so as to minimize the movement of liquids through the impoundment, promote drainage, minimize erosion of the cover, accommodate settling and subsidence, and function with minimal maintenance. The cover must have a permeability rate not greater than that of the bottom liner system or the natural subsoils. In addition, if waste residues or contaminated materials are to be left in place, the owner or operator must comply with the postclosure requirements discussed in Chapter 9 of this book.

If an impoundment that was subject to the standard for a single liner failed to comply with that standard, then the closure plan for the impoundment must include a plan for closure by removing wastes and waste residues, and a plan for closing in place any contaminated soils that cannot be practicably removed at closure. In addition, a contingent postclosure plan must be developed in the event that not all contaminated soils can be practicably removed at closure. In such case, the closure and postclosure care cost estimates must include the costs of the contingent closure plan and the contingent postclosure plan, but these estimates need not include the cost of closure by removal.

Ignitable or reactive wastes may not be placed in a surface impoundment unless the owner or operator complies with the Land Disposal Restrictions and (1) treats the waste before placement in the impoundment so that the residue is no longer ignitable or reactive and general requirements for reactive or ignitable wastes are met; (2) protects

---

[58]*Id.* § 264.228.

the waste from any material or condition that would cause it to ignite or react; or (3) uses the impoundment solely for emergencies.[59] Incompatible wastes may not be placed together in an impoundment unless the general requirements for incompatible waste are met.[60]

Hazardous wastes bearing the waste codes F020, F021, F022, F023, F026, and F027 may not be placed in a surface impoundment without the approval of the permitting authority. That approval must take into account the characteristics of the waste (including migration potential through soil), the attenuative properties of the surrounding soils or material, the mobilizing properties of material in contact with the wastes, and the effectiveness of treatment, design, or monitoring techniques.[61]

Finally, operation of the surface impoundment must also comply with the applicable requirements of the air emission standards in 40 C.F.R. 264 Subparts BB and CC.[62]

The interim status standards for surface impoundments are found at 40 C.F.R. Sections 265.220 through 265.231. A surface impoundment that is subject to the interim status standards must meet the standard for a double liner and leachate collection system with respect to any new unit on which construction commences after January 29, 1992, replacement of an existing unit that is to commence reuse after July 29, 1992, or lateral extension of an existing unit on which construction commences after July 29, 1992. The permitting authority must be given 60 days' notice of the use of such new, replacement, or extended unit, and a Part B permit application must be filed within six months of the the permitting authority's receipt of that notice. If an owner or operator installs a liner and leachate collection system in good-faith compliance with the interim status standards, the permitting authority will be precluded from requiring a different liner and leachate collection system when the first permit is issued unless it has reason to believe that the liner is leaking.[63]

Interim status impoundments must be operated with enough freeboard to prevent overtopping by overfilling, wave action, or a storm. The amount of freeboard must be at least two feet unless a qualified engineer certifies that alternative design features or operating plans will prevent overtopping the dike. The dikes must also have some protective cover to minimize wind and water erosion.

---

[59]*Id.* § 264.229.
[60]*Id.* § 264.230.
[61]*Id.* § 264.231.
[62]*Id.* § 264.232.
[63]*Id.* § 265.221.

Chapter 11: Land Disposal Facilities   275

Before treating a new hazardous waste in an interim status impound-ment or using a new treatment process, the owner or operator must con-duct waste analyses and trial treatment tests or document that simi-lar waste was treated under similar circumstances to show compliance with the general requirements for reactive, ignitable, and incompatible wastes.[64] The owner or operator of an interim status impoundment must inspect the freeboard level daily and inspect the impoundment weekly for evidence of leaks, deterioration, or failure.[65]

The owner or operator may not place ignitable or reactive wastes in a surface impoundment unless it complies with the Land Disposal Restrictions and (1) treats the waste before placing it in the impound-ment so that the residue is no longer ignitable or reactive and general requirements for reactive or ignitable wastes are met; (2) protects the waste from any material or condition that would cause it to ignite or react; or (3) uses the impoundment solely for emergencies.[66] Incompati-ble wastes may not be placed together in an impoundment unless the general requirements for incompatible waste are met.[67] Finally, operation of the surface impoundment must also comply with the applicable requirements of the air emission standards in 40 C.F.R. 265 Subparts BB and CC.[68]

To close an interim status surface impoundment, the owner or oper-ator must remove or decontaminate all waste residues, contaminated containment system components, contaminated soils, and contaminated structures and equipment, and close the impoundment in compliance with the requirements for closing a landfill. Additionally, free liquids must be eliminated or solidified, and the remaining residues must be stabilized sufficiently to be able to bear the final cover.[69]

B. Waste Piles

The permitting standards for waste piles are found at 40 C.F.R. Sections 264.250 through 264.269. The term "pile" is defined to mean "any non-containerized accumulation of solid, non-flowing hazardous waste that is used for treatment or storage."[70] A waste pile that is located inside a building or other structure is not subject to these technical standards,

---

[64]*Id.* § 265.225.
[65]*Id.* § 265.226.
[66]*Id.* § 265.229.
[67]*Id.* § 265.230.
[68]*Id.* § 265.231.
[69]*Id.* § 265.228.
[70]*Id.* § 260.10.

provided that no liquids are placed on the pile, surface run-on is diverted from the pile, wind dispersal of the pile is controlled by some means other than wetting, and the pile will not generate leachate through decomposition or other reactions.[71] Such a waste pile might be reclassified as a containment building.

A waste pile is required to have a liner (except for that portion existing at the time the pile is first subject to regulation) that is designed, constructed, and installed to prevent the migration of wastes from the pile into soil, groundwater, or surface water. The liner must be constructed of materials that will prevent failure due to pressure gradients, physical contact with the wastes, climatic conditions, stress of installation, and the stress of daily operation. In addition, the liner must be constructed on a foundation that can support the liner and resist pressure from above and below in order to prevent liner failure due to settlement, uplift, or compression. A leachate collection system must be installed above the liner, be operated so that the depth of leachate above the liner does not exceed 30 centimeters (1 foot), be chemically resistant to the waste and leachate, and be strong enough to prevent collapse. The permitting authority may grant an exemption from the liner requirement if the owner or operator can demonstrate that alternative design and operating practices and the location of the pile will prevent the migration of hazardous constituents into the groundwater or surface water.[72]

Any new waste pile on which construction commences after January 29, 1992, each replacement of an existing waste pile unit that is to commence reuse after July 29, 1992, and each lateral extension of a waste pile unit on which construction commences after July 29, 1992, must have two liners with a leachate collection system above and between those liners.[73] The standards for the liners and leachate collection system (including the action leakage rate and response action plan) are similar to the standards for surface impoundments.

The waste pile must have a run-on control system that will prevent rainwater flow onto the pile during peak discharge from a 25-year storm. The pile must also have a runoff management system that can collect and control the volume of water resulting from a 24-hour, 25-year storm. Any tanks or containment systems used to satisfy these requirements must be emptied expeditiously after a storm to assure design capacity of the system. Finally, any pile that contains particulate matter subject to wind dispersal must have a cover or be managed to prevent such dispersal.[74]

---

[71]*Id.* § 264.250.
[72]*Id.* § 264.251(a)–(b).
[73]*Id.* § 264.251(c).
[74]*Id.* § 264.251(g)–(j).

Liner and cover systems must be inspected during construction for uniformity, damage, and imperfections. Immediately after installation, synthetic liners and covers must be inspected for tight seams and joints, as well as the absence of tears, punctures, and blisters. Soil-based and admixed liner and cover systems must be inspected immediately after installation for imperfections that could cause an increase in the permeability of the liner or cover.[75]

During operation, the waste pile must be inspected weekly and after storms for evidence of failure of the run-on and runoff control systems, proper functioning of the wind dispersal control system, and the presence of leachate in and proper operation of the leachate collection system.[76]

The owner or operator may not place ignitable or reactive wastes in a waste pile unless it complies with the Land Disposal Restrictions and (1) treats the waste is treated prior to placement in the pile so that the residue is no longer ignitable or reactive, and general requirements for reactive or ignitable wastes are met; or (2) protects the waste from any material or condition that would cause it to ignite or react.[77] Incompatible wastes may not be placed together in a waste pile unless the general requirements for incompatible waste are met. If incompatible wastes are stored nearby in containers, other piles, open tanks, or surface impoundments, the waste pile must be separated from those other materials by a dike, berm, wall, or other device. Furthermore, if incompatible wastes were previously stored on a waste pile, the base must be decontaminated prior to further use.[78]

Upon closure of a waste pile, the owner or operator must remove or decontaminate all waste residues, contaminated containment system components, contaminated soils, and contaminated structures and equipment. If not all of the contaminated soils can be practicably removed or decontaminated, the owner or operator must close the waste pile in compliance with the closure standards for a landfill.[79]

If a waste pile that was subject to the liner standard failed to comply with that standard, then the closure plan for the pile must include a plan for closure by removing wastes and waste residues and a plan for closing in place any contaminated soils that cannot be practicably removed at closure. In addition, a contingent postclosure plan must be developed in case not all contaminated soils can be practicably removed at closure. In that case, the closure and postclosure care cost estimates must include

---

[75]*Id.* § 264.254.
[76]*Id.*
[77]*Id.* § 264.256.
[78]*Id.* § 264.257.
[79]*Id.* § 264.258.

278 THE RCRA PRACTICE MANUAL

the costs of the contingent closure plan and the contingent postclosure plan, but the estimates need not include the cost of closure by removal.[80]

Hazardous wastes bearing the waste codes F020, F021, F022, F023, F026, and F027 may not be placed in a waste pile without the approval of the permitting authority. The approval must take into account the characteristics of the waste (including migration potential through soil), the attenuative properties of the surrounding soils or material, the mobilizing properties of material in contact with the wastes, and the effectiveness of treatment, design, or monitoring techniques.[81]

The interim status standards for waste piles are found at 40 C.F.R. Sections 265.250 through 265.258. Interim status waste piles may either comply with the following requirements or be managed as landfills.[82] A pile containing waste subject to wind dispersal must be covered or managed to control such dispersal.[83] A representative sample of each waste added to the pile must be analyzed unless the only wastes that are subject to piling are compatible.[84] If leachate from the pile is a hazardous waste, the pile must be placed on an impermeable base, and there must be run-on and runoff protection that meets the permitting standards. Alternatively, the pile must be protected from precipitation and run-on by some other means, and no liquids may be placed on the pile.[85]

The owner or operator may not place ignitable or reactive wastes in a waste pile unless it complies with the Land Disposal Restrictions and (1) addition of the waste to the pile removes the characteristic, and general requirements for reactive or ignitable wastes are met; or (2) the waste is protected from any material or condition that would cause it to ignite or react.[86] Incompatible wastes may not be placed together in a waste pile unless the general requirements for incompatible waste are met. If incompatible wastes are stored nearby in containers, other piles, open tanks, or surface impoundments, the waste pile must be separated from such other materials by a dike, berm, wall, or other device. Furthermore, if incompatible wastes were previously stored on a waste pile, the base must be decontaminated before further use.[87]

Interim status waste piles on which construction commences after January 29, 1992, replacements of existing units that are to commence reuse after July 29, 1992, or lateral extensions of existing units on which

---

[80]*Id.*

[81]*Id.* § 264.259.

[82]*Id.* § 265.250.

[83]*Id.* § 265.251.

[84]*Id.* § 265.252.

[85]*Id.* § 265.253.

[86]*Id.* § 265.256.

[87]*Id.* § 265.257.

construction commences after July 29, 1992, are subject to the same liner and leachate collection system requirements as permitted waste piles.[88]

At closure, the owner or operator must remove or decontaminate all residues, contaminated containment system components, contaminated soils, and contaminated structures and equipment. If not all contaminated soil can be practicably removed, the pile must be closed in compliance with the standards for a landfill.[89]

C. Land Treatment

The permitting standards for land treatment units are found at 40 C.F.R. Sections 264.270 through 264.283. A land treatment facility is "a facility or part of a facility at which hazardous waste is applied onto or incorporated into the soil surface; such facilities are disposal facilities if the waste will remain after closure."[90] A land treatment program must be designed to ensure that hazardous constituents placed in the treatment zone are degraded, transformed, or immobilized within that treatment zone. The treatment zone cannot extend more that five feet below the soil surface, and it must be at least three feet above the seasonal high-water table. The elements of an approved treatment program will be specified in the facility's permit.[91]

Before application of a particular waste, the owner or operator must demonstrate that the hazardous constituents will be degraded, transformed, or immobilized in the treatment zone. In making the demonstration, the owner or operator can rely on field tests (which would require their own permit), laboratory tests, available data, or operating data (if available). Any field or laboratory test used to make the demonstration must adequately simulate the characteristics and operating conditions of the proposed program and be conducted in a manner that is protective of human health and the environment.[92]

The permit will specify operating conditions for the program, including rate and method of waste application, control of soil pH, measures to enhance microbial or chemical reactions, and measures to control the moisture content of the treatment zone. The treatment zone must be designed, constructed, and operated to minimize the runoff of hazardous constituents during the life of the unit. The unit must have a run-on control system that will prevent flow onto the treatment zone during

---

[88]*Id.* §§ 265.254–.255.
[89]*Id.* § 265.258.
[90]*Id.* § 260.10.
[91]*Id.* § 264.270.
[92]*Id.* § 264.272.

280 THE RCRA PRACTICE MANUAL

peak discharge from a 25-year storm. The unit must also have a runoff management system that is capable of collecting and controlling the volume of water resulting from a 24-hour, 25-year storm. Any tanks or containment systems used to satisfy these requirements must be emptied expeditiously after a storm to assure design capacity of the system. Finally, any unit that contains particulate matter subject to wind dispersal must be managed to prevent such dispersal.[93]

Food-chain crops may be grown in the treatment zone only under limited circumstances. The owner or operator must demonstrate that hazardous constituents (other than cadmium) will not be transferred to the food or feed portions and otherwise be ingested by food-chain animals, or will not occur in greater concentrations than in the food portion of such crops grown in untreated soils under similar conditions. Such demonstration can be based on field or greenhouse studies (which would require a permit), available data, or operating data (if available). If cadmium is present in the waste, there are specific limits on the rate of application, depending on the crop grown and on the operating conditions. The specific limitations may be found at 40 C.F.R. Section 264.276(c).

The owner or operator must also implement an unsaturated-zone-monitoring program to determine whether hazardous constituents have migrated out of the treatment zone.[94] The hazardous constituents that the permitting authority determines must be degraded, transformed, or immobilized in the treatment zone must be monitored in the soil and soil pore liquid. The background levels of each hazardous constituent to be monitored must be determined, and monitoring immediately below the treatment zone must be undertaken. The permit will specify the sampling location and frequency.

If the monitoring program demonstrates a statistically significant increase (using procedures specified in the permit) in the level of hazardous constituents below the treatment zone, the owner or operator must notify the permitting authority, in writing, within seven days of determining that there is such an increase. Then, within 90 days, the owner or operator must file an application for a permit modification to modify the operating program to maximize the level of degradation, transformation, or immobilization in the treatment zone. The owner or operator may, in addition to or in place of the permit modification, demonstrate that a source other than the land treatment unit caused the increase or that the increase was caused by an error in sampling, analysis, or evaluation. Making such a demonstration does not relieve the owner or operator of the obligation to make a permit modification unless

---

[93]*Id.* § 264.273.
[94]*Id.* § 264.278.

Chapter 11: Land Disposal Facilities   281

he or she successfully demonstrates that the increase was caused by another source or by an error in sampling, analysis, or evaluation. An owner or operator making the demonstration must also submit a permit application within 90 days of determining the increase in hazardous constituents that modifies the unsaturated-zone-monitoring program at the facility (if appropriate). In any event, the owner or operator must continue the unsaturated-zone-monitoring program.

During closure, the owner or operator must continue all operations necessary to maximize degradation, transformation, or immobilization of hazardous constituents in the treatment zone and continue the runoff and run-on practices described earlier. Also, the wind dispersal, food-chain crop restrictions, and unsaturated-zone-monitoring program must continue. (The soil pore liquid monitoring may be discontinued 90 days after the last application of waste.) Finally, the owner or operator must establish a vegetative cover that requires little maintenance and does not substantially impede the degradation, transformation, or immobilization of hazardous constituents in the treatment zone.[95]

Upon completion of closure, an independent, qualified soil scientist must certify that closure was completed in compliance with the approved closure plan. During postclosure care, all of the operations and systems required during closure must continue. The owner or operator can be relieved of the postclosure care and vegetative cover obligations upon demonstrating that the level of hazardous constituents in the treatment zone does not exceed background levels. Upon making that demonstration, and if the unsaturated-zone-monitoring program indicates that hazardous constituents have not migrated beyond the treatment zone, the owner or operator will not be subject to Subpart F of Part 264.[96]

The owner or operator may not apply ignitable or reactive wastes to the treatment zone unless the Land Disposal Restrictions are complied with and (1) the material is immediately incorporated into the soil so that the mixture no longer exhibits the characteristic and general requirements for reactive or ignitable wastes; or (2) the waste is protected from any material or condition that would cause it to ignite or react.[97] Incompatible wastes may not be placed together in the treatment zone unless the general requirements for incompatible waste are met.[98]

Hazardous wastes bearing the waste codes F020, F021, F022, F023, F026, and F027 may not be placed in a land treatment unit without the approval of the permitting authority. This approval must take into

---

[95]*Id.* § 264.280.
[96]*Id.*
[97]*Id.* § 264.281.
[98]*Id.* § 264.282.

account the characteristics of the waste (including migration potential through soil), the attenuative properties of the surrounding soils or material, the mobilizing properties of material in contact with the wastes, and the effectiveness of treatment, design, or monitoring techniques.[99]

The interim status standards for land treatment units are found at 40 C.F.R. Sections 265.270 through 265.282. Interim status land treatment units must have run-on, runoff, and wind dispersal systems that meet the same standards as permitted units and can apply only wastes capable of being made less hazardous or nonhazardous by degradation, transformation, or immobilization in the soil.[100] Also, the owner or operator must determine the concentration of (1) any substance that exceeds the maximum concentration specified in the toxicity characteristic; (2) any substance that caused the waste to be listed (if so listed); or (3) arsenic, cadmium, lead, and mercury, if food crops are grown.[101] If food crops are grown, the permitting authority must be notified within 60 days after the unit is subject to regulation. To grow food-chain crops, the owner or operator must show that hazardous constituents (other than cadmium) will not be transferred to the food or feed portions or otherwise be ingested by food-chain animals, or will not occur in greater concentrations than in the food portion of such crops grown in untreated soils under similar conditions. If cadmium is present in the waste, additional limitations apply; these may be found at 40 C.F.R. Section 264.276(c).

The owner or operator may not apply ignitable or reactive wastes to the treatment zone unless the Land Disposal Restrictions are complied with and (1) the material is immediately incorporated into the soil so that the mixture no longer exhibits the characteristic and general requirements for reactive or ignitable wastes; or (2) the waste is protected from any material or condition that would cause it to ignite or react.[102] Incompatible wastes may not be placed together in the treatment zone unless the general requirements for incompatible waste are met.[103] Finally, an interim status land treatment unit must comply with unsaturated-zone-monitoring requirements.[104]

Closure and postclosure of an interim status land treatment unit must address control of migration of hazardous waste and hazardous constituents into the groundwater and take into consideration the type

---

[99]*Id.* § 264.283.
[100]*Id.* § 265.272.
[101]*Id.* § 265.273.
[102]*Id.* § 265.281.
[103]*Id.* § 265.282.
[104]*Id.* § 265.278.

Chapter 11: Land Disposal Facilities   283

and amount of hazardous wastes treated in the unit, as well as other location-specific parameters. Consideration must be given to removing contaminated soils, providing a cover, and groundwater monitoring. Additional requirements are found at 40 C.F.R. Section 265.280.

D. Landfills

The permitting standards for landfills are found at 40 C.F.R. Sections 264.300 through 264.317. A landfill is defined as "a disposal facility or part of a facility where hazardous waste is placed in or on land and which is not a pile, a land treatment facility, a surface impoundment, an underground injection well, a salt dome formation, a salt bed formation, an underground mine, or a cave."[105]

As with surface impoundments, landfills are subject to minimum technological requirements. Landfills on which construction commences after January 29, 1992, each replacement of an existing landfill that is to commence reuse after July 29, 1992, and each lateral extension of an existing landfill unit on which construction commences after July 29, 1992, must have two or more liners with a leachate collection system above and between the liners. The standards for the liners and leachate collection system (including the action leakage rate and response action plan) are similar to the standards for surface impoundments.[106]

Landfills that were in operation on November 8, 1984, are required to have installed a single liner for all portions of the landfill except the then-existing portions.[107] The liner must be designed to prevent wastes from migrating into the liner and must be constructed of materials that will prevent failure due to pressure gradients, contact with the waste, climatic conditions, stress of installation, and stress of daily operation. In addition, the liner must be placed on a foundation capable of providing support and preventing failure due to settlement, compression, or uplift. A leachate collection system must be installed above the liner, be operated so that the depth of leachate above the liner does not exceed 30 centimeters (1 foot), be chemically resistant to the waste and leachate, and be strong enough to prevent collapse. The permitting authority may grant an exemption from the liner requirement if the owner or operator can demonstrate that alternative design and operating practices and the location of the landfill will prevent the migration of hazardous constituents into the groundwater or surface water.[108]

---

[105]*Id.* § 260.10.
[106]*Id.* §§ 264.301(c), .302, .304.
[107]*Id.* § 264.301(a).
[108]*Id.* § 264.301(b).

The landfill must have a system to control run-on sufficient to prevent flow onto the active portion of the landfill during peak discharge from a 25-year storm. The landfill must also have a runoff management system that is capable of collecting and controlling the volume of water resulting from a 24-hour, 25-year storm. Any tanks or containment systems used to satisfy these requirements must be emptied expeditiously after a storm to assure design capacity of the system. Finally, any landfill that contains particulate matter subject to wind dispersal must have a cover or be managed to prevent such dispersal.[109]

Liner and cover systems must be inspected during construction for uniformity, damage, and imperfections. Immediately after installation, synthetic liners and covers must be inspected for tight seams and joints and the absence of tears, punctures, and blisters. Soil-based and admixed liner and cover systems must be inspected immediately after installation for imperfections that could cause an increase in the permeability of the liner or cover.[110]

During operation, the landfill must be inspected weekly and after storms for evidence of failure of the run-on and runoff control systems, proper functioning of the wind dispersal control system, and presence of leachate in and proper operation of the leachate collection system.[111]

The operating record must contain a map indicating the exact location and depth of each cell in relation to permanently surveyed benchmarks. The operating record must also contain a record of the contents of each cell and the approximate location of each hazardous waste within each cell.[112]

At closure of the landfill or any cell thereof, the owner or operator must place a final cover on the landfill or cell that will minimize migration of liquids through the closed portion, function with minimum maintenance, promote drainage and minimize erosion of the cover, accommodate settling and subsidence, and have a permeability rate not greater than that of the bottom liner or natural subsoils. After closure, the owner or operator is subject to the general postclosure requirements discussed in Chapter 9. In addition, the owner or operator must maintain and repair the final cover, operate the leachate collection system until leachate is no longer detected, maintain the groundwater-monitoring program as required, prevent run-on and runoff from damaging the cover, and maintain surveyed benchmarks referred to above.[113]

---

[109]*Id.* § 264.301(g)–(j).
[110]*Id.* § 264.303.
[111]*Id.*
[112]*Id.* § 264.309.
[113]*Id.* § 264.310.

Chapter 11: Land Disposal Facilities 285

The owner or operator may not place ignitable or reactive waste in a landfill unless the Land Disposal Restrictions are complied with and (1) the resulting waste no longer exhibits the characteristic and the general requirements for reactive and ignitable wastes; or (2) the waste is managed in containers and is disposed in a manner that protects the waste from material or conditions that may cause it to ignite or react.[114] Incompatible wastes may not be placed together in the same landfill cell unless the general requirements for incompatible wastes are met.[115]

The placement of bulk or containerized liquids in landfills is prohibited in 40 C.F.R. Section 264.314. Furthermore, placement of a nonhazardous liquid in a landfill is prohibited unless the owner or operator demonstrates that the only reasonably available alternative is another landfill or an unlined surface impoundment that does or will contain hazardous waste, and placement of the liquid in the landfill will not present a risk of contamination of an underground source of drinking water.

Containers must be at least 90 percent full when placed in a landfill unless they are very small (such as an ampule) or are crushed, shredded, or reduced in volume to the maximum practical extent. Small containers may be placed in overpacked drums and placed in a landfill if the Land Disposal Restrictions are complied with and the following conditions are met:

- the inside containers must be sealed, nonleaking, and meet applicable Department of Transportation (DOT) requirements;
- the outer container must be an open head, DOT-specification metal shipping container no larger than 110 gallons and packed with enough absorbent material to completely absorb all of the liquid contents of the inside containers;
- the absorbent material must be compatible with the waste materials;
- incompatible waste cannot be placed in the same outer container; and
- except for cyanide- and sulfide-bearing wastes, reactive wastes must be rendered nonreactive before packaging.[116]

Hazardous wastes bearing the waste codes F020, F021, F022, F023, F026, and F027 may not be placed in a landfill without the approval of the permitting authority. The approval must take into account the characteristics of the waste (including migration potential through soil), the

[114]*Id.* § 264.312.
[115]*Id.* § 264.313.
[116]*Id.* § 264.317.

286   THE RCRA PRACTICE MANUAL

attenuative properties of the surrounding soils or material, the mobilizing properties of material in contact with the waste, and the effectiveness of treatment, design, or monitoring techniques.[117]

The interim status standards for landfills are found at 40 C.F.R. Sections 265.300 through 265.316. Any new unit on which construction commences after January 29, 1992, replacement of an existing unit that is to commence reuse after July 29, 1992, or lateral extension of an existing unit on which construction commences after July 29, 1992, is subject to the same standard for a double liner and leachate collection system as a permitted unit.[118]

The permitting authority must be given 60 days' prior notice of the use of such new, replacement, or extended unit, and a Part B permit application must be filed within six months of the date the permitting authority receives that notice. If an owner or operator installs a liner and leachate collection system in good-faith compliance with the interim status standards, the permitting authority may not require a different liner and leachate collection system when the first permit is issued, unless it has reason to believe that the liner is leaking. An interim status landfill must be provided with run-on, runoff, and wind dispersal control systems required under the permitting standards.[119]

Such facilities must also comply with the same standards as permitted units for surveying and record keeping; ignitable, reactive, and incompatible wastes; the prohibition on bulk and containerized liquids; the requirements for containers; and the requirements for small containers in overpacked drums.[120] Additionally, upon closure, the owner or operator of an interim status landfill must comply with the same closure requirements as in the standards for permitted units.[121]

E. Miscellaneous Units

Any land disposal unit that does not meet the definition of surface impoundment, waste pile, land treatment unit, or landfill is permitted under 40 C.F.R. 264 Subpart X, Miscellaneous Units. Because of the diversity of potential units covered under Subpart X, the regulations do not attempt to define precise technological standards for miscellaneous units, but rather set forth performance-based criteria. In general, "a miscellaneous unit must be located, designed, constructed, operated, maintained,

---

[117]*Id.*

[118]*Id.* §§ 265.301–.304.

[119]*Id.* § 265.301.

[120]*Id.* §§ 265.309, .312–.316.

[121]*Id.* § 265.310.

and closed in a manner that will ensure protection of human health and the environment."[122] Protection of human health and the environment includes the prevention of any releases that would harm human health and the environment through the migration of waste constituents through environmental media.[123]

Monitoring, testing, analytical data, inspections, response, and reporting procedure and frequencies must be sufficient to ensure protection of human health and the environment, and ensure compliance with the general facility standards for monitoring, testing, analytical data, inspections, response, and reporting procedure and frequencies found in 40 C.F.R. 264 Subparts A through F.

V. Conclusion

In addition to the usual requirements for RCRA units (for example, monitoring, waste analysis, closure and postclosure requirements and requirements for special types of wastes), the technical standards for land disposal units are particularly designed to assure protection of groundwater. As a result, the owner or operator of a land disposal unit will need to pay close attention to the groundwater-monitoring requirements, as well as the special construction requirements for liners and leachate collection and removal systems.

---

[122]*Id.* § 264.601.
[123]*Id.*

CHAPTER 12

Land Ban Disposal Restrictions

STEVEN E. SILVERMAN

The Resource Conservation and Recovery Act (RCRA) land ban (or, more precisely, the land disposal restrictions [LDR] program) is conceptually relatively simple. The program does not ban the land disposal of hazardous wastes. It does, however, prohibit the land disposal of hazardous wastes until they meet pretreatment standards established by the Environmental Protection Agency (EPA or the Agency). The wastes do not have to be pretreated if they are being disposed of into units from which there will be no migration of hazardous constituents for as long as the wastes remain hazardous. These requirements apply not only to hazardous wastes disposed of in conventional land disposal units such as landfills, but also to wastes placed in surface impoundments, underground injection wells, short-term storage piles, land treatment, or other units where waste is placed on the land.

This is a significant and far-reaching scheme. The LDR program alters traditional methods of hazardous waste management by making land disposal the waste management method of last rather than first resort. Less immediately obvious are the ways in which the LDR program interacts with other parts of the RCRA program—in particular, the question of when wastes are hazardous and whether subtitle C regulation ceases when wastes are no longer hazardous—as well as on the regulatory programs of the Clean Water Act, Safe Drinking Water Act, and remedial programs under RCRA and the Comprehensive Environmental Response, Compensation, and Liability Act (CERCLA).

This chapter will begin with a discussion of the LDR statutory and regulatory scheme, and later address in more detail the treatment standards and how they are implemented, the temporary and permanent

290   THE RCRA PRACTICE MANUAL

alternatives to treatment, and conclude with an examination of the interface between the LDR program and other statutory and regulatory programs.

I. Relevant Statutory and Regulatory Provisions

In the 1984 amendments to RCRA, Congress recognized that land disposal could not guarantee perpetual containment of hazardous wastes, and therefore added provisions to minimize reliance on land disposal. Accordingly, Congress enacted the land ban, which requires that before hazardous wastes are land disposed, they meet either treatment standards established by EPA or be disposed of in a land disposal unit from which there will be no migration for as long as the waste remains hazardous (a so-called no-migration unit).[1] Hazardous wastes subject to these controls are often referred to as "prohibited" hazardous wastes.

The treatment standards are the most important part of the statutory scheme. They require EPA to establish "levels or methods of treatment, if any, which substantially diminish the toxicity of the waste or substantially reduce the likelihood of migration of hazardous constituents from the waste so that short-term and long-term threats to human health and the environment are minimized." (A "hazardous constituent" is any of the chemicals listed in appendix VIII to Part 261.) These standards have to be met *before* the wastes are land disposed.[2] As discussed in more detail in the next section, the fact that the Section 3004(m) standard is more strict than the standard for determining if a waste is hazardous has striking ramifications for the types of wastes to which the land disposal prohibitions and treatment standards can apply.

The prohibitions and treatment standards were phased in on a congressionally mandated schedule. The first wastes to be prohibited (by November 8, 1986) were listed solvent and dioxin-containing wastes.[3] A select list of other wastes were barred from land disposal on July 8, 1987 (so-called California list wastes).[4] (The prohibition dates are somewhat later for these wastes when disposed into deep injection wells or when they are generated as contaminated soil and debris in the course of CERCLA response actions or RCRA corrective action.[5]) All remaining

---

[1]RCRA §§ 3004(d), (e), and (g).
[2]API v. EPA, 906 F.2d 726, 73436 (D.C. Cir. 1990) (hazardous wastes must be fully treated before being placed in land treatment units, notwithstanding that further treatment might occur in those units).
[3]RCRA § 3004(e).
[4]*Id.* § 3004(d).
[5]*Id.* §§ 3004(d)(3), (e)(3), and (f).

wastes identified or listed as hazardous at the time of the 1984 amendments were then ranked on the basis of their intrinsic hazard and the volume generated annually, and divided into three parts. EPA was required to establish prohibitions and treatment standards for each successive third of the list on August 8, 1988, June 8, 1989, and May 8, 1990, respectively.[6] Characteristic hazardous wastes were in the final "third" ("third third") of the schedule and hence were prohibited in the May 8, 1990, rule making. If EPA had failed to promulgate prohibitions for these wastes by specified dates, the wastes would be prohibited from land disposal by operation of law—the so-called hammer provisions.[7] EPA is to promulgate prohibitions and treatment standards for wastes identified or listed after the date of the 1984 amendments within six months of the identification or listing taking effect,[8] but there is no automatic prohibition if the Agency fails to act by the required date. At this time, EPA has promulgated prohibitions and treatment standards for all of the wastes in the original schedule and for certain wastes newly listed since 1984. The largest categories of hazardous wastes not presently covered by prohibitions and treatment standards are wastes exhibiting the toxicity characteristic (and that do not exhibit the old Extraction Procedure (EP) characteristic), and wastes (such as spent potliners from primary aluminum production) removed from coverage of the Bevill amendment after 1984.

The prohibition on "land disposal" of hazardous wastes covers a wide range of activities. "Land disposal," for purposes of the LDR program, is defined "to include, but not be limited to, any placement of such hazardous waste in a landfill, surface impoundment, waste pile, injection well, land treatment facility, salt dome formation, salt bed formation, or underground mine or cave."[9]Thus, the land ban can potentially affect hazardous wastes that are going to be disposed of in virtually any manner that involves placement of the waste on the land. A prime example, besides the familiar situation of landfill or surface impoundment disposal, is disposal by underground injection (notwithstanding that the practice is also regulated by the Safe Drinking Water Act).[10] Additionally, wastes do not have to remain permanently in the land disposal unit for the land ban to apply.[11] Storage involving placement of wastes on the

---

[6]*Id.* § 3004(g)(5).
[7]*Id.* § 3004(g)(6)(C).
[8]RCRA § 3004(g)(4)
[9]RCRA § 3004(k).
[10]*Id.* §§ 3004(f) and (g).
[11]*Id.* § 3004(k).

land followed by removal of the wastes is nevertheless land disposal for purposes of the land disposal prohibitions, and so prohibited wastes must normally meet the treatment standards before such storage occurs. On the other hand, there are many types of waste management activities that are not affected by the ban because no land disposal occurs. For example, if hazardous wastewaters are managed in tanks (such as clarifiers) and then discharged into publicly owned treatment works (POTWs) or navigable waters, they do not have to be treated to meet the Section 3004(m) standards because they are never land disposed.

Land disposal prohibitions normally take effect immediately.[12] In order for there to be a legal means of disposal, therefore, EPA promulgates the Section 3004(m) treatment standards at the same time as the prohibitions.[13] The implementing regulations thus contain both prohibitions,[14] a statement that the prohibitions do not apply to wastes that meet the treatment standards,[15] and the treatment standards themselves.[16]

The effective date of the land disposal prohibitions (and hence the date when wastes must be pretreated before being land disposed) can be postponed for up to two years if EPA grants a national capacity variance from the otherwise applicable effective date based on "the earliest date on which adequate alternative treatment, recovery, or disposal capacity which protects human health and the environment will be available."[17] This date can be extended for individual applicants for one additional year, renewable for one year, provided the applicant shows that treatment capacity is unavailable and the applicant has a binding contract to create or otherwise utilize treatment capacity.[18] Thus, when EPA promulgates a land disposal prohibition and treatment standard, compliance can be delayed no longer than four years.

In addition to prohibiting the land disposal of hazardous wastes, Congress also prohibited storage of any waste that is prohibited from land disposal unless "such storage is solely for the purpose of the accumulation of such quantities of hazardous waste as are necessary to facil-

---

[12]RCRA § 3004(h)(1).

[13]*Id.* § 3004(m)(1).

[14]40 C.F.R. §§ 268.30–35

[15]*Id.* § 268.33(e)(1)

[16]*Id.* §§ 268.41, .42, and .43.

[17]RCRA § 3004(h)(2).

[18]*Id.* § 3004(h)(3).

[19]RCRA § 3004(j); 40 C.F.R. § 268.50 (codifying the provision and stating further that if prohibited wastes are stored for over one year, the person storing has the burden of proving that storage is nevertheless for the purpose of accumulating sufficient amounts of waste to facilitate proper management; prior to one year, EPA has the burden of proving that the storage is occurring for the wrong reason).

itate proper recovery, treatment or disposal."[19] The purpose of the storage prohibition is to prevent use of long-term storage to circumvent the pretreatment requirements.[20] In practice, however, the prohibition also adversely affects persons storing prohibited wastes for extended periods because treatment is simply unavailable (such as persons storing certain type of mixed wastes or dioxin wastes).[21]

These prohibitions are implemented by means of a waste-tracking program somewhat analogous to the hazardous waste manifest system. These provisions, contained largely in 40 C.F.R. Section 268.7, require generators and treatment facilities to provide tracking documents with each shipment of wastes potentially subject to a land disposal prohibition. The tracking document must identify the waste and its treatment standard, indicate whether the waste meets that treatment standard, or show why the waste is subject to an exception from the requirement of meeting the treatment standard before land disposal (for example, existence of a national capacity variance). Generators can determine from their own knowledge whether the wastes meet the treatment standard, but treatment and disposal facilities must conduct tests (although not necessarily of each waste shipment) to determine if the treatment standards have been satisfied. These distinctions are explained and sustained in *Hazardous Waste Treatment Council v. EPA*.[22]

II. The Section 3004(m) Treatment Standards

A. The Statute, Applicable Regulations, and Means of Achieving the Standards

The Section 3004(m) treatment standards have been aptly called "the heart of RCRA's hazardous waste management program."[23] EPA is to promulgate "levels or methods of treatment, if any, which substantially diminish the toxicity of the waste or substantially reduce the likelihood of migration of hazardous constituents from the waste so that short-term and long-term threats to human health and the environment are minimized."

The treatment standards are found in 40 C.F.R. Sections 268.41, .42, and .43, listed and cross-referenced by waste code. (In the event mix-

---

[20]129 CONG. REC. H8139 (daily ed. Oct. 6, 1983).
[21]55 Fed. Reg. at 22,672 (1990); *see also* Edison Electric Institute v. EPA, 996 F.2d 326 (D.C. Cir. 1993) (construing storage prohibition).
[22]886 F.2d 355, 370 (D.C. Cir. 1989), *cert. denied*, 111 S. Ct. 139 (1990) and Chemical Waste Management v. EPA, 976 F.2d 2, 31 (D.C. Cir. 1992), *cert. denied*, 61 U.S.L.W. 3731 (1993).
[23]Chemical Waste Management v. EPA, 976 F.2d 23 (D.C. Cir. 1992).

294 THE RCRA PRACTICE MANUAL

tures of prohibited wastes are treated, the strictest treatment standard for each common constituent applies.[24]) The treatment standards can be expressed as either numerical levels for hazardous constituents (e.g., benzene in waste code K048 must be at a level of 14 ppm before it can be land disposed) or as a mandated method of treatment (e.g., recovery of lead for hazardous lead acid batteries). The numerical standards can be measured in either an extract from the waste (normally obtained by using the toxicity characteristic leaching procedure) (these standards are found in 40 C.F.R. Section 268.41), or measured in the waste itself.[25]

Since the wastes can occur as either liquids or solids, which are amenable to different types of treatment technologies with differing levels of performance, the numerical treatment standards typically take the form of one set of standards for wastewaters and another for nonwastewaters. Residues from treating the wastes must typically meet the treatment standard for the waste from which they are generated. For example, incinerator ash from treating waste code F001 solvent still bottoms must meet the treatment standards for waste code F001 nonwastewaters, and scrubber water from incinerating the still bottoms must meet the standards for waste code F001 wastewaters. (This is an example of the so-called waste code carry-through principle whereby residues from treating listed wastes retain the same waste code as the underlying waste and remain subject to the treatment standards for that waste code. The waste code carry-through principle is an example of how the derived-from rule and the land ban rules interact.)

A treatability variance is available for those waste matrices for which a treatment standard is legitimately unachievable or for which the treatment technology is inappropriate.[26] These variances may be granted by rule making or by site-specific administrative action.[27] Grant of a variance means that the waste in question must be treated to an alternative level (or by an alternative method) established in the variance proceeding. The numerical treatment standards need not be met by treating the waste if it already meets the treatment standards as generated. In addition, unless EPA mandates a method of treatment, the wastes can be treated by any permissible means to achieve the numerical standard.

The impermissible method of achieving numerical standards is by diluting the wastes. This prohibition is contained in 40 C.F.R. Section 268.3 and states that dilution "as a substitute for adequate treatment . . . , to circumvent the effective date of a prohibition . . . , or to circumvent

---

[24]*Id.* § 268.41(b).
[25]*Id.* § 268.43.
[26]40 C.F.R. § 268.44.
[27]*Id.* §§ 268.44(e) and (h).

Chapter 12: Land Ban Disposal Restrictions 295

a [statutory prohibition]" is illegal. EPA based this regulatory prohibition on explicit legislative history,[28] but the D.C. Circuit showed that it also comes directly from the treatment standard provision itself: Section 3004(m) requires that hazardous constituents be substantially destroyed, removed, or reduced in mobility, which cannot be achieved by dilution.[29]

The Agency has provided some guidance in preambles as to what types of activities constitute impermissible dilution. The most difficult issue involves determining when centralized wastewater treatment, which necessarily involves dilution of some wastes in the form of aggregation of wastes before introduction into a centralized treatment unit, may constitute impermissible dilution. The Agency has indicated that combination of wastes for centralized treatment is acceptable where the centralized treatment covers all of the combined wastes. Thus, for example, aggregation of wastes containing hazardous organic constituents for centralized biological treatment would normally be permissible because biological treatment effectively treats organics. On the other hand, aggregation of wastes containing significant concentrations of both metals and organics for centralized biological treatment would not normally be permissible because the metals are not adequately treated by such treatment. To the extent their concentrations are reduced, it is through the effects of dilution, and, therefore, impermissible.[30]

B. Issues Involving the Treatment Standards

1. *Technology Versus Risk-Based Standards and at What Point Must Treatment Cease?*

EPA has based the treatment standards on the performance of best demonstrated available technology (BDAT), based largely on explicit legislative history that this is how Congress expected the provision to be implemented. It has been argued, however, that the treatment standards must be risk based. That is, EPA cannot compel wastes to be treated to a level below which insignificant risk is present. The D.C. Circuit substantially agreed with both approaches, holding that standards based on performance of BDAT (i.e., technology-based standards) were legally permissible, but that treatment could not occur beyond the point at which "threats to human health and the environment are minimized."[31] The court held further that the existing treatment standards for solvent wastes

---

[28]Found in S. REP. NO. 284, 98th Cong., 1st Sess. 17 (1983).
[29]Chemical Waste Management v. EPA, 976 F.2d 16 (D.C. Cir. 1992).
[30]55 Fed. Reg. at 22,666 (1990).
[31]Hazardous Waste Treatment Council v. EPA, 886 F.2d at 363 (HTWC), quoting § 3004(m)(1).

296 THE RCRA PRACTICE MANUAL

were valid notwithstanding that they were lower than the characteristic level that would define the wastes as hazardous, and notwithstanding that, in some instances, they were lower than delisting levels. This is because the "minimize threat" standard in Section 3004(m) is a stricter standard than required to identify wastes as hazardous.[32] EPA has confessed to being unable at this time to determine precisely what generic "minimize threat" levels are.[33] Indeed, the quest for these levels has become the Holy Grail of the RCRA program.[34] The *HWTC* court has agreed that minimize-threat levels are elusive when assessing land disposal of hazardous wastes, and that this very uncertainty is what motivated Congress to enact the land ban in the first place.[35] Consequently, treatment must presently occur to the full extent of the existing technology-based treatment standards, and those standards are not capped by risk-based determinations purporting to show that further treatment is unnecessary.

2. Must Wastes Be Treated If They Are No Longer Hazardous Wastes When They Are Disposed?

The minimize threat treatment standard is more strict than the test for identifying wastes as hazardous, a fact that has very significant ramifications. One might think that once a waste is no longer hazardous, it is no longer subject to subtitle C regulation of any type, including having to satisfy land ban treatment standards. This would mean that characteristic hazardous wastes would only have to be treated to remove the characteristic, notwithstanding that the wastes might still contain significant concentrations of untreated hazardous constituents (for example, the cyanide in reactive cyanide wastes would remain if only the characteristic property of reactivity were removed). This is because characteristic wastes are no longer hazardous wastes when they stop exhibiting a characteristic property.[36]

The Agency recognized that this approach would result in ineffective treatment of characteristic wastes, without any significant policy or legal justification. Why, it might be asked, would Congress have wanted characteristic wastes to be subject to a less rigorous treatment standard than listed wastes? EPA accordingly maintained that so long as a waste is hazardous at the point it is generated, it must be treated to the full

---

[32]886 F.2d at 363.
[33]55 Fed. Reg. 6640 (1990).
[34]57 Fed. Reg. 49,280 (1992).
[35]886 F.2d at 362.
[36]40 C.F.R. § 261.3(d)(1).

extent of the Section 3004(m) treatment standard before it can be land disposed, notwithstanding that it may no longer be a hazardous waste at the point it is land disposed. In the jargon of the land ban, the prohibitions and treatment requirements attach at the point of waste generation, so that if a waste exhibits a characteristic at the point it is generated, it cannot be land disposed until it is treated to meet the Section 3004(m) standard. Thus, in the example above of reactive cyanide wastes, land disposal of the waste could not occur until the cyanide wastes were adequately treated, whether or not the waste still exhibited the characteristic of reactivity. The D.C. Circuit upheld this interpretation as permissible in *Chemical Waste Management v. EPA*.[37] However, as discussed below, the point of generation theory has potentially far-reaching implications for centralized wastewater management of characteristic wastes, implications with which the Agency is now grappling.

Before ending discussion in this area, it is important to note that there are certain situations where the point of generation approach does not apply, at least under present rules. The first is when characteristic wastes are treated in tanks and then discharged to POTWs where they are subsequently managed in surface impoundments and then discharged. In this case, EPA does not believe that the POTW is affected by LDR requirements, so long as the wastes are commingled with domestic sewage before reaching the POTW. This is because the domestic sewage exclusion in RCRA Section 1004(27) and 40 C.F.R. Section 261.4(a)(1) cut off applicability of the land disposal prohibitions.[38] In addition, EPA presently interprets the Bevill amendment as cutting off applicability of the land disposal prohibitions. Thus, if a Bevill device coprocesses prohibited hazardous wastes along with Bevill raw materials (for example, a cement kiln that processes normal raw materials and also burns hazardous waste fuel) and generates a waste otherwise covered by the Bevill amendment (as determined by the tests in 40 C.F.R. Section 266.112), the residues do not have to meet land ban treatment standards.

III. Temporary and Permanent Alternatives to Treatment

Even after EPA promulgates prohibitions and treatment standards for a hazardous waste, wastes need not meet those standards either temporarily or permanently under certain circumstances. These are discussed below.

---

[37]976 F.2d at 14, 16 (D.C. Cir. 1992).
[38]55 Fed. Reg. 22,660–61 (1990).

298 THE RCRA PRACTICE MANUAL

A. National Capacity Variances and Case-by-Case Capacity Variances

As noted above, the land disposal prohibitions are to be effective immediately unless EPA finds that there is insufficient alternative protective treatment, recovery, or disposal capacity for the wastes.[39] In fact, this has frequently proven to be the case, and EPA has thus postponed the effective dates of many of the prohibitions and treatment standards for the two years allowed by statute.[40] During the duration of the national capacity variance, the wastes do not require treatment in order to be land disposed. If they are disposed of in a landfill or surface impoundment, however, that unit must meet the minimum technology requirements of RCRA Section 3004(o) (essentially double liners, leachate collection systems, and groundwater monitoring).[41]

EPA is also authorized to grant up to a one-year extension, renewable for another one year, of a prohibition effective date on a case-by-case basis.[42] Applicants must demonstrate that adequate alternative treatment, recovery, or disposal capacity for the petitioner's waste cannot reasonably be made available by the effective date due to circumstances beyond the applicant's control, and that the petitioner has entered into a binding contractual commitment to construct or otherwise provide such capacity.[43] During the period of the extension, the waste can be disposed of untreated; but if an impoundment or landfill is used for disposal, it must meet the RCRA Section 3004(o) minimum technology requirements.

B. Special Provisions for Surface Impoundments

Congress also created an exception that allows the placement of untreated wastes in surface impoundments.[44] Under this provision, the hazardous wastes may be placed in impoundments provided the impoundments meet the minimum technology requirements and provided that any sludges in the impoundments that do not meet the treatment standard for that waste are removed within one year. (Since these impoundments are receiving hazardous wastes, they must, of course, meet all other applicable subtitle C regulatory standards.)

---

[39]RCRA § 3004(h)(2).
[40]40 C.F.R. § 268.35(c), (d), and (e) (two-year variance for certain "third third" wastes).
[41]RCRA § 3004(h)(4) and 40 C.F.R. § 268.5(h).
[42]RCRA § 3004(h)(3).
[43]40 C.F.R. § 268.5.
[44]RCRA § 3005(j)(11), implemented in 40 C.F.R. § 268.4.

There is a slight twist for subtitle C impoundments receiving wastes newly identified or listed after the date of the 1984 amendments. RCRA Section 3005(j)(6) allows such impoundments up to four years to retrofit to meet the minimum technology requirements or to close. On the other hand, EPA could conceivably promulgate land disposal prohibitions for that waste which, in some circumstances, could have the effect of nullifying the RCRA Section 3005(j)(6) retrofitting period, either by virtue of RCRA Section 3005(j)(11) or 3004(h)(4).[45] Interpreting these potentially conflicting provisions, the Agency determined that impoundments receiving newly identified and listed wastes would have four years to close or retrofit under all circumstances. Consequently, if EPA were, for example, to promulgate prohibitions for the toxicity characteristic (TC) wastes before March 29, 1994 (the date of the four-year retrofit period allowed by RCRA Section 3005(j)(6)), persons would still have until that date to close or retrofit the impoundments, and could still manage TC wastes not treated to meet the treatment standard until that time.

C. Disposal in No-Migration Units

The only permanent exception to the pretreatment requirement is for prohibited wastes that are disposed of in so-called no-migration units. These are land disposal units from which "it has been demonstrated to the Administrator, to a reasonable degree of certainty, that there will be no migration of hazardous constituents from the disposal unit or injection zone for as long as the wastes remain hazardous."[46] The test must be satisfied based solely on the hydrogeology and other naturally occurring conditions at the unit. The no-migration standard cannot be satisfied based on artificial barriers, such as liners or other containment mechanisms.[47] Implementing regulations for surface disposal units are found at 40 C.F.R. Section 268.6 and for underground injection wells at 40 C.F.R. Section 148.20.

EPA has interpreted this language to mean that the test is satisfied so long as the concentration of hazardous constituents at the boundary of the land disposal unit is less than a health-based level established by EPA.[48] This could be compared to a drinkable-leachate/eatable soil at the unit boundary test. The interpretation was narrowly upheld by the D.C. Circuit in *NRDC v. EPA*, over the strong dissent of Judge Wald, who

---

[45]56 Fed. Reg. 37,194 (1992).
[46]RCRA §§ 3004(d)(1), (e)(1), and (g)(5).
[47]S. Rep. No. 284, 98th Cong., 1st Sess. 15.
[48]53 Fed. Reg. 28,122 (1988).

300 THE RCRA PRACTICE MANUAL

pointed out logically that the Agency was reading "no migration of hazardous constituents to mean some migration of hazardous constituents."[49]

It is difficult for surface disposal units such as landfills, land treatment units, and surface impoundments to meet even the Agency's version of the no-migration standard. Meeting health-based levels at the unit boundary means that for a land treatment unit, for example, health-based levels for volatile organic hazardous constituents must be achieved essentially at the very surface of the unit. The test has been met relatively frequently, however, by class I hazardous deep injection wells. In part, this is because the unit boundary for these deep wells includes the entire injection zone, an area far larger than that available for surface units, so that injected wastes have ample time and area for attenuation and immobilization before reaching the unit boundary.

D. Other Bars to Applicability of the LDRs

Section 268.1(b) of the regulations states that wastes that are excluded or exempted from regulation under the part 261 regulations are also not subject to the land disposal prohibitions. Thus, for example, small quantity generator wastes generated in quantities under 100 kg per month are not subject to the LDRs. Nor, as noted above, are hazardous wastes that are commingled with domestic sewage and sent to a POTW that treats the wastes in a surface impoundment (unless the wastes exhibit a characteristic when placed in the impoundment).[50]

IV. Interface between the LDR Rules and Other Statutory and Regulatory Programs

A. LDR and the Clean Water Act

Hazardous wastewaters are often treated in surface impoundments followed by ultimate discharge to a navigable water or POTW. The content of these discharges is controlled under the Clean Water Act, Sections 402 and 307. If the wastes are hazardous when they are placed in the surface impoundment, they need not be pretreated first due to the exception in Section 3005(j)(11).

However, what if the wastes are hazardous when they are generated (for example, an ignitable wastewater) and are nonhazardous when they reach the surface impoundment? Assume further that the waste is non-

---

[49]907 F.2d 1146, 115962 (D.C. Cir. 1990).
[50]55 Fed. Reg. 22,660–61 (1990).

Chapter 12: Land Ban Disposal Restrictions 301

hazardous because it has been diluted rather than undergoing treatment that destroys or removes hazardous constituents. This is the critical fact pattern of the "third third" rule and the subsequent *Chemical Waste Management* opinion. The fact pattern indeed is that of ordinary centralized wastewater treatment using a surface impoundment, and the dilution occurs due to an aggregation step that is necessary to equalize wastewater flows into a treatment unit.

EPA maintained that under these circumstances, in order to avoid undermining the parallel treatment regimes adopted to satisfy the Clean Water Act, the land disposal prohibitions need not apply.[51] The D.C. Circuit agreed only partially, holding that once the LDR prohibitions attached to a waste at the point it is generated, the waste remains subject to that prohibition even if it no longer exhibits a characteristic. It therefore must be treated to remove or destroy hazardous constituents.[52] Although treatment must normally precede land disposal, to accommodate the parallel treatment scheme of the Clean Water Act, the court further held that the treatment need not occur before the decharacterized waste is placed in a surface impoundment, but rather can be achieved as part of the total treatment the waste undergoes: "the material that comes out of CWA treatment facilities that employ surface impoundments must remove the hazardous constituents to the same extent that any other treatment facility that complies with RCRA does."[53] (Since these wastes are no longer hazardous when disposed of, the impoundments receiving the wastes are subtitle D impoundments and so ordinarily would not comply with the conditions of Section 3005(j)(11).) EPA is presently wrestling with this language to determine if it merely requires that end-of-pipe discharge standards for persons treating decharacterized wastes in impoundments must be adjusted to conform to the potentially different RCRA treatment standards, or if the court also meant to require further controls to preclude leakage and excess volatilization from the impoundments plus treatment of any sludges generated in the impoundments (as a means of ensuring that hazardous constituents are being treated rather than diluted).[54] At the least, this uneasy melding of the Clean Water Act and LDR program has the potential to alter commonly utilized treatment practices adopted to comply with the act's discharge limits. Certainly, any facility that is generating characteristically

---

[51] 55 Fed. Reg. 22,657 (1990).

[52] 976 F.2d at 20, 22.

[53] 976 F.2d at 23.

[54] 58 Fed. Reg. 4972 (1993) and 58 Fed. Reg. 29,860 (1993) (emergency rule replacing those treatment standards vacated by the court, but deferring action on the issues remanded by the court, including those relating to the equivalence standard).

302 THE RCRA PRACTICE MANUAL

hazardous wastewaters and treating them in surface impoundments must take the "third third" rule and *Chemical Waste Management* opinion into account, no matter how many nonhazardous streams are mixed in before treatment.

B. LDR and the Safe Drinking Water Act

Underground injection is a form of land disposal.[55] Thus, hazardous wastes being injected must either be pretreated or the injection well must obtain a no-migration variance in order to comply with the LDRs. Following the "third third" court decision, this also appears to be true even if the wastes are no longer hazardous at the time they are injected. Thus, for example, if a facility generates an ignitable waste, mixes it with other nonhazardous wastes, and injects the decharacterized mixture into a class I nonhazardous well, the ignitable wastes would likely either have to be pretreated or the well would have to obtain a no-migration variance (notwithstanding that it is not injecting hazardous waste).[56] In so ruling, the court rejected EPA's position that it could choose to apply the land ban prohibitions to class I deep wells only to wastes that were hazardous at the point of disposal (so that class I nonhazardous injection wells were unaffected),[57] and that the generally protective nature of the Safe Drinking Water Act regulatory program for class I wells made it unnecessary to also apply the RCRA prohibitions.[58]

As with the parallel situation of centralized treatment in impoundments of decharacterized wastes, the *Chemical Waste Management* decision is likely to have significant impact on underground injection of formerly characteristic wastes.

C. LDR and Remedial Programs under RCRA and CERCLA

Wastes that are disposed before they are identified or listed as hazardous nevertheless become RCRA hazardous wastes when they are identified or listed.[59] (Thus, a listed spent solvent disposed of in 1979 is a hazardous waste after the date it is listed.) The wastes do not become subject to RCRA regulatory requirements, however, unless they are actively man-

---

[55]RCRA § 3004(f), (k).
[56]976 F.2d at 25–26.
[57]*Id.* at 23,
[58]*Id.* at 2526.
[59]53 Fed. Reg. 31,148 (1988); upheld in Chemical Waste Management v. EPA, 869 F.2d 1526, 153637 (D.C. Cir. 1989).

Chapter 12: Land Ban Disposal Restrictions 303

aged after they are identified or listed.[60] However, active management of previously disposed wastes can frequently occur in the context of remedial activities such as those adopted pursuant to CERCLA or RCRA corrective action. One issue then becomes whether these wastes become subject to the land disposal restrictions if they are exhumed and then disposed of again in the course of these remedial activities.

RCRA indicates explicitly that soil and debris that are contaminated with hazardous wastes and that are generated during CERCLA remedial activities or RCRA corrective action are subject to the land ban.[61] Thus, at least under some circumstances, the land ban can apply, either as a direct regulatory requirement or as an applicable requirement under CERCLA Section 121. However, the Agency has also stated that in some circumstances, management of wastes in a remedial setting can be viewed as movement of wastes within an existing land disposal unit, which movement does not trigger the land ban.[62] (Movement of hazardous waste within an area of contamination is essentially movement of wastes within a single landfill where the waste never crosses the unit boundary and therefore land disposal prohibitions do not apply). More recently, the Agency has promulgated a new rule allowing a Regional Administrator of EPA, in the context of a RCRA corrective action or CERCLA remedial action, to designate a "corrective action management unit" (CAMU—a concept undoubtedly influenced by the existential French author whose name it bears) at a remediation site. Management of hazardous wastes within that designated unit would not be considered to be land disposal, even if, for example, wastes within the unit are exhumed, treated, and disposed of on the land within the CAMU.[63] A number of petitions for review have been filed challenging this regulation.

---

[60]53 Fed. Reg. 31,149 (1988).
[61]RCRA § 3004(d)(3) and (e)(3).
[62]55 Fed. Reg. at 8760 (1990)
[63]58 Fed. Reg. 8658 (1993).

CHAPTER 12

UPDATE FOR SECOND EDITION

Land Ban Disposal Restrictions

STEVEN SILVERMAN

I. Introduction

The land disposal restriction (LDR) program has emerged from a turbulent childhood into a sober and staid maturity. Basic issues relating to applicability and scope of the program now appear well settled, and many of the program's features are now standardized. The issue that remains somewhat dynamic is the relationship between the LDR and remediation programs. This update discusses the resolution of issues posed by the D.C. Circuit's opinion in *Chemical Waste Management v. EPA*,[1] relating to LDR applicability, EPA's standardization of treatment standards, and EPA's establishment and application of the principle that LDR requirements should not be applied in a way that leads to environmentally counterproductive results, one result being a separate treatment regime for remediation wastes.

II. Resolution of Issues Relating to LDR Applicability: *Update of* Chemical Waste Management v. EPA

A. Applicability to CWA/SDWA Systems

The D.C. Circuit's *Chemical Waste Management* opinion had three major prongs:

1. Wastes that are hazardous at the point they are generated cannot be land-disposed until they satisfy treatment standards sufficient

---

[1]976 F.2d 2 (D.C. Cir. 1992).

305

306 THE RCRA PRACTICE MANUAL

to minimize threats posed by the wastes' land disposal, even if the wastes cease being hazardous wastes before land disposal occurs.

2. This principle applies even if land disposal of the no longer hazardous waste occurs in units subject to parallel management regimes under the Clean Water Act or Safe Drinking Water Act.

3. Threats posed by so-called underlying hazardous constituents—hazardous constituents that are present in the waste but do not cause the waste to exhibit a hazardous waste characteristic—must be minimized before land disposal can occur.[2]

The first two principles—treatment requirements continue to apply to wastes hazardous at their point of generation but no longer hazardous when disposed (typically because the waste no longer exhibits a hazardous waste characteristic) and treatment requirements apply to underlying hazardous constituents—are now firmly established.[3]

However, Congress amended the statute in 1996 to nullify the portions of the opinion dealing with the interface of LDR with Clean Water Act treatment systems containing impoundments and Safe Drinking Water Act class I injection wells (essentially reenacting EPA's June 1, 1990, third third rule on this point). RCRA Section 3004(g)(7)[4] thus provides that LDRs do *not* apply to characteristic wastes that are decharacterized by any means (including dilution) and then treated in a land-based treatment system that is a direct or indirect discharger under applicable Clean Water Act provisions or (if a zero discharger) that provides treatment equivalent to that provided by a direct or indirect discharger. The exception is for wastes for which the treatment standard is a specified method of treatment, including reactive cyanide wastes, identified in 40 C.F.R. Section 261.23(a)(5).[5] Wastes that exhibit a characteristic when generated, become decharacterized by any means, and are then injected into a class I injection well are not subject to LDRs at all.[6] This means that LDRs do not apply in either of these two paradigm fact patterns:

1. facility generates characteristic wastewater, commingles it with other wastewaters so as to be amenable to centralized waste-

---

[2]*See generally* RCRA PRACTICE MANUAL at pp. 167, 169–70.

[3]*See, e.g.,* 60 Fed. Reg. 11,702, 11,706–08 (Mar. 2, 1995); 61 Fed. Reg. 15,566, 15,568 (Apr. 8, 1996); 63 Fed. Reg. 28,556, 28,560 (May 26, 1998).

[4]42 U.S.C. § 6924(g)(7).

[5]RCRA § 3004(g)(8).

[6]RCRA § 3004 (g) (9); *see also* 40 C.F.R. §§ 268.1(c)(3)–(4), 268.40 n.8–9, codifying these provisions.

EPA was further required to do a study of risks to human health and the environment posed by these modes of waste management, and whether these potential

continued

Chapter 12: Land Ban Disposal Restrictions   307

water treatment in the course of which commingling the waste no longer exhibits a characteristic, commingled wastewaters are treated in a surface impoundment before discharge;

2. same facts except that the decharacterized wastewater is injected into a class I injection well.

B. Treatment of Underlying Hazardous Constituents

As far-reaching as the holding that LDRs can apply to wastes that are no longer hazardous is the corollary principle that such wastes must satisfy treatment standards for all hazardous constituents the wastes contain that might pose a threat when land-disposed.[7] This holding is implemented by 40 C.F.R. Section 268.40(e), which requires that a prohibited characteristic hazardous waste cannot be land-disposed unless it meets the treatment standards for all underlying hazardous constituents that may be present. An "underlying hazardous constituent" is defined as any constituent for which EPA has established a Universal Treatment Standard (see below) "which can reasonably be expected to be present at the point of generation of the hazardous waste at a concentration above the constituent-specific treatment standards."[8] Although sampling and analysis may be necessary to ascertain the presence of underlying hazardous constituents in some instances, generator knowledge may be used in lieu of sampling and analysis in appropriate circumstances.[9]

There is no inherent bar to an underlying hazardous constituent requirement also applying to listed wastes. The reason EPA has not done

---

risks are better addressed under other regulatory authorities. RCRA § 3004(g)(10). In its study, *Industrial Surface Impoundments in the United States,* EPA found little risk to human health and the environment from surface impoundments that manage non-hazardous wastewaters. To the extent there was any risk, EPA concluded that such risk is not widespread but may exist at a facility-specific level. In addition, EPA in its study concluded that although there are some limited gaps in regulatory coverage of surface impoundments managing nonhazardous waste, EPA did not find any serious risks that are unaddressed by existing programs. The surface impoundment study is available at http://www.epa.gov/apaoswer/hazwaste/ldr/icr/ldr-impd .htm.

The *Study for Congress on the Risks Associated with Class I Underground Injection Wells* (Mar. 2001) concluded that current injection practices offer multiple safeguards against any well failures, and that the Class I UIC regulations in place ensure adequate protection of human health and the environment from the disposal of hazardous and nonhazardous wastewaters. The study is posted at http://www .epa.gov/safewater/uic.html.

[7]*See, e.g.,* 976 F.2d at 16–18.

[8]40 C.F.R. § 268.2 (i), which also establishes that fluoride, sulfides, selenium, vanadium, and zinc are not underlying hazardous constituents.

[9]60 Fed.Reg. 43,654, 43,675 (Aug. 22, 1995); 63 F.R. 28,556, 28,576 (May 26, 1998).

308   THE RCRA PRACTICE MANUAL

so is that the agency conducted a comprehensive waste analysis for listed wastes when developing treatment standards for them, so the treatment standards already apply to all hazardous constituents likely to be present in such wastes. (The notable exceptions are the listed solvent wastes, Hazardous Wastes F001 through F005.[10]) Soils contaminated with listed wastes, however, are an exception, since such soils are likely to be cross-contaminated with all sorts of wastes unrelated to the generating process.[11] The tailored treatment standards for contaminated soils (see below) consequently require the soils to satisfy treatment standards for underlying hazardous constituents, whether the soils exhibit a characteristic or are contaminated with listed hazardous waste.[12]

C. Wastes Not Hazardous at Their Point of Generation

LDRs do not attach to wastes that are not hazardous at the point they are generated. This principle seems intuitive but sometimes applies in ways not immediately obvious. For example, LDRs do not apply to wastes covered by the Bevill Amendment, even if such wastes are the partial product of hazardous waste management. A specific instance is cement kiln dust generated by a cement kiln that burns hazardous waste fuel, where one determines whether the dust is covered by the Bevill Amendment (according to the "substantially affected" principle set out in 40 C.F.R. Section 266.112) at the point the dust is generated.[13] Another example is contaminated soils, which can be covered by LDRs if they contain listed wastes (a term of art discussed later) or exhibit a characteristic, when excavated—excavation being the relevant point of generation.[14] However, if the soils do not "contain" hazardous waste when excavated (even if hazardous waste may have been spilled on or otherwise came into contact with the soil at some time), LDRs would not apply. Now pending in litigation is the issue of whether a contingent listing (that is, x is a hazardous waste when managed by method y) that allows a waste to be land-disposed without meeting LDRs (because this

---

[10]*See* 65 Fed. Reg. 37,932, 37,947 (June 19, 2000).

[11]63 Fed. Reg. 28,609.

[12]40 C.F.R. § 268.49(d).

[13]Horsehead Res. Dev. Co. v. EPA, 16 F.3d 1246, 1261 (D.C. Cir. 1994) (upholding the "substantially affected" principle and further holding that EPA permissibly interpreted the statute to say that LDRs do not apply to wastes covered by the Bevill amendment which are the partial product of hazardous waste management).

[14]63 Fed. Reg. 28,617–19 (and see further below).

Chapter 12: Land Ban Disposal Restrictions 309

is not a management method covered by the listing) is valid.[15] These issues should all turn on the question of the LDR point of generation.[16]

III. Standardization of Treatment Standards

A. Universal Treatment Standards

EPA's 1986–1992 treatment standards contained different numerical standards for each hazardous constituent in each hazardous waste. Thus, for example, the treatment standard for benzene in waste *a* was (typically) different than the treatment standards for benzene in waste *b*. The result was many hundreds of different numerical standards, often differing one from the other only minutely (and often just reflecting a different analytical detection level for the waste matrix, rather than an actual difference in performance).

EPA has significantly simplified this regime. In a conscious effort to make the treatment standards as uniform as possible, but still adhering to the fundamental requirement that the standard must minimize threats to human health and the environment, EPA developed the Universal Treatment Standards.[17] The Universal Treatment Standards match their name: most hazardous constituents now have the same treatment standard, no matter what waste they are found in, whether listed or characteristic, whether or not a constituent is one for which there is an enumerated treatment standard, and whether or not it is an underlying hazardous constituent. In the example above, the standard for benzene in waste *a* would thus be the same as the standard for benzene in waste *b*.[18] The Universal Treatment Standards have been a signal success in implementation, not only simplifying the whole treatment regime, but also eliminating most disputes relating to analytic detection levels.

B. Exceptions to Universal Treatment Standards

EPA has developed separate treatment standards—that is, treatment standards other than the Universal Treatment Standards—for two wastes: contaminated debris and spent potliners from primary aluminum pro-

---

[15]Sierra Club v. EPA, No. 01-1057 (D.C. Cir.).

[16]*See* 55 Fed. Reg. 22,520, 22,661 (June 1, 1990); 62 Fed. Reg. 25,998, 26,006 (May 12, 1997); 63 Fed. Reg. 28,623–24 (general guidance on LDR point of generation questions).

[17]59 Fed. Reg. 47,980, 47,988–48,002 (Sept. 19, 1994).

[18]*See* 40 C.F.R. §§ 268.48 (the Universal Treatment Standards themselves), 268.40 tbl. (the treatment standards for each hazardous waste, almost all of which incorporate the Universal Treatment Standards).

duction (hazardous waste K088). Contaminated debris is debris that "contains" a listed hazardous waste (either on its surface or in interstices).[19] The standards for contaminated debris actually allow entities the option of treating to meet the Universal Treatment Standards or treating the debris by a method designated in the rule.[20] These methods of treatment generally involve extraction of the waste from the debris, destruction of the waste, or immobilization of the entire matrix (waste plus debris).[21] Residue from treating the debris by a designated method must then be physically separated from the debris and must be further treated to meet any applicable waste-specific treatment standard (the Universal Treatment Standards) before such residue can be land-disposed, except for certain enumerated types of treatment residues that no longer exhibit a characteristic of hazardous waste, which may be land-disposed without further treatment.[22] The debris itself may be land-disposed after it has been treated by a designated method of treatment.

The rules establishing treatment standards for contaminated debris marked the first codification of the so-called "contained in" and "contained out" principles. These principles state that media (such as soil or debris) that is not itself a waste can be a hazardous waste if it "contains" a listed hazardous waste (or if it exhibits a hazardous waste characteristic). EPA initially developed these principles as an interpretive gloss on the mixture and derived-from rules.[23] Determining whether such media contain a hazardous waste involves a case-by-case determination that hazardous constituents are not present in the media at concentrations posing significant risk.[24] Section 268.45(a) now indicates expressly that it applies to "hazardous debris," defined as debris that contains a listed waste or exhibits a hazardous waste characteristic.[25] Moreover, the rules provide means for classifying contaminated debris as nonhazardous ("contained out"). Debris that has been treated by an extraction or destruction technology and no longer exhibits a characteristic is no longer considered to contain hazardous waste, so it is not subject any

---

[19]57 Fed. Reg. 37,194, 37,225 (Aug. 18, 1992).

[20]40 C.F.R. § 268.45(a), n.1.

[21]See id. § 268.45 tbl.1 (menu matching appropriate treatment methods with types of debris and hazardous constituents).

[22]Id. § 268.45(d).

[23]See Chem. Mfrs. Ass'n v. EPA, 869 F.2d 1526, 1536–37 (D.C. Cir. 1989) (upholding this interpretation).

[24]57 Fed. Reg. 37,226; 63 Fed. Reg. 28,622 (discussing relationship of contained-in principle and the core LDR requirement that hazardous wastes cannot be land disposed until threats posed by their disposal have been minimized).

[25]40 C.F.R. §§ 268.45(a), 268.2(h).

Chapter 12: Land Ban Disposal Restrictions 311

longer to any of the Subtitle C rules.[26] The Regional Administrator may also make a case-by-case "contained out" determination for any contaminated debris.[27]

Spent potliners from producing primary aluminum (Hazardous Waste K088) now have a customized (non-Universal) treatment standard for arsenic following a complicated history full of sound and fury that in the end signified little. EPA initially established the Universal Treatment Standards as the treatment standards for this waste, plus a treatment standard for fluoride, a non-Appendix VIII constituent present in this waste in high concentrations and linked to groundwater contamination in a number of damage incidents involving improper potliner disposal.[28] Virtually all of the treatment capacity for this waste was provided by a single facility, using a process that, among other things, increased the pH of the treatment residue to alkaline levels. As it happens, arsenic and fluoride are amphoteric (significantly more soluble in alkaline conditions than in acidic ones). The Universal Treatment Standards, however, use the TCLP to measure compliance for arsenic (and other metals; the TCLP was also used to measure compliance with the fluoride treatment standard for K088). The TCLP uses a slightly acidic extractant. Thus, the TCLP was not mirroring a worst-case management scenario for the alkaline K088 treatment residue, as demonstrated by actual events. A dedicated landfill for K088 treatment residue, exposed only to rainwater, began leaching high concentrations of arsenic and fluoride (consistent with their solubility profiles), even though the treatment residue was in compliance with LDR standards. Faced with these facts, EPA initially extended the national capacity variance for K088 but eventually declined to extend the variance on the theory that some treatment standard was better than none.[29] The D.C. Circuit found this action to be arbitrary and capricious, holding that the TCLP was not a proper model for ascertaining successful treatment performance.[30] EPA reads this decision narrowly: Because all commercial treatment capacity was provided by a single facility using a single process and disposing of all treatment residue at a single location, the TCLP was demonstrably and seriously underreporting leaching potential of the waste 100 percent of the time and so was not a proper model.[31] The decision thus does not call into question

---

[26]*Id.* §§ 268.45(c), 261.3(f)(1) (which also assigns the burden of proof in an enforcement action to the party claiming this exclusion).

[27]*Id.* § 261.3(f)(2).

[28]61 Fed. Reg. 15,566, 15,585 (Apr. 8, 1996).

[29]62 Fed. Reg. 37,694 (July 14, 1997).

[30]Columbia Falls Aluminum v. EPA, 139 F.3d 914, 923 (D.C. Cir. 1998).

[31]63 Fed. Reg. 28,571–72.

312 THE RCRA PRACTICE MANUAL

the normal principle that models need not be entirely accurate to be applied legitimately.

The ironic upshot of the *Columbia Falls* decision is that EPA, at the court's invitation,[32] promulgated interim treatment standards for K088 that were slightly less stringent than the ones the court vacated, lacking a fluoride standard and having an arsenic standard that measures total rather than leachable arsenic.[33] These standards were challenged by the *Columbia Falls* petitioners as inconsistent with the opinion's mandate, but the court denied the motion to enforce the mandate. These interim standards remain in effect because these same petitioners, after much ballyhooing of alternative, superior treatment technologies, now acknowledge (in comments to treatment standards EPA proposed[34]) that nothing superior to existing treatment is now available. The treatment standards for K088 thus remain the Universal Treatment Standards for most metals, organics, and cyanide but a separate (non-Universal) standard for arsenic.

IV. Assuring That LDRs Do Not Lead to Environmentally Inappropriate Results and Modifying LDRs to Encourage Aggressive Remediation

An emerging principle, now codified and judicially ratified, is that the LDRs should not be applied in a way that leads to environmentally inappropriate results, and LDRs may be adjusted to avoid this result. The issue arises in situations where hazardous wastes have already been disposed and there is no ready means to compel their excavation.[35] Examples include not just CERCLA cleanups and RCRA corrective action where remedy requirements allow a balancing of treatment and containment strategies, but also RCRA closures (choice between clean closure and closure with waste in place) and situations where rules (or relevant policies) allow wastes to remain within an "area of contamination."[36] In these situations, it may be desirable to excavate the wastes and manage them more securely elsewhere. However, LDRs can create a disincentive to such action because the LDR treatment requirements attach at the point of excavation—the LDR point of generation for remediation wastes (see earlier discussion of LDR point of generation). EPA has promulgated

---

[32]*Columbia Falls, supra* note 30, 139 F.3d at 924.
[33]63 Fed. Reg. 51,254 (Sept. 24, 1998).
[34]65 Fed. Reg. 42,937 (July 12, 2000).
[35]*See generally* 63 Fed. Reg. 28,603–04.
[36]Descriptions of many of these and other relevant policies and regulations, including references, are included in the memorandum Management of Remediation Waste under RCRA, EPA 530-F-98-026 (Oct. 1998).

Chapter 12: Land Ban Disposal Restrictions 313

a series of rules to reduce or eliminate this disincentive, all resting on the principle that LDRs can be adjusted to avoid the environmentally inappropriate result of discouraging aggressive remediation.

A. Treatment Variances

The first explicit codification of this principle came in the somewhat out-of-the-way context of LDR treatment variances. Motivated initially by a situation where a facility had a choice between closing a large surface impoundment in place or clean closing it, EPA amended the treatment variance rules to provide that treatment variances can be granted "for remediation waste only if [petitioners demonstrate that] treatment to the specified level or by the specified method is environmentally inappropriate because it would likely discourage aggressive remediation."[37] A corollary principle, announced in the preamble to this regulation, is that in determining whether an alternative treatment standard granted through a treatment variance is sufficient to minimize threats posed by land disposal, "EPA (or the authorized State) may consider risks posed by land disposal not only of the treated residue, but also the risks posed by the continuation of any existing land disposal of the untreated waste, that is, the risks posed by leaving previously land disposed waste in place."[38] The D.C. Circuit sustained both the rule and the interpretive principle as "plainly reasonable" interpretations of RCRA Section 3004(m).[39]

B. Special Standards for Contaminated Soils

EPA applied this same principle, in the so-called Phase IV rule, to support promulgation of alternative treatment standards for contaminated soil.[40] Again, on the grounds that requiring contaminated soil to be treated to meet LDRs could be environmentally inappropriate (and sometimes technically inappropriate as well), EPA allowed the option of treatment to a level of either ten times the applicable Universal Treatment Standard (UTS) or 90 percent reduction in hazardous constituent levels (measured in either a TCLP extract (for most metals) or totals (for most organics).[41] This requirement applies to hazardous constituents reasonably likely to be present in any contaminated soil at concentrations exceeding ten times the Universal Treatment Standard, thus including

---

[37]40 C.F.R. § 268.44(a)(2)(ii), (h)(2)(ii).
[38]62 Fed. Reg. 64,504, 64,506 (Dec. 5, 1997).
[39]La. Envtl. Action Network v. EPA, 172 F.3d 65, 72 (D.C. Cir. 1999).
[40]63 Fed. Reg. 28,602–22.
[41]40 C.F.R. § 268.49(c).

314 THE RCRA PRACTICE MANUAL

underlying hazardous constituents (called "constituents subject to treatment" in the rule).[42] The one exception is PCBs found in contaminated soils exhibiting the Toxicity Characteristic (TC) for metals. The agency deferred the requirement that PCBs be considered a constituent subject to treatment (that is, an underlying hazardous constituent) in this class of contaminated soils due to the possibility that the PCB treatment requirement was impeding ongoing remediations.[43] A further gloss on this exception for PCBs is that PCB levels of 1,000 milligrams per kilogram in such soil (or less if the soil contains other halogenated organic compounds) would still require treatment pursuant to the California list treatment requirement for halogenated organic compounds, found in RCRA Section 3004(d)(2)(E) (codified with respect to TC metal contaminated soils at section 268.32).

The Phase IV rules also indicate when LDRs apply to contaminated soil, taking into account whether LDRs applied when the waste was first disposed, and whether they apply when the waste is regenerated (that is, excavated). This, in turn, requires that the contained-in principle be taken into account, since the contained-in principle is used to determine whether the soil is considered to be hazardous (contains a listed hazardous waste) upon excavation (assuming the soil does not exhibit a characteristic). The following principles determine LDR applicability to contaminated soil (and, for that matter, to other comparable remediation waste as well):

- LDRs only attach to contaminated soils that are generated and placed in a land disposal unit.
- Even after soil is generated and re-land-disposed, LDRs only apply to soil that, at that point, contains a hazardous waste (that is, exhibits a characteristic, or contains environmentally significant concentrations of hazardous constituents from listed hazardous wastes); see the earlier discussion of the contained-in principle in the context of debris and LDR point of generation.
- Once LDR standards attach (at the point of excavation), they continue to apply until the treatment standards are met, per the D.C. Circuit's *Chemical Waste Management* decision.

LDRs thus continue to apply to excavated soils that "contain" hazardous waste when they are generated (that is, excavated) but no longer

---

[42]*Id.* § 268.49(d).

[43]*See generally* 65 Fed. Reg. 81,373 (Dec. 26, 2000); 40 C.F.R. § 268.49(d) (final sentence).

Chapter 12: Land Ban Disposal Restrictions 315

do so before they are re-land disposed.[44] These principles are codified in the rules in the tabular matrix that appears at Section 268.49(a).

An exception to these principles arises if an applicant can demonstrate to EPA, on a site-specific basis, that hazardous constituent levels in soil are below those necessary to minimize threats to human health and the environment.[45] These site-specific minimize threat levels could be the same as "contained out" levels but could conceivably be lower.[46] The standards for granting a site-specific minimize threat treatment variance for soils are that, at a minimum, risks posed by carcinogenic hazardous constituents under a reasonable maximum exposure scenario not exceed a lifetime risk range of 10^{-4} to 10^{-6}.[47] For threshold hazardous constituents, constituent concentrations should not exceed levels causing "appreciable risk of deleterious effect" during lifetime exposure.[48] In promulgating this risk-based minimize threat site-specific treatment variance for soils, EPA explained that the goal of generally applicable risk-based variances remains elusive[49] but that EPA is able to adopt them on a site-specific basis for soils, given the remediation context where a great deal is known about the individual site and soil matrix.[50]

C. Special Standards for Hazardous Wastes Placed in *Corrective Action Management Units (CAMUs)*

EPA's 1993 CAMU rule created a special type of hazardous waste management unit—a corrective action management unit (CAMU)—to be used only for on-site treatment, storage, and disposal of hazardous wastes managed for implementing cleanup. The theory of the rules vis-à-vis LDRs is that consolidation or placement of cleanup wastes into a CAMU is not considered land disposal, so it does not trigger RCRA's LDR requirements.[51] Overseeing agencies then had flexibility to tailor waste treatment requirements (and also design, operating, closure, and postclosure requirements) to site- and waste-specific conditions.

EPA has recently amended the 1993 rule to establish (among other things) a new framework for treatment of wastes placed in CAMUs.[52]

---

[44]63 Fed. Reg. 28,617–19.

[45]40 C.F.R. § 268.44(h)(3); 63 Fed. Reg. 28,606–08.

[46]63 Fed. Reg. 28,628, 28,622.

[47]40 C.F.R. § 268.44(h)(i)(A).

[48]*Id.* § 268.44(h)(3)(i)(B).

[49]*See* THE RCRA PRACTICE MANUAL, at p. 166 (referring to the "quest for these levels" as "the Holy Grail of the RCRA program").

[50]63 Fed. Reg. 28,607.

[51]40 C.F.R. § 264.552(a)(1).

[52]*See* 67 Fed. Reg. (Jan. 2002) (signed December 21, 2001).

316 THE RCRA PRACTICE MANUAL

Under this new framework, "principal hazardous constituents"[53] (PHCs) must meet either minimum national treatment standards adapted from the LDR Phase IV soil treatment standards—the 90 percent reduction or ten times UTS levels—or, in specific circumstances, site-specific treatment standards based on defined adjustment factors. These treatment standards apply to both soil and nonsoil wastes, including sludges and debris. (CAMU-eligible debris that contains PHCs must be treated using the current LDR treatment standards for hazardous debris at 40 C.F.R. Section 264.45 or the CAMU treatment standards, whichever the Regional Administrator deems appropriate.) CAMU-eligible wastes must also be treated to remove the characteristics of ignitability, corrosivity, or reactivity. In addition, the treatment standard requirement applies only when wastes will be placed in a CAMU for permanent disposal, so the treatment requirement does not apply when wastes are placed in CAMUs for storage and/or treatment solely. Finally, the rule does not require that treatment standards be met before placement. Treatment may occur either before or after wastes are placed in a CAMU.

The rule further provides for a number of adjustments to these treatment standards. First, the TCLP need not be used in all instances for measuring compliance with the treatment standards for metals. The rule provides that a regulatory agency may require the use of a test other than the TCLP when it finds that the test is available for use and that it reflects conditions at the site that affect leaching more accurately than the TCLP.[54] The rule further sets out five factors that outline circumstances under which Regional Administrators may adjust the minimum national treatment standards on a site-specific basis: technical impracticability, consistency with site cleanup standards, community views, short-term risks, and protection offered by engineering controls under specified circumstances.[55] When one or more of the adjustment factors are applied, the rule requires that the resulting site-specific treatment standard be "protective of human health and the environment."

---

[53]PHCs are defined in 40 C.F.R. § 264.552(e)(4)(i)(C) as constituents that "pose a risk to human health or the environment that is substantially higher than the cleanup levels or goals at the site." The Regional Administrator selects PHCs from constituents that would otherwise be subject to treatment under the RCRA LDR treatment standards for as-generated waste. The rule further provides that "in general, the Regional Administrator will designate as principal hazardous constituents: carcinogens that pose a potential direct risk from ingestion or inhalation at the site at or above 10^{-3}; and non-carcinogens that pose a potential direct risk from ingestion or inhalation at the site an order of magnitude or greater over their reference dose." The rule also provides authority to designate additional PHCs based, generally, on risk considerations.

[54]40 C.F.R. § 264.552(e)(4)(iv)(F).

[55]See id. § 264.552(e)(4)(v)(A)–(E).

Chapter 12: Land Ban Disposal Restrictions   317

Finally, again to encourage aggressive remediation, the rule allows CAMU-eligible waste to be placed in off-site Subtitle C landfills and meet the treatment standards from the CAMU rule, rather than the normal LDR treatment standards.[56] Should this occur, the treatment adjustment factors differ slightly from those in the rest of the rule to reflect the different circumstances of disposal in an off-site landfill.[57]

D. Exceptions to the Principle of Modifying LDRs to Encourage Aggressive Remediation

EPA has noted that not every type of remediation involving excavation and treatment warrants modification of LDR requirements. The notable example to date is the end disposition of the treated remediation waste involving a so-called use constituting disposal—that is, recycling of the material involving placement on the land, either directly or in the form of a waste-derived product that is placed on the land. Thus, the rules provide that the special standards for contaminated soils (90 percent reduction or ten times UTS) do not apply if the soil is to be used in a manner constituting disposal.[58] EPA was unable to find that the special soil standards were sufficient to minimize threats posed by land disposal of the contaminated soils if the soils were to be used in a manner constituting disposal because of the uncertainties associated with this mode of recycling: Waste-derived products used in a manner constituting disposal can be placed virtually anywhere, "compounding potential release mechanisms, exposure pathways, and human and environmental receptors."[59] For the same reason, EPA does not necessarily feel warranted in encouraging this type of remediation.[60] These points were all endorsed by the D.C. Circuit when it upheld the rule making contaminated soils used in a manner constituting disposal ineligible for the special standards for contaminated soils.[61]

For the same reasons, EPA has cautioned that in considering treatment variances, special consideration should be given to whether the treated waste will be used in a manner constituting disposal.[62] If this is the end disposition of the waste, it may not be possible to find that threats to human health and the environment will still be minimized at treatment variance levels.[63]

---

[56]*See id.* § 264.555.
[57]*Id.* § 264.555(a)(2).
[58]63 Fed. Reg. 28,609–10.
[59]*Id.* at 28,610.
[60]*Id.*
[61]Ass'n of Battery Recyclers v. EPA, 208 F.3d 1047, 1059–60 (D.C. Cir. 2000).
[62]40 C.F.R. § 268.44(m) (final sentence).
[63]62 Fed. Reg. 64,506.

CHAPTER 13

Corrective Action Requirements

JAMES T. PRICE AND KARL S. BOURDEAU

I. Overview of the Statutory Scheme and Regulatory Background

The corrective action program under the Resource Conservation and Recovery Act (RCRA) imposes substantial obligations on owners and operators of RCRA hazardous waste management facilities to investigate and clean up on-site and off-site contamination caused by current and historic activities. Much like the cleanup program under the Comprehensive Environmental Response, Compensation, and Liability Act (CERCLA),[1] to which corrective action often is compared, the corrective action program has been subjected to blistering criticism from representatives of most significant stakeholder groups. Industry has criticized the program as being overly expansive, unwieldy, unworkable, and too expensive. Environmental groups and congressional overseers have criticized the program for being too slow to address and clean up contaminated sites. States have criticized the program for usurping their power and granting too little flexibility. As with CERCLA, however, recent administrative reforms promise a more streamlined and "results-oriented" program.

The corrective action program was established with the Hazardous and Solid Waste Amendments of 1984 (HSWA). Unlike CERCLA, which for the past ten years has been subjected to proposals for statutory change, RCRA corrective action largely has escaped significant proposals for legislative amendment. It has, however, been the subject of numerous regulatory proposals and guidance to implement, interpret, revise, and sometimes abandon key program provisions. Accordingly,

---

[1] 42 U.S.C. § 9601 et seq.

320 THE RCRA PRACTICE MANUAL

the most significant details on RCRA corrective action program elements are found not in RCRA but in regulations, proposed regulations, and guidance, all of which have undergone dramatic changes over time. Additionally, many states now are authorized to operate state-led corrective action programs under authorization from EPA, further adding to the myriad of potentially authoritative provisions. This chapter does not address more expanded state requirements or interpretations of RCRA corrective action.

Before HSWA, many persons argued that EPA did not have substantial authority under RCRA to require remediation of historical contamination at facilities that currently manage hazardous wastes. RCRA Section 3013 authorized EPA to issue orders requiring testing and analysis of certain releases of hazardous wastes, and RCRA Section 7003 authorized EPA to either issue administrative orders or seek court orders to abate imminent and substantial dangers posed by hazardous or solid wastes. Despite these provisions, RCRA essentially was a prospective statute addressing current waste management practices. HSWA added key corrective action provisions, providing clear authority for corrective action as a consequence of both current and past waste-handling activities at permitted facilities;[2] corrective action beyond the boundary of a treatment, storage, and disposal facility (TSDF);[3] and corrective action for interim status TSDFs.[4]

The program is expansive and expensive. According to EPA estimates, approximately 6,400 facilities with more than 80,000 solid waste management units (SWMUs) potentially are subject to RCRA corrective action authorities—more facilities than the core Superfund program.

Essentially, the RCRA corrective action program has passed through three phases, each with a distinct emphasis. These are reviewed in detail in Section III below. The latest—and current—phase emphasizes what EPA calls its "results-based" approach to corrective action. Under this approach, much of the current focus of the RCRA corrective action program is on achieving two so-called "environmental indicators" (EIs): human exposures under control and migration of contaminated groundwater under control. Demands to achieve those EIs at each of more than 1,700 sites designated by EPA drives much of the corrective action program today. EIs are discussed in Section IV, below.

---

[2]RCRA § 3004(u), 42 U.S.C. § 6924(u).
[3]RCRA § 3004(v), 42 U.S.C. § 6924(v).
[4]RCRA § 3008(h), 42 U.S.C. § 6928(h).

II. Jurisdictional Reach of the Program

Perhaps not surprisingly, EPA takes a broad view of its authority. EPA even has interpreted corrective action as extending to certain releases of hazardous chemicals associated with manufacturing activities beyond typical waste management activities, to merely suspected or potential future releases, and to releases of hazardous constituents into any environmental medium, not just soil and groundwater.

A. Permit and Interim Status Corrective Action

Corrective action authority applies to TSDFs that have a RCRA permit or are subject to the RCRA interim status provisions. (As discussed elsewhere in this book, "interim status" refers to the status conferred upon an active hazardous waste management facility that authorizes it to treat, store, or dispose of hazardous waste until it receives a final RCRA permit.) The permit or interim status authorization may exist under either EPA regulations or the program of a state that EPA has authorized to conduct its own hazardous waste program in lieu of the federal program.

Section 3004(u) of RCRA requires every facility seeking a RCRA Section 3005 permit after November 8, 1984, to undertake corrective action for all releases of hazardous wastes and hazardous constituents of nonhazardous solid wastes from SWMUs at the facility, regardless of when the waste was placed in the unit involved. Section 3004(u) also provides for schedules of compliance in RCRA permits for undertaking corrective action and requires financial responsibility assurances for completing such action. Section 3004(v) of RCRA requires that corrective action be undertaken beyond the facility's property boundary to address off-site contamination where necessary to protect human health and the environment, assuming access from adjoining property owners can be secured. Section 3005(i) states that certain corrective action requirements are to be imposed upon designated hazardous waste management units that received hazardous waste after July 26, 1982. RCRA Section 3005(c)(3) requires that RCRA permits contain all conditions necessary to protect human health or the environment. This so-called "omnibus authority" is used, *inter alia*, to require corrective action at so-called "areas of concern" (AOCs). (AOCs are areas of a facility that may not qualify as SWMUs but still present environmental concerns associated with releases of hazardous constituents. AOCs and omnibus authority are discussed in Section II.B.2, below.) Finally, RCRA Section 3008(h) authorizes EPA to issue administrative corrective action orders or institute civil judicial actions where a release of hazardous waste into the environment requires a response.

Sections 3004(u) and 3008(h) apply only to facilities that have obtained, or are required to obtain, a RCRA hazardous waste permit or interim status. Generators, transporters, and those that store hazardous wastes in containers or tanks for no more than the time limit allotted by applicable federal or state regulation without triggering a hazardous waste permit requirement (typically 90 days) generally are not subject to these authorities by virtue of those activities alone. These classes of parties, however, must exercise care in their hazardous waste activities to avoid engaging in actions that unwittingly will subject them to the corrective action program.

Some facilities that fear they are subject to corrective action may not be. An example is a facility that generates hazardous waste and sometime in the past applied for interim status to protect itself from potential liability for exceeding storage time limits, but never actually operated or used that interim status authority. EPA guidance indicates that those so-called "protective filers" were not "authorized to operate" under interim status and are not subject to corrective action.[5]

On the other hand, EPA has indicated that a facility that actually operated subject to interim status (regardless of whether the facility applied for such status) is subject to corrective action jurisdiction. EPA takes a similar position on facilities that have ceased using their interim status, whether or not they officially have requested that EPA revoke it. In EPA's view, moreover, facilities that lose their interim status by operation of law for failing to submit a Part B permit application also remain subject to RCRA Section 3008(h) interim status corrective action jurisdiction. Accordingly, prospective purchasers of property are well advised to determine whether activities were conducted at the property that subjected it to corrective action requirements, which may be imposed on current property owners.

B. Types of Units Subject to Corrective Action Authorities

Numerous EPA guidance documents and decisions on administrative appeals of corrective action permit conditions demonstrate the agency's intention to apply its corrective action authorities to a broad universe of facilities and to address contamination from a wide range of historical activities conducted at those facilities. As the agency has implemented the RCRA Subtitle C corrective action program, it has swept into that

---

[5]*See* 50 Fed. Reg. 38,946 (1985); 54 Fed. Reg. 41,000, 41,006 (1989); 53 Fed. Reg. 23,981 (1988).

Chapter 13: Corrective Action Requirements 323

program a diverse spectrum of contaminated areas not traditionally associated with solid waste management activities.

1. *Releases of "Solid Waste"*

Theoretically, corrective action pursuant to Section 3004(u) (which refers to releases from *solid waste* management units) and Section 3008(h) (referring to releases of *hazardous waste*) is limited to waste management units, thus excluding releases of other, nonwaste materials such as products and the like. The meaning of the phrase "solid waste" should limit EPA's corrective action jurisdiction.

RCRA's definition of solid waste is discussed elsewhere in this book. The following discussion will provide a mere overview as this definition relates to corrective action. EPA defined solid waste at length in its regulations identifying and listing hazardous wastes.[6] EPA has discussed the meaning of the term in regulatory preambles relating to hazardous waste identification and corrective action. Moreover, the courts have had occasion to define what materials constitute RCRA solid wastes. In *American Mining Congress v. EPA (AMC I)*,[7] the court held that a material must be discarded to constitute a waste. According to the *AMC I* court, certain by-products of a production process that were recycled into a continuous ongoing manufacturing process were not "discarded" and therefore not subject to RCRA regulation.

Two later cases refine the D.C. Circuit's view of the definition of "solid waste" in the context of recycled by-products. The D.C. Circuit has made clear that the mere possibility that a material may be recycled into a production process does not mean the material is not discarded.[8] The general approach employed by the D.C. Circuit in those cases to determine whether a material has been discarded is whether it has become a part of the "waste disposal problem."[9] The court, however, has left EPA room to resolve whether materials in different recycling situations have become part of the waste disposal problem and thus are within RCRA jurisdiction.[10]

EPA has stated its view in guidance that leakage from raw material and product storage or transfer areas and other types of "units" associated with production processes will be considered releases from SWMUs

---

[6]40 C.F.R. § 261.2.

[7]824 F.2d 1177 (D.C. Cir. 1987).

[8]Am. Mining Cong. v. EPA, 907 F.2d 1179 (D.C. Cir. 1990) (*AMC II*); Am. Petroleum Inst. v. EPA, 906 F.2d 729 (D.C. Cir. 1990).

[9]*Id.*

[10]*AMC II, supra* note 8, 907 F.2d at 1186–87.

324 THE RCRA PRACTICE MANUAL

subject to corrective action if the leaks or releases are "routine and systematic," thereby suggesting that the material involved has become "discarded" and is thus a solid waste.[11] This interpretation of the scope of Section 3004(u) has been upheld in a number of administrative permit appeal decisions.[12] Although the agency has indicated that it does not intend routinely to examine a facility's production, handling, and storage areas during corrective action investigations,[13] as a practical matter, the identification of possible releases from such areas during EPA inspections often has resulted in the owner or operator being required to investigate further to verify releases and to address any such releases under corrective action.

2. Areas of Concern and Omnibus Authority

Despite its acknowledgment that one-time or episodic spills or releases from raw material or product storage areas, manufacturing processes, and transportation incidents at facilities otherwise subject to corrective action authorities are not "routine and systematic"[14] and statements early in its implementation of the program that such releases were not subject to Section 3004(u) authorities, EPA nonetheless requires investigation and remediation of releases from such so-called areas of concern (AOCs) in corrective action permits. Although the AOC concept is not found anywhere in RCRA or its implementing regulations, EPA regions routinely seek to require facilities to address non-SWMU contaminated areas of a facility where evidence is lacking of routine and systematic releases of hazardous constituents.

These jurisdictional reaches by EPA regional offices generally have been upheld in administrative RCRA permit appeal decisions as proper exercises of the "omnibus" permit authority of RCRA Section 3005(c)(3), which authorizes EPA and states with authorized RCRA permit programs to impose such terms and conditions in permits as they deem necessary to protect human health and the environment.[15]

---

[11]See, e.g., Draft National RCRA Corrective Action Strategy (National Strategy), OSWER Directive 9502.00-6, (Oct. 14, 1986), pp. 3–4, 25; Subpart S Proposed Corrective Action Rule (Subpart S Proposed Rule), 55 Fed. Reg. 30,798 at 30,808–09 (proposed July 1990).

[12]In re Am. Cyanamid Co., RCRA Appeal No. 89-8 (June 20, 1991); See, e.g., In re Chevron USA, Inc., RCRA Appeal No. 89-26 (Dec. 31, 1990).

[13]See National Strategy, supra note 11, at 9–10; Am. Cyanamid, supra note 12 (corrective action reference to "entire plant" too broad as potentially encompassing production facilities).

[14]55 Fed. Reg. 30,808 (1990).

[15]See, e.g., Am. Cyanamid, supra note 12; In re LCP Chems.–N.C., Inc., RCRA Appeal No. 90-4 (Feb. 14, 1991); In re Amerada Hess Corp., RCRA Appeal No. 88-10 (Aug. 15, 1989); In re Morton Int'l, Inc., RCRA Appeal No. 90-17 (Feb. 28, 1992) (rejecting the facility's argument that omnibus authority under Section 3005(c)(3) extends only to units that also qualify as SWMUs).

Chapter 13: Corrective Action Requirements   325

Although these decisions hold that Section 3005(c)(3) provides a broad grant of jurisdictional authority to address AOCs, they also indicate that the omnibus permit authority may be invoked for that purpose only where "an adequate nexus" of the AOC to solid or hazardous waste at the facility has been demonstrated and the administrative record supporting the permit demonstrates, on a site-specific basis, that the permit condition imposed is necessary to protect human health and the environment.[16] In other words, findings in the initial RCRA facility assessment or other investigation performed by the agency must be sufficient to support a conclusion that (1) addressing the AOC or nonwaste material in it is necessary or desirable to properly regulate solid or hazardous waste management activities reasonably associated with the AOC or nonwaste material, and (2) the AOC poses a sufficient human health or environmental concern to warrant the type of corrective action the agency seeks to impose.

C. Extent of the Facility Subject to Corrective Action

For purposes of RCRA corrective action, EPA defines a RCRA "facility" to include all contiguous property, from fenceline to fenceline, owned by the owner of the TSDF.[17] This is a broader application of the term "facility" than EPA uses in other aspects of the RCRA regulations.[18] Where the facility owner and operator are different entities, EPA says corrective action authority extends to all the property owner's contiguous property, regardless of whether that property is occupied by the TSDF operator, is leased to and occupied by others, or is currently used for waste management.

The effect of EPA's broad definition of "facility" is to require fenceline-to-fenceline corrective action assessments, investigations, and remediations, even if the RCRA-regulated unit is found in only one small portion of a larger facility. This approach has presented concerns for manufacturing facilities, which naturally question why the cumbersome corrective action process should apply to slightly contaminated portions of manufacturing facilities on which some isolated, historical SWMUs are present. The problem has been even more significant at RCRA corrective action sites with redevelopment potential—so-called "brownfields." At such sites, facility owners, operators, potential buyers, and

---

[16]*See, e.g., In re* BP Chems. Am., Inc., RCRA Appeal No. 89-4 (Aug. 20, 1992); *In re* Sandoz Pharm. Corp., RCRA Appeal No. 91-14 (July 9, 1992); *Morton Int'l., supra* note 15.

[17]40 C.F.R. § 260.10.

[18]*See* Mobil Oil Corp. v. EPA, 871 F.2d 149 (D.C. Cir. 1989) (approving EPA's interpretation of "facility" to encompass only a particular waste management unit in applying the RCRA minimum technology requirement for facilities that receive certain wastes).

326 THE RCRA PRACTICE MANUAL

potential lenders have found this fenceline-to-fenceline corrective action policy hinders transactions and redevelopment of uncontaminated portions of larger tracts. As a result of EPA's results-based corrective action initiatives, in recent years at some sites EPA regions have been willing to allow the sites to be subdivided or some portions declared "clean" and no longer subject to corrective action. Such decisions have proceeded on a pilot or case-by-case basis, however, and often require cumbersome modifications of RCRA permits, corrective action orders, or other legal documents. In February 2003, EPA issued its "Guidance on Completion of Corrective Action Activities at RCRA Facilities" to help facility owners and prospective purchasers determine when EPA considers corrective action at such sites to be complete.[19]

D. Types of Releases Subject to Corrective Action Authorities

EPA also has interpreted its corrective action authorities broadly with respect to the types of releases they cover. Even though Sections 3004(u) and 3008(h) appear on their face to cover only actual releases, EPA has taken the position that those authorities also extend to suspected or *potential future* releases (for example, buried drums that, although not currently leaking, could leak in the future).[20] Consistent with 1986 amendments to CERCLA that extended the definition of "release" under that statute to include abandonment of closed receptacles containing hazardous substances, EPA has stated that in the absence of a definition of "release" in RCRA, it will interpret "release" for Section 3004(u) purposes to encompass that situation as well.[21]

EPA also has sought to assert jurisdiction over releases regulated under other environmental laws.[22] Examples include stack emissions from solid waste incinerators with state air permits; wastewater discharges to surface waters consistent with a Clean Water Act National Pollutant Discharge Elimination System (NPDES) permit; and at times,

---

[19]*See* 68 Fed.Reg. 8757 (Feb. 25, 2003).

[20]*See, e.g., In re* GSX Servs. of S.C., Inc., RCRA Permit Appeal No. 89-22 (Dec. 29, 1992); *Sandoz, supra* note 16; *In re* Marathon Petroleum Co., RCRA Permit Appeal No. 88-24 (Nov. 16, 1990); *In re* Envirosafe Servs. of Idaho, Inc., RCRA Permit Appeal No. 88-41 (Apr. 3. 1990) (relating to future releases where no current releases suspected). *But see* 55 Fed. Reg. 30,874 (1990) (requiring that a release be "likely"); *In re* Caribe Gen. Elec. Prods., Inc., RCRA Appeal No. 98-3 (Feb. 4, 2000) (requiring EPA to demonstrate that hazardous constituents are migrating or have migrated to an off-site area before it can require such an area to be addressed pursuant to RCRA corrective action).

[21]55 Fed. Reg. 30,808 (1990).

[22]*See, e.g.,* 55 Fed. Reg. 30,808 (1990); *In re* S.D. Warren Co., RCRA Appeal No. 89-35 (Nov. 29, 1991).

Chapter 13: Corrective Action Requirements   327

manufacturing worker exposure to indoor air releases well below thresholds set by the Occupational Safety and Health Administration (OSHA).

In sum, EPA has chosen to extend its jurisdictional reach with respect to both the universe of facilities and units subject to corrective action authorities and the releases of hazardous constituents at such facilities that are within the scope of these authorities. The agency's positions raise a number of statutory interpretation issues that eventually may have to be decided by federal courts.

III. The Corrective Action Process

A. Interim Status Corrective Action Orders

Corrective action requirements often are imposed under an interim status corrective action order from EPA. The order will govern corrective action activities unless and until those activities are incorporated as requirements of the RCRA permit.

EPA usually first seeks to enter a consent order with the facility owner and operator. If the parties cannot negotiate an acceptable consent order, EPA unilaterally may issue a corrective action order to the facility. The procedures for issuing such orders are set forth at 40 C.F.R. Part 24. The recipient has an opportunity to appeal, which involves a hearing followed by a final agency decision made by the Regional Administrator of EPA.[23]

B. Corrective Action under RCRA Permits

In addition, EPA can impose corrective action requirements on a facility when the facility's RCRA permit is renewed. EPA's RCRA permit regulations allow it to modify a permit when "the standards or regulations on which the permit was based have been changed by statute."[24] EPA can impose corrective action requirements on a permitted facility under this authority.[25] Finally, EPA will impose corrective action requirements on interim status facilities when they obtain permits. Unless the state is authorized to implement RCRA corrective action requirements, EPA will issue and supervise the corrective action portion of the permit. At times, EPA has sought to impose additional corrective action requirements in

---

[23]40 C.F.R. §§ 24.18–24.20.

[24]*Id.* § 270.41(a)(3).

[25]*But see In re* Gen. Motors Corp., RCRA Consolidated Appeal Nos. 90-24, 90-25 (Nov. 6, 1992) (limitations upon EPA's permit modification authority).

328 THE RCRA PRACTICE MANUAL

federal permits even after a state receives authorization. In other situations EPA has commented on draft state corrective action permit requirements in a manner that preserves EPA's ability to enforce conditions it seeks beyond those imposed by the state.[26]

C. The Basic Steps of Corrective Action

The corrective action process undertaken by a facility owner and operator generally consists of three steps: (1) a RCRA facility investigation (RFI); (2) a corrective measures study (CMS); and (3) corrective measures implementation. An intermediate step called interim measures, discussed later in Section III.D of this chapter, may be used to stabilize the contamination and slow down or prevent further migration and exposure while studies are ongoing. Interim measures now are common components of corrective action activities and often are required to achieve compliance with Environmental Indicators discussed in Section IV.C.

Before corrective action begins, an EPA contractor frequently has performed a RCRA facility assessment (RFA), which describes the nature of the facility, its SWMUs and AOCs, and whether further investigation is needed for such units in order to address releases of hazardous constituents.

1. RCRA Facility Investigations

EPA will require facilities to conduct an RFI if the initial RFA indicates that a release of hazardous constituents under 40 C.F.R. Part 261, Appendix VIII or Part 264, Appendix IX is occurring, has occurred, or is likely to have occurred. The RFI is similar to a CERCLA remedial investigation. The RFI will identify releases that will require corrective action. Some such releases already may have been identified in the RFA.

The RFI process typically begins with submittal to EPA of a description of current conditions, which presents in summarized form available information on facility waste management practices. Based in part on the level of current knowledge and the EPA-approved scope of work, the facility owner or operator prepares an RFI work plan delineating the scope of the RFI work. The RFI work plan provides an early and effective means to define the scope of the corrective action program for the facility.

An RFI for a facility consists of an assessment of active or inactive SWMUs to determine whether they ever received hazardous wastes or hazardous constituents. For most such SWMUs, the facility owner or

---

[26]*See, e.g.,* 40 C.F.R. § 271.19, 270.2 (definition of "Director").

operator must assess their conditions and evaluate whether they adequately could contain the waste. The agency may require additional investigation to determine whether releases have occurred. If potential pathways for releases are identified, the facility owner or operator must investigate to determine whether such releases have occurred, are likely, or are suspected. Where releases or potential releases are confirmed, the facility must conduct additional investigation to determine the extent of the releases and their effect on the environment.

EPA's "RCRA Facility Investigation Guidance," including its risk assessment methodologies, has been used by EPA regions to determine the adequacy of remedy investigations proposed by facilities. Unfortunately, EPA regions tend to follow this guidance strictly, notwithstanding the admonition of the 1996 advance notice proposed rule making (ANPR) (discussed below in Section IV.C) against "process laden" corrective action. The regions at times are unwilling to tailor the investigatory tasks to site-specific conditions and information. Although permittees (and other recipients) can sometimes convince regional officials to tailor investigation requirements significantly, often they have to challenge a region's refusal to do so. Because a successful challenge must demonstrate that the region's requirements were clearly erroneous, these challenges can prove difficult.[27]

At the conclusion of the RFI, the facility owner or operator submits a report to EPA. EPA typically reserves the right to comment on and require modifications to the RFI report. Once the RFI report is final, and assuming EPA concludes that corrective measures are warranted, the corrective measures study begins.

2. Corrective Measures Studies

A corrective measures study (CMS) is similar in objective to a CERCLA feasibility study. It is intended to identify and evaluate appropriate cleanup alternatives to eliminate or reduce the risks posed by releases of hazardous wastes or hazardous constituents discovered during the RFI. Inherent in this activity is establishing the goals of the cleanup, colloquially called the "how clean is clean?" question.

The trigger for a CMS typically is a release exceeding an "action level." EPA has stated generally that the level of effort required for a CMS should be geared to the level of risk and complexity of cleanup posed by the contamination at a particular facility. Potentially this focus can reduce the range of remedial alternatives that would need to be

---

[27]*See, e.g., In re* Gen. Elec. Co., RCRA Appeal No. 91-7 (Nov. 6, 1992); *Gen. Motors Corp., supra* note 25.

evaluated. EPA in some situations has embraced the use of a focused CMS if a proper corrective measure is readily identifiable and the facility's future use is both clear and consistent with that measure. This is one technique to streamline the corrective action process used at ongoing manufacturing facilities or redevelopment projects.

In light of the agency's frequent willingness to gear the scope of a CMS to the nature and extent of contamination at a RCRA facility, many facility owners and operators consider early data-gathering efforts of their own to characterize SWMU releases. Often such data is part of an earlier state-led (but not RCRA corrective action) investigation. If properly gathered, such data can influence the direction and scope of both further investigatory and remedial alternatives analysis that the agency will require. (If a facility owner or operator expects to use earlier-acquired data during the RFI process, that should be written into scopes of work and, where applicable, consent orders.)

In most permits and orders, the requirement to complete a corrective measures study depends upon completing the RFI process. Nevertheless, owners and operators commonly begin work on some aspects of the corrective measures study during the RFI. This approach allows CMS work to be performed while technically related RFI work is ongoing and may help the facility owner meet its CMS deadlines.

D. Interim Measures

Consistent with EPA's stated goal of early cleanup activities to address the most significant risks at corrective action sites, the agency in 1991 issued a guidance document, "Managing the Corrective Action Program for Environmental Results: The RCRA Facility Stabilization Effort."[28] Under the stabilization strategy in this guidance, EPA directed its regional offices to make more frequent use of interim actions to achieve near-term reductions in risks posed by the most significant problems at corrective action sites. Although final comprehensive remedies along the lines summarized above remain the ultimate objective of the agency's program, this stabilization initiative has encouraged the regions to take action before RFIs have fully characterized site conditions in order to prevent the further spread of contamination.

Interim measures are the corrective action activities used to achieve these stabilization objectives, and as noted above, they have become common in corrective action permits and orders. Even where individual interim measures are not specified in permits or orders, the regions have

---

[28]This document was issued on Oct. 25, 1991.

Chapter 13: Corrective Action Requirements   331

sought to establish broad authorities in permit and order conditions to enable them readily to require such measures during the course of the permit or order. Administrative permit appeal decisions have concluded that the regions need not necessarily demonstrate an immediate and significant threat in order to impose such measures. Although the use of interim measures must somehow account for the immediacy and magnitude of the threat involved, that determination properly may weigh the amount of time needed to implement permanent corrective action measures in determining whether interim measures are appropriate.[29]

Interim measures present the prospect of significant expenditures for corrective action measures, even before the risks posed by conditions at the facility have been fully characterized and an overall remedy for the site determined. Despite the broad discretion typically accorded the regions to make such technical determinations, EPA regional offices must nonetheless provide a sufficient, site-specific factual basis in the record to sustain a decision that risks are immediate and large enough to warrant interim measures. Failing to do so has resulted in the remand of interim measure determinations for further consideration.[30]

A key challenge regarding interim measures is drafting permit or order provisions that balance the need for flexibility, the ability to respond to new conditions as they are discovered, the need to be protective, and the need to ensure the facility owner has a meaningful opportunity to resolve disputes that arise. In *In re Rohm and Haas Co.*,[31] the Environmental Appeals Board approved the region's interim measures provision in a final permit where the region agreed to incorporate permit language proposed by the facility owner to restrict use of interim measures to situations involving imminent threats. Notably, the region addressed the permittee's concerns by incorporating into the final permit nine guidance factors for employing interim measures taken directly from EPA's 1990 Subpart S Proposed Rule that had been proposed yet withdrawn. (The Subpart S Proposed Rule is discussed in Section IV.B below.) Similarly, in *In re Caribe General Electric Products, Inc.*,[32] the Environmental Appeals Board approved interim measures in a final permit over the objection of the permittee, who argued that the permit's broad interim measures provisions could lead the region to require additional cleanup activity without undertaking notice and comment requirements of a permit modification. The board approved the region's proposal to

---

[29]*Gen. Motors Corp., supra* note 25, at 15–16; *In re* B.F. Goodrich Co., RCRA Appeal No. 89-20 (Dec. 19, 1990).

[30]*Gen. Elec. Co., supra* note 27, at 16–23.

[31]RCRA Appeal No. 98-2 (Oct. 5, 2000).

[32]RCRA Appeal No. 98-3 (Feb. 4, 2000).

332 THE RCRA PRACTICE MANUAL

limit its discretion to impose interim measures based on the factors set forth in the Subpart S Proposed Rule. The board held that the permit's dispute resolution provision gave the permittee sufficient due process if disputes arose.[33]

IV. Implementation of the Corrective Action Program

As noted above, EPA's corrective action program can be divided roughly into three distinct phases. It is useful to examine the historical development of the program because it is so dependent on regulations, proposed regulations, and guidance. Certain key decisions made in the program's infancy continue in effect today. This is true especially of EPA's decisions regarding the scope of its authority and its jurisdiction. Moreover, much implementation is on a case-by-case basis by EPA regional offices utilizing these guidance documents and rules. In most instances, the regions have interpreted their mandate broadly, and they are not always in tune with EPA headquarters' current approaches.

A. Initial Regulatory Implementation

The corrective action program's first phase ran from HSWA passage in 1984 until the Subpart S Proposed Rule was issued in July 1990.[34] During this phase, EPA set out a wide range of basic applicability and jurisdictional decisions. Most have continued to the present day. Key documents during this period explaining EPA's own view of its corrective action authority include the following:

- First Codification Rule, 50 Fed. Reg. 28,702 (1985);
- Memorandum from J. Winston Porter and Courtney M. Price to Regional Administrators *et al.*, Interpretation of Section 3008(h) of the Solid Waste Disposal Act (December 16, 1985) (EPA Section 3008(h) Memo);
- National RCRA Corrective Action Strategy (October 14, 1986); and
- Second Codification Rule, 52 Fed. Reg. 45,788 (1987).

In its First Codification Rule implementing HSWA, EPA codified certain corrective action authorities and related permit requirements. That rule making provided, among other things, EPA's broad definitions of "facility" (encompassing all land within the plant's contiguous property boundaries); "release" (covering virtually all ways in which a hazardous

---

[33]In doing so, the board cited *Gen. Elec. Co., supra* note 27.
[34]55 Fed. Reg. 30,798 (July 27, 1990).

Chapter 13: Corrective Action Requirements   333

constituent may enter any environmental medium, and without the CER-CLA statutory exemptions from the definition of that term); and solid waste management unit, or SWMU (extending to virtually any discernible area where solid wastes were ever managed and from which a hazardous constituent *might* migrate, but excluding transportation spills). The First Codification Rule also set forth EPA's interpretation that RCRA Section 3004(u) applies not only to facilities required to obtain operating permits, but also to facilities subject to RCRA "postclosure" permits and certain "permits-by-rule,"[35] and certain agency legal interpretations of the scope of Section 3008(h) orders.[36]

In judicial challenges to that rule making, the D.C. Circuit Court of Appeals upheld EPA's view that Section 3004(u) applies to (1) any facility obtaining merely a permit-by-rule for certain underground injection control (UIC) wells or a postclosure permit, and (2) all SWMUs anywhere within the property boundary of the plant, not merely SWMUs within that portion of property currently used for hazardous waste management.[37]

In its Second Codification Rule, EPA addressed permit application information requirements regarding releases from SWMUs and the nature of the obligation to undertake cleanup beyond the facility property boundary. In further detail and with some modifications, the rule also covered the applicability of the postclosure permit requirement and of RCRA Section 3004(u) to facilities that have ceased active management of hazardous wastes but nonetheless must obtain postclosure permits, or only manage UIC wells receiving permits-by-rule. Finally, the rule addressed the applicability of Section 3004(u) to special "study" wastes identified under Section 3001(b) of RCRA (for example, certain fossil fuel combustion wastes, mining wastes, cement kiln dust wastes, and oil and gas wastes).

In a judicial challenge to this rule making, the D.C. Circuit affirmed its earlier decision upholding the application of Section 3004(u) to facilities required to obtain only UIC permits-by-rule or postclosure permits. The court also upheld EPA's decision to apply Section 3004(u) to SWMUs containing only special "study" wastes.[38] These rulings, together with those resulting from the challenge to the First Codification Rule, broadened

---

[35]40 C.F.R. § 270.1(c).

[36]*See* EPA Section 3008(h) memo.

[37]United Techs. Corp., Pratt & Whitney Group v. EPA, 821 F.2d 714 (D.C. Cir. 1987).

[38]Am. Iron & Steel Inst. v. EPA, 886 F.2d 390 (D.C. Cir. 1989), *cert. denied sub nom.* Am. Mining Cong. v. EPA, 497 U.S. 1003 (1990). *Accord* Inland Steel Co. v. EPA, 901 F.2d 1419 (7th Cir. 1990) (exemption from RCRA definition of "solid waste" for point source discharges subject to permit requirement under Section 402 of the Clean Water Act does not exempt UIC wells from Section 3004(u)).

334 THE RCRA PRACTICE MANUAL

EPA's authority to require investigation into past waste management practices at RCRA permitted facilities and the potential impacts and costs of this program's requirements.

B. EPA's 1990 Subpart S Proposed Rule

In July 1990, EPA published its "Subpart S Proposed Rule," a key corrective action proposal that set forth the structure of the agency's intended approach to corrective action at that time.[39] The Subpart S Proposed Rule would have created a new Subpart S of 40 C.F.R. Part 264. The proposal presented detailed requirements for corrective action responses at individual facilities and the procedural and technical requirements for conducting RCRA facility investigations, evaluating remedial alternatives, and selecting and implementing remedies.

This proposal never was finalized. Although some of the most important portions of the rule (notably, the Corrective Action Management Unit and Temporary Unit concepts) eventually were finalized, the Subpart S Proposed Rule as a whole proved to be too cumbersome, lacked significant flexibility and opportunity to tailor decisions to the needs of particular sites, and was subjected to a barrage of criticism. EPA finally and formally withdrew its proposal on October 7, 1999,[40] thus essentially closing out the second phase of the corrective action program.

The rationale EPA advanced for withdrawing large portions of the Subpart S Proposed Rule was that it was more appropriate to implement many of the proposal's concepts by guidance rather than by regulation. In many instances, superseding guidance has yet to be issued, however. Thus, the Subpart S Proposed Rule continues in the life of the corrective action program as project managers and regions adhere to its terms even though they need not and, in many instances, should not.[41]

Corrective action practitioners, therefore, frequently turn to the "withdrawn" Subpart S Proposed Rule because it still contains the last authoritative EPA headquarters pronouncement on some important issues. Although sometimes superseded by later pronouncements and guidance, the 1990 Subpart S Proposed Rule addressed such issues as the "trigger" and "target" levels for site studies and cleanup actions; possible adjustment to, or waiver of, cleanup standards; the point of

---

[39] 55 Fed. Reg. 30,798 (July 27, 1990).

[40] *See* 64 Fed. Reg. 54,604.

[41] *See, e.g., In re* Rohm & Haas Co., RCRA Appeal No. 98-2 (Oct. 5, 2000) (noting that even though the Subpart S Proposed Rule was withdrawn, it would continue to provide guidance for corrective action implementation for appropriate portions of the proposal not replaced or superseded, and proceeding to employ that proposal in approving permit corrective action interim measures provisions).

compliance for meeting cleanup standards; permissible use of institutional controls in lieu of active remedial measures; use of conditional remedies that permit on-site corrective measures to be undertaken over time based on likelihood of exposure to hazardous constituents; the factors used to employ interim measures; and the role that cost considerations may play in cleanup activities.

During the nearly ten years the Subpart S Proposed Rule was pending, the EPA regions used it religiously as guidance. It developed a negative reputation for its heavy process orientation; its drawn-out process of data collection, analysis, and reports; its ponderous decision-making process; and its lack of flexibility on both process and cleanup decisions. Indeed, EPA's current results-oriented approach to corrective action generally is viewed as a reaction to this reputation of the Subpart S Proposed Rule.

The Subpart S Proposed Rule drew many of its defining characteristics from another key document published during this time, the RCRA Corrective Action Plan,[42] sometimes referred to simply as "the CAP." This document set forth detailed provisions regarding how RCRA corrective action investigations and cleanups should proceed. Originally issued as interim final guidance in June 1988, the CAP was finalized in May 1994. The CAP's methodical, step-by-step approach to gathering information, preparing reports, and making decisions, coupled with the similar approach articulated in the Subpart S Proposed Rule, in large measure set the tone for the approach of the corrective action program during its first two phases.

As noted above, although the Subpart S Proposed Rule never was adopted in its entirety, several of its significant components were. EPA's regulations adopted in 1993 establishing Corrective Action Management Units (CAMUs) and temporary units[43] were based on components of the Subpart S Proposed Rule. They created new types of waste management units designed to promote speedier cleanups by removing obstacles posed by certain unnecessary requirements for management of remediation wastes at corrective action sites. These are discussed below in Section V.

C. Results-Based Corrective Action

EPA's current results-based approach to corrective action largely is the result of two factors. First, as noted above, it is a reaction to the ponderous, rigid, and process-oriented approach of the Subpart S Proposed

---

[42]OSWER Directive 9902.3-2A (May 1994).
[43]55 Fed. Reg. 8,658 (Feb. 16, 1993).

336 THE RCRA PRACTICE MANUAL

Rule and the CAP. Second, it fosters EPA's implementation of the Government Performance and Results Act of 1993 (GPRA)[44] as it relates to the corrective action program.

EPA's first significant steps toward results-based corrective action began in May 1996, when EPA issued its ANPR, "Corrective Action for Solid Waste Management Units at Hazardous Waste Management Facilities."[45] In the ANPR, EPA articulated its plan to revise the then-still-pending Subpart S Proposed Rule and solicited stakeholder comments on the ANPR's proposals. Although the ANPR's proposals in certain respects were similar to the Subpart S Proposed Rule, in other respects, the ANPR represented a fundamental shift in the direction of the corrective action program, advancing many concepts that later would come to be known as results-based corrective action. In sum, EPA stated that it intended to base corrective action decisions on site-specific risk and to focus program implementation on results rather than on process. The ANPR stated that EPA would emphasize interim actions and stabilization measures and that states primarily should implement the corrective action program.

EPA has stated that the ANPR should be used as guidance for implementing the corrective action program. As a result, EPA's subsequent corrective action proposals and guidance have increased their emphasis on facility-wide evaluations in place of SWMU-by-SWMU approaches; site-specific data collection and reports; site-specific agency oversight; and guidance rather than rule making to implement corrective action. On September 28, 2000, EPA issued notice of its draft results-based approaches to corrective action guidance that now sets forth current agency strategies for implementing corrective action.[46] Key elements of the draft guidance are performance standards, targeted data collection, tailored oversight, presumptive remedies, phased approaches to cleanup, and interim action and stabilization.

The GPRA requires agencies to set, track, and achieve objective and quantifiable performance goals. In applying the GPRA to the corrective action program, EPA has sought to document the goals of the program and develop a system to measure progress toward those goals. To chart the corrective action program's progress and ensure that short-term goals are achieved at high-priority sites, EPA introduced two Environmental Indicators (EIs): Current Human Exposures under Control (CA725) and Migration of Contaminated Groundwater under Control (CA750). The first is intended to determine whether unacceptable human exposures to hazardous constituents exist from current conditions at a

---

[44]Pub. L. No. 103-62, 107 Stat. 285 (1993).
[45]61 Fed. Reg. 19,432 (May 1, 1996).
[46]*See* 65 Fed. Reg. 58,275.

facility. The second seeks to determine whether groundwater contamination is continuing to migrate in concentrations deemed of concern.

EPA maintains an Environmental Indicators Web site at http://www .epa.gov/epaoswer/hazwaste/ca/eis.htm. As corrective action sites achieve a passing mark in these two categories, EPA charts their progress and that of the corrective action program. On February 5, 1999, EPA issued an Interim Final Guidance advising regional policy managers on the criteria for a site to receive a passing mark. EPA has continued to refine those criteria, especially for risks posed by discharge of contaminated groundwater to surface water and by vapor intrusion from soil into buildings.

As part of its RCRA cleanup reforms effort, EPA has identified approximately 1,700 "high-priority" facilities used to chart RCRA corrective action progress. These sites are known collectively as the RCRA Cleanup Baseline and sometimes are referred to simply as the "GPRA sites." These facilities are assessed with regard to whether they pass the criteria set forth by the EI guidance. As part of long-term GPRA goals, the RCRA corrective action program intends by 2005 to have human exposures under control at 95 percent of sites and migration of contaminated groundwater under control at 70 percent of the sites. The program's progress toward reaching these goals is reported annually and can be viewed in a document on EPA's Web site at http://www.epa.gov/ epaoswer/hazwaste/ca/lists/base_sta.pdf.

V. Managing Remediation Wastes

For much of the history of the corrective action program, EPA and stakeholders have struggled to establish and comply with RCRA rules that govern the management of hazardous wastes generated during environmental cleanups. Over the last ten years, much of EPA's efforts to improve the program have been devoted to determining and streamlining those rules so that hazardous waste management requirements ill-suited to remediation do not hamper timely, protective cleanups.

Corrective action measures typically generate additional solid waste, some of which may be characterized as hazardous under hazardous waste identification principles such as the retroactive application of hazardous waste listings, the derived-from rule, and the contained-in principle, discussed elsewhere in this book. If deemed hazardous and absent an applicable regulatory exemption, such wastes generally must be managed subject to RCRA Subtitle C requirements, including the land disposal restrictions (LDRs) and minimum technology requirements (MTRs) set forth in Section 3004(d)–(m) and (o) of RCRA. If nonhazardous, the wastes typically would be subject to less onerous RCRA Subtitle D requirements unless EPA determined that additional controls were necessary to protect human health and the environment. In either case, other applicable federal, state, and local requirements could impose additional management controls. In contrast to CERCLA on-site response actions, these controls can include permit requirements. EPA also could seek to use its omnibus regulatory authority under Section 3005(c)(3) or general statutory authority under Section 3004(u) to impose additional protective requirements it found necessary under the circumstances.[47]

EPA recognizes that strict adherence to potentially applicable hazardous waste requirements in all cases could hinder timely and effective corrective action. In an effort to address this concern, EPA for more than ten years has worked on a series of proposals to make it somewhat easier to manage remediation wastes without invoking many of the rules that were developed to apply to manufacturing process wastes. A discussion follows of some of the key policies EPA has developed.

A. Contained-in Policy

Contaminated environmental media (or debris) is subject to RCRA regulation if it "contains" hazardous waste, pursuant to EPA's contained-in policy. If contaminated media contains hazardous waste, it is subject to all applicable RCRA requirements until it no longer contains the hazardous waste. EPA considers contaminated media to no longer contain hazardous waste when it no longer exhibits a characteristic of hazardous waste and when concentrations of hazardous constituents from listed hazardous waste are below health-based levels. Ordinarily, contaminated media that no longer contains hazardous waste is not subject to RCRA Subtitle C requirements, although under some circumstances it may be subject to LDR treatment requirements. It is EPA policy that such "contained out" determinations for media containing listed hazardous wastes must be approved by EPA or a RCRA authorized state. EPA's contained-in policy has been presented and discussed in a number of *Federal Register* preambles and guidance. A detailed discussion appears in the preamble to the proposed Hazardous Waste Identification Rule for Contaminated Media,[48] discussed below.

B. Area of Contamination Policy

EPA interprets RCRA to allow certain contiguous "areas of contamination" to be considered RCRA waste management units. This allows con-

---

[47]*But see Gen. Motors Corp., supra* note 25, at 20–21 (EPA without unilateral authority under Section 3005(c)(3) to modify corrective action permit provisions without observing the permit modification requirements in 40 C.F.R. Section 270.41).

[48]61 Fed. Reg. 18,795 (Apr. 29, 1996).

solidation and *in situ* treatment of hazardous waste within the area of contamination without creating a separate point of RCRA hazardous waste generation. Under this interpretation wastes may be consolidated or treated in situ within an area of contamination without triggering RCRA's LDRs or MTRs. The area of contamination policy has been discussed in preambles to the CERCLA National Oil and Hazardous Substances Pollution Contingency Plan (NCP) and in EPA guidances.[49]

C. Corrective Action Management Units (CAMUs)

The concept of corrective action management units is similar to EPA's area of contamination policy, but it allows the waste to be removed from the "RCRA unit," treated ex situ, and then placed into a CAMU without triggering RCRA LDRs or MTRs. Other hazardous waste requirements may apply, however. The differences between CAMUs and AOCs are discussed in the March 13, 1996, EPA guidance, "Use of the Area of Contamination Concept during RCRA Cleanups." CAMUs may be located in uncontaminated portions of a facility in some circumstances, and they may be used to consolidate wastes from areas that are not contiguous. CAMUs must be approved by EPA or an authorized state, and they must be designated in a permit or corrective action order. Public review and comment may be required.

The CAMU concept was introduced and discussed at length in the Subpart S Proposed Rule in 1990. It was included in regulations issued in 1993 adopting targeted portions of that proposed rule. The CAMU rule was extensively revised in 2002, in part to settle a lawsuit challenging the CAMU rule, *Environmental Defense Fund v. EPA*,[50] by amending the rule to establish, among other things, CAMU-specific treatment and design standards.[51]

D. Temporary Units

A temporary unit is another type of special RCRA waste management unit established specifically to manage remediation wastes. Temporary units are part of the CAMU regulations, and the specific regulations covering them are found at 40 C.F.R. Section 264.553. These regulations allow EPA and authorized states to modify design, operating, and closure standards for temporary tank and container units used to treat or store

---

[49]*See, e.g.,* 53 Fed. Reg. 51,444 (Dec. 21, 1988), 55 Fed. Reg. 8758–60 (Mar. 8, 1990); EPA Guidance, Use of the Area of Contamination Concept During RCRA Cleanups (Mar. 13, 1996) (available at http://www.epa.gov/oswer/oswerpolicy.htm (OSWER Policy Database No. 3074)).

[50]No. 93-1316 (D.C. Cir.).

[51]67 Fed. Reg. 2962 (Jan. 22, 2002). The current CAMU concept is codified at 40 C.F.R. §§ 264.500–.552.

certain hazardous remediation wastes. Temporary units may operate for only one year, with an opportunity for a one-year extension. They must be approved by EPA or an authorized state in a permit or corrective action order.

Like CAMUs, temporary units were discussed extensively in the Subpart S Proposed Rule and were adopted as part of the 1993 package of corrective action regulations that finalized only limited portions of the original 1990 proposal.[52]

E. The HWIR-Media Rule

In November 1998, EPA issued its final Hazardous Waste Identification Rule for Contaminated Media (the HWIR-Media Rule).[53] The rule made it easier to obtain permits to treat, store, or dispose of RCRA hazardous remediation waste, and provided that such permits, in and of themselves, would not subject the owner or operator to facility-wide corrective action. The rule also created a new type of unit, called a "staging pile," that increased flexibility in storing remediation waste during cleanup, excluded dredged materials from RCRA Subtitle C if they are managed under other permitting requirements, and streamlined the process for states to receive federal authorization of their RCRA programs and to incorporate certain revisions to federal RCRA regulations.

Originally intended to institute broader reforms to RCRA regulation of hazardous remediation wastes, this rule was the result of extensive discussions among EPA, industry, and various other stakeholder groups after the Subpart S Proposed Rule was withdrawn. As proposed in 1996, the HWIR-Media Rule had been designed to address the major RCRA Subtitle C management requirements considered to be the biggest causes of problems and delays for cleanups, including land disposal restrictions, minimum technology requirements, and RCRA permitting procedures. As proposed, the HWIR-Media Rule would have replaced the then-existing CAMU rules. However, certain stakeholder groups were concerned that the proposal was overly lenient; as a result, the final rule was truncated and did not adopt EPA's broad proposed reforms. EPA, instead, retained the CAMU rule as the CAMU rule existed at 40 C.F.R. Section 264.552.

F. LDR Treatment Standards for Contaminated Soils

On May 26, 1998, EPA issued RCRA land disposal restriction treatment standards for contaminated soils, sometimes referred to as the "LDR

---

[52]*See* 58 Fed. Reg. 8677 (Feb. 16, 1993).
[53]63 Fed. Reg. 65,873 (Nov. 30, 1998).

Phase IV Final Rule."[54] These treatment standards require contaminated soils being land-disposed and subject to LDRs for listed hazardous wastes to be treated to reduce concentrations of hazardous constituents by 90 percent or to meet hazardous constituent concentrations no more than ten times universal treatment standards applicable to process wastes, whichever is greater. Contaminated soil exhibiting a hazardous characteristic (ignitability, reactivity, toxicity, or corrosivity) must also have that characteristic eliminated.

At the same time, EPA promulgated a new LDR treatment variance for contaminated soils. Under 40 C.F.R. Section 268.44(h)(3), variances from otherwise applicable LDR treatment standards may be approved if compliance with the treatment standards would result in treatment beyond the point at which threats to human health and the environment are minimized. This allows site-specific, risk-based determinations to supersede technology-based LDR treatment standards under certain circumstances.

G. Guidance on Managing Remediation Waste

EPA has published a guidance document, "Management of Remediation Waste under RCRA,"[55] and an accompanying chart dated October 15, 1998, summarizing the requirements applicable to managing hazardous remediation wastes. This guidance is particularly helpful in that it collects in one place the various regulatory exemptions that may ease the management of remediation wastes. The guidance addresses a number of other policies and programs, as well.

The guidance and other EPA documents discussed in this section are available on the EPA Web site at http://www.epa.gov/correctiveaction. *Federal Register* notices published after 1994 are available at http://www .access.gpo.gov/nara.

VI. Other Technical Issues

RCRA corrective action cleanups often present a number of intricate and thorny issues that might be referred to as "technical issues." In actuality, they are "technical" only in the sense that they affect the manner in which a corrective action cleanup proceeds. They are very much "legal" issues in the sense that they deal with jurisdictional requirements, the interrelationship between RCRA corrective action and other legal authorities, and related matters.

---

[54] 63 Fed. Reg. 28,556 (May 26, 1998).
[55] Oct. 14, 1998.

342 THE RCRA PRACTICE MANUAL

A. Relationship to the Superfund Program

Because cleanup and waste management standards under RCRA become potentially applicable or relevant and appropriate requirements (ARARs) governing the nature and extent of cleanups under CERCLA Section 121(d),[56] EPA's corrective action requirements can play an influential role in shaping response actions under that statute as well. For facilities potentially subject to both RCRA and CERCLA, EPA generally seeks to minimize distinctions between the two programs in an effort to reduce any advantage by proceeding under one statute or the other. In any event, the agency seems intent on handling contamination problems associated with SWMUs at active RCRA facilities under RCRA rather than CERCLA except in unusual circumstances.[57]

On September 24, 1996, EPA headquarters issued a memorandum, "Coordination between RCRA Corrective Action and Closure and CERCLA Site Activities," that described EPA's plans to try to coordinate the CERCLA and RCRA cleanup programs. EPA also addressed RCRA-CERCLA integration issues in the May 1, 1996, ANPR and in other guidance documents.

B. Key Additional Guidances

In 1999, EPA issued guidance, "Use of Monitored Natural Attenuation at Superfund, RCRA Corrective Action, and Underground Storage Tank Sites,"[58] describing the circumstances under which monitored natural attenuation could be used to remediate contaminated soil and groundwater at RCRA corrective action and other sites. This guidance discusses the circumstances under which EPA would consider monitored natural attenuation an appropriate remedy. Among other points, the guidance states that natural attenuation should not be considered a default or presumptive remedy at any contaminated site and should be thoroughly and adequately supported with site-specific characterization data and analysis. EPA stated, moreover, that it expected natural attenuation would be most appropriate when used with other remedial measures such as source control or groundwater extraction, or as a follow-up to active remediation measures.

In September 2000, EPA issued the guidance, "Institutional Controls: A Site Manager's Guide to Identifying, Evaluating and Selecting Institutional Controls at Superfund and RCRA Corrective Action Cleanups."[59]

---

[56]42 U.S.C. § 9621(d).

[57]50 Fed. Reg. 47,912 (1985); 54 Fed. Reg. 41,004 (1989) (EPA policies for listing of RCRA facilities on the CERCLA National Priorities List of top-priority sites).

[58]OSWER Directive No. 9200.4-17P (Apr. 21, 1999).

[59]OSWER Directive No. 9355.0-74FS-P (Sept. 2000).

This guidance discusses a wide variety of types of institutional controls (ICs) and reviews the circumstances under which ICs might be considered as an element of a cleanup under RCRA corrective action or other programs. On February 19, 2003, EPA issued draft supplemental guidance, "Institutional Controls: A Guidance to Implementing, Monitoring, and Enforcing Institutional Controls at Superfund, Brownfields, Federal Facility, UST and RCRA Corrective Action Cleanups." This guidance focuses on a number of issues associated with implementing and enforcing ICs. Both guidances are available at http://www.epa.gov/superfund/action/ic/index/htm. The use of institutional controls and the means to ensure both their protectiveness and their enforceability continue to receive close scrutiny by EPA.

In September 2001, EPA issued its "Handbook of Groundwater Protection and Cleanup Policies for RCRA Corrective Action."[60] The handbook presents EPA's strategies for addressing contaminated groundwater at RCRA corrective action facilities and reiterates EPA's long-standing expectation that final cleanups will return usable groundwater to its maximum beneficial use where practicable. The handbook also identifies short-term and intermediate goals that could be components of a phased approach to addressing contaminated groundwater. The handbook describes varying points of compliance for groundwater cleanups that might be appropriate, depending on whether the facility and regulators are pursuing short-term, intermediate, or final cleanup goals. Notably, this guidance also conveys EPA's expectation that facilities will control sources to reduce or eliminate, to the extent practicable, further releases of hazardous waste or hazardous constituents to the environment.

EPA has also issued rules and guidance to help ensure public participation in the RCRA decision-making process, including RCRA corrective action decisions. EPA's RCRA Public Participation Manual explains how public participation works in the RCRA permitting and corrective action processes and how interested persons can participate in agency decision making. The public participation manual followed EPA's final RCRA Expanded Public Participation Rule.[61]

VII. Expediting Corrective Action

As this chapter has noted, the RCRA corrective action program has been criticized for being cumbersome, expensive, and too focused on process and not enough on practical, achievable environmental results. EPA and stakeholders alike have sought to improve the program by expediting

---

[60]*See* 66 Fed. Reg. 52,762 (Oct. 17, 2001).
[61]*See* 60 Fed. Reg. 63,417 (Dec. 11, 1995).

corrective action. This chapter has discussed several methods to do just that. For example, EPA's results-based corrective action seeks, above all, to focus on results rather than on process and to incorporate into the RCRA decision-making process risk analysis based on an assessment of realistic risk- and reasonably anticipated land uses.

Although these efforts have been only partially successful, EPA Region 5 has pioneered an innovative approach. In certain corrective action documents, EPA and the respondents simplified substantially the formats of their agreements, choosing to write them in general terms rather than including a great deal of specifics. The intent is that the parties will work through the process of investigation and cleanup in a streamlined, results-oriented fashion, collaborating at key decision points to determine the next steps appropriate based on site-specific information gathered to that point. In this fashion, they hope to avoid most of the obstacles created by the typical corrective action process.

Similarly, in a January 2, 2001, guidance, "Enforcement Approaches for Expediting RCRA Corrective Action," EPA headquarters identified several key steps that regulators and stakeholders can use to streamline corrective action. Some suggestions are heavily oriented toward enforcement. These include the aggressive use of schedules and deadlines in corrective action orders and permits, establishing strict time limits for negotiating key corrective action documents, and establishing strict schedules of compliance with administrative penalties for missing deadlines. Other suggestions are more innovative and collaborative. These include the use of flexible compliance schedules, voluntary facility-initiated agreements, streamlined consent orders, unilateral letter orders, and other techniques.

VIII. Conclusion

The RCRA corrective action program imposes substantial "fenceline-to-fenceline and beyond" obligations on facilities subject to it. Accordingly, facility owners and operators, prospective purchasers, and their lawyers need to understand how EPA has chosen to implement the program.

Since first being introduced, the corrective action program has undergone numerous significant changes. EPA's most recent changes seek to streamline the program, make it less rigid and cumbersome, and emphasize results rather than process. Futher refinement of the program can be expected as EPA continues to seek to achieve GPRA goals and promote redevelopment of dormant portions of RCRA corrective action facilities. Only time will tell whether this latest direction will be a permanent policy change or merely another in a series of interim revisions.

CHAPTER 14

Regulation of Underground Storage Tanks

JOHN C. CHAMBERS, CHRIS S. LEASON, MICHAEL D. HOCKLEY, AND BENJAMIN T. CLARK

I. Introduction

Eight years after passing the Resource Conservation and Recovery Act (RCRA), Congress amended RCRA by enacting the Hazardous and Solid Waste Amendments (HSWA) of 1984. One major portion of HSWA is Subtitle I, which mandates the establishment of a comprehensive program for the regulation of underground storage tanks (USTs) containing regulated substances other than RCRA hazardous wastes. While the scope of this chapter is limited to the federal UST program, most states have separate UST programs that may differ in requirements from the federal program. Once a state has been authorized to administer the UST program, the state requirements operate in lieu of federal requirements.

Subtitle I reflects a national awareness that the widespread existence of leaking USTs may constitute a threat to human health and groundwater resources. The UST program establishes requirements for leak detection, leak prevention, financial responsibility, and corrective action for owners and operators of USTs containing regulated substances. While the program does not extend to aboveground storage tanks per se, Subtitle I applies to any tank whose volume is at least 10 percent belowground, if it contains regulated substances and is not otherwise excluded from regulations.

A. Scope of the Problem

EPA estimates that the underground storage tank regulations will affect over 2 million UST systems located at over 700,000 facilities nationwide.[1] The major cause of underground storage tank and piping failure is corrosion. In 1984, it was estimated that 85 percent of the 2 million underground storage tanks containing regulated substances (petroleum or hazardous substances) were made of steel without corrosion protection. Based on these startling figures, Senate hearings on USTs, and segments on the television programs *60 Minutes* and *Good Morning, America* concerning the effects of leaking underground storage tanks in the Northeast, the time was ripe for UST legislation.

B. Statutory Authority

On November 8, 1984, President Reagan signed into law the Hazardous and Solid Waste Amendments of 1984.[2] The statute describes an underground storage tank as:

> any one or combination of tanks (including underground pipes connected thereto) which is used to contain an accumulation of regulated substances, and the volume of which (including the volume of the underground pipes connected thereto) is *10 per centum* or more beneath the surface of the ground.[3]

The statutory requirements of Subtitle I apply only to underground storage tanks "used to contain an accumulation of regulated substances."[4] Regulated substances are defined to include:

> (A) any substance defined in section [101 (14) of the Comprehensive Environmental Response, Compensation, and Liability Act (CERCLA)] (*but not including any substance regulated as a hazardous waste under subtitle [C]*), and
> (B) petroleum.[5]

In enacting Subtitle I, Congress exempted certain types of tanks that would otherwise be included within the definition of an underground storage tank. Nine types of tanks are excluded from the definition of an underground storage tank:

---

[1] 53 Fed. Reg. 37,082, 37,083 (1988).
[2] Pub. L. No. 98-616, 1984 U.S.C.C.A.N. (98 Stat.) 3221 (codified as amended in scattered sections of 15, 20, 33, 42, and 44 U.S.C.).
[3] 42 U.S.C. § 6991(1) (emphasis added).
[4] *Id.* § 6991(1).
[5] *Id.* § 6991(2) (emphasis added).

1. farm or residential tanks of 1100-gallons-or-less capacity used for storing motor fuel for noncommercial purposes;
2. tanks used for storing heating oil for consumptive use on the premises where stored;
3. septic tanks;
4. pipeline facilities (including gathering lines) that are regulated under the Natural Gas Pipeline Safety Act of 1968, the Hazardous Liquid Pipeline Safety Act of 1979, or are intrastate pipeline facilities regulated under comparable state laws;
5. surface impoundments, pits, ponds, or lagoons;
6. stormwater or wastewater collection systems;
7. flow-through process tanks;
8. liquid trap or associated gathering lines directly related to oil or gas production and gathering operations; or
9. storage tanks situated in an underground area (such as a basement, cellar, mineworking drift, shaft, or tunnel) if the storage tank is situated upon or above the surface of the floor.[6]

Subtitle I requires EPA to promulgate, under notice and comment rule making, release detection, prevention, and corrective action regulations applicable to all owners and operators of underground storage tanks as are necessary to protect human health and the environment.[7] Further, EPA is required to promulgate new tank performance standards including guidelines for design, construction, installation, release detection, and compatibility standards.[8]

As originally enacted, Subtitle I gave EPA discretion to establish a financial responsibility program for underground storage tanks.[9] The Superfund Amendments and Reauthorization Act of 1986 (SARA)[10] amended RCRA *requiring* EPA to promulgate financial responsibility regulations.[11] SARA also established a response program for releases from petroleum underground storage tanks.

The response program includes a $500 million Leaking Underground Storage Tank (LUST) Trust Fund to pay for corrective action when it is necessary to protect human health and the environment. As of September 1999, although the fund was nearly $1 billion, EPA's annual appropriations have been minimal. For example, the appropriations equaled

---

[6]*Id.* § 6991(1).
[7]*Id.* § 6991b(a).
[8]*Id.* § 6991b(e).
[9]*Id.* § 6991b(d).
[10]Pub. L. No. 99-499, 1986 U.S.C.C.A.N. (100 Stat.) 2835.
[11]42 U.S.C. § 6991b(c)(6).

348　THE RCRA PRACTICE MANUAL

approximately $65 million for fiscal year 1998. Moreover, in recent years, Congress has often appropriated less money from the fund to EPA than the president requested.

EPA is authorized to institute enforcement actions and assess penalties against violators of the UST technical and financial responsibility requirements.[12] Further, EPA is authorized to issue administrative orders requiring compliance with the UST requirements.[13] EPA may assess a civil penalty up to $10,000 for each tank per day for violation.[14] EPA may also institute judicial enforcement actions to compel compliance with an administrative order and may also assess penalties up to $25,000 for each day of noncompliance with an administrative order.[15] In addition, owners who knowingly violate the notification rules may be assessed a civil penalty up to $10,000 for each tank.[16] The maximum penalties cited above, as indexed for inflation, currently are $11,000, $27,500, and $11,000, respectively.[17]

Finally, EPA is authorized to approve state UST programs to implement and enforce the federal regulations; a state program may be approved only if its standards are no less stringent than the federal requirements and the program contains adequate enforcement measures.[18]

II. EPA Underground Storage Tank Regulations

A. Introduction

On September 23, 1988, EPA published final regulations to implement the UST program, including release detection, release prevention, and corrective action requirements and requirements for the approval of state programs.[19] EPA supplemented the UST program again in 1988 by promulgating final regulations concerning financial responsibility requirements for petroleum USTs.[20] Finally, in 1993 EPA published financial responsibility requirements and compliance mechanisms for local governments with petroleum USTs.[21]

---

[12]*Id.* § 6991e.
[13]*Id.* § 6991e(a).
[14]*Id.* § 6991e(d)(2).
[15]*Id.* § 6991e(a).
[16]*Id.* § 6991e(d)(1).
[17]40 C.F.R. § 19.4, tbl.1.
[18]42 U.S.C. § 6991c.
[19]53 Fed. Reg. 37,082 (1988) (codified at 40 C.F.R. §§ 280.10–.74); 53 Fed. Reg. 37,212 (1988) (codified at 40 C.F.R. §§ 281.10–.61).
[20]53 Fed. Reg. 43,322 (1988) (codified at 40 C.F.R. §§ 280.90–.116).
[21]58 Fed. Reg. 9026 (1993) (codified at 40 C.F.R. pt. 280, subpt. H–Financial Responsibility).

B. Definition of a Regulated Substance

In promulgating the UST regulations, EPA codified the statutory definition of a regulated substance contained in RCRA Section 9001. A regulated substance includes any substance defined in Section 101(14) of CERCLA (but not including any substance regulated under RCRA Subtitle C as a hazardous waste) or petroleum, including crude oil or a fraction thereof that is liquid at standard conditions of temperature and pressure.[22]

C. Definition of an Underground Storage Tank

EPA codified the definition of an underground storage tank found in RCRA Section 9001 as any tank, or series of tanks and connected piping, that contains a regulated substance in which the volume is 10 percent or more beneath the surface of the ground.[23] Therefore, an owner or operator of a UST system containing a regulated substance will be subject to the requirements contained in 40 C.F.R. Section 280 unless one of the exclusions, exemptions, or deferrals discussed below applies.

D. Exemptions or Exclusions from Regulation

The EPA regulations codify the nine underground storage tank exemptions contained in RCRA Section 9001.[24] Further, EPA specifically excludes by regulation the following UST systems from regulation as an underground storage tank:

1. UST systems holding hazardous wastes;
2. wastewater treatment tank systems that are part of a wastewater treatment facility regulated under Section 402 or Section 307(b) of the Clean Water Act;
3. equipment or machinery containing regulated substances for operational purposes, such as hydraulic lift tanks and electrical equipment tanks;
4. UST systems with a capacity of 110 gallons or less;
5. UST systems that contain a de minimis concentration of regulated substances; and
6. any emergency spill or overflow containment UST system that is expeditiously emptied after use.[25]

---

[22] 40 C.F.R. § 280.12.
[23] Id. § 280.12.
[24] Id.
[25] Id. § 280.10(b).

350   THE RCRA PRACTICE MANUAL

In support of these regulatory exclusions, EPA cited RCRA Section 9003(a) as providing congressional authorization to establish UST programs "as may be necessary to protect human health and the environment."[26] As further support for the regulatory exclusions cited above, EPA cited RCRA Section 9003(b), which permits the EPA Administrator to consider factors such as tank size and quantity of substances stored when establishing the necessary technical requirements.[27]

E. Deferrals and Limitations

In promulgating the final UST regulations, EPA chose to defer certain requirements for select underground storage tank systems. For example, the following UST systems are excluded from compliance with the requirements in Subparts B, C, D, E, and G of the UST regulations (relating to installation, operating, release detection, release reporting, out-of-service UST systems, and closure requirements):

1. wastewater treatment tank systems;
2. any UST system containing radioactive material regulated under the Atomic Energy Act of 1954;
3. any UST system that is part of an emergency generator system at a nuclear power generation facility regulated by the Nuclear Regulatory Commission under 10 C.F.R. Part 50, Appendix A;
4. airport hydrant fuel distribution systems; and
5. UST systems with field-constructed tanks.[28]

Further, EPA chose not to apply the release detection requirements of Subpart D to any underground storage tank system that stores fuel solely for use by emergency power generators.[29]

III. Performance Standards, Operating Requirements, and Release Detection

EPA is required under RCRA Section 9003 to promulgate regulations concerning "release detection, prevention, and corrective action regulations applicable to all owners and operators of underground storage tanks, as may be necessary to protect health and the environment."[30] In

---

[26]42 U.S.C. § 6991b(a).
[27]*Id.* § 6991b(b).
[28]40 C.F.R. § 280.10(c).
[29]*Id.* § 280.10(d).
[30]42 U.S.C. § 6991b(a).

Chapter 14: Regulation of Underground Storage Tanks   351

accordance with this mandate, EPA regulations dictate performance standards, operating requirements, and release detection requirements for new and existing UST systems containing regulated substances. The specific requirements for new and existing systems are discussed in detail below. In general, all tanks must meet four requirements; they must be: (1) designed, constructed, and installed in accordance with national codes of practice; (2) protected from corrosion; (3) equipped with spill and overfill protection devices; and (4) equipped with release detection devices. The methods for compliance and dates of compliance vary depending on whether the tank is new or existing and whether it stores petroleum or hazardous substances.

A. New Underground Storage Tanks

All new underground storage tanks—that is, those installed after December 22, 1988—are required to be designed and constructed in accordance with a national code of practice and equipped with corrosion protection, leak detection, and spill and overflow devices *at the time of installation*.[31] These requirements are the same for petroleum and hazardous substance USTs with the exception of the release detection requirements, which will be discussed individually below for petroleum and hazardous substance USTs.

1. Design and Construction Requirements
Unlike the proposed regulations, which contained specific technical requirements for new UST systems, the final regulations require USTs to be designed, constructed, and installed in accordance with a code of practice developed by a nationally recognized association or independent testing laboratory.[32]

For tanks and piping, the construction must be of fiberglass-reinforced plastic, cathodically protected steel, steel-fiberglass-reinforced-plastic composite, or bare steel (provided the soil conditions for the tank satisfy regulatory requirements as determined by a corrosion expert).[33]

2. Corrosion Protection
New underground storage tanks must be protected from corrosion using certain fabrication techniques, unless a corrosion expert has determined that the installation site is not corrosive enough to cause a release due to corrosion during the operational life of the system. The following

---

[31]40 C.F.R. §§ 280.20, 280.40–.42.
[32]*Id.* § 280.20(a), (d).
[33]*Id.* § 280.20.

352 THE RCRA PRACTICE MANUAL

fabrication techniques are authorized by the regulations: (1) fiberglass-reinforced plastic; (2) cathodically protected steel; (3) steel-fiberglass-reinforced-plastic composite; or (4) another suitable method determined by the implementing agency.[34]

Steel underground storage tank systems equipped with corrosion protection equipment must be operated and maintained continuously to provide corrosion protection to the metal components of the tank that routinely contain regulated substances and are in contact with the ground.[35] Cathodic protection systems must be inspected by a qualified tester and tested within six months of installation and at least every three years thereafter.[36] For impressed current cathodic protection systems, inspection must be conducted every 60 days.[37] The inspection criteria to be utilized by the cathodic protection tester must be in accordance with a code of practice developed by a nationally recognized association.[38] Finally, records must be kept that demonstrate compliance with these inspection requirements.[39]

3. Spill and Overfill Control

EPA's studies of UST releases indicate that spills and overfills are the most frequent causes of releases; therefore, the regulations require owners and operators of new underground storage tank systems to install spill prevention and overfill protection equipment.[40] Spill prevention equipment must prevent product release when the transfer hose is detached from the fill pipe (for example, spill catchment basin).[41] Further, overfill protection equipment must automatically shut off the flow into the tank when the tank is no more than 95 percent full or warn the transfer operator when the tank is 90 percent full.[42] On October 13, 1991, EPA issued a set of performance standards that can be used as an alternative to the existing overfill prevention design standards. These standards allow use of equipment capable of (1) restricting flow 30 minutes before overfill; (2) alerting the operator with a high-level alarm one minute before overfilling; or (3) automatically shutting off flow into the tank so that none of the fittings located on top of the tank are exposed to product due to overfilling.[43]

---

[34]*Id.* § 280.20(a).
[35]*Id.* § 280.31(a).
[36]*Id.* § 280.31(b).
[37]*Id.* § 280.31(c).
[38]*Id.* § 280.31(b)(2).
[39]*Id.* §§ 280.31(d), 280.34(b)(2).
[40]*Id.* § 280.30.
[41]*Id.* § 280.20(c)(1)(i).
[42]*Id.* § 280.20(c)(1)(ii).
[43]56 Fed. Reg. 38,342 (1991) (codified at 40 C.F.R. § 280.20(c)(1)(ii)(B)–(C)).

Chapter 14: Regulation of Underground Storage Tanks 353

Owners and operators are exempt from the spill and overfill prevention requirements if either alternative equipment is used that the state-implementing agency determines is no less protective of human health and the environment than existing EPA requirements, or the UST system is filled by transfers of no more than 25 gallons at a time.[44]

4. Release Detection

All new UST systems are required to maintain a release detection method. Every release detection device must be

- capable of detecting a release from any portion of the UST system, including any connected underground piping that routinely contains product;
- installed, calibrated, operated, and maintained in accordance with the manufacturer's instructions, including routine maintenance and service checks for operability or running condition;
- capable of meeting the performance requirements for tanks and piping in 40 C.F.R. Section 280.43 or 280.44, with any performance claims and their manner of determination described in writing by the equipment manufacturer or installer; and
- capable of detecting the leak rate or quantity specified for that method of release detection with a probability of detection of 0.95 and a probability of false alarm of 0.05.[45]

Specific release detection requirements for new petroleum and hazardous substance USTs are discussed below.

a. Petroleum Underground Storage Tanks. Generally, new petroleum USTs must be monitored at least every 30 days for releases using one or a combination of the following methods: (1) automatic tank gauging; (2) vapor monitoring; (3) interstitial monitoring; (4) groundwater monitoring; or (5) another approved state method so long as the method is as effective as any of the preceding methods.[46]

As an alternative to monthly monitoring, tanks that meet the performance standards (corrosion protection and spill prevention/overfill protection) may use monthly inventory control combined with tank tightness testing at least every five years until ten years after the tank is installed. At the end of the ten-year period, one of the monthly monitoring methods specified above must be used.[47] Tanks with a capacity of 550

---

[44]40 C.F.R. § 280.20(c)(2).
[45]*Id.* § 280.40(a).
[46]*Id.* §§ 280.41(a), 280.43(d)–(h).
[47]*Id.* § 280.41(a)(1).

354 THE RCRA PRACTICE MANUAL

gallons or less may use weekly manual tank gauging as the sole method of release detection.[48]

b. Hazardous Substance Underground Storage Tanks. The release detection requirements for new hazardous substance USTs differ significantly from the requirements for new petroleum USTs. Hazardous substance USTs must have secondary containment for release detection. The secondary containment system must be designed, constructed, and installed to (1) contain a substance release from the UST until the release is detected and removed; (2) prevent releases to the environment during the operational life of the UST system; and (3) be checked for evidence of a release at least every 30 days.[49]

The secondary containment requirement may be satisfied by using one or more of the following devices: a doubled-walled UST, a concrete vault in which the UST is situated, or a natural or synthetic liner in the excavation area surrounding the UST. The regulations permit the use of other methods of release detection if the state implementing agency determines that the alternative method works as effectively as the monitoring methods specifically approved in the regulations.[50]

B. New Underground Storage Tank Piping

1. Corrosion Protection

New UST piping must be protected from corrosion, unless a corrosion expert has determined that the installation site is not corrosive enough to cause a release due to corrosion during the operational life of the system. One of the following fabrication techniques must be used: fiberglass-reinforced plastic, cathodically protected steel, or another suitable method as determined by the implementing agency.[51] For cathodically protected steel piping, the piping must first be coated with a dielectric material. Further, cathodically protected systems must be operated in accordance with 40 C.F.R. Section 280.31.

2. Release Detection

a. Petroleum Underground Piping. Release detection requirements for new underground piping containing petroleum are prescribed based on whether the piping is pressurized or suction. For new pressurized pip-

---

[48]*Id.* § 280.41(a)(3).
[49]*Id.* § 280.42(b)(1)(i)–(iii).
[50]*Id.* § 280.42(b)(5).
[51]*Id.* § 280.20(b).

Chapter 14: Regulation of Underground Storage Tanks 355

ing, the piping must be equipped with an automatic line leak detector and have either annual line-tightness tests or monthly monitoring.[52] Acceptable methods of monthly monitoring include vapor monitoring, groundwater monitoring, interstitial monitoring; or another method approved by the state implementing agency and as effective as any of the preceding methods.[53]

For new suction piping, acceptable methods of release detection include line tightness tests every three years, monthly monitoring, or systems designed so that the piping operates at less than atmospheric pressure, the piping is sloped so that the contents of the piping will flow back into the UST if the suction is released, and one check valve is included in the line as close as practical to the suction pump.[54]

b. Hazardous Substance Underground Piping. New underground piping containing a hazardous substance must be equipped with secondary containment that will contain a hazardous substance release until the release is detected and removed, prevent releases to the environment during the operational life of the UST system, and be checked for evidence of a release at least every 30 days. Further, pressurized piping must have an automatic line leak detector.[55] As with the release detection requirements for new hazardous substance USTs, the regulations permit the use of other methods of release detection for piping if the state implementing agency determines that the alternative method works as effectively as the methods prescribed by the regulations for hazardous substance UST piping.[56]

C. Existing Underground Storage Tanks

1. Ten-Year Upgrade Requirements

While new underground storage tanks must comply with the EPA's UST requirements at installation, owners and operators of existing underground storage tanks had until December 22, 1998, to comply with the applicable new UST performance standards (as previously discussed), upgrade according to the regulations, or close.[57] An existing UST is defined as a tank containing a regulated substance for which installation commenced on or before December 22, 1988.[58]

---

[52]*Id.* § 280.41(b)(1).
[53]*Id.* § 280.44.
[54]*Id.* § 280.41(b)(2).
[55]*Id.* § 280.42(b)(4).
[56]*Id.* § 280.42(b)(5).
[57]*Id.* § 280.21(a).
[58]*Id.* § 280.12.

356   THE RCRA PRACTICE MANUAL

If upgrading an existing underground storage tank is the selected means of compliance, the following methods are authorized by 40 C.F.R. Section 280.21(b): (1) addition of an interior liner; (2) installation of cathodic protection; or (3) installation of both an interior liner and cathodic protection. Each of these alternatives requires compliance with specific technical, installation, and inspection requirements. Finally, the system was required to comply with the spill and overfill prevention equipment requirements required for new UST systems by December 22, 1998.[59]

December 22, 1998, was the deadline for petroleum and hazardous substance storage tanks to have installed corrosion protection, leak detection, and spill and overflow prevention devices for tanks and piping installed before December 1988. The passage of this deadline received wide media attention, particularly on local service station owners who were required to shut down because their USTs had not been replaced or upgraded. For example, the *Chicago Sun-Times* reported that a gas station owner who had been in business for over 20 years was forced to shut down because he couldn't afford the $50,000 needed to replace his tanks. Such stories should not have been surprising, considering a poll conducted by the Petroleum Equipment Institute two months before the compliance deadline. This poll found that with only two months before the compliance deadline, 45 percent of underground storage tanks did not meet 1998 standards.

Although EPA did not extend the December 22, 1998, deadline, it did announce that certain facilities would be low priority for enforcement for six months after the deadline. EPA announced that it would not focus its federal inspection resources on two types of UST facilities: (1) small UST facilities (generally four or fewer tanks) owned and operated by one person not owning or operating other regulated UST facilities; and (2) USTs owned or operated by local governments and states (including public service entities such as school districts, fire departments, and police departments).

2. *Release Detection*

a. Petroleum Underground Storage Tanks. Release detection requirements for existing petroleum USTs are similar to those for new petroleum USTs; however, the requirements for existing petroleum tanks were phased in based upon the year the UST was installed according to the following schedule:

---

[59]*Id.* § 280.21(d).

Year UST Installed	Date Release Detection Required
Before 1965 or unknown	December 22, 1989
1965–1969	December 22, 1990
1970–1974	December 22, 1991
1975–1979	December 22, 1992
1980–1988	December 22, 1993

Source: 40 C.F.R. Section 280.40(c).

These requirements mandate that petroleum USTs be monitored at least every 30 days, starting on the date above, for releases using one of the following methods: automatic tank gauging, vapor monitoring, interstitial monitoring, groundwater monitoring, or another state-approved method.[60]

b. Hazardous Substance Underground Storage Tanks. Existing hazardous substance USTs must meet the same release detection requirements for existing petroleum USTs based on the year the UST was installed, according to the schedule above, and, by December 22, 1998, these tanks were required to also meet the release detection requirements for new hazardous substance USTs—namely, secondary containment and interstitial monitoring.[61]

D. Existing Underground Storage Tank Piping

1. Corrosion Protection

By December 22, 1998, all existing metal underground piping was required to be upgraded with cathodic protection, replaced with fiberglass-reinforced-plastic piping or replaced with dielectrically coated, cathodically protected piping.[62]

2. Release Detection

a. Petroleum Underground Piping. The detection requirements for underground piping are contingent on whether the piping is pressurized or suction. By December 22, 1990, all existing pressurized piping was required to have an automatic line leak detector and annual line tightness tests or monthly monitoring.[63] Leak detection for suction piping follows

---

[60]*Id.* § 280.43(d)–(h).
[61]*Id.* § 280.42(a).
[62]*Id.* §§ 280.20(b), 280.21(c).
[63]*Id.* §§ 280.40(c), 280.41(b).

the same schedule as the leak detection schedule for its associated UST.[64] For existing suction piping, acceptable methods of release detection include line tightness tests every three years, monthly monitoring, or systems designed so that the piping operates at less than atmospheric pressure, the piping is sloped so that the contents of the piping will flow back into the UST if the suction is released, and one check valve is included in the line as close as practical to the suction pump.[65]

b. Hazardous Substance Underground Piping. Existing hazardous substance underground piping must be upgraded according to the same requirements and deadlines as for petroleum underground piping.[66] Further, by December 22, 1998, all piping was required to have secondary containment and interstitial monitoring.[67]

IV. Notification Requirements

Each owner that brings a tank into use after May 8, 1986, must submit the notification form prescribed in the regulations to the designated agency within 30 days.[68] EPA has prepared notification forms, which are published at 40 C.F.R. Part 280, Appendix I. The form should be submitted to the agency identified in 40 C.F.R. Part 280, Appendix II. Forms prepared by a state may be submitted in lieu of the federal form if they satisfy the requirements of RCRA Section 9002.[69] In addition, under 40 C.F.R. Section 280.22(c), owners are permitted to submit a single notification form for multiple tanks, provided that the tanks are at a single location.

Owners and operators of USTs that were in the ground on May 8, 1986, unless taken out of operation before January 1, 1974, were required to notify the agency designated by EPA[70] by May 8, 1986, on a form published by EPA in the November 8, 1985, *Federal Register*, unless notice was previously given pursuant to CERCLA Section 103(c).[71] Owners and operators that have not already complied with the notification requirements may use the notification form contained in Appendix I of the regulations.[72]

---

[64]*Id.* § 280.40(c).
[65]*Id.* § 280.41(b)(2).
[66]*Id.* § 280.42(a).
[67]*Id.* § 280.42(b)(4).
[68]*Id.* § 280.22(a).
[69]*Id.* § 280.22(b).
[70]*Id.* pt. 280, app. II.
[71]*Id.* § 280.22(a).
[72]*Id.*

Chapter 14: Regulation of Underground Storage Tanks 359

All owners of new UST systems must certify on the notification form that the following provisions of the technical requirements were satisfied: installation of tanks and piping; cathodic protection of steel tanks and piping; financial responsibility; and release detection.[73] Also, the installer must certify that the installation method complied with the regulations.[74]

Any person who sells a UST is required to inform the purchaser of the obligation to notify the appropriate regulatory agency within 30 days of bringing a tank into use. The form provided in Appendix III of the regulations may be used to comply with this requirement.[75]

V. Release Reporting and Response

Owners and operators of USTs must investigate, report, abate, and remedy releases of regulated substances to the environment. The regulations include corrective action requirements for both an immediate and long-term response.

A. Identification and Confirmation

Upon discovering the release of regulated substances at the site or surrounding area, unusual operating conditions indicating that a release may have occurred, or monitoring results from a release detection method indicating that a release may have occurred, owners and operators must report that discovery to the implementing agency within 24 hours or another reasonable time period specified by the implementing agency.[76] Owners and operators must immediately investigate and confirm all suspected releases within seven days by conducting a system check, site check, or other procedure approved by the implementing agency.[77]

B. Initial Response

The regulations require three specific responses to a release within 24 hours of the release or within a reasonable period of time determined by the implementing agency. The three responses are: (1) report the release to the implementing agency; (2) immediately stop the release or spill

---

[73]*Id.* § 280.22(e).
[74]*Id.* § 280.22(f).
[75]*Id.* § 280.22(g).
[76]*Id.* § 280.50.
[77]*Id.* § 280.52.

360 THE RCRA PRACTICE MANUAL

and ensure that human health and safety are not endangered; and (3) identify and mitigate fire, explosion, and vapor hazards.[78]

Spills or overfills of petroleum that are less than 25 gallons (unless they cause a sheen on nearby surface water) or of hazardous substances that are less than the CERCLA reportable quantity do not need to be reported, provided the spill or overfill is contained and cleaned up within 24 hours.[79]

C. Initial Abatement Measures and Site Characterization

After their initial response to a release, owners and operators must perform abatement measures. They must remove as much of the regulated substance from the system as necessary to prevent further release to the environment. In addition, owners and operators must assemble site characterization information, including an estimate of the nature and quantity of the release and the location of wells, sewer lines, and surrounding populations.[80] Within 20 days after release confirmation, owners and operators must submit a report to the implementing agency, summarizing the initial abatement steps taken and any resulting data.[81] If the abatement measures performed indicate the presence of free product, owners and operators must remove the free product to the maximum extent practicable.[82] Within 45 days, owners and operators must submit site characterization information to the implementing agency.[83]

D. Corrective Action

The implementing agency may require owners and operators to develop a corrective action plan for responding to contaminated soils and groundwater.[84] The implementing agency will approve the plan only after ensuring that it will adequately protect human health, safety, and the environment in light of (1) the physical and chemical characteristics of the spilled substance; (2) the hydrogeologic characteristics of the facility and surrounding area; (3) the proximity and uses of nearby water; (4) the potential effects of residual contamination of surface and groundwater; (5) an exposure assessment; and (6) any other relevant information

---

[78]*Id.* §§ 280.53(a), 280.61.
[79]*Id.* § 280.53(b).
[80]*Id.* §§ 280.62(a), 280.63(a).
[81]*Id.* § 280.62(b).
[82]*Id.* § 280.64.
[83]*Id.* § 280.63(b).
[84]*Id.* § 280.66(a).

Chapter 14: Regulation of Underground Storage Tanks   361

discovered during the release investigation.[85] After the implementing agency has approved the plan, the owner and operator are responsible for the cleanup.[86] Public notice of, and access to, the corrective action plan must be provided.[87]

EPA has proposed to reduce the burden on persons cleaning up petroleum-contaminated soil and debris by exempting these wastes from RCRA hazardous waste requirements by deferring application of the toxicity characteristic to such wastes.[88]

VI. Closure

A. Temporary Closure

If a tank system is temporarily closed or taken out of service, the owner and operator must continue to comply with the corrosion protection, release detection, release reporting, and response requirements. However, release detection is not required as long as the system is empty. A tank is empty when all materials have been removed so that no more than 2.5 centimeters of residue, or 0.3 percent by weight of the total capacity of the system, remain in the system.[89] When a tank system is temporarily closed for three months or more, owners and operators also must ensure that vent lines are left open and functioning and that all other lines, pumps, manways, and ancillary equipment are capped and secured.[90]

If the tank is temporarily closed for more than 12 months and does not meet either the performance standards for new tanks or the upgrade requirements for existing tanks (except the spill and overfill requirements), it must be permanently closed. The implementing agency may provide an extension following the submission of a site assessment by the owner or operator.[91]

B. Permanent Closure or Change in Service

An owner or operator must notify the implementing agency of its intent to permanently close or change-in-service a tank at least 30 days before

---

[85]*Id.* § 280.66(b).
[86]*Id.* § 280.66(c).
[87]*Id.* § 280.67.
[88]55 Fed. Reg. 11,798 (1990).
[89]40 C.F.R. § 280.70(a).
[90]*Id.* § 280.70(b).
[91]*Id.* § 280.70(c).

362 THE RCRA PRACTICE MANUAL

beginning permanent closure or change-in-service, or within another reasonable time period determined by the agency, unless the action is in response to corrective action.[92] To permanently close the tank, the owner or operator must empty and clean the tank by removing all liquids and accumulated sludges, and must either remove the tank or fill it with an inert solid material.[93] A change-in-service of a UST occurs when the owner or operator continues to use the UST to store a nonregulated substance.[94] To change-in-service, the owner or operator must empty and clean the tank.[95]

C. Site Assessment

A site assessment must be conducted whenever an owner or operator desires to close permanently a system or have a change-in-service. This site assessment must measure for the presence of a release where contamination is most likely to be present at the UST site.[96] If contaminated soil, contaminated groundwater, or free product is discovered, the owner or operator must begin corrective action.[97] In addition, for at least three years, records must be maintained demonstrating compliance with the closure requirements and the results of the site assessment.[98]

VII. Financial Responsibility for Petroleum Underground Storage Tank Systems

EPA published financial responsibility requirements for petroleum USTs on October 26, 1988.[99] Further, on February 18, 1993, EPA published additional financial responsibility mechanisms for governmental petroleum USTs.[100] These regulations require owners and operators of both new and existing petroleum USTs to ensure that there will be sufficient financial resources available to pay for the costs associated with a petroleum leak.

---

[92]*Id.* § 280.71(a).
[93]*Id.* § 280.71(b).
[94]*Id.* § 280.71(c).
[95]*Id.* § 280.71(e).
[96]*Id.* § 280.72(a).
[97]*Id.* § 280.72(b).
[98]*Id.* § 280.74(b).
[99]53 Fed. Reg. 43,322 (codified at 40 C.F.R. pt. 280, subpt. F).
[100]58 Fed. Reg. 9026 (1993) (codified at 40 C.F.R. pt. 280, subpt. F).

A. Schedule of Compliance

The final rule phased in compliance in five stages based on the number of tanks owned by petroleum marketing firms, net worth for nonpetroleum marketing firms, or promulgation of financial mechanisms for local governments owning or operating petroleum USTs:

Compliance Date

Date	Petroleum Marketing Firms	Nonpetroleum Marketing Firms
January 24, 1989	1,000 or more tanks	Tangible net worth of $20 million or more reported to the Securities & Exchange Commission, Dun and Bradstreet, the Energy Information Administration, or the Rural Electrification Administration
October 26, 1989	100–999 tanks	None
April 26, 1991	13–99 tanks at more than one facility	None
December 31, 1993	1–12 tanks or only one facility with fewer than 100 tanks	Tangible net worth of less than $20 million, including all local government entities
February 18, 1994	Local government entities and Indian tribes	
December 31, 1998	Indian tribes with USTs on Indian lands	

Source: 40 C.F.R. Section 280.91.

For petroleum marketing firms, EPA based the phase-in on the total number of USTs owned to make clear at what time USTs that are owned and operated by different entities were required to be in compliance with the final rule.[101]

B. Amount of Coverage

RCRA requires coverage for petroleum tank owners and operators to be not "less than $1 million for each occurrence with an appropriate aggregate requirement."[102] The final regulations require owners or operators of petroleum USTs that are located at facilities engaged in petroleum production, refining, or marketing or that handle more than 10,000 gallons of petroleum per month to have a minimum of $1 million of "per occurrence" coverage.[103] RCRA permits the EPA Administrator to set

---

[101]53 Fed. Reg. 43,332.
[102]42 U.S.C. § 6991b(d)(5)(A).
[103]40 C.F.R. § 280.93(a)(1).

limits lower than $1 million for USTs at facilities not engaged in petroleum production, refining, or marketing and that are not used to handle substantial quantities of petroleum.[104] Accordingly, the final regulations require owners or operators of USTs that are not located at facilities engaged in petroleum production, refining, or marketing, or that handle 10,000 gallons or less of petroleum per month, to have a minimum of $500,000 of coverage.[105]

Aggregate requirements, set forth in 40 C.F.R. Section 280.93(b)(1)–(2), specify that facilities with 1 to 100 tanks have $1 million in coverage and that facilities with 101 or more tanks have $2 million in coverage.

C. Allowable Mechanisms and Combinations of Mechanisms

Owners and operators may use a single mechanism or a combination of mechanisms to obtain the required amount of financial assurance so long as both corrective action and third-party compensation are fully covered.[106]

1. Financial Test for Self-Insurance

The final rule includes a financial test that owners or operators may use to self-insure. The test requires the owner or operator to meet the financial assurance requirements using one of two methods. The first method requires that:

- the firm must have a tangible net worth equal to at least ten times the amount of aggregate assurance required for UST financial assurance (if the firm is also using a financial test to meet the financial responsibility requirements for the costs of closure, post-closure, liability coverage, and/or corrective action at a Subtitle C facility or for the costs of plugging and abandonment of a class I hazardous waste injection well, the firm must have a tangible net worth equal to at least ten times the sum of these costs plus the required aggregated coverage for its USTs);
- the firm must have a tangible net worth of at least $10 million;
- the firm must have a letter signed by the chief financial officer and worded as specified in the regulations;
- the firm must either file annual financial statements with the Securities and Exchange Commission (SEC), the Energy Information Administration (EIA), or the Rural Electrification Administration (REA) or report annually the firm's tangible net worth to

---

[104]42 U.S.C. § 6991b(d)(5)(B).
[105]40 C.F.R. § 280.93(a)(2).
[106]*Id.* § 280.94.

Chapter 14: Regulation of Underground Storage Tanks   365

Dun and Bradstreet, which must have assigned the firm a financial strength rating of 4A or 5A; and
- the firm's year-end financial statements, if independently audited, may not include an adverse auditor's opinion, disclaimer of opinion, or "going concern" qualification.[107]

The second method, which was added in the final rule, allows firms to substitute the requirement that the firm have a tangible net worth equal to at least ten times the amount of aggregate assurance required for UST financial assurance with a tangible net worth of at least six times their UST obligations if they also have:

- at least 90 percent of their assets in the United States or U.S. assets at least six times their UST obligations;
- either net working capital at least six times the required amount of UST aggregate coverage or a current Standard and Poor's or Moody's bond rating at a certain level; and
- if financial statements are not submitted annually to the SEC, EIA, or REA, a special auditor's report that compares the financial information reported in the test submission with the firm's financial statements and certifies that there are no material differences between the two.[108]

The financial test information must be completed within 120 days after the end of the firm's reporting year.[109] Firms must obtain alternative coverage within 150 days of the end of the year reported in their financial statements if the statements indicate they no longer meet the financial test criteria.[110] Finally, if the firm fails to obtain alternate assurance within 150 days, or within 30 days of notification by the director of the implementing agency that the firm no longer qualifies, the firm must notify the director of such failure within ten days.[111]

2. Guarantees

The final rule permits only one form of financial assurance by which a firm promises to pay the specified amounts for corrective action or third-party liability for another—a guarantee.[112] A guarantee may be

---

[107]*Id.* § 280.95(b)(1)–(5).
[108]*Id.* § 280.95(c)(1)–(5).
[109]*Id.* § 280.95(d).
[110]*Id.* § 280.95(e).
[111]*Id.* § 280.95(g).
[112]*Id.* § 280.96.

366   THE RCRA PRACTICE MANUAL

provided by related firms or by unrelated firms that have a substantial business relationship with the owner or operator. Guarantors must demonstrate that they are qualified to provide financial assurance by satisfying the financial test described above.[113] The guarantee can be used only if it is certified as valid and enforceable by the attorney general of the state where the USTs covered by the mechanism are located.

3. Insurance and Risk Retention Groups

The final rule allows UST owners and operators to demonstrate financial responsibility through the purchase of insurance. The rule specifies conditions that each insurance policy must contain, including on-site corrective action coverage (but not coverage for routine maintenance of the tank site or site restoration and enhancement), sudden and nonsudden occurrences coverage, first-dollar coverage, a six-month extended reporting period in certain circumstances, and exclusion of legal defense costs.[114]

The rule permits claims-made policies that provide coverage only for releases reported during the policy period and that begin subsequent to the policy's retroactive date, which is generally the same as the effective date. A ten-day notification period for cancellation of insurance for nonpayment of premium or misrepresentation is required; 60 days is required in all other cases.[115]

Lastly, 40 C.F.R. Section 280.97(c) requires both insurers and risk retention groups (RRGs) to be licensed to transact the business of insurance or be eligible to provide insurance as an excess or surplus lines insurer in one or more states.

4. Surety Bond

RCRA Section 9003(d)(1) specifically lists surety bonds as one mechanism for EPA to consider in promulgating financial assurance requirements.[116] The final rule allows owners or operators to use surety bonds to satisfy the financial assurance requirements, and it specifies the language the surety bond must contain, including exclusionary language that limits the type and circumstances of third-party liability for when a surety bond can be used.[117]

The rule requires that any surety company issuing a bond be listed as an acceptable surety on federal bonds in the latest circular 570 of the

---

[113]*Id.* § 280.96(a)–(c).
[114]*Id.* § 280.97(a)–(b).
[115]*Id.* § 280.97(b).
[116]42 U.S.C. § 6991b(d)(1).
[117]40 C.F.R. § 280.98(b).

Chapter 14: Regulation of Underground Storage Tanks   367

U.S. Department of Treasury.[118] The surety bond can be used only if it is certified as valid and enforceable by the attorney general of the state where the USTs covered by the mechanism are located.

5. Letters of Credit

RCRA Section 9003(d)(1) also lists letters of credit as a mechanism EPA is to consider in establishing financial assurance requirements.[119] The final rule allows owners or operators to use letters of credit to satisfy the financial assurance requirements.[120] The issuing institution must be an entity that has the authority to issue letters of credit in each state where used and the letter-of-credit operations must be regulated and examined by a federal or state agency.[121] The final rule specifies the required terms for the letter of credit including certain irrevocability on exclusionary language that limits the type and circumstances of third-party liability for which a letter of credit can be used.[122]

6. State-Required Mechanisms

According to the final rule, owners or operators in states that do not have authorized UST programs but do have financial responsibility requirements may use equivalent state-required financial assurance mechanisms to meet the federal financial assurance requirements.[123] A state, an owner or operator, or any other interested party may petition the EPA Regional Administrator to accept a state-required mechanism as equivalent.[124] While the Regional Administrator evaluates the equivalency of a state-required mechanism, the owners and operators using that mechanism will be deemed to be in compliance for USTs covered by the mechanism.[125]

7. State Funds

RCRA Section 9004(c)(1) authorizes the use of "[c]orrective action and compensation programs administered by State or local agencies" as mechanisms to meet the financial assurance requirements.[126] Accordingly, the final rule permits UST owners or operators to use state funds

---

[118]*Id.* § 280.98(a).
[119]42 U.S.C. § 6991b(d)(1).
[120]40 C.F.R. § 280.99.
[121]*Id.* § 280.99(a).
[122]*Id.* § 280.99(b), (d).
[123]*Id.* § 280.100.
[124]*Id.* § 280.100(c).
[125]*Id.* § 280.100(e).
[126]42 U.S.C. § 6991c(c)(1).

368 THE RCRA PRACTICE MANUAL

or other state assurance programs to meet the financial responsibility obligations. The rule does not, however, require any state to establish an assurance program.[127]

The state must submit a description of the fund and a list of the classes of USTs covered by the fund to the Regional Administrator of EPA for a determination that the covered class of USTs is in compliance. Pending review, the owner or operator of a covered class of USTs will be deemed to be in compliance.[128] Upon notification by the Regional Administrator of acceptance of the state fund, the state is required to provide a letter or certificate regarding the state's assumption of responsibility to the owner or operator.[129]

State assurance programs may not provide complete financial responsibility for UST owners or operators. Accordingly, if a UST owner or operator uses a state program that does not provide complete coverage, it also must use other financial assurance mechanisms to demonstrate compliance with the financial responsibility requirements.

8. Trust Fund

The final rule designates a trust fund as an allowable financial assurance mechanism. To ensure that the fund will provide adequate financial assurance, the rule requires the fund to be either fully funded for the amount of required coverage, or partially funded and used in combination with another allowable mechanism that provides the remaining amount of required coverage.[130]

The rule requires the trustee to be an entity that has the authority to act as a trustee and whose trust operations are regulated and examined by a federal agency or an agency of the state in which the fund is established.[131]

9. Standby Trust Fund

The final rule establishes a standby trust fund as the depository mechanism that an owner or operator must put in place upon acquiring a guarantee, surety bond, or letter of credit. Funds drawn under any of these instruments in accordance with instructions from EPA or the implementing agency must be deposited directly into the fund by the institution making the payment.[132]

---

[127]40 C.F.R. § 280.101(a).
[128]Id. § 280.101(c).
[129]Id. § 280.101(d).
[130]Id. § 280.102(c).
[131]Id. § 280.102(a).
[132]Id. §§ 280.96(d), 280.98(d), 280.99(c).

Chapter 14: Regulation of Underground Storage Tanks   369

The trustee must be an entity that has authority to act as a trustee and whose trust operations are regulated by a federal or state agency. The wording of the standby trust agreement must be identical to the wording provided in the regulations.[133] The final rule allows the owner or operator to establish one trust for all funds assured in compliance with the financial assurance requirements.[134]

D. Financial Mechanisms for Local Governments

As noted earlier, local governments that own and operate petroleum underground storage tanks currently must have financial assurance mechanisms in place by February 18, 1994.[135] To demonstrate financial responsibility for USTs, local governments may use any one, or a combination, of the preceding mechanisms.[136] Further, on February 18, 1993, EPA added four additional mechanisms that local governments may use to satisfy the financial responsibility requirements: a bond rating test, a local government financial test, a governmental guarantee, and maintenance of a fund balance.[137]

E. Substitution of Financial Assurance Mechanisms

An owner or operator may substitute alternative financial assurance provided that an effective mechanism or combination thereof that satisfies the financial assurance requirements exists at all times.[138]

F. Cancellation or Nonrenewal by a Provider

Generally, providers of insurance, RRG coverage, and state-backed coverage must provide 60 days' notice before canceling or terminating of coverage. In the event of nonpayment of premium or misrepresentation by an insured, providers must provide ten days' notice. Owners or operators that fail to obtain alternate coverage within 60 days after receipt of a cancellation or termination notice must notify the implementing agency. Providers of local government guarantees, guarantees, letters of

---

[133]*Id.* § 280.103(a)–(b).
[134]*Id.* § 280.103(d).
[135]*Id.* § 280.91(e).
[136]*Id.* § 280.94(a)(1).
[137]58 Fed. Reg. 9026 (to be codified at 40 C.F.R. §§ 280.104–.107).
[138]40 C.F.R. § 280.108.

370 THE RCRA PRACTICE MANUAL

credit, or surety bonds must provide 120 days' notice of cancellation or termination of coverage.[139]

G. Reporting/Record-Keeping Requirements

1. Reporting

An owner or operator must submit the appropriate documentation of financial responsibility to the implementing agency under any of the following circumstances:

- when notifying the state or local agency of the existence of a new UST;
- within 30 days of a release required to be reported to the implementing agency;
- if the owner or operator fails to obtain alternative coverage within 30 days after notice of commencement of bankruptcy proceedings by a provider of financial assurance, suspension or revocation of the provider's authority to issue financial assurance, a guarantor's failure to meet the requirements of the financial test, or other incapacity of a provider;
- if financial assurance is canceled and the owner or operator is unable to obtain alternate financial assurance within 60 days; or
- if the owner or operator fails to meet the requirements of the financial test.[140]

2. Record Keeping

Copies of financial assurance instruments must be maintained at the owner's or operator's UST site or place of business.[141] However, off-site records must be made available upon request of the implementing agency.

If a financial test or guarantee, a local government financial test, or a local government guarantee supported by the local government financial test is used, a copy of the chief financial officer's letter based on year-end financial statements for the most recent year must be on file within 120 days after the close of the financial reporting year.[142] If a guarantee, surety bond, or letter of credit is used, a copy of the signed standby trust fund agreement and copies of any amendments thereto

---

[139]*Id.* § 280.109.
[140]*Id.* § 280.110.
[141]*Id.* § 280.111.
[142]*Id.* § 280.111(b)(2).

Chapter 14: Regulation of Underground Storage Tanks 371

must be maintained.[143] If an insurance policy or RRG coverage is used, a copy of the signed insurance policy or RRG coverage policy with the endorsement or certificate of insurance and any amendments to the agreement must be maintained.[144] Lastly, if coverage is provided by a state fund, a copy of any evidence of coverage provided by the state must be maintained.[145]

H. Bankruptcy

An owner or operator must notify the implementing agency and a guarantor must notify the owner or operator within ten days after commencement of a voluntary or involuntary bankruptcy proceeding.[146] In the event of bankruptcy or incapacity of a provider, or suspension or revocation of the authority of a provider to issue financial assurance, any owner that demonstrates financial responsibility by means other than the financial test is deemed to be without financial assurance.[147] If the owner or operator does not obtain alternate coverage within 30 days, it must notify the implementing agency.[148] Similarly, if the owner or operator receives notice that a state fund has become incapable of assuring costs, the owner or operator must obtain alternative financial assurance.[149]

I. Release from Financial Assurance Requirements

Owners or operators need only maintain financial responsibility until date of closure, or until corrective action is completed if a release is found at the time of closure.[150]

J. Leaking Underground Storage Tank Fund

The leaking UST (LUST) fund was established by SARA, which added Section 9003(h) to RCRA, to be used in special circumstances, where there is an emergency situation involving an UST containing petroleum and the owner of the tank has insufficient funds to pay for an emergency cleanup.[151] RCRA describes "allowable corrective action" to include

---

[143]*Id.* § 280.111(b)(3).
[144]*Id.* § 280.111(b)(7).
[145]*Id.* § 280.111(b)(8).
[146]*Id.* § 280.114(a)–(b).
[147]*Id.* § 280.114(e).
[148]*Id.*
[149]*Id.* § 280.114(f).
[150]*Id.* § 280.113.
[151]42 U.S.C. § 6991b(h).

372 THE RCRA PRACTICE MANUAL

temporary or permanent relocation of residents, provision of alternative household water supplies, and the undertaking of an exposure assessment.[152] The fund, which is financed by excise taxes on motor fuels, does not relieve the responsible party of the financial responsibility for cleanup. EPA will file a cost recovery action against a party whose failure to comply with the financial responsibility regulations requires the fund to pay for corrective action. The fund will pay for corrective action costs if any one of the following conditions exists:

1. no responsible owner/operator is found within 90 days (a shorter period if necessary to protect public health);
2. prompt action by EPA or a state is necessary to protect public health;
3. corrective action costs exceed financial responsibility requirements; or
4. the owner or operator has failed to comply with a corrective action order.[153]

EPA implements the program through cooperative agreements with states that require the state to pay contractors to perform cleanups. The state then attempts to recoup the cleanup costs from tank owners and may use the recovered funds to pay for additional cleanups. In some instances, the cooperative agreement may limit use of the funds to a particular site.

VIII. Financial Responsibility for Hazardous Substance Underground Storage Tank Systems

Subtitle I of RCRA provides for the establishment of a regulatory program for USTs containing hazardous substances, including requirements for maintaining evidence of financial responsibility.[154] On February 9, 1988, EPA published an advance notice of proposed rule making (ANPR), which discussed the financial responsibility requirements for USTs containing hazardous substances and requested comments.[155]

The ANPR focuses on several issues: exemptions, deferrals, amount of required coverage, and approaches to setting coverage. EPA plans to exempt state and federal owners or operators from the financial responsi-

---

[152]*Id.* § 6991b(h)(5).
[153]*Id.* § 6991b(h)(2).
[154]*Id.* § 6991b(c)(6).
[155]53 Fed. Reg. 3818 (1988).

Chapter 14: Regulation of Underground Storage Tanks 373

bility requirements and may exempt local government entities.[156] EPA will exempt local governments if it determines that they are sufficiently permanent, stable, and possess adequate financial strength; it has not yet determined whether Indian tribes should be subject to the financial responsibility requirements. EPA may also defer financial responsibility requirements for the categories of UST systems for which the technical requirements are deferred until there is sufficient information available to determine appropriate per-occurrence and aggregate levels of coverage.[157]

Owners of USTs containing hazardous substances should expect that the amount of required coverage will exceed the required coverage for USTs containing petroleum. EPA projects that the average corrective action costs for a release of a hazardous substance exceed the average corrective action costs for a release of petroleum.[158] EPA's data indicate that UST releases of hazardous substances are more likely to contaminate groundwater and result in liability to third parties than releases of petroleum.[159]

EPA has not yet determined whether per-occurrence coverage should be uniform or should vary depending on UST characteristics, site characteristics, or the type of substance contained in the UST. Although the uniform approach would be easier to administer, EPA recognizes that the costs associated with releases from different hazardous substance USTs will vary significantly. Further, coverage that varies according to UST characteristics provides an incentive for owners or operators to upgrade or retrofit their USTs.[160]

EPA intends to provide a wide variety of mechanisms for proving financial responsibility that should be similar to the mechanisms provided for establishing assurance in the case of USTs containing petroleum.[161]

IX. Lender Liability

On September 7, 1995, EPA issued a final rule exempting banks and other creditors holding a security interest in USTs from the corrective action, technical, and financial responsibility requirements of the federal UST regulations.[162] In issuing this rule, EPA recognized that most businesses with USTs required loans to finance the work necessary to comply with

---

[156]53 Fed. Reg. 3820.
[157]*Id.*
[158]*Id.* at 3821.
[159]*Id.*
[160]*Id.* at 3822.
[161]*Id.* at 3824.
[162]60 Fed. Reg. 46,692 (Sept. 7, 1995); *see also* 40 C.F.R. § 280.200 (2002).

374 THE RCRA PRACTICE MANUAL

regulations. Many lending institutions, however, were reluctant to accept the environmental responsibility if a tank owner defaulted on a loan. EPA hoped the rule would increase the availability of credit for tank owners, helping them meet the 1998 tank upgrade and other regulatory requirements. Under the lender liability rule, a lender may qualify for an exemption, both before and after foreclosure, from compliance with all RCRA Subtitle I requirements for a UST owner or operator if the lender (1) holds an ownership interest in a UST, or in a property on which a UST is located, in order to protect its security interest; (2) does not take part in petroleum production, refining and marketing; and (3) does not participate in the management or operation of the UST. In addition, a lender must empty the UST within 60 days after the foreclosure and either permanently or temporarily close the UST unless a current operator is at the site and can be held responsible with UST regulatory requirements. The lender liability rule also applies to trustees and fiduciaries in addition to lenders.

X. *Authorization of State Programs*

On September 23 and October 26, 1988, EPA promulgated final regulations for the approval of state UST programs to implement the UST standards.[163] States with approved programs must have standards that are no less stringent than the federal requirements and contain adequate enforcement measures. UST owners and operators should expect states to impose fees, either in the form of a license fee or a tax, since state program approval requires the existence of an adequate funding mechanism.[164]

According to EPA, state implementation of the UST program is necessary to provide a long-term solution to the problem of contamination from leaking tanks. To encourage state participation, EPA may link the availability of LUST funds to a state's reasonable progress toward submitting a completed application for state program approval.[165] To date, 28 states have approved UST programs, including Alabama, Arkansas, Connecticut, Delaware, Georgia, Iowa, Kansas, Louisiana, Maine, Maryland, Massachusetts, Mississippi, Montana, Nevada, North Carolina, New Hampshire, New Mexico, North Dakota, Oklahoma, Rhode Island, South Dakota, Tennessee, Texas, Utah, Vermont, Virginia, Washington,

---

[163]53 Fed. Reg. 37,212 (1988) (codified at 40 C.F.R. §§ 281.10–.61); 53 Fed. Reg. 43,322 (1988) (codified at 40 C.F.R. § 281.37).
[164]40 C.F.R. § 281.21.
[165]53 Fed. Reg. 37,240.

Chapter 14: Regulation of Underground Storage Tanks 375

and West Virginia. In addition, the District of Columbia and Puerto Rico have received final authorization from EPA to operate UST programs in lieu of the federal UST program.

XI. The USTfields Program

In November 2000, EPA announced grants for ten communities pursuant to a new program to clean up abandoned underground petroleum tanks. This program, entitled USTfields, will provide grants to states for local pilot projects to plan cleanups, stop contamination of groundwater, allow for future economic development of the sites, and protect human health.

Similar to brownfields, USTfields are underutilized or abandoned commercial and industrial areas in need of redevelopment. The USTfields program is intended to address petroleum contamination from abandoned tanks typically excluded from brownfields redevelopment. Using federal grant money, local communities may entice developers and citizens in helping plan cleanup of these tanks, and leverage new funds to complete the job and move on to future developments that would not otherwise be possible. In awarding grants, special consideration is given to cities experiencing difficulties from MTBE contamination, a fuel additive that poses risks to groundwater.

In 2001, EPA announced that it would spend $4 million from the Leaking Underground Storage Tank (LUST) trust fund to fund up to 40 additional USTfields redevelopment projects in its second phase of the USTfields program.[166]

XII. Enforcement

Pursuant to RCRA Section 9006, EPA is authorized to institute enforcement actions and assess penalties against violators of the UST technical and financial responsibility requirements.[167] RCRA Section 9006(a) authorizes EPA to issue administrative orders requiring compliance with these requirements.[168] EPA may assess a civil penalty up to $10,000 for each tank per day of violation.[169] Under RCRA Section 9006(a), EPA may also institute judicial enforcement actions to compel compliance with an administrative order.[170] Penalties up to $25,000 for each day of noncom-

---

[166]*See* 66 Fed. Reg. 44,345 (Aug. 23, 2001).

[167]42 U.S.C. § 6991e.

[168]*Id.* § 6991e(a).

[169]*Id.* § 6991e(d).

376 THE RCRA PRACTICE MANUAL

pliance with an administrative order may be assessed.[171] Finally, owners that knowingly violate the notification rules may be assessed a civil penalty up to $10,000 for each tank.[172]

On December 31, 1996, EPA issued a final rule that increased civil monetary penalties by 10 percent to adjust for inflation.[173] The Debt Collection Improvement Act of 1996 requires all federal agencies to adjust civil monetary policies for inflation on a periodic basis. For example, EPA may now assess a civil penalty up to $11,000 for each tank per day of violation. Penalties up to $27,500 for each day of noncompliance with an administrative order also may be assessed.[174]

In July 1990, EPA issued its *UST/LUST Enforcement Procedures Guidance Manual*,[175] which guides EPA regional personnel in taking enforcement action for violations of the UST technical and corrective action requirements. In November 1990, EPA issued its Penalty Guidance for Violations of UST Regulations,[176] which guides regional personnel in calculating civil penalties against owners and operators of USTs that violate the UST technical and financial responsibility requirements.

EPA issued its Final Policy on Compliance Incentives for Small Businesses on June 3, 1996.[177] This policy applies to facilities owned by small businesses, defined as "a person, corporation, partnership, or other entity who employs 100 or fewer individuals (across all facilities and operations owned by the entity)." The policy can mitigate penalties sought against a small business if the business demonstrates that (1) it has not previously violated the specific requirement within the past three years and was not the subject of two or more enforcement actions for violating any environmental rule within the past five years; (2) it must correct the violation within the corrections period, not to exceed 180 days; and c) the violation must not involve criminal conduct and must not cause a significant health, safety, or environmental harm or threat. Penalty reductions apply only to violations that were identified as part of a facility-conducted audit or part of a government agency's on-site compliance assistance visit to the facility. If a small business does not satisfy the criteria listed above but has otherwise made a good-faith effort to comply, EPA has discretion to refrain from seeking civil penalties.

---

[170]*Id.* § 6991e(a)(1).
[171]*Id.* § 6991e(a)(3).
[172]*Id.* § 6991e(d)(1).
[173]61 Fed. Reg. 69,630 (Dec. 31, 1996).
[174]40 C.F.R. § 19.4 (2002).
[175]Office of Solid Waste and Emergency Response (OSWER) Directive No. 9610.11.
[176]OSWER Directive No. 9610.12.
[177]61 Fed. Reg. 27,984 (June 3, 1996).

A. Section 9003 Corrective Action Orders

EPA has promulgated regulations for the issuance of UST administrative corrective action orders and administrative hearings conducted pursuant to such orders.[178] The agency elected to adopt the more streamlined 40 C.F.R. Part 24 hearing for review of UST corrective action orders, stating that streamlined procedures are appropriate since Part 24 addresses whether a *release* has occurred and the corrective measures necessary, but does not address whether a *violation* has occurred.[179] Given these considerations, EPA concluded that full-blown hearing procedures with discovery, examination, and cross-examination were unnecessary and, in fact, contrary to the statutory objective of prompt cleanup.[180]

EPA bifurcated the Part 24 procedures into Subparts B and C. Subpart B procedures, which are the least formal and least time-consuming, are used when the order recipient is asked to undertake studies related to a release. Subpart C is to be utilized when the order recipient is directed to undertake cleanup activities.[181]

B. Significant Case Law

In April 1991, the Department of Justice filed the first civil suit under RCRA Subtitle I, seeking injunctive relief and civil penalties against Ownbey Enterprises for noncompliance with a consent order.[182] The consent order required Ownbey to remediate soil and groundwater contamination linked to two underground storage tanks owned by Ownbey. Later, Ownbey refused to comply with the consent order, claiming that (1) EPA withheld information of other possible sources of the contamination; (2) EPA did not follow its own operating procedures for investigating the contamination; and (3) new data suggest Ownbey's tanks could not have been the source of contamination.[183]

Cross-motions for summary judgment were denied by the District Court for the Northern District of Georgia on March 27, 1992.[184] While the court refused Ownbey's request to modify the consent order at this stage of the litigation, it did leave open the possibility that Ownbey

---

[178]56 Fed. Reg. 49,376 (1991).

[179]*Id*. at 49,378.

[180]*Id*. at 49,379.

[181]*Id*.

[182]United States v. Ownbey Enters., Inc., 789 F. Supp. 1145, 1148 (N.D. Ga. 1992).

[183]*Id*. at 1148.

[184]*Id*. at 1145.

378 THE RCRA PRACTICE MANUAL

could be excused from "remedy[ing] a problem it did not create" if it shows it is not responsible for *any* of the contamination.[185]

The case of *Zands v. Nelson* involves a RCRA citizen suit by current landowners against prior owners and operators of a gas station located on the land.[186] The District Court for the Southern District of California held that leaking gasoline is a solid waste, supporting a citizen suit under RCRA.[187] Further, the court found that leaking gasoline constitutes an "imminent and substantial endangerment to health or the environment."[188] The court found that "individuals who own or operate gas stations are responsible for gasoline that leaks from the piping system or the gas tanks themselves," and that gas station owners or operators are responsible for spillage caused by parties delivering gasoline to the station's tanks.[189]

Because the recovery of response costs for releases of petroleum products is not available under CERCLA, due to the petroleum product exclusion,[190] a number of private parties filed citizen suits seeking recovery of response costs related to leaking petroleum USTs. In *Meghrig v. KFC Western, Inc.*, the U.S. Supreme Court held that the citizen suit provision of RCRA does not allow private citizens to recover the costs of cleaning up petroleum contamination that, at the time of the lawsuit, no longer presented a danger to health or environment.[191] In its unanimous opinion, the Court reversed a ruling by the U.S. Court of Appeals for the Ninth Circuit. The Court stated that the citizen suit provision allows suits seeking injunction relief against people responsible for waste that still "may present an imminent and substantial endangerment to health or the environment." Private parties, however, cannot file citizen suits seeking reimbursement of response costs after they have already cleaned up the contamination.

---

[185]*Id.* at 1153.

[186]Zands v. Nelson, 797 F. Supp. 805 (S.D. Cal. 1992); *see* 42 U.S.C. § 6972(a)(1)(B) (permitting citizen suits under RCRA against parties who contributed or must have contributed to "the past or present handling, storage, treatment, transportation, or disposal of any solid waste or hazardous waste which may present an imminent and substantial endangerment to health or the environment").

[187]*Zands, supra* note 186, 797 F. Supp. at 809.

[188]*Id.*

[189]*Id.* at 810.

[190]42 U.S.C. § 9601(14).

[191]Meghrig v. KFC W., Inc., 516 U.S. 479 (1996).

Chapter 14: Regulation of Underground Storage Tanks 379

XIII. Using the Internet to Research UST Issues

Those interested in obtaining further background information on USTs or other issues mentioned in this chapter may find the Internet to be a helpful resource. To obtain comprehensive information on the UST program, the reader may want to examine EPA's Web page located at http://www.epa.gov/swerust1/pubs/index.htm. In addition, the following address provides direct access to the RCRA hotline: http://www.epa.gov/epaoswer/hotline/index.htm. This site provides a list of frequently asked questions about RCRA, the UST program, EPCRA, and CERCLA. Finally, for free federal legislative information, the reader should visit Thomas, a site created by the 104th Congress. This site, located at http://thomas.loc.gov, provides the status of bills, text from the *Congressional Record*, and the text of bills before Congress.

XIV. Conclusion

The federal regulatory program for USTs is comprehensive in its coverage of USTs that are not otherwise excluded from regulation. Owners and operators of USTs must be cognizant of these regulatory requirements or their state equivalents to avoid situations of noncompliance that could result in substantial penalties being assessed by administrative agencies. Compliance with the monitoring, operating, and release detection requirements will also help avoid potential civil liability, which could be sought by parties who might otherwise be harmed by leaks that in the past may have gone undetected for years. Additionally, the financial assurance requirements attempt to ensure that funds will be available to conduct cleanup activities if and when a release occurs. On balance, considering the aging population of underground tanks, the UST program serves an important purpose in protecting the environment.

CHAPTER 15

Regulation of Nonhazardous Waste under RCRA

ROBERT B. McKINSTRY JR.

I. Introduction

Although the principal focus of the Resource Conservation and Recovery Act (RCRA) is the regulation of hazardous waste, the largest volume of waste generated within the United States is nonhazardous waste, which is either governed by Subtitle D, 42 U.S.C. Sections 6941 through 6949a, or excluded from regulation under RCRA altogether. In 1987, approximately 13 billion tons of this nonhazardous waste was generated, of which 195.7 million tons was municipal solid waste (MSW), and 12.8 billion tons was mining, agricultural, and nonhazardous industrial waste (including wastewater).[1] Both the volumes and per capita generation rates of nonhazardous waste generated have continued to grow. In 1999, sources in the United States produced 229.9 million tons of MSW, or 4.62 pounds per person, compared with 88 million tons or 2.7 pounds per person in 1960.[2] EPA further reported that, as of 2002, an additional 7.6 billion tons of industrial nonhazardous waste was managed in land disposal units.[3]

---

[1]Report to Congress, Solid Waste Disposal in the United States (hereinafter "Report to Congress"), vols. I and II, EPA No. 530-88-011 and -011B; NTIS PB89-110381 and 110399 (1988); 1987 NAT'L BIENNIAL RCRA HAZARDOUS WASTE REP., EPA 530SW91061, NTIS PBI-220293 (July 1991); Characteristics of Municipal Solid Waste in the United States, 1992 Update, EPA 530R-92-019, NTIS PB92-207166 (July 1992).

[2]Introduction to RCRA Solid Waste Programs, in RCRA, SUPERFUND & EPCRA CALL CENTER TRAINING MODULE, EPA530-K-02-0191, at p.2 (Oct. 2001).

[3]EPA, Industrial Waste Management, at http://www.epa.gov/industrial waste.

382   THE RCRA PRACTICE MANUAL

Although some of these nonhazardous wastes pose threats to human health and the environment as great as those of regulated hazardous wastes, historically regulation under Subtitle D was characterized by very little federal involvement and limited federal technical standards for the protection of human health and the environment. Without a federal floor, state standards varied dramatically, with some very strict and others virtually nonexistent. In contrast, characterization of a waste as a regulated hazardous waste under the RCRA Subtitle C regulatory program resulted in the regulation of virtually all aspects of its handling from cradle to grave. This disparity in federal regulation under RCRA has been adjusted to a certain degree by the adoption of somewhat more stringent permitting and technical requirements for MSW landfills pursuant to changes required by the Hazardous and Solid Waste Amendments of 1984 (HSWA)[4] and for nonmunicial, nonhazardous waste landfills receiving conditionally exempt small-quantity generator waste.[5] However, the largest volume of nonhazardous solid waste regulated under RCRA Subtitle D falls outside of the regulatory framework of these provisions.

Significant volumes of waste generated within the United States fall outside of both Subtitle D and Subtitle C. To be regulated under Subtitle D, a waste must be a "solid waste" as defined in 40 C.F.R. Section 261.2 and not excluded from all RCRA regulation under 40 C.F.R. Section 261.4(a). Thus, as under Subtitle C, wastewaters discharged to a publicly owned treatment works (POTW) or to a treatment plant regulated as a point source discharge under Section 402 of the Clean Water Act,[6] materials subjected to in situ mining techniques, and a wide variety of materials that are recycled or used in a process are exempt from regulation under RCRA altogether. The conditional inclusions in the latter category of materials such as sludges, by-products and spent materials from the mineral-processing industry,[7] various scrap metals,[8] a variety of oil-refining wastes and used oil,[9] and various paper-making and wood-products industry wastes,[10] result in perhaps the largest volume of wastes generated in the United States being regulated solely under alternative programs such as the Clean Water Act[11] or the Surface Mining Control and Reclamation Act[12] or escaping federal regulation altogether.

---

[4]40 C.F.R. pt. 258.
[5]*Id.* pt. 257, subpt. B.
[6]33 U.S.C. § 1342.
[7]*Id.* § 261.4(a)(17).
[8]*Id.* § 261.4(a)(13)–(14).
[9]*Id.* § 261.4(a)(12).
[10]*Id.* § 261.4(a)(6), (9).
[11]33 U.S.C. §§ 1251–1387.
[12]30 U.S.C. §§ 1201–1328.

Chapter 15: Regulation of Nonhazardous Waste under RCRA   383

The nonhazardous solid wastes that are subject to limited regulation under Subtitle D encompass a wide variety of waste streams, identified in 40 C.F.R. Section 261.4(b). Many of these so-called nonhazardous waste streams include materials that create environmental hazards virtually indistinguishable from those created by wastes that are regulated as hazardous wastes. For example, MSW generated by households, institutions, and hospitals, like lunchroom and plant trash generated by industries, includes household hazardous waste and small-quantity generator waste. If these same wastes were generated by another party, they would be regulated as hazardous wastes. Subtitle D also addresses wastes that are not MSW, such as nonhazardous industrial sludges, other process wastes, and agricultural wastes. The most voluminous of these are mining wastes and fossil fuel combustion wastes, many of which would otherwise be considered hazardous but for the Bevill Amendment.[13] Other significant Subtitle D wastes include certain wastes for which special handling requirements apply, such as sewage sludge and used oil.

These nonhazardous wastes are managed in a variety of ways. Generally, there are four management alternatives for MSW and other types of nonhazardous waste: source reduction, recycling, combustion, and landfilling. EPA has established a hierarchy of preferred alternatives for management of nonhazardous waste. Source reduction is the most highly preferred method, followed by recycling, then combustion, and finally, landfilling.[14]

Source reduction involves the design or use of materials to prevent their entry into the waste stream. This involves methods such as designing materials, such as packaging, to reduce waste or promote reuse, reusing the materials, or managing organic wastes through composting on site. In 1992 EPA measured 630,000 tons of MSW that was source reduced, and by 1999 that number had grown to 50,042,000,[15] although the extent to which this involved better measurement, as opposed to actual reductions, is unclear.

---

[13]42 U.S.C. § 6921(b)(3); see 40 C.F.R. § 261.4(b)(3) (mining overburden), (4) (fossil fuel combustion wastes), (7) (wastes from the extraction, beneficiation, and processing of ores and minerals); Chem. Mfrs. Ass'n v. EPA, 673 F.2d 507, 509 (D.C. Cir. 1982); Envtl. Def. Fund v. EPA, 852 F.2d 1309 (D.C. Cir. 1988), cert. denied sub nom. Am. Mining Cong. v. Envtl. Def. Fund, 489 U.S. 1011, 103 L. Ed. 2d 183, 109 S. Ct. 1120 (1989); Envtl. Def. Fund v. EPA, 852 F.2d 1316 (D.C. Cir. 1988), cert. denied sub nom. Am. Mining Cong. v. Envtl. Def. Fund, 489 U.S. 1011, 103 L. Ed. 2d 183, 109 S. Ct. 1120 (1989).

[14]The Solid Waste Dilemma: Solutions for the Nineties (preliminary draft for focus group comment, USEPA OSW Mun. Solid Waste Program Aug. 1990) (hereinafter "Agenda for Action"); Municipal Solid Waste in the United States: 1999 Facts and Figures (EPA, OSWER 2001), at http://www.epa.gov/epa/oswer/non-hw/muncpl/msw99.htm#link (hereinafter "1999 Facts and Figures") at 12–13.

[15]1999 Facts and Figures at 13.

384   THE RCRA PRACTICE MANUAL

Recycling involves the separation of materials from the waste stream (a process known as "source separation") for recovery, as well as various recovery techniques. These techniques include community-level composting (as opposed to on-site composting) and the use of recovered materials such as paper, glass, and plastic in manufacturing processes. Source separation and materials recovery may be facilitated by the construction of materials recovery facilities (MRFs).[16] Compost manufactured from sewage sludge, leaves and grass, and other organic components of MSW results in a product that can be applied to land as soil conditioner. Sewage sludge also is often applied directly to land as a fertilizer.

The combustion of waste may involve a variety of technologies. Combustion for energy recovery is a preferred alternative to simple incineration. Waste-to-energy technologies include both "mass burn" technologies and various refuse-derived fuel (RDF) technologies. In mass burn technologies, all municipal waste is burned in a single chamber to generate steam. In facilities that employ RDF technologies, the combustible portion of MSW is separated from the inert portion and processed into pellets or "fluff"; the pellets or "fluff" may be burned in boilers or other devices for recovery of the energy component.

Landfilling remains the predominant disposal method for MSW, particularly in sparsely populated or rural areas and in communities where resource recovery facilities are not feasible or have not been constructed. Landfilling is required for the ultimate disposal of ash or other "residue" from incineration facilities, including energy recovery facilities.

II. State Planning and Open Dumping Requirements of Subtitle D

Where Subtitle C contemplates a comprehensive federal system of regulation based upon a permit system that may be implemented through the states, Subtitle D contemplates primarily state and local regulation developed through plans approved by EPA. Subtitle D expressly seeks to encourage the development of state and regional solid waste management plans with the stated purposes of "maximiz[ing] the utilization of valuable resources including energy and materials which are recoverable from solid waste and . . . encourag[ing] resource conservation."[17] The focus of these plans is the maximization of recycling and other forms of resource recovery,[18] and the elimination of "open dumps" and the prac-

---

[16]Agenda for Action at 5–7.
[17]42 U.S.C. § 6941.
[18]*Id.* §§ 6941–6942.

Chapter 15: Regulation of Nonhazardous Waste under RCRA   385

tice of "open dumping" as defined in federal guidelines established under Sections 1008(a) and 4004(a) of RCRA.

A. Section 1008 Guidelines

The planning required under Subtitle D is founded upon guidelines published by EPA under RCRA Section 1008. Section 1008 requires EPA to develop guidelines that:

- "provide a technical and economic description of the level of performance that can be obtained by various available solid waste management practices (including operating practices) which provide for the protection of public health and the environment";
- describe levels of performance for protecting groundwater, surface water, air, safety, disease control, and aesthetics; and
- most importantly, define open dumping.

These guidelines are recommended only for the private sector and state and local governments, but Section 6004 of RCRA makes the guidelines binding upon federal agencies and contractors operating any federal property or facility. The guidelines can be enforced against federal agencies or such contractors in a citizen suit brought pursuant to Section 7002 of RCRA.[19]

Although EPA developed many of its guidelines under Section 1008 either before or shortly after the enactment of RCRA, the agency has recently removed outdated guidelines and updated other guidelines significantly, particularly for landfills and recycled products. The current guidelines deal with thermal processing,[20] storage and collection,[21] and recycling issues, namely, source separation for materials recovery, and procurement of products that contain recycled material.[22] EPA has relied upon Section 1008 as well as Section 4004 of RCRA to prescribe enforceable open dumping criteria applicable to MSW landfills[23] and other disposal facilities.[24]

B. State and Regional Solid Waste Plans

State solid waste management plans are the centerpiece of the Subtitle D program. Through its plan, a state establishes an overall strategy for

---

[19]Blue Legs v. Bureau of Indian Affairs, 867 F.2d 1094 (8th Cir. 1989).
[20]40 C.F.R. pt. 240.
[21]*Id.* pt. 243.
[22]*Id.* pts. 246–247.
[23]*Id.* pt. 258.
[24]*Id.* pt. 257.

386   THE RCRA PRACTICE MANUAL

protecting human health and the environment from the potentially adverse effects of solid waste disposal. State plans also specify programs for encouraging resource conservation and recovery, formulate plans for providing adequate disposal capacity, and describe how a state will implement its programs.[25]

Section 4002 of RCRA calls for the establishment of federal guidelines for solid waste plans, and Section 4003 sets forth the criteria EPA is to use in approving such plans. Section 4006 then requires states to develop solid waste management plans. States must follow the guidelines established pursuant to Section 4002 and meet the criteria in Section 4003. These plans must receive federal approval under Section 4007.

The purposes of these plans are set forth in the standards that govern EPA approval of state plans. Above all, the plans must call for the closing of "open dumps," prohibit the establishment of new open dumps, and assure that all solid waste is either utilized for resource recovery or disposed in regulated "sanitary landfills."[26] A plan cannot be approved unless it accomplishes these goals, provides the regulatory powers to do so,[27] and eliminates state law barriers that might prevent a municipality from entering into long-term contracts necessary to finance a state-of-the-art resource recovery facility.[28]

Generally, the federal guidelines require states to designate administrative and planning regions.[29] In establishing these regions and developing their plans, states are required to consider all of the environmental, technical, social, and legal factors that will determine the amounts and types of waste generated, and the technologies that will maximize resource recovery and environmental protection.[30] EPA guidelines call for the establishment of a region large enough, where possible, to achieve economies of scale and maximize resource recovery, considering transportation costs and availability, political boundaries, and geologic, hydrologic, climatic, and constraining factors.[31] RCRA specifically encourages the establishment of regional and even interstate plans, suggesting that, where feasible, regional water quality planning agencies designated under Section 208 of the Clean Water Act[32] be utilized for solid waste planning.[33] To aid in interstate planning and enforcement, Section 1005 of

---

[25]Report to Congress, vol. II.
[26]42 U.S.C. § 6943(a)(2), (3).
[27]*Id.* § 6943(a)(4).
[28]*Id.* § 6943(a)(5).
[29]*Id.* § 6946(a).
[30]*Id.* § 6943(c).
[31]40 C.F.R. §§ 255.10–.11.
[32]33 U.S.C. § 1288.
[33]42 U.S.C. § 6946(b)(1).

Chapter 15: Regulation of Nonhazardous Waste under RCRA 387

RCRA encourages interstate cooperation and gives advance congressional consent to interstate compacts, if approved by EPA and Congress.[34]

In response to these guidelines and statutory directives, states most frequently designate counties as local solid waste planning and administrative units. However, recognizing that in many cases counties will contain insufficient population to support state-of-the-art treatment and disposal facilities, states frequently provide an opportunity for counties to develop joint plans.

The state plans must also include "methods for achieving the objectives of environmentally sound management and disposal of solid and hazardous waste, resource conservation, and maximum utilization of valuable resources."[35] The plans must address physical environmental factors relevant to the protection of air and water quality. They must address solid waste collection, storage, treatment and disposal technologies, and their effects. Population and economic factors relevant to solid waste generation; political, financial, and other management systems; and markets for recovered (that is, recycled) materials and energy must all be considered.[36]

C. Prohibition of Open Dumping

The closure of open dumps is both the central goal of the planning provisions of Subtitle D and the focus of the only substantive provision of that subtitle. Sections 4002 and 4003 require state plans to define and prohibit open dumps and the practice of open dumping. Section 4007 prohibits approval of a state solid waste management plan unless it provides for the elimination of open dumps and dumping, and contains provisions for revision whenever the federal open dumping criteria are modified.

The classification of solid waste facilities as open dumps and their prohibition are governed by Sections 4004 and 4005 of RCRA. Section 4004 distinguishes between and defines "open dumps" and "sanitary landfills." It requires EPA to "promulgate regulations containing criteria for determining which facilities shall be classified as sanitary landfills and which shall be classified as open dumps." The regulations, "[a]t a minimum, . . . shall provide that a facility may be classified as a sanitary landfill and not an open dump only if there is no reasonable probability of adverse effects on health or the environment from disposal of solid waste at such facility." Effective six months after the promulgation of

---

[34]*Id.* § 6904(b).
[35]40 C.F.R. § 256.01(a).
[36]42 U.S.C. § 6942(c).

388 THE RCRA PRACTICE MANUAL

these regulations, each state plan must prohibit the establishment of open dumps and require disposal of solid waste in sanitary landfills.

Section 4005(a) imposes the principal substantive requirement of Subtitle D by prohibiting the practice of open dumping as defined pursuant to Section 1008, except in cases where the facility is operating under a compliance schedule. Section 4005(a) further provides that its prohibition may be enforced in a citizen suit. The prohibition is prospective only and does not apply to disposal activity that took place before the promulgation of the criteria.[37]

Section 4005(b) calls for a national inventory of open dumps. Each state plan must require all open dumps on the inventory to comply with measures "to eliminate health hazards and minimize potential health hazards." Where a facility is unable to comply with such measures, the state plan must include a compliance schedule to bring the facility into compliance within five years.

EPA has consistently chosen to promulgate the criteria for defining open dumps and sanitary landfills under Section 4004 and the criteria for defining the practices constituting open dumping under Section 1008 in a single set of regulations. This is true both of the original Part 257 open dumping criteria promulgated in 1979[38] and the revised Part 258 criteria for landfills promulgated in 1991 in response to HSWA.[39] The practice of open dumping defined under Section 1008, which is prohibited by Section 4005, has been defined identically with criteria for defining open dumps and sanitary landfills. This has practical implications, in that the Section 4005 prohibition is enforceable in a citizen suit under Section 7002, while the Section 4004 criteria are to be implemented and enforced through state plans and might not otherwise be directly enforceable.[40]

D. Modifications to the Open Dumping Criteria Required by HSWA

The regulatory and enforcement model originally adopted by Congress in Subtitle D called primarily for state implementation of plans, coupled with limited substantive criteria directly enforceable through citizen suits. This model differed from the comprehensive federal permitting and enforcement scheme established under Subtitle C and regulation schemes typically seen in many other federal environmental laws. In

---

[37]Jones v. Inmont Corp., 584 F. Supp. 1425 (S.D. Ohio 1984).

[38]44 Fed. Reg. 53,460 (1979).

[39]56 Fed. Reg. 50,978 (1991).

[40]O'Leary v. Moyer's Landfill, Inc., 523 F. Supp. 642 (E.D. Pa. 1981).

Chapter 15: Regulation of Nonhazardous Waste under RCRA 389

1984, HSWA modified RCRA's regulatory and enforcement model as applied to landfills that accept household hazardous waste or small-quantity generator waste. HSWA also mandated the development of a federally enforceable state permit system designed to implement federal open dumping criteria at these landfills.

Section 4010, added by HSWA, required EPA to conduct a study to determine the extent to which the Section 1008 and 4004 criteria and guidelines applicable to nonhazardous waste management facilities, in general, and landfills and surface impoundments, in particular, were sufficient to protect groundwater. EPA was required to submit a report to Congress on the results of the study. This section also required EPA to reevaluate and to revise its open dumping criteria applicable to facilities that receive household hazardous waste and small-quantity generator waste. EPA was directed to establish:

> criteria . . . necessary to protect human health and the environment and . . . tak[ing] into account the practicable capability of such facilities. At a minimum such revisions for facilities potentially receiving such wastes should require groundwater monitoring as necessary to detect contamination, establish criteria for the acceptable location of new or existing facilities, and provide for corrective action as appropriate.[41]

In response to these dictates, in October 1988, EPA submitted a report to Congress.[42] In 1991 EPA then promulgated new criteria for all landfills receiving MSW under 40 C.F.R. Part 258, based, in part, on that report.[43] Although those standards were largely upheld on appeal,[44] the reviewing court noted, in dicta, that those standards were incomplete in that they failed to address non-MSW landfills receiving conditionally exempt small-quantity generator (CESQG) waste and that EPA's failure to promulgate standards for non-MSW facilities by the statutory deadline of March 31, 1988, was unlawful. EPA subsequently promulgated a new Subpart B to Part 257, applying to industrial waste landfills receiving CESQG waste.[45] Finally, in 1998, EPA adopted regulations, codified at 40 C.F.R. Part 239, specifying the criteria and procedures for approval of the state permit systems required to implement these requirements.[46]

---

[41]42 U.S.C. § 6949a(c).

[42]*See* Report to Congress.

[43]56 Fed. Reg. 50,978 (1991).

[44]Sierra Club v. EPA, 992 F.2d 337, 345–47 (D.C. Cir. 1993).

[45]40 C.F.R. pt. 257, subpt. B, 61 Fed. Reg. 34,269 (July 1, 1996).

[46]63 Fed. Reg. 57,040 (Oct. 23, 1998).

390 THE RCRA PRACTICE MANUAL

To assure more effective and uniform enforcement of the open dumping criteria, Section 4005(c), added by HSWA, requires the establishment of a federally enforceable permit system. Specifically, each state is required to develop and to implement a permit program for all solid waste management facilities that may receive household hazardous waste or small-quantity generator waste. Section 4005(c) further requires that states amend and implement a permit system to enforce the revisions to the open dumping criteria required by HSWA within 18 months of the promulgation of revised criteria.

Where EPA finds that a state has failed to adopt a permit system incorporating these revised open dumping criteria, EPA is authorized to use Sections 3007 and 3008 of RCRA to enforce those criteria. This represents the only instance in which EPA may take enforcement action under RCRA at a nonhazardous waste facility, other than the authorization to take action in response to an imminent hazard under Section 7003.

III. The Substantive Requirements of the Open Dumping Criteria

A. The Part 257, Subpart A, Open Dumping Criteria

The first open dumping criteria promulgated by EPA under Sections 1008(a)(3) and 4004(a) of RCRA are set forth in 40 C.F.R. Part 257, Subpart A, and first became effective in 1979. Those regulations generally apply to nonhazardous waste management practices and facilities, with certain stated exceptions. These include exemptions for facilities regulated under Subpart C of RCRA. As originally adopted and as they apply today, the Part 257 regulations did not apply to agricultural operations or mining operations where the waste was intended to be returned to the mine site. In addition, irrigation return flows, septage, sewage treatment plant discharges, discharges regulated under National Pollutant Discharge Elimination System (NPDES) permits, and underground injection wells regulated under the Safe Drinking Water Act[47] all fell outside the original scope of coverage of these standards.[48]

In some cases where EPA has adopted updated or more specific standards for hazardous waste facilities and various specific types of nonhazardous solid waste facilities, it has exempted those facilities from regulation under the more general and outdated Part 257 requirements contained in Subpart A. Thus, in adopting the Part 258 municipal solid

---

[47]42 U.S.C. § 300(f) *et seq.*
[48]40 C.F.R. § 257.1.

Chapter 15: Regulation of Nonhazardous Waste under RCRA   391

waste landfill (MSWLF) criteria pursuant to HSWA in 1991, EPA removed MSWLFs from coverage under Part 257.[49] In enacting sewage sludge use and disposal guidelines under Section 405 of the Clean Water Act,[50] EPA similarly excluded sites for the land disposal of sewage sludge (other than industrially generated sludge) from Part 257 coverage. All other MSW management facilities, including waste piles, impoundments, land application sites, and incinerators, remained subject to the Part 257 standards, now contained in Subpart A. All other nonhazardous, nonmunicipal waste disposal facilities and operations also remain subject to the Part 257 standards. In 1993, when EPA adopted additional location, groundwater-monitoring, and corrective action requirements for nonhazardous industrial waste landfills receiving CESQG waste, it added those requirements as a new Subpart B and redesignated the original Part 257 regulations as Subpart A. In this case, EPA established additional standards in Subpart B for non-MSW nonhazardous waste facilities accepting CESQG wastes but required these facilities to comply with certain Part 257, Subpart A requirements.[51]

The original Part 257, Subpart A criteria remain general and fail to address many issues known to be of concern today. They contain specific requirements applicable to floodplains, endangered species, surface water, groundwater, application to land used for production of food-chain crops, disease vectors, air, and safety.[52]

For the most part, the requirements of Part 257, Subpart A, unlike Subtitle C regulations, do not contain specific technical requirements and often do little more than reference requirements imposed under other federal environmental laws. By way of example, the surface water standard[53] generally requires compliance with the requirements for permits under Sections 402 and 404 of the Clean Water Act; and the air standard simply prohibits the practice of open burning and requires compliance with state implementation plans under the Clean Air Act.[54]

In some limited instances, the Part 257 requirements do impose siting, design, and operating requirements in addition to those imposed by other federal laws. This is true of both the land application[55] and disease vector[56] requirements, which provide limited protection and standards

---

[49]56 Fed. Reg. 51,016 (Oct. 9, 1991).
[50]33 U.S.C. § 1345.
[51]*See* 40 C.F.R. § 257.5(a).
[52]*Id*. §§ 257.3-1 to -8.
[53]*Id*. § 257.3-3.
[54]*Id*. § 257.3-6.
[55]*Id*. § 257.3-5.
[56]*Id*. § 257.3-6.

392 THE RCRA PRACTICE MANUAL

not imposed under other federal laws. The water standard similarly prohibits non-point source pollution in violation of an otherwise unenforceable water quality management plan adopted under Section 208 of the Clean Water Act.[57] The groundwater requirement[58] prohibits contamination of groundwater by certain specified substances at the facility boundary at levels exceeding the maximum contaminant level (MCL) for those substances under the Safe Drinking Water Act. Finally, the safety standard requires control of methane gas to maintain levels below 25 percent of the lower explosive limit (LEL) and requires certain facilities to take measures to prevent bird hazards to airports.[59]

B. Part 258 Open Dumping Criteria for MSWLFs

HSWA required revision of the open dumping criteria for municipal solid waste landfills ("MSWLFs") that accept household hazardous waste or small-quantity generator waste. Revised criteria promulgated pursuant to this requirement are contained in 40 C.F.R. Part 258 and became effective on October 9, 1993.[60] These revised criteria contain far more detailed technical and procedural requirements than the original Part 257 criteria; and, in many cases, the Part 258 requirements are similar to those developed under Subtitle C. The Part 258 criteria apply to virtually all MSWLFs that accepted any waste after October 9, 1991,[61] with certain exceptions. MSWLFs that ceased accepting all waste before October 9, 1993, are exempt from all requirements other than the requirement to apply final cover.[62] As permitted by a RCRA amendment adopted in 1996,[63] certain MSWLFs accepting less than 20 tons of waste per year in remote or inaccessible areas may be exempt from the liner and groundwater-monitoring and corrective action requirements.[64]

The Part 258 criteria were crafted to simplify federal and citizen enforcement, regardless of whether a state develops and implements an adequate regulatory program. Section 258.1(h) criteria expressly provide that any facility not in compliance with Part 258 will be considered an open dump prohibited under Section 4005 of RCRA, and if the facility contains sewage sludge, it will violate Sections 309 and 405(e) of the Clean Water Act.[65]

---

[57] 33 U.S.C. § 1288; 40 C.F.R. § 257.3-3.
[58] *Id.* § 257.3-4.
[59] *Id.* § 257.3-8.
[60] *Id.* § 258.1(j).
[61] *Id.* § 258.1.
[62] *Id.* § 258.1(d).
[63] 42 U.S.C. § 6949a(c).
[64] *Id.* § 258.1(f).
[65] 33 U.S.C. §§ 1319, 1345(e); 40 C.F.R. § 258.1(i).

The applicable criteria are simple to determine under Part 258 and do not allow, in most cases, for exceptions that might otherwise be raised as defenses in an enforcement action. Exceptions to the criteria and reliance upon certain performance-based standards rather than specified technology are allowed only where the state has developed a permit program so that the exception or alternative standards can be reflected in permit conditions, which themselves can then be readily ascertained. By way of example, new MSWLFs and lateral expansions must be designed with a single composite liner, and the liner requirement may be waived only in limited circumstances by the director of an approved state program or by EPA upon the petition of a director in an unapproved state.[66] Similarly, new MSWLFs and expansions are flatly prohibited in wetlands,[67] within 200 feet of a Holocene fault,[68] or in a seismic impact zone,[69] unless a director in an *approved* state authorizes a limited waiver. Waivers from methane gas control measures[70] and suspension of groundwater-monitoring requirements[71] are authorized only where an approved state program is in place.

Part 258 includes far more detailed and extensive substantive requirements than Part 257. As with the Subtitle C regulations, the Part 258 regulations include requirements for siting, design, operation, groundwater monitoring, corrective action, closure and postclosure care, financial assurance, and record keeping.

The location criteria prohibit or severely constrain the siting of MSWLFs within or near airports, floodplains, or unstable areas such as karst terrains or unstable slopes. New units or lateral expansions are similarly limited within wetlands, seismic impact zones, or known Holocene fault areas.[72] The design criteria generally require a composite liner. However, where expressly approved by the director of an approved state or through the grant of an EPA waiver upon state application, an alternative system providing equivalent protection may be utilized.[73] Coupled with the liner requirement are requirements for groundwater monitoring, detection monitoring, and corrective action. Remedial action requirements are similar to those required under Subtitle C. The remedy selection process resembles that required under the corrective action program.[74]

---

[66]40 C.F.R. § 258.40.
[67]*Id.* § 258.12.
[68]*Id.* § 258.13.
[69]*Id.* § 258.14.
[70]*Id.* § 258.23(c)(4).
[71]*Id.* § 258.50(b).
[72]40 C.F.R. §§ 258.10–.16.
[73]*Id.* § 258.40.
[74]*Id.* §§ 258.50–.58.

394 THE RCRA PRACTICE MANUAL

Operating criteria include both the requirements contained in Part 257 and additional measures. The Part 258 operating criteria require the establishment of programs, including training, to exclude hazardous waste. Control of disease vectors, placement of daily and final cover, access control, and general compliance with the Clean Air and Clean Water Acts are required. Methane gas levels must be monitored and controlled to below 25 percent of the LEL. Open burning and the disposal of bulk liquids are prohibited. Systems to control run-on and runoff must be implemented.[75]

Closure and postclosure care requirements include the requirement for a final cap with permeability the lesser of 10^{-5} centimeters per second or the permeability of the bottom liner. A closure and postclosure plan must be prepared. Thirty years of postclosure care, including continued groundwater and methane gas monitoring and remediation, erosion and access control, and a deed notification, are required.[76] The financial assurance requirements apply to municipalities and private owners and operators, but not to state or federal governments. They require the establishment of financial assurance in the form of a trust fund, surety bond, letter of credit, insurance, or state-funded mechanism to assure funds for closure, postclosure care, and corrective action.[77]

Owners or operators of a MSWLF must keep records to demonstrate compliance with most substantive requirements. Generally, each owner or operator must develop and maintain an operating record[78] and submit various notifications to the state director as key records demonstrating compliance are developed.[79]

C. Part 257, Subpart B, Requirements for Industrial Waste Landfills Receiving Conditionally Exempt Small-Quantity Generator Waste

Three years after the U.S. Court of Appeals for the District of Columbia noted, in dicta, that the failure to promulgate groundwater-monitoring requirement for non-MSW, nonhazardous waste landfills receiving conditionally exempt small-quantity generator (CESQG) waste was unlawful,[80] EPA promulgated a new subpart to Part 257, applying to industrial

---

[75]*Id.* §§ 258.20–.29.
[76]*Id.* §§ 258.60–.61.
[77]*Id.* §§ 258.70–.74.
[78]*Id.* § 258.29.
[79]*See, e.g., id.* §§ 258.29(b) (notification of establishment of operating record), 258.51(c)(1) (notification of establishment of groundwater monitoring system).
[80]*See* Sierra Club v. EPA, 992 F.2d 337, 345–47 (D.C. Cir. 1993).

waste landfills receiving CESQG waste.[81] These regulations apply to non-municipal nonhazardous waste land disposal facilities receiving CESQG wastes after January 1, 1998.[82] Like the Part 258 requirements, these regulations contain far more detailed technical and procedural requirements than do those found in Part 257, Subpart A. They mirror the Part 258 standards in many respects.

The regulations impose new, additional location restrictions for floodplains[83] and wetlands.[84] The wetlands requirement prohibits location of landfills in wetlands that result in wetland degradation or a net loss in wetlands.

Most notably the Part 257, Subpart B standards include requirements for groundwater monitoring and corrective action paralleling and, for the most part, identical to those found in Part 258 for MSW landfills.[85] Those monitoring requirements apply for the life of the facility plus 30 years. Owners and operators may obtain an exemption from the groundwater-monitoring requirements by demonstrating that there is no potential for migration of hazardous constituents from the unit to the uppermost aquifer during the active life of the facility plus 30 years.[86]

The Part 257, Subpart B standards further include requirements to maintain records relating to demonstrations of eligibility for regulatory exemptions and the groundwater-monitoring and corrective action requirements.[87] On the other hand, with the exception of the requirement for monitoring, the Subpart B standards lack the standards for closure and postclosure care and financial assurance found in the Part 258 standards. The Part 257, Subpart B standards also lack design standards and many of the operating standards contained in Part 258. (Some operating standards are contained in Part 257, Subpart A, and apply to landfills accepting CESQG waste.)

IV. Bevill/Bentson Wastes

While the addition of Part 258 and the Part 257, Subpart B regulations redressed somewhat the incongruity of regulating municipal and industrial wastes under Subtitle C instead of Subtitle D of RCRA, the largest volume of solid wastes generated in the United States remains subject to

---

[81]40 C.F.R. pt. 257, subpt. B, 61 Fed. Reg. 34,269 (July 1, 1996).

[82]40 C.F.R. § 257.5(a).

[83]*Id.* § 257.8.

[84]*Id.* § 257.9.

[85]*Id.* §§ 257.21–.28.

[86]*Id.* § 257.21(b).

[87]*Id.* § 258.30.

396 THE RCRA PRACTICE MANUAL

only minimal levels of regulation. Even though many of these wastes would be characteristic hazardous wastes, the largest quantity of wastes generated in the United States are governed by regulatory exemptions contained in or authorized by the Bevill and Bentson amendments to RCRA. Congress adopted these amendments to deal with wastes that were hazardous but whose large volumes and remote locations had originally led EPA to propose they be treated as "special wastes" with an intermediate level of regulation under Subtitle C. When EPA withdrew this proposal, Congress, in the 1980 amendments to RCRA, adopted two amendments providing a "temporary" exemption from regulation for these large-volume wastes. The Bevill Amendment to RCRA, adopted in the 1980 amendments to the act, created an exemption from regulation of wastes from the "extraction, beneficiation, and processing of ores and minerals," utility wastes, and cement kiln dust as hazardous wastes until six months after EPA conducted certain studies under Section 6982(f), (n), (o), or (p). That section required studies of the volumes, disposal methods, impacts, alternatives, and costs of mining wastes (Section 6982(f)), utility (fossil fuel combustion) wastes (Section 6982(n)), cement kiln dust (Section 6982(o)), and mineral-processing waste (Section 6982(p)).[88] The Bentson Amendment[89] gave a parallel exemption to oil, gas, and geothermal production wastes.[90]

EPA completed a study of the early stages of mineral processing—extraction and beneficiation—on December 31, 1985.[91] Although the 1985 report found that 755 million metric tons of the 1.3 billion metric tons of mining waste produced annually would qualify as hazardous waste, it determined that extraction and beneficiation wastes should be regulated under a special Subtitle D program. EPA therefore simultaneously withdrew a determination that certain mineral-processing wastes did not fall within the Bevill Amendment.[92] EPA's determination to regulate wastes from the extraction and beneficiation stages under Subtitle D was upheld on appeal, with the court noting its "decision today does not license the agency to ignore safety or relieve the agency from its duty to effectuate the underlying purpose of the RCRA provisions governing

---

[88]*See* Envtl. Def. Fund v. EPA ("*EDF I*"), 852 F.2d 1309 (D.C. Cir. 1988), *cert. denied sub nom.* Am. Mining Cong. v. Envtl. Def. Fund, 489 U.S. 1011, 103 L. Ed. 2d 183, 109 S. Ct. 1120 (1989); Envtl. Def. Fund v. EPA ("*EDF II*"), 852 F.2d 1316 (D.C. Cir. 1988), *cert. denied sub nom.* Am. Mining Cong. v. Envtl. Def. Fund, 489 U.S. 1011, 103 L. Ed. 2d 183, 109 S. Ct. 1120 (1989).

[89]42 U.S.C. §§ 6921(b)(2)(A), 6982(m).

[90]*See* Am. Iron & Steel Inst. v. EPA, 886 F.2d 390 (D.C.Cir. 1989), *cert. denied sub nom.* Am. Mining Cong. v. EPA, 497 U.S. 1003, 111 L. Ed. 2d 748, 110 S. Ct. 3237 (1990).

[91]*See EDF I, supra* note 88, 852 F.2d at 1312.

[92]*EDF I, supra* note 88; *EDF II, supra* note 88.

Chapter 15: Regulation of Nonhazardous Waste under RCRA 397

mining wastes—protection of health and environment in a cost effective manner."[93] In a companion case, *EDF II*, the same court reversed EPA's decision to withdraw an interpretation that would treat six smelter (mineral-processing) wastes as hazardous. EPA subsequently issued a series of determinations finding that certain mineral-processing wastes should be regulated as hazardous under Subtitle C, but that the majority remained regulated under Subtitle D.[94]

EPA subsequently supplemented the 1985 mining waste report with additional data.[95] Nevertheless, EPA has yet to develop a regulatory program for mining wastes under Subtitle D. These wastes, representing the most voluminous and hazardous wastes under Subtitle D, remain either completely unregulated under RCRA when at or returned to the mine site[96] or minimally regulated under Part 257.

The first required study of wastes from fossil-fuel-fired plants was completed in February 1988.[97] EPA supplemented that report with additional research[98] and, on August 9, 1993, issued a regulatory determination regarding high-volume wastes from the combustion of coal by utilities.[99] In this first utility waste determination, EPA stated that it would maintain the Bevill Amendment exclusion for these high-volume wastes and would regulate their disposal by way of regulations that it intended to develop under Subtitle D. Seven years later, EPA issued a second determination regarding low-volume utility wastes.[100] In this second determination, EPA concluded that all wastes from combustion of fossil fuel should remain exempt from regulation under Subtitle C of RCRA. EPA further announced its intention to develop regulations under Subtitle D of RCRA governing disposal of coal combustion wastes in landfills or surface impoundments and to develop either Subtitle D regulations or regulations under the Surface Mining Control and Reclamation Act (SMCRA)[101] to address disposal of coal combustion wastes in mines and in mine reclamation. EPA announced that it did not intend to regulate other beneficial uses of coal combustion wastes under RCRA or to

---

[93]*EDF I, supra* note 88, 852 F.2d 1309 at 1316.

[94]*See* Solite Corp. v. EPA, 952 F.2d 473 (D.C. Cir. 1991); 54 Fed. Reg. 36,592 (Sept. 1, 1989); 55 Fed. Reg. 2322 (Jan. 23, 1990); 55 Fed. Reg. 32,135 (Aug. 7, 1990); 56 Fed. Reg. 27,300 (June 13, 1991); 61 Fed. Reg. 2338 (Jan. 25, 1996).

[95]*See* 60 Fed. Reg. 11,089 (Mar. 1, 1995).

[96]40 C.F.R. § 257.1(c)(2).

[97]EPA Report to Congress: Wastes from the Combustion of Coal by Electric Utility Power Plants, EPA/SW-88-002 (Feb. 1988).

[98]*See* 58 Fed. Reg. 8273 (Feb. 12, 1993).

[99]58 Fed. Reg. 42,466 (Aug. 9, 1993).

[100]65 Fed. Reg. 32,214 (May 22, 2000).

[101]30 U.S.C. §§ 1201–1328.

398 THE RCRA PRACTICE MANUAL

regulate disposal of other types of fossil fuel combustion wastes (wastes from oil and natural gas). EPA further designated which wastes it would consider "uniquely associated" with the Bevill wastes and entitled to the continuing exemption and which wastes were not uniquely associated (for example, boiler blowdown), so that characteristic hazardous wastes would be subject to regulation under Subtitle C. EPA has not issued regulations for this category of waste, either.

EPA's proposed handling of cement kiln dust (CKD) represents a unique hybrid approach. After completing a study on CKD in January 1994[102] and gathering additional data,[103] EPA determined that it would develop a RCRA Subtitle C program to address releases to groundwater from that waste, but that it would retain the Bevill Amendment exemption until that program was complete.[104] In 1999 EPA proposed adopting an intermediate approach—a regime under which it would exempt properly managed CKD from regulation under Subtitle C but would treat mismanaged cement kiln dust as a hazardous waste, under a proposed Subpart I to Part 266.[105] EPA proposed management standards to be promulgated as detailed regulations at 40 C.F.R. Part 259, which would define the standards for distinguishing between properly managed "unregulated" wastes and mismanaged hazardous waste. The proposed management standards include location, design, operation, monitoring, corrective action, closure, and financial assurance requirements for landfills to prevent releases to groundwater and to prevent releases of fugitive CKD. Handling and storage areas would also be required to manage the cement kiln dust to prevent releases of fugitive emissions. Finally, the proposed regulations include standards for agricultural use of CKD. EPA expressed a preference for this hybrid approach as a means to allow it to address violations directly, using its enforcement powers under Subtitle C. EPA solicited comments on this regulatory approach and is considering whether to adopt it or one of several other approaches discussed in the proposal, including regulation under Subtitle D.

Thus, the Bevill/Bentson wastes represent an area where additional categories of Subtitle D and possibly hybrid types of regulations will be emerging. In the meantime, these wastes will remain subject to substantially lower levels of regulation than equally hazardous or less hazardous but less voluminous wastes. This does not mean that these wastes remain unregulated. In addition to Part 257 requirements, corrective

---

[102]59 Fed. Reg. 709 (Jan. 6, 1994).
[103]59 Fed. Reg. 47,133 (Sept. 14, 1994).
[104]60 Fed. Reg. 7366 (Feb. 7, 1995).
[105]64 Fed. Reg. 45,632 (Aug. 20, 1999).

action and imminent hazard requirements may be triggered by disposal of these wastes. In addition, owners and operators may inadvertently bring Bevill/Bentson units into the Subtitle C regime by mixing associated waste streams that are not "uniquely associated" with waste streams clearly subject to the exemption.

V. Resource Recovery: Recovery of Energy and Materials from MSW

In setting forth the objectives of RCRA, Congress specified that it was seeking to encourage *all* types of resource recovery, including the recovery of both "valuable materials and energy from solid waste."[106] These objectives are mirrored in the congressional findings supporting Subtitle D.[107] The definition of "resource recovery" encompasses both recovery of materials and energy from waste.[108] This intent to encourage both recovery of materials (through recycling) and energy (through waste-to-energy facilities) appears throughout Subtitle D and other provisions of RCRA governing nonhazardous waste.

A. Treatment of Waste-to-Energy Facilities

RCRA specifically seeks to encourage development of waste-to-energy facilities. However, Congress also suggests that recovery of energy from waste should not interfere with recycling, which, in the statute, appears to represent a more favored technology. EPA has expressly stated that its policy is to favor recycling over waste-to-energy. The agency has established a hierarchy in which source reduction represents the first preferred alternative, followed by recycling, then combustion with resource recovery, and finally, landfilling.[109]

One of the central purposes of the planning required under Subtitle D is the encouragement of resource recovery generally, namely, recovery of both energy and materials from waste. RCRA seeks to accomplish this first by eliminating legal and institutional barriers to the financing of facilities. Resource recovery facilities in general, and waste-to-energy facilities in particular, require large investments of capital. Such facilities are usually funded with long-term bonds that are often repaid with

---

[106] 42 U.S.C. § 6902(a)(10), (11).

[107] *Id.* § 6941(a).

[108] *Id.* § 6903(22); *see also id.* § 6903(23) (definition of "resource recovery system") and (24) (definition of "resource recovery facility").

[109] *See* Agenda for Action.

400 THE RCRA PRACTICE MANUAL

revenues from the facilities. Accordingly, financing will usually require contracts for waste disposal and energy or materials sales that will produce the needed revenues throughout the life of the bonds. RCRA seeks to remove barriers to financing these facilities by requiring that each plan provide that no state or local government:

> shall be prohibited under State or local law from negotiating and entering into long-term contracts for the supply of solid waste to resource recovery facilities, from entering into long-term contracts for the operation of such facilities, or from securing long-term markets for material and energy recovered from such facilities.[110]

In provisions added in the Solid Waste Disposal Act Amendments of 1980 with the intent of expressly encouraging waste-to-energy facilities, RCRA further makes federal aid available to communities for feasibility planning required for facilities to conserve or recover energy and materials under the state plan.[111]

On the other hand, critics of waste-to-energy facilities have suggested such facilities may discourage recycling of flammable materials such as paper and plastics, particularly where put-or-pay contracts are also used to promote consistent cash flow. Accordingly, HSWA added to Section 4003 a provision requiring that, in any Subtitle D planning, "the present and reasonably anticipated future needs of the recycling and resource recovery interest" within the service area be considered when "determining the size of the waste-to-energy facility."[112]

RCRA also facilitates the development of waste-to-energy projects with provisions that are intended to shield waste-to-energy facilities from regulation under Subtitle C and thereby remove other perceived barriers to financing. These provisions address concerns that these facilities could be deemed hazardous waste facilities due to inadvertent acceptance of regulated hazardous waste, or that they could face higher disposal costs for ash if it is classified as a hazardous waste.

Most notably, Section 3001(i) of RCRA provides that a waste-to-energy facility that (1) receives and burns only household waste and industrial or commercial solid waste not containing hazardous wastes; (2) does not accept any hazardous waste; and (3) has established contractual or other notification and inspection procedures to assure that

---

[110]42 U.S.C. § 6943(a)(5).

[111]*Id.* §§ 6943(c), 6948.

[112]*Id.* § 6943(d).

Chapter 15: Regulation of Nonhazardous Waste under RCRA   401

hazardous wastes are not accepted or burned, "shall not be deemed to be treating, storing, disposing of, or otherwise managing hazardous wastes for the purposes of regulation under this subchapter."[113] On its face, this provision protects owners and operators of waste-to-energy facilities from the adverse consequences that might arise from inadvertently receiving or burning regulated hazardous waste. Thus, if an owner or operator satisfies the requirements of Section 3001(i) but inadvertently receives hazardous waste at its facility, it will not be "penalized" for storing, treating, or disposing of hazardous waste. Also, the residue of the burning process will not automatically be deemed hazardous by virtue of the derived-from rule.[114]

For many years the issue of whether ash from the burning of MSW in incinerators and resource recovery may be a "characteristic" hazardous waste remained unsettled. EPA reversed itself several times on the issue, and the courts of appeal split. Some courts have found that, under Section 3001(i), ash derived from the burning of exempt materials was nonhazardous even where it exhibited hazardous characteristics.[115] In *City of Chicago v. Environmental Defense Fund, Inc.*,[116] the Supreme Court settled the issue and held that Section 3001(i) did not require that wastes from incineration of MSW or mixtures of MSW and nonhazardous commercial wastes be automatically deemed nonhazardous. Rather, the Supreme Court found that that section required that ash be evaluated under conventional procedures to determine whether it is a characteristic hazardous waste. Accordingly, facilities managing waste deemed to be hazardous were required to file Part A applications.[117] Although analysis of grab samples of ash can show individual samples to be characteristic hazardous wastes, MSW is a heterogeneous substance, and when composite samples are taken, most wastes from incineration of MSW have been found to be nonhazardous wastes subject to regulation under Subtitle D.

B. Recycling and Procurement Guidelines

Because RCRA generally encourages resource recovery and, in most instances, does not distinguish between recovery of energy and recovery of materials, all of the planning provisions encouraging resource recovery

---

[113]*Id.* § 6921(i).

[114]40 C.F.R. § 261.3(c)(2).

[115]*See, e.g.*, Envtl. Def. Fund v. Wheelabrator Techs., Inc., 931 F.2d 211 (2d Cir.), *cert. denied*, 112 S. Ct. 453 (1991).

[116]511 U.S. 328, 114 S. Ct. 1588, 128 L. Ed. 2d 302 (1994).

[117]59 Fed. Reg. 29,372 (June 7, 1994).

402 THE RCRA PRACTICE MANUAL

in Subtitle D also relate to recycling. Moreover, as also noted above, there is at least some statutory authority supporting EPA's policy favoring recycling over waste-to-energy.

Although many states have adopted laws mandating separation of recyclables from waste (known as source separation) and recycling, there are no comparable provisions in RCRA. As noted above, EPA has, however, adopted guidelines pursuant to Section 1008 of RCRA, requiring recycling at federal facilities. These guidelines have been consolidated and updated in 40 C.F.R. Part 246. They require source separation and recovery of high-grade office paper, newsprint, glass and cans, and corrugated paper for most federal facilities.[118] These include both required and recommended procedures.

RCRA further seeks to encourage recycling by creating a federal market for goods manufactured from "recovered materials." Recovered materials are defined to include both "postconsumer materials" and certain "manufacturing, forest residues and other wastes" such as paper wastes and other fibrous waste materials.[119] Section 6002(e) of RCRA requires EPA to promulgate procurement guidelines for use by federal agencies that "designate those items which are or can be produced with recovered materials" and "set forth recommended practices with respect to procurement of recovered materials and items containing such materials."[120]

After such item-specific guidelines are published, Section 6002(c) of RCRA requires each agency procuring any items designated in those guidelines to "procure such items composed of the highest percentage of recovered materials practicable . . . consistent with maintaining a satisfactory level of competition, considering such guidelines."[121] This requirement pertains in all cases where the purchase price of the item exceeds $10,000 or where more than $10,000 was spent to purchase a quantity of the item or functionally equivalent items during the preceding fiscal year.[122] The procuring agency may decide not to procure items composed of recycled goods governed by such a guideline only when such goods (1) are not reasonably available within a reasonable time; (2) do not meet reasonable performance standards; or (3) "are only available at an unreasonable price."[123] To implement this requirement, RCRA further requires that, in bids, vendors estimate the percentage of recycled materials that they will use to complete the contract and certify that the

---

[118]40 C.F.R. pt. 246.
[119]42 U.S.C. § 6962(h).
[120]*Id.* § 6962(e).
[121]*Id.* § 6962(c).
[122]*Id.* § 6962(a).
[123]*Id.* § 6962(c).

Chapter 15: Regulation of Nonhazardous Waste under RCRA 403

materials that they will supply will meet the minimum requirements set forth in EPA guidelines.[124]

The promulgation of procurement guidelines triggers a requirement that each procuring agency develop a procurement program including a recovered materials preference program. The agency may adopt either a case-by-case approach or minimum content standards.[125] In addition to compliance with these EPA guidelines, RCRA requires all federal agencies with responsibility for drafting and reviewing specifications to review their specifications and eliminate any requirements that would exclude the use of recovered materials or require the purchase of items manufactured from virgin materials.[126] Section 6002(i) of RCRA gives procuring agencies up to one year after promulgation of procurement guidelines to develop an affirmative procurement program to assure that the items composed of recovered materials "will be purchased to the maximum extent practicable."[127]

From the time of its original enactment in 1976, Section 6002 of RCRA had called for the promulgation of federal procurement guidelines. However, "[f]or many years, EPA simply refused to issue the guidelines required by RCRA."[128] By 1984, when HSWA was enacted, only one set of guidelines had been promulgated, governing the procurement of fly ash.[129] Reacting to this "incredible" failure, Congress, in HSWA, enacted Section 6002(e) and required EPA to prepare final guidelines for paper products by May 7, 1985, and for three additional product categories (including tires) by October 1, 1985.[130] Although EPA failed to meet these deadlines, by the end of the decade it had promulgated four additional guidelines governing paper and paper products containing recovered materials, retread tires, lubricating oils containing re-refined oil, and building insulation products.

During the Clinton Administration, EPA implemented a Comprehensive Procurement Guideline (CPG) program pursuant to Section 6002 and Executive Orders 12873 and 13101. In 1995, EPA promulgated the Comprehensive Procurement Guidelines for Products Containing Recovered Materials.[131] This first CPG covered the original five procurement guidelines and added 19 products. Executive Order 13101 further required

---

[124]*Id.* § 6962(c)(3).

[125]*Id.*

[126]*Id.* § 6962(d).

[127]*Id.* § 6962(i).

[128]Nat'l Recycling Coalition v. Reilly, 884 F.2d 1431 (D.C. Cir. 1989) (Wald, dissenting).

[129]40 C.F.R. pt. 249.

[130]42 U.S.C. § 6962(e)(2).

[131]40 C.F.R. pt. 257, 60 Fed. Reg. 21,381 (May 1, 1995).

404 THE RCRA PRACTICE MANUAL

two-year updates of CPGs and significantly expanded the scope of the program. An update published in November 1997 added 12 items,[132] and the second update in January 2000 designated another 18 items.[133] Thus, a total of 49 items were added from 1995 to 2000, compared with five during the 20 previous years.[134] Supplementing this program are EPA's Recovered Materials Advisory Notices, which recommend recycled-content levels for CPG items. Although the CPG program is directed at federal agencies, the information is also provided for the use of state and local agencies and private parties.

EPA initially construed its authority to encourage procurement of recycled products narrowly, to the extent that it was unclear whether the initial guidelines provided any real preference. For example, EPA specified minimum content percentages for purchases of recycled paper to be used in the preference program. However, EPA indicated that if other paper were available at a lower price, the recycled paper could be deemed "not to be available at a reasonable price," and the procuring agency would be excused from meeting the percentage guidelines.[135] The result of this interpretation was that the preference program applied only in the case of a tie in bids. By regulation, EPA also excluded "incidental purchases" from its recycled content requirements. Thus, for example, a building contractor on a federal project would not be required to meet the standards for retreaded tires or recycled oil in machinery used for the project. This exception was also challenged and upheld in *National Recycling Coalition, Inc. v. Browner*.[136]

Executive Order 13101, entitled *Greening the Government through Waste Prevention, Recycling, and Federal Acquisition*,[137] significantly expanded the scope of the procurement guidelines program and the efficacy of the programs. An interagency task force was created, a waste reduction and recycling strategic plan and biennial progress reports to the president were required, and agency reporting and assessment procedures established. Most notably, every agency was required to establish an affirmative procurement program under Section 6002. This included a requirement that each agency was required to "ensure that their affirmative procurement programs require 100 percent of their purchases of products . . . meet or exceed the EPA guideline unless written justification is provided that a product is not available competitively within a reason-

---

[132] 62 Fed. Reg. 60,973 (Nov. 13, 1997).

[133] 65 Fed. Reg. 3080 (Jan. 19, 2000).

[134] *See* http://www.epa.gov/cpg/about.htm.

[135] *See* Nat'l Recycling Coalition Inc. v. Reilly, 884 F.2d 1431, *reh. en banc denied*, 890 F.2d 1242 (D.C. Cir. 1989).

[136] 984 F.2d 1243 (D.C. Cir. 1993).

[137] 63 Fed. Reg. 49,673 (Sept. 16, 1998).

able time frame, does not meet appropriate performance standards, or is only available at an unreasonable price."[138] As noted, this EO and its predecessor have already resulted in a vast expansion of the procurement guidelines program.

VI. Planning Restrictions on Interstate Flow of Waste and Waste Flow Control for Financing and the Commerce Clause

The imposition of state and local control over the "flow" of waste within jurisdictions and between jurisdictions has been the subject of many challenges under the Commerce Clause of the Constitution.[139] In many cases, these restrictions are imposed as part of the planning required under RCRA. The interstate flow of waste may be "regulated" in two distinct ways in planning—by "waste flow restrictions" and by "waste flow control." Waste flow restrictions *prevent* the importation of waste into a planning jurisdiction. It has been argued that these restrictions are essential to allow the entity charged with plan implementation to determine the size of a waste facility and schedule its construction. Waste flow control requires that all waste from within a jurisdiction go to a particular facility. Waste flow controls have often been imposed to promote facility viability. Although the Supreme Court has "settled" the issue in a series of decisions prohibiting both general prohibitions on interstate waste flow importation and interstate waste flow controls, exceptions to the scope of Commerce Clause restrictions, coupled with state and municipal obligations, under Subtitle D and state law, to develop and implement plans to meet the disposal needs of their residents, have resulted in a patchwork of regulatory programs. Often, the effect is to eliminate interstate commerce in waste altogether and replace it with municipal monopolies.

In *Fort Gratiot Sanitary Landfill v. Michigan*,[140] the Supreme Court held that import restrictions imposed by a county as a part of its planning scheme violated the Commerce Clause, under the rationale of *City of Philadelphia v. New Jersey*.[141] In *Philadelphia*, the Supreme Court invalidated New Jersey's flat ban on the importation of waste, holding that solid waste was an article of commerce and that a state could not prohibit its interstate flow under the "dormant" restriction of the Commerce Clause. The Michigan law invalidated in *Fort Gratiot* had forbidden

---

[138]*Id.* § 403(c).
[139]U.S. CONST. art. I, § 8, cl. 3.
[140]504 U.S. 353, 112 S. Ct. 2019, 119 L. Ed. 2d 139 (1992).
[141]437 U.S. 617 (1978).

406 THE RCRA PRACTICE MANUAL

private landfills from disposing of waste not generated outside of the county where they were located unless permitted by the county solid waste management plan. Neither the *Fort Gratiot* decision nor the *Philadelphia* decision addressed the issue of whether restrictions upon the interstate flow of waste imposed as a part of the planning required under RCRA Subtitle D would violate the Commerce Clause. Neither decision addressed the issue of waste flow controls.

In *C & A Carbone, Inc. v. Town of Clarkstown, New York*,[142] the Supreme Court held that waste flow control in the form of an ordinance requiring disposal of all MSW generated in a New York town at a local waste transfer facility was a "local processing requirement" that discriminated against interstate commerce. Because the Court also found that the town had failed to articulate a legitimate state interest that could not be addressed by other means, the Court found that assuring the economic viability of that local facility was not a legitimate purpose. The RCRA planning requirements were not addressed by the majority opinion. However, recognizing that Congress may authorize states to impose restrictions on commerce,[143] Justice O'Connor, in a concurring opinion, examined the RCRA Subtitle D requirements and concluded:

> I agree with *amicus* NABL that these references [to RCRA] indicate that Congress expected local governments to implement some form of flow control. Nonetheless, they neither individually nor cumulatively rise to the level of the "explicit" authorization required by our dormant Commerce Clause decisions.[144]

Notwithstanding the Supreme Court rejection of the argument based upon RCRA in *Carbone*, it is difficult to implement the Subtitle D requirements for MSW planning without the same ability to impose waste flow restrictions or waste flow controls. If a local government is required to develop a plan that will assure that adequate facilities will be available to meet the needs of its residents and encourage recovery of resources from waste, some mechanism must be used to assure that the disposal capacity is not exhausted prematurely. Similarly, sound waste planning requires facilities that will be economically viable. Subtitle D therefore specifically requires state plans to address financing and economic issues. Often, the most environmentally advanced facilities are more capital intensive than facilities that incorporate less than state-of-the-art controls. For example, landfills with liners and leachate collection

---

[142]511 U.S. 383, 114 S. Ct. 1677, 128 L. Ed. 2d 399 (1994).
[143]*South-Central Timber Development Inc. v. Wunnicke*, 467 U.S. 82, 87–88 (1984).
[144]*Fort Gratiot, supra* note 140, 504 U.S. at 410 (O'Connor, concurring).

Chapter 15: Regulation of Nonhazardous Waste under RCRA 407

and treatment systems require a larger capital investment and have higher operating costs than unlined facilities such as those grandfathered under the Part 258 standards. Resource recovery facilities, particularly waste-to-energy facilities, require even larger initial investments. To recover these larger capital and operating expenses, state-of-the-art facilities often need to charge higher "tipping fees" (disposal charges) than grandfathered facilities or facilities not employing resource recovery. Without some planning to assure that waste is actually delivered to a planned state-of-the-art facility, there is a significant danger that waste will be diverted to less costly and less environmentally protective facilities in other jurisdictions. Accordingly, the financing for many resource recovery facilities and many state-of-the-art landfills has required some waste flow control mechanism to be employed to assure that waste will be delivered to the facility for the life of the bonds required for the facility. Revenues from tipping fees of this waste are necessary to repay the interest and principal of the bonds. This waste flow can be secured by a variety of means. These means, before *Carbone*, included "put-or-pay" contracts, waste flow ordinances, "hybrids" of ordinances and contracts such as franchises (which by ordinance create contractual rights to waste flow), and most typically, combinations of mechanisms. Because of these financing needs, Subtitle D, as originally enacted in 1976, requires that no state or local government may be "prohibited under State or local law from negotiating and entering into long-term contracts for the supply of solid waste to resource recovery facilities."[145] In 1980 Congress further amended RCRA to provide grants to help states and localities develop the various institutional mechanisms necessary generally to assure delivery of waste to resource recovery facilities and to allow their financing.[146]

In light of these concerns, states and localities following *Carbone* have resorted to a number of means to secure waste flow controls and restrictions that either exempt interstate commerce or take advantage of the "market participant" exception[s] to the interstate Commerce Clause restriction that allows states and municipalities to provide services to or contract exclusively with their residents.[147] Although these alternatives often result in greater inhibition of interstate commerce than the type of waste flow controls invalidated by the Supreme Court, many of these restrictions have withstood Commerce Clause challenges in the courts of appeals. As contemplated by the Supreme Court decisions, the courts of appeals have upheld laws uniformly banning all landfill operation

---

[145]42 U.S.C. § 6943(a)(5).

[146]Pub. L. No. 96-482, § 32(f), 94 Stat. 2355, codified at 42 U.S.C. § 6948(d)(3)(B)–(C).

[147]*See* Reeves v. Stake, 447 U.S. 383, 100 S. Ct. 1083, 128 L. Ed. 2d 429 (1980).

within a municipality[148] and a municipality's ability to restrict disposal of waste within a municipally owned facility to the municipality's residents.[149] Similarly, a law requiring that all public entities implement a solid waste management plan and haul all waste collected or generated by the public entities to a facility designated by the plan has been held valid under the market participant exception.[150] So has a law requiring that all waste collected by a town or a franchised hauler be disposed at a designated resource recovery facility pursuant to a contract with an authority.[151] Programs in two states where laws and waste flow ordinances require that waste disposed of within the state be sent to designated facilities but allow disposal of waste outside of the state without restriction have been upheld as nondiscriminatory.[152] The Third Circuit has held that a state scheme designating particular disposal facilities and requiring that all waste be disposed in those facilities will withstand a Commerce Clause challenge as long as out-of-state operators are given an even chance to compete for the opportunity to process the state's or district's waste.[153] The Sixth Circuit has also upheld a designation of specific facilities that was made freely available to in-state and out-of-

---

[148]Gary D. Peake Excavating, Inc. v. Town Bd. of the Town of Hancock, N.Y., 93 F.3d 68 (2d Cir. 1996).

[149]Red River Serv. Corp. v. City of Minot, N.D., 146 F.3d 583 (8th Cir. 1998).

[150]Nat'l Solid Waste Mgmt. Ass'n v. Williams, 146 F.3d 595 (8th Cir.), *cert. denied*, 525 U.S. 1012, 142 L. Ed. 2d 441, 119 S. Ct. 531 (1998).

[151]Sal Tinnerello & Sons, Inc. v. Town of Stonington, 141 F.3d 46 (2d Cir.), *cert. denied*, 525 U.S. 923, 142 L. Ed. 2d 230, 119 S. Ct. 278 (1998) (upholding scheme under test for both market participant and market regulator); *see also* United Haulers Ass'n v. Oneida-Herkimer Solid Waste Mgmt. Auth., 261 F.3d 245 (2d Cir. 2001), *cert. denied*, 151 L. Ed. 2d 699, 122 S. Ct. 815 (2002) (holding that law requiring delivery to municipally owned transfer stations, unlike privately owned station at issue in *Carbone*, required analysis under the balancing test in *Pike v. Bruce Church, Inc.*, 397 U.S. 137, 90 S. Ct. 844, 25 L. Ed. 2d 174 (1970), rather than test for discriminatory laws and remanding); *contra* Huish Detergents, Inc. v. Warren County, Ky., 214 F.3d 707 (6th Cir. 2000) (striking down ordinance and franchise agreement that required collection by franchised haulers, delivery to city-owned transfer station, and disposal in landfill licensed by host state).

[152]United Waste Sys. v. Wilson, 189 F.3d 762 (8th Cir. 1999); Ben Oehrleins & Sons & Daughter, Inc. v. Hennepin County, 115 F.3d 1372 (8th Cir.), *cert. denied*, 522 U.S. 1029, 139 L. Ed. 2d 609, 118 S. Ct. 629 (1997).

[153]*Compare* Harvey & Harvey, Inc. v. County of Chester, 68 F.3d 788 (3d Cir. 1995), *cert. denied sub nom.* Tri-County Indus. v. Mercer County, 516 U.S. 117, 134 L. Ed. 2d 213, 116 S. Ct. 1265 (1996) (remanding two waste flow ordinances for consideration of whether opportunity for designations open to out-of-state interests) *and* Atlantic Coast Demolition & Recycling, Inc. v. Bd. of Chosen Freeholders of Atl. County, 112 F.3d 652 (3d Cir. 1997), *cert. denied sub nom.* Essex County Utils. Auth. v. Atl. Coast Demolition & Recycling, 522 U.S. 966, 139 L. Ed. 2d 316, 118 S. Ct. 412, 118 S. Ct. 413 (1997) (invalidating New Jersey's comprehensive statewide waste flow regulations for failure to provide opportunity to out-of-state operations).

Chapter 15: Regulation of Nonhazardous Waste under RCRA 409

state facilities to administer collection of a fee to fund recycling, reuse and waste minimization activities, as well as other county activities incident to implementation of its solid waste plan. However, a fee imposed on all waste disposal that exempts waste disposed at a county-designated facility has been invalidated on Commerce Clause grounds.[154]

The Supreme Court decisions have resulted in numerous attempts to amend RCRA to provide authorization for various permutations of waste flow restrictions or controls. In light of RCRA's requirements for state and local solid waste planning and the continuing confusion in "regulation" of this area by the judicial branch, congressional action directing a consistent approach would be helpful and is likely in the future.

VII. Other Nonhazardous Wastes to Which Special Handling Requirements Apply

A number of wastes in addition to the Bevill/Bentson wastes are classified as nonhazardous and have been singled out for additional or different regulation than that applied generally to nonhazardous waste under Subtitle D. These wastes include used oil, sewage sludge, and medical waste. The establishment of the program for used oil and the now "dormant" program for medical waste, like the requirements for facilities that accept household hazardous waste and small-quantity generator waste, reflects congressional recognition that in many cases the sharp dichotomy between detailed cradle-to-grave regulation under Subtitle C and virtually no regulation under Subtitle D is inappropriate. In these programs, Congress has required regulatory programs more closely tailored to the nature of the waste and the risk it poses (or is perceived to pose). As noted in connection with the discussion of Bevill/Bentson wastes, such special or hybrid approaches can be expected to expand in the future.

A. Used Oil

Congress has amended RCRA twice in an attempt to minimize the environmental damage associated with improper handling of used oil. First, Congress enacted the Used Oil Recycling Act of 1980,[155] which directed EPA to promulgate "regulations establishing such performance standards and other requirements as may be necessary to protect the public health and the environment from hazards associated with recycled oil," and to determine whether the tests for hazardous waste characteristics

---

[154]Waste Mgmt. v. Metro. Gov't, 130 F.3d 731 (6th Cir. 1997), *cert. denied*, 523 U.S. 1094, 140 L. Ed. 2d 792, 118 S. Ct. 1560 (1998).

[155]Pub. L. No. 96-463, 94 Stat. 2055 (1980).

410   THE RCRA PRACTICE MANUAL

apply to used oil.[156] When EPA failed to do either by 1984, Congress again focused on used oil in HSWA, requiring EPA to decide whether "to list or identify used automobile and truck crankcase oil as hazardous waste."[157] To promote the dual goals of protection of health and encouragement of recycling, HSWA directed EPA to establish standards for generation and transportation of used oils and, in so doing, to "take into account the effect of such regulations on environmentally acceptable types of oil recycling."[158]

Congress also created a conditional exemption from manifesting, transportation, and permitting requirements under Subtitle C of RCRA for recycled used oil.[159] Specifically, a generator is exempt if it recycles used oil at a permitted (or permit-by-rule) facility, does not mix the oil with other hazardous wastes, and keeps such records relating to the oil as EPA deems appropriate. An oil-recycling facility is exempted from the hazardous waste permitting requirements if it satisfies the technical standards for recycling that EPA was required to promulgate under Section 3004. EPA was given the right to require a permit for those recycling facilities, but only after promulgating the regulations. These exemptions and the permit-by-rule apply even when the oil is a characteristic hazardous waste.

In response to these requirements, EPA initially proposed to list used oil as a hazardous waste.[160] However, EPA received public comments strongly opposing this proposal on the basis that it would discourage recycling. After the rule-making proposal, Congress amended Section 3008 of RCRA[161] to grant EPA enforcement powers with respect to regulation of oil as a nonhazardous waste in the Superfund Amendments and Reauthorization Act of 1986 (SARA).[162] Based on these comments and the change in the law, EPA found that a hazardous waste designation would destroy the market for recyclable oil and decided not to list used oil.[163] This determination was challenged. The U.S. Court of Appeals for the District of Columbia Circuit held that EPA could not refuse to list used oil on this ground alone, and remanded the issue to EPA for additional rule making.[164]

---

[156]42 U.S.C. § 6935(a).

[157]*Id.* § 6935(b).

[158]*Id.* § 6935(c).

[159]*Id.* § 6935(c)–(d).

[160]50 Fed. Reg. 49,258 (1985).

[161]42 U.S.C. § 6928.

[162]Pub. L. No. 99-499, tit. II, § 205(k), 100 Stat. 1703 (1986).

[163]51 Fed. Reg. 41,900 (1986).

[164]Hazardous Waste Treatment Council v. EPA, 861 F.2d 270 (D.C. Cir. 1988), *cert. denied,* 490 U.S. 1106, 104 L. Ed. 2d 1020, 109 S. Ct. 3157 (1989).

Chapter 15: Regulation of Nonhazardous Waste under RCRA   411

On remand, after further study, EPA published a final rule in which it again declined to list used oil as a hazardous waste.[165] EPA concluded that used oil frequently did not satisfy the criteria for listing and that the existing federal regulations, particularly the toxicity characteristic leaching procedure (TCLP), which had been promulgated in June 1990,[166] adequately regulated the disposal of any used oils that might exhibit a characteristic of hazardous waste.[167] This determination addressed only oil that was to be disposed of and did not address oil to be recycled. The rule, therefore, did not address processing, refining, or the residuals from those operations.

Oil to be recycled was addressed in a separate rule making; a few months later, EPA promulgated its Recycled Used Oil Management Standards.[168] Here, EPA issued a decision not to list as a hazardous waste most of the used oil designed for recycling. When used oil is mixed with a hazardous waste, it is not exempt from full Subtitle C regulation. However, to simplify enforcement of this restriction, EPA adopted a rebuttable presumption that oil having greater than 1,000 parts per million but no more than 4,000 parts per million total halogen was considered to have been mixed with solvents, thus shifting the burden to the used-oil recyclers to prove otherwise.

Despite this decision not to list used oil as a hazardous waste, EPA nevertheless was still required by statute to establish management standards for used oil exhibiting a hazardous characteristic. To simplify recycling and protect the environment, EPA elected to establish management standards applying to all oil to be recycled, both hazardous and nonhazardous. Thus, like the expanded requirements applicable to MSWLF under Subtitle D, used oil represents another area where management standards are used in place of a cradle-to-grave regulatory program.

Although EPA has elected to list oil as a nonhazardous waste, the used-oil management regulations are adopted under Subtitle C. Accordingly, regulations go into effect in an authorized state only after it revises its program to adopt EPA's rules under state law.[169]

The used-oil regulations provide standards required under Section 3014(a) and (c)[170] for generators, transporters, and processors of used oil. Generators must keep storage tanks and containers in good condition, label storage tanks "used oil," clean up any used-oil spills or leaks to the

---

[165]57 Fed. Reg. 21,524 (1992).
[166]55 Fed. Reg. 11,876 (1990).
[167]57 Fed. Reg. 21,524 (1992).
[168]40 C.F.R. pt. 279, 57 Fed. Reg. 41,566 (1992).
[169]57 Fed. Reg. 41,605.
[170]42 U.S.C. § 6935.

412   THE RCRA PRACTICE MANUAL

environment, and use a transporter with an EPA identification number.[171] Transporters, in turn, must obtain an EPA identification number and follow maintenance, labeling, and storage requirements, including limiting the duration of used-oil storage to 35 days at transfer facilities.[172] Processors must obtain an EPA identification number, maintain storage tanks in good condition and label them "used oil," process and store used oil in areas with oil-impervious flooring and secondary containment structures, clean up any used-oil spills, track incoming used oil and outgoing recycled used-oil products, keep records, and make biennial reports.[173]

B. Sewage Sludge

Although sewage sludge is another type of nonhazardous solid waste regulated under the original Part 257 regulations, sewage sludge disposal has been regulated under the Clean Water Act as well. Specifically, Section 405 of the Clean Water Act,[174] as amended by Congress in 1987, required EPA to establish a comprehensive program for reducing the potential environmental risks and maximizing the beneficial use of sewage sludge. After years of consideration, EPA issued regulations implementing such a program,[175] electing to regulate sewage sludge primarily under the Clean Water Act, except in cases where the sludge is disposed of in a facility accepting both MSW and sewage sludge.

These Clean Water Act regulations provide standards for the use and disposal of sewage sludge, taking into account the potential for pollutants in the sludge to affect public health and the environment through various routes of exposure. Substantive requirements are codified at 40 C.F.R. Parts 257, 403, and 503. The amendment of Part 257 removes sewage sludge subject to the standards in Part 503 from any of the Part 257 requirements.

C. Medical Waste

Medical waste represents a nonhazardous waste that briefly motivated a legislative response, which expired with waning interest. Responding to concerns over the lack of regulation of medical waste, triggered by scenes of medical waste washing up on beaches, Congress enacted the Medical Waste Tracking Act of 1988 (MWTA). The principal perceived risk posed by medical waste was unauthorized dumping, which the MWTA sought

---

[171]40 C.F.R. pt. 279, subpt. C.
[172]*Id.* pt. 279, subpt. E.
[173]*Id.* pt. 279, subpt. F.
[174]33 U.S.C. § 1345.
[175]58 Fed. Reg. 9248 (1993).

Chapter 15: Regulation of Nonhazardous Waste under RCRA   413

to address through manifesting and other record-keeping requirements. The MWTA added a new Subtitle J to RCRA[176] and directed EPA to establish a limited duration, demonstration program of "medical waste" regulation in New York, New Jersey, Connecticut, the states contiguous to the Great Lakes, and any other states that decided to opt in.[177] This program has since terminated, and there is no sign that it will be revived. Most of the affected states, however, retain medical waste regulatory programs.

VIII. Special Issues in Enforcement of Subtitle D Requirements and Other Requirements Relating to Nonhazardous Waste

Although enforcement under RCRA generally is the subject of a separate chapter, allocation of authority to the federal government to enforce the requirements of Subtitle D differs so dramatically from that under Subtitle C that it warrants separate discussion. Specifically, citizens and state and local governments, in most cases, have greater authority to enforce the open dumping criteria under Subtitle D than does the federal government.

Indeed, before the adoption of the MSWLF criteria in Part 258, the federal government had virtually no power to enforce the open dumping criteria, and there is still no federal authority to enforce Part 257.[178] Thus, before the adoption of the Part 258 MSWLF criteria, EPA's power under RCRA to address the problems caused by improper MSW operations was largely limited to its powers to address imminent hazards under Section 7003 of RCRA.

Federal power to enforce Subtitle D was expanded somewhat by HSWA, but it remains limited. In cases where a state does not obtain approval of a permit program to implement Part 258 within 18 months of its adoption (April 19, 1993), Section 4005(c)(2)(a)[179] authorizes EPA to enforce those criteria pursuant to the full panoply of enforcement mechanisms available under Sections 3007 and 3008 of RCRA.[180] Nevertheless, the federal government remains powerless to enforce these requirements in any state where a state program has been approved, or until a state has missed the deadline for establishing a program in a nonapproved state.

---

[176]42 U.S.C. §§ 6992–6992k.

[177]*Id.* § 6992(a).

[178]*See* Thompson v. Thomas, 680 F. Supp. 1, 2 (D.D.C. 1987); Blue Legs v. Bureau of Indian Affairs, 867 F.2d 1094 (8th Cir. 1989).

[179]42 U.S.C. § 6945(c)(2)(a).

[180]*Id.* §§ 6927–6928.

414 THE RCRA PRACTICE MANUAL

Congress intended that the states would take the principal role in implementing and enforcing the Subtitle D requirements through state permit programs adopted pursuant to the requirement of Section 4005(c) of RCRA.[181] It was not until 1998, however, that EPA adopted regulations, codified at 40 C.F.R. Part 239, specifying the requirements applicable to its approval of such state programs.[182]

Federal and state governments are not the only RCRA enforcers. The broadest authority to bring an enforcement action under RCRA with respect to nonhazardous waste management arises under Section 7002.[183] This citizen suit provision authorizes enforcement actions to enforce the Subtitle D criteria and to abate imminent hazards caused by any solid waste. The citizen suit provision of RCRA, like other federal citizen suit provisions, is intended to vest individual citizens with the authority to act as "private attorneys general," subject to prefiling notification and waiting period restrictions and governmental inactivity. Because "person" is defined under RCRA to include not only individual and juridical persons but also any "association, State, municipality, commission, political subdivision of a State, or any interstate body,"[184] individuals, environmental groups, Indian tribes, and virtually any municipality or municipal-type entity[185] may bring a citizen suit.[186]

Section 4005(a) of RCRA[187] expressly provides that the "prohibition [against open dumping] . . . shall be enforceable under section 6972 of this title against persons engaged in the act of open dumping." Thus, the open dumping criteria under both Part 257 and Part 258 may be enforced in a citizen suit. Virtually all courts have found that the open dumping criteria are enforceable in a citizen suit.[188] Only one court has held that a citizen suit cannot be brought to enforce the open dumping

---

[181]*Id.* § 6945(c). *See* Ringbolt Farms Homeowners Ass'n v. Town of Hull, 714 F. Supp. 1246 (D. Mass. 1989).

[182]63 Fed. Reg. 57,040 (Oct. 23, 1998).

[183]42 U.S.C. § 6972.

[184]*Id.* § 6903(15).

[185]*Id.* § 6903(13).

[186]*See* O'Leary v. Moyer's Landfill, Inc., 523 F. Supp. 642 (E.D. Pa. 1981); Middlesex County Bd. of Chosen Freeholders v. NJDEP, 645 F. Supp. 715 (D.N.J. 1986).

[187]42 U.S.C. § 6945(a).

[188]Dague v. City of Burlington, 732 F. Supp. 458 (D. Vt. 1989), *aff'd*, 935 F.2d 1343 (2d Cir. 1991); Blue Legs v. Bureau of Indian Affairs, 867 F.2d 1094 (8th Cir. 1989); Jones v. Inmont Corp., 584 F. Supp. 1425 (S.D. Ohio 1984); *O'Leary, supra* note 185; *see also* Williams v. Allied Auto., Autolite Div., 704 F. Supp. 782 (N.D. Ohio 1988) (finding that both hazardous waste and open dumping allegations could be brought); Lutz v. Chromatex, Inc., 718 F. Supp. 413 (M.D. Pa. 1989); Fishel v. Westinghouse Elec. Corp., 617 F. Supp. 1531 (M.D. Pa. 1985) (finding counts alleging hazardous waste and open dumping violations inconsistent in that open dumping applies only to nonhazardous waste, but allowing both to stand pending evidentiary proofs), *later proceeding*, 640 F. Supp. 442 (M.D. Pa. 1986).

criteria.[189] That case has been criticized[190] and was expressly overruled by Congress in HSWA.[191] Thus, in adopting Part 258, EPA stated:

> Citizens may seek enforcement of the revised Criteria, independent of any State enforcement program, by means of citizen suits under section 7002 of RCRA . . . . Once the self-implementing criteria in today's rule become effective, they constitute the basis for citizen enforcement actions brought in Federal court against facilities that fail to comply.[192]

Of course, the federal government retains full enforcement power under Section 3008 at any nonhazardous waste facility that accepts regulated hazardous waste. This dichotomy of enforcement power was largely reponsible for EPA's proposal for the hybrid regulations it is considering for cement kiln dust, which violation of the standards would make the waste a hazardous waste subject to federal enforcement. The other non-Bevill Amendment "special" wastes discussed above are generally governed by different enforcement requirements that may be utilized by the federal government. Violations of requirements relating to nonhazardous used oil may be enforced directly under Section 3008, as a result of amendments adopted as part of SARA.[193] The sludge regulations are enforceable under the Clean Water Act.

IX. Conclusion

Nonhazardous wastes are diverse, and RCRA employs a variety of regulatory mechanisms to address the problems posed by these wastes. The primacy of state and local regulation and the use of planning to address particular problems and to coordinate programs remain the dominant themes with respect to regulation of nonhazardous waste. However, recent administrative initiatives to implement congressional objectives have sought to encourage recycling and resource recovery activities with guidelines, grants, procurement, and special exemptions. Congress and EPA have also addressed certain "problem" wastes, such as household hazardous waste and small-quantity generator hazardous wastes in landfills, used oil, and sewage sludge with federal regulations tailored to the

---

[189]City of Gallitin v. Cherokee County, 563 F. Supp. 940 (E.D. Tex. 1983).
[190]Jones v. Inmont Corp., 584 F. Supp. 1425 (S.D. Ohio 1984).
[191]*See Blue Legs, supra* note 187.
[192]Preamble, 56 Fed. Reg. 50,995 (1991).
[193]Pub. L. No. 99-499, tit. II, § 205(k), 100 Stat. 1703.

416 THE RCRA PRACTICE MANUAL

particular waste types. It is proposing hybrid approaches for some of the large-quantity Bevill/Bentson wastes. These waste-specific tailored regulations may reflect the growing consensus that the all-or-nothing, cradle-to-grave approach under Subtitle C is an inappropriate response to materials as diverse as those encompassed by the definition of solid waste. This waste-specific approach will continue to evolve for the other nonhazardous wastes that EPA will address in the future. In the meantime, the largest volume of wastes generated, including mining wastes, most nonhazardous industrial wastes, and agricultural wastes, still remain unregulated or weakly regulated.

CHAPTER 16

Civil and Criminal Enforcement

MICHAEL W. STEINBERG
AND KENNETH D. WOODROW

I. Introduction

The Resource Conservation and Recovery Act (RCRA) is enforced by the Environmental Protection Agency (EPA), the Department of Justice (DOJ), the states, and private citizens, all of whom have access to an imposing array of legal tools. The dominant feature of the current enforcement climate is that severe sanctions—including criminal sanctions—are being imposed on a growing number of violators each year. Companies found to have violated RCRA may face broad injunctive relief that curtails their waste management activities, imposes court-supervised environmental auditing programs, and affects other aspects of their business operations. Both corporate violators and individual offenders commonly pay substantial civil or criminal penalties, with individual offenders increasingly facing imprisonment as well.

This chapter will first highlight the growing challenge that RCRA enforcement presents for American business. It will then describe the structure of the enforcement teams at EPA and the Department of Justice. Each of the tools in the RCRA enforcement arsenal will then be examined: information gathering; civil proceedings, both administrative and judicial; criminal proceedings; and imminent and substantial endangerment orders. Finally, this chapter will review citizen suits and enforcement at federal facilities.

417

418 THE RCRA PRACTICE MANUAL

A. The Challenge of RCRA Enforcement

The current enforcement climate is of particular concern for the thousands of companies that actively manage hazardous wastes in the course of their business operations. Few areas of environmental regulation excite the public and the media as much as hazardous waste management. Unfortunately, despite the growing pressure for tougher enforcement, most companies find that "perfect compliance" with RCRA is an unattainable goal. The RCRA hazardous waste program, more than any other EPA program, is built on a foundation of ambiguous regulations, obscure interpretations, and unpublished guidance documents.

RCRA has justifiably been described as a "mind-numbing" statute.[1] The basic EPA regulations alone now occupy some 1,000 pages in the *Code of Federal Regulations*; the background documents, interpretative material, and guidance documents for those rules would fill an entire room. As EPA's top-ranking hazardous waste official remarked in 1991: "RCRA is a regulatory cuckoo land of definition. . . . I believe we have five people in the agency who understand what 'hazardous waste' is."[2] All of this tends to make "perfect compliance" an unattainable goal, even for the most well-intentioned company.

In the not-too-distant past, the unattainability of "perfect compliance" did not carry the severe repercussions that it does today. The law drew a bright line between conduct that called for purely civil penalties and conduct that warranted the harsher sanctions of the criminal code. Even in the environmental area, where civil penalties are often imposed for "innocent" or "unavoidable" violations, the dividing line between civil and criminal violations seemed fairly clear, and relatively few violations were deemed serious enough to justify criminal prosecution.

Unfortunately, those days are gone. Most EPA statutes, including RCRA, now authorize criminal sanctions for many violations of environmental standards and regulations. The law does little to distinguish between violations that are appropriate for criminal prosecution and those that should be handled through civil penalties only. In the case of RCRA, Congress has said that only "knowing" violations can be punished criminally. But as we will see, the protection afforded by that limitation is largely illusory: One need not even know that he or she is performing an unlawful act in order to be convicted of a "knowing" violation!

---

[1]Am. Mining Cong. v. EPA, 824 F.2d 1177, 1189 (D.C. Cir. 1987).
[2]Special Supp. to XIV LEGAL TIMES OF WASH., Dec. 16, 1991, at 52.

Another feature that aggravates this situation is the growing tendency of federal and state enforcement officials to target individuals, rather than corporations, for criminal enforcement. As one recent assistant attorney general for environment and natural resources explained: "It has been, and will continue to be, Justice Department policy to conduct environmental criminal investigations with an eye toward identifying, prosecuting, and convicting the highest ranking truly responsible corporate officials."[3]

The bottom line can be stated simply. Federal, state, and local enforcement officials have declared open season on companies and individuals involved in the handling of hazardous waste. In doing so, these public servants tend to respond to the strong public sentiment and political pressure for tougher enforcement. They do not always stop to consider whether a particular company has a good overall compliance record, or whether the violations at issue resulted in any actual environmental harm. Instead, they bring cases one at a time, selecting their targets with a narrow perspective, seeking to obtain a conviction or a major fine, and then move on.

The impact of this increased emphasis on RCRA enforcement is reflected not only in the record number of prison sentences imposed, but also in the record penalty amounts being imposed in some civil and criminal cases. Notable examples include:

- $18 million in criminal fines under a plea agreement with Rhodia Inc. at Silver Bow, Montana;
- 17-year prison sentence for an Idaho fertilizer manufacturer convicted of knowingly exposing his employees to cyanide gas; and
- $3.38 million in administrative penalties, plus establishment of a $1 million trust fund for environmental education, paid by Formosa Plastics Corporation.

EPA's aggressive enforcement shows no signs of abating. In the face of this challenge, there is no easy solution. The best defense—in this case—is a good defense, in the form of a rigorous program of compliance auditing, coupled with a clear understanding of the RCRA enforcement process.

---

[3]Habicht, *The Federal Perspective on Environmental Criminal Enforcement*, 17 ENVTL. L.REP. (ELI) 10,478, 10,480 (1987).

420 THE RCRA PRACTICE MANUAL

B. Statutory Enforcement Authorities

The tools used to enforce RCRA are contained in six of its sections, which can logically be grouped as follows: information gathering; administrative, civil, and criminal provisions; remedial authority; citizen suits; and compliance of federal facilities. These sections are briefly outlined here and are discussed more fully below.

EPA's information-gathering authority is contained in two sections of RCRA. Section 3007 grants EPA access to, and the authority to obtain information and samples from, facilities that treat, store, or dispose of hazardous waste. Section 3013 authorizes EPA to order a facility presenting a substantial hazard to conduct monitoring, testing, and analysis, and to report the results to EPA.

Section 3008 authorizes EPA to issue compliance orders, assess civil penalties, and revoke or suspend permits for violations of hazardous waste management regulations or noncompliance with EPA's enforcement orders. EPA may also refer a case to DOJ for filing in court as a civil or criminal enforcement action. Section 3008 authorizes criminal penalties for "knowing" violations of many requirements and for "knowing endangerment."

Section 7003 provides EPA with administrative authority to order remedial action for waste-related situations "that may present an imminent and substantial endangerment." Alternatively, EPA can refer a civil action to DOJ for appropriate relief, including an injunction to compel cleanup or an order assessing penalties for violations of EPA orders.

Citizens can act as "private attorneys general" under Section 7002. Subject to several important limitations, citizens can bring suit in federal district court against any person that violates any RCRA permit, regulation, or order. Citizens can also sue to abate any waste-related situation "that may present an imminent and substantial endangerment."

Finally, Section 6001 subjects federal facilities to all federal, state, and local environmental requirements. These facilities are subject to both injunctive relief and civil penalties.

II. The Enforcing Agencies

RCRA enforcement is carried out primarily by two federal agencies and dozens of state agencies. Within any one of those federal or state agencies, however, there may be multiple divisions or offices with overlapping jurisdiction and conflicting positions. Companies facing enforcement actions need to understand how the agencies are organized and how they share responsibility for RCRA enforcement.

Chapter 16: Civil and Criminal Enforcement 421

A. Environmental Protection Agency

Although most RCRA enforcement cases begin in one of EPA's ten regional offices, the Office of Enforcement and Compliance Assurance (OECA) at EPA headquarters also has significant management responsibility for enforcement of RCRA. A major reorganization in late 1993 divided OECA into six offices, most of which are actively involved in RCRA enforcement.

Administrative and civil enforcement is handled by the Office of Regulatory Enforcement, which includes a RCRA Enforcement Division as one of its key components. RCRA corrective action cases (along with Superfund cases) are assigned to the Office of Site Remediation Enforcement. Criminal enforcement is handled by the Office of Criminal Enforcement. Cases involving federal facilities (including government contractors) are the responsibility of the Office of Federal Activities, whose mission and authority remain the subject of considerable controversy. Finally, the National Enforcement Investigations Center in Denver, Colorado, supports OECA's cases by collecting evidence and providing technical assistance.

B. Department of Justice

While EPA can initiate administrative actions on its own, it lacks independent litigating authority under RCRA. As a result, EPA must refer to DOJ those RCRA enforcement cases requiring litigation in the federal courts. Pursuant to a memorandum of understanding between EPA and DOJ, the assistant attorney general in charge of the Environment and Natural Resources Division makes the final decision whether to proceed with a RCRA enforcement case referred by EPA. In addition, any proposed settlement of civil or criminal RCRA enforcement litigation must be approved by both EPA and DOJ.

Within the Department of Justice, the responsibility for RCRA enforcement is shared, sometimes uneasily, between the Environment and Natural Resources Division (ENRD) at DOJ headquarters and the 95 U.S. attorney's offices around the country. At DOJ headquarters, ENRD's Environmental Enforcement Section, with over 125 lawyers, handles all civil RCRA enforcement actions referred by EPA. Criminal RCRA enforcement actions are handled by the Environmental Crimes Section within ENRD, which has over 30 lawyers on its staff.

In addition, the 95 U.S. attorney's offices have become increasingly active, and increasingly independent, in the area of environmental enforcement, particularly criminal enforcement. This growing independence presents a serious problem for many companies facing RCRA enforcement actions, as the U.S. attorney's offices are typically more political than the ENRD at DOJ headquarters. Moreover, the assistant U.S. attorneys in the field often lack the RCRA expertise of their colleagues at DOJ headquarters. The combined result may be that the lead prosecutor in a particular case lacks a complete understanding of how EPA has interpreted the relevant RCRA regulations, a perspective on the significance of the alleged violations, or both.

In 1999 DOJ issued two enforcement policies addressing the investigation, prosecution, and settlement of parallel civil and criminal proceedings. The *Global Settlement Policy* provides that criminal plea agreements should be negotiated separately from civil settlements, so that defendants may not achieve reduced criminal penalties by agreeing to accept enhanced civil relief. The *Integrated Enforcement Policy* provides that civil and criminal investigators should share evidence early in their cases—subject to legal and ethical constraints—and that any information obtained as the result of legitimate civil discovery may be freely shared with criminal enforcement. The policy acknowledges, however, that civil and administrative discovery should not be used as a pretext to obtain information for a criminal investigation, and that the threat of criminal prosecution should not be used to extract a settlement in a civil case.

C. The States

Although EPA and DOJ play extremely important roles, the enforcement of RCRA is primarily the work of the states. Virtually all states now administer their own EPA-authorized RCRA programs, in whole or in part, in lieu of the federal program. These states have primary enforcement authority for RCRA within their own borders. Significantly, the RCRA regulations applicable to facilities within a given state are generally those contained in the state's own EPA-authorized RCRA program, which may differ significantly from the RCRA regulations found in Title 40 of the *Code of Federal Regulations*.

EPA also retains the right to enforce the states' authorized RCRA programs. Under the memorandum of agreement commonly signed by EPA and the authorized state, EPA reserves the right to take direct enforcement action if the state is "unwilling or unable" to take "timely and appropriate" enforcement action. Thus, even if the state files an enforcement action, EPA can "overfile" if it believes the state action is too little or comes too late. Note that even in an overfiling situation, EPA is enforcing the state's authorized RCRA program, which (as noted above) may not be identical to EPA's RCRA rules.

The law on EPA's authority to "overfile" on RCRA violations in authorized states is still developing. In 1999, in *Harmon Industries, Inc. v.*

Browner, the Eighth Circuit held that EPA may overfile only when: (1) EPA has provided notice to the state and the state declines or fails to initiate an action; or (2) EPA withdraws its authorization of the state's program.[4] In 2001, however, the Ninth Circuit declined to follow *Harmon*, holding that EPA retains both its civil and criminal enforcement powers in authorized states because a state program authorized under RCRA supplants only the federal permitting scheme, not its enforcement authority.[5]

Two important exceptions to this basic division of federal-state authority bear emphasis here. The first concerns state RCRA requirements that are either "more stringent" or "broader in scope" than the corresponding EPA regulations. EPA has traditionally taken the position that a "more stringent" state RCRA requirement submitted to EPA for approval (for instance, a requirement that a hazardous waste disposal facility maintain higher dollar amounts for liability insurance) becomes part of the state's authorized RCRA program and thereafter becomes enforceable by EPA (as well as by private citizens under Section 7002). On the other hand, EPA maintains that where a state requirement is "broader in scope," such as a listing of additional wastes as hazardous, the requirement does not become part of the authorized state RCRA program, so it is not enforceable by EPA. The distinction between "more stringent" and "broader in scope" is admittedly something of a quagmire, but one that bears watching.

Second, the federal-state relationship is further complicated by the enactment of the Hazardous and Solid Waste Amendments of 1984. Under those amendments, a number of important new regulations, such as the land disposal restrictions and accompanying treatment standards, took effect as a matter of federal law even in authorized states. EPA therefore retained primary enforcement authority for those specific provisions until the states eventually revised their programs and obtained new authorizations to cover those provisions. The practical result is that in most states, EPA retains primary enforcement authority for at least some important RCRA regulations.

Finally, EPA not only oversees state enforcement of RCRA in particular cases, but also actively encourages a greater overall level of criminal enforcement activity by the states. Four regional environmental enforcement networks now provide training and assistance on criminal enforcement techniques to a total of 46 states, with two-thirds of the funding for these networks coming from EPA.

---

[4]Harmon Indus., Inc. v. Browner, 191 F.3d 894 (8th Cir. 1999).
[5]United States v. Elias, 269 F.3d 1003 (9th Cir. 2001).

424 THE RCRA PRACTICE MANUAL

III. Information Gathering

Sections 3007 and 3013 of RCRA authorize EPA to gather information on facilities that handle hazardous waste. These provisions are powerful tools for developing future enforcement actions.

A. Section 3007

Section 3007 allows EPA to request information from any person that generates, transports, stores, treats, disposes, or otherwise handles or has handled hazardous waste. EPA need not suspect that a violation has occurred before requesting this information, so long as the information sought will assist in the development of future regulations.

Under Section 3007, EPA may also inspect facilities and obtain samples. EPA must make all collected information and samples available to the public, subject only to "satisfactory" claims of business confidentiality. In addition, EPA must inspect all permitted treatment, storage, and disposal (TSD) facilities biennially.

EPA can request an ex parte administrative search warrant if the owner or operator of the facility refuses to allow access. While probable cause is needed to obtain the warrant, the standard is less rigorous than that applied in criminal cases. EPA need not demonstrate any actual releases, and in fact few requests are considered too broad. As a result, "reasonable" requests, such as requests to obtain background samples, may be honored even if they ultimately yield no useful information or if they disrupt business operations. Information requests can also be enforced in federal district court under the authority of Section 3008(g), which now authorizes civil penalties of up to $32,500 per day. (All maximum civil penalty amounts described in this chapter reflect the 2004 increases pursuant to the 1996 Debt Collection Improvement Act.)

B. Section 3013

If EPA believes that the presence or release of a hazardous waste at a site "may present a substantial hazard" to human health and the environment, Section 3013 authorizes EPA to order such monitoring, testing, and analysis as is "reasonable to ascertain the nature and extent of [the] hazard." The order can apply to the present owner or operator of the facility, or to the previous owner or operator if the facility is not in operation and the present owner or operator reasonably has no knowledge of the presence of hazardous waste. If EPA determines that no one can satisfactorily conduct the sampling, it can perform the work and issue an order requiring reimbursement of its costs. Reimbursement is not available, however, where the facility owner or operator dutifully per-

Chapter 16: Civil and Criminal Enforcement 425

forms the testing required by a Section 3013 order and EPA's additional testing merely serves to confirm the results of the earlier testing.

Section 3013 provides EPA with a relatively easy standard to justify the issuance of an order. First, a release of hazardous waste need not be found; the mere presence of such waste will suffice. Second, because of the section's "may present" language, EPA need only show that the waste is a potential hazard. Third, the term "substantial hazard" requires a lesser showing than the "imminent endangerment" language found in Section 7003 (discussed below). Finally, the requirement that requests be "reasonable" is essentially identical to that for information requests under Section 3007, described earlier.

Unlike Section 3007, however, Section 3013 itself specifically authorizes penalties for noncompliance with monitoring orders. EPA can go to court to obtain injunctive relief or civil penalties of up to $6,500 for each day of noncompliance.

The few challenges to EPA's authority to issue and enforce monitoring orders have met with little success. "Pre-enforcement" judicial review of such monitoring orders is typically denied. The recipient of such an order therefore cannot challenge the order unless and until EPA seeks to enforce it.

IV. Civil Enforcement Proceedings

As noted earlier, EPA can choose from several different enforcement routes when it believes a violation of RCRA has occurred. EPA can issue an administrative order or may refer a civil action to DOJ for filing.

Administrative actions are used in some 70 percent of all civil cases. EPA prefers them to civil judicial actions, because administrative actions require no DOJ involvement and often proceed more swiftly. But EPA will refer a civil judicial action to DOJ if it believes that: (1) the hazardous waste handler is a chronic violator or is not expected to comply with an order; (2) the handler is in violation of a compliance schedule, order, agreement, or decree; or (3) an intentional violation of the regulations has occurred and a criminal action is not contemplated. Commonly, EPA issues one or more notices of violation before referring a matter to DOJ, but EPA is not required to do so.

A. Administrative Orders and Hearings

1. Scope

Under Section 3008, EPA may issue a compliance order, revoke or suspend a permit, and/or assess penalties of up to $32,500 per day for any

426 THE RCRA PRACTICE MANUAL

violation of RCRA, including (as described earlier) any state law requirement that is part of an EPA-authorized state RCRA program.

2. Procedure

The process typically begins when the regional enforcement attorney issues an administrative complaint. The complaint must describe the alleged violation, explain the proposed penalty amount and the manner in which it was calculated, and inform the alleged violator (called "the respondent") of the right to request a hearing before an administrative law judge.

From that point on, the administrative enforcement procedures are governed by EPA's Consolidated Rules of Practice, found at Part 22 of Title 40, *Code of Federal Regulations*. The Part 22 rules govern such matters as answers to the complaint, default judgments, intervention and participation of amici curiae, discovery, informal settlement conferences, prehearing conferences, posthearing submissions, and appeals. Litigators accustomed to federal court practice will find that these rules provide relatively limited opportunities for defendants to obtain discovery or early rulings on key legal issues.

EPA encourages settlement and usually offers to hold an informal settlement conference at about the same time as the respondent must answer the complaint. Any settlement agreed to by the regional enforcement staff must then be submitted to the Regional Administrator of EPA for approval. Final settlements are typically incorporated into so-called consent orders that simply call for payment of a specified amount in civil penalties. Although these settlements are public documents, they provide little insight into administrative enforcement, because they do not explain the derivation of the final penalty amount.

If no settlement is reached, an administrative hearing is held before an administrative law judge (ALJ). If the ALJ decides that a civil penalty should be assessed, he or she calculates the amount by considering EPA's proposed penalty amount, as well as EPA's RCRA Civil Penalty Policy (discussed below), but he or she is not bound by either. The ALJ's final decision following the hearing becomes effective 45 days after it is issued, unless a timely motion is made to reopen the hearing because new evidence is available or further administrative appeal is granted within the agency.

Historically, the only administrative appeal from an ALJ decision was to the EPA Administrator. In practice, the cases were delegated to EPA's Chief Judicial Officer, who actually wrote the final decisions for the Administrator. In 1992, however, due to the growing volume of appeals from regional enforcement and permit decisions, the Environmental

Appeals Board was established to hear all such appeals. The three-judge board decides matters by majority vote, with final decisions reviewable in federal district court in accordance with RCRA and/or the Administrative Procedure Act. Note that the actual amount of a civil penalty is typically reviewable only for abuse of discretion.

3. Relief and Penalties

Section 3008, which governs civil penalties, directs EPA to consider the seriousness of the violation and any good-faith efforts to comply in determining the amount of the penalty to be assessed. EPA's 1990 RCRA Civil Penalty Policy spells out EPA's approach to calculating penalties as follows:

Penalty amount = Gravity-based component x Multiday component
+ Adjustments + Economic benefit

The gravity-based component is based on EPA's assessment of the potential for harm and the extent of the deviation from regulatory requirements. According to EPA's policy, the gravity-based component will vary from $110 to $550 per day, for minor harm and minor deviations, to $22,000 to $27,500 per day, for major harm and major deviations.

EPA then calculates the multiday component based on the number of days that EPA believes it can document noncompliance. Depending on EPA's view of the seriousness of the factors used in the gravity-based component, the multiday component may be discretionary in some cases.

After the gravity component is multiplied by the multiday component, further adjustments can increase or decrease the penalty amount. Six factors can be considered:

1. good—or bad—faith efforts to comply;
2. degree of willfulness and/or negligence;
3. history of noncompliance;
4. ability to pay;
5. beneficial environmental projects sponsored by the violator; and
6. other unique factors.

The final step in the process is consideration of the economic benefit of noncompliance, which is defined as the economic advantages from cost avoidance and delayed cost. Economic benefit is calculated by means of the BEN model, a mathematical computer model designed to estimate the economic benefit of noncompliance. In EPA's view, the final penalty amount must always be at least as high as any economic benefit that was realized due to the RCRA violation. Recovering the economic benefit of noncompliance is meant to "level the playing field" for those that comply and those that do not.

4. Enforcement of Administrative Orders

If the recipient of a Section 3008(a) administrative compliance order fails to comply with that order, Section 3008(c) authorizes EPA to assess civil penalties of up to $32,500 per day of noncompliance and to suspend or revoke the facility's permit, even if it is a state-issued permit. EPA can also repair to federal district court for injunctive relief and civil penalties.

5. Statute of Limitations

At least one court of appeals held that the general five-year federal statute of limitations applicable to government enforcement actions applies to RCRA administrative enforcement actions. In an unpublished opinion, the Sixth Circuit applied the general five-year statute of limitations to a RCRA administrative enforcement case, holding that EPA's motion to amend its administrative compliant to add a party was timely filed because it was filed within five years of the alleged violation.[6]

B. Civil Judicial Enforcement

1. Scope

Upon referral of an enforcement case by EPA, DOJ may file a civil action in federal district court in the judicial district where the alleged violations occurred. Such suits are often filed when administrative remedies have been or are expected to be ineffectual.

2. Relief and Penalties

a. Equitable Relief. A civil action may be brought to obtain temporary restraining orders or other injunctive relief. RCRA explicitly provides for temporary and permanent injunctions.

While RCRA enforcement still applies the three-pronged test for granting permanent injunctive relief (that is, inadequate legal remedies, risk of irreparable injury, and balancing of the equities), the standard is somewhat less stringent than for injunctions sought by private litigants. First, it has been held that EPA need not show inadequate legal remedies, because RCRA specifically authorizes injunctions. Second, in dealing with public health statutes such as RCRA, the emphasis shifts somewhat from irreparable injury to concern for the general public interest.

---

[6]Shillman v. United States, 2000 U.S. App. LEXIS 15800 (6th Cir. June 29, 2000).

Finally, balancing of the equities may not be required when the plaintiff is the sovereign and the activity to be enjoined may endanger the public health.

Thus, for a defendant, the issue may not be so much whether an injunction can issue, but rather its terms. In some cases, the courts have ordered relief as severe as loss of interim status or permanent closure of hazardous waste facilities.

b. Civil Penalties. Section 3008(g) authorizes the federal district courts to impose civil penalties of up to $32,500 per day for each violation. The courts, in exercising their discretion, have used the factors in EPA's RCRA Civil Penalty Policy or a similar set of factors. Penalties can be severe, such as the $1.23 million assessed for operating two surface impoundments after they had lost interim status. On the other hand, penalties can be reduced by mitigating factors, such as reliance on advice given by state officials, discovery by means of a voluntary compliance audit, or minimal potential for future environmental harm.

3. Other Issues

Two additional issues in civil judicial proceedings deserve at least brief mention: the right to a jury trial and the statute of limitations.

a. Right to a Jury Trial. The first issue is whether a defendant has a right to a jury trial to determine liability for civil penalties. The U.S. Supreme Court ruled in 1987 that the defendant in a Clean Water Act enforcement action for civil penalties is entitled to a jury trial on the question of liability, but not on the amount of the penalty. This could provide a basis for defendants in civil RCRA cases to obtain jury trials on the issue of liability.

b. Statute of Limitations. The second issue, which has several facets, concerns the applicable statute of limitations. Because RCRA contains no statute of limitations, courts apply the general five-year federal statute of limitations. Two subsidiary issues then emerge: When does the claim first accrue, and do administrative enforcement actions toll the statute?

The date on which claims first accrue is often hard to determine because violations may occur on private property and may not be immediately detected by enforcement authorities. Two theories can be used for determining when the claim first accrues: the continuing violation theory and the discovery rule.

Under the continuing violation theory, every day that the violation continues is a new violation. Thus, alleged violations committed more than five years before the claim is filed are not actionable; only violations committed in the last five years can be used in calculating a penalty. For violations involving the failure to obtain a permit, EPA has taken the position that the violation continues from the day the permit was required until the illegal conduct is complete. In the RCRA criminal context, at least one district court found that the failure to obtain a permit for the storage of hazardous waste was a continuing violation. However, several district courts reached a different position in the context of the Clean Air Act, holding instead that the failure to obtain a construction permit is a violation that accrues only once. In addition, to avoid excessive penalties, EPA has been reluctant to impose multiday penalties for each of the daily and continuing violations.

The discovery rule has not been directly applied to RCRA, but it has been used in Clean Water Act cases. Under the discovery rule, the claim first accrues on the date that the government discovers (or should have discovered) the violation. However, courts have been reluctant to extend the discovery rule in the context of the Clean Air Act and Toxic Substances Control Act. Certainly, it could be argued that if Congress had wanted to use the discovery rule in RCRA, it could have inserted provisions to that effect.

The next issue is whether administrative enforcement proceedings toll the statute, so that EPA, after pursuing administrative enforcement, can file an action in district court more than five years after the RCRA violation occurred. In situations where administrative actions are required as a prerequisite to judicial action, the courts have held that the statute is tolled, but RCRA does not require EPA to exhaust its administrative remedies first.

Where administrative proceedings are not required as a prerequisite to judicial action, the courts are split on whether the statute is tolled by such proceedings. Several courts have held that there is no tolling. The rationale, borrowed from Clean Water Act cases, is that such proceedings are not equivalent to a court proceeding because there are fewer constitutional safeguards, the tribunal has no powers of enforcement or penalty assessment, and there are no provisions for public participation.

On the other hand, EPA might argue that administrative enforcement under RCRA should toll the statute of limitations for two reasons. First, RCRA administrative enforcement proceedings are more similar to court proceedings than those under the Clean Water Act. EPA does have powers of enforcement and penalty assessment, and there are provisions for public participation through intervention. Second, Congress provided for RCRA administrative enforcement actions to avoid clogging the courts, so the proceedings were intended to function as a court.

4. Defenses

Five defenses that have been raised in RCRA civil enforcement proceedings will be discussed here: (1) impossibility; (2) the invalidity of the underlying regulation; (3) equitable estoppel; (4) EPA's permit-as-shield rule; and (5) good-faith efforts to comply.

a. Impossibility. The impossibility defense has typically been unsuccessful, because the courts believe there is always at least one alternative to continuing to violate RCRA—to cease operations. In the same vein, the D.C. Circuit upheld an EPA regulation requiring treatment of certain wastes for which no lawful treatment capacity exists, making compliance literally impossible. The court reasoned that the affected companies should have made other arrangements to deal with their wastes long before the EPA rule was adopted.[7]

b. Invalidity of Underlying Regulations. Defendants in enforcement actions may wish to raise substantive or procedural challenges to the validity of the underlying RCRA regulations. Importantly, Section 7006(a)(1) of RCRA requires that challenges to EPA regulations be filed within 90 days of their promulgation, which typically means within 90 days after publication in the *Federal Register*. The statute goes on to address untimely challenges: "[A]ction of the Administrator with respect to which review could have been obtained [within 90 days] shall not be subject to judicial review in civil or criminal proceedings for enforcement."

The sole statutory exception to this rule is a narrow one. The defendant must show that the challenge is based on "grounds arising after" the 90th day.

Where an EPA regulation is challenged in a timely manner, however, and the challenge succeeds, the implications for enforcement actions can be dramatic. For example, the sweep of EPA's enforcement authority was curtailed by *Shell Oil Co. v. EPA*[8] and its aftermath. The *Shell Oil* decision vacated EPA's 1980 mixture and derived-from rules as unlawful, due to inadequate notice and opportunity for public comment. Although EPA later reinstated the rules on an interim final basis, effective February 18, 1992, and then on a final basis, effective May 16, 2002, the 1980 rules were held to be void ab initio and thus unenforceable.[9]

---

[7]Edison Elec. Inst. v. EPA, 996 F.2d 326 (D.C. Cir. 1993).
[8]950 F.2d 741 (D.C. Cir. 1991).
[9]United States v. Goodner Bros. Aircraft, 966 F.2d 380 (8th Cir. 1992).

432   THE RCRA PRACTICE MANUAL

c. Equitable Estoppel. The defense that the government is equitably estopped has generally been unsuccessful. One court ruled that a company was not relieved of the burden of complying with federal RCRA standards for surface impoundments even when there was an agreement between the state and the company that state closure standards for surface impoundments had been satisfied. Another court held that reliance on EPA's RCRA/Superfund telephone "hot line," which was set up to provide guidance on difficult interpretative questions involving RCRA, was no defense to an enforcement action.[10]

d. EPA's Permit-as-Shield Rule. EPA's permit-as-shield rule is another potential shelter from enforcement actions. It states that compliance with a RCRA permit is considered to be compliance, for purposes of enforcement, with all hazardous waste regulations, except for statutory provisions added after issuance of the permit and for land disposal restriction (LDR) requirements.[11]

e. Good-Faith Efforts to Comply. Good-faith efforts to comply have generally been held not to be a defense to violations of RCRA. Such efforts are relevant to mitigating penalties, not to liability.

V. Criminal Enforcement

Section 3008(d) lists the categories of "knowing" violations that are subject to criminal prosecution. Perhaps the most commonly cited are Subsections (d)(1) (knowing transportation of hazardous waste to a facility that does not have a permit) and (d)(2) (knowing treatment, storage, or disposal of hazardous waste without a permit or in violation of a permit or of interim status requirements). The other listed offenses involve reporting, record keeping, manifesting waste shipments, exporting hazardous waste, and handling of used oil.

One important area of ambiguity is criminal enforcement of violations of the Part 268 land disposal restrictions, which are not specifically mentioned in Section 3008(d). EPA could argue, however, that these land disposal restrictions are permit conditions enforceable under Section 3008(d)(2) because, like all hazardous waste regulations, they are routinely incorporated by reference in the boilerplate of RCRA permits.

The penalties for committing the offenses in Section 3008(d) are fines of up to $50,000 per day, imprisonment of up to five years (two years for

---

[10]EPA v. Envtl. Waste Control, Inc., 917 F.2d 327, 334 (7th Cir. 1990).
[11]40 C.F.R. § 270.4(a) (1992).

Chapter 16: Civil and Criminal Enforcement   433

violations other than those in Section 3008(d)(1) and (2)), or both. A repeat offender is subject to double the maximum penalties applicable to first-time offenders. Special enhanced penalties are provided for the separate offense of "knowing endangerment," as described below.

A. "Persons" Subject to Prosecution

The term "person," as used in Section 3008(d), is defined at Section 1004(15) and includes individuals, firms, corporations, partnerships, states, and municipalities. These "persons" may face prosecution as direct actors, as responsible corporate officers, or on a theory of respondeat superior.

Direct actors have been held to include individuals directly committing the violation, directly supervising the act, approving general plans for the act, and implicitly directing the act. Such direct actors have ranged from the president and principal stockholder of the company to the lower-level employees who may have known that the facility did not have a permit and were not authorized to obtain one for the facility. Federal employees prosecuted as individuals, and not as agents of the federal government, also have been convicted.

Individual corporate officers also have been held liable under the "responsible corporate officer" doctrine. Under this doctrine, a responsible corporate officer can be convicted of willfully or negligently causing a crime based on the willfulness or negligence imputed to him or her from a lower-level employee. EPA is not required to prove that the officers had, in fact, exercised authority over the employees who committed the acts.

Corporations and other organizations can be held indirectly liable under the collective knowledge theory or respondeat superior. Under the former approach, the corporation is considered to have acquired the collective knowledge of its employees within the scope of their employment, and is responsible for their illegal acts. Under the latter approach, the corporation is held accountable for the acts of its employees committed within the scope of their employment. Corporations are attractive targets for prosecutors because of their assets and their lack of protection from self-incrimination under the Fifth Amendment.

B. What Is a "Knowing" Violation?

Congress did not define the term "knowing" in Section 3008(d), and the courts continue to grapple with its meaning. Most defendants have

434 THE RCRA PRACTICE MANUAL

found that this term offers far less protection than one might have anticipated.

Under Section 3008(d)(1), for example, the courts have readily upheld convictions for "knowingly" transporting hazardous waste to a facility without a permit. They have required EPA to prove only that the defendant knew the facility receiving the hazardous waste did not have a permit. Even this limited "knowing" element can be proved either circumstantially or by showing a willful failure to determine the permit status of the receiving facility. Significantly, EPA did not have to prove that the defendant knew the material in question was classified as a "waste" under RCRA or knew the material in question was classified as "hazardous" under RCRA.

The standard of proof is less clear under Section 3008(d)(2), which concerns treatment, storage, or disposal without a permit, because the statutory language itself is less clear. The majority rule is the that the defendant need not "know" the legal status of the waste, so long as he or she knew the waste was potentially harmful. Several cases following this approach have also held that the defendant need not "know" that the facility did not have a permit to treat, store, or dispose of hazardous waste. The minority rule, followed in the Third Circuit, is that the defendant must "know" that: (1) the material was classified as a hazardous waste; (2) disposal requires a permit; and (3) the facility lacked a permit.

C. "Knowing Endangerment"

Section 3008(e) creates a series of enhanced "knowing endangerment" offenses. The maximum penalty for an individual is a $250,000 fine and 15 years' imprisonment; for an organization, the maximum penalty is $1 million. To date, only a few defendants have been convicted under Section 3008(e).

The essence of the knowing endangerment offense is (1) the commission of any "knowing" violation listed in Section 3008(d), (2) where the violator also "knows" that he or she is thereby placing another person in imminent danger of death or seriously bodily injury. For purposes of these special offenses, a person is responsible only for the actual awareness or belief he or she possessed, not for knowledge attributed to him or her, although circumstantial evidence of the person's awareness or belief can be used. Two affirmative defenses are explicitly provided; they involve consent given for (1) dangers that were reasonably foreseeable hazards of an occupation, profession, or business, or (2) medical treatment or scientific experimentation conducted by a professional, with the risk explained to the subject.

D. Defenses

A wide array of defenses has been asserted in criminal enforcement cases. They include the running of the statute of limitations, challenges to the validity and scope of the RCRA regulations at issue, assertions that elements of the offense were not satisfied, and various equitable defenses.

Because RCRA contains no statute of limitations, as noted above, the general five-year statute of limitations for federal offenses is used. This limitations period would be overcome, as also noted above, if the violation is a continuing one.

Challenges to the validity of the regulations, on substantive or procedural grounds, would be unsuccessful if untimely. As with a civil enforcement action, such challenges must be made within 90 days of promulgation, with few exceptions. In some circumstances, the Constitution may restrict the application of this doctrine to bar the assertion of such a defense.[12]

A related defense is a due process argument that a particular RCRA requirement is unconstitutionally vague as applied. Such arguments were asserted, without success, as to the definition of reactive hazardous waste and the exemption for small-quantity generators.

The last group of defenses involves various equitable arguments based on government conduct: equitable estoppel, collateral estoppel, misrepresentation, and laches. To date, estoppel defenses have not been successfully litigated in the context of RCRA criminal enforcement. One criminal defendant successfully asserted that EPA misrepresented the contamination at issue. Finally, it remains to be seen whether the doctrine of laches applies to enforcement actions brought by the government.

E. Fines and Sentencing: Federal Sentencing Guidelines

The Federal Sentencing Guidelines, which took effect November 1, 1987, substitute mandatory sentencing guidelines for a system of indeterminate sentencing based on court discretion. The guidelines frequently result in harsher sentences and fines for environmental crimes, including sentences for white-collar criminals.

The guidelines currently cover all aspects of sentencing for individuals convicted of environmental crimes. As recently supplemented, the guidelines also address fines, probation, and restitution for convicted organizations.

The legislation authorizing the guidelines allows the imposition of criminal fines far in excess of the levels set out in Section 3008(d) of

---

[12]*See generally* Adamo Wrecking Co. v. United States, 434 U.S. 275 (1978).

436 THE RCRA PRACTICE MANUAL

RCRA. Specifically, fines up to $250,000 per violation for individuals, and up to $500,000 per violation for organizations, are permitted.

The guidelines use numeric penalty levels, which are calculated for each offense. The sentencing judge must begin with penalty levels for base offenses, such as knowing endangerment or mishandling hazardous or toxic substances, and then enhance the level for such factors as threat of serious bodily injury, continuous or repetitive releases, evacuation of the community, and substantial environmental damage. The level can be reduced for simple record-keeping or reporting violations.

F. Self-Auditing

Fear of criminal prosecution has discouraged self-auditing efforts by many companies that handle hazardous waste. DOJ has attempted to promote self-auditing by announcing that it will view self-auditing as a mitigating factor in evaluating environmental crimes, subject to the following factors:

- voluntary disclosure;
- cooperation;
- preventive measures and compliance programs;
- pervasiveness of noncompliance;
- internal disciplinary action; and
- subsequent compliance efforts.

The DOJ policy is useful but falls far short of the assurance most companies want before engaging in self-auditing. The problem is illustrated by a Ninth Circuit case holding that absent an express promise not to sue, there was no misconduct when the government prosecuted after receiving a voluntary disclosure.[13]

VI. Imminent and Substantial Endangerment

Section 7003 of RCRA contains its own unique, potent, and potentially draconian enforcement provisions. They are not keyed to any regulatory requirements or to any published standards. Instead, Section 7003 authorizes EPA to issue a unilateral administrative order or to bring suit for injunctive relief, to abate any situation that "may present an imminent and substantial endangerment to human health and the environment." No hazardous waste need be involved, so long as some solid waste is involved. These orders can be enforced by a district court with fines of up to $6,500 per day.

---

[13]United States v. Rockwell Int'l Corp., 924 F.2d 928, 934–35 (9th Cir. 1991).

Before enactment of the federal Superfund law in 1980, EPA and DOJ used Section 7003 to seek injunctions compelling the cleanup of contaminated sites. Today, even after the enactment of Superfund, Section 7003 remains the key statutory authority for cleanup of petroleum product spills and any other materials that may not be "hazardous substances" as defined in CERCLA.

To obtain relief under Section 7003, there must be a finding made that (1) conditions at the site may present an imminent or substantial endangerment; (2) the endangerment stems from handling any solid waste or hazardous waste; and (3) the defendant has contributed or is contributing to the activities in (2).

Importantly, the courts have defined "imminent and substantial endangerment" as future risk of harm or exposure, not actual harm or even current exposure. Thus, a situation posing some risk of possible future exposure to hazardous wastes might well be deemed to present an "imminent and substantial endangerment."

Courts have also chosen the broader statutory definitions of "solid waste" and "hazardous waste" over the somewhat narrower regulatory definition. The statutory definition contains the concept of "discarded material" but does not contain the additional qualifiers of "abandonment" and "disposal" contained in the EPA regulations. As a result, material not defined by EPA as a "solid waste" or "hazardous waste" under the RCRA regulations may nevertheless be deemed a "solid or hazardous waste" in a Section 7003 action for imminent and substantial endangerment.

The "contributed to" language requires a showing of causation, which has been broadly construed. Causation includes past acts as well as a failure to act. Because liability is strict, the government does not have to prove the defendant's control over the activities. The 1984 amendments to RCRA expanded the reach of Section 7003 to nonnegligent off-site generators and transporters.

Relief under Section 7003 may come in the form of administrative orders or injunctions, and may include performing studies, ceasing or modifying operations, and taking remedial actions. Because of the equitable nature of relief, several equitable defenses have been raised in Section 7003 actions: collateral estoppel, laches, and unclean hands.

VII. Citizen Suits

Another significant source of enforcement litigation is Section 7002 of RCRA, which provides for citizen suits. The number of citizen suits filed under RCRA never approached the number filed under the Clean Water Act. Nevertheless, the federal cause of action provided by Section 7002, with its explicit fee-shifting provision, remains attractive to potential plaintiffs.

Section 7002(a)(1)(A) authorizes suits against any person, including the federal government, for violations of solid and hazardous waste regulations and permits. An action can also be maintained under Section 7002(a)(1)(B) against past and present waste handlers for an "imminent and substantial endangerment." Plaintiffs must provide notice before commencing actions—except for violations of hazardous waste regulations—and such actions will be precluded by ongoing "diligent prosecution" by EPA or the state. Relief includes civil penalties and injunctions.

In several respects, the citizen suit provisions in RCRA are broader than those found in other environmental statutes. First, actions can be maintained to abate imminent and substantial endangerments, as well as to abate violations of regulations and permits. Thus, a district court in New Jersey ordered the excavation of chrome ore processing waste at an estimated cost of $400 million. Second, civil penalties can be recovered. Third, there is no lengthy notice period before filing for violations of hazardous waste regulations.

On the other hand, the RCRA citizen suit provisions are narrower than those found under other statutes, in that they cannot be used to challenge siting and permitting decisions. In addition, the practical evidentiary burdens facing a plaintiff are greater under RCRA because the regulatory program is so much more complex.

A. Scope

1. Who May Sue and Who Can Be Sued

Any "person," including individuals, states, corporations, and municipalities, can sue for relief under the citizen suit provisions. Standing to sue in such cases has been granted liberally, both for individuals and for organizations. However, an out-of-state corporation lacks standing to sue its economic competitor for alleged RCRA violations in a state where the plaintiff has no facilities.[14]

A suit can also be commenced against any "person." States can only be sued as a handler of hazardous waste, not as an administrator of a hazardous waste regulatory program. In addition, actions against states will only be permitted to the extent allowed by the Eleventh Amendment.

2. Actionable Violations and Endangerment

The citizen suit provisions can be used to sue a person that violates any "permit, standard, regulation, condition, requirement, prohibition, or

---

[14]Goldendale Aluminum Co. v. Reynolds Metals Corp., 1997 U.S. Dist. LEXIS 21709 (W.D. Ark. 1997).

Chapter 16: Civil and Criminal Enforcement 439

order" issued under the authority of RCRA. The violations must be continuing, at least in part, rather than wholly in the past. This could potentially include past illegal hazardous waste disposal if the waste remains where it was deposited and can still damage the environment.

Section 7002 also allows actions in response to imminent and substantial endangerment. Because this language is almost identical to the "imminent and substantial endangerment" language of Section 7003, there need be no showing of actual harm; threatened or potential harm will suffice.

B. Notice Provisions

To afford EPA or the state the chance to obtain compliance and the alleged violator the opportunity to comply, a person must file notice of intent to litigate with EPA, the state, and the person being sued. An action under Section 7002(a)(1)(A) for violating regulations and orders can be commenced 60 days after notice is given. The waiting period in an action to abate imminent and substantial endangerment is 90 days. If the alleged violation involves hazardous waste management, even if it also involves other violations or imminent and substantial endangerment, the suit may be filed immediately after serving notice.

The U.S. Supreme Court has held that the statutory notice requirement is jurisdictional and must be followed strictly.[15] Procedures for serving notice can be found at 40 C.F.R. Part 254.

C. Preclusion by Government Enforcement

One of the purposes of the notice provisions discussed above is to allow the government time to decide whether it wishes to take the lead in enforcing against the alleged violator. To that end, Section 7002(b) precludes any citizen suit over a violation of any RCRA requirement if the federal or state government is already "diligently prosecuting" that violation in a civil or criminal enforcement action. The federal or state enforcement authorities can thus deny jurisdiction to a citizen suit by commencing an action during the waiting period.

The next issue is what constitutes "diligent prosecution." Courts have generally held that administrative actions are not "court actions" for purposes of preclusion. As a result, the following actions have not been considered diligent prosecution: EPA compliance orders, state administrative actions, and negotiations between the state and the alleged violator. Courts are split on whether agreements between the state and the alleged violator, even if they have been filed in state court, constitute diligent prosecution.

---

[15]Hallstrom v. Tillamook County, 493 U.S. 20 (1989).

440   THE RCRA PRACTICE MANUAL

Various governmental actions taken under the federal Superfund law will serve to preclude a citizen suit to abate an "imminent and substantial endangerment." The provisions of Section 7002(b) are fairly detailed in this regard but still leave considerable room for creative lawyering. For example, one district court held that EPA's placement of a site on CERCLA's National Priority List, and the conduct of a remedial investigation and feasibility study by the private defendant, barred a citizen suit even in the face of allegations that these actions were insufficient.

Citizen suits will not be precluded, however, if deadlines are not being met and the government is not acting to ensure timely compliance. Actions also may not be precluded if the scope or duration of the government's action does not match those of the citizen suit. For example, if EPA has left the site and there is merely the possibility of future EPA action, or if government action is directed at contaminated groundwater and a citizen suit is directed at surface waters, an action may be maintained.

D. Other Jurisdictional Issues

The courts are split on whether federal courts can hear citizen suits alleging violations of hazardous waste regulations in states with EPA-authorized RCRA programs. Courts rejecting such suits reason that the alleged violations are exclusively a matter of state law, even if state law is closely patterned after, or identical to, the federal RCRA provisions. Courts allowing such suits cite the statutory language that an authorized state RCRA program operates "in lieu of" the federal program, which they read to mean that federal jurisdiction is retained.

Intervention in citizen suits is liberally granted. RCRA grants intervention as a matter of right in suits for violations of regulations or standards. It also allows intervention as a matter of right in suits for imminent and substantial endangerment, using a test similar to that found in Rule 24(a)(2) of the Federal Rules of Civil Procedure.

Federal courts will sometimes hear pendent state claims in citizen suits. If the state claims are based on the state's RCRA hazardous waste program, for example, then the court may hear those claims. On the other hand, pendent state common law claims, such as those for nuisance, negligence, trespass, and strict liability, are typically dismissed by federal courts.

E. Relief and Penalties

The district courts are authorized to grant four forms of relief: (1) assessing civil penalties under Sections 3008(a) and (g); (2) requiring compliance with permits, regulations, or standards; (3) restraining persons con-

Chapter 16: Civil and Criminal Enforcement 441

tributing to imminent and substantial endangerment due to handling of solid or hazardous waste; and (4) requiring such persons to take any necessary actions.

The equitable relief that can be granted in citizen suits is very broad. For example, the court may order immediate compliance with regulations or permanent closure of a facility. As in civil judicial enforcement, the three-pronged test for granting a permanent injunction is less stringent than requests for such injunctions in private actions.

Some plaintiffs have tried to use RCRA citizen suits as a cost recovery vehicle, seeking an injunction ordering payment as a form of restitution. This was seen as a potentially attractive alternative to Superfund litigation in many cases. The Supreme Court later foreclosed RCRA cost recovery actions with respect to past cleanup costs,[16] and the lower courts have continued to whittle away at it, even with regard to future cleanup costs.

RCRA is silent as to who receives any civil penalties assessed against the defendant. Several courts have ruled that such penalties must be paid directly to the U.S. Treasury, perhaps to seek a balance between promoting private enforcement and not paying bounty hunters. Courts have also held that Section 7002 does not create a private cause of action for damages.

Section 7002(e) grants courts the discretion to order the payment of costs, including reasonable attorney fees, to the substantially prevailing party. Courts have awarded costs to citizen suit plaintiffs and to intervenors in actions brought by EPA. Some courts have use the relatively intuitive test of whether the citizen group materially altered the legal relationship of the parties or simply affected the behavior of the defendant, even if the relief sought was not granted by the court. But recent Supreme Court jurisprudence under other fee-shifting statutes suggests that these "catalyst theory" awards may be a thing of the past. Finally, costs are not granted for all activities of the prevailing party, such as opposing the defendant in a related enforcement action under the Clean Water Act, challenging local procedural rules, or making an appearance at the defendant's bankruptcy proceedings.

VIII. Federal Facility Enforcement

Congress has waived sovereign immunity for federal facilities managing solid and hazardous wastes. Under Section 6001 of RCRA, as amended by the Federal Facility Compliance Act of 1992, federal facilities are subject

---

[16]*Meghrig v. KFC W., Inc.*, 516 U.S. 479 (1996).

to the substantive requirements and the enforcement sanctions of all federal, state, interstate, and local laws. This includes both injunctive relief and civil penalties, including coercive and punitive fines. In this regard, the Federal Facility Compliance Act overturned a prior Supreme Court ruling that federal facilities were subject only to coercive fines.

The president may exempt an entity from regulatory requirements for one-year periods if it is in the national interest. Lack of appropriations is not a defense to noncompliance, unless the president asks for appropriations and Congress rejects the request. Government-owned contractor-operated facilities are to be treated as private facilities.

IX. Conclusion

Congress gave EPA, DOJ, the states, and private citizens a variety of powerful tools to use in enforcing RCRA, tools that are being used with increasing frequency and severity. The courts have further enhanced this enforcement arsenal with rulings favorable to EPA on the very limited degree of "knowledge" needed for a criminal conviction under RCRA. As a result, virtually any violation of the RCRA regulations can now be successfully prosecuted as a felony offense, regardless of its environmental significance.

This relentless criminalization of RCRA violations has certainly caught the attention of corporate America. It is neither the fairest nor the most appropriate way to encourage compliance with a set of extraordinarily complex rules that have generated tens of thousands of telephone requests to EPA for guidance. But the current enforcement climate makes it absolutely imperative that companies handling hazardous waste remain extraordinarily attentive to their RCRA compliance status.

CHAPTER 17

The Federal-State Relationship under RCRA

MARCIE R. HOROWITZ
AND MICHAEL T. SCANLON

I. Introduction

Pollution control in the United States was once primarily a state or local concern. Even the first wave of major federal environmental legislation in the early 1970s emphasized "the primary responsibilities and rights of States to prevent, reduce, and eliminate pollution." The federal role was envisioned as important but limited, consisting mainly of technical services and financial aid.

The passage of RCRA in 1976 marked a subtle but significant shift in the federal-state relationship. Retreating from its earlier policy to preserve the states' primary role, Congress tipped RCRA's balance in favor of federal control:

> [W]hile the collection and disposal of solid wastes should continue to be primarily the function of State, regional, and local agencies, the problems of waste disposal as set forth above have become a matter national in scope and in concern and necessitate Federal action through financial and technical assistance and leadership in the development, demonstration, and application of new and improved methods and processes to reduce the

444 THE RCRA PRACTICE MANUAL

amount of waste and unsalvageable materials and to provide for proper and economical solid waste disposal practices.[1]

One of RCRA's stated objectives was to establish a "viable Federal-State partnership" to carry out the purposes of the act.[2] This chapter examines several key facets of that partnership.

II. *Authorization of State Hazardous Waste Programs*

RCRA places the primary burden of hazardous waste regulation on the federal government. The statute directs EPA to identify the characteristics of hazardous waste, list particular wastes subject to regulation, establish hazardous waste management standards, and require permits for treatment, storage, and disposal facilities. These tasks form the heart of RCRA, and the statute provides few avenues for state involvement in these fundamental aspects of the program.

While the states' role in *developing* national hazardous waste policy is limited, their role in *administering* this policy can be significant. At their option, states may seek authorization from EPA to "administer and enforce" their own hazardous waste program.[3] Once authorized, a state program operates "in lieu of" the federal program, and the state—not EPA—is responsible for running it.[4] Authorization can be withdrawn if EPA determines, after a public hearing, that a state is not administering and enforcing its program in accordance with RCRA's requirements.[5]

Part 272 of 40 C.F.R. sets forth some of the state hazardous waste management programs that have been authorized by EPA and incorporates the state statutes and regulations by reference into the federal RCRA program. Significantly, Part 272 does not include all authorized state programs; indeed, many authorized state programs are *not* listed in Part 272. The decision to codify the state authorizations in Part 272 is made individually by each EPA regional office, and certain regions have been more aggressive in this regard than others.

A. Authorization Requirements

RCRA provides two means by which states can administer the RCRA program. *Interim authorization* was initially available to states whose

---

[1] 42 U.S.C. § 6901(a)(4).

[2] *Id.* § 6902(a)(7).

[3] *Id.* § 6926(b).

[4] *Id.; see also* Northside Sanitary Landfill, Inc. v. Thomas, 804 F.2d 371, 382 (7th Cir. 1986).

[5] 42 U.S.C. § 6926(e).

Chapter 17: The Federal-State Relationship under RCRA 445

existing hazardous waste programs were "substantially equivalent" to the federal program.[6] *Final authorization* is available to states whose programs are "equivalent" to the federal program. More precisely, the statute provides that authorization shall be granted *unless* EPA finds, after notice and opportunity for a public hearing, that

- the state program is "not equivalent" to the federal program;
- the state program is "not consistent" with the federal or state programs applicable in other states; or
- the program "does not provide adequate enforcement of compliance."[7]

The state program need not be an exact replica of the federal program. RCRA's "savings clause"—added in 1980—allows states to impose requirements that are "more stringent" than those imposed by the federal RCRA program.[8]

EPA's implementing regulations specify the elements that must be present in an authorized state program.[9] Basically, an approvable state program must include provisions equivalent to 40 C.F.R. Part 261 (identification and listing of waste), Part 262 (generator standards), Part 263 (transporter standards), Parts 264 and 266 (hazardous waste management facilities), and Part 270 (permitting requirements). In addition, the state program must have procedures for compliance evaluation, including inspection and surveillance procedures. Finally, the state program must provide specific enforcement authority, including the ability to enjoin unauthorized activity, sue to recover appropriate civil penalties, and seek criminal remedies.

EPA's regulations describe three circumstances in which a state program may be deemed "inconsistent" with the federal program or other state programs. First, any aspect of the state program that unreasonably restricts, impedes, or bans the interstate movement of hazardous waste for treatment, storage, or disposal is deemed inconsistent.[10] Any aspect of the state program that has no basis in protection of human health or the environment, and acts to prohibit the treatment, storage, or disposal of hazardous waste in the state, *may* be deemed inconsistent.[11] Finally, if

---

[6]*Id.* § 6926(c)(1).
[7]*Id.* § 6926(b).
[8]*Id.* § 6929.
[9]40 C.F.R. §§ 271.9–.16.
[10]*Id.* § 271.4(a).
[11]*Id.* § 271.4(b).

446   THE RCRA PRACTICE MANUAL

the state manifesting system does not meet federal requirements, the state program is deemed inconsistent.[12]

Except for the matters addressed in 40 C.F.R. Section 271.4, state requirements may be "more stringent" or "broader in scope" than the federal requirements.[13] Requirements that are broader in scope than the federal program are not part of the federally approved program and are therefore not enforceable by EPA. State requirements that are deemed more stringent than the federal requirements become part of the authorized program and may be enforced by EPA.[14]

EPA has issued guidance for determining whether a particular state provision is "more stringent" or "broader in scope" than the federal RCRA requirements.[15] Basically, if the imposition of the state requirement *increases the size of the regulated community* beyond that of the federal program or does not have a direct counterpart in the federal regulatory program, EPA considers the state requirement "beyond the scope" of the federal program and therefore not federally enforceable. For example, if a state lists a waste that is not on the federal list, that requirement would be considered broader in scope because it increases the size of the regulated community. Similarly, if the state imposes licensing requirements on transporters or requires the preparation of an environmental impact statement or siting board approval as part of the permit issuance process, such requirements are broader in scope than the federal program because they have no direct counterparts in the federal program.

In contrast, if the state requirement has a direct federal counterpart and does not increase the size of the regulated community, the requirement is deemed "more stringent" than the corresponding federal provision and is, therefore, *part* of the federally authorized program. The EPA guidance provides three examples of requirements that would be more stringent than the federal program:

- limited financial assurance options for facility closure;
- submittal of annual rather than biennial report for generators; and
- expiration of permits after five years instead of ten.

---

[12]*Id.* § 271.4(c).

[13]*Id.* § 271.1(i).

[14]*See* Memorandum from William A. Sullivan Jr., EPA Enforcement Counsel, to Regional Administrators and Counsels, EPA Enforcement of RCRA-Authorized State Hazardous Waste Laws and Regulations (Mar. 15, 1982) (available at http://www.epa.gov/rcraonline).

[15]*See* Memorandum from Lee M. Thomas, EPA Assistant Administrator for Solid Waste and Emergency Response, Determining Whether State Hazardous Waste Management Requirements Are Broader in Scope or More Stringent Than the Federal RCRA Program (May 21, 1984) (available at http://www.epa.gov/rcraonline).

B. Withdrawal of Authorization

When a state program is inconsistent with the federal program, its authorization may be withdrawn.[16] This is what the petitioners in *Hazardous Waste Treatment Council v. Reilly*[17] tried but failed to do in a case challenging North Carolina's authorized RCRA program. At issue was a state statute limiting the discharge of wastewater from commercial hazardous waste treatment facilities. As a result of this law, petitioners were precluded from constructing a large treatment facility in Laurinburg, North Carolina; a smaller facility, with less discharge, would comply with the law but would be uneconomical. Petitioners claimed that this statute made North Carolina's hazardous waste program "inconsistent" under 40 C.F.R. Section 271.4(b) because it operated effectively as a "prohibition" on hazardous waste treatment in the state and had no basis in human health or environmental protection. They therefore petitioned EPA to withdraw authorization of North Carolina's hazardous waste program.

EPA declined to withdraw North Carolina's program. It concluded that the state law did not *prohibit* the treatment, storage, or disposal of hazardous waste. EPA's rationale was that a large facility could be built elsewhere in the state and a smaller facility could be built in Laurinburg.

The court of appeals upheld EPA's determination. The court construed EPA's decision "to mean that a state law 'acts as a prohibition' on the treatment of hazardous wastes when it effects a total ban on a particular waste treatment technology within a State," and found that this construction was reasonable and merited deference.[18]

III. The Hazardous and Solid Waste Amendments of 1984

When RCRA was enacted, the state authorization mechanism was designed to yield complete control of the hazardous waste program to the authorized states. Once a state became authorized, subsequent rule makings by EPA would not take effect in that state until the state itself adopted the new regulations. Of course, because the authorized states needed to maintain programs equivalent to the federal program, they were compelled to revise their programs each time EPA promulgated a new federal rule. But as a result of the inevitable lag time, nonauthorized states would feel the immediate impact of a new federal regulation, while for the authorized states, such impact could be delayed for months.

---

[16]42 U.S.C. § 6926(e).
[17]938 F.2d 1390 (D.C. Cir. 1991).
[18]*Id.* at 1395, 1397.

448   THE RCRA PRACTICE MANUAL

The Hazardous and Solid Waste Amendments of 1984 (HSWA) significantly changed this aspect of the federal-state relationship. HSWA mandated that EPA develop major new regulatory initiatives to supplement the existing RCRA regime, and provided that this new round of federal rule making would go into effect simultaneously in both authorized and nonauthorized states. EPA would carry out the so-called HSWA-driven regulations in each state until the state gained authorization to do so. Tables 1 and 2 of 40 C.F.R. Section 271.1(j) set forth the federal regulations implementing HSWA and HSWA's self-implementing statutory provisions. These HSWA provisions include several key components of the RCRA program, including the expanded toxicity characteristic, land disposal restrictions, and corrective action.

HSWA has muddied the already complicated federal-state relationship under RCRA. In most states, the RCRA base program is administered by the state, but many HSWA-driven requirements are still administered by EPA. As a result, the regulated community serves two masters. Permits are typically written in two parts, one by EPA and the other by the authorized state. (Closure of a treatment, storage, or disposal facility may be overseen by the state, for example, while corrective action at the same facility is directed by EPA.) For updated information on the status of state authorization, see EPA's Web site at http://www.epa.gov/epaoswer/hazwaste/state/index.htm.

IV. Effects of State Authorization on EPA Enforcement Power

In a state with an authorized program, federal law is "displaced by state law"; the federal program is "superseded" by the state program. Indeed, federal hazardous waste regulations that are not HSWA-driven have no force or effect in a state with an authorized program.[19]

Since the federal program has no force and effect in an authorized state, does EPA have the power to *enforce* the authorized state requirements? In the past few years, this question has provoked lively debate and conflicting judicial opinions. The controversy has focused on two related issues: (1) EPA's right to bring a civil enforcement action in an authorized state and, in particular, its right to "overfile"—that is, to bring an enforcement action when an authorized state has already taken some action against an alleged violator; and (2) the jurisdiction of the federal courts to hear criminal enforcement cases in an authorized state.

---

[19]40 C.F.R. § 264.1(f).

A. Civil Enforcement and EPA's Right to Overfile

Section 3008(a)(1) of RCRA provides that EPA may issue a compliance order or commence a civil action against any person who "has violated or is in violation of any requirement of this subchapter."[20] Section 3008(a)(2) then continues:

> In the case of a violation of any requirement of this subchapter where such violation occurs in a State which is authorized to carry out a hazardous waste program under section 6926 of this title, the [EPA] Administrator shall give notice to the State in which such violation has occurred prior to issuing an order or commencing a civil action under this section.[21]

Section 3008(a) is widely interpreted to mean that, while an authorized state is primarily responsible for enforcing its hazardous waste program, EPA retains the power to act when the state fails to do so.[22] RCRA's legislative history supports this view:

> This legislation permits the states to take the lead in the enforcement of the hazardous wastes laws. However, there is enough flexibility in the act to permit the Administrator, in situations where a state is not implementing a hazardous waste program, to actually implement and enforce the hazarodus [sic] waste program against violators in a state that does not meet the federal minimum requirements. Although the Administrator is required to give notice of violations of this title to the states with authorized state hazardous waste programs *the Administrator is not prohibited from acting in those cases where the state fails to act, or from withdrawing approval of the state hazardous waste plan and implementing the federal hazardous waste program pursuant to title III of this act.*[23]

---

[20]42 U.S.C. § 6928(a)(1).

[21]*Id.* § 6928(a)(2).

[22]*See, e.g.,* United States v. Conservation Chem. Co., 660 F. Supp. 1236, 1245 (N.D. Ind. 1987) ("Because the state has chosen not to act, there is no prohibition to the EPA bringing this independent enforcement action"); *see also* Wyckoff Co. v. EPA, 796 F.2d 1197, 1200 (9th Cir. 1986) (in upholding EPA's power to issue RCRA Section 3013 orders in an authorized state, court observed that the notification provision in Section 3008(a)(2) made it "clear that Congress did not intend, by authorizing a state program 'in lieu of the Federal program,' to preempt federal *regulation* entirely") (emphasis in original).

[23]H.R. Rep. No. 94-1491, pt. I, 94th Cong., 2d Sess. 31 (1976), *reprinted in* 1976 U.S.C.C.A.N. 6238, 6269 (emphasis added).

450   THE RCRA PRACTICE MANUAL

The more difficult question, and the one that has prompted so much recent controversy, is whether EPA may "overfile"—that is, whether it may bring a competing enforcement action to supplement action already taken by an authorized state. In 1999, the Eighth Circuit concluded that EPA did not have overfiling authority.[24] "The plain 'in lieu of' language contained in the RCRA reveals a congressional intent for an authorized state program to supplant the federal hazardous waste program in all respects including enforcement," stated the court.[25] The court held that if the state fails to initiate *any* enforcement action, the EPA may act, as long as it provides notice to the state under Section 3008(a)(2). If, however, the state acts but the EPA deems the state's action inadequate, EPA can initiate its own enforcement action only if it first withdraws the state's RCRA authorization pursuant to Section 3006(e).[26]

The *Harmon* decision sent shock waves throughout the RCRA legal community, and subsequent decisions in other jurisdictions have not followed its lead. In *United States v. Power Engineering Co.*,[27] for example, the Tenth Circuit rejected outright the Eighth Circuit's reasoning and holding in *Harmon*. The court concluded that RCRA was ambiguous on the overfiling issue, and deferred to EPA's "reasonable interpretation" of the statute.[28]

EPA, too, has taken steps to limit *Harmon*'s adverse impact on its enforcement authority. Among other things, EPA developed new model Federal Register Notice language to be used in the state authorization process. The language, which is not meant for inclusion in states within the Eighth Circuit, states that EPA retains the authority to "take enforcement actions regardless of whether the State has taken its own actions." EPA's model language may be found on its Web site at http://www.epa.gov/epaoswer/hazwaste/state/revision/program.htm#moa. Additional EPA guidance addressing the agency's position on overfiling (all issued pre-*Harmon*) may be found in several memoranda and their accompanying attachments: "Guidance on RCRA Overfiling," by A. James Barnes[29] and its attachment, "Effect on EPA Enforcement of Enforcement Action Taken by State with Approved RCRA Program," by Francis S. Blake; and "EPA Enforcement of RCRA-Authorized State Hazardous Waste Laws and Regulations," by William A. Sullivan Jr.[30] These documents are

---

[24]Harmon Indus., Inc. v. Browner, 191 F.3d 894 (8th Cir. 1999).
[25]*Id.* at 899.
[26]42 U.S.C. § 6926(e).
[27]303 F.3d 1232 (10th Cir. 2002).
[28]*See also* United States v. Murphy Oil USA, Inc., 143 F. Supp. 2d 1054 (W.D. Wis. 2001).
[29]May 19, 1986.
[30]Mar. 15, 1982.

Chapter 17: The Federal-State Relationship under RCRA   451

included in EPA's *RCRA Enforcement Policy and Compendium* (http://cfpub.epa.gov/compliance/resources/policies/civil/rcra).

B. Criminal Enforcement Authority

EPA's criminal enforcement authority under RCRA differs from its civil enforcement authority in one crucial respect: Section 3008(a) expressly grants EPA only the authority to issue a *civil* compliance order or commence a *civil* action in the federal court. Section 3008(d), which sets out RCRA criminal penalties, is silent on EPA's role, if any, in prosecuting such cases in federal court.

Nonetheless, efforts to oust the federal court of jurisdiction in RCRA criminal cases have generally failed. The courts have concluded that the federal government retains criminal enforcement authority under Section 3008(d) in an authorized state. *United States v. MacDonald & Watson Waste Oil Co.*[31] is an early appellate case in this area. There, the appellants appealed their convictions under Section 3008(d), arguing that the district court lacked jurisdiction over the case because "Rhode Island's authorized state program displaced the federal program, leaving no federal crime and ousting the federal court of jurisdiction."[32] The First Circuit rejected this argument, holding that "[t]he language of the challenged federal criminal provision, 42 U.S.C. § 6928(d), does not limit prosecutions thereunder to those who deal with facilities lacking a *federal* permit. The statute criminalizes 'Any person' who acts without, or in respect to facilities lacking, 'a permit under this subchapter.' A permit under this subchapter is one issued by the Administrator of the EPA or by an authorized state."[33] Subsequent decisions have followed the First Circuit's lead.[34]

V. Citizen Suits in Authorized States

RCRA's citizen suit provision, Section 7002, gives "any person" the right to bring a civil action against any person "alleged to be in violation of any permit, standard, regulation, condition, requirement, prohibition, or order which has become effective pursuant to [RCRA]"[35] (a "Subsection A" suit). A person may also bring a citizen suit regarding waste practices that "may present an imminent and substantial endangerment to

---

[31] 933 F.2d 35 (1st Cir. 1991).
[32] *Id.* at 43 (footnote omitted).
[33] *Id.* at 44 (emphasis in original).
[34] *See, e.g.*, United States v. Elias, 269 F.3d 1003, 2001; United States v. Flanagan, 126 F. Supp. 2d 1284 (C.D. Cal. 2000).
[35] 42 U.S.C. § 6972(a)(1)(A).

452   THE RCRA PRACTICE MANUAL

health or the environment"[36] (a "Subsection B" suit). Over the past decade or so, many federal courts have considered whether their jurisdiction extended to RCRA citizen suits brought in an authorized state.

1. "Subsection A" citizen suits alleging violations of *federal* RCRA requirements in an authorized state have often been dismissed for lack of subject matter jurisdiction. Recall that under RCRA Section 3006, the authorized state program operates "in lieu of" the federal program, which has no force or effect in an authorized state.[37] Plaintiffs who allege violations of the *superseded* federal requirements generally have had no success in the federal court. Rather, they have been limited to bringing an action under state law or petitioning EPA to withdraw authorization of the state program.[38] In most states, some federal requirements (for example, HSWA-driven federal rules) remain in effect and coexist with the authorized state program. A citizen suit alleging violations of these federal requirements will likely pass jurisdictional muster in the federal court.[39]

2. "Subsection A" citizen suits alleging violations of the authorized *state* RCRA requirements have met with mixed success in the federal courts. The question here is whether RCRA's citizen suit provision can be used in the federal court to enforce *state* statutes and regulations promulgated under the state's authorized hazardous waste program. For the most part, the courts have willingly stretched their jurisdiction to encompass such citizen suits. They reason that when a state program is authorized by EPA under RCRA Section 3006, it becomes "effective pursuant to RCRA," thus making a citizen suit proper.[40] Many of these courts

---

[36]*Id.* § 6972(a)(1)(B).

[37]*Id.* § 6926(b).

[38]*See, e.g.,* Dague v. City of Burlington, 935 F.2d 1343 (2d Cir. 1991), *rev'd on other grounds sub nom.* City of Burlington v. Dague, 505 U.S. 557 (1992); Clorox Co. v. Chromium Corp., 158 F.R.D. 120 (N.D. Ill. 1994); City of Heath v. Ashland Oil, Inc., 834 F. Supp. 971 (S.D. Ohio 1993); Williamsburgh-Around-the-Bridge Block Ass'n v. N.Y. DEC, 1989 U.S. Dist. LEXIS 9961, 30 Env't Rep. Cas. (BNA) 1188 (N.D.N.Y. 1989); Thompson v. Thomas, 680 F. Supp. 1 (D.D.C. 1987). *See also* Lutz v. Chromatex, Inc., 725 F. Supp. 258 (M.D. Pa. 1989), and Sierra Club v. Chem. Handling Corp., 824 F. Supp. 195 (D. Colo. 1993).

[39]*See, e.g., City of Heath, supra* note 41, 834 F. Supp. at 979 (court willing to consider plaintiff's claims based on alleged violation of federal RCRA regulations still in effect in Ohio, an authorized state).

[40]*See, e.g.,* Long Island Soundkeeper Fund, Inc. v. N.Y. Athletic Club, 1996 U.S. Dist. LEXIS 3383, 42 Env't Rep. Cas. (BNA) 1421 (S.D.N.Y. 1996); Evco Assoc. v. C.J. Saporito Plating Co., 1995 U.S. Dist. LEXIS 13964 (N.D. Ill. 1995); Sierra Club v. Chem. Handling Corp., 824 F. Supp. 195 (D. Colo. 1993); Lutz v. Chromatex, Inc., 725 F. Supp. 258 (M.D. Pa. 1989).

have been influenced by EPA's position on the issue; EPA has expressly supported the rights of citizens to sue under RCRA Section 7002 in an authorized state.[41] When an authorized state program does not precisely match its federal counterpart, the analysis of this issue becomes a bit more complicated. As discussed above, a state program may be *more stringent than* the federal program, or it may be *broader in scope*. A state program that is more stringent than the federal program is nonetheless part of the federally approved program and, arguably, can be enforced through a citizen suit under Section 7002. A state program that is broader in scope than the federal program, however, does not become part of the federally approved program. A federal court may be unwilling to hear a citizen suit brought to enforce portions of a state program that are broader in scope than their federal counterpart.[42]

3. "Subsection B" citizen suits alleging "imminent and substantial endangerment" do not pose the jurisdictional problems faced by a Subsection A plaintiff. Subsection B "is more general, and allows a direct cause of action against those whose activities 'may present an imminent and substantial endangerment to health or the environment'. Thus, a subsection B suit does not depend on any specific [RCRA] subchapter III provision, nor is it superseded by a state program."[43]

VI. Constitutional Issues

A. Commerce Clause

The Commerce Clause grants Congress the power to regulate interstate commerce.[44] It also has a "negative" or "dormant" aspect that prohibits states from discriminating against or unduly burdening the free flow of commerce. Congress may override the so-called dormant Commerce Clause, but its intent to do so "must be unmistakably clear."[45]

---

[41]*See, e.g., Lutz, supra* note 40, 725 F. Supp. at 261 (quoting 45 Fed. Reg. 85,016, 85,020–21 (1980)).

[42]Glazer v. Am. Ecology Envtl. Serv. Corp., 894 F. Supp. 1029 (E.D. Tex. 1995) (raising, but not deciding, the issue); *cf.* Ashoff v. City of Ukiah, 130 F.3d 409 (9th Cir. 1997) (in a RCRA Subtitle D context, the court held that RCRA does not authorize citizen suits based on state standards that exceed the federal criteria; the court's articulation of its holding is unfortunate, as it appears to mix the "broader in scope" and "more stringent than" concepts).

[43]*Dague, supra* note 38, 935 F.2d at 1352–53; *accord Clorox, supra* note 38, 158 F.R.D. at 124.

[44]U.S. Const. art. I, § 8, cl. 3.

[45]South-Central Timber Dev., Inc. v. Wunnicke, 467 U.S. 82, 91 (1984).

454 THE RCRA PRACTICE MANUAL

The Commerce Clause has long been applied to the interstate flow of waste.[46] Thus, while state attempts to discriminate against out-of-state waste may be wildly popular with the local citizenry, such discrimination rarely, if ever, survives a Commerce Clause challenge.

In such challenges, courts have generally rejected state claims that RCRA authorizes the states to discriminate against out-of-state waste. In *Environmental Technology Council v. Sierra Club*,[47] for example, the State of South Carolina argued that through enacting RCRA and other environmental statutes, "Congress created a federal scheme to address the disposal of hazardous wastes which authorized the [discriminatory] state laws . . . , thus displacing the dormant Commerce Clause."[48] The court rejected this argument. It held that Congress had not "expressly contemplated or authorized" discrimination by the states when it enacted RCRA, and that South Carolina's efforts to discriminate against out-of-state hazardous waste were therefore unconstitutional.[49] Similarly, the Fifth Circuit held that a Louisiana statute barring the importation and management of hazardous waste from foreign nations violated the Commerce Clause.[50] The court noted that, far from indicating congressional intent to permit states to burden interstate commerce, "RCRA could be read to *prohibit* state hazardous-waste legislation that burdens interstate commerce."[51]

B. Supremacy Clause and Federal Preemption

Like the dormant Commerce Clause, the Supremacy Clause is often invoked by litigants attempting to invalidate state and local environmental laws. The Supremacy Clause provides that federal law is the "supreme Law of the Land";[52] a federal law will preempt state or local law when Congress intends—explicitly or implicitly—for it to do so. There are three types of preemption:

> (1) express preemption, where the [federal] statute contains "explicit pre-emptive language," (2) field preemption, "where the scheme of federal regulation is so pervasive as to make reasonable

---

[46]*See, e.g.*, Chem. Waste Mgmt., Inc. v. Hunt, 504 U.S. 334 (1992); City of Philadelphia v. New Jersey, 437 U.S. 617 (1978).

[47]98 F.3d 774 (4th Cir. 1996).

[48]*Id.* at 782.

[49]*Id.* at 784.

[50]Chem. Waste Mgmt., Inc. v. Templet, 967 F.2d 1058 (5th Cir. 1992).

[51]967 F.2d at 1059 (emphasis in original).

[52]U.S. CONST., art. VI, cl. 2.

Chapter 17: The Federal-State Relationship under RCRA   455

the inference that Congress left no room for the States to supplement it," and (3) conflict preemption, "where compliance with both federal and state regulations is a physical impossibility, or where state law stands as an obstacle to the accomplishment and execution of the full purposes and objectives of Congress."[53]

Nothing in RCRA expressly preempts state or local law. Nor is the RCRA scheme "so pervasive" as to imply that Congress intended the RCRA statute to occupy the entire field, leaving the states no room to act. On the contrary, Congress intended RCRA to establish a "viable Federal-State partnership" to carry out the regulation of solid and hazardous waste[54] and to establish a "cooperative effort" among the federal, state, and local governments.[55] RCRA also contains a "savings clause," which expressly allows states and their political subdivisions to impose requirements that are "more stringent than" the federal requirements.[56]

While RCRA does not preempt all state and local regulation of hazardous waste disposal, state requirements that conflict with federal law will be nullified. The Tenth Circuit's decision in *Blue Circle Cement, Inc. v. Board of County Commissioners*[57] provides a useful overview and analysis of this issue. After considering the relevant precedent, the court summarized its understanding of preemption analysis under RCRA:

> First, ordinances that amount to an explicit or de facto total ban of an activity that is otherwise encouraged by RCRA will ordinarily be preempted by RCRA. Second, an ordinance that falls short of imposing a total ban on encouraged activity will ordinarily be upheld so long as it is supported by a record establishing that it is a reasonable response to a legitimate local concern for safety or welfare. Significant latitude should be allowed to the state or local authority. However, if the ordinance is not addressed to a legitimate local concern, or if it is not reasonably related to that concern, then it may be regarded as a sham and nothing more than a naked attempt to sabotage federal RCRA policy of encouraging the safe and efficient disposition of hazardous waste materials.[58]

---

[53]Boyes v. Shell Oil Prod. Co., 199 F.3d 1260, 1267 (11th Cir. 2000) (*quoting* Gade v. Nat'l Solid Wastes Mgmt. Ass'n, 505 U.S. 88, 98 (1992)).

[54]42 U.S.C. § 6902(a)(7).

[55]*Id.* § 6902(a)(11).

[56]*Id.* § 6929.

[57]27 F.3d 1499 (10th Cir. 1994).

[58]27 F.3d at 1508 (footnotes and citations omitted).

456   THE RCRA PRACTICE MANUAL

Applying the appellate court's instructions upon remand of the case, the district court struck down a local ordinance, concluding that the ordinance amounted to a de facto ban on the burning of hazardous waste fuels and thus "thwart[ed] the federal policy in a material way."[59]

Preemption may also apply where a remedy approved by the federal government conflicts with the remedy sought by the state or local government or by a private party. In *Feikema v. Texaco, Inc.*,[60] for example, the plaintiff homeowners brought nuisance and trespass claims to redress petroleum contamination that had migrated onto their properties. The defendant had previously entered into an administrative consent order with EPA to remediate the problem. The court held that RCRA preempted the plaintiffs' claim for injunctive relief, because the relief requested conflicted with the remedial measures already selected and supervised by EPA pursuant to the consent order. (The homeowners' damages claims, in contrast, were not preempted by RCRA.) Similarly, the court in *People v. Teledyne, Inc.*[61] refused to order the defendant to remove certain hazardous wastes from two disposal sites. EPA had previously issued an administrative order under RCRA Section 3008(h) directing the defendant to contain and treat the waste in place, but the state and county wanted the waste removed. The court distinguished the establishment of more stringent environmental *standards*—which was protected by RCRA's savings clause—from the imposition of different *remedies*, which was not.[62]

Federal preemption is inappropriate if a state imposes requirements that, although more stringent than the federal standards, are consistent

---

[59]Blue Circle Cement, Inc. v. Bd. of County Comm'rs, 917 F. Supp. 1514, 1520 (N.D. Okla. 1995) [*quoting Blue Circle Cement, Inc.*, 27 F.3d at 1509]; *see also Boyes, supra note 53,*199 F.3d at 1260 (unapproved state underground storage tank program is preempted to the extent it conflicts with federal program); ENSCO, Inc. v. Dumas, 807 F.2d 743 (8th Cir. 1986) (county ordinance that prohibited the storage, treatment, or disposal of acute hazardous waste within county boundaries "subvert[ed]" federal policies regarding the management of hazardous waste and was preempted); Ogden Envtl. Servs. v. San Diego, 687 F. Supp. 1436 (S.D. Cal. 1988) (city's denial of conditional use permit was preempted because it was based on generalized environmental or health and safety concerns that had already been evaluated, and found acceptable, by EPA); City of Jacksonville v. Arkansas DPCE, 824 S.W.2d 840 (Ark. 1992) (local ordinances prohibiting transportation of waste directly conflict with and frustrate the purpose of RCRA and are preempted).

[60]16 F.3d 1408 (4th Cir. 1994).

[61]599 N.E.2d 472 (Ill. App. Ct. 1992).

[62]599 N.E.2d at 477. *Accord* Hermes Consol. Inc. v. Wyoming, 849 P.2d 1302 (Wyo. 1993).

with RCRA. As the Third Circuit has noted, "RCRA sets a floor, not a ceiling, for state regulation of hazardous wastes."[63]

VII. Conclusion

RCRA has a well-deserved reputation as one of the most arcane of the federal environmental programs. The standards governing the treatment, storage and disposal of hazardous waste are complex and can provoke hours of debate even among seasoned practitioners. Overlying these substantive issues, however, is the intricate state-federal "partnership" that was devised to develop and implement RCRA's regulatory scheme. This is one of the recurring themes in RCRA, and it regularly finds its way into the courts. Litigants and the regulated community alike would be well advised to remain alert to state-federal issues.

---

[63]Old Bridge Chems. Inc. v. N.J. DEP, 965 F.2d 1287, 1296 (3d Cir. 1992). *See, e.g.,* N. Haven Planning & Zoning Comm'n v. Upjohn Co., 753 F. Supp. 423, 431 (D. Conn. 1990), (upholding a local zoning ordinance in the face of a preemption challenge, and noting that "this would seem to be the exact sort of site selection process, or application of more stringent standards, envisioned by the savings clause"), *aff'd,* 921 F.2d 27 (2d Cir. 1990) Lafarge Corp. v. Campbell, 813 F. Supp. 501 (W.D. Tex. 1993) (upholding state siting statute and dismissing federal preemption challenge because state statute did not result in an absolute prohibition of a type of technology or prohibit importation of hazardous waste).

TABLE OF CASES

Adamo Wrecking Co. v. United States, 434 U.S. 275 (1978), 435n.12

Am. Chemistry Council v. EPA, 337 F.3d 1060 (D.C. Cir. 2003), 56n.10

Am. Iron & Steel Inst. v. EPA, 886 F.2d 390 (D.C. Cir. 1989), *cert. denied sub nom.* Am. Mining Cong. v. EPA, 497 U.S. 1003 (1990), 333n.38, 396n.90

Am. Mining Cong. v. Envtl. Def. Fund, 489 U.S. 1011 (1989), 383n.13, 396n.88

Am. Mining Cong. v. EPA, 497 U.S. 1003 (1990), 333n.38, 396n.90

Am. Mining Cong. v. EPA, 824 F.2d 1177 (D.C. Cir. 1987), 3n.10, 418n.1

Am. Mining Cong. v. EPA (AMC I), 824 F.2d 1177 (D.C. Cir. 1987), 39, 39n.26, 323, 323n.7

Am. Mining Cong. v. EPA (AMC II), 907 F.2d 1179 (D.C. Cir. 1990), 3n.10, 39, 39n.28

Am. Petroleum Inst. v. EPA, 216 F.3d 50 (D.C. Cir. 2000), 3n.10, 40n.30

Am. Petroleum Inst. v. EPA, 906 F.2d 729 (D.C. Cir. 1990), 39, 39n.27

API v. EPA, 906 F.2d 726, (D.C. Cir. 1990), 290n.2

Ashoff v. City of Ukiah, 130 F.3d 409 (9th Cir. 1997), 453n.42

Ass'n of Battery Recyclers v. EPA, 208 F.3d 1047 (D.C. Cir. 2000), 3n.10, 40, 40n.29, 317n.61

Atl. Coast Demolition & Recycling, Inc. v. Bd. of Chosen Freeholders of Atl. County, 112 F.3d 652 (3d Cir. 1997), *cert. denied sub nom.* Essex County Utils. Auth. v. Atl. Coast Demolition & Recycling, 522 U.S. 966 (1997), 408n.153

Ben Oehrleins & Sons & Daughters, Inc. v. Hennepin County, 115 F.3d 1372 (8th Cir.), *cert. denied,* 522 U.S. 1029 (1997), 408n.152

Blue Circle Cement, Inc. v. Bd. of County Comm'rs, 27 F.3d 1499 (10th Cir. 1994), 455, 455n.47, 455n.58

Blue Circle Cement, Inc. v. Bd. of County Comm'rs, 917 F. Supp. 1514 (N.D. Okla. 1995), 456n.59

Blue Legs v. Bureau of Indian Affairs, 867 F.2d 1094 (8th Cir. 1989), 314n.178, 385n.19, 414n.188, 415n.191

Boyes v. Shell Oil Prod. Co., 199 F.3d 1260 (11th Cir. 2000), 455n.53

C & A Carbone, Inc. v. Town of Clarkstown, N.Y., 511 U.S. 383 (1994), 119n.79, 406–407, 406n.142

Chem. Mfrs. Ass'n v. EPA, 673 F.2d 507 (D.C. Cir. 1982), 383n.13

Chem. Mfrs. Ass'n v. EPA, 869 F.2d 1526 (D.C. Cir. 1989), 310n.23

Chem. Waste Mgmt., Inc. v. EPA, 976 F.2d (D.C. Cir. 1992), *cert. denied,* 113 S. Ct. 1961 (1993), 19, 19n.23, 20, 20n.24, 20n.25, 23, 24n.51, 24n.52, 295n.29

460 TABLE OF CASES

Chem. Waste Mgmt., Inc. v. Hunt, 504 U.S. 334 (1992), 119n.78, 454n.46

Chem. Waste Mgmt., Inc. v. Templet, 967 F.2d 1057 (5th Cir. 1992), 454n.50

Chem. Waste Mgmt. v. Armstrong World Indus., 669 F. Supp. 1285 (E.D. Pa. 1987), 29n.75

Chem. Waste Mgmt. v. EPA, 869 F.2d 1526 (D.C. Cir. 1989), 302, 302n.59

Chem. Waste Mgmt. v. EPA, 976 F.2d 2 (D.C. Cir. 1992), *cert. denied*, 61 U.S.L.W. 3731 (1993), 293n.22, 305, 305n.1, 314

Chem. Waste Mgmt. v. EPA, 976 F.2d 14 (D.C. Cir. 1992), 9n.62, 297, 297n.37

Chem. Waste Mgmt. v. EPA, 976 F.2d 23 (D.C. Cir. 1992), 293n.23

Ciba-Geigy Corp. v. Sidamon-Eristoff, 3 F.3d 40 (2d Cir. 1993), 134n.24

City of Burlington v. Dague, 505 U.S. 557 (1992), 452n.38

City of Chicago v. Envtl. Def. Fund, Inc., 511 U.S. 328 (1994), 401, 401n.116

City of Gallitin v. Cherokee County, 563 F. Supp. 940 (E.D. Tex. 1983), 415n.189

City of Heath v. Ashland Oil, Inc., 834 F. Supp. 971 (S.D. Ohio 1993), 452n.38

City of Jacksonville v. Arkansas DPCE, 824 S.W.2d 840 (Ark. 1992), 456n.59

City of Philadelphia v. New Jersey, 437 U.S. 617 (1978), 405–406, 405n.141, 454n.46

Clason v. Indiana, 306 U.S. 439 (1939), 119n.77

Clorox Co. v. Chromium Corp., 158 F.R.D. 120 (N.D. Ill. 1994), 452n.38

Colorado Pub. Utils. Comm'n v. Harmon, 951 F.2d 1571 (10th Cir. 1991), 118n.70

Columbia Falls Aluminum v. EPA, 139 F.3d 914 (D.C. Cir. 1998), 311n.30, 312, 312n.32

Dague v. City of Burlington, 732 F. Supp. 458 (D. Vt. 1989), *aff'd*, 935 F.2d 1343 (2d Cir. 1991), 414n.188

Dague v. City of Burlington, 935 F.2d 1343 (2d Cir. 1991), *rev'd on other grounds sub nom.* City of Burlington v. Dague, 505 U.S. (1992), 452n.38

Edison Elec. Inst. v. EPA, 996 F.2d 326 (D.C. Cir. 1993), 293n.21, 431n.7

Ensco, Inc. v. Dumas, 807 F.2d 743 (8th Cir. 1986), 116n.59, 456n.59

Envtl. Def. Fund v. EPA (EDF I), 852 F.2d 1309 (D.C. Cir. 1988), *cert. denied sub nom.* Am. Mining Cong. v. Envtl. Def. Fund, 489 U.S. 1011 (1989), 383n.13, 396n.88

Envtl. Def. Fund v. EPA (EDF II), 852 F.2d 1316 (D.C. Cir. 1988), *cert. denied sub nom.* Am. Mining Cong. v. Envtl. Def. Fund, 489 U.S. 1011 (1989), 383n.13, 396n.88

Envtl. Def. Fund v. EPA, No. 93-1316 (D.C. Cir.), 339, 339n.50

Envtl. Def. Fund v. Lamphier, 714 F.2d 331 (4th Cir. 1990), 129n.18

Envtl. Def. Fund v. Wheelabrator Techs., Inc., 931 F.2d 211 (2d Cir.), *cert. denied*, 112 S. Ct. 453 (1991), 401n.115

Envtl. Tech. Council v. Sierra Club, 98 F.3d 774 (4th Cir. 1996), 454, 454n.47, 454n.48, 454n.49

EPA v. Envtl. Waste Control, Inc., 917 F.2d 327 (7th Cir. 1990), 432n.10

Essex County Utils. Auth. v. Atl. Coast Demolition & Recycling, 522 U.S. 966 (1997), 408n.153

Evco. Assoc. v. C.J. Saporito Plating Co., 1995 U.S. Dist. LEXIS 13964 (N.D. Ill. 1995), 452n.40

Evergreen Waste Sys. v. Metro. Serv. Dist., 820 F.2d 1482 (9th Cir. 1987), 120n.81

Table of Cases 461

Feikema v. Texaco., Inc., 16 F.3d 1408 (4th Cir. 1994), 456, 456n.60

Fishel v. Westinghouse Elec. Corp., 617 F. Supp. 1531 (M.D. Pa. 1985), *later proceeding,* 640 F. Supp. 442 (M.D. Pa. 1986), 414n.188

Fort Gratiot Sanitary Landfill v. Michigan, 504 U.S. 353 (1992), 405–406, 405n.140, 406n.144

Gade v. Nat'l Solid Wastes Mgmt. Ass'n, 505 U.S. 88 (1992), 455n.53

Gary D. Peake Excavating, Inc. v. Town Bd. of the Town of Hancock, N.Y., 93 F.3d 68 (2d Cir. 1996), 408n.148

Glazer v. Am. Ecology Envtl. Serv. Corp., 894 F. Supp. 1029 (E.D. Tex. 1995), 453n.42

Goldendale Aluminum Co. v. Reynolds Metals Corp., 1997 U.S. Dist. LEXIS 21709 (W.D. Ark. 1997), 438n.14

Greenpeace v. Waste Techs. Indus., 1993 W.L. 128,732 (N.D. Ohio 1993), 236, 236n.24, 236n.25, 236n.26

H.P. Hood & Sons, Inc. v. DuMond, 336 U.S. 525 (1949), 119n.75

Hallstrom v. Tillamook County, 493 U.S. 20 (1989), 439n.15

Hardage v. Atkins, 582 F.2d 1264 (10th Cir. 1978), 119n.76

Harmon Indus., Inc. v. Browner, 191 F.3d 894 (8th Cir. 1999), 422–423, 423n.4, 450, 450n.24, 450n.25

Harvey & Harvey, Inc. v. County of Chester, 68 F.3d 788 (3d Cir. 1995), *cert. denied sub nom.* Tri-County Indus. v. Mercer County, 516 U.S. 117 (1996), 408n.153

Hazardous Waste Treatment Council v. EPA, 861 F.2d 270 (D.C. Cir. 1988), *cert. denied,* 490 U.S. 1106 (1989), 410n.164

Hazardous Waste Treatment Council v. EPA, 886 F.2d 355 (D.C. Cir. 1989), *cert. denied,* 61 U.S.L.W. 3731 (1993), 293, 293n.22, 295n.31

Hazardous Waste Treatment Council v. Reilly, 938 F.2d 1390 (D.C. Cir. 1991), 447, 447n.17, 447n.18

Hermes Consol. Inc. v. Wyoming, 849 P.2d 1302 (Wyo. 1993), 456n.62

Horsehead Res. Dev. Co. v. EPA, 16 F.3d 1246 (D.C. Cir. 1994), 308n.13

Horsehead Res. Dev. Co. v. EPA, 16 F.3d 1246 (1994), *cert. denied,* (U.S.) 115 S. Ct. 72 (1994), 248, 248n.45

Houlton Citizens' Coalition v. Town of Houlton, 175 F.3d 178 (1st Cir. 1999), 120n.81

Huish Detergents, Inc. v. Warren County, Ky., 214 F.3d 707 (6th Cir. 2000), 608n.151

In re Wheland Foundry, 1993 W.L. 426,029 (EPA), 248, 248n.44

Inland Steel Co. v. EPA, 901 F.2d 1419 (7th Cir. 1990), 333n.38

Jones v. Inmont Corp., 584 F. Supp. 1425 (S.D. Ohio 1984), 388n.37, 416n.190

La. Envtl. Action Network v. EPA, 172 F.3d 65 (D.C. Cir. 1999), 313n.39

Lafarge Corp. v. Campbell, 813 F. Supp. 501 (W.D. Tex. 1993), 457n.63

Long Island Soundkeeper Fund., Inc. v. N.Y. Athletic Club, 1996 U.S. Dist. LEXIS 3383 (S.D.N.Y. 1996), 452n.40

462   TABLE OF CASES

Louisiana-Pacific Corp. v. Asarco, Inc., 6 F.3d 1332 (9th Cir. 1993), 248, 248n.43
Lutz v. Chromatex, Inc., 718 F. Supp. 413 (M.D. Pa. 1989), 414n.188
Lutz v. Chromatex, Inc., 725 F. Supp. 258 (M.D. Pa. 1989), 452n.38, 452n.40

Mardan Corp. v. CGC Music, Ltd., 600 F. Supp. 1049 (D. Ariz. 1984), *aff'd*, 804 F.2d 1454 (9th Cir. 1986), 29n.75
Marine Shale Processors, Inc. v. EPA, 81 F.3d 1371 (5th Cir. 1996), 38n.25
Meghrig v. KFC Western, Inc., 516 U.S. 479 (1996), 378, 441n.16
Middlesex County Bd. of Chosen Freeholders v. NJDEP, 645 F. Supp. 715 (D.N.J. 1986), 414n.186
Mobil Oil Corp. v. EPA, 871 F.2d 149 (D.C. Cir. 1989), 325n.18

N. Haven Planning & Zoning Comm'n v. Upjohn Co., 753 F. Supp. 423 (D. Conn. 1990), 457n.63
Nat'l Recycling Coalition, Inc. v. Browner, 984 F.2d 1243 (D.C. Cir. 1993), 404, 404n.136
Nat'l Recycling Coalition, Inc. v. Reilly, 884 F.2d 1431, *reh. en banc denied*, 890 F.2d 1241 (D.C. Cir. 1989), 403n.128, 404n.135
Nat'l Solid Waste Mgmt. Ass'n v. Williams, 146 F.3d 595 (8th Cir.), *cert. denied*, 525 U.S. 1012 (1998), 408n.150
Nat'l Solid Waste Mgmt. Assoc. v. Ala. Dept. of Envtl. Mgmt., 729 F. Supp. 792 (N.D. Ala.), *vacated*, 910 F.2d 713 (11th Cir. 1990), *modified*, 942 F.2d 1001 (11th Cir.), *cert. denied*, 111 S. Ct. 2800 (1991), 116n.59, 119n.76
New York *ex rel.* Dep't of Envtl. Conservation v. U.S. Dep't of Transp., 37 F. Supp. 2d 152 (N.D.N.Y. 1999), 118n.71
Northside Sanitary Landfill, Inc. v. Thomas, 804 F.2d 371 (7th Cir. 1986), 444n.4
NRDC v. EPA, 907 F.2d 1146 (D.C. Cir. 1990), 299–300, 300n.49

Ogden Envtl. Servs. v. San Diego, 687 F. Supp. 1436 (S.D. Cal. 1988), 456n.59
Old Bridge Chems. Inc. v. N.J. DEP, 965 F.2d 1287 (3d Cir. 1992), 457n.63
O'Leary v. Moyer's Landfill, Inc., 523 F. Supp. 642 (E.D. Pa. 1981), 388n.40, 414n.186
Or. Waste Sys., Inc. v. Dep't of Envtl. Quality, 511 U.S. 93 (1994), 119n.79

Palumbo v. Waste Techs. Indus., 989 F.2d 156 (4th Cir. 1993), 236, 236n.27
People v. Teledyne, Inc., 599 N.E.2d 472 (Ill. App. Ct. 1992), 456, 456n.61, 456n.62
Philadelphia v. New Jersey, 437 U.S. 617 (1978), 116, 116n.58, 118n.73, 119, 120n.84
Pike v. Bruce Church, Inc., 397 U.S. 137 (1970), 120, 120n.82, 120n.83, 408n.151

Red River Serv. Corp. v. City of Minot, N.D., 146 F.3d 583 (8th Cir. 1998), 408n.149
Reeves v. Stake, 447 U.S. 383 (1980), 407n.147
Ringbolt Farms Homeowners Ass'n v. Town of Hull, 714 F. Supp. 1246 (D. Mass. 1989), 414n.181
Rollins Envtl. Servs., Inc. v. EPA, 937 F.2d 649 (D.C. Cir. 1991), 221, 221n.8
Rollins Envtl. Servs., Inc. v. Iberville Parish Police Jury, 371 So. 2d 1127 (La. 1979), 116n.59

Table of Cases   463

Sal Tinnerello & Sons, Inc. v. Town of Stonington, 141 F.3d 46 (2d Cir. 2001), *cert. denied*, 525 U.S. 923 (1998), 408n.151

Shell Oil Co. v. EPA, 950 F.2d 741 (D.C. Cir. 1991), 4, 4n.23, 54, 54n.6, 431, 431n.8

Shillman v. United States, 2000 U.S. App. LEXIS 15800 (6th Cir. 2000), 428n.6

Sierra Club v. Chem. Handling Corp., 824 F. Supp. 195 (D. Colo. 1993), 452n.38, 452n.40

Sierra Club v. EPA, 992 F.2d 337 (D.C. Cir. 1993), 389n.44, 394n.80

Sierra Club v. EPA, No. 01-1057 (D.C. Cir.), 309n.15

Solite Corp. v. EPA, 952 F.2d 473 (D.C. Cir. 1991), 397n.94

South-Central Timber Dev., Inc. v. Wunnicke, 467 U.S. 82 (1984), 406n.143, 453n.45

Thompson v. Thomas, 680 F. Supp. 1 (D.D.C. 1987), 413n.178, 452n.38

Tri-County Indus. v. Mercer County, 516 U.S. 117 (1996), 408n.153

U & I Sanitation v. City of Columbus, 205 F.3d 1063 (8th Cir. 2000), 119n.80

United Haulers Ass'n v. Oneida-Herkimer Solid Waste Mgmt. Auth., 261 F.3d 245 (2d Cir. 2001), *cert. denied*, 122 S. Ct. 815 (2002), 408n.151

United States v. Colorado, 990 F.2d 1565 (10th Cir. 1993), 28n.72

United States v. Conservation Chem. Co., 660 F. Supp. 1236 (N.D. Ind. 1987), 449n.22

United States v. Elias, 269 F.3d 1003 (9th Cir. 2001), 423n.5, 451n.34

United States v. Flanagan, 126 F. Supp. 2d 1284 (C.D. Cal. 2000), 451n.34

United States v. Goodner Bros. Aircraft, 966 F.2d 380 (8th Cir. 1992), 431n.9

United States v. MacDonald & Watson Waste Oil Co., 933 F.2d 35 (1st Cir. 1991), 451, 451n.31, 451n.32, 451n.33

United States v. Murphy Oil USA, Inc., 143 F. Supp. 2d 1054 (W.D. Wis. 2001), 430n.28

United States v. Ownbey Enters., Inc., 789 F. Supp. 1145 (N.D. Ga. 1992), 377n.182

United States v. Power Eng'g Co., 303 F.3d 1232 (10th Cir. 2002), 430, 430n.27

United States v. Rockwell Int's Corp., 924 F.2d 928 (9th Cir. 1991), 436n.13

United States v. Rohm & Haas Co., No. 92-1517 (3d Cir. 1993), 29n.75

United Techs. Corp., Pratt & Whitney Group v. EPA, 821 F.2d 714 (D.C. Cir. 1987), 10n.71, 333n.37

United Waste Sys. v. Wilson, 189 F.3d 762 (8th Cir. 1999), 408n.152

Waste Mgmt. v. Metro. Gov't, 130 F.3d 731 (6th Cir. 1997), *cert. denied*, 523 U.S. 1094 (1998), 409n.154

Williams v. Allied Auto, Autolite Div., 704 F. Supp. 782 (N.D. Ohio 1988), 414n.188

Williamsburgh-Around-the-Bridge Block Ass'n v. N.Y. DEC, 1989 U.S. Dist. LEXIS 9961 (N.D.N.Y. 1989), 452n.38

Wyckoff Co. v. EPA, 796 F.2d 1197 (9th Cir. 1986), 449n.22

Zands v. Nelson, 797 F. Supp. 805 (S.D. Cal. 1992), 378, 378n.186

TABLE OF STATUTES

Pub. L. No. 93-633, tit. I, 88 Stat. 2156 (1975), 111n.40

Pub. L. No. 94-580, 90 Stat. 2395, 1n.3

Pub. L. No. 96-463, 94 Stat. 2055 (1980), 409n.155

Pub. L. No. 96-482, § 32(f), 94 Stat. 2355, 407n.146

Pub. L. No. 98-616, 1984 U.S.C.C.A.N. (98 Stat.) 3221, 346n.2

Pub. L. No. 98-616, 98 Stat. 3221, 2n.6

Pub. L. No. 99-499, 1986 U.S.C.C.A.N. (100 Stat.) 2835, 347n.10

Pub. L. No. 99-499, tit. II, § 205(k), 100 Stat. 1703 (1986), 410n.162, 415n.193

Pub. L. No. 103-62, 107 Stat. 285 (1993), 336n.44

5 U.S.C. § 558(c), 142n.37

7 U.S.C. § 136 et seq., 17n.10

15 U.S.C. § 2601 et seq., 16n.5, 129n.16

15 U.S.C. § 2604, 24n.54

15 U.S.C. § 2605(e), 24n.57

15 U.S.C. § 2607, 24n.56

15 U.S.C. § 2612, 24n.55

30 U.S.C. §§ 1201–1328, 382n.12, 397n.101

33 U.S.C. § 257.3–.4, 392n.58

33 U.S.C. § 257.3–.8, 392n.69

33 U.S.C. § 258.1, 392n.61

33 U.S.C. § 258.1(d), 392n.62

33 U.S.C. § 258.1(f), 392n.64

33 U.S.C. § 258.1(j), 392n.60

33 U.S.C. § 261.4(a)(6), (9), 382n.10

33 U.S.C. § 261.4(a)(12), 382n.9

33 U.S.C. § 261.4(a)(13)–(14), 382n.8

33 U.S.C. § 261.4(a)(17), 382n.7

33 U.S.C. § 1251 et seq., 15n.1

33 U.S.C. §§ 1251–1387, 382n.11

33 U.S.C. § 1288, 386n.32, 392n.57

33 U.S.C. §§ 1319, 1345(e), 392n.65

33 U.S.C. § 1342, 382n.6

33 U.S.C. § 1345, 12n.90, 391n.50, 412n.174

33 U.S.C. § 1401 et seq., 17n.9

42 U.S.C. § 300(f) et seq., 16n.4, 390n.47

42 U.S.C. § 6901 et. seq., 1n.1, 1n.2

42 U.S.C. § 6901(a)(4), 444n.1

42 U.S.C. § 6902(a)(7), 444n.2, 455n.54

42 U.S.C. § 6902(a)(10), (11), 399n.106

42 U.S.C. § 6902(a)(11), 455n.55

42 U.S.C. § 6903(13), 414n.185

42 U.S.C. § 6903(15), 414n.184

42 U.S.C. § 6903(22), (23), (24), 399n.108

42 U.S.C. § 6903(27), 2n.7, 16n.3, 17n.12, 20n.28, 33n.1, 34n.4

42 U.S.C. § 6904(b), 387n.34

42 U.S.C. § 6905(b), 16n.8

42 U.S.C. § 6921(b), 3n.13

42 U.S.C. § 6921(b)(2), (3), 3n.18

42 U.S.C. §§ 6921(b)(2)(A), 6982(m), 396n.89

42 U.S.C. § 6921(b)(3), 383n.13

42 U.S.C. § 6921(d), 4n.27

42 U.S.C. § 6921(f), 4n.20

42 U.S.C. § 6921(i), 401n.113

42 U.S.C. § 6922(a), 5n.33

42 U.S.C. § 6922(b), 5n.32

466 TABLE OF STATUTES

42 U.S.C. § 6924(a), 6n.42, 21n.30, 161n.1
42 U.S.C. § 6924(a)(1)–(7), 161n.2
42 U.S.C. § 6924(d), (e)(1), (g)(5), 8n.60
42 U.S.C. § 6924(g)(7), 306n.4
42 U.S.C. § 6924(h)(2), 9n.63
42 U.S.C. § 6924(k), 23n.44
42 U.S.C. § 6924(m)(1), 19n.20
42 U.S.C. § 6924(m), (o), 8n.61
42 U.S.C. § 6924(n), 21n.31
42 U.S.C. §§ 6924(o), 6925(j), 8n.57
42 U.S.C. § 6924(o)(1), 256n.2
42 U.S.C. § 6924(o)(2), 256n.4
42 U.S.C. § 6924(o)(3), 257n.9
42 U.S.C. § 6924(q)(1), 8n.56
42 U.S.C. § 6924(u), 9n.68, 133n.23, 320n.2
42 U.S.C. § 6924(v), 9n.69, 320n.3
42 U.S.C. § 6925, 6n.30, 125n.1, 143n.43
42 U.S.C. § 6925(a), 129n.17
42 U.S.C. § 6925(c), 136n.26, 144n.48
42 U.S.C. § 6925(c)(3), 142n.36
42 U.S.C. § 6925(e), 6n.40, 163n.11
42 U.S.C. § 6925(j)(1), 256n.3
42 U.S.C. § 6925(j)(2), 256n.6
42 U.S.C. § 6925(j)(3), 256n.7
42 U.S.C. § 6925(j)(4), 256
42 U.S.C. § 6925(j)(6)(B), 257n.8
42 U.S.C. § 6925(j)(11), 9n.64
42 U.S.C. § 6925(j)(11)(B), 271n.50
42 U.S.C. § 6926(b), 6n.41, 444n.3, 444n.4, 445n.7, 452n.37
42 U.S.C. § 6926(c), 144n.49
42 U.S.C. § 6926(c)(1), 445n.6
42 U.S.C. § 6926(e), 444n.5, 447n.16, 450n.26
42 U.S.C. §§ 6927–6928, 413n.180
42 U.S.C. § 6928, 410n.161
42 U.S.C. § 6928(a)(1), 449n.20
42 U.S.C. § 6928(a)(2), 449n.21
42 U.S.C. § 6928(d), 70n.50, 451
42 U.S.C. § 6928(h), 9n.70, 320n.4
42 U.S.C. § 6929, 445n.8, 455n.56

42 U.S.C. § 6935, 411n.170
42 U.S.C. § 6935(a), 410n.156
42 U.S.C. § 6935(b), 410n.157
42 U.S.C. § 6935(c), 410n.158
42 U.S.C. § 6935(c)–(d), 410n.159
42 U.S.C. § 6938, 85n.129
42 U.S.C. § 6939b(a), 23n.45
42 U.S.C. § 6941, 384n.17
42 U.S.C. § 6941(a), 399n.107
42 U.S.C. §§ 6941–6942, 384n.18
42 U.S.C. §§ 6941–6949a, 381
42 U.S.C. § 6942(c), 387n.36
42 U.S.C. § 6943, 12n.82
42 U.S.C. § 6943(a)(2), (3), 386n.26
42 U.S.C. § 6943(a)(4), 386n.27
42 U.S.C. § 6943(a)(5), 386n.28, 400n.110, 407n.145
42 U.S.C. § 6943(c), 386n.30, 400n.111
42 U.S.C. § 6943(d), 400n.112
42 U.S.C. § 6945(a), 12n.84
42 U.S.C. § 6945(c)(2)(a), 413n.180
42 U.S.C. § 6946(a), 386n.29
42 U.S.C. § 6946(b)(1), 386n.33
42 U.S.C. § 6948, 400n.111
42 U.S.C. § 6949(a), 12n.85
42 U.S.C. § 6949a(c), 389n.41, 392n.63
42 U.S.C. § 6962(a), 402n.122
42 U.S.C. § 6962(c), 402n.121, 402n.123
42 U.S.C. § 6962(c)(3), 405n.124, 405n.125
42 U.S.C. § 6962(d), 405n.126
42 U.S.C. § 6962(e), 402n.120
42 U.S.C. § 6962(e)(2), 403n.130
42 U.S.C. § 6962(h), 402n.119
42 U.S.C. § 6962(i), 403n.127
42 U.S.C. § 6972, 414n.183
42 U.S.C. § 6972(a)(1)(A), 451n.35
42 U.S.C. § 6972(a)(1)(B), 452n.36
42 U.S.C. § 6973, 9n.67
42 U.S.C. § 6976, 29n.74
42 U.S.C. § 6991, 11n.76
42 U.S.C. § 6991(1), 11n.77, 11n.81, 346n.3, 346n.4, 347n.6
42 U.S.C. § 6991(2), 346n.5
42 U.S.C. § 6991(a)(2), 11n.79

Table of Statutes 467

42 U.S.C. § 6991(b), 11n.80
42 U.S.C. § 6991b(a), 347n.7, 350n.26, 350n.30
42 U.S.C. § 6991b(b), 350n.27
42 U.S.C. § 6991b(c)(6), 347n.11, 372n.154
42 U.S.C. § 6991b(d), 347n.9
42 U.S.C. § 6991b(d)(1), 366n.116, 367n.119
42 U.S.C. § 6991b(d)(5)(A), 363n.102
42 U.S.C. § 6991b(d)(5)(B), 364n.104
42 U.S.C. § 6991b(e), 347n.8
42 U.S.C. § 6991b(h), 371n.151
42 U.S.C. § 6991b(h)(2), 372n.153
42 U.S.C. § 6991b(h)(5), 372n.152
42 U.S.C. § 6991c, 348n.18
42 U.S.C. § 6991c(c)(1), 367n.126
42 U.S.C. § 6991e, 348n.12, 375n.167
42 U.S.C. § 6991e(a), 348n.13, 348n.15, 375n.168
42 U.S.C. § 6991e(a)(1), 376n.170
42 U.S.C. § 6991e(a)(3), 376n.171
42 U.S.C. § 6991e(d), 375n.169
42 U.S.C. § 6991e(d)(1), 348n.16, 376n.172

42 U.S.C. § 6991e(d)(2), 348n.14
42 U.S.C. § 6992 *et seq.*, 12n.87
42 U.S.C. §§ 6992–6992k, 413n.176
42 U.S.C. § 6992(a), 413n.177
42 U.S.C. § 7401 *et seq.*, 15n.2
42 U.S.C. § 7412(n)(7) (West Supp. 1990), 20n.27
42 U.S.C. § 9601 *et seq.*, 16n.7, 76n.87, 319n.1
42 U.S.C. § 9601(14), 26n.66, 378n.190
42 U.S.C. § 9621(d), 342n.56
42 U.S.C. § 11,001 *et seq.*, 231n.17
42 U.S.C.A. § 6921(3)(A), 247n.40
42 U.S.C.A § 6923, 110n.37
42 U.S.C.A. § 6923(b), 104n.2

49 U.S.C. § 1801 *et. seq.*, 6n.38, 16n.6
49 U.S.C. § 5125(a), 116n.60
49 U.S.C.A. § 1804, 1811(a), 118
49 U.S.C.A. § 5101 *et seq.*, 111n.38
49 U.S.C.A. § 5103(a), 111n.39
49 U.S.C.A. § 5125(e), 116n.61

TABLE OF REGULATIONS

Code of Federal Regulations

10 C.F.R. pt. 50, app. A, 350

29 C.F.R. pt. 1910, subpt. H, 62, 67

40 C.F.R. § 19.4 (2002), 376n.174
40 C.F.R. § 19.4, tbl. 1, 348n.17
40 C.F.R. §§ 24.18–.20, 327n.23
40 C.F.R. § 124.19, 134, 141
40 C.F.R. § 124.71–.91, 134
40 C.F.R. § 144.14, 23n.47, 162n.5
40 C.F.R. § 148.1(d), 23n.49
40 C.F.R. § 148.20, 299
40 C.F.R. § 164.112(b), 185n.9
40 C.F.R. § 171.1, 112n.43
40 C.F.R. § 171.15, 112
40 C.F.R. § 252.53, 106
40 C.F.R. § 252.81(k), 107n.19
40 C.F.R. §§ 255.10–.11, 386n.31
40 C.F.R. § 256.01(a), 387n.35
40 C.F.R. § 257.1, 390n.48
40 C.F.R. § 257.1(c)(2), 397n.96
40 C.F.R. §§ 257.21–.28, 395n.85
40 C.F.R. § 257.21(b), 395n.86
40 C.F.R. §§ 257.3-1 to -8, 391n.52
40 C.F.R. § 257.3-3, 391n.53, 392n.57
40 C.F.R. § 257.3-5, 391n.55
40 C.F.R. § 257.3-6, 391n.54, 391n.56
40 C.F.R. § 257.5(a), 391n.51, 395n.82
40 C.F.R. § 257.8, 395n.83
40 C.F.R. § 257.9, 395n.84
40 C.F.R. § 258.1(i), 392n.65
40 C.F.R. §§ 258.10–.16, 393n.72
40 C.F.R. § 258.12, 393n.67
40 C.F.R. § 258.13, 393n.68
40 C.F.R. § 258.14, 393n.69
40 C.F.R. §§ 258.20–.29, 394n.75
40 C.F.R. § 258.29, 394n.78

40 C.F.R. § 258.29(b), 394n.79
40 C.F.R. § 258.30, 395n.87
40 C.F.R. § 258.40, 383n.73, 393n.66
40 C.F.R. §§ 258.50–.58, 383n.74
40 C.F.R. § 258.50(b), 383n.71
40 C.F.R. § 258.51(c)(1), 393n.79
40 C.F.R. §§ 258.60–.61, 394n.76
40 C.F.R. §§ 258.70–.74, 394n.77
40 C.F.R. §§ 260–281 (1993), 2n.5
40 C.F.R. § 260.10, 11n.75, 19n.19,
    37n.19, 62n.4, 63n.5, 65n.17, 128,
    184n.4, 184n.5, 218, 220n.4, 222n.9,
    224, 232n.18, 232n.19, 232n.20, 240,
    241, 241n.32, 241n.33, 270n.43,
    275n.70, 279n.90, 283n.105, 325n.17
40 C.F.R. § 260.20, 4n.20
40 C.F.R. § 260.22, 4n.20, 22n.42, 48
40 C.F.R. § 260.32, 241
40 C.F.R. §§ 261–265, 268, 270, 220
40 C.F.R. § 261, subpt. D, 64
40 C.F.R. § 261.1(c)(3), 37n.17
40 C.F.R. § 261.2, 3n.9, 64, 323n.6, 382
40 C.F.R. § 261.2(a)(2), 34n.5
40 C.F.R. § 261.2(a)(2)(ii), 35n.10
40 C.F.R. § 261.2(b), 34n.7
40 C.F.R. § 261.2(c)(4), 261.1(c)(8),
    261.2(c), tbl. 1, 38n.24
40 C.F.R. § 261.2(c), tbl. 1, 37n.15,
    37n.16, 37n.18, 37n.20
40 C.F.R. § 261.2(c)–(e), 38n.23
40 C.F.R. § 261.2(d), 34n.6
40 C.F.R. § 261.2(e), 3n.12, 38n.22,
    64n.14
40 C.F.R. § 261.2(f), 35n.11
40 C.F.R. § 261.3, 64, 55
40 C.F.R. § 261.3(a)(2)(iv), 4n.21, 52
40 C.F.R. § 261.3(c)(2), 22n.43, 401n.114

40 C.F.R. § 261.3(c)(2)(i),52

40 C.F.R. § 261.3(c), (d), (f), 83

40 C.F.R. § 261.3(d)(1), 296n.36

40 C.F.R. § 261.3(f)(2), 311n.27

40 C.F.R. § 261.3(g)(1), 55

40 C.F.R. § 261.4, 3n.9, 64, 83, 128

40 C.F.R. § 261.4(a), 41n.33, 41n.34, 382

40 C.F.R. § 261.4(a)(1), 3n.11, 297

40 C.F.R. § 261.4(a)(1)(i), (4), 41n.32

40 C.F.R. § 261.4(a)(1)(ii), 17n.13

40 C.F.R. § 261.4(a)(1)(ii), (2), 41n.31

40 C.F.R. § 261.4(a)(2) comment, 18n.15

40 C.F.R. § 261.4(a)(8), 3n.12, 37

40 C.F.R. § 261.4(b), 383

40 C.F.R. § 261.4(b)(1), 64n.8

40 C.F.R. § 261.4(b)(1), (2), 3n.17

40 C.F.R. § 261.4(b)(3), 383n.13

40 C.F.R. § 261.5, 81n.94, 177n.116, 128, 200n.70

40 C.F.R. § 261.5(a), 81n.97

40 C.F.R. § 261.5(b), 261.6(a)(3), 69n.45

40 C.F.R. § 261.5(b), (g), 5n.28

40 C.F.R. § 261.5(e)–(f), 81n.95

40 C.F.R. § 261.5(g)(1), 81n.96

40 C.F.R. § 261.5(g)(2), 81n.98

40 C.F.R. § 261.5(g)(3), 81n.99, 81n.100

40 C.F.R. § 261.5(h), 82n.101

40 C.F.R. § 261.6, 64n.15

40 C.F.R. § 261.6(a), 42n.35

40 C.F.R. § 261.6(a)(1), 36n.12

40 C.F.R. § 261.6(b), (c), 36n.13

40 C.F.R. § 261.6(c), 36n.14

40 C.F.R. § 261.6(j), 82n.102

40 C.F.R. § 261.7, 65n.16, 83n.111, 220n.7

40 C.F.R. § 261.8, 25n.59, 52n.4, 83n.112

40 C.F.R. § 261.9, 83n.113

40 C.F.R. § 261.10(a)(2)(i), 64n.10

40 C.F.R. § 261.11(c)(2), 64n.11

40 C.F.R. § 261.21, 228

40 C.F.R. §§ 261.21–.24, 3n.14

40 C.F.R. § 261.23, 50

40 C.F.R. § 261.23(a)(5), 51, 51n.3, 306

40 C.F.R. § 261.24, 22n.41, 52

40 C.F.R. § 261.31, 18n.17, 47, 48

40 C.F.R. §§ 261.31–.33, 3n.16

40 C.F.R. § 261.32, 21n.29, 47

40 C.F.R. § 261.33, 220

40 C.F.R. § 261.33(e), 67

40 C.F.R. § 261.38, 38

40 C.F.R. § 262, 106

40 C.F.R. § 262.11, 64n.9

40 C.F.R. § 262.11(d), 64n.12

40 C.F.R. §§ 262.12, 262.30–.44, 174n.89

40 C.F.R. § 262.12(a), 69n.46, 104n.3

40 C.F.R. § 262.12(b), 69n.47

40 C.F.R. § 262.12(c), 70n.48

40 C.F.R. § 262.20, 70n.49, 104, 107

40 C.F.R. § 262.20(a), 107, 175n.90

40 C.F.R. § 262.20(b), 71n.53, 175n.91

40 C.F.R. § 262.20(c), 71n.54, 175n.92

40 C.F.R. § 262.20(d), 71n.55

40 C.F.R. § 262.20(e), 82n.104, 108

40 C.F.R. §§ 262.20–.22, 176n.102

40 C.F.R. §§ 262.20–.23, 4n.26, 106

40 C.F.R. § 262.21(a), 73n.61

40 C.F.R. § 262.21(b), 73n.62

40 C.F.R. § 262.21(c), 70n.51, 73n.63

40 C.F.R. § 262.22, 72n.57

40 C.F.R. § 262.23, 175n.96, 228

40 C.F.R. § 262.23(a), 71n.56

40 C.F.R. § 262.23(a)(1)–(2), 175n.93

40 C.F.R. § 262.23(b), 175n.90

40 C.F.R. § 262.23(c), 175n.99

40 C.F.R. § 262.23(c)–(d), 72n.60

40 C.F.R. § 262.23(d)(1), 175n.97

40 C.F.R. § 262.23(d)(3), 175n.98

40 C.F.R. § 262.30, 108

40 C.F.R. §§ 262.30–.33, 4n.25, 26n.64, 73n.64

40 C.F.R. §§ 262.30–.44, 174n.89

40 C.F.R. § 262.32, 73n.69

40 C.F.R. § 262.34, 65n.18, 66, 128

40 C.F.R. § 262.34(a), 5n.30

40 C.F.R. § 262.34(a)(1), 65n.19, 200n.69

40 C.F.R. § 262.34(a)(1)(ii), 66n.24

40 C.F.R. § 262.34(a)(1)(iii), 66n.31

40 C.F.R. § 262.34(a)(2)(3), 65n.20

40 C.F.R. § 262.34(a)(4), 67n.33, 67n.36

40 C.F.R. § 262.34(a)(iii)(A)–(B), 66n.32

40 C.F.R. § 262.34(b), 67n.35

40 C.F.R. § 262.34(c), 5n.31

40 C.F.R. § 262.34 (c)(1), 67n.37

40 C.F.R. § 262.34(c)(1)(i)–(ii), 67n.38

40 C.F.R. § 262.34(c)(2), 67n.39

40 C.F.R. § 262.34(d), 5n.29, 82n.105, 200n.70

40 C.F.R. § 262.34(d)(5), 83n.107, 83n.108

40 C.F.R. § 262.34 (d)–(f), 82n.103

40 C.F.R. § 262.34(e), 83n.109

40 C.F.R. § 262.34(f), 83n.110

40 C.F.R. § 262.34(g), 68

40 C.F.R. § 262.34(h), 68, 69n.43

40 C.F.R. § 262.40, 74n.70

40 C.F.R. § 262.40(a), 74n.72

40 C.F.R. § 262.40(b), 74n.73

40 C.F.R. § 262.40(c), 74n.74

40 C.F.R. § 262.40(d), 74n.75

40 C.F.R. § 262.41(a), 75n.77

40 C.F.R. § 262.41(a)(1)–(5), 75n.78

40 C.F.R. § 262.41(a)(6)–(7), 75n.79

40 C.F.R. § 262.41(b), 75n.81

40 C.F.R. § 262.42, 88

40 C.F.R. § 262.42(a)(1), 72n.58

40 C.F.R. § 262.42(a)(2), 72n.59, 76n.82

40 C.F.R. § 262.42(a)(2)(i)–(ii), 76n.83

40 C.F.R. § 262.42(a)(8), 75n.80

40 C.F.R. § 262.42(b), 76n.84, 76n.85, 76n.86

40 C.F.R. § 262.42, subpt. H, 88–89

40 C.F.R. § 262.43, 74n.71

40 C.F.R. § 262.44, 5n.29

40 C.F.R. § 262.52, 106n.12

40 C.F.R. § 262.52(c), 176n.100

40 C.F.R. § 262.53, 85n.131, 106, 106n.13

40 C.F.R. § 262.53(a), 86n.133

40 C.F.R. § 262.53(b), 86n.132

40 C.F.R. § 262.53(c), 86n.134

40 C.F.R. § 262.53(c)–(f), 87n.135

40 C.F.R. § 262.54, 87n.137, 106n.14

40 C.F.R. § 262.54(a)–(d), (f), (h), 87n.138

40 C.F.R. § 262.54(e), 88n.141

40 C.F.R. § 262.54(g), 87n.139

40 C.F.R. § 262.54(i), 88n.140

40 C.F.R. § 262.55, 88n.143

40 C.F.R. §§ 262.55–.57, 88n.142

40 C.F.R. § 262.56, 75n.76, 107n.15

40 C.F.R. §§ 262.56–.57, 88n.144

40 C.F.R. § 262.57, 107n.16

40 C.F.R. § 262.58(a)(1), 89

40 C.F.R. § 262.60(b), 85n.126

40 C.F.R. § 262.80, 107n.18

40 C.F.R. §§ 262.80–.89, 89n.145

40 C.F.R. § 262.82, 107n.20

40 C.F.R. § 262.90, 129

40 C.F.R. § 263.10(a), 104n.1

40 C.F.R. § 263.10(a) comment, 26n.65

40 C.F.R. § 263.10(b), 6n.36, 109n.26

40 C.F.R. § 263.10(c), 108n.25

40 C.F.R. § 263.12, 5n.35, 108n.24

40 C.F.R. § 263.20, 5n.34, 176n.101

40 C.F.R. § 263.20(a)–(c), 105n.4

40 C.F.R. § 263.20(c), 110n.32

40 C.F.R. § 263.20(d), 105n.5

40 C.F.R. § 263.20(e), 105n.6

40 C.F.R. § 263.20(f), 106n.8

40 C.F.R. § 263.20(f)(2), 106n.9

40 C.F.R. § 263.20(f)(3), (5), 106n.10

40 C.F.R. § 263.20(f)(4), 106n.11

40 C.F.R. § 263.20(g), 107n.17

40 C.F.R. § 263.20(h), 107n.21

40 C.F.R. § 263.21(a), 109n.30

40 C.F.R. § 263.21(b), 109n.31

40 C.F.R. § 263.22(a), 108n.22

40 C.F.R. § 263.22(b), 105n.7

40 C.F.R. § 263.22(c), 106, 107

40 C.F.R. § 263.22(e), 108n.23

40 C.F.R. §§ 263.30–.31, 6n.37

40 C.F.R. § 263.30(a), 110n.34

40 C.F.R. § 263.30(b), 110n.36

40 C.F.R. § 263.30(c)(2), 26n.64

40 C.F.R. § 263.31, 110n.35

472 TABLE OF REGULATIONS

40 C.F.R. § 264, 64, 223
40 C.F.R. § 264, app. VI, 168n.46
40 C.F.R. § 264, subpts. AA, BB, 21n.34
40 C.F.R. § 264.1 (2001), 161n.3
40 C.F.R. § 264.1(c) comment, (e) comment, 162n.7
40 C.F.R. § 264.1(c), (e), 162n.4
40 C.F.R. § 264.1(d), 23n.46, 162n.6
40 C.F.R. § 264.1(f), 162n.8, 448n.19
40 C.F.R. § 264.1(g)(6), 270.1(c)(2)(v), 18n.18
40 C.F.R. § 264.1(j)(13), 179
40 C.F.R. § 264.3, 234n.22
40 C.F.R. § 264.10(a), 170n.64
40 C.F.R. § 264.10(a)(2), 169n.59
40 C.F.R. § 264.10(b), 168n.52
40 C.F.R. § 264.11, 163n.13
40 C.F.R. § 264.12(a), 164n.14
40 C.F.R. § 264.12(b), 164n.16
40 C.F.R. § 264.12(c), 164n.15
40 C.F.R. § 264.13, 149
40 C.F.R. § 264.13(a)(1), 164n.17
40 C.F.R. § 264.13(a)(2) comment, 13(a)(1), 164n.18
40 C.F.R. § 264.13(a)(3), 165n.21
40 C.F.R. § 264.13(a)(4), 164n.19
40 C.F.R. § 264.13(b), 165n.22
40 C.F.R. § 264.13(b)(5), (c), 165n.23
40 C.F.R. § 264.14(a), 165n.24, 165n.25
40 C.F.R. § 264.14(b), 165n.26
40 C.F.R. § 264.14(b)(3)–(4), 166n.32
40 C.F.R. § 264.14(c), 165n.27, 165n.28
40 C.F.R. §§ 264.14(d)(3), 209n.105
40 C.F.R. § 264.15(a), 165n.30
40 C.F.R. § 264.15(a)(1), 205n.87
40 C.F.R. § 264.15(b)(1), 166n.31
40 C.F.R. § 264.15(b)(4), 166n.33, 166n.34
40 C.F.R. § 264.15(d), 165n.29
40 C.F.R. § 264.16(a)(1), (b), 166n.36
40 C.F.R. § 264.16(a)(1) comment, 167n.40
40 C.F.R. § 264.16(a)(3), 167n.41

40 C.F.R. § 264.16(b), 166n.37
40 C.F.R. § 264.16(c), 166n.38
40 C.F.R. § 264.16(e), 167n.39
40 C.F.R. § 264.17, 164n.20
40 C.F.R. § 264.17(a), 167n.42
40 C.F.R. § 264.17(a)(1), 176n.103
40 C.F.R. § 264.17(b), 167n.43
40 C.F.R. § 264.18(a), 167n.44
40 C.F.R. § 264.18(a) comment, 168n.45
40 C.F.R. § 264.18(b), 168n.52, 168n.53
40 C.F.R. § 264.18(b)(i), 168n.54
40 C.F.R. § 264.18(b) comment, 168n.54
40 C.F.R. §§ 264.18(b)(ii)(A)–(D), 169n.55
40 C.F.R. § 264.18(c), 169n.56
40 C.F.R. § 264.19, 169n.57, 169n.58
40 C.F.R. § 264.19(b), 169n.60
40 C.F.R. § 264.19(c), 169n.61
40 C.F.R. § 264.19(c)(2), 170n.62
40 C.F.R. § 264.19(d), 170n.63
40 C.F.R. § 264.31, 170n.65
40 C.F.R. § 264.32, 171n.66
40 C.F.R. § 264.33, 171n.67
40 C.F.R. § 264.34(a), 171n.68
40 C.F.R. § 264.34(a)–(b), 171n.71
40 C.F.R. § 264.34(b), 171n.69
40 C.F.R. § 264.35, 171n.70, 171n.71
40 C.F.R. § 264.37(b), 172n.73
40 C.F.R. § 264.37(c), 172n.72
40 C.F.R. § 264.45, 316
40 C.F.R. § 264.51(a), 172n.74
40 C.F.R. § 264.51(b), 172n.75
40 C.F.R. § 264.52, 172n.75
40 C.F.R. § 264.52(c), 173n.76
40 C.F.R. § 264.52(d), 173n.77
40 C.F.R. § 264.52(e), 173n.78
40 C.F.R. § 264.52(f), 173n.79
40 C.F.R. § 264.55, 173n.80, 173n.81
40 C.F.R. § 264.55(e)(4)(i)(C), 316n.53
40 C.F.R. § 264.56(a)–(c), 173n.82
40 C.F.R. § 264.56(d), 27n.67
40 C.F.R. § 264.56(d)(1), 173n.83
40 C.F.R. § 264.56(d)(2), 174n.84

Table of Regulations 473

40 C.F.R. § 264.56(d), pt. 264, subpt. J, 27n.68

40 C.F.R. § 264.56(d), pt. 280, 27n.69

40 C.F.R. § 264.56(e), 174n.85

40 C.F.R. § 264.56(f), 174n.86

40 C.F.R. § 264.56(g), 174n.87

40 C.F.R. § 264.56(h)–(j), 174n.88

40 C.F.R. § 264.71(1)(4), (b)(4), 177n.115

40 C.F.R. § 264.71(a)(1), (a)(3), (b)(1), (b)(3), 176n.106

40 C.F.R. § 264.71(a)(2), 176n.104

40 C.F.R. § 264.71(a)(2), (b)(2), 177n.108

40 C.F.R. § 264.71(a)(2) comment, (b)(2) comment, 177n.112

40 C.F.R. § 264.71(a)(5), (b)(5), 176n.107

40 C.F.R. § 264.71(b)(1)–(2), 176n.105

40 C.F.R. § 264.72(a)(1), 177n.109, 177n.110, 177n.111

40 C.F.R. § 264.72(b), 177n.113, 177n.114

40 C.F.R. § 264.73(a)–(b), 178n.120

40 C.F.R. § 264.73(b)(1)–(2), 178n.121

40 C.F.R. § 264.73(b)(2), 178n.122, 178n.123

40 C.F.R. § 264.73(b)(3)–(6), 178n.124

40 C.F.R. § 264.73(b)(7)–(9), 178n.125

40 C.F.R. § 264.73(b)(10)–(16), 179n.128

40 C.F.R. § 264.73(b)(17), 179n.129

40 C.F.R. § 264.74, 166n.35

40 C.F.R. § 264.74(a), 179n.130

40 C.F.R. § 264.75, 179n.131

40 C.F.R. § 264.75(a)–(g), 179n.132

40 C.F.R. § 264.75(h)–(i), 179n.133

40 C.F.R. § 264.75(j), 179n.134

40 C.F.R. § 264.76, 177n.118

40 C.F.R. § 264.76(a)–(g), 178n.119

40 C.F.R. § 264.76 comment, 177n.117

40 C.F.R. § 264.77, 179n.135

40 C.F.R. §§ 264.90–.101, 257n.13

40 C.F.R. § 264.90(b), 262n.28

40 C.F.R. § 264.90(f), 185

40 C.F.R. § 264.92, 264n.34

40 C.F.R. § 264.94, 264n.35

40 C.F.R. § 264.95, 264n.36

40 C.F.R. § 264.96, 263n.29, 264n.37

40 C.F.R. § 264.97, 265n.38

40 C.F.R. § 264.98, 263n.31, 265n.39

40 C.F.R. § 264.99, 263n.32, 267n.40

40 C.F.R. § 264.100, 7n.46, 263n.33, 268

40 C.F.R. § 264.100(c), 268n.41

40 C.F.R. §§ 264.110–.120, 265.110–.120, 184n.2

40 C.F.R. § 264.110(b), 7n.48, 189n.29

40 C.F.R. § 264.110(c), 185, 195n.49, 269n.42

40 C.F.R. § 264.111, 184n.1

40 C.F.R. § 264.112, 7n.47

40 C.F.R. § 264.112(b)(1), 184n.3, 185n.10

40 C.F.R. § 264.112(b)(2)–(3), 185n.11

40 C.F.R. § 264.112(b)(4), 185n.12

40 C.F.R. § 264.112(b)(5), 185n.13

40 C.F.R. § 264.112(b)(6), 185n.14

40 C.F.R. § 264.112(b)(7), 185n.15

40 C.F.R. § 264.112(b)(8), 185n.16

40 C.F.R. § 264.112(c), 186n.18

40 C.F.R. § 264.112(d), 187n.21

40 C.F.R. § 264.113, 188n.25

40 C.F.R. § 264.113(b)–(e), 188n.26

40 C.F.R. § 264.113(e)(7), 189n.27

40 C.F.R. § 264.113(e)(7)(v), 189n.28

40 C.F.R. § 264.115, 186n.19

40 C.F.R. § 264.116, 1186n.20

40 C.F.R. § 264.117, 7n.49

40 C.F.R. § 264.117(a), 146, 189n.30

40 C.F.R. § 264.117(a)(2), 190n.31

40 C.F.R. § 264.117(c), 191n.38

40 C.F.R. § 264.118(a), 190n.32, 190n.34

40 C.F.R. § 264.118(d), 190n.35

40 C.F.R. § 264.119(a), 192n.39

40 C.F.R. § 264.119(b), 192n.40

40 C.F.R. § 264.119(c), 192n.41, 192n.42

40 C.F.R. § 264.120, 192n.43

40 C.F.R. § 264.136, 231
40 C.F.R. § 264.140(d), 185
40 C.F.R. §§ 264.141(g), 203n.80,
203n.81, 203n.82
40 C.F.R. §§ 264.141(h), 207n.96
40 C.F.R. §§ 264.142, 200n.72, 201n.74
40 C.F.R. §§ 264.142(b), 201n.75
40 C.F.R. §§ 264.143–.145, 7n.51
40 C.F.R. §§ 264.143(a), 204n.86
40 C.F.R. §§ 264.143(a)(10), 205n.88
40 C.F.R. § 264.143(b)(3), 209n.101
40 C.F.R. § 264.143(b)–(c), 208n.99
40 C.F.R. § 264.143(c), 209n.102
40 C.F.R. § 264.143(d), 209n.103
40 C.F.R. § 264.143(e), 210n.106
40 C.F.R. § 264.143(f), 206n.89, 207n.95
40 C.F.R. § 264.143(f)(1)(i)(A), 206n.91
40 C.F.R. § 264.143(f)(1)(ii), 206n.92
40 C.F.R. § 264.143(f)(6), 207n.94
40 C.F.R. § 264.143(f)(10), 208n.98
40 C.F.R. § 264.143(g), 211n.107
40 C.F.R. § 264.143(g)–(h), 204n.85
40 C.F.R. § 264.143(h), 212n.108
40 C.F.R. § 264.143(i), 204n.84
40 C.F.R. § 264.144, 200n.73, 202n.76
40 C.F.R. § 264.146, 211n.107
40 C.F.R. § 264.147, 202n.77
40 C.F.R. § 264.147(a), 214n.112
40 C.F.R. § 264.147(a)(1)(i), 204n.83
40 C.F.R. § 264.147(a)(2)–(5), 214n.113
40 C.F.R. § 264.147(a)(6), 214n.114
40 C.F.R. § 264.147(a)(7), 214n.115
40 C.F.R. § 264.147(c), 202n.78
40 C.F.R. § 264.147(d), 203n.79
40 C.F.R. § 264.147(f), 206n.90
40 C.F.R. § 264.147(h), 214n.116
40 C.F.R. § 264.149, 212n.109
40 C.F.R. § 264.151, 207n.93
40 C.F.R. § 264.151(b), 208n.100
40 C.F.R. § 264.151(d), 209n.104
40 C.F.R. § 264.151(f), (h), 208n.97
40 C.F.R. § 264.172, 220n.5
40 C.F.R. § 264.173, 219n.3
40 C.F.R. § 264.174, 219n.2
40 C.F.R. § 264.175, 8n.52, 218

40 C.F.R. § 264.177, 220n.6
40 C.F.R. § 264.178, 195n.50, 221
40 C.F.R. § 264.190, 222
40 C.F.R. § 264.191, 226
40 C.F.R. §§ 264.191–.196, 265.191–.196,
8n.53
40 C.F.R. § 264.192, 226n.11, 227
40 C.F.R. § 264.193, 223, 224, 225n.10,
228, 230n.15
40 C.F.R. §§ 264.193–.194, 264.197,
8n.54
40 C.F.R. § 264.194, 227
40 C.F.R. § 264.195, 227
40 C.F.R. § 264.195(b), 166n.35
40 C.F.R. § 264.196, 230, 231n.16
40 C.F.R. § 264.197, 189, 195n.51, 229
40 C.F.R. § 264.197(c), 196n.52
40 C.F.R. § 264.198, 228n.12
40 C.F.R. § 264.199, 229n.13
40 C.F.R. § 264.220, 8n.59
40 C.F.R. §§ 264.220–232, 269
40 C.F.R. § 264.221, 270n.44
40 C.F.R. § 264.221(d), 256n.4, 271n.48
40 C.F.R. § 264.221(e)(2)(i)(A),
257n.10, 257n.11
40 C.F.R. § 264.221(g)–(h), 270n.45
40 C.F.R. § 264.222, 270n.46
40 C.F.R. § 264.222(e)(2)(i)(B)–(C),
257n.12
40 C.F.R. § 264.223, 270n.47
40 C.F.R. § 264.226, 271n.52
40 C.F.R. § 264.226(b), 166n.35
40 C.F.R. § 264.227, 272n.57
40 C.F.R. § 264.228, 196n.53, 273n.58
40 C.F.R. § 264.228(1), 196n.55
40 C.F.R. § 264.228(c)(1)(ii), 190n.33
40 C.F.R. § 264.229, 272n.54, 274n.59
40 C.F.R. § 264.230, 272n.55, 274n.60
40 C.F.R. § 264.231, 272n.56, 274n.61
40 C.F.R. § 264.232, 271n.53, 274n.62
40 C.F.R. § 264.250, 276n.71
40 C.F.R. §§ 264.250–.269, 275
40 C.F.R. § 264.250(c), 262
40 C.F.R. § 264.250(c), pt. 264, subpt.
F, 262n.27

Table of Regulations 475

40 C.F.R. § 264.251(a)–(b), 276n.72
40 C.F.R. § 264.251(c), 276n.73
40 C.F.R. § 264.251(g)–(j), 276n.74
40 C.F.R. § 264.254, 277n.75, 277n.76
40 C.F.R. § 264.254(b), 166n.35
40 C.F.R. § 264.256, 277n.77
40 C.F.R. § 264.257, 277n.78
40 C.F.R. § 264.258, 197n.57, 277n.79, 278n.80
40 C.F.R. § 264.259, 278n.81
40 C.F.R. § 264.270, 279n.91
40 C.F.R. §§ 264.270–.283, 279
40 C.F.R. § 264.272, 279n.92
40 C.F.R. § 264.273, 280n.93
40 C.F.R. § 264.276(c), 280
40 C.F.R. § 264.280, 197n.58, 281n.95, 281n.96
40 C.F.R. § 264.280(b), 198n.60
40 C.F.R. § 264.280(c), 197n.59, 198n.61
40 C.F.R. § 264.280(d), 198n.62
40 C.F.R. § 264.281, 281n.97
40 C.F.R. § 264.282, 281n.98
40 C.F.R. § 264.283, 282n.99
40 C.F.R. §§ 264.300–.317, 283
40 C.F.R. §§ 264.301, 265.301, 8n.58
40 C.F.R. § 264.301(a), 283n.107
40 C.F.R. § 264.301(b), 283n.108
40 C.F.R. § 264.301(c), 283n.106
40 C.F.R. § 264.301(g)–(j), 284n.109
40 C.F.R. § 264.302, 283n.16
40 C.F.R. § 264.302(e)(2)(i)(A), 257n.10, 257n.11
40 C.F.R. § 264.302(e)(2)(i)(B)–(C), 257n.12
40 C.F.R. § 264.303, 284n.110, 284n.111
40 C.F.R. § 264.303(b), 166n.35
40 C.F.R. § 264.304, 283n.106
40 C.F.R. § 264.309, 284n.112
40 C.F.R. § 264.310, 199n.66, 230, 284n.113
40 C.F.R. § 264.312, 285n.114
40 C.F.R. § 264.313, 285n.115
40 C.F.R. § 264.314, 164n.20, 285
40 C.F.R. § 264.317, 285n.116, 286n.117

40 C.F.R. § 264.341, 164n.20
40 C.F.R. § 264.342, 152
40 C.F.R. § 264.343, 152, 236, 237, 237n.28, 238
40 C.F.R. §§ 264.343–.347, 8n.55
40 C.F.R. § 264.345, 237
40 C.F.R. § 264.347, 238
40 C.F.R. § 264.347(b), 166n.35
40 C.F.R. § 264.351, 199n.67, 239
40 C.F.R. §§ 264.500–.552, 339n.51
40 C.F.R. § 264.552, 340
40 C.F.R. § 264.552(a)(1), 315n.51
40 C.F.R. § 264.552(e)(4)(iv)(F), 316n.54
40 C.F.R. § 264.552(e)(4)(v)(A)–(E), 316n.55
40 C.F.R. § 264.553, 339
40 C.F.R. § 264.555, 317n.56
40 C.F.R. § 264.555(a)(2), 317n.57
40 C.F.R. § 264.575, 199n.67
40 C.F.R. § 264.575(b), 199n.68
40 C.F.R. § 264.601, 287n.122, 287n.123
40 C.F.R. § 264.602, 166n.35
40 C.F.R. § 264.603, 199n.67
40 C.F.R. § 264.1033(f)(3), 166n.35
40 C.F.R. § 264.1034(d), 164n.20
40 C.F.R. § 264.1052(a)(1)–(2), 166n.35
40 C.F.R. § 264.1058(a), 166n.35
40 C.F.R. § 264.1102, 189
40 C.F.R. § 265, 64
40 C.F.R. § 265, subpts. A–F, 255n.1
40 C.F.R. § 265, subpt. I, 67
40 C.F.R. § 265, subpt. W, 66
40 C.F.R. §§ 265.11–.16., 6n.43
40 C.F.R. § 265.13, 149, 234
40 C.F.R. § 265.16, 67
40 C.F.R. §§ 265.17–.18, 7n.44
40 C.F.R. §§ 265.90–.91, 7n.45
40 C.F.R. §§ 265.90–.94, 257n.13, 258n.14
40 C.F.R. § 265.90(c), 258n.15
40 C.F.R. § 265.90(e), 258n.16
40 C.F.R. § 265.90(f), 185
40 C.F.R. § 265.91, 258
40 C.F.R. § 265.92, 259

476 TABLE OF REGULATIONS

40 C.F.R. § 265.92(d), 260n.18
40 C.F.R. § 265.92(e), 260n.19
40 C.F.R. § 265.93(a), 260n.17
40 C.F.R. § 265.93(b), 260n.21
40 C.F.R. § 265.93(d), 260n.22, 261n.23
40 C.F.R. § 265.93(e), 261n.24
40 C.F.R. § 265.93(f), 260n.20
40 C.F.R. § 265.94, 261n.25
40 C.F.R. § 265.94(b), 261n.26
40 C.F.R. § 265.110(b), 7n.48, 189n.29
40 C.F.R. § 265.110(d), 185, 195n.49, 269n.42
40 C.F.R. § 265.111, 184n.1
40 C.F.R. § 265.112, 7n.47
40 C.F.R. § 265.112(1)(2), 197n.56
40 C.F.R. § 265.112(a), 184n.6
40 C.F.R. § 265.112(a), (d), 184n.7
40 C.F.R. § 265.112(b), 185n.9
40 C.F.R. § 265.112(b)(1), 184n.3, 185n.10
40 C.F.R. § 265.112(b)(2)–(3), 185n.11
40 C.F.R. § 265.112(b)(4), 185n.12
40 C.F.R. § 265.112(b)(5), 185n.13
40 C.F.R. § 265.112(b)(6), 185n.14
40 C.F.R. § 265.112(b)(7), 185n.15
40 C.F.R. § 265.112(b)(8), 185n.16
40 C.F.R. § 265.112(c), 186n.17, 186n.18
40 C.F.R. § 265.112(d), 187n.21, 187n.22
40 C.F.R. § 265.112(d)(3), 187n.23
40 C.F.R. § 265.112(d)(4), 188n.24
40 C.F.R. § 265.113, 188n.25
40 C.F.R. § 265.113(b)–(e), 188n.26
40 C.F.R. § 265.113(e)(7), 189n.27
40 C.F.R. § 265.113(e)(7)(v), 189n.28
40 C.F.R. § 265.115, 186n.19
40 C.F.R. § 265.116, 1186n.20
40 C.F.R. § 265.117, 7n.49
40 C.F.R. § 265.117(a), 146, 189n.30
40 C.F.R. § 265.117(a)(2), 190n.31
40 C.F.R. § 265.117(c), 191n.38
40 C.F.R. § 265.118(a), 190n.32, 190n.34
40 C.F.R. § 265.118(d), 190n.35

40 C.F.R. § 265.118(e), 191n.36
40 C.F.R. § 265.118(f), 191n.37
40 C.F.R. § 265.119(a), 192n.39
40 C.F.R. § 265.119(b), 192n.40
40 C.F.R. § 265.119(c), 192n.41, 192n.42
40 C.F.R. § 265.120, 192n.43
40 C.F.R. § 265.121, 194n.47
40 C.F.R. § 265.140(d), 185
40 C.F.R. § 265.141(g), 203n.80, 203n.81, 203n.82
40 C.F.R. § 265.141(h), 207n.96
40 C.F.R. § 265.142, 200n.72, 201n.74
40 C.F.R. § 265.142(b), 201n.75
40 C.F.R. §§ 265.143–.145, 7n.51
40 C.F.R. § 265.143(a), 204n.86
40 C.F.R. § 265,143(a)(10), 205n.88
40 C.F.R. § 265.143(b), 208n.99
40 C.F.R. § 265.143(c), 209n.103
40 C.F.R. § 265.143(c)(6), 207n.94
40 C.F.R. § 265.143(d), 210n.106
40 C.F.R. § 265.143(e), 206n.89, 207n.95
40 C.F.R. § 265.143(e)(1)(i)(A), 206n.91
40 C.F.R. § 265.143(e)(1)(ii), 206n.92
40 C.F.R. § 265.143(e)(10), 208n.98
40 C.F.R. § 265.143(f), 211n.107
40 C.F.R. § 265.143 (f)–(g), 204n.85
40 C.F.R. § 265.143(g), 212n.108
40 C.F.R. § 265.143(h), 204n.84
40 C.F.R. § 265.144, 200n.73, 202n.76
40 C.F.R. § 265.146, 211n.107
40 C.F.R. § 265.147, 202n.77
40 C.F.R. § 265.147(a), 214n.112
40 C.F.R. § 265.147(a)(2)–(5), 214n.113
40 C.F.R. § 265.147(a)(6), 214n.114
40 C.F.R. § 265.147(a)(7), 214n.115
40 C.F.R. § 265.147(c), 202n.78
40 C.F.R. § 265.147(d), 203n.79
40 C.F.R. § 265.147(f), 206n.90
40 C.F.R. § 265.147(h), 214n.116
40 C.F.R. § 265.149, 212n.109
40 C.F.R. § 265.151(c)(3), 209n.105
40 C.F.R. § 265.171, 66n.21
40 C.F.R. § 265.172, 66n.22, 220n.5

40 C.F.R. § 265.173, 219n.3
40 C.F.R. §§ 265.173–.174, 66n.22
40 C.F.R. § 265.173(b), 66n.21
40 C.F.R. § 265.174, 66n.25, 219n.2
40 C.F.R. § 265.177, 66n.23, 220n.6
40 C.F.R. § 265.178, 221
40 C.F.R. § 265.190, 222
40 C.F.R. § 265.191, 226
40 C.F.R. § 265.192, 223, 226n.11, 227
40 C.F.R. § 265.193, 224, 225n.10, 230n.15
40 C.F.R. § 265.194, 66n.26
40 C.F.R. § 265.195, 44n.28, 227
40 C.F.R. § 265.196, 66n.27, 230, 231, 231n.16
40 C.F.R. § 265.197, 189, 195n.51, 229
40 C.F.R. § 265.197(b), 200n.71
40 C.F.R. § 265.197(c), 66n.29, 196n.52
40 C.F.R. § 265.198, 228n.12
40 C.F.R. § 265.199, 229n.13
40 C.F.R. § 265.200, 66n.30, 229n.14
40 C.F.R. § 265.201, 83n.106
40 C.F.R. § 265.220, 148
40 C.F.R. §§ 265.220–.231, 274
40 C.F.R. § 265.221, 274n.63
40 C.F.R. § 265.221(c), 256n.5
40 C.F.R. § 265.225, 275n.64
40 C.F.R. § 265.226, 275n.65
40 C.F.R. § 265.228, 196n.53, 275n.69
40 C.F.R. § 265.228(b), 196n.54
40 C.F.R. § 265.229, 275n.66
40 C.F.R. § 265.230, 275n.67
40 C.F.R. § 265.231, 275n.68
40 C.F.R. § 265.250, 278n.82
40 C.F.R. §§ 265.250–.258, 278
40 C.F.R. § 265.251, 278n.83
40 C.F.R. § 265.252, 278n.84
40 C.F.R. § 265.253, 278n.85
40 C.F.R. §§ 265.254–.255, 279n.88
40 C.F.R. § 265.256, 278n.86
40 C.F.R. § 265.257, 278n.87
40 C.F.R. § 265.258, 197n.57, 279n.89
40 C.F.R. §§ 265.270–.282, 282
40 C.F.R. § 265.272, 282n.100
40 C.F.R. § 265.273, 282n.101

40 C.F.R. § 265.278, 282n.104
40 C.F.R. § 265.280, 197n.58, 283
40 C.F.R. § 265.280(a), 198n.63
40 C.F.R. § 265.280(b), 187n.64
40 C.F.R. § 265.280(l), 198n.65
40 C.F.R. § 265.281, 282n.102
40 C.F.R. § 265.282, 282n.103
40 C.F.R. §§ 265.300–.316, 286
40 C.F.R. § 265.301, 286n.119
40 C.F.R. §§ 265.301–.304, 286n.118
40 C.F.R. §§ 265.309, 265.312–.316, 286n.120
40 C.F.R. § 265.310, 199n.66, 286n.121
40 C.F.R. § 265.341, 234n.23
40 C.F.R. § 265.345, 238n.30
40 C.F.R. § 265.347, 238
40 C.F.R. § 265.351, 199n.67, 239
40 C.F.R. § 265.352, 238n.29
40 C.F.R. § 265.404, 199n.67
40 C.F.R. § 265.445, 199n.67
40 C.F.R. § 265.445(b), 199n.68
40 C.F.R. § 265.1102, 189
40 C.F.R. § 266, subpt. H, 21n.33
40 C.F.R. § 266.100, 8n.56, 242
40 C.F.R. § 266.100 et seq., 240, 241
40 C.F.R. § 266.101, 242n.34
40 C.F.R. § 266.102, 243, 245
40 C.F.R. § 266.102(b), 247, 247n.38
40 C.F.R. § 266.103, 243, 245
40 C.F.R. § 266.103(j), 247, 247n.39
40 C.F.R. § 266.104, 243n.35
40 C.F.R. § 266.105, 244n.36
40 C.F.R. § 266.108, 242
40 C.F.R. § 266.111, 245n.37, 249
40 C.F.R. § 266.112, 242n.34, 247, 247n.42, 248, 297, 308
40 C.F.R. § 266.220, 8n.59
40 C.F.R. § 266.225, 58
40 C.F.R. § 266.230, 58
40 C.F.R. § 268, 64
40 C.F.R. § 268.1, 64n.13
40 C.F.R. § 268.1(c)(3), 23n.49
40 C.F.R. § 268.2(c)(3)–(4), 306n.6
40 C.F.R. § 268.2(i), 307n.8
40 C.F.R. § 268.3, 294

40 C.F.R. § 268.3(b), 19n.22
40 C.F.R. § 268.4, 9n.65, 298n.44
40 C.F.R. § 268.5, 298n.43
40 C.F.R. § 268.5(h), 298n.41
40 C.F.R. § 268.6, 9n.66, 299
40 C.F.R. § 268.7, 293
40 C.F.R. § 268.7(a)(5), 67
40 C.F.R. § 268.8, 164n.20
40 C.F.R. § 268.23(c)(4), 393n.70
40 C.F.R. §§ 268.30–.35, 292n.14
40 C.F.R. § 268.32(a)(2)–(3), 25n.63
40 C.F.R. § 268.33(e)(1), 292n.15
40 C.F.R. § 268.35(c), (d), (e), 298n.40
40 C.F.R. § 268.40, 306n.6
40 C.F.R. § 268.40 tbl., 309n.18
40 C.F.R. § 268.40(e), 307
40 C.F.R. § 268.41, 292n.16, 293, 294
40 C.F.R. § 268.42, 292n.16, 293
40 C.F.R. § 268.43, 292n.16, 293
40 C.F.R. § 268.44, 294n.26
40 C.F.R. § 268.44(a)(2)(ii), (h)(2)(ii), 313n.37
40 C.F.R. §§ 268.44(e), (h), 294n.27
40 C.F.R. § 268.44(h)(3), 315n.45, 341
40 C.F.R. § 268.44(h)(3)(i)(B), 315n.48
40 C.F.R. § 268.44(h)(i)(A), 315n.47
40 C.F.R. § 268.44(m), 317n.62
40 C.F.R. § 268.45 tbl. 1, 310n.21
40 C.F.R. § 268.45(a), 268.2(h), 310n.25
40 C.F.R. § 268.45(a), 310n.20
40 C.F.R. § 268.45(c), 311n.26
40 C.F.R. § 268.45(d), 310n.22
40 C.F.R. § 268.48, 309n.18
40 C.F.R. § 268.49(c), 313n.41
40 C.F.R. § 268.49(d), 308n.12, 314n.42, 314n.43
40 C.F.R. § 268.50, 292n.19
40 C.F.R. § 270.1(c), 28n.70, 193n.44, 333n.35
40 C.F.R. § 270.1(c)(1), 137n.27
40 C.F.R. § 270.1(c)(2), (3), 128
40 C.F.R. § 270.1(c)(2)(i), 128n.7
40 C.F.R. § 270.1(c)(2)(ii), 128n.8
40 C.F.R. § 270.1(c)(2)(iii), 128n.9
40 C.F.R. § 270.1(c)(2)(iv), 128n.10

40 C.F.R. § 270.1(c)(2)(v), 128n.11
40 C.F.R. § 270.1(c)(2)(vi), 129n.12
40 C.F.R. § 270.1(c)(2)(vii), 129n.13, 129n.14
40 C.F.R. § 270.1(c)(3), 129n.15
40 C.F.R. § 270.1(c)(5), 143n.41, 194n.45, 263n.30
40 C.F.R. § 270.1(c)(6), 194n.46
40 C.F.R. § 270.1(c)(7), 195n.48
40 C.F.R. § 270.2, 128, 328n.26
40 C.F.R. § 270.4, 125n.2, 126, 126n.3
40 C.F.R. § 270.4(a) (1992), 432n.11
40 C.F.R. § 270.6, 130
40 C.F.R. § 270.10, 65
40 C.F.R. § 270.10(3), 144n.46
40 C.F.R. § 270.10(b), 130, 130n.20
40 C.F.R. § 270.10(c), 142
40 C.F.R. § 270.10(e), 130, 145n.50
40 C.F.R. § 270.10(e)(i), 143n.44
40 C.F.R. § 270.10(e)(ii), 143n.45
40 C.F.R. § 270.10(f), 130
40 C.F.R. § 270.10(f)(2), 130n.19
40 C.F.R. § 270.10(f)(3), 129n.17
40 C.F.R. § 270.10(h), 142n.38
40 C.F.R. § 270.11(a)(1), 133n.22
40 C.F.R. § 270.13, 140
40 C.F.R. § 270.14, 28n.73
40 C.F.R. § 270.14(b)(11), 168n.47
40 C.F.R. § 270.14(b)(11)(ii)(B), 168n.48, 168n.49, 168n.50
40 C.F.R. § 270.14(b)(11)(ii)(B) comment, 168n.51
40 C.F.R. § 270.14(b)(13), 184n.8
40 C.F.R. § 270.14, pt. 124, 29n.74
40 C.F.R. § 270.21, 140
40 C.F.R. § 270.28, 146
40 C.F.R. § 270.29, 138
40 C.F.R. §§ 270.30–.31, 136n.25
40 C.F.R. § 270.30(h)(10), 126n.4
40 C.F.R. § 270.41, 338n.47
40 C.F.R. § 270.41(a)(3), 327n.24
40 C.F.R. § 270.42, 140n.31
40 C.F.R. § 270.42, app. I, 140
40 C.F.R. § 270.42(a), 140
40 C.F.R. § 270.42(b)(6), 140n.32

Table of Regulations 479

40 C.F.R. § 270.42(c), 141
40 C.F.R. § 270.42(d), 141n.33
40 C.F.R. § 270.42(f)(2), 141n.34
40 C.F.R. § 270.42(f)(3), 141n.35
40 C.F.R. § 270.42(g), 142
40 C.F.R. § 270.43, 143n.42
40 C.F.R. § 270.50, 146n.51
40 C.F.R. § 270.50(a), 142n.36
40 C.F.R. § 270.51, 142n.37
40 C.F.R. § 270.51(a)(2), 142n.39
40 C.F.R. § 270.51(d), 142n.40
40 C.F.R. § 270.60, 130
40 C.F.R. § 270.60(b), 23n.48, 137
40 C.F.R. § 270.60(c), 137
40 C.F.R. § 270.61, 129, 138n.29
40 C.F.R. § 270.61(b)(5), 138n.30
40 C.F.R. § 270.62, 140, 235
40 C.F.R. § 270.63, 140
40 C.F.R. § 270.64, 137n.28
40 C.F.R. § 270.65, 130, 149
40 C.F.R. § 270.70(c), 144n.47
40 C.F.R. § 270.73, 144n.48
40 C.F.R. § 271.1(i), 271.4, 163n.9,
   446n.13
40 C.F.R. § 271.1(j), tbls. 1, 2, 448
40 C.F.R. § 271.4, 446
40 C.F.R. § 271.4(a), 445n.10
40 C.F.R. § 271.4(b), 445n.11, 447
40 C.F.R. § 271.4(c), 446n.12
40 C.F.R. §§ 271.9–.16, 445n.9
40 C.F.R. § 271.19, 328n.26
40 C.F.R. § 272.70, 128
40 C.F.R. § 273.9, 83n.115
40 C.F.R. § 273.12, 84n.116
40 C.F.R. § 273.13, 274.33, 84n.118
40 C.F.R. § 273.14, 273.34, 84n.119
40 C.F.R. § 273.15, 273.35, 84n.120
40 C.F.R. § 273.16, 273.36, 84n.121
40 C.F.R. § 273.17, 273.37, 84n.122
40 C.F.R. § 273.19, 273.39, 84n.123
40 C.F.R. § 273.20, 84n.124, 87n.136
40 C.F.R. § 273.32, 84n.117
40 C.F.R. § 273.40, 84n.124, 87n.136
40 C.F.R. § 274.278, 280n.94
40 C.F.R. § 279.11, 43

40 C.F.R. § 280, 349
40 C.F.R. §§ 280.10–.74, 348n.19
40 C.F.R. § 280.10(b), 349n.25
40 C.F.R. § 280.10(c), 350n.28
40 C.F.R. § 280.10(d), 350n.29
40 C.F.R. § 280.12, 11n.77, 349n.22,
   349n.23, 349n.24, 355n.58
40 C.F.R. § 280.20, 351n.31, 351n.33
40 C.F.R. § 280.20(a), 352n.34
40 C.F.R. § 280.20(a), (d), 351n.32
40 C.F.R. § 280.20(b), 354n.51, 357n.62
40 C.F.R. § 280.20(c)(1)(i), 352n.41
40 C.F.R. § 280.20(c)(1)(ii), 352n.42
40 C.F.R. § 280.20(c)(1)(ii)(B)–(C),
   352n.43
40 C.F.R. § 280.20(c)(2), 353n.44
40 C.F.R. § 280.21(a), 355n.57
40 C.F.R. § 280.21(b), 356
40 C.F.R. § 280.21(c), 357n.62
40 C.F.R. § 280.21(d)1, 356n.59
40 C.F.R. § 280.22(a), 358n.68, 358n.71
40 C.F.R. § 280.22(a)3, 58n.72
40 C.F.R. § 280.22(b), 358n.69
40 C.F.R. § 280.22(c), 358
40 C.F.R. § 280.22(e), 359n.73
40 C.F.R. § 280.22(f), 359n.74
40 C.F.R. § 280.22(g), 359n.75
40 C.F.R. § 280.30, 352n.40
40 C.F.R. § 280.31, 354
40 C.F.R. § 280.31(a), 352n.35
40 C.F.R. § 280.31(b), 352n.36
40 C.F.R. § 280.31(b)(2), 352n.38
40 C.F.R. § 280.31(c), 352n.37
40 C.F.R. § 280.31(d), 352n.39
40 C.F.R. § 280.34(b)(2), 352n.39
40 C.F.R. §§ 280.40–.42, 351n.31
40 C.F.R. § 280.40(a), 353n.45
40 C.F.R. § 280.40(c), 357n.63, 358n.64
40 C.F.R. § 280.41(a), 353n.46
40 C.F.R. § 280.41(a)(1), 353n.47
40 C.F.R. § 280.41(a)(3), 354n.48
40 C.F.R. § 280.41(b), 357n.63
40 C.F.R. § 280.41(b)(1), 355n.52
40 C.F.R. § 280.41(b)(2), 355n.54,
   358n.65

480 TABLE OF REGULATIONS

40 C.F.R. § 280.42(a), 357n.61, 358n.66

40 C.F.R. § 280.42(b)(1)(i)–(iii), 354n.49

40 C.F.R. § 280.42(b)(4), 355n.55, 358n.67

40 C.F.R. § 280.42(b)(5), 354n.50, 355n.56

40 C.F.R. § 280.43, 280.44, 353

40 C.F.R. § 280.43(d)-(h), 353n.46, 357n.60

40 C.F.R. § 280.44, 355n.53

40 C.F.R. § 280.50, 359n.76

40 C.F.R. § 280.52, 359n.77

40 C.F.R. § 280.53(a), 360n.78

40 C.F.R. § 280.53(b), 360n.79

40 C.F.R. § 280.61, 360n.78

40 C.F.R. § 280.62(a), 360n.80

40 C.F.R. § 280.62(b), 360n.81

40 C.F.R. § 280.63(a), 360n.80

40 C.F.R. § 280.63(b), 360n.83

40 C.F.R. § 280.64, 360n.82

40 C.F.R. § 280.66(a), 360n.84

40 C.F.R. § 280.66(b), 361n.85

40 C.F.R. § 280.66(c), 361n.86

40 C.F.R. § 280.67, 361n.87

40 C.F.R. § 280.70(a), 361n.89

40 C.F.R. § 280.70(b), 361n.90

40 C.F.R. § 280.70(c), 361n.91

40 C.F.R. § 280.71(a), 362n.92

40 C.F.R. § 280.71(b), 362n.93

40 C.F.R. § 280.71(c), 362n.94

40 C.F.R. § 280.71(e), 362n.95

40 C.F.R. § 280.72(a), 362n.96

40 C.F.R. § 280.72(b), 362n.97

40 C.F.R. § 280.74(b), 362n.98

40 C.F.R. §§ 280.90–.116, 348n.20

40 C.F.R. § 280.91(e), 369n.135

40 C.F.R. § 280.93(a)(1), 363n.103

40 C.F.R. § 280.93(a)(2), 364n.105

40 C.F.R. § 280.93(b)(1)–(2), 364

40 C.F.R. § 280.94, 364n.106

40 C.F.R. § 280.94(a)(1), 369n.136

40 C.F.R. § 280.95(b)(1)–(5), 365n.107

40 C.F.R. § 280.95(c)(1)–(5), 365n.108

40 C.F.R. § 280.95(d), 365n.109

40 C.F.R. § 280.95(e), 365n.110

40 C.F.R. § 280.95(g), 365n.111

40 C.F.R. § 280.96, 365n.112

40 C.F.R. § 280.96(a)–(c), 366n.113

40 C.F.R. § 280.96(d), 368n.132

40 C.F.R. § 280.97(a)–(b), 366n.114

40 C.F.R. § 280.97(b), 366n.115

40 C.F.R. § 280.97(c), 366

40 C.F.R. § 280.98(a), 367n.118

40 C.F.R. § 280.98(b), 366n.117

40 C.F.R. § 280.98(d), 368n.132

40 C.F.R. § 280.99, 367n.120

40 C.F.R. § 280.99(a), 367n.121

40 C.F.R. § 280.99(b), (d), 367n.122

40 C.F.R. § 280.99(c), 368n.132

40 C.F.R. § 280.100, 367n.123

40 C.F.R. § 280.100(c), 367n.124

40 C.F.R. § 280.100(e), 367n.125

40 C.F.R. § 280.101(a), 368n.127

40 C.F.R. § 280.101(c), 368n.128

40 C.F.R. § 280.101(d), 368n.129

40 C.F.R. § 280.102(a), 368n.131

40 C.F.R. § 280.102(c), 368n.130

40 C.F.R. § 280.103(a)–(b), 369n.133

40 C.F.R. § 280.103(d), 369n.134

40 C.F.R. §§ 280.104–.107, 369n.137

40 C.F.R. § 280.108, 369n.138

40 C.F.R. § 280.109, 370n.139

40 C.F.R. § 280.110, 370n.140

40 C.F.R. § 280.111, 370n.141

40 C.F.R. § 280.111(b)(2), 370n.142

40 C.F.R. § 280.111(b)(3), 371n.143

40 C.F.R. § 280.111(b)(7), 371n.144

40 C.F.R. § 280.111(b)(8), 371n.145

40 C.F.R. § 280.113, 371n.150

40 C.F.R. § 280.114(a)–(b), 371n.146

40 C.F.R. § 280.114(e), 371n.147, 371n.148

40 C.F.R. § 280.114(f), 371n.149

40 C.F.R. § 280.200 (2002), 373n.162

40 C.F.R. §§ 281.10–.61, 374n.163, 349n.19

40 C.F.R. § 281.10 *et seq.*, 11n.78

40 C.F.R. § 281.21, 374n.164

40 C.F.R. § 281.37, 374n.163

40 C.F.R. § 300.430(e)(9), 30n.80

Table of Regulations 481

40 C.F.R. § 300.700(c)(3), 29n.77, 30n.78
40 C.F.R. § 302.6, 76n.88
40 C.F.R. pt. 24, 327, 377
40 C.F.R. pt. 124, 134, 138, 143
40 C.F.R. pt. 239, 389, 414
40 C.F.R. pt. 240, 385n.20
40 C.F.R. pt. 243, 385n.21
40 C.F.R. pt. 246, 402, 402n.118
40 C.F.R. pt. 249, 403n.129
40 C.F.R. pt. 254, 439
40 C.F.R. pt. 256, 75
40 C.F.R. pt. 257, 12n.83, 385n.24, 403n.131
40 C.F.R. pt. 257, subpt. A, 390
40 C.F.R. pt. 257, subpt. B, 382n.5, 389n.45, 395n.81
40 C.F.R. pt. 258, 12n.86, 382n.4, 385n.23, 389, 392
40 C.F.R. pt. 259, 398
40 C.F.R. pt. 261, 445
40 C.F.R. pt. 261, app. II, 3n.15
40 C.F.R. pt. 261, app. VIII, 47, 328
40 C.F.R. pt. 261, subpt. D, 47, 55
40 C.F.R. pt. 261.31, 219
40 C.F.R. pt. 262, 61n.1, 70, 104, 108, 112, 445
40 C.F.R. pt. 262, subpt. D, 75n.76
40 C.F.R. pt. 262, subpt. E, 85n.128
40 C.F.R. pt. 262, subpt. F, 84n.125
40 C.F.R. pt. 263, 103, 104, 107
40 C.F.R. pt. 264, 75, 126, 132, 217, 445, 151
40 C.F.R. pt. 264, app. IX, 328
40 C.F.R. pt. 264, subpts. A–F, 287
40 C.F.R. pt. 264, subpt. B, § 264.18, 149
40 C.F.R. pt. 264, subpt. O, 21n.32
40 C.F.R. pt. 264, subpt. S, 334
40 C.F.R. pt. 264, subpt. X, 255n.1, 286
40 C.F.R. pt. 264, subpts. AA, BB, 22n.38
40 C.F.R. pt. 264, subpts. BB, CC, 271, 274
40 C.F.R. pt. 265, 65, 81, 144, 149, 163n.12, 217

40 C.F.R. pt. 265 (AA), (BB), (CC), 126
40 C.F.R. pt. 265, subpts. C, D, 67
40 C.F.R. pt. 265, subpt. F, 149
40 C.F.R. pt. 265, subpt. H, 148
40 C.F.R. pt. 265, subpt. M, 150
40 C.F.R. pt. 265, subpt. N, 150
40 C.F.R. pt. 265, subpt. P, 150
40 C.F.R. pt. 265, subpt. Q, 149
40 C.F.R. pt. 265, subpt. R, 255n.1
40 C.F.R. pt. 265, subpts. BB, CC, 275
40 C.F.R. pt. 266, 42, 75, 217, 445
40 C.F.R. pt. 266, subpts. C, F, G, 42n.37, 42n.38
40 C.F.R. pt. 266, subpt. H, 42, 42n.36
40 C.F.R. pt. 268, 126
40 C.F.R. pt. 269, 65
40 C.F.R. pt. 270, 75, 81, 445
40 C.F.R. pt. 270, subpt. C, 134
40 C.F.R. pt. 270, subpt. D, 138
40 C.F.R. pt. 271, 62n.2, 81, 142
40 C.F.R. pt. 272, 444
40 C.F.R. pt. 273, 59, 83, 107
40 C.F.R. pt. 279, 411n.168
40 C.F.R. pt. 279, subpt. C, 12n.89, 412n.171
40 C.F.R. pt. 279, subpt. E, 12n.89, 412n.172
40 C.F.R. pt. 279, subpt. F, 12n.89, 412n.173
40 C.F.R. pt. 279, subpts. G, H, 43
40 C.F.R. pt. 279, subpt. I, 43n.39
40 C.F.R. pt. 280, 11n.80
40 C.F.R. pt. 280, app. I, 358
40 C.F.R. pt. 280, app. II, 358n.70
40 C.F.R. pt. 280, subpt. F, 362n.99, 362n.100
40 C.F.R. pt. 280, subpt. H, 349n.21
40 C.F.R. pt. 300, 29n.40, 110n.33
40 C.F.R. pt. 761, 24n.58
40 C.F.R. pts. 124 and 270, 125, 127n.5
40 C.F.R. pts. 246–247, 385n.22
40 C.F.R. pts. 257, 403, and 503, 12n.91, 412, 412
40 C.F.R. pts. 260, 264, 265, 266, 125

482 TABLE OF REGULATIONS

40 C.F.R. pts. 264 and 265, 6, 65, 108, 255

40 C.F.R. pts. 264 and 265, §§ .1054, .1057, 34

40 C.F.R. pts. 264, 265, subpts. A–H, 255

40 C.F.R. pts. 264 and 265, subpt. G, 150

40 C.F.R. pts. 264 and 265, subpt. H, 7n.50, 148

40 C.F.R. pts. 264 and 265, subpt. J, 149

40 C.F.R. pts. 265, 265, subpt. O, 150

40 C.F.R. pts. 270 and 124, 147

40 C.F.R. subpt. G, 143n.43

40 C.F.R. subpts. 264, 265, 270, 67n.34, 68n.42

49 C.F.R. § 171.2, 109n.27

49 C.F.R. § 171.8, 112n.41, 112n.42

49 C.F.R. §§ 171.15–.16, 112n.44

49 C.F.R. § 171.15(a), 112n.45, 112n.46

49 C.F.R. § 171.16(a), 113n.47

49 C.F.R. § 172.3, 113n.48

49 C.F.R. § 172.101(c)(10), 113n.49

49 C.F.R. § 172.300, 113n.50

49 C.F.R. § 172.304, 73n.68

49 C.F.R. § 172.500(b), 114n.51

49 C.F.R. § 173.2–.2a, 114n.52

49 C.F.R. § 173.22, 114n.53

49 C.F.R. § 173.24, 114n.54

49 C.F.R. § 173.28, 173.29, 173.3, 173.4, 173.6, 173.12, 173.150–.156, 173.306, 114n.55

49 C.F.R. pt. 171, 6

49 C.F.R. pt. 172, 73n.66

49 C.F.R. pt. 172, subpt. F, 73n.67

49 C.F.R. pts. 171–180, 110

49 C.F.R. pts. 173, 178, 179, 73n.65

Federal Register

38 Fed. Reg. 11,176 (1993), 117n.65

42 Fed. Reg. 12,722, 33,066 (1980), 1n.4

44 Fed. Reg. 53,460 (1979), 388n.38

45 Fed. Reg. 7200 (1991), 34n.2

45 Fed. Reg. 12,746 (1988), 69n.44

45 Fed. Reg. 33,084, 33,097 (1980), 18n.14

45 Fed. Reg. 33,096 (1980), 4n.22

45 Fed. Reg. 33,098, 18n.16

45 Fed. Reg. 51,645 (1980), 114n.56

45 Fed. Reg. 71,026–27, 73n.6

45 Fed. Reg. 72,026–28 (1980), 63n.6

45 Fed. Reg. 76,633 (1980), 144n.46

45 Fed. Reg. 85,016, 85,020–21 (1980), 453n.41

50 Fed. Reg. 641 (1985), 2n.8

50 Fed. Reg. 28,702 (1985), 332

50 Fed. Reg. 38,946 (1985), 322n.5

50 Fed. Reg. 47,912 (1985), 342n.57

50 Fed. Reg. 49,258 (1985), 410n.160

51 Fed. Reg. 5472 (1986), 48n.2

51 Fed. Reg. 24,496 (1986), 3n.19

51 Fed. Reg. 28,664, 28,682 (1986), 85n.129, 85n.130

51 Fed. Reg. 37,854, 37,855 n.2 (1986), 212n.110, 213n.111

51 Fed. Reg. 41,900 (1986), 410n.163

52 Fed. Reg. 45,788 (1987), 332

53 Fed. Reg. 3818 (1988), 372n.155

53 Fed. Reg. 3820, 373n.156, 373n.157

Table of Regulations 483

53 Fed. Reg. 3821, 373n.158, 373n.159
53 Fed. Reg. 3822, 373n.160
53 Fed. Reg. 3824, 373n.161
53 Fed. Reg. 17,578–86 (1988), 57n.11
53 Fed. Reg. 23,981 (1988), 322n.5
53 Fed. Reg. 25,446 (1988), 3n.19
53 Fed. Reg. 28,122 (1988), 299n.48
53 Fed. Reg. 31,148 (1988), 302n.59
53 Fed. Reg. 31,149 (1988), 303n.60
53 Fed. Reg. 37,082 (1988) (codified at
   40 C.F.R. §§ 280.10–.74), 348n.19
53 Fed. Reg. 37,082, 37,083 (1988),
   346n.1
53 Fed. Reg. 37,212 (1988) (codified at
   40 C.F.R. §§ 281.10–.61), 349n.19,
   374n.163
53 Fed. Reg. 37,240, 374n.165
53 Fed. Reg. 43,322 (1988), 374n.163,
   348n.20, 362n.99
53 Fed. Reg. 51,444 (1988), 339n.49

54 Fed. Reg. 3845 (1989), 80n.93
54 Fed. Reg. 36,592 (1989), 397n.94
54 Fed. Reg. 41,000, 41,006 (1989),
   322n.5
54 Fed. Reg. 41,004 (1989), 342n.57

55 Fed. Reg. 2322 (1990), 397n.94
55 Fed. Reg. 6640 (1990), 296n.33
55 Fed. Reg. 8658 (1993), 335n.43
55 Fed. Reg. 8758–60 (1990), 339n.49
55 Fed. Reg. 8760 (1990), 303n.62
55 Fed. Reg. 11,798 (1990), 3n.15,
   361n.88
55 Fed. Reg. 11,798, 11,841 (1990),
   25n.60, 25n.61, 25n.62
55 Fed. Reg. 11,876 (1990), 411n.166
55 Fed. Reg. 22,520 (1990), 9n.62
55 Fed. Reg. 22,657, 19n.21, 301n.51
55 Fed. Reg. 22,658–59, 23n.50
55 Fed. Reg. 22,660–61 (1990),
   297n.38, 301n.54
55 Fed. Reg. 22,661 (1990), 309n.16
55 Fed. Reg. 22,666 (1990), 295n.30
55 Fed. Reg. 22,671 (1990), 35n.8

55 Fed. Reg. 22,672 (1990), 293n.21
55 Fed. Reg. 22,676–78 (1990), 17n.11
55 Fed. Reg. 30,798 (1990), 10n.71,
   332n.55, 334n.39
55 Fed. Reg. 30,808 (1990), 324n.14,
   326n.21, 326n.22
55 Fed. Reg. 30,808–09 (proposed July
   1990), 324n.11
55 Fed. Reg. 30,817 (1990), 22n.40
55 Fed. Reg. 30,824, 30n.79
55 Fed. Reg. 30,853, 28n.71
55 Fed. Reg. 30,874 (1990), 326n.20
55 Fed. Reg. 32,135 (1990), 397n.94
55 Fed. Reg. 39,409 (1990), 129n.18

56 Fed. Reg. 7134 (1991), 247n.41
56 Fed. Reg. 7137 (1991), 21n.35,
   21n.36, 21n.37
56 Fed. Reg. 7200 (1991), 34n.3
56 Fed. Reg. 7849 (1991), 80n.93
56 Fed. Reg. 27,300 (1991), 397n.94
56 Fed. Reg. 37,194 (1992), 299n.45
56 Fed. Reg. 38,342 (1991) (codified at
   40 C.F.R. § 280.20(c)(1)(ii)(B)–(C),
   352n.43
56 Fed. Reg. 49,376 (1991), 377n.178
56 Fed. Reg. 49,378 (1991), 377n.179
56 Fed. Reg. 49,379 (1991), 377n.180,
   377n.181
56 Fed. Reg. 50,978 (1991), 388n.39,
   389n.43
56 Fed. Reg. 50,995 (1991), 415n.192
56 Fed. Reg. 51,016 (1991), 391n.49

57 Fed. Reg. 12 (1992), 48n.1
57 Fed. Reg. 7628 (1992), 54n.7
57 Fed. Reg. 21,450 (1992), 55n.8
57 Fed. Reg. 21,524 (1992), 12n.88,
   411n.165, 411n.167
57 Fed. Reg. 31,114 (1993), 77n.90
57 Fed. Reg. 32,726 (1992), 118n.69
57 Fed. Reg. 37,218–21 (1992), 271n.49
57 Fed. Reg. 37,221, 271n.51
57 Fed. Reg. 37,225 (1992), 310n.19
57 Fed. Reg. 37,226, 310n.24

484   TABLE OF REGULATIONS

57 Fed. Reg. 41,566 (1992), 411n.168
57 Fed. Reg. 41,605, 411n.169
57 Fed. Reg. 49,280 (1992), 296n.34
57 Fed. Reg. 58,848 (1992), 117n.63
57 Fed. Reg. 62,608 (1992), 22n.39

58 Fed. Reg. 4802 (1993), 80n.93
58 Fed. Reg. 4972 (1993), 301n.54
58 Fed. Reg. 8273 (1993), 397n.98
58 Fed. Reg. 8658 (1993), 11n.75,
  31n.81, 303n.63
58 Fed. Reg. 8677 (1993), 340n.52
58 Fed. Reg. 9026 (1993), 349n.21,
  362n.100, 369n.137, 412n.175
58 Fed. Reg. 9248 (1992), 12n.91
58 Fed. Reg. 29,860 (1993), 301n.54
58 Fed. Reg. 29,863 (1993), 20n.26
58 Fed. Reg. 29,864 (1993), 24n.53
58 Fed. Reg. 31,114 (1993), 77
58 Fed. Reg. 32,149 (1993), 117n.64
58 Fed. Reg. 42,466 (1993), 397n.99

59 Fed. Reg. 709 (1994), 398n.102
59 Fed. Reg. 6186 (1994), 117n.66
59 Fed. Reg. 29,372 (1994), 401n.117
59 Fed. Reg. 47,133 (1994), 398n.103
59 Fed. Reg. 47,988–48,002 (1994),
  309n.17
59 Fed. Reg. 62,896 (1980), 68n.40

60 Fed. Reg. 7366 (1995), 398n.104
60 Fed. Reg. 11,089 (1995), 397n.95
60 Fed. Reg. 11,706–08 (1995), 306n.3
60 Fed. Reg. 15,970 (1997), 117n.68
60 Fed. Reg. 21,381 (1995), 403n.131
60 Fed. Reg. 25,492 (1995), 83n.114
60 Fed. Reg. 43,675 (1995), 307n.9
60 Fed. Reg. 46,692 (1995), 373n.162
60 Fed. Reg. 63,417 (1995), 343n.61

61 Fed. Reg. 2338 (1996), 397n.94
61 Fed. Reg. 15,568 (1996), 306n.3
61 Fed. Reg. 15,585 (1996), 311n.28
61 Fed. Reg. 18,795 (1996), 338n.48
61 Fed. Reg. 19,432 (1996), 336n.45

61 Fed. Reg. 27,984 (1996), 376n.177
61 Fed. Reg. 34,269 (1996), 389n.45,
  395n.81
61 Fed. Reg. 59,932, 68n.41
61 Fed. Reg. 69,630 (1996), 376n.173

62 Fed. Reg. 26,006 (1997), 309n.16
62 Fed. Reg. 37,694 (1997), 311n.29
62 Fed. Reg. 60,973 (1997), 404n.132
62 Fed. Reg. 64,506 (1997), 313n.38,
  317n.63

63 Fed. Reg. 28,556 (1998), 10n.74,
  341n.54
63 Fed. Reg. 28,560 (1998), 307n.9
63 Fed. Reg. 28,571–72, 311n.31
63 Fed. Reg. 28,576 (1998), 307n.9
63 Fed. Reg. 28,602–22, 313n.40
63 Fed. Reg. 28,603–04, 312n.35
63 Fed. Reg. 28,606–08, 315n.45
63 Fed. Reg. 28,607, 315n.50
63 Fed. Reg. 28,609, 308n.11
63 Fed. Reg. 28,609–10, 317n.58
63 Fed. Reg. 28,610, 317n.59, 317n.60
63 Fed. Reg. 28,617–19, 308n.14,
  315n.44
63 Fed. Reg. 28,622, 310n.24, 315n.46
63 Fed. Reg. 28,623–24, 309n.16
63 Fed. Reg. 43,332, 363n.101
63 Fed. Reg. 49,673 (1993) § 403 (c),
  404n.137, 405n.138
63 Fed. Reg. 51,254 (1998), 312n.33
63 Fed. Reg. 57,040 (1998), 389n.46,
  414n.182
63 Fed. Reg. 65,873 (1998), 340n.53

64 Fed. Reg. 45,632 (1999), 398n.105
64 Fed. Reg. 54,604 (1999), 10n.73,
  334n.40

65 Fed. Reg. 3080 (2000), 404n.133
65 Fed. Reg. 32,214 (2000), 397n.100
65 Fed. Reg. 37,947 (2000), 308n.10
65 Fed. Reg. 42,937 (2000), 312n.34
65 Fed. Reg. 58,275, 336n.46

Table of Regulations   485

65 Fed. Reg. 61,251 (2001), 109n.29
65 Fed. Reg. 81,373 (2000), 314n.43

66 Fed. Reg. 27,266 (2001), 53n.5
66 Fed. Reg. 28,240 (2001), 175n.94
66 Fed. Reg. 37,089 (2001), 117n.67
66 Fed. Reg. 37,092 (2001), 117n.62
66 Fed. Reg. 44,345 (2001), 375n.166
66 Fed. Reg. 46,162 (2001), 175n.94
66 Fed. Reg. 50,332, 4n.24, 56n.9

66 Fed. Reg. 52,191, 127n.6
66 Fed. Reg. 52,762 (2001), 343n.60
66 Fed. Reg. 61,251 (2001), 109n.29

67 Fed. Reg. 2962 (2002), 339n.51
67 Fed. Reg. 6968, 239n.31
67 Fed. Reg. (2002), 315n.52

68 Fed. Reg. 8757 (2003), 326n.19
68 Fed. Reg. 73,539 (2003), 175n.94,
  175n.95

INDEX

NOTE: Boldface numbers refer to figures or tables.

Abandoned materials, in defining solid waste, 34–35
Accidental or infrequent production of hazardous waste, 63–64
Accidents, accidental occurrence, financial responsibility and, 203
Accumulation of wastes, 5, 65–69
Acknowledgment of Consent papers, 85–87
  export of hazardous wastes and, 85, 86, 87
  transport of hazardous wastes and, 106
Action or trigger levels for corrective action, 10, 327, 329–330
Action, 27–31
Administrative orders and hearings, enforcement of RCRA and, 425–428
Administrative Procedure Act (APA), hazardous wastes and, 54
Advanced notice of proposed rule making (ANPR), 372–373
Agricultural waste, 3
Air emission/pollution, 15
  boilers and industrial furnaces (BIFs) and, 244–245
  generators of hazardous wastes and, 68
  incinerators and, 237
Air quality, 8
Alabama
  transport of hazardous wastes and, 119
  underground storage tank (UST) regulation in, 374
Alarm requirements for TSD facilities, 171
Alaska, location of TSD facilities in, regulations, 168
Alternatives to treatment, land disposal restrictions (LDRs) and, temporary and permanent, 297–300
Aluminum processing, Universal Treatment Standards and, 311
Analysis of waste, 164–165
Appeal process for permits, 138, **139**, 141
Application procedure for permits under RCRA, 130–133, **131**
Areas of concern (AOC), corrective action and, 321–322, 324–325, 328

"Areas of contamination" policy, corrective action and, 338–339
Arizona, location of TSD facilities in, regulations, 168
Arkansas, underground storage tank (UST) regulation in, 374
As-is secondary materials in recycling, 36, 37–38
Atomic Energy Act, solid wastes and, 41
Authorization of state hazardous waste programs, 444–447

Bankruptcy of owner/operator, 371
Barnes, A. James, 450
Batteries, universal waste rule for, 58–59
Bentson wastes (*see also* Bevill wastes), 395–399, 409–413
Benzene, TCLP thresholds for, **53**
Bergeson, Lynn L., 45
Best demonstrated available technology (BDAT), 8–9
  land disposal restrictions (LDRs) and, 295
Bevill wastes, 56, 247, 248, 297, 383, 395–399, 409–413
Beyond RCRA/Prospects for Waste and Materials Management . . . 2020, 60
Biennial report requirements, 75, 179
Blake, Francis S., 450
Boilers and industrial furnaces (BIFs), 7–8, 240–249
  Bevill amendments and, 247, 248
  boiler defined, 240–241
  carbon monoxide emission and, 244
  Clean Air Act and, 21
  destruction and removal efficiencies (DREs) of, 243
  dioxins and, 243
  documentation requirements for, 250–253
  efficiency rating of, 243
  emissions from, 244–245
  energy recovery and, 241
  exemptions to regulations pertaining to, 240, 241–243
  feed of waste into, 245, 249
  heat requirements of, 245–246
  industrial furnace defined, 241

488 INDEX

Boilers and industrial furnaces (BIFs), (*continued*)
  interim status facilities and, 243, 245–246
  maintenance of, 246–247
  metal recovery furnaces in, 242
  metals, hydrogen chloride, chlorine gas emissions, 244–245
  operating requirements for, 245–247
  P-listed wastes, 242
  permits for, 243–245
  residues from, treatment of, 247–249
  small quantity generators (SQGs) and, 242
  smelting, melting, refining furnaces in, 242
  standards for, 217, 240–249
Bond ratings, financial responsibility and, 206–207
Bond requirements
  financial responsibility and, 208–209
  transport of hazardous wastes and, 117–118
Bourdeau, Karl S., 319
By-product regulation, 3, 24, 35, 37, 41

California
  location of TSD facilities in, regulations, 168
  transport of hazardous wastes and, 118
California-listed hazardous wastes, 25, 290
Capacity variances, land disposal restrictions (LDRs) and, national and case-by-case, 298
Capping of hazardous sites (*see also* Closure; Postclosure), 30–31, 191–193, 196–199
Carbon filtration systems, 34
Carbon monoxide, 8
Carbon tetrachloride, TCLP thresholds for, **53**
Cement kiln dust (CKD), 398
Certificate of Liability Insurance, 214
Cessation of treatment guidelines, land disposal restrictions (LDRs) and, 295–296
Chambers, John C., 345
Characteristic hazardous wastes, 3, 45, 49–52, 64, 291
Chlordane, TCLP thresholds for, **53**
Chlorine gas (Cl_2), 244–245
Chlorobenzene, TCLP thresholds for, **53**
Chloroform, TCLP thresholds for, **53**
Citizen suits and RCRA enforcement, 437–441
Civil and criminal enforcement (*see* Enforcement, civil and criminal)
Civil suits in authorized states, 451–453
Clark, Benjamin T., 345

Class 1 modifications to permit, 138, 140
Class 2 modifications to permit, 138, 140
Class 3 modifications to permit, 140–141
Clean Air Act, 15, 20–22
  boilers or industrial furnaces (BIFs) under, 21
  CERCLA and, 26
  dust and sludges produced by scrubbers, 20–21
  hazardous air pollutants (HAPs) and, 20–22
  Hazardous Organics Standard and, 22
  Hazardous Waste Combustion Strategy (Draft) and, 22
  incinerators and, 21, 232
  nonhazardous wastes and, 391, 394
  treatment, storage, disposal (TSD) facilities and, 21
Clean Water Act, 3, 12, 15, 16, 17–20
  CERCLA and, 26
  corrective action and, 326–327
  dilution and antidilution rules in, 19–20
  domestic sewage and, 17–18
  impoundment or storage of wastewater under, 19–20
  industrial wastewater and, 18
  land disposal restrictions (LDRs) and, 19–20, 289, 300–302, 305–307
  nonhazardous wastes and, 382–383, 391, 392, 394, 412, 415
  pretreatment standards of, 17, 18–19
  publicly owned treatment works (POTWs) and, 17
  sewage sludge and, 19, 412, 415
  tanks or tank systems in, 18–19
  underground storage tanks (USTs) and, 349
Cleanup process, CERCLA vs. RCRA, 30–31
Closed-loop reclamation, 35, 40–41
Closure of TSD facilities (*see also* Financial responsibility), 184–189, 204
  certification of, 186
  containers and tanks and, 195–196, 221–222, 229–230
  conversion to nonhazardous waste handling and, 188–189
  cost estimate for, 200–204
  delay of, 188–189
  drip pads and, 199
  financial assurance for, 199–215
  groundwater protection and, 262–263
  impoundments and, 273
  incinerators and, 199, 239
  interim status facilities and, 185–186, 198
  land treatment units and, 197–198, 281, 282–283
  landfills and, 198–199, 284
  plan for, 184–186
  post- (*see* Postclosure)

runoff and runoff control in, 197–198
surface impoundments and, specifications for, 196–197
timing of, 187–188
underground storage tanks (USTs) and, 361–362
waste piles and, 197, 277–278
Co-products, 35
Coking operations, 41
Colorado
location of TSD facilities in, regulations, 168
transport of hazardous wastes and, 118
Columbia Falls decision, Universal Treatment Standards and, 312
Commerce Clause
enforcement of RCRA and, 453–454
interstate flow of wastes vs., 405–409
state and local regulation of transport, 118–120
Communications requirements for TSD facilities, 171
Compliance Incentives for Small Businesses, underground storage tanks (USTs) and, 376
Compliance monitoring, groundwater protection and, 267–268
Comprehensive Environmental Response, Compensation, and Liability Act (CERCLA/Superfund), 11, 16, 17, 26–31
"areas of contamination" policy in, 339
capping of hazardous sites under, 30–31
Clean Air Act and, 26
Clean Water Act and, 26
cleanup process under, 30–31
corrective action and, 319–320, 326, 338, 342
corrective action management units, 31
covered sites under, 27–28
definition of hazardous waste under, 26
emergency reporting under, 76
enforcement of RCRA and, 437
enforcement scheme and cost recovery under, 28
feasibility studies under, 329
financial responsibility and, 215
land disposal restrictions (LDR) program, 31, 289, 290, 302, 312
liability under, 29–30
National Contingency Plan (NCP) and, 29–30
National Oil and Hazardous Substances, 339
National Response Centers and, 26–27
overlap of RCRA regulation and, 26–27
Preliminary Assessment/Site Investigation, 30

Remedial Investigation and Feasibility Study, 30
reporting requirements of, 26–27
response action of, vs. RCRA corrective, 27
solid waste management units (SWMUs) and, 28
Superfund Amendments and Reauthorization, 231, 239
Toxic Substances Control Act (TSCA) and, 26
treatment, storage, and disposal (TSD), 28
underground storage tanks (USTs) and, 27, 347, 349, 360, 378
Comprehensive Procurement Guidelines (CPG), nonhazardous wastes and, 403–404
Concentration-based exemption criteria (CBEC), hazardous wastes and, 54–55
Conditionally exempt small quantity generators (CESQGs), 42, 80–82
nonhazardous wastes and, 389, 391, 394–395
used oil, 42
volume limits for, 81–82
Connecticut, underground storage tank (UST) regulation in, 374
Constitutional issues in enforcement, 453–457
Construction quality assurance (CQA) program, operation and design of TSDs, 169–170
Contained-in policy, hazardous wastes, 52–57, 310, 338
land disposal restrictions (LDRs) and, 310, 338
Contained liquids and gases (as solid waste), 2, 33–34
Containers and tanks (see also Underground storage tanks), 7–8, 218–222
age of, secondary containment and, 223–226
Clean Water Act and, 18–19
closure and postclosure regulations and, 195–196, 221–222, 229–230
corrosion protection for, 351–352, 354, 357
design requirements for, 218–219
empty, residues of wastes in, 59, 220–221
F-listed, 219
Flammable and Combustible Liquids Code, 228–229
ignitable and reactive wastes in, 228–229
incompatible wastes and, 229
inspection of, 227–228
interim status facilities and, 222–223, 229

490 INDEX

Containers and tanks (*continued*)
labeling of, 64–65, 73, 113–114
landfills and, 285
leak detection systems for, 225–226, 228
maintenance of, 66, 219–220, 227–228
polychlorinated biphenyls (PCBs) and, 221
Practical Guide for Inspection of Refinery Equipment, 228
return to service, 231
secondary containment requirements for, 223–226
specific wastes and, specifications for, 220, 228–229
spill and overfill control for, 225, 230–231, 351–352
standards for, 218–222
storage areas for, 218–219
Superfund Amendments and Reauthorization Act of 1986 (SARA) and, 231
tank systems, 222–231
  age of, secondary containment and, 223–226
  ancillary equipment and, 225
  certification of, 226
  closure and postclosure regulations and, 229–230
  definition of tank in, 222
  design and component requirements for, 223–227
  dual wall, 224
  exemptions to rules governing, 222–223
  existing systems, requirements for, 226
  Flammable and Combustible Liquids Code, 228–229
  ignitable and reactive wastes in, 228–229
  incompatible wastes and, 229
  inspection of, 227–228
  interim status facilities and, 222–223, 229
  leak detection systems for, 225–226, 228
  liners for, 224
  maintenance of, 227–228
  new systems, requirements for, 226–227
  return to service, 231
  secondary containment requirements for, 223–226
  specific wastes and, specifications for, 228–229
  spills from, 225, 230–231
  Superfund Amendments and Reauthorization Act of 1986 (SARA) and, 231
  vault systems for, 224

triple rinsing protocol for, 59, 221
underground (USTs), 11–12, 27
waste piles and, 276
Contaminated Debris Rule, impoundments and, 271
Contingency plan for TSD facilities, 172–174
Corporate guarantee of financial responsibility, 207–208
Corrective action management units (CAMUs), 9, 10–11, 335, 339, 340
CERCLA and, 31
land disposal restrictions (LDRs) and, 303, 315–317
Corrective action plan (CAP), 335
Corrective action under RCRA, 9–11, 27–31, 319–344
  "areas of contamination" policy in, 338–339
  action levels for, 329–330
  action orders for, 327
  applicability of, types of units subject to, 322–325
  areas of concern (AOC) and, 321–322, 324–325, 328
  CERCLA and, 27–31, 319–320, 326, 338, 342
  Clean Water Act and, 326–327
  contained-in policy for, 338
  corrective action management units (CAMUs) and, 335, 339, 340
  corrective action plan (CAP) and, 335
  corrective measures study (CMS) in, 328, 329–330
  current human exposures under control (CA725) and, 336–337
  enforcement of, 343–344
  environmental indicators (EIs) and, 320, 336–337
  expediting, 343–344
  extent of the facility subject to, 325–326
  financial responsibility and, 212–213
  First Codification Rule of, 332–333
  Government Performance and Results Act of 1993 (GPRA) and, 336–337
  groundwater protection and, 263, 268–269, 343
  Hazardous and Solid Waste Amendments (HSWA) and, 319–320, 332
  HWIR for Contaminated Media (HWIR-Media) regulation and, 340
  implementation of, 328, 332–337
  initial regulatory implementation of, 332–334
  institutional control (IC) and, 343
  interim measures under, 330–332
  interim status facilities and, 321–322, 327
  jurisdictional reach of, 321–327

Index   491

key additional guidance for, 342–343
land disposal restrictions (LDRs) and, 290, 337–338, 340–341
migration of contaminated groundwater under control (CA750) and, 336–337
National Pollutant Discharge Elimination System (NPDES) and, 326–327
Occupational Safety and Health Administration (OSHA) and, 327
omnibus authority under, 324–325
permit requirements of RCRA and, 133, 321–322, 327–328
prioritization of facilities for, 337
process of, 327–332
protective filers and, 322
public participation in, 343
RCRA facility assessment (RFA) in, 328
RCRA facility investigation (RFI) in, 328–329
releases subject to, 326–327
remediation waste management and, 337–341
results-based, 335–337
Second Codification Rule of, 333
soil contamination and, 340–341
solid waste management units (SWMUs) and, 320, 321, 323–324, 328, 330, 333
solid waste releases and, 323–324
statutory scheme and regulatory background for, 319–320
steps in, 328–330
Subpart S proposed rule (EPA) and, 334–335
technical issues related to, 341–343
temporary units and, 339–340
treatment, storage, disposal (TSD) facilities and, 320
underground storage tanks (USTs) and, 342, 360–361, 377
Corrective Measures Study (CMS), 30, 328, 329–330
Corrosion protection, underground storage tanks (USTs) and, 351–352, 354, 357
Corrosivity, in defining hazardous waste, 3, 50, 64
Cost estimate of closure/postclosure, 200–204
Cost recovery, CERCLA vs. RCRA, 28–30
Cresol, TCLP thresholds for, 53, **53**
Criminal enforcement proceedings, 432–436, 451
Current human exposures under control (CA725), 336–337
Cyanides, 50, 51

"Decharacterized" hazardous wastes, Safe Drinking Water Act (SDWA) and, 23–24
Defenses against RCRA enforcement, 431–432, 435
Definition of hazardous waste under CERCLA, 26
Definition of hazardous waste under RCRA (*see also* Hazardous wastes), 2–4, 16, 26, 45–60, 64–65
Del Piano, Anthony J., 61
Delaware, underground storage tank (UST) regulation in, 374
Delisting of hazardous wastes, 4, 48–49
Denny, S., 121–124
Department of Justice, 421–422
Department of Transportation (DOT), 5
coordination with EPA by, 114–115
Hazardous Materials Transportation Act (HMTA) and, 25–26
Memorandum of Understanding (MOU) with EPA in, 114–115
transport of hazardous wastes and, 103–104, 110
Derived-from rule, hazardous wastes and, 4, 52–57, 310
Design of TSDs (*see* Standards for operation and design of TSDs)
Destruction and energy recovery (DER) rate, incinerators and, 236
Destruction and removal efficiencies (DREs), 235
boilers and industrial furnaces (BIFs) and, 243
incinerators and, 235
Detection monitoring, groundwater protection and, 265–267
Dichlorobenzene, TCLP thresholds for, **53**
Dichloroethane, TCLP thresholds for, **53**
Dichloroethylene, TCLP thresholds for, **53**
Dielectric fluids (*see also* Polychlorinated biphenyls), 25, 52
Dilution and antidilution rules, 19–20
Clean Water Act and, 19–20
Safe Drinking Water Act (SDWA) and, 23
Dinitrotoluene, TCLP thresholds for, **53**
Dioxins, 34, 243
Direct reuse, 35
Direct use exclusions, 38
"Discarded material," in defining solid waste, 34–41
Disposal of hazardous wastes, 6–9
Disposal of nonhazardous wastes under RCRA, 12
Documentation, 203–204
boilers and industrial furnaces (BIFs), 250–253

492 INDEX

Documentation (*continued*)
financial responsibility and, 203–204, 207
Drip pads, 66, 199
Dual-wall tanks, 224
Dust and sludges produced by air scrubbers, Clean Air Act and, 20–21

Education in handling of wastes, 67
Efficiency rating, boilers and industrial furnaces (BIFs) and, 243
Emergency coordinator, 173
Emergency permits, 130, 136, 137–138
Emergency reporting, generators of hazardous wastes and, 76
Emergency response, 67, 172–174
emergency coordinator role and, 173
financial responsibility and, 203
fire and rescue, local, 171–172
National Response Center, 174
operation and design of TSDs, 170–174
spills, 230–231
transport of hazardous wastes and, 113
underground storage tanks (USTs) and, 359–360
Emissions (*see* Air emission/pollution)
Empty containers, residues in, 59, 220–221
Endangerment, imminent and substantial, 436–437
Endangerment, knowing, 434
Energy recovery, 241
boilers and industrial furnaces (BIFs) and, 241
incinerators and, 236
nonhazardous wastes and, 399–405
Enforcement of RCRA, civil and criminal, 417–442, 448–451
administrative orders and hearings in, 425–428
agencies responsible for, 420–423
CERCLA and, 437
challenges to, 418–419
citizen suits and, 437–441
civil judicial, 428–432
civil proceedings in, 425–432
civil suits in authorized states and, 451–453
Commerce Clause and, 453–454
constitutional issues in, 453–457
criminal proceedings in, 432–436, 451
defenses against, 431–432, 435
Department of Justice and, 421–422
Environment and Natural Resources Division (ENRD) of DOJ and, 421
EPA and, 421
equitable relief and, 428–428
estoppel defense against RCRA enforcement, 432

federal facilities and, 441–442
fines and sentencing under, federal guidelines for, 435–436
Global Settlement Policy for, 422
good faith efforts to comply and, 432
imminent and substantial endangerment and, 436–437
impossibility defense against, 431
information gathering for, 424–425
Integrated Enforcement Policy for, 422
invalidity of underlying regulations defense against, 431
jury trial and, 429
knowing endangerment and, 434
knowing violation under, 433–434
land disposal restrictions (LDRs) and, 432
Office of Criminal Enforcement and, 421
Office of Enforcement and Compliance Assurance (OECA) and, 421
Office of Federal Activities and, 421
Office of Regulatory Enforcement and, 421
Office of Site Remediation Enforcement and, 421
overfile right of EPA, in civil enforcement, 449–451
permit as shield rule and, 432
persons subject to prosecution under, 433
RCRA Enforcement Policy and Compendium, 451
relief and penalties in, 427–429
self auditing and, 436
state authorization and, 448–451
state based, 422–423
statute of limitations in, 428, 429–430
statutory authority for, 420
Supremacy Clause and federal preemption in, 454–457
Enforcement scheme and cost recovery, CERCLA vs. RCRA, 28–30
Environment and Natural Resources Division (ENRD) of DOJ, 421
Environmental indicators (EIs), corrective action and, 320, 336–337
Environmental Protection Agency (EPA), 1, 3, 33
Beyond RCRA/Prospects for Waste and Materials Management...2020, 60
corrective action and, Subpart S proposed rule and, 334–335
DOT Memorandum of Understanding (MOU) with, 114–115
enforcement of RCRA and, 421
generators of hazardous wastes and, defining, 63
land disposal restrictions (LDRs) and, 289–303
Office of Enforcement and Compliance Assurance, 86

Office of Solid Waste (OSW), 51
permit requirements of RCRA and,
standardization of, 127
RCRA integration by, 16–17
state authorization and enforcement
power of, 448–451
EPA identification number (EPA ID), 163
generators of hazardous wastes and, 63,
69–70, 84–85, 87, 88, **95–96**
transport of hazardous wastes and,
104–108, 110
*EPA Manual for Waste Minimization
Opportunity Assessments*, 77–79,
97–101
Equipment requirements for TSD facilities,
170–171
Equitable estoppel defense against RCRA
enforcement, 432
Equitable relief, enforcement of RCRA
and, 428–429
Estoppel defense against RCRA
enforcement, 432
Eugster, Matthew B., 125
Ex-process reuse, 35
Exception reports, 75–76
Expanded characteristic option (ECHO),
hazardous wastes and, 55
Explosive materials (*see also* Reactivity in
defining hazardous waste), 50–51
Export of hazardous wastes, 85–89,
106–107
Acknowledgment of Consent papers for,
85, 86, 87
Customs requirements for, 88
manifest requirements for, 87–88
notification requirements for, 85–87
Organization for Economic Cooperation
and Development (OECD) and,
88–89, 107
reporting requirements for, 88–89
transport requirements for, 106–107

F-listed hazardous wastes, 3, 34, 38, 47–48,
219, 238, 272, 274, 278, 281–282,
285–286, 294, 308
Facilities, 28
Feasibility study, CERCLA, 329
Federal facilities, enforcement of RCRA
and, 441–442
Federal Facility Compliance Act of 1992,
441–442
Federal Highway Administration
(FHWA), transport of hazardous
wastes and, 115
Federal Insecticide, Fungicide, and
Rodenticide Act (FIFRA), 17
Federal Transit Act of 1998 (FTA), 111
Federal Water Pollution Control Act (*see*
Clean Water Act)

Federal-state relationship under RCRA,
443–457
authorization of state hazardous waste
programs and, 444–447
civil suits in authorized states and,
451–453
Commerce Clause and, 453–454
constitutional issues in, 453–457
criminal enforcement and, 451
EPA enforcement power and, 448–451
Hazardous and Solid Waste
Amendments (HSWA) of 1984 and,
447–448
interim facilities and, 444–445
overfile right of EPA, in civil
enforcement, 449–451
*RCRA Enforcement Policy and
Compendium*, 451
Supremacy Clause and federal
preemption in, 454–457
withdrawal of authorization and, 447
Financial responsibility (*see also* Closure;
Postclosure), 183, 199–215
accidents, accidental occurrence and, 203
bankruptcy of owner/operator and, 371
bond ratings and, 206–207
CERCLA and, 215
Certificate of Liability Insurance, 214
corporate guarantee of, 207–208
corrective action and, paying for,
212–213
cost estimates and, closure/postclosure,
200–204
documentation of, 203–204, 207
generator classification and, 200
guarantees, 365–366
Hazardous Waste Facility Liability
Endorsement, 214
implications of, 214–215
insurance for, 203–204, 210–211,
363–364, 366, 369–370
interim status facilities, 200
lender liability and, 373–374
letter of credit for, 209–210, 367
liability requirements of, 213–214
local government and, 369
multiple mechanisms and facilities,
211–212
risk retention groups and, 366
self-insurance, 364
state mechanisms, 212
"substantial business relationship"
defined in, 207–208
surety bond for, 208–209, 366–367
test of, 206–207
trust funds for, 204–206, 368–369
underground injection systems and, 206
underground storage tanks (USTs) and,
347, 348, 362–373

494 INDEX

Fines and sentencing, enforcement of RCRA and, federal guidelines for, 435–436
First Codification Rule, corrective action and, 332–333
Flammable and Combustible Liquids Code, 228–229
Floodplains, 168–169
  hazardous wastes and, 7
  nonhazardous wastes and, 393
Fuel, refuse-derived fuel (RDF) using, nonhazardous wastes and, 384
Furans, 34
Furnaces (*see* Boilers and industrial furnaces; Incinerators and furnaces)

Garbage, 2
Garrett, Theodore L., 1
Generators of hazardous waste, 4–5, 61–89, 174–175
  accidental or infrequent production of, 63–64
  accumulation and storage requirements for, 65–69
  air emission control standards and, 68
  biennial reports by, 75
  CERCLA reporting requirements for, 76
  certifications for manifest and, 71
  conditionally exempt small quantity generators (CESQGs), 42, 80–82
  container and tank maintenance by, 66, 219–220, 227–228
  emergency reporting by, 76
  emergency response requirements of, 67
  EPA identification number (EPA ID) for, 63, 69–70, 84–85, 87, 88, **95–96**
  EPA Manual for Waste Minimization Opportunity Assessments, 77–79, **97–101**
  exception reports by, 75–76
  exemptions for, 64, 80–84
  export of hazardous wastes by, 85–89
  financial assurance of, 199–215
  hazardous waste defined for, 64–65
  import of hazardous wastes by, 84–85
  labeling of container and tanks in, 64–65, 73, 113–114
  land disposal restrictions (LDRs) and, 293
  large quantity handler of universal waste (LQHUW) and, 83–84
  liability in, 63
  manifest system to track waste handling and, 70–73, 87–88, 104–108, 174–178
  minimization of wastes by, 77–80
  notification to EPA of hazardous waste activities by, 69
  permit requirements of RCRA and, exclusions, 128

  permitting requirements of, 67
  pretransportation requirements of, 73
  record keeping and reporting requirements for, 73–76
  recyclable materials and, 64–65
  small quantity (SQGs), 82–84
  small quantity handler of universal waste (SQHUW) and, 83–84
  training and education in handling wastes and, 67
  transport of hazardous wastes and, 108
  Uniform Hazardous Waste Manifest for, 70–73, **93–94**, 174–178, **181**
  volume limits for storage by, 68–69
  wastewater and sludge, 68
Generic recycle exclusions, 36–39
Georgia, underground storage tank (UST) regulation in, 374
Global Settlement Policy, 422
Good faith efforts to comply, enforcement of RCRA and, 432
Government Performance and Results Act of 1993 (GPRA), 336–337
"Grandfathering" in permitting, 143–145
Greening the Government through Waste Prevention, Recycling, Federal Acquisition, 404–405
Groundwater protection, 257–269
  assessment program for, 260–261
  closure and postclosure of TSD facilities and, 262–263
  compliance monitoring and, 267–268
  compliance period for, 264
  corrective action and, 263, 268–269, 343
  detection monitoring and, 265–267
  general standards for, 258–259
  hazardous wastes and, 7
  indicator evaluation program for, 259–260
  interim status facilities and, 257–261
  landfills and, 283
  migration of contaminated groundwater under control (CA750) and, 336–337
  nonhazardous wastes, 12, 393
  permit modification rules for, 266–267
  permits for, 262–269
  postclosure of TSD facilities and, 194
  recordkeeping and reporting requirements for, 261
  release of hazardous materials and, 263
  Safe Drinking Water Act and, 264
  sampling and analysis in, 259
  standards for, 264–265
  underground injection control (UIC) permitting and, 22, 23, 137
Guarantees, 365–366
Guidance Manual for the Location Standards, 168

Index 495

Halogen acid wastes, 34
Halogenated organic compounds (*see also* Polychlorinated biphenyls), 25
Hawaii, location of TSD facilities in, regulations, 168
Hazardous air pollutants (HAPs), Clean Air Act and, 20–22
Hazardous and Solid Waste Amendment (HSWA) of 1984, 11
  corrective action and, 319–320, 332
  enforcement of RCRA and, 447–448
  interim status facilities and, 144–145
  land disposal facilities and, 255
  nonhazardous wastes and, 382, 410, 413, 415
  postclosure of TSD facilities and permits, 193–194
  underground storage tanks (USTs) and, 345, 346
  used oil and, 410–413
Hazardous materials regulations (HMRs) of DOT, 111–114
  definitions under, 111
  emergency response, training, and mixtures in, 113
  enforcement of, 111
  Federal Transit Act of 1998 (FTA) and, 111
  Hazardous Materials Transportation Act of 1975 (HMTA) and, 111
  Hazardous Materials Transportation Authorization Act of 1994 (HMTAA) and, 111
  Hazardous Materials Transportation Uniform Safety Act of 1990 (HMTUSA) and, 111, 116
  Hazardous Waste Manifest Requirements (EPA) and, 112
  history of, 111
  Intermodal Safe Container Transportation Amendments Act of 1996 (ISCTAA) and, 111
  labeling and placard requirements of, 113–114
  notice requirements of, 112–113
  packaging requirements for, 114
  scope of, 111–114
  those regulated by, 112
Hazardous Materials Transportation Act (HMTA), 6, 25–26, 16, 109, 111, 115–118
Hazardous Materials Transportation Authorization Act of 1994 (HMTAA), 111
Hazardous Materials Transportation Uniform Safety Act of 1990 (HMTUSA), 111, 116–117
Hazardous Organics Standard, 22

Hazardous Solid Waste Amendments of 1984 (HSWA), 2
Hazardous Waste Combustion Strategy (Draft), 22
Hazardous Waste Facility Liability Endorsement, 214
Hazardous Waste Manifest Requirements (EPA), 112
Hazardous wastes, 281–282
  accidental or infrequent production of, 63–64
  accumulation of wastes and, 5, 65–69
  Administrative Procedure Act (APA) and, 54
  analysis of, 164–165
  authorization of state programs for, 444–447
  Bentson wastes (*see also* Bevill wastes), 395–399, 409–413
  Bevill wastes and, 56, 247, 248, 297, 383, 395–399, 409–413
  California-listed, 25, 290
  categories of, 3
  characteristic wastes defined under, 3, 45, 49–52, 64, 291
  concentration-based exemption criteria (CBEC) and, 54–55
  contained-in policy for, 52–57, 310, 338
  corrosivity in, 3, 50, 64
  definition of, under CERCLA, 26
  definition of, under RCRA, 2–4, 16, 26, 45–60, 64–65
  delisting of, 4, 48–49
  derived-from rule for, 4, 52–57, 310
  empty containers and residues of wastes in, 59, 220–221
  excluded wastes, 46
  expanded characteristic option (ECHO) in, 55
  F-listed, 3, 34, 38, 47–48, 219, 238, 272, 274, 278, 285–286, 294, 308
  generators of, obligations under RCRA, 4–5, 61–89
  HWIR for Contaminated Media (HWIR-Media) regulation and, 57, 340
  HWIR92 proposal for, 54–55
  ignitability in, 3, 49–50, 64, 84–85, 167, 228–229, 273–275, 277, 281, 285
  K-listed, 3, 47–48, 55–56
  land disposal restrictions (LDRs) and, 296–297
  listed hazardous wastes, 3, 45, 47–49, 141–142
  low level mixed wastes (LLMW) and, 57–58
  manifest system to track waste handling and, 70–73, 87–88, 104–108, 174–178
  minimization of, 77–80
  mixed waste exemption in, 57–58

496 INDEX

Hazardous wastes (*continued*)
mixture rule for, 4, 52–57, 310
naturally occurring/accelerator-
produced radioactive material
(NARM) in, 57–58
nonspecific sources of, 47
notification of EPA of, 69
P-listed, 3, 25, 35, 38, 47–48, 55–56, 242
polychlorinated biphenyls (PCBs) and,
24–25, 52, 129, 221, 314
pretransportation requirements of, 73
reactivity in, 3, 50–51, 64, 167, 228–229,
273–275, 277, 281, 285
recycling, 35–36
small generator exemption, 4–5
specific sources of, 47
spills of (*see also* spills and
overfills), 47
toxic constituents in, 47–48
Toxic Substances Control Act (TSCA)
and, 24–25, 52
Toxicity Characteristic Leaching
Procedure (TCLP) and, 52, **53**, 311,
313–315, 316, 411
toxicity in, 3, 51–52, 64
transport of, 5–6
treatment, storage, and disposal
of, 6–9
U-listed, 3, 25, 35, 38, 47–48, 55–56
underground storage tanks (USTs) and,
354, 355, 357, 358, 372–373
underlying hazardous constituents,
LDRs and, 307–309
universal waste rule for, 58–59,
83–84
unused discarded commercial chemical
products and, 47
used oil containing, 42–43
Hearings, enforcement of RCRA and,
425–428
Heat requirements, boilers and industrial
furnaces (BIFs) and, 245–246
Heptachlor, TCLP thresholds for, **53**
Hexachlorobenzene, TCLP thresholds
for, **53**
Hexachlorobutadiene, TCLP thresholds
for, **53**
Hexachloroethane, TCLP thresholds
for, **53**
Hockley, Michael D., 345
Horowitz, Marcie R., 443
Hotline, RCRA, 65
Household waste, 3
HWIR for Contaminated Media (HWIR-
Media) regulation, 57, 340
HWIR92 proposal for hazardous wastes,
54–55
Hydrogen chloride (HCl), 244–245
Hydrogen sulfide, 51

Idaho, location of TSD facilities in,
regulations, 168
Ignitability, in defining hazardous waste,
3, 49–50, 64, 167, 228–229, 273–275,
277, 281, 285
Imminent and substantial endangerment
and, 436–437
Import of hazardous wastes, 84–85,
106–107
Impossibility defense against RCRA
enforcement, 431
Impoundments (*see also* Land disposal
facilities), 256–257, 269–275
Clean Water Act and, 19–20
closure and postclosure of TSD facilities
and, 196–197
closure of TSD facilities and, 273
Contaminated Debris Rule and, 271
F-listed wastes and, 272, 274
ignitable or reactive wastes in, 273–275
inspection, 272
interim status facilities and, 197,
274–275
land disposal restrictions (LDRs) and,
275, 298–299
leak detection and, 272
liners and covers for, 271
return to service after failure, 272–273
technical standards for, 269–275
In-process reuse, 35
"Inadvertent" TSD facility status, permit
requirements of RCRA and, 145
Incidental report requirements, 179
Incinerators, 3, 7–8, 232–240
Clean Air Act and, 21, 232
closure and postclosure of TSD facilities
and, 199, 239
Combustion of Hazardous Wastes draft
proposal (EPA) and, 233
definition of, 232
destruction and energy recovery (DER)
rate in, 236
destruction and removal efficiencies
(DREs) of, 235
efficiency standards for, 232, 235
emissions standards for, 237
evaluation of, 233
exemption from regulation of,
233–234
existing systems, 233
F-listed wastes, 238
Hazardous Waste Combustion Strategy
(Draft) and, 22
inspection of, 238–239
interim status facilities and, 238
mobile type, 239–240
NESHAP rules for, 239
operating requirements for, 237–238
permitting of, 233, 236–237

Index 497

plasma arc type, 232
policy issues and, 232–233
principal organic hazardous constituent
(POHC) analysis for, 235, 236
standards for, 217, 232–240
Superfund Amendments and
Reauthorization Act of 1986
(SARA) and, 239
trial burns in, 235–236, **252–253**
waste analysis for, 234–235
waste monitoring requirements for, 239
Incompatible wastes, in containers and
tanks, 229
Industrial nonhazardous wastes, 394–395
Industrial wastewater, 3, 18, 68
Information gathering, enforcement of
RCRA and, 424–425
Inherently waste-like and abandoned mate-
rials, in defining solid wastes, 34–35
Inspection requirements for TSD facilities,
165–166
containers and tanks and, 227–228
impoundments and, 272
incinerators and, 238–239
landfills and, 284
*Practical Guide for Inspection of Refinery
Equipment*, 228
waste piles and, 277
Institutional control (IC), corrective action
and, 343
Insurance, 203–204, 210–211
Certificate of Liability Insurance, 214
Hazardous Waste Facility Liability
Endorsement, 214
hazardous wastes and, TSDFs and, 7
liability requirements of, 213–214
self-, 364
underground storage tanks (USTs) and,
363–364, 366, 369–370
Integrated Enforcement Policy, 422
Interim measures, corrective action and,
330–332
Interim status facilities, 6, 10
boilers and industrial furnaces (BIFs)
and, 243, 245–246
closure plans for, 185–186, 198
containers and tanks and, 217, 222–223,
229
corrective action and, 321–322, 327
enforcement of RCRA and, 444–445
financial responsibility and, 200
groundwater protection and, 257–261
Hazardous and Solid Waste
Amendments of 1984 (HSWA) and,
144–145
impoundments as, 197, 274–275
incinerators and, 238
landfills and, 286
loss of, 144–145

Notification of Hazardous Waste
Activity by, 144
permit requirements of RCRA and,
143–145
postclosure of TSD facilities and, 191, 194
waste piles and, 278–279
Intermodal Safe Container Transportation
Amendments Act of 1996
(ISCTAA), 111
Interstate flow of wastes, 405–409
Invalidity of underlying regulations defense
against RCRA enforcement, 431
Iowa, underground storage tank (UST)
regulation in, 374
Irrigation return flow, 41

Jacus, John R., 103
Jurisdictional reach of RCRA, 15–17
Jury trial, enforcement of RCRA and, 429

K-listed hazardous wastes, 3, 47–48,
55–56
Kaleta, J., 121–124
Kansas, underground storage tank (UST)
regulation in, 374
Kastner, Kenneth M., 33
Knowing endangerment, 434
Knowing violation, 433–434
Kok, Andrew J., 125

Lagoons and ponds for landfills, 8
Lamps, universal waste rule for, 58–59
Land ban, 8–9
Land disposal facilities (*see also*
Impoundments; Landfills; Land
treatment units; Waste piles),
255–287
Contaminated Debris Rule and, 271
defining, 255
exemptions to technological
requirements for, 256–257
groundwater monitoring and, 257–269
Hazardous and Solid Waste
Amendments (HSWA) of 1984
and, 255
impoundments as, 256–257, 269–275
land treatment units in, 279–283
landfills as, 256–257, 283–286
minimum technological requirements
for, 256–257
miscellaneous units and, 286–287
monofills, 257
National Pollutant Discharge Elimination
System (NPDES) and, 257
technical standards for, 269–287
waste piles and, 275–279
Land disposal restrictions (LDRs),
289–303, 305–317
activities covered by, 291–292

498 INDEX

Land disposal restrictions (LDRs)
(*continued*)
alternatives to treatment under,
temporary and permanent, 297–300
applicability of, 305–309
applicability of, bars to, 300
best demonstrated available technology
(BDAT) in, 295
Bevill wastes and, 297
California list wastes and, 290
capacity variances, national and case-
by-case, 298
CERCLA and, 31, 289, 290, 312
cessation of treatment guidelines in,
295–296
characteristic wastes and, 291
Clean Water Act and, 19–20, 289,
300–302, 305–307
Columbia Falls decision and, 312
contained-in policy and, 310, 338
contaminated soil and, 313–315
corrective action and, 290, 337–338
corrective action management unit
(CAMUs) and, 303, 315–317
criteria for treatable wastes under,
296–297
derived-from rule and, 310
effective date for, 292
enforcement of RCRA and, 432
EPA and, 289
F-listed wastes and, 294, 308
generators of hazardous wastes and, 293
implementation of, 293
impoundments and, 275
inappropriate results from, 312–317
interface between other statutory/
regulatory programs and, 300–303
land treatment units and, 282
landfills and, 285
mixture rule and, 310
modification of, exceptions to, 317
no-migration disposal units and,
299–300
nonhazardous wastes and, at point of
generation, 308–309
polychlorinated biphenyls (PCBs)
and, 314
principal hazardous constituents (PHCs)
and, 316
publicly owned treatment works
(POTWs) and, 292, 297, 300
RCRA and, 302–303
remediation programs and, 312–317
Safe Drinking Water Act and, 289,
291–292, 302, 305–307
Section 3004(m) treatment standards for,
293–297
soil contamination and, 340–341
solid wastes and, 294

standardization of treatment standards
for, 309–312
statutory and regulatory provisions of,
290–293
storage of wastes and, 291–293
surface impoundment and, 298–299
technology vs. risk-based standards in,
295–296
underlying hazardous constituents and,
treatment of, 307–309
Universal Treatment Standards and,
307, 309–312
updated material for, 305–317
variances for treatment methods and,
294–295, 313
waste piles and, 278
waste tracking system for, 293
Land treatment units, 279–283
closure and postclosure of TSD facilities
and, 197–198, 281, 282–283
F-listed wastes in, 281–282
food chain crops and, 280
ignitable and reactive wastes in, 281
land disposal restrictions (LDRs)
and, 282
monitoring for, 280–281
permitting for, 279–280
Land use, postclosure of TSD facilities
and, 192
Landfills (*see also* Land disposal facilities),
8, 256–257, 283–286
closure and postclosure of TSD facilities
and, 198–199, 284
containers and tanks in, 285
F-listed wastes in, 285–286
groundwater protection and, 283
hazardous wastes and, 7
ignitable or reactive wastes in, 285
inspection for, 284
interim status facilities and, 286
land disposal restrictions (LDRs)
in, 285
leachate and, 3
leachate collection systems and, 283
liners and cover systems for, 283
nonhazardous waste, 12
permitting for, 286
recordkeeping requirements for, 284
runoff control and, 284
technological requirements for,
283–286
Toxicity Characteristic Leaching
Procedure (TCLP) and, 52, **53**, 411
Large quantity handler of universal waste
(LQHUW), 83–84
Leachate, 3, 8
landfills and, 283
Toxicity Characteristic Leaching
Procedure (TCLP) and, 52, **53**, 411

Lead paint, 35
Leak detection, leak testing, 8
containers and tanks and, 225–226, 228
impoundments and, 272
underground storage tanks (USTs) and,
350–358
Leaking Underground Storage Tank
(LUST) Trust Fund, 347–348,
371–372
Leason, Chris S., 345
Legitimate vs. sham recycling criteria,
38–39
Lender liability, underground storage
tanks (USTs) and, 373–374
Letter of credit, 209–210, 367
Liability requirements, 63, 213–214
Liners and cover systems, 8
containers and tanks and, 224
impoundments and, 271
landfills and, 8, 283
waste piles and, 276, 277
Listed hazardous wastes, 3, 45, 47–49
newly, 141–142
Litigation, 213–214
Location of TSD facilities, 167–169
Louisiana, underground storage tank
(UST) regulation in, 374
Love Canal, 2
Low level mixed wastes (LLMW), 57–58
Lowrance, Sylvia, 38–39

Maine, underground storage tank (UST)
regulation in, 374
Maintenance of boilers and industrial
furnaces (BIFs), 246–247
Maintenance of containers and tanks, 66,
219–220, 227–228
Manifest system to track waste handling
(*see also* Tracking system), 70–73,
87–88, 104–108, 174–178
Marine Protection, Research and
Sanctuaries Act, 16–17
Maryland
transport of hazardous wastes and, 117
underground storage tank (UST)
regulation in, 374
Massachusetts
transport of hazardous wastes and, 117
underground storage tank (UST)
regulation in, 374
Materials recovery facilities (MRFs), 384
Maximum contaminant level goals
(MCLGs), Safe Drinking Water Act
(SDWA) and, 22
Maximum contaminant levels (MCLs),
Safe Drinking Water Act (SDWA)
and, 22
McKinney, John A., Jr., 61
McKinstry, Robert B., Jr., 381

McQuaid, Janet L., 161
Medical Waste Tracking Act (MWTA) of
1988, 412–413
Medical wastes, 12, 412–413
Memorandum of Understanding (MOU),
DOT/EPA, 114–115
Metal recovery operations, 41, 242
Methyl ethyl ketone, TCLP thresholds
for, **53**
Methylene chloride, 48
Michigan, transport of hazardous wastes
and, 117
Migration of contaminated groundwater
under control (CA750), 336–337
Miller, Dean C., 103
Mineral extraction/processing, 3
Minimization of wastes, 77–80
*EPA Manual for Waste Minimization
Opportunity Assessments, 77–79,
97–101*
Miscellaneous units, land disposal,
286–287
Mississippi, underground storage tank
(UST) regulation in, 374
Missouri, transport of hazardous wastes
and, 117
Mixed-waste exemption, hazardous
wastes and, 57–58
Mixture rule, hazardous wastes and, 4,
52–57, 310
Mixtures, transport of hazardous wastes
and, 113
Mobile incinerators, 239–240
Modifications to permits, 138–142
Monofills, 257
Montana
location of TSD facilities in,
regulations, 168
underground storage tank (UST)
regulation in, 374
Montgomery, Michael D., 183, 255
Municipal solid waste (MSW) (*see also*
Nonhazardous wastes), 381
Municipal solid waste landfill (MSWLF),
nonhazardous wastes and,
390–394, 413

National Contingency Plan (NCP),
CERCLA and, 29–30
National Fire Protection Association,
228–229
National Oil and Hazardous Substances
Pollution Contingency Plan (NCP),
29–30, 110, 339
National Pollutant Discharge Elimination
system (NPDES), 41
corrective action and, 326–327
nonhazardous wastes and, 390
permits under, 41

500 INDEX

National Response Center, 26–27, 76, 174
National Technical Information
    Service, 146
Naturally occurring/accelerator-produced
    radioactive material (NARM),
    57–58
NESHAP rules, incinerators and, 239
Nevada
    location of TSD facilities in,
        regulations, 168
    underground storage tank (UST)
        regulation in, 374
New Hampshire, underground storage
    tank (UST) regulation in, 374
New Jersey, transport of hazardous wastes
    and, 116, 119
New Mexico
    location of TSD facilities in,
        regulations, 168
    underground storage tank (UST)
        regulation in, 374
New York, transport of hazardous wastes
    and, 117
Nitrobenzene, TCLP thresholds for, **53**
No-migration disposal units, land disposal
    restrictions (LDRs) and, 299–300
Nonhazardous wastes, 12, 381–416
    Bentson wastes (*see also* Bevill wastes),
        395–399, 409–413
    Bevill wastes and, 383, 395–399,
        409–413
    cement kiln dust (CKD) as, 398
    Clean Air Act and, 391, 394
    Clean Water Act and, 382–383, 391, 392,
        394, 412, 415
    closure of TSD facilities and,
        188–189
    Comprehensive Procurement Guidelines
        (CPG) for, 403–404
    conditionally exempt small quantity
        generators (CESQGs) and, 389, 391,
        394–395
    dangers and threats posed by, 382
    design criteria for, 392–394
    Greening the Government through Waste
        Prevention, Recycling, Federal
        Acquisition for, 404–405
    Hazardous and Solid Waste
        Amendment (HSWA) and, 382, 410,
        413, 415
    industrial waste as, 394–395
    interstate flow of, 405–409
    land disposal restrictions (LDRs) and, at
        point of generation, 308–309
    location of dumps for, 393
    materials recovery facilities (MRFs)
        and, 384
    medical wastes and, 412–413

    municipal solid waste (MSW) as, 381
    municipal solid waste landfill (MSWLF)
        and, 390–394, 413
    National Pollutant Discharge Elimina-
        tion System (NPDES) and, 390
    open dumping of, 384–395, 414–415
    operating criteria for, 394
    publicly owned treatment works
        (POTWs) and, 382
    recycling and procurement guidelines
        for, 401–405
    recycling of, 383, 384
    refuse-derived fuel (RDF) using, 384
    regulation of, 383
    resource recovery programs for, 399–405
    Safe Drinking Water Act and, 392
    sewage sludge, 412, 415
    source reduction programs for, 383
    special handling requirements for some,
        409–413
    special issues in enforcement of Subtitle
        D requirements, etc., 413–415
    state planning and, 384–390
    Superfund Amendment and
        Reauthorization Act (SARA),
        410, 415
    Surface Mining Control and
        Reclamation Act and, 382–383
    types of wastes in, 382–383
    used oil as, 409–412
    volume of wastes generated in U.S.,
        382–383
Nonspecific sources of hazardous
    wastes, 47
North Carolina, underground storage tank
    (UST) regulation in, 374
North Dakota, underground storage tank
    (UST) regulation in, 374
Nuclear Regulatory Commission
    (NRC), 58
Nuclear wastes, 57–58
    naturally occurring/accelerator-
        produced radioactive material
        (NARM) in, 57–58
    Nuclear Regulatory Commission
        (NRC), 58

Occupational Safety and Health
    Administration (OSHA), 67, 327
Office of Criminal Enforcement, 421
Office of Enforcement and Compliance
    Assurance (OECA), 86, 421
Office of Federal Activities, 421
Office of Regulatory Enforcement, 421
Office of Site Remediation Enforcement, 421
Office of Solid Waste (OSW), 51
Office of Solid Waste and Emergency
    Response (OSWER), 146

Index   501

Oil and gas exploration, 3
Oil, lubricants as waste (*see* Used oil)
Oklahoma, underground storage tank
  (UST) regulation in, 374
Omnibus authority, corrective action and,
  324–325
On-site transportation, 109
Open dumping of nonhazardous wastes,
  384–395, 414–415
Operation of TSDs (*see* Standards for
  operation and design of TSDs)
Organics, 22
  Hazardous Organics Standard and, 22
  Toxicity Characteristic Leaching
    Procedure (TCLP) thresholds for,
    53, **53**
Organization for Economic Cooperation
  and Development (OECD), export
  of hazardous wastes and, 88–89, 107
Overfile right of EPA, in civil enforcement,
  449–451
Overfill controls, underground storage
  tanks (USTs) and, 352–353

P-listed hazardous wastes, 3, 25, 35, 38,
  47–48, 55–56, 242
Packaging requirements, transport of
  hazardous wastes and, 114
Penalties, enforcement of RCRA and,
  427–429
Pennsylvania, transport of hazardous
  wastes and, 117
Pentachlorophenol, TCLP thresholds for, **53**
Permit requirements of RCRA, 6, 10,
  28–29, 125–147, 162, 163
  appeal process for, 138, **139**, 141
  applicability determination for, 127–129
  application procedure for, 130–133, **131**
  boilers and industrial furnaces (BIFs)
    and, 243–245
  case-by-case conditions for, 136
  change in owner or operator and, 140
  Class 1 modifications to permit in,
    138, 140
  Class 2 modifications to permit in,
    138, 140
  Class 3 modifications to permit in,
    140–141
  corrective action and, 133, 321–322,
    327–328
  definition of, 125–126
  denial of permit in, 138
  duration of permit, 142
  emergency permits under, 130, 136,
    137–138
  EPA issuance of, 142
  EPA standardization of, 127
  exclusions to, 128–129

form for, **153–159**
generators of hazardous wastes and, 67
"grandfathering" in, 143–145
groundwater protection and, 262–269
"inadvertent" TSD facility status and, 145
incinerators and, 233, 236–237
interim status facilities and, 143–145
land treatment units and, 279–280
landfills and, 286
mobile incinerators, 239–240
modifications to permit in, 138–142
newly regulated wastes and hazardous
  waste management units in,
  141–142
Notification of Hazardous Waste
  Activity and, 144
obtaining permits under, 130–133
operation and design of TSDs, 163
Part A application for, 130
Part B application for, 132–133
permits by rule under, 136, 137
polychlorinated biphenyls (PCBs)
  and, 129
postclosure of TSD facilities and, 146,
  193–195
processing of application for,
  133–134, **135**
publicly owned treatment works
  (POTW) and, 137
purpose of, 125–126
RCRA Facility Assessment (RFA) in, 133
reference materials for, 146, 158–152
renewal of permit, 142
"shield" effect of, 126, 432
special permits under, 136–138
standard conditions for 134–136
standardization of, 127
state issuance of, 142
storage of wastes and, 67
temporary modification authorization
  for, 141
termination of permit in, 142–143
treatment, storage, disposal (TSD)
  facilities and, 125–126
underground injection control (UIC)
  permits and, 137
waste piles and, 275–276
water/ocean disposal vessels and, 137
Permits by rule, 136, 137
Pesticides, universal waste rule for,
  58–59
Petroleum products, 40–41
  recycling of, 40
  underground storage tanks (USTs) and,
    353–357, **357**
Pinto, Vito A., 61
Piping, for underground storage tanks
  (USTs), 354–355, 357–358

Placard requirements, transport of hazardous wastes and, 113–114
Plasma arc incinerators, 232
Pollution Contingency Plan (NCP) and, 339
Polychlorinated biphenyls (PCBs), 24–25, 52, 129
 containers and tanks and, 221, 314
 land disposal restrictions (LDRs) and, 314
 permit requirements of RCRA and, 129
Porter, J. Winston, 332
Postclosure of TSD facilities (*see also* Closure of TSD facilities; Financial responsibility), 189–195
 care of facility, cover, caps during, 191–193
 certification of, 192–193
 containers and tanks in, 195–196, 221–222
 cost estimate for, 200–204
 drip pads and, 199
 enforcement documents for, 195
 financial assurance for, 199–215
 groundwater monitoring and, 194, 262–263
 incinerators and furnaces, 199, 239
 insurance coverage and, 203–204, 210–211
 interim status facilities and, 191, 194, 198
 land treatment units and, 197–198, 281, 282–283
 landfills and, 198–199, 284
 period of, 189–190
 permits for, 146, 193–195
 plans for, 190–191
 removal of wastes, 192
 runoff and runoff control in, 197–198
 surface impoundments and, specifications for, 196–197
 waste piles and, 197, 277–278
 zoning and land use after, 192
Practical Guide for Inspection of Refinery Equipment, 228
Preliminary Assessment/Site Investigation (PA/SI), 30
Preparedness and prevention standards, operation and design of TSDs, 170–172
Preston, David E., 125
Pretransportation requirements, 73
Pretreatment, wastewater, 17–19
Prevention standards, operation and design of TSDs, 170–172
Price, Courtney M., 332
Price, James T., 319
Primary vs. secondary materials in recycling, 36–39
Principal hazardous constituents (PHCs), 316

Principal organic hazardous constituent (POHC) analysis, incinerators and, 235, 236
Protective filers, corrective action and, 322
Publicly owned treatment works (POTW), 41
 Clean Water Act and, 17
 land disposal restrictions (LDRs) and, 292, 297, 300
 nonhazardous wastes and, 382
 operation and design of TSDs, 162
 permit requirements of RCRA and, 137
Pulping processes, 41
Pyridine, TCLP thresholds for, **53**

Rail transport, 105–106
RCRA Enforcement Policy and Compendium, 451
RCRA Facility Assessment (RFA), 30, 133, 328
RCRA Facility Investigation (RFI), 30, 328–329
RCRA Hotline, 65
RCRA Permit Policy Compendium, 146
RCRA Policy Documents/Finding Your Way Through the Maze..., 13
Reactivity, in defining hazardous waste, 3, 50–51, 64, 167, 228–229, 273–275, 277, 281, 285
Reclamation, 3
 minimization of wastes through, 79
 small quantity generators (SQGs) and, 107–108
Record keeping requirements, 178–179
 generators of hazardous wastes and, 73–76
 groundwater protection and, 261
 landfills and, 284
 transport of hazardous wastes and, 108
 underground storage tanks (USTs) and, 370–371
Recyclable materials, 2, 3, 33, 35–36
 Comprehensive Procurement Guidelines (CPG) for, 403–404
 court cases pertaining to, 39–41
 direct use exclusions in, 38
 F-listed wastes in, 38
 generators of hazardous wastes and, 64–65
 generic exclusions for, 36–39
 Greening the Government through Waste Prevention, Recycling, Federal Acquisition for, 404–405
 hazardous waste and, 35–36
 legitimate vs. sham recycling criteria in, 38–39
 minimization of wastes through, 78–79
 nonhazardous wastes and, 383, 384, 401–405

Index   503

petroleum refining and, 40
P-listed wastes in, 38
primary vs. secondary materials in
    recycling, 36–39
RCRA regulation of, 42
U-listed wastes in, 38
Reference materials for permit process,
    146, 148–152
Refuse, 2
Refuse-derived fuel (RDF), 384
Release detection, underground storage
    tanks (USTs) and, 350, 353–357, **357**
Releases subject to corrective action,
    326–327
Relief and penalties, enforcement of
    RCRA and, 427–429
Remedial Investigation and Feasibility
    Study (RI/FS), CERCLA, 30
Remediation programs, 312–317
    corrective action and, 337–341
    land disposal restrictions (LDRs) and,
        312–317
Reporting requirements, 26–27
    export of hazardous wastes and, 88–89
    generators of hazardous wastes and,
        73–76
    groundwater protection and, 261
    operation and design of TSDs, 179
    RCRA vs. CERCLA, 26–27
    underground storage tanks (USTs) and,
        359–361, 370–371
Research and Special Programs
    Administration (RSPA), transport of
    hazardous wastes and, 109
Residues from BIFs, treatment of,
    247–249
Residues of wastes in empty containers,
    59, 220–221
Resource Conservation and Recovery Act
    (RCRA), 1–13
    accumulation of wastes and, 5, 65–69
    boiler and industrial furnace (BIF)
        standards under, 217, 240–249
    capping of hazardous sites under,
        30–31, 191–193, 196–199
    categories of hazardous wastes under
        (F, K, P, U), 3
    CERCLA and, 17, 302–303
    characteristic wastes defined under, 3,
        45, 49–52, 64
    Clean Air Act and, 15, 20–22, 391, 394
    Clean Water Act and, 15–20, 289,
        300–302, 305–307, 349, 382–383, 391,
        392, 394, 412, 415
    cleanup process under, 30–31
    Comprehensive Environmental
        Response, Compensation, and
        Liability Act (CERCLA) and, 11, 16,
        26–31, 289, 290, 312, 326, 338, 342

container and tank standards under,
    217, 218–222
corrective action management units
    (CAMUs) and, 31, 315–317
corrective action requirements under,
    9–11, 27–31, 133, 212–213, 319–344
Corrective Measures Study (CMS)
    and, 30
covered sites under, for corrective
    action, 27–28
definition of hazardous waste under,
    2–4, 16, 26, 45–60
enforcement of, civil and criminal,
    28–30, 417–442
Environmental Protection Agency (EPA)
    integration of, 16–17
Federal Insecticide, Fungicide, and
    Rodenticide Act (FIFRA) and, 17
federal-state relationship under, 443–457
generators of hazardous wastes and,
    obligations of, 4–5, 61–89
Government Performance and Results
    Act of 1993 (GPRA) and, 336–337
Hazardous and Solid Waste
    Amendments of 1984 (HSWA) and,
    2, 11
Hazardous Materials Transportation Act
    (HMTA) and, 6, 16, 25–26, 115–118
Hazardous Organics Standard and, 22
Hazardous Waste Combustion Strategy
    (Draft) and, 22
incinerator and furnace standards
    under, 217, 232–240
jurisdictional reach of, 15–17
land disposal restrictions (LDR)
    program, 31, 289–303
listed hazardous wastes, 3, 45, 47–49
Marine Protection, Research and
    Sanctuaries Act and, 16–17
National Pollutant Discharge Elimination
    System (NPDES) and, 257
nonhazardous waste disposal and, 12,
    381–416
overview of, 1–13
permit requirements of, 6, 10, 28–29,
    125–147, 162, 163
RCRA Facility Assessment (RFA) and,
    30, 133
RCRA Facility Investigation (RFI)
    and, 30
recyclable materials regulation under, 42
relationship to other laws of, 15–31
reporting requirements of, 26–27
Safe Drinking Water Act (SDWA) and,
    16, 17, 22–24, 162, 289, 291–292, 302,
    305–307, 392
small generator exemption and, 4–5
solid waste defined for, 2–3, 15–16,
    33–43

504 INDEX

Resource Conservation and Recovery Act
(RCRA) (*continued*)
Solid Waste Disposal Act and, 15
solid waste management units
(SWMUs) and, 28
state implementation of, 2, 443–457
Superfund Amendments and
Reauthorization Act of 1986
(SARA) and, 231, 239
Toxic Substances Control Act (TSCA)
and, 16, 24–25
transport of hazardous waste and, 5–6,
103–120
treatment, storage, and disposal (TSD)
facilities and, 28, 161
treatment, storage, and disposal of
hazardous wastes under, 6–9
underground storage tanks (USTs) and,
11–12, 27, 345–379
used oil regulation under, 42–43
Resource recovery programs,
nonhazardous wastes and, 399–405
Results-based corrective action, 335–337
Return to service, impoundments, 272–273
Reuse, 35
minimization of wastes through, 79
Rhode Island
enforcement of RCRA and, 451
underground storage tank (UST)
regulation in, 374
Risk retention groups, 366
Risk-based standards, land disposal
restrictions (LDRs) and, 295–296
Runoff and runoff control
closure and postclosure of TSD facilities
and, 197–198
landfills and, 284
waste piles and, 276

Sadler, Susan J., 217
Safe Drinking Water Act (SDWA), 16, 17,
22–24
"decharacterized" hazardous wastes
and, 23–24
dilution and antidilution rules in, 23
groundwater protection and, 264
land disposal restrictions (LDRs) and,
289, 291–292, 302, 305–307
maximum contaminant level goals
(MCLGs) and, 22
maximum contaminant levels (MCLs)
in, 22
nonhazardous wastes and, 392
toxicity characteristic levels (TCLs)
and, 22
treatment, storage, disposal (TSD)
facilities and, 23
underground injection control (UIC)
permitting and, 22, 23, 206

Sampling, groundwater protection and, 259
Satellite accumulation of wastes, 5
Scanlon, Michael T., 443
Second Codification Rule, corrective
action and, 333
Secondary containment requirements,
tank systems, 223–226
Section 3004(m) treatment standards for,
293–297
Security requirements for TSD
facilities, 165
Seismic faults, 7, 167–168, 393
Self-auditing, enforcement of RCRA
and, 436
Self-insurance, underground storage tanks
(USTs) and, 364
Sentencing, enforcement of RCRA and,
federal guidelines for, 435–436
Sewage sludge, 2, 3, 12, 35, 37, 41, 412, 415
Clean Water Act and, 19
publicly owned treatment works
(POTW), 41
Sewage, domestic, 17–18
Sham recycling criteria, 38–39
Silverman, Steven E., 289, 305
Site Identification Form (RCRA Subtitle
C), **90–92**
Sludge (*see also* Dust and sludges
produced by air scrubbers; Sewage
sludge), 20, 35, 37, 41
Small generator exemption, 4–5
Small quantity generators (SQGs), 82–84
boilers and industrial furnaces (BIFs)
and, 242
reclamation exemption for, 107–108
transport of hazardous wastes and,
reclamation exemption for,
107–108
Small quantity handler of universal waste
(SQHUW), 83–84
Smelting, melting, refining furnaces, 242
Soil contamination, 10–11
corrective action and, 340–341
land disposal restrictions (LDRs) and,
313–315, 340–341
Solid Waste Disposal Act, 1, 15
Solid waste management units (SWMUs),
28, 320, 321, 323–324, 328, 330, 333
Solid wastes, 2–3, 15–16, 33–43
as-is secondary materials in, 36, 37–38
contained liquids and gases as, 2, 33–34
corrective action and, releases of,
323–324
definition of, 2–3, 15–16, 33–43
direct use exclusions in, 38
"discarded material" as definition of,
34–41
exclusions specific from, 41
generic recycle exclusions and, 36–39

Index   505

inherently waste-like and abandoned
materials in definition of, 34–35
legitimate vs. sham recycling criteria in,
38–39
National Pollutant Discharge
Elimination System (NPDES)
permits and, 41
Office of Solid Waste (OSW), 51
physical form of, in defining, 33–34
primary vs. secondary materials in
recycling, 36–39
recycled materials in definition of, 35–36
sewage sludge and, 41
wastewater and, 41
SONREEL, 13
Source reduction programs for
nonhazardous wastes, 383
South Carolina, enforcement of RCRA
and, 454
South Dakota, underground storage tank
(UST) regulation in, 374
Special permits, 136–138
Specific sources of hazardous wastes, 47
Speculative accumulation, 35
Spills, 8, 34–35
containers and tanks and, 225, 230–231
hazardous wastes and, 47
National Oil and Hazardous Substances
Pollution Contingency Plan (NCP)
and, 110, 339
notification of National Response
Center for, 109–110
underground storage tanks (USTs) and,
352–353
Squire, Daniel H., 15
Standards for containers, tanks,
incinerators etc. (*see* Boilers;
Containers and tanks; Incinerators
and furnaces), 217
Standards for operation and design of
TSDs, 161–180
biennial report requirements, 179
communications and alarm
requirements for, 171
construction quality assurance (CQA)
program in, 169–170
contingency plan procedures in, 172–174
emergency coordinator role and, 173
emergency response in, 170–174
EPA identification number (EPA ID)
and, 163
equipment requirements for, 170–171
general facility standards in, 163–170
general scope of, 162–163
general waste analysis in, 164–165
generators of hazardous waste and,
174–175
ignitable, reactive or incompatible
wastes in, 167

incidental report requirements, 179
inspection requirements for, 165–166
location standards and 167–169
manifest system, record keeping and
reporting requirements in, 174–179
new vs. existing facilities in, 163
notification to EPA of intended
operations, 164
permit requirements of RCRA and, 163
preparedness and prevention standards
for, 170–172
publicly owned treatment works
(POTWs) and, 162
record keeping requirements for, 178–179
security requirements for, 165
state and local authorities,
arrangements with, 171–172
testing requirements for, 170–171
training and education of personnel
and, 166–167
transporters, 175
underground injection-sites exempted
from, 162
water/ocean disposal vessels exempted
from, 162
Standby trust fund, 368–369
State implementation of RCRA, 2,
422–423, 443–457
authorization of state hazardous waste
programs and, 444–447
civil suits in authorized states and,
451–453
Commerce Clause and, 453–454
constitutional issues in, 453–457
criminal enforcement and, 451
enforcement of RCRA and, 422–423
EPA enforcement power and, 448–451
financial responsibility and, 212
Hazardous and Solid Waste
Amendments (HSWA) of 1984 and,
447–448
interim facilities and, 444–445
interstate flow of wastes and, 405–409
operation and design of TSDs, 171–172
overfile right of EPA, in civil
enforcement, 449–451
permit requirements of RCRA and, 142
*RCRA Enforcement Policy and
Compendium*, 451
Supremacy Clause and federal
preemption in, 454–457
transport of hazardous wastes and,
Commerce Clause limitations on,
118–120
transport of hazardous wastes and,
federal preemption in, 115–118
underground storage tanks (USTs) and,
367–368, 374–375
withdrawal of authorization and, 447

506 INDEX

Statute of limitations, enforcement of
RCRA and, 428, 429–430
Steel Tank Institute, 224
Steinberg, Michael W., 417
Storage of hazardous wastes, 6–9, 65–69
air emission control standards
and, 68
closure of TSD facilities and, 188–189
closure, postclosure specifications for,
195–196
conditionally exempt small quantity
generators (CESQGs), 81–82
containers and tanks and, 218–219
drip pads and, 66
education in handling of wastes in, 67
emergency response and, 67
labeling of containers and tanks, 64–65,
73, 113–114
land disposal restrictions (LDRs) and,
291–293
large quantity handler of universal
waste (LQHUW) and, 83–84
maintaining tanks for, 66, 219–220,
227–228
permitting requirements for, 67
small quantity generators (SQGs), 82–84
small quantity handler of universal
waste (SQHUW) and, 83–84
Uniform Hazardous Waste Manifest for,
70–73, **93–94**, 174–178, **181**
volume limits for, 68–69
Subpart S proposed rule (EPA) and,
334–335
"Substantial business relationship,"
financial responsibility and,
207–208
Sulfides, 50, 51
Sulfuric acid, 41
Sullivan, William A., Jr., 450
Superfund (*see also* Comprehensive
Environmental Response,
Compensation, and Liability Act),
1, 2, 9, 16
Superfund Amendment and
Reauthorization Act (SARA) of
1986, 231, 239
nonhazardous wastes and, 410, 415
underground storage tanks (USTs)
and, 347
used oil and, 410
Supremacy Clause and federal
preemption, enforcement of RCRA
and, 454–457
Surety bond, 208–209, 366–367
Surface impoundments (*see* Impoundment
of wastewater)
Surface Mining Control and Reclamation
Act, 382–383

Tanks (*see* Containers and tanks)
Technology vs. risk-based standards, land
disposal restrictions (LDRs) and,
295–296
Temporary units, corrective action and,
339–340
Tennessee, underground storage tank
(UST) regulation in, 374
Testing requirements for TSD facilities,
170–171
Tetrachloroethylene, TCLP thresholds
for, **53**
Texas, underground storage tank (UST)
regulation in, 374
Thermostats, universal waste rule for,
58–59
Toxic constituents, hazardous wastes and,
47–48
Toxic Substances Control Act (TSCA), 16,
24–25
by-product regulation and, 24
California-listed hazardous wastes
under, 25
CERCLA and, 26
P- and U-listed hazardous wastes
under, 25
polychlorinated biphenyls (PCBs) and,
24–25, 52, 129
small quantity generators (SQGs) and, 83
Toxicity characteristic (TC), 314
Toxicity Characteristic Leaching Procedure
(TCLP), 3, 52, **53**, 311
contaminated soil and, 313–315
principal hazardous constituents (PHCs)
and, 316
used oil, 411
Toxicity characteristic levels (TCLs), Safe
Drinking Water Act (SDWA)
and, 22
Toxicity, in defining hazardous waste, 3,
51–52, 64
Tracking system, land disposal restrictions
(LDRs) and, 293
Training and education
generators of hazardous wastes,
obligations of, 67
operation and design of TSDs, 166–167
transport of hazardous wastes and, 113
Transport of hazardous waste, 5–6,
103–120, 175–176
Acknowledgment of Consent papers
for, 106
bond requirements for, 117–118
Commerce Clause limitations on state
and local regulation of, 118–120
Department of Transportation (DOT)
coordination with EPA in, 103–104,
110, 114–115

Index 507

emergency response in, 113
EPA identification number (EPA ID) and, 104–108, 110
export of hazardous wastes and, 85–89, 106–107
Federal Highway Administration (FHWA) and, 115
federal preemption of local and state regulations in, 115–118
Federal Transit Act of 1998 (FTA) and, 111
fee schedules vs. Commerce Clause in, 119–120
generators of wastes and TSD requirements, 108
hazardous materials regulations (HMRs) of DOT and, 111–114
Hazardous Materials Transportation Act (HMTA) and, 109, 111, 115–118
Hazardous Materials Transportation Authorization Act of 1994 (HMTAA) and, 111
Hazardous Materials Transportation Uniform Safety Act of 1990 (HMTUSA) and, 111, 116–117
import of hazardous wastes, 84–85, 106–107
Intermodal Safe Container Transportation Amendments Act of 1996 (ISCTAA) and, 111
labeling and placard requirements for, 113–114
manifest system to track waste handling and, 70–73, 87–88, 104–108, 174–178
mixtures of hazardous materials, 113
National Oil and Hazardous Substance Contingency Plan and, 110
nonhazardous wastes and, interstate, 405–409
notification requirements for, 85–87
on-site transportation in, 109
operation and design of TSDs, 175–176
Organization for Economic Cooperation and Development (OECD), 107
packaging requirements for, 114
pretransportation requirements of, 73
"public highway" defined, 121–124
rail transport and, 105–106
record retention for, 108
Research and Special Programs Administration (RSPA) program for, 109
Site Identification Form (RCRA Subtitle C), **90–92**
small quantity generators (SQGs) and, reclamation exemption for, 107–108
spills during, National Response Center notification of, 109–110

substantive requirements for, 109–110
training and education of personnel in, 113
Uniform Hazardous Waste Manifest for, 70–73, **93–94**, 174–178, **181**
unmanifested wastes, 177–178
water transport and, bulk shipments, 105
Treatment of hazardous wastes, 6–9
land disposal restrictions (LDRs) and, Section 3004(m), 293–297
Treatment, storage, and disposal facilities (TSDFs), 6–9, 10
CERCLA and, 28
Clean Air Act and, 21
closure of, 184–189
corrective action and, 320
enforcement of RCRA and, 424–425
"inadvertent" status of, 145
permit requirements for (*see also* Permit requirements of RCRA), 125–126
postclosure regulations for, 189–195
Safe Drinking Water Act (SDWA) and, 23
standards for operation and design of (*see* Standards for operation and design of TSDs)
transport of hazardous wastes and, 108
Trial burn regulations, incinerators and, 235–236, **252–253**
Trichloroethylene, TCLP thresholds for, **53**
Trichlorophenol, TCLP thresholds for, **53**
Trigger levels for corrective action (*see* Action or trigger levels)
Triple rinsing protocol for waste residues, 59, 221
Trust funds, 204–206, 368–369

U-listed hazardous wastes, 3, 25, 35, 38, 47–48, 55–56
Underground caves, mines, 169
Underground injection control (UIC) program, 162
corrective action and, 342
financial responsibility and, 206
permit requirements of RCRA and, 22, 23, 137
Underground storage tanks (USTs), 2, 11–12, 345–379
advanced notice of proposed rule making (ANPR) for, 372–373
bankruptcy of owner/operator and, 371
case law pertaining to, 377–378
CERCLA and, 27, 349, 360, 378
Clean Water Act and, 349
closure of (temporary and permanent), 361–362
Compliance Incentives for Small Businesses and, 376

508 INDEX

Underground storage tanks (USTs) (*continued*)
compliance with regulations concerning, 348, 363, **363**
corrective action and, 360–361, 377
corrosion protection for, 351–352, 354, 357
deferrals and limitations to regulation of, 350
definition of, 349
design and construction requirements for, 351
emergency response and, 359–360
enforcement of regulations concerning, 348
enforcement/penalties for regulations pertaining to, 375–378
exemptions to regulations concerning, 346–347, 349–350
existing tanks in, 355–357
financial responsibility for, 347, 348, 362–373
Hazardous and Solid Waste Amendments (HSWA) and, 345, 346
hazardous substances in, 354, 355, 357, 358, 372–373
initial abatement measures and site characterization for, 360
insurance coverage for, 363–364, 366, 369–370
Internet resources for research on, 379
Leaking Underground Storage Tank (LUST) Trust Fund and, 347–348, 371–372
lender liability and, 373–374
letters of credit for, 367
local government and financial responsibility, 369
new tanks and, 351–354
notification requirements for, 358–359
performance standards, operating requirements, 350–358
petroleum containing, 353–357, **357**
piping for, 354–355, 357–358
recordkeeping requirements for, 370–371
regulated substances in, 349
regulations pertaining to, 348–350
release detection in, 350, 353–357, **357**
reporting requirements for, 359–361, 370–371
risk retention groups and, 366
scope of installation, problems with, 346
site assessment for, 362
spill and overfill control for, 352–353
state funds for, 367–368
state program authorizations and, 374–375
state required financial responsibility rules for, 367

statutory authority over, 346–348
Superfund Amendment and Reauthorization Act (SARA) and, 347
surety bonds for, 366–367
trust funds for, 368–369
upgrade requirements for, ten-year, 355–356
UST/LUST Enforcement Procedures Guidance Manual for, 376
USTfields program for, 375
Underlying hazardous constituents, land disposal restrictions (LDRs) and, treatment of, 307–309
Universal Treatment Standards (UTSs), 307
aluminum processing and, 311
Columbia Falls decision and, 312
contained-in, derived-from, and mixture rules in, 310
exemptions to, 309–312
land disposal restrictions (LDRs) and, 307, 309–312
soil contamination and, 313–315
Toxicity Characteristic Leaching Procedure (TCLP) and, 311, 313–315
Universal waste rule, 58–59
large quantity handler of universal waste (LQHUW) and, 83–84
small quantity generators (SQGs) and, 83–84
small quantity handler of universal waste (SQHUW) and, 83–84
Unmanifested Waste Report, 178
Unmanifested wastes, 177–178
Unused discarded commercial chemical products, 47
Upgrade requirements for underground storage tanks (USTs), ten-year, 355–356
Use constituting disposal, 35
Used oil, 12, 42–43, 409–412
conditionally exempt small quantity generators (CESQGs) and, 42
hazardous wastes and, 42–43
"off specification," 43
Used Oil Recycling Act of 1980, 409
UST/LUST Enforcement Procedures Guidance Manual, 376
USTfields program, 375
Utah
location of TSD facilities in, regulations, 168
underground storage tank (UST) regulation in, 374

Variances for treatment methods, land disposal restrictions (LDRs) and, 294–295, 313

Index 509

Vault systems, 224
Vermont, underground storage tank (UST)
  regulation in, 374
Vinyl chloride, TCLP thresholds for, **53**
Violations, knowing, 433–434
Virginia, underground storage tank (UST)
  regulation in, 374
Volume limits for storage of hazardous
  wastes, 68–69
  conditionally exempt small quantity
    generators (CESQGs), 81–82
  large quantity handler of universal
    waste (LQHUW) and, 83–84
  small quantity generators (SQGs), 82–84
  small quantity handler of universal
    waste (SQHUW) and, 83–84

Washington
  location of TSD facilities in,
    regulations, 168
  underground storage tank (UST)
    regulation in, 374
Waste analysis, incinerators and, 234–235
Waste Minimization National Plan, 80
Waste piles, 275–279
  closure and postclosure of TSD facilities
    and, 197, 277–278
  containers and tanks for, 276
  F-listed wastes in, 278
  ignitable or reactive wastes in, 277

inspections for, 277
interim status facilities and, 278–279
land disposal restrictions (LDRs)
  and, 278
liners and covers, 276, 277
nonhazardous wastes and, open
  dumping and, 384–395, 414–415
permitting for, 275–276
runoff control and wind dispersal
  from, 276
Wastewater, 41
Wastewater, industrial (*see* Industrial
  wastewater)
Water discharges, 15
Water transport, bulk shipments, 105
Water/ocean disposal, 8–9, 162
  permit requirements of RCRA and,
    vessels and, 137
West Virginia, underground storage tanks
  (USTs) and, 375
Wilkinson, Robert F., 183, 255
Withdrawal of authorization, enforcement
  of RCRA and, 447
Wood preservative processes, 41
Woodrow, Kenneth D., 417
Wyoming, location of TSD facilities in,
  regulations, 168

Zoning, postclosure of TSD facilities
  and, 192